PRENTICE HALL SERIES PTR ON MICROSOFT® TECHNOLOGIES

BizTalk

IMPLEMENTING BUSINESS-TO-BUSINESS E-COMMERCE

James G. Kobielus

PH
PTR

Prentice Hall PTR, Upper Saddle River, NJ 07458
www.phptr.com

ISBN 0-13-089159-2

- Windows 2000 Hardware and Disk Management
  Simmons

- Windows 2000 Server: Management and Control, Third Edition
  Spencer, Goncalves

- Creating Active Directory Infrastructures
  Simmons

- Windows 2000 Registry
  Sanna

- Configuring Windows 2000 Server
  Simmons

- Supporting Windows NT and 2000 Workstation and Server
  Mohr

- Zero Administration Kit for Windows
  McInerney

- Tuning and Sizing NT Server
  Aubley

- Windows NT 4.0 Server Security Guide
  Goncalves

- Windows NT Security
  McInerney

CERTIFICATION

- Core MCSE: Windows 2000 Edition
  Dell

- Core MCSE: Designing a Windows 2000 Directory Services Infrastructure
  Simmons

- Core MCSE
  Dell

- Core MCSE: Networking Essentials
  Keogh

- MCSE: Administering Microsoft SQL Server 7
  Byrne

- MCSE: Implementing and Supporting Microsoft Exchange Server 5.5
  Goncalves

- MCSE: Internetworking with Microsoft TCP/IP
  Ryvkin, Houde, Hoffman

- MCSE: Implementing and Supporting Microsoft Proxy Server 2.0
  Ryvkin, Hoffman

- MCSE: Implementing and Supporting Microsoft SNA Server 4.0
  Mariscal

- MCSE: Implementing and Supporting Microsoft Internet Information Server 4
  Dell

- MCSE: Implementing and Supporting Web Sites Using Microsoft Site Server 3
  Goncalves

- MCSE: Microsoft System Management Server 2
  Jewett

- MCSE: Implementing and Supporting Internet Explorer 5
  Dell

- Core MCSD: Designing and Implementing Desktop Applications with Microsoft Visual Basic 6
  Holzner

- Core MCSD: Designing and Implementing Distributed Applications with Microsoft Visual Basic 6
  Houlette, Klander

- MCSD: Planning and Implementing SQL Server 7
  Vacca

- MCSD: Designing and Implementing Web Sites with Microsoft FrontPage 98
  Karlins

Library of Congress Cataloging-in-Publication Data
Kobielus, James G.
  BizTalk: implementing business-to-business electronic commerce/James G. Kobielus
    p. cm.
  Includes index.
  ISBN 0-13-089159-2
  1. Microsoft BizTalk.   2. Electronic commerce.   I. Title.
  HF5548.32.K63 2000
  658.8'4—dc21   00-060695

Editorial/Production Supervision: *Kerry Reardon*
Acquisitions Editor: *Jill Pisoni*
Project Coordinator: *Anne Trowbridge*
Cover Design Director: *Jerry Votta*
Cover Designer: *Nina Scuderi*
Manufacturing Manager: *Alexis R. Heydt*
Manufacturing Buyer: *Maura Zaldivar*
Series Design: *Gail Cocker-Bogusz*
Marketing Manager: *Bryan Gambrel*
Art Director: *Gail Cocker-Bogusz*

 © 2001 by Prentice Hall PTR
Prentice-Hall, Inc.
Upper Saddle River, New Jersey 07458

Prentice Hall books are widely used by corporations and government agencies for
training, marketing, and resale. The publisher offers discounts on this book when
ordered in bulk quantities. For more information, contact:

  Corporate Sales Department,
  Prentice Hall PTR
  One Lake Street
  Upper Saddle River, NJ 07458
  Phone: 800-382-3419; FAX: 201-236-7141
  E-mail (Internet): corpsales@prenhall.com

Printed in the United States of America

10   9   8   7   6   5   4   3   2   1

ISBN 0-13-089159-2

Prentice-Hall International (UK) Limited, *London*
Prentice-Hall of Australia Pty. Limited, *Sydney*
Prentice-Hall Canada Inc., *Toronto*
Prentice-Hall Hispanoamericana, S.A., *Mexico*
Prentice-Hall of India Private Limited, *New Delhi*
Prentice-Hall of Japan, Inc., *Tokyo*
Pearson Education Asia, Pte. Ltd.
Editora Prentice-Hall do Brasil, Ltda., *Rio de Janeiro*

DEDICATION

To my wife Egidia,
who helped me block out time for this project,
and my children, Jason and Sonya,
who read much of this technology stuff
standing over my shoulder
and will someday
understand
more than me

TALK OF BILLIONS
We are
both of us
sitting in the same chair
six thousand miles
apart.

We are
six billion
sitting in one
and the same room.

We talk at the same time,
sip from the same drink,
and watch the same screen
materialize.

James Kobielus

CONTENTS

What Makes an Electronic Marketplace Tick?

We live in the most dynamic, productive, and innovative society the world has ever known.

Today's economy pulses with electronic vibrancy. We have created an engine of nonstop wealth generation, drawing power from the flow of cheap, easy, instantaneous transactions on the World Wide Web. In the few short years since we first commercialized the Web, this new mass medium has become a familiar presence in offices and households worldwide. Millions of us are venturing out onto the Web to browse for goods and services. The thought of transmitting our credit card numbers to a merchant's distant server no longer seems so scary. Buying online has become so commonplace that we hardly think twice anymore. E-commerce is simply how we shop and work in this new millennium.

Electronic marketplaces are the backbone of our new economy. We are all familiar with business-to-consumer (B2C) e-marketplaces, in the form of mass-market portals, online retailers, auction sites, and the like. Just as important are business-to-business (B2B) e-marketplaces, which build upon companies' long experience with electronic data interchange (EDI) and provide various Internet-based commerce services tailored to the needs of particular industries. Trading partners may establish B2B connections through online intermediaries, often called commerce "hubs" or "exchanges," or through secure "extranets" implemented between their respective internal networks. However implemented, these are environments where dozens, thousands, or millions of buyers and sellers can meet to transact business.

E-marketplaces rely, of course, on networks, software, and the technical wizardry that keeps it all operating around the clock, day in and day out, across all trading partners. But what makes B2B e-marketplaces really tick, down deep, are agreements on the ground rules for transactions among trading partners. This is where B2B trading environments build on traditional EDI, with its emphasis on secure, guaranteed, electronic delivery of standardized business documents. This is also where Microsoft's BizTalk initiative fits into the world of B2B e-commerce.

The beauty of BizTalk is in the simplicity of the concept and the richness of its potential B2B applications. At its core, BizTalk defines a standard electronic message "envelope" for routing e-commerce transactions between companies. You can transmit this BizTalk message over standard e-mail systems, over the Web, and over other underlying network "protocols." You can process this BizTalk message over any operating environment, using programs developed in any computer language, without the need for sending and receiving applications to be online at the same time or otherwise in direct communication.

BizTalk is several things. It is a Microsoft-championed strategic e-commerce initiative. It is a Microsoft-dominated e-commerce industry consortium, repository, and clearinghouse. It is a set of Microsoft-developed e-commerce interoperability specifications. It is a set of Microsoft and third-party products and services that implement these interoperability specifications. And it is a core infrastructure for the Microsoft .NET initiative.

Fundamentally, BizTalk supports development of ever more sophisticated "marketectures" for industry segments and the economy as a whole. You can build new e-commerce services by developing new business rules to manage the routing and processing of BizTalk messages and their precious cargo: structured business documents. Change the business rules for handling BizTalk messages and you change the ground rules of the e-marketplace. Change the business rules on your extranet and you reengineer the supply chain.

The details of Microsoft's multifaceted BizTalk initiative are the substance of this book. Microsoft has defined an ambitious roadmap for its own products and services that implement the BizTalk "framework." However, BizTalk is not just limited to Microsoft's offerings. Indeed, BizTalk will have failed as an industry initiative if Microsoft doesn't enlist a broad range of other software vendors and service providers to implement its technical framework.

BizTalk: Implementing Business-to-Business E-Commerce is a business book that will help you think through a host of management and technical issues before investing precious corporate resources on BizTalk-enabled products and services. We have developed this book primarily to serve two groups of professionals:

- *Nontechnical management:* business professionals who have a basic understanding of computer and telecommunications concepts and are responsible for B2B e-commerce projects

- *Technical management:* information systems and telecommunications professionals who have a basic understanding of management issues and are responsible for B2B e-commerce infrastructure planning, deployment, and operations within their organizations

We provide a detailed technical discussion of Microsoft's BizTalk Server 2000 product and how it integrates with Windows 2000, Commerce

Server 2000, SQL Server 2000, Host Integration Server 2000, Visual Studio, and other Microsoft products, services, and technologies. We show you how BizTalk Server 2000 might figure into the architectures of hubbed e-marketplaces, extranets, and intranets. And we discuss how BizTalk figures into Microsoft's business plans and into those of some of Microsoft's strategic partners.

We have organized the book into four principal parts, each of which consists of several chapters.

Part One discusses BizTalk fundamentals. What is BizTalk? What value does BizTalk contribute to e-commerce? Who developed, manages, and oversees the BizTalk initiative's many facets? How does BizTalk differ from other e-commerce initiatives? Which vendors are implementing and supporting BizTalk? What are the basic standards and technologies behind BizTalk? How mature are BizTalk-compliant products and services? How open is the BizTalk Framework?

Part Two provides a comprehensive overview of BizTalk applications in B2B e-commerce. Most of the discussion addresses potential applications, since Microsoft had not yet released the commercial BizTalk Server 2000 product at the time this book was written. We describe three integration scenarios into which enterprises and service providers will deploy BizTalk Server 2000:

* *Hubbed marketplace integration*: integrating your internal business processes indirectly, via external trading hubs and exchanges, with trading partners (TPs)

* *Extranet supply-chain integration*: integrating your internal business processes directly, via extranets, with trading partners

* *Enterprise application integration*: integrating your internal "back-end" business applications with your e-commerce site

Part Three discusses commercial BizTalk-enabled products and services that have been announced for availability in 2000. We examine on Microsoft's two-pronged strategy for rolling out BizTalk-enabled offerings: as server-based software products and as portal-based e-commerce services. We provide an in-depth discussion of Microsoft's BizTalk Server 2000 product and its integration with Windows 2000, Windows DNA 2000 application servers, and other Microsoft products and services.

Part Four discusses the various technologies, standards, and products that support a full deployment of BizTalk Server 2000 in a corporate or service provider network. In particular, we discuss the following BizTalk-related topics:

* *Operating environment*: How does BizTalk Server 2000 integrate with Microsoft Windows 2000?

* *Markup technologies*: How does BizTalk Server 2000 parse, produce, and process messages and documents encoded in the industry-standard Extensible Markup Language (XML)?

- *Document mapping and transformation technologies*: How does BizTalk Server 2000 use the industry-standard Extensible Stylesheet Language Transformations (XSLT) specification to map and transform XML-encoded messages and documents?

- *Schema definition technologies*: How does BizTalk Server 2000 make use of the industry standard XML Namespaces and XML Schemas specifications, and Microsoft's own XML Data Reduced specification, in validating XML-encoded messages and documents?

- *Database technologies*: How does BizTalk Server 2000 integrate with Microsoft SQL Server?

- *Directory technologies*: How does BizTalk Server 2000 integrate with Windows 2000's Active Directory and with third-party directories via the industry standard Lightweight Directory Access Protocol (LDAP).

- *Security technologies*: How does BizTalk Server 2000 integrate with Windows 2000's public key infrastructure (PKI) features?

- *Object technologies*: How does BizTalk Server 2000 integrate with Microsoft's Component Object Model (COM), Distributed COM (DCOM), and COM+ object technologies and work with the Microsoft-developed Simple Object Access Protocol (SOAP)?

- *Message-brokering technologies*: How does BizTalk Server 2000 integrate with Microsoft Message Queue Server (MSMQ) and other message-brokering technologies, including IBM's MQSeries?

- *Transaction technologies*: How does BizTalk Server 2000 integrate with Microsoft Transaction Server (MTS).

- *Application development technologies*: How does BizTalk Server 2000 integrate with Microsoft's Visual Studio development tools?

- *System management technologies*: How does BizTalk Server 2000 integrate with Microsoft Management Console?

We also provide a comprehensive glossary of technical terms that appear in the book. You will find this book an invaluable resource in high-visibility e-commerce integration projects over the coming years. BizTalk-compliant products and services will become widespread in B2B projects in the near future, riding on the coattails of the popular Windows 2000 operating environment.

The bottom line is that if your boss doesn't ask you to get up to speed on BizTalk, before long your trading partners almost certainly will.

Okay, you've taken a critical step. You've got this book in your hands. Now what's your next move?

With all the hyperbole and nonsense flying around the topic of e-business and Web marketplaces, you're really going to need the insights, ideas, and directions this invaluable book provides.

This is not some glib exhortation to "E!" your business.

The world has plenty of pundits chanting the "E-everything!" mantra. Those sparkling Masters of the Obvious—denizens of the rubber chicken and resort conference scene—aren't telling you anything new. You already know just how big the e-business opportunity is and you're already feeling enough pressure to retool your workflow, and sales and supply processes, right?

Besides, it's only a matter of time before these digital heralds move on to the naysaying phase of business-to-business (B2B). They overdid it on business-to-consumer (B2C) e-commerce and now they're gnawing on the corpses of those B2C pioneers who dropped by the wayside, providing hindsight-enriched "analysis" of why the plans unraveled.

What James Kobielus has done is far more ambitious and far more practical.

In this book, you'll find a comprehensive exploration of what's involved in really Web-enabling your business, from back-end information technology (IT) to the electronic marketplaces where business partners exchange information, products and services. Whether you are a business manager or an IT professional, this book will guide you to a clearer understanding of the real scope of the e-business opportunity and just what has to be done to take advantage of market shifts facing your industry and every other sector of the economy.

Through the prism of Microsoft's BizTalk initiative, Kobielus shows you how e-business and e-marketplaces will evolve, and what you and your key suppliers need to do to achieve success. This is part textbook, part roadmap and part crystal ball—all mixed skillfully, thanks to Kobielus' eye for detail and his clear, direct prose.

Kobielus is a long-time columnist for my publication, Network World, and our readers have benefited from his knowledge and insight. Some columnists make you laugh, some pound a political drum, some take the human interest angle. But my favorite columnists are the ones who make you think.

Like Kobielus.

Jim helps you look at the world in a new way and he helps you formulate a clearer vision of where the industry is going. That's a pretty tall order in this rapidly changing, Internet-supercharged world.

Whether you come at this from a business or technology angle, preparing for the e-marketplace of the future is the biggest challenge you face today. Be glad you have someone like Kobielus to help you face that challenge.

Hold on tight and turn the page.

John Gallant
Editorial Director
Network World

James Kobielus is an analyst for The Burton Group, focusing on e-business and collaboration technologies. He is a recognized authority on strategic telecommunications and information systems topics. He has been a contributing editor with Network World since 1987 and writes its popular "Above the Cloud" column. He authored the 1997 IDG Books title, *Workflow Strategies*.

Kobielus lives in Alexandria, Virginia with his wife, Egidia, and children, Jason and Sonya.

PART ONE

BIZTALK FUNDAMENTALS

Part One discusses BizTalk fundamentals. What is BizTalk? What value does BizTalk contribute to e-commerce? Who developed, manages, and oversees the BizTalk initiative's many facets? How does BizTalk differ from other e-commerce initiatives? Which vendors are implementing and supporting BizTalk? What are the basic standards and technologies behind BizTalk? How mature are BizTalk-compliant products and services? How open is the BizTalk Framework?

What Is BizTalk?

BizTalk defines an environment for interorganizational workflows in support of electronic commerce and supply-chain integration.

At its most basic level, BizTalk—understood as a framework of interoperability specifications—is not much different from traditional EDI, which is just intercompany workflow by another name. Workflow refers to the flow of information and control in a business process. When a business process crosses corporate boundaries, the corresponding workflow does as well. A B2B workflow usually involves transmission of several standard business documents in a predetermined sequence between various functional groups within participating companies.

B2B workflows can spell the difference between the success or failure of an enterprise or industry. Increasingly, companies are establishing extranets that link them to customers, distributors, suppliers, and other trading partners. Sustainable competitive advantage lies in an organization's ability to use information technologies to respond rapidly to new challenges by modifying internal workflows and external links to trading partners. We've entered an era in which companies must escalate business process reengineering to the B2B level in order to survive. The extranet and the e-marketplace are the platforms for meaningful industry-wide reengineering.

1.1 BizTalk, EDI, and Workflow

As with traditional B2B EDI, BizTalk applications support information flows between companies engaged in routine online transactions, such as purchasing, inventory control, and logistical coordination. The flow of control in such transactions follows the procedures that allow one company to interface its internal processes to those of its trading partners, including customers, contractors, distributors, and suppliers. These procedures, in turn, follow business rules codified in the trading partners' various business contracts, operating agreements, and internal policies. And these business rules come to life in the programming code upon which the trading partners build their e-commerce and supply-chain applications.

Figure 1-1 shows the usual flow of point-to-point B2B EDI connections, in which corporations map data to and from a common format for transmission between their otherwise incompatible back-end applications. Notice that traditional EDI applications often use traditional X.25 or frame-relay value-added networks (VANs), rather than the Internet or Internet Protocol (IP)–based extranets.

BizTalk doesn't replace traditional B2B EDI so much as supplement it and take it to a new level of openness, flexibility, and Internet orientation. The BizTalk Framework uses the EDI and workflow feature set of Microsoft's existing Site Server Commerce Edition as a baseline. The BizTalk Framework defines a standardized electronic envelope for routing and handling structured and unstructured business documents. Each BizTalk message may contain two or more linked business documents to be processed as a unit. A BizTalk-enabled B2B workflow, in turn, may involve one or more BizTalk messages transmitted as e-mail attachments, riding on the Internet's ubiquitous Simple Mail Transfer Protocol (SMTP). However, BizTalk-enabled transactions could just as easily ride over the Web's HyperText Transfer Protocol (HTTP), File Transfer Protocol (FTP), or any other network "transport" protocol. Each transport protocol that carries a BizTalk message wraps it a second time within an envelope appropriate to that transport. Consequently, a BizTalk-enabled workflow or transaction can run over several transports.

Figure 1-1   *A typical end-to-end EDI application involves one trading partner mapping and translating from its proprietary data format to an EDI standard format, such as ANSI X12 or EDIFACT transaction sets, and transmitting the transaction sets over EDI VANs to the recipient, who translates and maps the information back into its own proprietary data format.*

The essence of BizTalk—what makes it a powerful alternative to "EDI as usual"—is what's in the header of a BizTalk message envelope. The BizTalk message's header includes some simple fields that allow applications to specify how a particular business document, contained in the message, fits into a broader workflow (or, in Microsoft's term, into an "orchestration"). The header also allows the message to specify how the document is to be processed when it reaches its destination. As such, a BizTalk message can describe that message's precise role within an ongoing business transaction.

One might say that a BizTalk message makes the workflow of which it's a part "self-describing." We will discuss the precise syntax and structure of a BizTalk message, and the real-world limits of what it means to define a "self-describing" workflow, in greater detail later in this chapter.

Traditional EDI, by contrast, has never had anything resembling "self-describing" workflows. Rather, EDI has always focused on exchanging just the content of a transaction, encoded in standardized "transaction sets." There is rarely any "process state information" contained in EDI transaction sets that specifies where a particular document fits into a precise routing and processing sequence. All the state information in traditional EDI resides in the business applications that generate and receive the transaction sets.

One reason for this is that EDI has historically been a point-to-point solution, requiring any two companies to spend a great deal of time and money to establish specific connections and processes that apply to them and only them. Within each of the trading partners' networks and systems, the transaction sets usually follow a rigid chain of routing and processing steps involving one or more databases. Often, these internal processes are totally hidden from direct tracking by EDI trading partners.

EDI will not mature until it becomes part of a much broader, more general-purpose e-commerce infrastructure that applies to all companies, not just two big companies that can afford to build specific connections for a specific application. In such an environment, companies will be able to view each other's B2B workflow "process models" in a standardized format and merge, concatenate, and otherwise interface internal business processes to establish a new trading partner relationship. BizTalk will be a fundamental technology for establishing just such a general-purpose e-commerce infrastructure.

BizTalk will also be a catalyst for transforming traditional EDI into a full-fledged workflow management environment. A workflow management system is one that supports structured routing and tracking of documents and other information throughout a business process. For EDI to count as a true workflow management environment, it must support intercompany processes that specify the precise routing and processing sequence that a transaction follows. This would allow each company to track (and possibly control) a transaction path into and through its trading partners' systems.

Furthermore, BizTalk will be a catalyst for transforming traditional workflow systems into e-commerce environments. BizTalk's routing envelope addresses a gap in the workflow market that has heretofore stymied implementation of robust interorganizational workflow. There are no widely implemented standards in the workflow management market. As a result, workflow management tools have been applied primarily to intra-organizational business process reengineering, within intranets that revolve around a single vendor's proprietary workflow product.

Clearly, a single-vendor workflow solution is not a viable option for B2B EDI. You are not very likely to impose a single monolithic workflow solution on all your trading partners.

1.2 Microsoft as BizTalk Evangelist

The only reason why Microsoft stands any chance at success in defining a universal B2B workflow standard is because it's Microsoft. At this juncture in the evolution of distributed computing, only one vendor has the vision, clout, and determination to spearhead such an ambitious program.

Microsoft has become the mothership of modern distributed computing, covering most important enterprise software bases with market-leading or best-of-breed products. It has crafted a compelling Windows-centric marketecture that draws greater numbers of programmers, independent software vendors (ISVs), and integrators into its sphere of influence. And its business fundamentals put Microsoft in good stead for continued success. Sure, the regulators and politicians can put a crimp in Microsoft's story, but it is very likely to evolve its way out from any restrictions they impose.

The BizTalk initiative is yet another example of Microsoft taking a leadership role in an industry that delights at thumbing its nose at leaders. And Microsoft has subjected itself to considerable criticism in its efforts to catalyze the industry around this initiative and thereby strengthen its effective hegemony in the computing industry. Of course, Microsoft is not operating from altruistic motives in this endeavor.

To understand Microsoft's motives surrounding BizTalk, we should examine the genesis and scope of the initiative and identify how it fits into Microsoft's business strategies in the business software and application service provider markets.

1.3 BizTalk as Microsoft Strategic E-Commerce Initiative

Microsoft Chairman Bill Gates announced the BizTalk initiative on March 4, 1999, committing the company to a very broad, ambitious program. The BizTalk initiative is a sprawling vision of interoperable e-commerce environments based on new products, services, standards, and industry alliances.

The BizTalk announcement was the sort of bold Bill Gates gesture that grabs plenty of media attention and raises the hackles of Microsoft's competitors, not to mention the legal and regulatory establishment.

However, the BizTalk announcement was full of substance, far from the empty marketing-oriented initiatives that high-tech vendors (Microsoft included) often parade before a hungry press corps. From the start, Microsoft has defined the BizTalk initiative as consisting of three closely related, ongoing development efforts:

* E-commerce interoperability standards
* E-commerce industry coalition, schema repository, and developer community, and
* E-commerce products and services

Before we discuss each of these efforts in detail, we should explain how Microsoft is selling the BizTalk initiative to the industry at large and to its own employees and business partners. Microsoft has taken two approaches in explaining and justifying the BizTalk initiative to the industry at large: BizTalk the e-commerce brand and BizTalk the e-commerce philosophy.

1.3.1 BizTalk the Brand: Microsoft as Usual

First and foremost, the company has positioned BizTalk as its brand for e-commerce infrastructure products and services.

This is the familiar Microsoft posture: the sharp, aggressive player who stakes an early claim in a new market, thereby galvanizing its forces and striking fear into the hearts of competitors. Gates left no doubt that his company would place a top priority on rolling out BizTalk products and services in short order. Microsoft's multibillionaire cofounder also announced that the BizTalk initiative is an umbrella for development of other new products, such as Commerce Server and Small Business Commerce Services, as well as relevant feature enhancements for existing products such as SQL Server and Visual Studio. We will discuss Microsoft's specific plans for these products in Part Four of this book.

What's most significant about the BizTalk initiative, as regards Microsoft's strategic business directions, is that it positions the company to negotiate an industry paradigm shift now in full swing. Microsoft is attempting to extend the BizTalk brand across both of its principal business models—independent software vendor and application service provider (ASP)—and in the process integrate them into a powerful new business paradigm.

On the ISV side, BizTalk Server will ride on the considerable coattails of the Windows 2000 network operating system and Microsoft Server suite (formerly known as the "BackOffice" suite). On the ASP side, BizTalk Server will provide the e-commerce workflow engine for Microsoft's MSN family of portal-based B2B and B2C services. BizTalk software will be the building block for BizTalk-enabled e-marketplaces operated by Microsoft and strategic partners. Microsoft is positioned either to go on making most of its money from software licenses, or shift to collecting transaction fees from portal services if the much-anticipated sea change—toward software as a subscription service—washes away its old business model.

The synergies between the two business models don't stop there. One of the dominant themes of the BizTalk initiative is Microsoft's attempt to blur the boundaries between licensed software packages and subscription services. As Gates explained it, Microsoft's goal is to reduce "barriers to entry" that keep small and mid-sized customers from selling their products and services on the Web. The BizTalk initiative would support this goal by providing software tools that allow enterprise customers to easily configure an e-commerce site, integrate the site with internal applications and databases, and automatically register and advertise the site on a network-based e-marketplace service. The enterprise may even replicate its e-commerce catalog to an MSN-based hosting site, further blurring the boundary between BizTalk products and services.

Even more functional blurring could occur in cases where two or more trading partners deploy Microsoft's BizTalk Server and use its MSN e-commerce services. This environment could conceivably allow trading partners to offload some authentication, routing, translation, data storage, advertising management, payment processing, billing, and other functions to MSN when this arrangement promises greater reliability, performance, or cost-effectiveness.

In this way, Microsoft is using BizTalk and its online service to position itself as an important middleman for e-commerce transactions in the 21st century. The vendor is providing what could turn out to be the dominant e-commerce server suite—including the BizTalk Server, Commerce Server, and other Microsoft servers—for this new age. It already provides the dominant "thin client," the Internet Explorer browser, for accessing BizTalk-enabled e-commerce services.

So, once again, Microsoft is building a powerful new brand to help it evolve and thrive in a new era of distributed computing, an era in which electronic marketplaces will penetrate business processes to their very cores. BizTalk is a new page in Bill Gates's strategy of "Microsoft everywhere."

1.3.2 BizTalk the Philosophy: A New Microsoft?

Microsoft also presents BizTalk as a new philosophy for implementing multi-vendor e-commerce infrastructures.

This is unfamiliar territory for Microsoft, the company that has pressed a "Windows everywhere" party line for years. The BizTalk philosophy, by contrast, calls for an e-commerce environment that, on the surface, seems to depend on no one operating system. According to the philosophy, a BizTalk e-commerce infrastructure is multiplatform, relies on open Internet standards, and integrates applications through loosely coupled message-passing protocols.

The core of Microsoft's BizTalk philosophy is encapsulated in the slogan "no glue," which speaks more to a technical crowd than a general business audience. As expressed in a Microsoft white paper on the topic, the concept of "glue" permeates traditional attempts to bridge incompatible systems and applications. The paper defines glue as a paradigm for application integration that involves all of the following:

- Deployment of best-of-breed applications that are often incompatible in terms of their ability to share data and interface process logic
- Definition of an ad-hoc information model or schema common to the incompatible applications
- Use of a specific transport protocol for interfacing application components to each other across a network or across the bus in a particular machine
- Implementation of an intermediate layer of software adapters, either on the same or different machine as the communicating applications, for exposing the functionality of otherwise incompatible systems, translating objects and data shared by the systems, managing transfer of objects and data between the systems over appropriate protocols, and enforcing appropriate business rules in interactions between the systems

One advantage of the glue approach is that it allows companies to avoid rewriting existing applications in order to get them to work together. As a result, you can eliminate the delay, cost, and trouble of rewriting one or more applications. Instead, you implement an adapter layer—usually a communication gateway or format translation program—that adapts the outputs of one application to the inputs of the other, and vice versa. You might also use an object protocol—such as Common Object Request Broker Architecture (CORBA)—to allow dispersed applications to behave as if they were running on the same machine under the same operating system.

Another advantage of the glue approach is that it gives companies the flexibility to acquire best-of-breed software packages that run on different platforms or operating environments. So long as you can acquire or develop a software glue layer to interface best-of-breed applications, you can make incompatible environments play together to some extent. You don't necessarily need to run all applications under a single operating environment, such as Microsoft Windows 2000 or Sun Solaris, to get them to interoperate.

The great disadvantage of the glue approach is the maintenance burden on programmers and corresponding cost burden on companies that employ them. We can define the glue approach's maintenance burden through the following statements, which form a sort of "devil's syllogism" for software developers:

- The greater the range of applications to be integrated, the greater the need for upfront systems analysis and planning at a global level.
- The greater the range of applications to be integrated, the more system analyst hours needed to plan and oversee this integration.
- The greater the range of applications to be integrated, the broader the range of programming conventions, binary data types, security contexts, and methods that will be needed to be bridged among them.
- The greater the range of applications and programming conventions to be integrated, the more complex the range of potential interactions among them.
- The more complex the interactions, the more intricate and convoluted the glue code needs to be and the more often this code will have bugs and glitches.
- The more rapidly the various applications change, the more often the glue code needs to be modified.
- The more intricate the glue code is, the more often it has bugs and glitches, and the more often it needs to be modified, the more often it needs to be tested.
- The more often the glue code needs to be modified and tested, the more programmer hours needed to do this work.
- The more often the glue code has bugs and glitches, the more programmer-hours needed to diagnose, troubleshoot, and fix it.
- The broader the range of applications that this glue code interfaces, the broader the skill sets of analysts and programmers who work on this glue code, hence the more expensive the technical talent needed to keep it all running.

Microsoft rightly notes that the traditional glue approach will not scale up to this new age of universal e-commerce, which will require heretofore unheard of levels of end-to-end application integration across diverse companies and technical environments. The way out of the devil's syllogism of the glue paradigm, according to the BizTalk philosophy, is to implement more "loosely coupled" integration among communicating applications.

Under the BizTalk "no glue" paradigm, applications don't need to be aware of each other's calling conventions, such as programming parameters to be passed and data types and formats to be returned. Instead, you establish a universal communication infrastructure and interchange format that manages the flows of information between applications. This universal infrastructure and format will eliminate application dependencies on the locations of various software components, on the protocols that bridge these components, and on the object models and programming constructs that bind them into an integrated application service. As applications interface to a universal infrastructure and generate and consume the universal format, the less need there will be for intermediate glue code to help them interoperate.

One technical basis upon which Microsoft grounds the BizTalk philosophy is a fairly recent standard called the Extensible Markup Language (XML), which was ratified by the World Wide Web Consortium (W3C) in February 1998. Another technical linchpin for BizTalk is an older technology known alternately as message-oriented middleware (MOM) or message brokering. We will discuss XML and MOM and other BizTalk-enabling technologies in greater detail in Part Four of this book.

Let's focus on XML, since this is the core technology behind the BizTalk framework. Essentially, XML provides a flexible language for defining content that carries its own application context. A "self-describing" XML document, object, or message can contain all the content and context that two dissimilar systems or applications need to ensure interoperability. Communicating applications need not share a common object model, network protocol, operating system, database, or programming language as long as they can exchange and interpret messages formatted in XML. Senders and recipients of XML documents are free to process them as they wish, without being tightly coupled to each other.

That's XML's promise, and it's well on the way to fulfilling that promise, judging by the impressive range of vendors who are implementing it and vertical markets that have based their interoperability standards on it. Microsoft is certainly not the only software vendor singing the praises of XML these days. However, Microsoft's embrace of XML as the basis for its BizTalk framework has occasioned some industry cynicism about the company's motives. Some observers suspect that Microsoft has defined the BizTalk Framework in such a way as to build hidden "hooks" that constrain users to implementing these specifications exclusively over Windows environments. There are legitimate grounds for such cynicism, but the real story is not pure black and white. Shortly, we will discuss limitations and catches in the current version, 2.0, of the BizTalk Framework Independent Document Specification. Later in Part I of this book we will take up the broader issue of whether Microsoft's BizTalk initiative and framework are truly "open."

Microsoft says it has gotten religion on the issue of open standards, and offers the BizTalk Framework as testament to its newfound faith. The company says it based the BizTalk Framework on two guiding principles: Use standards wherever possible and make the process of defining the interoperability specifications as open as possible. The BizTalk Framework consists of the following components:

- Technical specification that defines mandatory and optional XML tags for a BizTalk "message envelope"
- Online repository (www.biztalk.org) containing vertical-market XML "schemas" for the e-commerce documents to be transmitted in the standard BizTalk message envelope

Microsoft claims that the BizTalk framework realizes the no glue philosophy in three ways, to be discussed shortly. However, the company has left the framework littered with caveats that could easily be interpreted as defining the need for a new generation of glue under the guise of XML-oriented middleware.

First, Microsoft states that BizTalk eliminates the need for applications to agree on a particular transport protocol in order to exchange BizTalk message envelopes, since the framework is protocol independent. Nevertheless, Microsoft strongly encourages the use of message-oriented middleware protocols, such as its own Microsoft Message Queue (MSMQ) protocol.

Second, Microsoft claims that BizTalk doesn't require applications to agree on or be aware of each other's calling conventions in order to exchange BizTalk message envelopes and process them successfully. However, the company has left undefined several state variables that require some knowledge of platform-specific application contexts, such as those under its Windows 2000 operating system (OS).

Third, Microsoft claims that BizTalk eliminates the need for special-purpose adapter software layers to support object and data mapping and interchange among multiple applications. However, the BizTalk Framework strongly suggests the need for a general-purpose e-commerce adapter layer such as that provided by its BizTalk Server product.

We won't argue the metaphysical and ultimately futile issue of what constitutes the complete absence of glue in a distributed application environment. However, one important point to remember is that Microsoft is overstating its case when it asserts that "BizTalk applications are essentially blind"—in other words, that they need no foreknowledge of the configuration or state of other applications in order to exchange and process BizTalk-wrapped e-commerce documents effectively. We've shown that the BizTalk envelope specification leaves large loopholes for platform-specific end-to-end implementations.

1.4 BizTalk as E-Commerce Interoperability Standards

In spite of its Microsoft-leaning bias, BizTalk Framework is a solid framework for developing interorganizational workflow applications.

As we've already discussed, BizTalk provides a standardized electronic envelope for routing and handling structured and unstructured business documents. To understand how this envelope fits into a broader e-commerce application environment, we need to understand BizTalk Framework 2.0, which Microsoft published in June 2000. This specification addresses fundamental BizTalk concepts: application model, schemas, documents, messages, workflows, and event model. The following discussion goes into detail on each of these topics.

1.4.1 BizTalk Application Model

The BizTalk application model includes three logical "layers": the application layer, the BizTalk server layer, and data communications services layer. (Note that the BizTalk specification uses the lowercase "s" to denote the "BizTalk server" logical layer and distinguish it from Microsoft's BizTalk Server 2000 product, which sports the uppercase "S.") These layers support transmission, processing, and receipt of BizTalk Messages, which we'll describe in greater detail in Section 1.4.4. Figure 1-2 depicts the layers graphically.

In a BizTalk environment, line-of-business applications communicate amongst themselves by exchanging documents through one or more intermediate BizTalk servers. Documents are encapsulated in electronic message envelopes defined under the Simple Object Access Protocol (SOAP) version 1.1 (which we'll discuss in greater detail in Chapter 14). Applications and BizTalk servers exchange SOAP-enveloped BizTalk documents over various data communications services or protocols, such as HTTP, FTP, or a message-brokering protocol such as MSMQ.

Under the BizTalk application model, an application is any system that fits all three of the following criteria. First, it stores and executes line-of-business data or processing logic. Second, it can generate and/or consume XML-formatted Business Documents, which we'll describe in greater detail in Section 1.4.3. Third, it can communicate with a BizTalk server via a data communications service or protocol. The application may use an adapter glue layer to process XML and communicate with BizTalk servers. The application may support XML as one of its native file formats, or interface with adapter software that converts between XML and one or more of the application's native file formats.

The line-of-business application, or its BizTalk adapter, generates XML-formatted Business Documents, according to the appropriate, application-

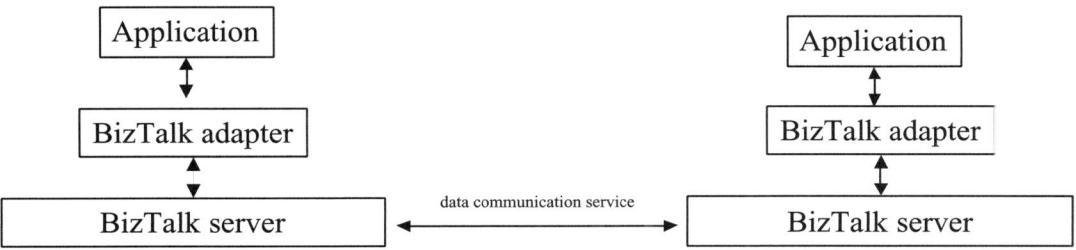

Figure 1-2   *The BizTalk Application Model involves three logical software layers on sending and receiving nodes: an application, a BizTalk adapter, and a BizTalk server.*

specific XML schema defined outside the BizTalk Framework. The application adapter then wraps Business Documents, and any associated binary file "attachments," with the XML "BizTags," both header and trailer, that define a "BizTalk Document," per BizTalk schema defined in the BizTalk Framework. (We'll discuss BizTalk Documents in greater detail in Section 1.4.3 and BizTalk Schemas in Section 1.4.2.) Then the application submits the BizTalk Document to an originating BizTalk server.

BizTags provide BizTalk servers with document handling and routing information, acting as an "envelope" for the business information to be transmitted. They are the set of XML tags (both mandatory and optional) that are used to specify the handling of a Business Document, which is contained in a BizTalk Document, which is in turn contained in a BizTalk Message. The BizTags are added as an XML envelope or wrapper around a Business Document by an application or BizTalk application adapter. BizTags are processed by the BizTalk server, or by other applications facilitating the document interchange.

BizTalk servers provide various processing services to applications, including validating, mapping, translating, encoding, encrypting, signing, routing, storing, forwarding, and delivering BizTalk Messages and BizTalk Documents. Any compliant BizTalk server can process any BizTag defined under BizTalk Framework 2.0. By contrast, the tags used to mark up business information within the BizTalk Message body are determined by application-specific XML document schemas. Application-specific document tags within a Business Document are not BizTags and are generally not processed directly by the BizTalk server.

An originating BizTalk server receives a BizTalk Document sent by an application and then wraps this document within an electronic envelope that defines a "BizTalk Message." The envelope of a BizTalk message—in other words, the specific non-BizTag headers and trailers used to enclose a BizTalk Document—are specific to each network transport protocol, such as HTTP, FTP, or MSMQ. As of the date this book was published, Microsoft had published the BizTalk transport "binding" to HTTP, but not to any other protocol.

Table 1-1 describes the typical end-to-end flow of a BizTalk Message, consisting of five principal processing steps (also depicted graphically in Figure 1-3).

BizTalk applications differ from one another in several critical respects. First, applications may differ in the set of business rules implemented at endpoint applications as well as intermediate BizTalk servers. Second, they may differ in the contents, schemas, and formats of Business Documents and binary file attachments they exchange. Third, they may differ in the end-to-end workflow process parameters encoded in BizTags in their BizTalk Documents. Fourth, they may differ in the platform-specific processing context in which each application or server processes a particular BizTalk Message or Document.

Table 1-1	Typical End-to-End Flow of a BizTalk Message

Step	Description
1	A commerce-relevant event occurs within an application, thereby triggering business rules that spur creation of one or more Business Documents and (optional) binary file attachments.
2	The application, or its BizTalk adapter, transforms these Business Documents into a BizTalk Document by wrapping them with BizTags defined in the BizTalk schema (per specifications at www.biztalk.org) and XML tags defined in application-specific schemas (per specifications defined at other industry schema-repository sites such as www.xml.org).
3	The originating application transmits the BizTalk Document to the originating BizTalk server.
4	The originating BizTalk server creates a BizTalk Message by wrapping transport-specific envelope information around one or more Business Documents. The originating server uses addressing information contained in BizTags to determine the correct transport-specific destination address or addresses. The originating server then transmits the BizTalk Message to the destination BizTalk server over the appropriate transport protocol.
5	The destination BizTalk server validates the BizTalk Message, extracts the BizTalk Document contained within, validates it, and routes it to destination applications. Destination applications extract the Business Documents and optional binary file attachments contained in BizTalk Documents. Applications then process these documents and attachments according to application-specific business rules.

Indeed, there is a broad range of implementation-specific issues that come into play when you're developing an end-to-end BizTalk application. Table 1-2 presents these implementation-specific issues.

Table 1-2	Implementation-specific Issues in Developing End-to-End BizTalk Application

ISSUE	DESCRIPTION
BizTalk server functionality	The BizTalk Framework does not specify the precise set of services to be provided by a generic BizTalk server. The scope of server functionality depends on the particular BizTalk server vendor's implementation. However, the BizTalk Framework strongly implies that these services will be provided to end-to-end applications from a homogeneous set of BizTalk servers, such as Microsoft's BizTalk Server 2000 product. We will discuss the functionality of Microsoft's BizTalk Server 2000 in greater detail in Part Three.
Physical hosting	The BizTalk Framework does not specify the physical deployment of applications and BizTalk servers. Applications and BizTalk servers usually reside on separate machines connected over local and wide-area networks. However, they may also run on the same machine and communicate via various protocols over its internal bus.

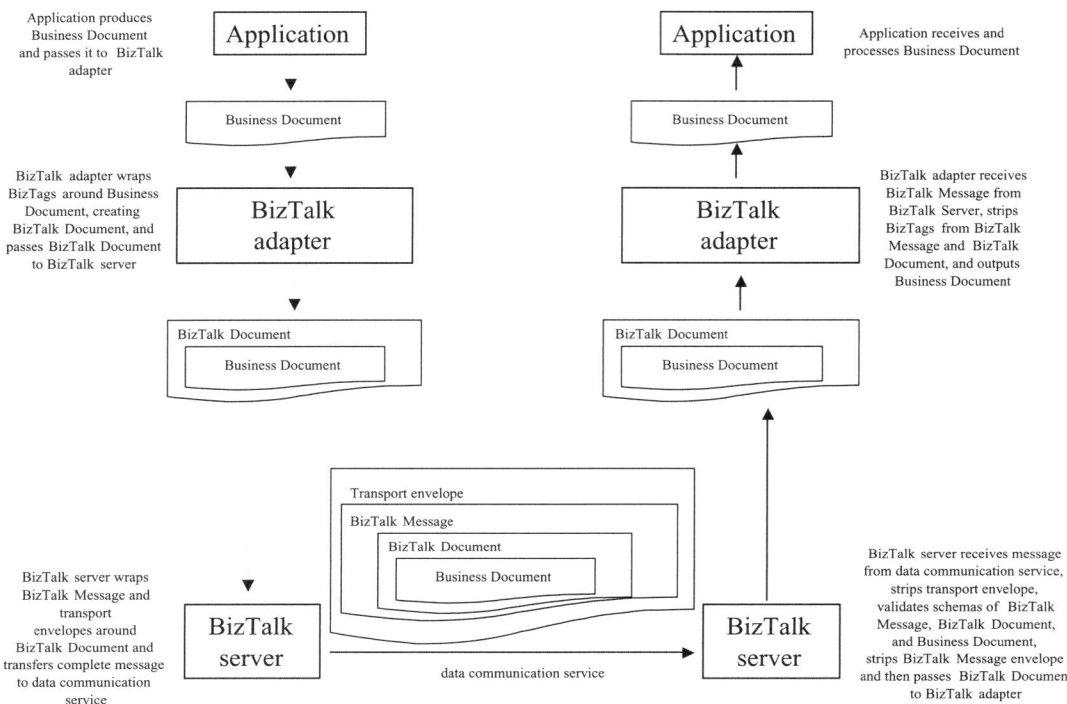

Application produces Business Document and passes it to BizTalk adapter

BizTalk adapter wraps BizTags around Business Document, creating BizTalk Document, and passes BizTalk Document to BizTalk server

BizTalk server wraps BizTalk Message and transport envelopes around BizTalk Document and transfers complete message to data communication service

Application receives and processes Business Document

BizTalk adapter receives BizTalk Message from BizTalk Server, strips BizTags from BizTalk Message and BizTalk Document, and outputs Business Document

BizTalk server receives message from data communication service, strips transport envelope, validates schemas of BizTalk Message, BizTalk Document, and Business Document, strips BizTalk Message envelope and then passes BizTalk Document to BizTalk adapter

Figure 1-3   *The typical end-to-end flow of a BizTalk Message involves transmission of documents from a business application through a BizTalk adapter software layer to a BizTalk server layer. Each layer adds additional header information into a message that gets routed over a data communication service to the recipient, whose BizTalk server and adapter layers strip the header information and deliver the "wrapped" document to recipient application.*

Table 1-2   *Implementation-specific Issues in Developing End-to-End BizTalk Application (cont.)*

ISSUE	DESCRIPTION
Transport protocols	The BizTalk Framework does not specify the communications protocols binding applications and BizTalk servers to one another. Applications and servers may use any data communications network or protocol to communicate amongst themselves.
Software interfaces	The BizTalk Framework does not specify the software interfaces among the application, BizTalk server, and data communications layers. These interfaces depend on the application programming interfaces (APIs), programming languages, and object models supported on the platforms on which these components are deployed.

Table 1-2	Implementation-specific Issues in Developing End-to-End BizTalk Application (cont.)
ISSUE	**DESCRIPTION**
Security mechanisms	The BizTalk Framework does not specify mechanisms for authentication, access control, encryption, tamperproofing, or nonrepudiation on BizTalk Messages and their contents. Security on end-to-end BizTalk transactions depends on implementation-specific agreements on these issues.
Application state information	The BizTalk Framework does not specify how applications and BizTalk servers are supposed to define and communicate state information on in-process interchanges. State information defines the context of a particular Business Document within an end-to-end e-commerce transaction. However, BizTalk Framework 2.0 provides several BizTalk Message header fields for input of implementation-specific state information. These header fields consist of type, handle, and process.
Operating environments	As noted previously, the BizTalk Framework does not specify the operating environments on which line-of-business applications, BizTalk application adapters, and BizTalk servers run. Operating environments constrain the physical-hosting, transport-protocol, software-interface, and state-information options available to BizTalk-enabled line-of-business applications. However, the framework strongly implies that BizTalk implementers will develop or optimize their applications to run on Windows 2000 and associated Microsoft server software, especially Internet Information Server (IIS), Commerce Server, Structured Query Language (SQL) Server, Microsoft Transaction Server (MTS), and MSMQ. In Part Three of this book, we will discuss the components of a full-fledged BizTalk Server deployment, in terms of the roles and integration of other Microsoft products.
Business document schemas	The BizTalk Framework does not specify the schema—or information model—implemented in the contents of Business Documents. Microsoft has deliberately and wisely chosen not to dictate the logical structure of application-specific or vertical-market documents. Instead, the BizTalk Framework defers to other industry initiatives to define the XML schemas of business documents. BizTalk Documents can contain documents defined in vertical-market initiatives, such as the RosettaNet program that has has defined XML schemas for business documents and online catalogs supporting the information-technology industry's supply chain. Similarly, the XML/EDI group is mapping existing American National Standards Institute (ANSI) X12 transaction sets to XML schemas. As we will discuss later in this chapter, Microsoft has established an industry clearinghouse at www.biztalk.org for others to post application-specific or vertical-market XML document schemas that can be encapsulated in BizTalk Documents and Messages.

Table 1-2	*Implementation-specific Issues in Developing End-to-End BizTalk Application (cont.)*

ISSUE	DESCRIPTION
Workflow process definition and execution	The BizTalk Framework does not contain specifications for defining end-to-end workflows involving BizTalk Messages. As a result, the framework does not live up to its promise of being able to encapsulate "self-describing" workflows within any given message transmitted between trading partners. The BizTalk Framework simply defines the header syntax of individual messages and the documents contained within them. These headers contain state information that hints at a BizTalk Message's role in a larger *interchange*, a term that is largely synonymous with workflow or business process. However, the headers by themselves do not specify the end-to-end sequence of processing steps through which one or more linked BizTalk Messages are to pass. If companies wish to implement interorganizational applications involving messages passed between two or more vendors' BizTalk servers, they will have to cobble together a very implementation-specific approach to defining, executing, and tracking these workflows. Note that Microsoft provides a tool and framework—the Commerce Interchange Pipeline—for defining e-commerce workflows involving a complex sequence of messages processed within a particular BizTalk server (Microsoft's own BizTalk Server 2000 product).
Event model and error messages	The BizTalk Framework does not specify the event model to be shared and error messages exchanged between BizTalk servers, BizTalk application-adapters, line-of-business applications, and data communications interfaces. The event model should include standard alerts for a server, adapter, or application's inability to validate or process a BizTalk Message, BizTalk Document, or Business Document. The error messages should be standard XML documents that can be processed by BizTalk servers and application-adapters. Until Microsoft defines the BizTalk event model and error messages, these important features will remain implement-specific (in other words, proprietary features of Microsoft's BizTalk products and services).

Clearly, BizTalk's application model, as laid out in BizTalk Framework 2.0, provides only a general development framework. It is not a specification to which independent developers can write code without first addressing a broad range of implementation-specific issues. Consequently, a BizTalk application will not be easily portable to application environments other than the one to which they were written. As we've seen, Microsoft provides just such an application environment, the centerpiece of which is its BizTalk Server 2000 product.

1.4.2 BizTalk Schemas

The term *schema* is one we've used repeatedly in the foregoing discussion but not defined fully. We need to differentiate between several uses of the term, ranging from general to specific.

The term *schema* in computer lingo generally refers to an information model of some application domain. This information model defines the logical relationships among the various entities, elements, and fields within that application domain. In directory services environments, for example, schemas refer to the information model applicable to various directory entities, as expressed through fields, attributes, and rows in the directory.

Specifically, an XML schema primarily addresses the information model instantiated in a particular XML document-type. In other words, the schema defines the relation of entities, elements, and fields within XML documents of that type. This is the primary sense in which BizTalk Framework 2.0 uses the term. An XML schema is an entity that defines the permissible elements, attributes, and values contained in an XML document-type. The entity defining the schema may be a separate, linked document or simply lines of XML code in the document that instantiates the schema. We will discuss XML schema-definition standards in greater detail in Part Four of this book.

The primary purpose of XML schemas is to help receiving applications automatically determine the prescribed logical relationship among items and thereby detect when some new item deviates from the permissible. For example, to ascertain whether an incoming item conforms to the BizTalk 2.0 document type, a BizTalk-enabled application invokes a "validating processor," which compares the document to the structure prescribed in the entity defining its schema. The BizTalk Message or Document is valid if it complies with the constraints expressed in the schema provided in BizTalk Framework 2.0.

Another way to look at XML schemas is that they provide human-readable "metadata" pertinent to a document and its elements. Metadata is simply data that comments on other data, and XML tags, which are terse and descriptive, perform this role in the context of an XML document.

The BizTalk XML schema defines the tags—BizTags—that describe the logical structure and content of a BizTalk Document, hence the core of a BizTalk Message (which includes an outer, non-XML envelope specific to the particular transport protocol over which it's being transmitted). Other XML schemas—such as those defined under such vertical-market initiatives as RosettaNet and Information and Content Exchange (ICE)—define XML tags specific to Business Documents that a BizTalk Document would contain.

Consequently, a typical BizTalk Message would reference at least one non-BizTalk schema in addition to the BizTalk schema. The destination BizTalk server and application would work together to validate these dual layers of schemas, according to the processing steps described in Table 1-3 and illustrated in the right side (receiving BizTalk server, BizTalk adapter, and application) in Figure 1-3.

Currently, the BizTalk Framework defines BizTalk document schemas in the XML Data Reduced (XDR) format. Microsoft developed XDR and submitted it as a proposal to the W3C in 1998, but it is not an industry standard nor is it on a W3C standards track. Acknowledging this fact and having committed to supporting open, ratified standards where available, Microsoft now identifies XDR solely as a transitional schema definition format for use within the BizTalk Framework. The company recognizes that the W3C's more recent XML Schema specifications are on a standards fast track and has committed to supporting them in a future version of the framework. W3C ratification of XML Schema as a formal Recommendation (i.e., a standard) is expected sometime in 2000 or early 2001.

Microsoft chose XDR over XML 1.0's native Document Type Definition (DTD) schema format due to XDR's support for more robust data typing and object-oriented functionality. The XML Schema specification draws on concepts and conventions developed in XDR and other schema definition proposals submitted to the W3C, including such proposals as Schema for Object-Oriented XML (SOX) and Document Content Description (DCD).

XDR renders document schemas through tagged XML element name-tags, rather than DTD declaration statements. XML parsers must recognize

Table 1-3	*Schema-Validation Steps in Processing of BizTalk Message*

Step	Description
One	A destination BizTalk server parses the structure of the incoming BizTalk Message's outer, non-XML-based transport envelope and validates that structure using procedures defined outside the BizTalk Framework specifications.
Two	The destination BizTalk server extracts the BizTalk Document from the BizTalk Message, parses the structure of the BizTalk Document's XML envelope, and validates that structure against the BizTalk schema.
Three	The destination BizTalk server sends the validated XML-formatted BizTalk Document to the destination application.
Four	The destination application extracts the Business Documents contained in the BizTalk Document, parses their XML structures, validates them against the relevant application-specific XML schemas, and processes the data contained in these documents according to application-specific business rules. According to the BizTalk Framework, some of these Business Documents may include non-XML data, in which case the destination application would have separate procedures for parsing, validating, and processing them.

XDR schemas in order to validate documents against them. XDR schemas include tags for declaring:

- Conceptual-graph and syntactical-tree schemas, plus rules for mapping between them
- DTD-like document constructs, such as elements, attributes, entities, and notations
- Object classes, such as class hierarchies, properties, constraints, and relationships
- Data types, including all highly popular data types, all built-in data types of popular database and programming languages, parsing rules, and implementation formats

The XDR specification identifies data types for particular elements through references to Web Uniform Resource Identifiers (URIs). The data type's URI refers to a part of the XML document's schema that declares the appropriate parser and storage format of the element.

XDR supports open content models in addition to the closed content models defined under XML 1.0. Open content models allow XML documents to contain subelements that were not explicitly listed in their schema declarations. A closed content model, by contrast, requires that all elements and attributes be listed explicitly and declares as invalid any XML document that includes undeclared content. XDR also defines tags for declaring elements as keys and foreign keys. This is useful for instantiating a conceptual data model among elements within an XML document and for supporting database-style joins.

As we've noted, XDR (and XML Schema) defines the schema or information model applicable to a valid XML document-type, such as a BizTalk Document. The BizTalk Document is an envelope around one or more application-specific Business Documents, some but not all of which need be in XML format. In order to validate the structure and contents of an XML-formatted Business Document, an XML-enabled application would have to access the XML schema appropriate to that document-type.

As we'll discuss later in this chapter, Microsoft has established an online repository where organizations may publish their application-specific Business Document schemas. The schema repository is available free of charge to all comers at www.biztalk.org, a nonprofit clearinghouse that we will discuss in more detail later in this chapter. Schemas for Business Documents do not contain any BizTags, but only those XML tags required to support the business transaction. Business Document schemas are designed by various companies, industry groups, and other implementing organizations, not by Microsoft. However, Microsoft has defined general requirements and guidelines for Business Document schema implementations and made them available at www.biztalk.org/Resources/schemasguide.asp.

1.4.3 BizTalk Documents

As noted previously, we must distinguish between BizTalk Documents and Business Documents. BizTalk Documents are the primary container and Business Documents the primary payload or "body" in a BizTalk transaction. The high-level nesting of content in a BizTalk Document is as follows:

- BizTalk Documents contain one or more Business Documents and zero or more binary file attachments. As noted previously, the BizTalk Framework prescribes the schema of BizTalk Documents, in terms of specifying the set of XML-based BizTags that may envelope Business Documents. BizTalk Documents "wrap" BizTags around the Business Documents and, by means of a "manifest" header tag, point to binary attachments that are transmitted (as Multipurpose Internet Mail Extensions body parts or other mechanisms) in the BizTalk Message envelope (to be discussed in greater detail later in this chapter).

- Business Documents contain XML markup tags; textual element, attributes, and values; and (optional) binary body parts. As noted previously, the BizTalk Framework does not prescribe the content or schema of individual XML-formatted Business Documents, which must be defined separately under the relevant application or vertical-market domains.

- Text and binary element values contain business transaction data, such as the fields of a standard purchase order, invoice, sales forecast, bill of lading, or other business document.

BizTalk Documents embed prescribed markup tags—BizTags--to define this content-nesting hierarchy. BizTags use Simple Object Access Protocol (SOAP) 1.1 conventions, declaring some attributes as in the SOAP "envelope" or SOAP "header" (per the discussion in Chapter 14). The BizTalk document-type is defined by various BizTags (per BizTalk's XDR document schema, as discussed previously). Table 1-4 presents the hierarchy of elements and attributes in a SOAP-enveloped BizTalk Document, plus the BizTags used to delimit these features in a BizTalk Document. We will discuss XML concepts in greater detail in Chapter 13 and SOAP concepts in Chapter 14.

The BizTalk Framework takes special care to describe mechanisms for encoding both BizTalk Documents and Business Documents. Both of these are well-formed XML document-types, per the XML 1.0 standard, which only supports Unicode, US-ASCII, or ISO 8859 text strings for markup and element values. However, BizTalk transactions will often be required to transmit binary and other non-Unicode information, such as computer application files, raster images, or other strings containing unsupported characters. XML processors would interpret binary information as unsupported characters, triggering processing errors. In order to

Table 1-4	Structure and BizTags of a SOAP-Enveloped BizTalk Document	
BizTalk Level	**Structure**	**BizTags**

BizTalk Document Envelope	Contained in SOAP 1.1 Envelope, which contains one instance of a SOAP 1.1 Header and one of a SOAP 1.1 Body as peer sub-elements
	
	Includes one instance each of the following mandatory attributes:
	⊛ SOAP namespace declaration
	⊛ SOAP encoding scheme
	⊛ XML Schema type declaration
	Contains one instance each of the following mandatory elements:
	⊛ BizTalk Document Header (SOAP 1.1 Header)
	⊛ BizTalk Document Body (SOAP 1.1 Body)
		SOAP 1.1 Envelope:
		  <SOAP-ENV:Envelope>
		  </SOAP-ENV:Envelope>
		SOAP namespace declaration:
		  xmlns:SOAP-ENV=http://schemas.xml soap.org/soap/ envelope/
		SOAP encoding scheme:
		  xmlns:SOAP-ENC=http://schemas. xmlsoap.org/soap/encoding/
		XML Schema type declaration:
		  xmlns:xsi="http://www.w3.org/1999/ XMLSchema-instance"

BizTalk Document Header	Contained in SOAP 1.1 Header
	Includes one instance of the following mandatory attribute:
	⊛ BizTalk namespace declaration
	Contains elements:
	⊛ Delivery (mandatory): Describes how a BizTalk Document is transmitted, routed, and handled. Includes one instance of BizTalk Framework 2.0 namespace declaration and one each of the following elements:
	  To (mandatory): Address of target application. Includes one instance of Address attribute
	  From (mandatory): Address of source application. Includes one instance of Address attribute
		SOAP 1.1 Header:
		  <SOAP-ENV:Header>
		  </SOAP-ENV:Header>
		Delivery:
		  <dlv:delivery>…
		  </dlv:delivery>
		BizTalk namespace declaration:
		  xmlns:dlv="http://schemas.biztalk.org/ btf-2-0/delivery"
		To:
		  <dlv:to…
		    <dlv:address
		    </dlv:address>
		  </dlv:to>
		From:
		  <dlv:from
		    <dlv:address
		    </dlv:address>
		  </dlv:from>

Table 1-4	Structure and BizTags of a SOAP-Enveloped BizTalk Document (cont.)	
BizTalk Level	**Structure**	**BizTags**

BizTalk Document Body	Reliability (optional): Indicates whether notification of reliable delivery is required. Includes one instance each of the sendReceiptTo and receiptRequiredBy attributes, both of which are mandatory if this element is used.	Reliability:
		   <dlv:reliability>
		   </dlv:reliability>
		 sendReceiptTo:
		   <dlv:sendReceiptTo>.
		   </dlv:sendReceiptTo>
		 receiptRequiredBy:
		   <dlv:receiptRequiredBy>
		   </dlv:receiptRequiredBy>

	• Properties (mandatory): Includes one instance each of the following attributes:	Properties:
		   <prop:properties
		   </prop:properties>

	Identity (mandatory): Universally unique URI reference that identifies BizTalk Document for purposes of logging, tracking, error handling, or other document processing and correlation requirements	Identity:
		   <prop:identity>
		   </prop:identity>

	SentAt (mandatory): Sending timestamp, reflecting the time at which the properties element was created.	SentAt:
		   <prop:sentAt>
		   </prop:sentAt>

	ExpiresAt (mandatory): Expiration timestamp of the Document, beyond which point in time the associated BizTalk Document is considered to have expired and must not be processed by the destination business entity.	ExpiresAt:
		   <prop:ExpiresAt>
		   </prop:ExpiresAt>

	Topic (mandatory): URI reference that uniquely identifies the overall purpose of the BizTalk Document, useful for publish/subscribe routing and for verifying the consistency of the BizTalk Document content with its intent.	Topic:
		   <prop:topic>
		   </prop:topic>
		 Manifest:
		   <fst:manifest
		   </fst:manifest>
		 Reference, URI, and description:
		   <fst:reference
		   fst:uri="#insurance_claim_document_id">
		   <fst:description>Insurance Claim</fst:description>
		   </fst:reference>

Table 1-4	Structure and BizTags of a SOAP-Enveloped BizTalk Document (cont.)	
BizTalk Level	**Structure**	**BizTags**
	• Manifest (optional): Document catalog that Includes references to both the Business Documents carried within the primary BizTalk Document in the BizTalk Message, as well as any additional attachments, such as images or binary data, that may be considered a part of the BizTalk Message. Includes one or more instances of the Reference element, each instance of which includes one instance each of the mandatory URI attribute and optional Description element.	Process management: <prc:process> </prc:process> Type: <prc:type> </prc:type> Instance: <prc:instance> </prc:instance> Handle: <prc:handle> </prc:handle> Receipt: <rct:receipt> </rct:receipt>
	• Process management (optional): Includes one instance each of the following elements:	
	Type (mandatory): URI reference that signifies the type of business process involved.	
	Instance (mandatory): URI reference that uniquely identifies a specific instance of the business process that this BizTalk Document is associated with.	
	Handle (optional): URI reference that provides further information that may be required to identify a step or an entry point within the business process instance.	
	• Receipt (optional): includes one instance of the receivedAt sub-element.	

Table 1-4	*Structure and BizTags of a SOAP-Enveloped BizTalk Document (cont.)*

BizTalk Level	Structure	BizTags
BizTalk Document Body	Contained in SOAP 1.1 Body Includes mandatory Business Document sub-element, which includes optional application-specific Business Document namespace and mandatory application-specific Business Document. Encloses XML tags (not BizTags) associated with the XML schemas of the one or more Business Documents. The Business Document implements an application-specific XML schema associated with its document-type. The Business Document's document-type, schema, and associated XML tag-set would be defined outside the BizTalk Framework—for example, by a vendor consortium associated with the commerce document type or e-commerce application.	BizTalk Document Body: <SOAP-ENV:Body> </SOAP-ENV:Body>

support transmission of this content, the BizTalk Framework defines two permissible encoding mechanisms: one for inline binary content and the other for separate binary file attachments.

To support transmission of inline binary element-values within a Business Document, the BizTalk Framework specifies "base-64" encoding of this content. The base-64 encoding scheme "hides" binary information from XML processors by representing the information with valid characters supported under XML 1.0. Receiving applications are responsible for decoding binary information as appropriate. This base-64 encoding scheme has the drawback of increasing the potential message size greatly, increasing the concomitant load on processing, network, and storage capacity throughout the BizTalk implementation. Another drawback is that it may run afoul of some XML processors that have design or platform limitations on the size of documents they can parse and process.

To support transmission of binary content as separate file attachments in a BizTalk Message, the framework specifies encoding of these attachments as separate MIME body parts. Some protocol-specific BizTalk implementations—such as HTTP and SMTP--may use "multipart" MIME to support transmissions of one or more BizTalk Documents along with one or more attached non-XML files. Microsoft has promised it will publish detailed protocol-specific implementation details as a follow-up to BizTalk Framework 2.0.

1.4.4 BizTalk Messages

It's easy to confuse BizTalk Messages with two different but closely related concepts: BizTalk Documents and Business Documents.

The BizTalk Message is the outer envelope in a BizTalk interchange. As noted in Section 1.4.3, a BizTalk Message encloses one BizTalk Document, which encloses one or more inline Business Documents. Figure 1-4 graphically depicts the nesting of Business Documents within BizTalk Documents within BizTalk Messages. The bulk of the process-relevant header information is contained in the BizTalk Document (hence Section 1.4.3's detailed discussion of BizTalk Document tags, elements, and attributes). The bulk of the

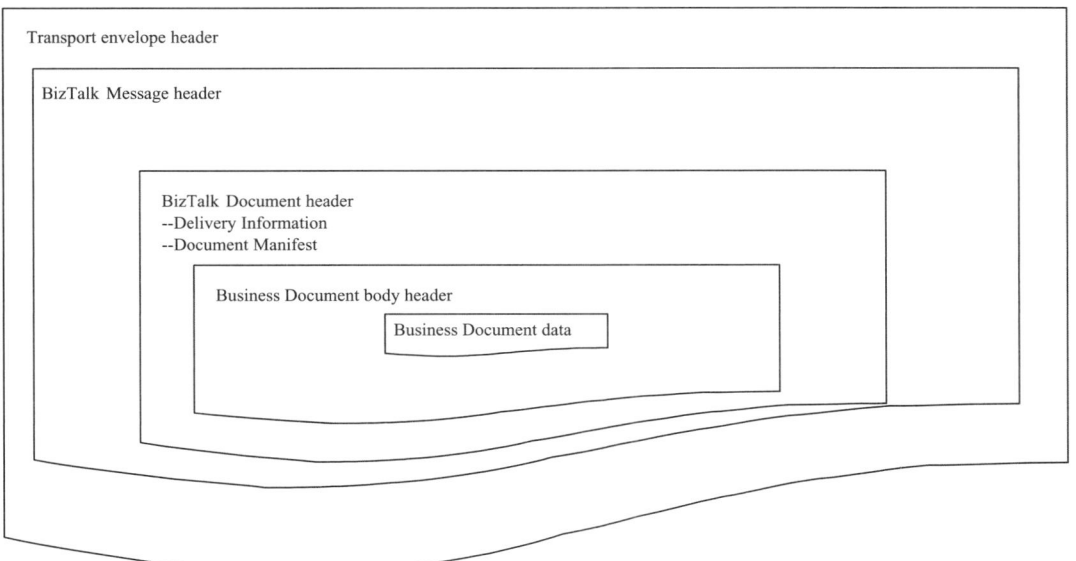

Figure 1-4   *A BizTalk interchange involves an outer-layer transport-specific envelope. Within this is a BizTalk Message, which contains a BizTalk Document. Within a BizTalk Document are one or more Business Documents.*

application-relevant content is contained in the Business Document. You will have to master this message structure and grasp its details as second nature in order to navigate the complexities of BizTalk application development and deployment.

Every BizTalk interchange consists of overlapping dialogues among three sets of e-commerce entities: BizTalk servers, BizTalk application adapters, and line-of-business applications. The headers of the three nested objects—BizTalk Messages, BizTalk Documents, and Business Documents—contain information that helps these entities to collectively route, validate, process, and handle the content within Business Documents. The content of the three overlapping dialogues is as follows:

- A BizTalk Message is what one BizTalk server exchanges with other BizTalk servers.
- A BizTalk Document is what one BizTalk application adapter exchanges with other BizTalk application adapters.
- A Business Document is what one line-of-business application exchanges with other line-of-business applications.

A BizTalk Message may also enclose one or more Attachments associated with the BizTalk Document, which are referenced in that document's "manifest." However, these Attachments often contain binary data files and are transmitted outside the BizTalk Document. One technique for transmitting Attachments is as separate MIME body parts of the BizTalk Message. This approach is necessary due to the fact that XML documents cannot contain nontext content.

The BizTalk Message's outer envelope will vary in structure according to the transport protocol used to transmit it. Unlike the BizTalk Document, which Microsoft has mapped out in fine detail (as we saw in Section 1.4.3), the structural details of the BizTalk Message's outer envelope are as yet undefined. However, it's clear that Microsoft is focusing on defining the BizTalk Message as a MIME body part for transmission over the leading Internet application-layer protocols: HTTP, Simple Mail Transfer Protocol (SMTP), and File Transfer Protocol (FTP). In addition, Microsoft is defining the BizTalk Message envelope for transmission over message-oriented middleware protocols such as its own proprietary MSMQ. The vendor has promised to publish transport-specific BizTalk Message implementation guides in a separate document.

1.4.5 BizTalk Workflows

The BizTalk Framework does not define a full-fledged, flexible workflow environment in all its details. Rather, it defines only one workflow process model: a point-to-point request/reply message flow that can potentially operate over various transports, including HTTP, SMTP, message brokering, file exchange, or batch jobs.

The framework distinguishes between logical URI addresses (contained in BizTalk Document headers) and physical transport-specific addresses (resolved from logical addresses by BizTalk servers). These addressing schemes provide BizTalk servers, BizTalk application-adapters, and line-of-business applications with the means to define more complex routing paths, based on business rules applied to the headers and contents of Business Documents.

Missing from the framework are specifications for defining more complex workflow process definitions that can be interchanged between components in a BizTalk interchange. These process definitions could be interchanged in the headers of BizTalk Messages or BizTalk Documents, or perhaps in the body of separate documents exchanged between BizTalk servers.

Microsoft recognizes that future versions of the BizTalk Framework will need to support additional workflow models. It lists the following models as candidates for support in future versions of the framework:

- Single sender distribution lists
- Independent sender and reply handlers
- Anonymous messaging or publish/subscribe

1.4.6 BizTalk Event Model

As noted earlier, the BizTalk Framework does not specify the event model to be shared and error messages exchanged between BizTalk servers, BizTalk application adapters, line-of-business applications, and data-communications interfaces. A full-fledged event model would include standard alerts for a server, adapter, or application's inability to validate or process a BizTalk Message, BizTalk Document, or Business Document.

In BizTalk Framework 2.0, Microsoft has hinted that it is developing just such an event model as well as the standard error and notification messages that implement such a model. The framework defines four types of errors to be handled through structured messages between components of the BizTalk application model, as described in Table 1-5.

1.5 BizTalk as E-Commerce Industry Coalition, Schema Repository, and Developer Community

Developing complex technical specifications such as the BizTalk Framework is a daunting challenge. Getting the industry to accept and implement them as standards—de facto or de jure—can be even harder.

Microsoft's politicking for its BizTalk Framework has so far been reasonably successful. The vendor has been an important catalyst for bringing various e-commerce industry players together to discuss common application and schema architectures.

Table 1-5	*Types of Error Messages in the BizTalk Event Model*
Type of Error	**Description**
Server-to-server	Occur between BizTalk servers or within a single BizTalk server. They fall into three categories. First, the destination server cannot parse the message. Second, the destination server parsed the message successfully, but determined it is not a valid BizTalk message. Third, the destination server parsed the message successfully, determined it is a valid BizTalk message, but no adapter was available to process the message.
Application-to-server	Occur in the communication between an application and a BizTalk server. For example, the source BizTalk server may receive an error from a destination line-of-business application when the source server attempts to invoke an invalid method or pass incorrect data.
Application-to-application	Occur between source and destination line-of-business applications, providing notifications of anomalous application events. For example, the destination application may notify the requesting application that a part number referenced in a Business Document was invalid. BizTalk support for application-to-application notifications requires future definition of error-message document schemas to support a wide range of application-level events, which may be processed by some combination of destination BizTalk server, application adapter, and line-of-business application.
Server-to-network	Occur when a server calls the data communications layer to transmit a message. These errors and the appropriate error messages depend upon the specific data communication capabilities and protocols.

Just as important, Microsoft has enlisted a broad e-commerce industry coalition that is committed to developing products and services in compliance with the BizTalk Framework. Microsoft has organized a nonprofit industry group, BizTalk.org, to manage the evolution of the BizTalk Framework. This group, overseen by Microsoft, has implemented a Web site that spreads the BizTalk gospel, supports an online repository for vertical-market XML document schemas, and hubs a growing community of developers writing software for BizTalk-enabled applications.

Bear in mind, however, that BizTalk.org is not the only organization on the Internet that has such aims. There are competing e-commerce standards frameworks, schema repositories, and developer communities. We will discuss these other initiatives in more detail in Chapter 2.

1.5.1 BizTalk Steering Committee

The nonprofit group that manages BizTalk.org and drives development of the BizTalk Framework is formally known as the BizTalk Steering Committee. Microsoft developed the BizTalk Framework in consultation with this committee, which includes representatives from the following firms:

- B2B e-commerce software vendors: Ariba Technologies Inc., Clarus Corp., Commerce One Inc., Concur Technologies Inc., New Era of Networks, Pivotal Corp.
- B2B industry consortia: RosettaNet, The Open Applications Group
- EDI standards group: Data Interchange Standards Association
- Enterprise resource planning (ERP) software vendors: The Baan Co., J.D. Edwards & Co., PeopleSoft Inc., SAP AG
- Financial services provider: Merrill Lynch & Co. Inc.
- Manufacturer: The Boeing Co.
- Trade association: American Petroleum Institute

The range of organizations on the committee is impressive. On the one hand, it includes firms with a vested interest in furthering industry adoption of B2B e-commerce, enterprise application integration, customer relationship management, and supply chain management solutions. On the other, it includes industry groups with an interest in promoting data-level standardization of e-commerce interchanges around XML.

Even more impressive, the BizTalk Steering Committee includes two software vendors—Ariba and Commerce One—that also are aggressively deploying Internet-based B2B e-marketplaces and have proposed XML-based e-commerce interoperability frameworks that to varying degrees overlap with BizTalk. In bringing all these firms into its camp, Microsoft has gained a critical mass of industry support for BizTalk early on, helping its chances of succeeding as a de facto set of standards. In other words, having Ariba and Commerce One on its side buys Microsoft some ready-made "street cred" in the emerging B2B e-marketplace industry.

Per BizTalk.org's formal philosophy statement, "The purpose of the steering committee is to provide guidance and insight to make **www.biztalk.org** an open and level playing field." The committee operates as a "built-in watchdog group" whose mandate is to "prevent anyone from subverting the BizTalk Framework or XML in proprietary ways that benefit one vendor or group of customers more than another." It is, according to the philosophy statement, a "hand-selected group" of organizations with "experience, insight, interest and commitment to the BizTalk Framework." Committee members are organizations committed to promoting the use of XML-based solutions for communication between applications and organizations.

In terms of internal structure and procedures, the steering committee is not a standards group and does not pretend to be one. It has no working groups or regular meetings. Instead, its representatives review proposed changes to BizTalk Framework specifications before they are posted to the www.biztalk.org Web site (which came online in September 1999). The committee gathers public comments on proposed specifications through e-mail and other feedback via the Web site. Then the group achieves consensus on the proposed specifications before publishing them as final.

Be that as it may, no one seriously doubts that Microsoft exercises predominant sway over the steering committee and its agenda. Whose hand selected the members of the group? In fact, every indication is that Microsoft sets the agenda and single-handedly develops the draft BizTalk Framework specifications.

The agenda that truly steers the committee comes to light in this telling excerpt from BizTalk.org's philosophy statement: "The purpose of the BizTalk Steering Committee is to provide the oversight and guidance that will make the BizTalk Server, the BizTalk Framework and **www.biztalk.org** an important part of your IT (information technology) strategy." Notice that the "S" in "BizTalk Server" is uppercase, denoting not the logical layer but the Microsoft product of that name.

Which is not surprising. However, the BizTalk Framework cannot be a truly open, vendor-neutral e-commerce initiative unless a sizable number of non-Microsoft vendors begin to develop their own BizTalk servers. Maybe this will require an open-source initiative similar to the Apache project that developed a vendor-neutral Web server or the Linux project that developed a vendor-neutral Unix server.

It will be interesting to see whether the BizTalk.org developer community develops along such lines, or whether an open-source BizTalk server project springs up outside the sway of the consortium and its lead player.

1.5.2 Online Schema Repository

It's important to note that industry support for the BizTalk Framework is not limited to Microsoft and its business allies on the BizTalk Steering Committee. Indeed, even a cursory glance at the news and other postings at www.biztalk.org gives ample evidence for its strong and growing support.

Microsoft and its BizTalk Steering Committee have gone to great lengths to define what goes into the header of a BizTalk Document. The repository they set up at www.biztalk.org takes the initiative to its logical next step: inviting the business world to define what goes into the body of a BizTalk Document. The success of BizTalk is not determined by the size or membership of the steering committee. BizTalk can succeed only if XML-format Business Documents become ubiquitous and companies choose to wrap these documents with BizTags and transmit them across networks of BizTalk servers.

The BizTalk.org repository promotes these ends by providing a free-of-charge clearinghouse for "publishers" of vertical-market and application-specific XML Business Documents. It is an open repository for the submission and publication of XML Business Document schemas. B2B schema publishers might be software developers exposing XML interfaces to their products and services, or user organizations exposing their Business Document formats to trading partners.

Publication of Business Document schemas enables trading partners to have a common reference specification for document interchange with agreed-upon meanings for each content element. Agreement on common Business Document schemas enables trading partners to map document contents to their respective internal database schemas and integrate this data with line-of-business applications.

As of the date this book was published, more than 150 organizations had registered as schema publishers on www.biztalk.org and had submitted more than 250 valid XML Business Document schemas. The posted schemas originate from 11 industry groups:

- Agriculture, forestry, and fishing
- Construction
- Educational services
- Finance and insurance
- Health care and social assistance
- Information
- Manufacturing
- Professional, scientific, and technical services
- Real estate, rental, and leasing
- Retail trade
- Wholesale trade

Schemas submitted to BizTalk.org do not become the intellectual property of the consortium, steering committee members, or Microsoft. They remain the possession of the schema "publisher" or author. In submitting to the repository, however, the publisher grants the public the right to use the schema free of charge within their applications. However, publishers also have the option of posting schemas to a secure area on the Web site for private use between them and their trading partners. The only processing that BizTalk.org performs on a schema prior to posting it in the repository is to validate that it is in the repository's only supported XML schema-definition format: XML Data Reduced (XDR). BizTalk.org does not wrap BizTags around Business Documents stored in the repository.

One restriction that BizTalk.org places on schema publishers is that the specifications they submit be associated with a product or service for which they are the registered owner of either a trademark or Internet domain name. BizTalk.org provides schema publishers with storage space on the repository server and access to schema design and editing tools. What publishers submit is a collection of documents that describe and categorize an XML schema. The repository makes schema submissions visible to BizTalk.org's members (who can join free of charge). BizTalk.org members can search posted schemas by author, company, product industry, process, and document type. Publishers control updates to their schemas on the repository and can measure how many other companies have accessed the schemas and what other information they've published. Publishers can also notify their customers automatically of impending or proposed changes to their schemas. Publishers can also share proposed changes with select individuals, and these "in-review" submissions are withheld from general viewing and search in the repository.

The repository resides under the "Library" table on www.biztalk.org's homepage. The library presents a query interface with drop-down option lists, allowing browsers to search for schemas by keyword, industry group, and submitting organization. The query result is a list of schemas meeting user-input criteria. For each schema, the list provides its name, a brief textual summary of the schema, the name and industry of the submitting organization, and the number of BizTalk.org members using the schema. Clicking one entry's on-screen "View Schemas" button presents a full-page view of information pertinent to that entry. In addition to the fields just mentioned, this page includes the BizTalk.org URI of the schema and the date and time it was published. It also includes clickable buttons for viewing and downloading the schema, a sample XML Business Document implementing the schema, and a textual description of the schema.

1.5.3 Developer Community

The www.biztalk.org site is also a portal that provides resources for the growing community of developers and other IT professionals implementing BizTalk-enabled B2B solutions. In addition to hosting the Business Document schema library, the site is an online reference for BizTalk Framework specifications, reference materials, tools, sample applications, and a community newsgroup.

Membership in the BizTalk.org developer community is free of charge and open to everyone. You can register online with the site and have your membership approved almost instantaneously. The community is designed to put B2B solutions developers in touch with B2B schema publishers in the private and public sectors. It is also designed to put B2B schema publishers in touch with their trading partners so that organizations can interface their respective business processes through the medium of standardized content within BizTalk Documents and Messages.

The Web site also supports online community discussion groups organized by topics of interest to BizTalk schema and application developers and implementers. Residing under the "Community" tab on the www.biztalk.org homepage, the discussion groups (as of the date this book was published) are as follows:

- ABCs of Schemas
- BizTalk Framework Q&A
- BizTalk Server Q&A
- Community Projects
- General

- Jumpstart Kit
- Newbies Corner
- Riots, Raves, and Rants
- Shhh. Welcome to the Library
- XML by industry
- XML Pub – Casual Discussions
- XML Schema – experts
- XML Schema - learners

Microsoft technical personnel manage, monitor, and participate in these discussion groups, which provide educational and support channels for BizTalk.org members. BizTalk.org administrators also plan to hold periodic online seminars using chat technologies, featuring experts from Microsoft and other companies. These various discussion forums provide an important channel for the industry to communicate with the companies that are developing the BizTalk Framework and BizTalk-compliant products and services.

Under the "Resources" tab on the www.biztalk.org homepage is an assortment of tools, white papers, specifications, and educational materials for perusal and download by the general public. There are also articles and news on BizTalk-based B2B solutions and BizTalk B2B integration projects.

These forums and resources can prove vital to developers or administrators who are involved in complex, time-stressed BizTalk integration projects. Under such circumstances, IT professionals often need to communicate right away with outside experts on how to configure software, set various parameters, and map data fields correctly to get everything up and running.

BizTalk.org provides special tools and services for BizTalk.org "Partner" companies. BizTalk.org Partner companies are organizations that have developed BizTalk-compliant solutions or published schemas and other information to the repository. Partners have access to the BizTalk Framework Publisher's Toolkit and can display the BizTalk logo on their solutions and marketing materials. The Publisher's Toolkit links customers of Partner companies who use products crafted with the toolkit directly into www.biztalk.org for the purpose of looking up Business Document schemas, accessing other resources, and participating in the BizTalk developer's community. Essentially, the Publisher's Toolkit provides a "shrink-wrapped" membership in BizTalk.org to the customers of Partner companies, thereby expanding the BizTalk.org developer community with every sale made by a Partner company.

1.6 BizTalk as B2B E-Commerce Products and Services

Starting in mid to late 2000, Microsoft and BizTalk Partner companies are rolling out products and services that implement the framework specifications. Perhaps the best way to track who is developing what is to check the "News" tab at the www.biztalk.org homepage regularly.

What drives every BizTalk Partner's development roadmap is, of course, Microsoft's own product and service strategy. We devote a considerable portion of Part Three to discussing the new products and services that form the centerpiece of Microsoft's strategy, including the BizTalk Server and Commerce Server components of the Microsoft Server suite and the commerce services component of the MSN portal environment. In Part Three, we will go in-depth on the technical integration among these new products and services, as well as integration points with existing Microsoft products such as Windows 2000 Server, Internet Information Server, SQL Server, Message Queue Server, Transaction Server, and Visual Studio. You may already deploy many of these products within your intranet and extranet and want to know how Microsoft's new BizTalk Server and Commerce Server products fit into the equation.

The BizTalk Server product will be the focus of all these discussions, since it is the architectural focus of Microsoft's total strategy—products and services—in the B2B e-commerce market. We will describe in detail various processing services that Microsoft's BizTalk Server provides to applications. These services include validating, mapping, translating, encoding, encrypting, signing, routing, storing, forwarding, and delivering BizTalk Messages and their component BizTalk Documents and Business Documents. Figure 1-5

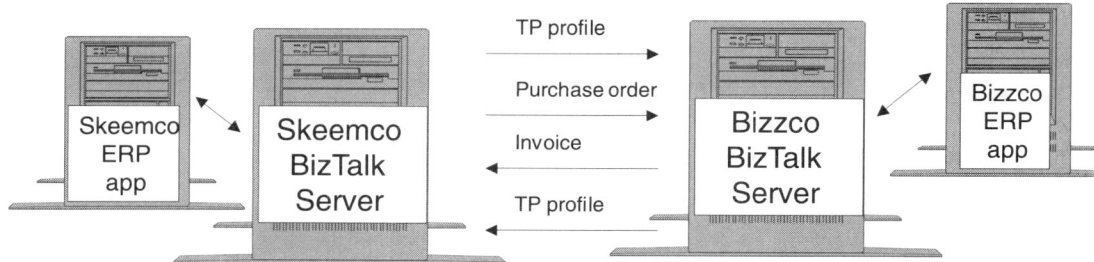

- Trading partner profile management
- Trading partner application integration
- Enterprise application integration
- Document mapping and translation tools
- Workflow tools
- Automated document interchange
- Digital certificates

Figure 1-5   *Microsoft BizTalk Server's core capabilities include managing TP profiles, mapping and translating documents between formats, wrapping documents in BizTags, and routing messages to and from other BizTalk servers and applications.*

provides a high-level overview of the capabilities of Microsoft BizTalk Server, both for trading-partner integration and for enterprise application integration.

No doubt you have EDI applications and EDI VANs that perform many of these services. BizTalk products and services are now on your radar screen. What you want to know is whether, when, and how to run your applications—EDI, e-commerce, supply-chain management, customer-relationship management, and e-marketplace—over BizTalk-compliant platforms. Those issues are the substance of this book.

How Does BizTalk Differ From Other E-Commerce Frameworks?

*E*lectronic commerce is a mosaic of many standards and interoperability specifications, each with its own architectural approach and functional scope.

BizTalk is one, but by no means the only, piece in that picture. The BizTalk Framework has a well-defined functional scope, which we presented exhaustively in the previous chapter. However, it is not the only industry initiative, framework, or repository for interoperable B2B e-commerce. Nor is it the first or most widely adopted set of B2B interoperability specifications. It does not have the broadest range of compliant products and services on the market. And it certainly does not address the full range and depth of applications, services, and functionality required by end-to-end B2B environments.

BizTalk is a "horizontal market" B2B framework, which means it applies broadly to many industries. Other horizontal market frameworks include CommerceXML (cXML), Open Buying on the Internet (OBI), Open Trading Protocol (OTP), the XML/EDI Group's initiative, the Commerce Business Library (CBL), and the Organization for the Advancement of Structured Information Standard's (OASIS) incipient Electronic Business XML (ebXML) effort. To varying degrees, these specifications use XML to define standard, horizontal market e-commerce data documents, messages, workflows, stores, and marketplaces. Many of these frameworks are complementary, and in several cases proponents are working together to converge them where appropriate.

However, the majority of e-commerce interoperability frameworks are "vertical market" oriented, which means they support the B2B requirements of particular industries. In this chapter we also discuss three such frameworks: Information and Content Exchange (online content syndicators), RosettaNet (IT supply chain automation), and Open Applications Group

Integration Specification (enterprise resource planning and supply chain management). Table 2-1 summarizes the leading horizontal and vertical market B2B interoperability frameworks, which we discuss in greater detail in this chapter.

BizTalk does not really compete with other horizontal and vertical market frameworks so much as supplement them. As we will discuss in this chapter, different frameworks have different architectural approaches and functional scopes, and are often used for different purposes within any given

Table 2-1	B2B E-Commerce Interoperability Frameworks
Framework	**Description**
BizTalk	Existing horizontal-market framework. Supports generalized order-fulfillment workflows. Defines XML-based B2B message envelope with some state information. Dominated by Microsoft. Has produced specification version 2.0.
cXML	Existing horizontal market framework. Supports generalized order-fulfillment workflows. Defines XML-based B2B message envelope with some state information. Dominated by Ariba. Has produced specification version 1.0.
OBI	Existing horizontal-market framework. Supports generalized order-fulfillment workflows. Defines non-XML-based B2B message envelope. Managed by multivendor consortium. Has produced specification version 2.0.
OTP	Existing horizontal-market framework. Supports generalized payment workflows. Defines XML-based B2B message envelope. Managed by multivendor consortium. Has produced specification version 1.0.
XML/EDI Group	Proposed horizontal-market framework. Will support generalized order-fulfillment workflows. Will define XML-based B2B message envelope with state and workflow information. Managed by multivendor consortium. Has not produced public specifications.
CBL	Existing horizontal-market reference library of reusable XML element- and attribute-tags for generating EDI documents. Not full B2B interoperability framework.
OASIS Electronic Business XML (ebXML)	Proposed horizontal-market framework. Will support generalized order-fulfillment workflows. Will define XML-based B2B message envelope with state and workflow information. Managed by multivendor consortium. Has begun to produce draft public specifications.
Information and Content Exchange (ICE)	Existing vertical-market B2B interoperability framework for online content syndication. Has produced detailed public specifications.
RosettaNet	Existing vertical-market B2B interoperability framework for IT supply chain automation. Has produced detailed public specifications.
Open Applications Group Integration Specification (OAGIS)	Existing vertical-market B2B interoperability framework for ERP and supply chain management automation. Has produced detailed public specifications.

e-commerce message, transaction, or trading environment. Microsoft has had great success in gaining support for BizTalk from other horizontal market B2B standards developers, such as Ariba Technologies, Commerce One, and the Data Interchange Standards Association (DISA), which shows that these organizations are addressing different problems and do not seriously conflict in their larger B2B market-development goals and ambitions.

What most B2B interoperability frameworks have in common are two things. First, they ground their specifications primarily in XML. Second, they are managed by various industry associations and/or strategic alliances (rather than formal standards bodies such as the Internet Engineering Task Force and World Wide Web Consortium).

As we showed in the previous chapter, BizTalk fits both of these criteria. The BizTalk Framework relies heavily on XML 1.0 and related standards, and it is managed by a nonprofit industry association dominated by a lead vendor, Microsoft. However, most B2B frameworks are more vendor-neutral than BizTalk, a point we will discuss throughout this chapter.

2.1 B2B Functional Reference Model

The best way to compare BizTalk with other B2B frameworks is in terms of breadth of support for an e-commerce interoperability "functional reference model." Table 2-2 shows the "layers" in the B2B functional reference model, which are needed to support end-to-end, interoperable B2B transactions.

We have presented these layers from lowest to highest, in terms of complexity. As we can see, the higher layers in the reference model contain and build upon the lower. The model's terminology echoes the BizTalk-specific discussion in the previous chapter, which described such entities as "BizTalk Documents," "BizTalk Messages," and "BizTalk Workflows." The term *store* suggests an e-commerce "storefront," such as what can be supported on Microsoft Commerce Server, but we use it more generally to refer to any online, shared, server-resident repository of data that plays a role in an e-commerce transaction. The term *marketplace* suggests an online trading hub managed by a particular organization, such as commerce services under MSN. However, we use the term more generally to refer to a complete transaction environment residing on a hub, extranet, or the Internet, regardless of whether any one organization manages that environment in its entirety.

This reference model allows us to characterize B2B standards frameworks by the scope of their ambitions. Microsoft's BizTalk initiative shows that the vendor addresses all five layers—from documents to marketplaces—and is developing commercial B2B products and services to address it all. Similarly, Ariba sells B2B software products and services and has established a horizontal-market framework, cXML, with a roughly equivalent functional scope.

Table 2-2	B2B Reference Model Functional Layers

Layer	Description
Document	A set of information elements or fields that contain business transaction data.
Message	An envelope for encapsulating business documents, routing them, and tracking their flow throughout a transaction.
Workflow	The flow of information and control in a business transaction, typically involving exchange of one or more messages among users, stores, and marketplaces in order to execute a specific end-to-end business transaction.
Store	Any repository or database of commercial information—such as product listings, descriptions, prices, contracts, customer profiles, digital certificates, and credit histories—that supports online transactional workflows.
Marketplace	An interchange environment involving one or more online stores—such as those maintained by merchants, trading hubs, financial institutions, and certification authorities—that must interoperate to support end-to-end e-commerce transactions. What defines a marketplace are the participants—human and automated—that interchange documents and data within that environment in order to buy and sell goods and services. The marketplace also includes a broad range of other participants whose jobs are to broker, facilitate, and otherwise support transactions and sustain relationships between buyers and sellers. In defining an e-marketplace, you first specify the participants, their roles and interfaces with respect to each other, and the services they provide.

The model also allows us to determine that the vast majority of XML-based e-commerce standardization efforts focus on the lowest layer. The e-commerce world's "schema wars" revolve around competing standards for XML-based business documents that address various vertical-market applications. Indeed, we can see that the battle between BizTalk.org and the Organization for the Advancement of Structured Information Standards (OASIS) over competing B2B schema repositories takes place almost entirely at the document level. Their repositories maintain a growing pool of XML-based vertical market business document schemas but do not host schemas for higher-order constructs such as messages, workflows, stores, and marketplaces. And this is as it should be: B2B depends most critically on document-level data-sharing standards. EDI, for example, has always run on such standards.

2.2 BizTalk and the B2B Reference Model

As we noted, Microsoft's BizTalk initiative addresses all five layers of the B2B reference model. Briefly revisiting the discussion in Chapter One, we size up the BizTalk initiative layer for layer in Table 2-3.

Table 2-3	BizTalk Framework per the B2B Reference Model

Layer	Description
Document	BizTalk Documents contain one or more Business Documents and zero or more binary file attachments. The BizTalk Framework prescribes the schema of BizTalk Documents (XDR or XML Schema format), in terms of specifying the set of XML-based BizTags that may envelope Business Documents. The BizTalk Framework does not prescribe the content or schema of individual XML-formatted Business Documents, which must be defined separately under the relevant application or vertical-market domains. Microsoft's BizTalk Server supports existing industry business document formats, such as any XML-based schema and EDI formats such as ASC X12 and UN EDIFACT.
Message	BizTalk Messages are the outer envelope in a BizTalk transaction. A BizTalk Message encloses one BizTalk Document, which encloses one or more inline Business Documents. The BizTalk Message's outer envelope will vary in structure according to the transport protocol used to transmit it.
Workflow	The BizTalk Framework defines a single workflow process model: a point-to-point request/reply message flow that can operate, potentially, over various transports, including HTTP, SMTP, message brokering, file exchange, or batch jobs. Microsoft's BizTalk Server provides a rule-based processing engine for managing the server-to-server request/reply-based workflow involving BizTalk Messages, BizTalk Documents, and Business Documents. In future versions of BizTalk Server, however, Microsoft plans to define a BizTalk-compatible message structure that supports more complex workflows and longer-lived transactions.
Store	The BizTalk Framework lacks schema definitions for online catalog contents, such as supplier profiles, product indexes, and contract information, though Microsoft and SAP are working together to define syntaxes for electronic catalogs under the BizTalk Framework. However, Microsoft's BizTalk Server makes use of several external data stores within the Microsoft Server environment. It uses Commerce Server's product catalog store; Windows 2000's file system for application data; Windows 2000's Active Directory for trading partner profiles, agreements, and public-key certificates; SQL Server for commerce transactional data; SQL Server Data Transformation Services for access to third-party data stores such as ERP applications; and SNA Server for access to mainframe data warehouses.
Marketplace	From a technical standpoint, the BizTalk Framework's application model essentially defines an e-marketplace as a set of stores and applications mediated by one or more BizTalk servers (constituting a logical layer, theoretically platform-neutral, that supports distributed routing, mapping, and transformation of business transactions). Collectively, the BizTalk servers provide a "workflow enactment service" or "orchestration' environment for the marketplace, enforcing business rules for interchanges and transactions. Organizations can establish extranet- or hub-based B2B e-marketplaces on one such BizTalk server: Microsoft's product of the same name. Or companies can subscribe to online B2B marketplace services—such as Microsoft is implementing in its MSN portal environment—which use the BizTalk Server product as the enabling platform. Microsoft is providing value-added marketplace services such as document routing, translation, profile interchange, advertising, promotion, and payment processing.

In 1999, the BizTalk initiative got its start at the lower end of the reference model: defining permissible document, message, and workflow types. These are the standards at the core of the BizTalk Framework.

In 2000, with the initial BizTalk standards published and stable, Microsoft has focused primarily on the upper two layers of the reference model. It has built and shipped the initial versions of BizTalk Server and Commerce Server, having integrated them with Windows 2000, SQL Server, and other data stores in the Microsoft Server suite. And it has begun to deploy commercial B2B e-marketplace services on MSN, running them over the scalable BizTalk Server and Commerce Server products. Part Three of this book focuses on Microsoft's efforts in developing, packaging, and marketing its BizTalk products and services in 2000. Part Four goes in-depth on the technical architecture and integration among the components of Microsoft's total commerce architecture, focusing on the central role of the BizTalk Server as a B2B workflow engine (or, in Microsoft's term, an "orchestration engine").

Over the next several years, Microsoft's efforts will probably focus increasingly on packaging new B2B workflow "orchestration" models to run seamlessly across its BizTalk-enabled products and services. Part Two of this book focuses on popular B2B business models—alternative commerce workflows, essentially—that we'll probably see running on BizTalk Servers in the future. That part gives the reader the conceptual framework necessary to identify potential applications of BizTalk-enabled products and services in their trading environments.

2.3 Ariba's Commerce XML (cXML)

Ariba released the cXML v. 1.0 specification—a horizontal market B2B framework—for industry review in August 1999. You can find the framework documents at www.cxml.org. We map Ariba's cXML initiative to the B2B reference model in Table 2-4.

In many ways, cXML competes directly with the BizTalk initiative. Like BizTalk, the cXML initiative specifies XML-based elements, documents, messages, protocols, online catalogs, workflow functionality, and transaction environments. However, Ariba sits on the BizTalk steering committee and has committed to converging cXML with Microsoft's framework. Ariba has focused CXML on specifying schemas for basic procurement document types, whereas BizTalk is strictly agnostic as regards the schemas of business documents contained in its routing envelope.

Ariba Technologies developed the cXML specification in conjunction with its e-commerce software and services business. It has also organized a nonprofit vendor consortium, at www.cxml.org, to maintain and extend cXML as an open standard for interoperability between e-commerce "buy-side," "sell-side," and marketplace solutions.

Unlike Microsoft, Ariba does not host an online clearinghouse and repository for XML-based e-commerce document schemas. Instead, Ariba has committed to publishing its cXML document schemas to the BizTalk repository at www.biztalk.org. In so doing, they will be wrapping BizTalk tags around their schemas to specify the default BizTalk namespace and attach BizTalk routing tags on their documents.

Table 2-4	CommerceXML (cXML) Per the B2B Reference Model
Layer	**Description**
Document	cXML 1.0 objects include basic data elements from the XML-Data Schema specification. The default cXML namespace governs all elements in a cXML-conforming entity. The specification includes two e-commerce document types: OrderRequest and OrderResponse. OrderRequest is analogous to a purchase order (PO) document, and OrderResponse to an acknowledgement that the supplier received a PO submission. Future versions of the cXML document will include new document types, such as charge orders, acknowledgments, status updates, and shipment and payment notifications.
Message	XML element tags define the envelope, header, and body of a cXML message. The message envelope specifies the cXML version supported; the payload ID for keeping track of lost or problem messages; and a timestamp of when the message was sent. The header contains authentication and addressing fields for the message. The body specifies whether the message represents a request or response and includes the corresponding request or response data, formatted as XML documents. If the message is a request, the body defines what type of data is expected in the response.
Workflow	There are two models for cXML transactions: request-response or one-way. Request-response transactions can run only over an HTTP 1.x transport mechanism, and include automated transactions between browser-based "shopping carts" and server-based online catalogs. One-way messages have no such transport protocol restrictions.
Store	The cXML specification defines three principal elements for online catalogs: supplier, index, and contract. The supplier element describes data about the supplier that the buyer may need to know, such as address, contact, and ordering information. The index element describes data about the supplier's inventory of goods and services, such as descriptions, part numbers, and classification codes. The contract element describes data about flexible attributes of the inventory negotiated between the buyer and supplier, such as price. Buyers may cache these data elements for persistent or cached use within their systems, or "punch out" as needed to access current information on the seller's Web site.
Marketplace	Ariba has already implemented cXML within its Operating Resource Management System (ORMS) e-commerce software and Ariba.com Network electronic marketplace service. ORMS automates the procurement workflow at the buyer's site and submits cXML OrderRequests to sellers over network connections. Ariba.com Network provides a full-fledged, online e-commerce transaction environment integrated with ORMS. The service supports online hosting and indexing of sellers' e-commerce catalogs. It also connects buyers to these sites, routes and tracks online purchases, and translates orders and acknowledgments into various document formats understood by trading partners.

2.4 Open Buying on the Internet

OBI is the oldest B2B interoperability framework (other than EDI, which has been around for well over a generation). The first version of OBI came out in June 1997, and version 2.0 followed in August 1999. You can find the OBI framework documents at www.openapplications.org.

OBI 2.0—like BizTalk and cXML—is a horizontal market B2B framework. It focuses on automating high-volume, low-dollar transactions among trading partners. Some e-commerce software vendors have implemented OBI in their products.

The OBI Consortium oversees development of the standard. Membership in the consortium is open to buying and selling organizations, technology companies, financial institutions, and other interested parties on an annual fee basis. Members (of which there were 67 as of December 8, 1999) include B2B software and service companies such as Ariba, Commerce One, Concur Technologies, Intelisys, and Microsoft. What this shows is that the three leading horizontal-market B2B frameworks have the same core supporters. However, OBI is more vendor-neutral than either BizTalk or cXML, since its development did not grow out of one B2B software vendor's effort to build industry interoperability specifications around its product.

We map OBI 2.0 to the B2B reference model in Table 2-5.

Figure 2-1 presents a typical OBI workflow. OBI, like cXML, specifies standard schemas for B2B documents and online catalogs. Consequently,

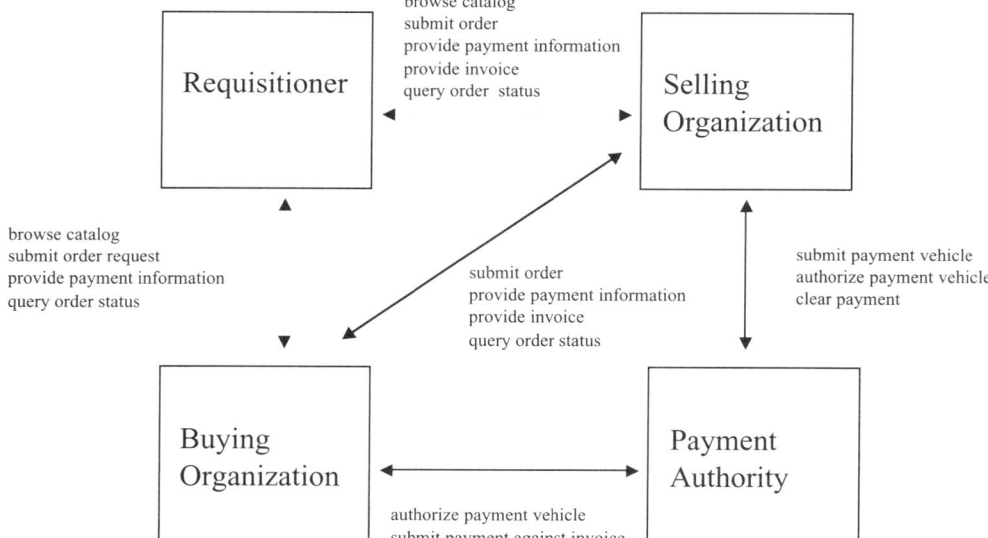

Figure 2-1   *A typical OBI workflow involves transactions among four marketplace participants: requisitioner, buying organization, selling organization, and payment authority.*

Table 2-5	*Open Buying on the Internet per the B2B Reference Model*
Layer	**Description**
Document	OBI 2.0 specifies use of ANSI X12 850 (version 3040) EDI transaction sets for Orders and Order Requests. X12 850 transactions sets describe purchase orders and purchase order requests. The OBI standard does not yet incorporate XML documents or schema. The consortium has stated that future versions of the standard may define mappings of additional EDI document formats to XML.
Message	OBI 2.0 specifies a standard envelope—an "OBI object"—for transmitting and routing order-related information. An OBI object is the standard data structure used to exchange order-related data between trading partners. An OBI object includes five fields: version, data length, OBI data (containing the OBI Order or Order Request in an OBI-specified X12 850 version 3040 format), signature length, and signature.
Workflow	OBI 2.0 defines a standard workflow under which requisitioners within buying organizations use their Web browsers to access OBI-compliant online catalogs within selling organizations. Requisitioners look up goods in the catalogs and populate their "shopping baskets" with their selections. If the requisitioner places an order, the selling organization transmits an order request to the buying organization's purchasing server for approval and/or additional information. The buying organization may approve or reject the order, through its own internal workflow and/or in communication with a validating external payment authority, and return an approved and completed order to the selling organization.
Store	OBI 2.0 specifies a standard feature set for online catalogs. OBI catalog servers must support Web-based sourcing, pricing, and ordering mechanisms that authenticate other entities via X.509 certificates and digital signatures and can generate and receive OBI-encapsulated document objects.
Marketplace	In the OBI architecture, there are four entities involved in an online purchasing process: requisitioners, buying organizations, selling organizations, and payment authorities. OBI focuses on aspects of this process that are the most critical to interoperability among trading partner systems. OBI specifies use of common technical standards available to all participants in the e-marketplace. HTML is the standard format for displaying all OBI objects and their contents. HTTP v. 1.0 is the standard application-layer protocol for all transactions. OBI security relies on X.509 certificates, SSL, digital signatures, and RSA Public Key Cryptographic Services (PKCS) to support user authentication, content authentication, content integrity, content confidentiality and nonrepudiation services.

both frameworks define specialized trading environments: ones that rely on the particular business documents and commerce stores specified in the standard. BizTalk, by contrast, defines a more general-purpose B2B environment by virtue of the fact that it does not specify the document or catalog schemas of BizTalk-based trading environments.

OBI differs from both cXML and BizTalk in specifying an end-to-end transactional workflow, not just a single client-server dialogue (request-response or one-way) within that workflow. One area where OBI is more limited than the other two horizontal-market frameworks is in its message envelope, the "OBI object," which contains no addressing information. The OBI object is designed to be transmitted only over a point-to-point HTTP connection between client and server, or between two servers.

Another area where OBI lags behind the other frameworks is its lack of support for XML-based business documents. OBI puts a new wrapper on old "payload": X12 EDI transaction sets.

2.5 Open Trading Protocol

OTP defines a horizontal-market framework for electronic payment over the Internet that is independent of any electronic payment protocol. OTP, managed by the financial industry OTP Consortium, provides a standard framework for encapsulating payment protocols such as Secure Electronic Transactions (SET) and DigiCash. You can find the framework documents at www.otp.org.

We map OTP to the B2B reference model in Table 2-6.

Table 2-6	*Open Trading Protocol (OTP) per the B2B Reference Model*
Layer	**Description**
Document	OTP documents, also known as "trading components" or "trading blocks," consist of elements formatted in XML 1.0.
Message	OTP messages consist of XML envelopes around OTP trading components or blocks. Message envelopes include "transaction reference blocks," which are XML elements that associate the message with an OTP transaction. Messages also include XML-formatted OTP "signature components," which use digital signature technologies.
Workflow	OTP defines request-response transaction protocols, which consist of a dialogue of messages between trading partners, otherwise referred to as "trading roles." The specification describes the content, format, and sequences of messages that pass among such trading roles as consumers, merchants, financial institutions, and customer care providers. Each payment scheme contains some message flows that are specific to that scheme. The OTP specification describes these payment-scheme-specific parts of the protocol.
Store	OTP defines a standardized mechanism of exposing merchant trading options to consumers. Trading options include payment methods, delivery modes, receipt formats, and invoices.
Marketplace	OTP defines a marketplace in which there are well-defined roles for consumers, merchants, financial institutions, and customer care providers. One or more parties perform the electronic merchant roles, such as shopping site, payment handler, delivery handler, and customer support provider. The framework defines mechanisms in support of online negotiation of parties' roles and responsibilities. It also defines mechanisms for offer presentment, payment, receipt modes, and delivery of goods and services. OTP supports such commercial transactions as purchases, refunds, value exchanges, authentication, withdrawals, deposits, and inquiries.

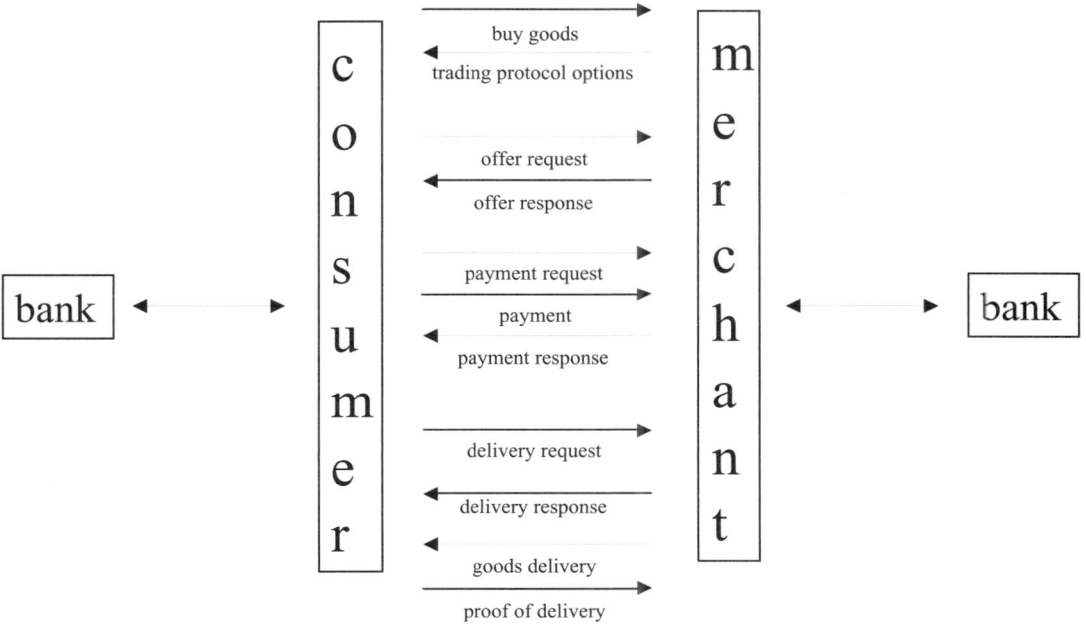

Figure 2-2 *A typical OTP workflow involves transactions between three marketplace participants: consumers, merchants, and banks.*

Figure 2-2 presents a typical OTP workflow. OTP differs from BizTalk, cXML, and OBI in one important way. OTP is a payment-oriented framework, while the others are order-oriented frameworks. Clearly, commerce cannot survive without both functions: ordering goods and paying for them. So OTP is clearly complementary to the other horizontal market B2B frameworks.

2.6 XML Electronic Data Interchange (XML/EDI) Group

Many e-commerce applications revolve around one type of object—the EDI "transaction set"—and many e-commerce initiatives adapt prior EDI formats into XML or create new EDI-like formats from scratch.

The XML/EDI Group is a nonprofit working group consisting primarily of XML tool vendors. The group is coordinating industry-wide development in the areas of XML/EDI integration, rule templates, automated commerce agents, global data dictionaries, and workflow design. It has published a timeline of standards development milestones from 2001 through 2003. You can find its current framework documents at www.xmledi.org.

The XML/EDI Group is also assisting standards bodies and industries with XML-related e-commerce projects. It is working with DISA to map existing Accredited Standards Committee (ASC) X12 EDI data elements, segments, and transaction sets to XML 1.0, making use of supplementary core standards such as Extensible Stylesheet Language (XSL) and XML Namespaces. The group's work is complementary to the OBI Consortium's e-commerce framework, since OBI specifies only a single EDI transaction set (ANSI X12 850 version 3040) and has not yet mapped this format to XML.

So far, the XML/EDI Group and ANSI ASC X12 have not issued any formal specifications for mapping EDI "data dictionaries" to XML. However, they have codeveloped a preliminary FAQ regarding how EDI data might be mapped to XML. Important issues that the organizations are addressing jointly include making use of XSL stylesheets to display EDI documents, integrating data-typing mechanisms into XML/EDI formats, representing repeating EDI data elements with XML, and linking XML objects to intelligent agents that can carry out workflow processes.

The XML/EDI Group has also published general, preliminary guidelines for using XML for EDI in interactive, forms-based, and batch applications, and for defining most of the application context necessary for self-describing e-commerce transactions. Table 2-7 maps the XML/EDI initiative into the various layers of the B2B reference model.

XML/EDI is potentially the most far-reaching of the horizontal-market B2B frameworks, since it defines a path for migrating traditional EDI to the new world of Internet-facing e-commerce. Unlike BizTalk, cXML, and OTP, XML/EDI focuses on populating the "document" layer of the reference model with content, in the form of XML mappings to today's vast range of X12 and EDIFACT transaction sets. In addition, the XML/EDI initiative has the most far-reaching vision for end-to-end workflow integration across companies, with an approach that defines mechanisms for storing workflow process models in repositories and also exchanging workflow rules with the objects being processed.

Table 2-7	*XML/EDI Initiative per the B2B Reference Model*
Layer	**Description**
Document	The group is working with DISA to map the ASC X12 EDI transaction sets to XML. It is also defining use of XML's XSL for mapping between different XML document schemas and translating documents between different presentation formats. XML/EDI documents will consist of the following formats: XML 1.0 document type definitions (DTDs), EDI segment and element definitions (such as ASC X12 and EDIFACT), business objects (transaction documents with embedded workflow and processing rules), and trading partner profiles.

Table 2-7	XML/EDI Initiative per the B2B Reference Model (cont.)

Layer	Description
Message	XML/EDI message objects will contain all the rules and data necessary to process them without reference to the originator for clarification. XML/EDI messages and the documents contained within them will be self-validating. The group has specified that XML/EDI documents may be exchanged through various protocols (such as SMTP, HTTP, and FTP), using various encodings (such as UTF-8, MIME, and Secure MIME), and supporting both interactive and batch processing modes. Documents may also be exchanged using an EDI message format such as EDIFACT to guide the transformation process at the receiving end (e.g., so that XML/EDI files in an EDIFACT message can be revalidated on receipt by an XML parser). The group has indicated it will integrate its "transaction delivery" specifications with those specified in the BizTalk and ICE frameworks. And it is defining requirements for message-store extensions to support complex workflows involving automated delivery and processing of XML/EDI messages. For example, a message store should not be able to acknowledge receipt of a message until its body and attachments have been parsed and validated as well-structured and valid XML documents.
Workflow	The group is defining data-manipulation agents (also known as "DataBots") that support automated routing and processing of XML/EDI documents and other objects. DataBots will be able to exchange "rule templates" to integrate their collective workflow and to support transparent access to one another's databases. In addition, DataBots will transmit XML/EDI "business objects" that contain transaction data plus the application logic specifying how receiving applications are to process that data. The XML/EDI message creator will be able to communicate process-related information in a format that is independent of the receiver's operating platform, native workflow environment, and data formats.
Store	The group is defining a standardized "lexicon repository" for storing XML-formatted business documents and online catalogs. This repository—a "global reference dictionary"—will store standardized data definitions in XML, X12, EDIFACT, and XML/EDI "business object" formats. The repository will also contain trading partner profiles and the "process templates" that encapsulate the end-to-end workflow process model associated with XML/EDI documents and business objects.
Marketplace	The group is defining the infrastructure for e-marketplaces consisting of rule-driven DataBots. As indicated above, DataBots will be able to search, broker, control, correct, and direct XML/EDI workflows; exchange data and process models; and take other independent actions under the control of programmable rule templates. In addition, DataBots will exchange authenticated trading partner profiles, maintained in the XML/EDI repository, to establish B2B relationships prior to exchange data and linking workflows.

Like BizTalk, the XML/EDI initiative also defines a "rules engine" layer for managing B2B workflows. BizTalk defines the need for interacting "BizTalk servers" for routing, mapping, and translating interchanges in accordance with a rule-based "commerce interchange pipeline." XML/EDI expresses this requirement in the form of rule-based, interacting DataBot agents.

Later in this chapter we will discuss this requirement more generally in terms of the need for a cross-platform B2B "workflow enactment service."

2.7 Organization for the Advancement of Structured Information Standards

OASIS is a nonprofit international consortium that promotes vendor-neutral standards for structured data, such as XML, HTML, and Standard Generalized Markup Language (SGML). Among other activities, the consortium assists businesses and industry organizations in designing vertical-market XML schema. It is also one of the primary sponsors of the ebXML effort discussed earlier, which aims to develop a full-features vendor-neutral B2B interoperability framework.

OASIS sits at just one level in the B2B reference model: the document layer. In May 1999, it announced plans to establish its own public XML schema registry, repository, and clearinghouse. The repository, at www.xml.org, will be in direct competition with Microsoft's BizTalk.org schema repository. Nevertheless, Microsoft is a member of OASIS, which also includes XML tool vendors such as DataChannel, POET Software, and SoftQuad and other enterprise computing vendors such as IBM, Novell, Oracle, and Sun Microsystems.

XML.org will be an open, vendor-neutral, public XML registry and repository providing automated public access to schemas, specifications, and other resources, such as DTDs, namespaces, and stylesheets. Industry groups will be able to submit, register, and manage their XML DTDs, schema, and resources and access XML resources necessary to develop new specifications, design software, or process an XML document.

Just as important as the XML.org repository will be OASIS's efforts to develop an architecture for distributed XML repositories maintained by other participating organizations. These distributed repositories will incorporate the same technical architecture as the "root" XML.org repository. This initiative will allow vendors to create interoperable versions of the registry for use within their intranets and extranets. The CommerceNet e-commerce vendor consortium, which belongs to OASIS, will integrate a branch XML.org repository into its member web site and use the shared environment for joint vendor collaboration on e-commerce projects.

2.8 Common Business Library

Commerce One is a B2B software vendor and e-marketplace service provider; consequently, it has a similar B2B business model to both Microsoft and Ariba. Commerce One has developed a reference library of reusable

XML element- and attribute-tags for generating EDI documents. The company's Common Business Library (CBL), currently in version 2.0, is an extensible collection of XML DTDs and modules that developers can customize and configure in crafting XML-based commerce applications. Commerce One has integrated CBL into its B2B software and MarketSite.Net electronic marketplace service offerings. You can find more information on CBL at www.commerceone.com.

As an initiative, CBL resides solely at the "document" layer in the B2B reference model. CBL's principal importance lies in the fact that it is a public set of commerce-oriented DTDs, available to developers for free through a nonprofit industry consortium. In September 1998, Commerce One submitted CBL to the eCo Framework Working Group of the CommerceNet consortium to encourage development of standard XML/EDI semantic elements and document formats.

As an e-commerce DTD/schema development environment, CBL is complementary to the ongoing work of the XML/EDI Group and ANSI ASC X12. CBL currently includes mappings to data elements analogous to those contained in some of the more popular ANSI X12 transaction sets. These mappings will almost certainly give way to any future mappings defined by ANSI ASC X12 and the XML/EDI Group, under the auspices of CommerceNet's eCo Framework Working Group. CommerceNet sponsors and oversees the work of the XML/EDI Group and is thereby in a position to incorporate that group's recommendations in updates to CBL.

CBL is also complementary to various vertical and horizontal market e-commerce frameworks. The CBL reference library includes XML mappings to document data elements defined within horizontal market frameworks (BizTalk, cXML, OBI, and OTP) and such vertical market frameworks as RosettaNet and Information and Content Exchange, to be discussed shortly. Developers can extend CBL's current mappings and incorporate new vertical and horizontal market document-types and elements within the library.

2.9 Vertical Market E-Commerce Frameworks

Many industries have already defined frameworks for XML-based e-commerce within their vertical-market domains. Some of the earliest such frameworks include Information and Content Exchange (online content syndication and subscription), RosettaNet (IT industry supply chain), and Open Applications Group Integration Specification (enterprise resource planning and supply chain management).

These specifications use XML to define vertical market e-commerce documents, messages, workflows, stores, and transaction environments, to varying degrees. These are by no means the only vertical market B2B interoperability frameworks. We have selected them to show how several industries are adapting XML to their own EDI-like requirements. We describe each effort in terms of the B2B reference model.

2.9.1 Information and Content Exchange

ICE defines a framework for automating online content exchange and reuse between the Web sites of publishers (also known as "syndicators") and those of their subscribers. Several vendors submitted ICE as a proposal to the W3C in September 1998. The specification forms the basis for Vignette's Syndication Server, its product for automating the distribution of digital assets, such as content, services, supplier information, and product catalogs, between affiliated Web sites. You can access the ICE standard document at www.vignette.com.

Table 2-8 maps ICE to the B2B reference model.

Table 2-8	Information and Content Exchange (ICE) per the B2B Reference Model
Layer	**Description**
Document	Developers define ICE data elements using declarations in XML 1.0. ICE defines the formats of XML documents that support subscription establishment, subscription management, content exchange, and event logging. One important XML-formatted document is the subscription offer, which includes such terms such as delivery policy, usage reporting, and presentation constraints.
Message	ICE messages are valid XML documents, with a structured hierarchy of tags describing ICE operations and data.
Workflow	ICE primarily supports a request-response transaction protocol between subscribers and syndicators. The entire ICE request/response exchange is contained in the body of the HTTP Post and its associated HTTP Response. ICE defines the dialogue of content exchange between syndicators and subscribers. A syndication relationship starts when the subscriber obtains a catalog of subscription offers from the syndicator and then subscribes to particular subscriptions, possibly engaging in protocol parameter negotiation to arrive at mutually agreeable delivery methods and schedules. The syndicator then delivers data to the subscriber per the terms of the subscription, using a package concept as a container mechanism for generic data items. Content exchanges utilize a "sequenced package model," which consists of a discrete set of packages delivered, in order, over a period of time. The ICE framework also defines push and pull data-transfer models; event-log transfer mechanisms; renegotiation of protocol parameters in established relationships; the ability to send unsolicited ad hoc notifications; and the ability to query and ascertain the state of the relationship.
Store	ICE defines the schema for a catalog of subscription offers that the syndicator provides to the subscriber.

Table 2-8	Information and Content Exchange (ICE) per the B2B Reference Model (cont.)
Layer	**Description**
Marketplace	ICE defines the roles and responsibilities of syndicators and subscribers and supports establishment, management, control, and auditing of content-syndication relationships among them. Subscribers consume content that is produced by Syndicators. Syndicators produce subscription offers. ICE content syndication assumes that the Syndicator and Subscribers have already agreed, through other channels, to have a relationship. ICE also assumes that these parties have already established the contractual, monetary, and business implications of their relationship through other channels.

ICE is an important B2B framework for two principal reasons. First, it is perhaps the most widely implemented XML B2B framework in actual shipping products. Second, it is a fundamental protocol for managing the distribution channel of one of the most important B2B services these days: live, fresh, online subscription content. The Web is the most powerful publishing medium ever invented, and ICE enables more efficient, manageable distribution of subscription content between sites.

2.9.2 RosettaNet

RosettaNet is a business consortium of information technology hardware and software vendors. With its XML-based Partner Interface Process (PIP) framework, RosettaNet seeks to automate and align procurement processes between trading partners throughout the IT supply chain. You can find its framework at www.rosettanet.org.

The RosettaNet consortium has defined a master EDI workflow schema—PIPs—for the entire IT supply chain. PIPs include interchange formats, protocols, and process models governing transactions among vendors, manufacturers, suppliers, distributors, resellers, and customers of computer hardware and software. Microsoft regards RosettaNet as one of many vertical market schema that can be wrapped in BizTalk Message and BizTalk Document tags and disseminated through its BizTalk.org schema repository. (Indeed, Microsoft is an active member of the RosettaNet Consortium.)

Table 2-9 shows how the RosettaNet consortium's major initiatives include map into the B2B reference model.

Figure 2-3 presents a graphical overview of the RosettaNet PIP architecture.

RosettaNet's framework is impressive in its technical scope and depth. The consortium has already defined a complete interoperability framework for the IT supply chain. This vertical market framework anticipates the XML/EDI Group's and ebXML group's long-awaited horizontal framework. RosettaNet's framework addresses all five layers of the B2B reference model very convincingly. It provides a powerful framework for defining self-describing workflows that wrap business content in a full envelope of B2B application context.

Table 2-9	RosettaNet per the B2B Reference Model

Layer	Description
Document	RosettaNet has defined an XML-based data dictionary that describes the elements of business documents. RosettaNet's dictionary includes sections addressing technical properties and business properties. The Technical Properties Dictionary includes properties of all IT product categories. The consortium has set its sights on expanding its data dictionary to cover 150 IT product categories.
Message	A RosettaNet business message consists of XML body-parts (preamble, header, and body) and is transported as a "multipart/related" MIME message. RosettaNet defines an outer Agent Protocol Message envelope understood by applications that implement RosettaNet agents (and the corresponding application-layer RosettaNet Agent Protocol over TCP/IP). Within the Agent Protocol Message is a Service Protocol Message. The header of the Service Protocol Message contains XML tags that describe how the message and content are to be processed by the receiving application and how they fit into a larger, multimessage transaction (i.e., a particular PIP). The body of the Service Protocol Message contains business documents in the XML schemas defined by the relevant PIP. Message body tags come from RosettaNet dictionaries, with each PIP having its own message XML DTDs or schemas. RosettaNet specifies that incoming messages go through grammar, sequence, schema, and content validations.
Workflow	Each PIP has one or more "actions"—business rules applied by recipients to message content—that are described by tags in the Service Protocol Message's header. The RosettaNet Implementation Framework provides a methodology for defining the supply chain and workflow between IT software companies. The guidelines define how computer systems cooperatively execute e-business processes in the IT supply chain. The framework defines class and sequence diagrams and validation tools for specifying PIPs in compliance with RosettaNet-standard interchange formats and protocols. The Object Management Group's (OMG) Unified Modeling Language (UML) is the basis for RosettaNet process models, which are transferable between trading partners and tools using OMG's XML Metadata Interchange (XMI) framework. The RosettaNet interchange protocol defines XML document-types that characterize services and messages involved in the PIP workflow among trading partners.
Store	RosettaNet defines a "service layer," which provides network resources that perform business-related functions, such as supporting an online catalog. In addition, the RosettaNet Business Properties Dictionary includes properties of online catalogs and trading partner profiles.
Marketplace	The RosettaNet Networked Application Architecture defines an "agent" layer that is analogous to the "DataBots" in XML/EDI or the "BizTalk server" under that framework. Automated RosettaNet agents in servers and applications manage an end-to-end PIP and execute business rules defined in Service Protocol Message headers. The RosettaNet e-marketplace is actually a supply chain defined under a PIP and implemented in PIP-specific message headers and contents. The RosettaNet Implementation Framework helps trading partners to define their business roles, processes, interactions, and information in the IT supply chain. This supply chain business model becomes the basis for a networked application execution process model, called a "PIP Blueprint." The PIP Blueprint specifies how software agents and services execute PIPs in a collaborative networked computer system. Automated agents and other service software components essentially constitute a distributed workflow enactment service for managing transactions under PIPs.

RosettaNet
framework
protocols

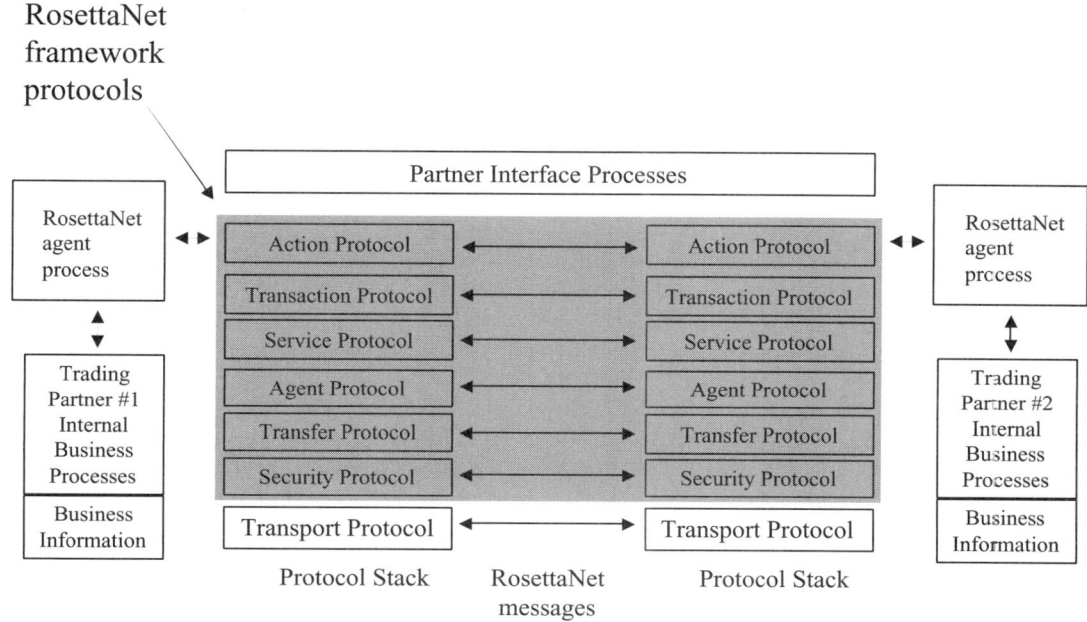

Figure 2-3   *The RosettaNet PIP architecture involves six layers of protocol transactions above the transport layer between RosettaNet agent processes in the systems of trading partners.*

2.9.3 Open Applications Group Integration Specification

The Open Applications Group is a nonprofit industry consortium that consists primarily of enterprise resource planning (ERP), supply-chain management (SCM), and application server software vendors (including Microsoft). Their OAGIS framework uses XML to define standardized interchanges among the components of several vendors' back-end business-automation software packages. You can access the framework documents at www.openapplications.org.

What's most noteworthy about the OAGIS framework is that it's not purely B2B in orientation, unlike ICE, RosettaNet, and most other vertical and horizontal market frameworks. OAGIS supports integration among ERP, SCM, and other software either on a inter- or intra-organizational basis, over a variety of hardware platforms, operating environments, and transport protocols, and on a loosely coupled basis. As such OAGIS's scope spans the worlds of B2B and enterprise application integration (EAI), raising the possibility of linking the extranet and intranet into a single, integrated, end-to-end e-marketplace.

Table 2-10 maps OAGIS to the B2B reference model.

Table 2-10	OAGIS per the B2B Reference Model

Layer	Description
Document	The OAGIS framework defines a "Business Object Document" (BOD). A BOD is a container of XML data that communicates a request from the originating business application to the destination business application; for example, for communicating requests from an order management module to a credit management module in a sell-side e-commerce application. Specifications have already been released for BODs interfacing between financial, human resources, manufacturing, and logistics software modules. Work is under way on BODs to define interoperability from these applications to supply chain and customer service applications. Each BOD includes supporting details to enable the destination business application to accomplish the requested action. Each BOD definition includes a noun and a verb: the former corresponds to an object handle and the latter to a method in object-oriented programming. These programming conventions enable software vendors to use BODs as "virtual object wrappers" supporting programmatic access to the functionality of their underlying applications.
Message	OAGIS does not specify technical message formats. OAGIS-compliant applications include one or more receiver addresses as parameters within the BOD. The transport mechanism uses these addresses in order to direct the BOD to its destination applications for final processing. The Open Applications Group intends to support all middleware transport mechanisms for transmission of BODs. OAGIS-compliant applications can use transport mechanisms associated with many business object invocation methods, which support communication between business software components. Common object invocation methods include Component Object Model, Distributed COM, Common Object Request Broker Architecture, Java Remote Method Invocation (RMI), message-oriented middleware, remote procedure calls (RPCs), and import/export functions. OAGIS focuses on data-level application integration and is strictly neutral to middleware issues, so it does not compete with the CORBA, DCOM, and other object technologies.
Workflow	OAGIS will support various workflows between business software components, including request/reply and publish/subscribe. Sending applications map their internal data structures and process models to BODs. Receiving applications map BODs to their internal data structures and process models, which may not be the same as the sender's. OAGIS uses BODs to address data synchronization between sending and receiving applications, either on a point-to-point, point-to-multipoint, or broadcast basis. The need to map to and from BODs imposes a standard core data and process model among communicating applications, which often represents a subset of their native functionality.
Store	OAGIS establishes a data dictionary of fields to be shared between OAGIS-compliant applications. The framework does not, however, specify a separate data store or warehouse to be shared among communicating applications. The specification supports synchronizing of data among applications but does not integrate business data across applications into a single data file or DBMS.
Marketplace	OAGIS-compliant applications can exchange BODs without need for automated agents, workflow engines, or any other such intermediary processor. However, OAGIS defines an optional "integration server" that manages routing, queuing, logging, and error handling on BOD transmissions between applications.

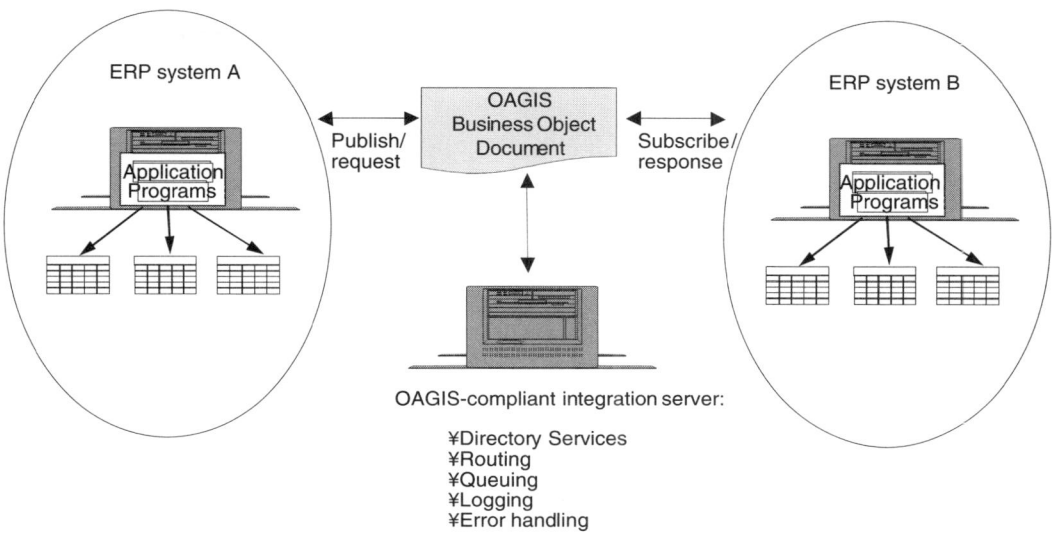

OAGIS-compliant integration server:

¥Directory Services
¥Routing
¥Queuing
¥Logging
¥Error handling

Figure 2-4   *An OAGIS-compliant integration server routes OAGIS Business Document Objects between heterogeneous ERP and other applications.*

Figure 2-4 illustrates the OAGIS integration server concept graphically.

OAGIS is an important B2B framework for three principal reasons. First, it supplies specifications for two or more organizations to directly interface their internal business processes, by means of ERP or SCM systems that exchange BODs. Second, it does so by exchanging standardized documents that instantiate standard models of business content and application context accepted and understood by the end applications. Third, it does so through a loosely coupled model that does not require a common operating environment, object model, middleware layer, or network protocol.

2.10 Synergies Between BizTalk and Other B2B Frameworks

How can we make sense of this plethora of B2B interoperability frameworks? Where does the BizTalk Framework fit into the picture? How can BizTalk-compliant products and services interoperate or coexist with applications that implement these other standards?

The fact that Microsoft sits on many other horizontal and vertical market B2B standards groups indicates that the competition from other frameworks is more apparent than real. The BizTalk Framework is still young, as

Table 2-11	*Likely Evolution of the BizTalk Framework Over the Next Several Years*
Layer	**Description**
Document	BizTalk-compliant applications and editing tools will probably employ CBL to generate BizTags to wrap around Business Documents supporting many XML document-types. OASIS's www.xml.org repository will be one of the sites from which BizTalk users will retrieve vertical-market Business Document schemas. As noted above, the BizTalk Framework is agnostic to the content of BizTalk Documents, which can encapsulate any well-formed XML document and reference separate non-XML document attachments. Consequently, BizTalk Documents can enclose content defined under cXML, OTP, XML/EDI, ICE, RosettaNet, OAGIS, and other standards. BizTalk Servers will be able to map and translate documents between these schemas and any other XML or non-XML format understood by end applications.
Message	Microsoft will probably give BizTalk Servers the ability to parse, validate, and route messages in cXML, OBI, OTP, XML/EDI, ICE, RosettaNet, OAGIS, and other envelopes. In other words, BizTalk Server will have to become more of a multiprotocol message gateway, in terms of processing application-level B2B envelopes (defined under various frameworks) in addition to transport-level envelopes (such as SMTP). In the process of routing messages to and from non-BizTalk B2B environments, BizTalk Server will also probably be able to convert message structures to fit the requirements of recipient systems.
Workflow	Microsoft will probably extend BizTalk Server's workflow process model by incorporating options from other B2B environments. BizTalk Server will probably be extended to support one-way, publish/subscribe, sequential, parallel, conditional, and broadcast workflows. The BizTalk Server will probably be enhanced in three ways to support these additional workflow options. First, Microsoft would have to extend the server's "commerce interchange pipeline" functionality to support these models. Second, Microsoft would have to give the servers the ability to exchange process models amongst themselves in specialized messages, defined no doubt under the BizTalk Framework. Third, Microsoft might also give the servers the ability to look into workflow variables contained in the documents themselves (and we fully expect BizTalk.org to extend its "delivery" tags to support complex workflow variables in the BizTalk Document header). In summary, the BizTalk Server will probably be transformed into a more full-featured workflow ("orchestration") engine to support its core role as a document-interchange processor. Enterprises will be able to easily deploy BizTalk Server for vertical-market B2B environments by loading workflow process definitions customized to those applications.
Store	In order to interface to online catalogs defined under other frameworks, the BizTalk Server would have to exchange documents and messages in formats supported by those environments. Alternately, BizTalk Server would interface programmatically to external (non-Microsoft) catalogs and data stores through COM, DCOM, MSMQ, MTS, SOAP, and other object technologies supported under Microsoft's Distributed interNetworking Architecture for Windows 2000. Another approach is for BizTalk Server to use SQL Server Data Transformation Services and SNA Server to access data in ERP applications and many other third-party stores.

Table 2-11	*Likely Evolution of the BizTalk Framework Over the Next Several Years*

Layer	Description
Marketplace	The BizTalk Server will expose its functionality to peer workflow agents and engines in other environments through COM, DCOM, and other object protocols, thereby enabling a sort of multivendor B2B workflow enactment service. The server will rely on Windows 2000's Active Directory to expose user identities, roles, profiles, and permissions to servers and applications running non-BizTalk-based B2B frameworks (by means of the Lightweight Directory Access Protocol), thereby extending the virtual bounds of the e-marketplace to other environments.

are Microsoft's BizTalk software and e-marketplace services. The company's presence in so many B2B standardization initiatives suggests that it is studying other frameworks to identify useful features and interfaces to bring into its own evolving strategy.

Microsoft's primary corporate commitment is not so much to the BizTalk Framework—though no one doubts that the company's commitment to its specifications is strong—but to its overall e-commerce product and service strategy. If success on the B2B front requires support for standards developed outside Microsoft, the company will no doubt build these interfaces into its offerings. Microsoft rapidly rearchitected its products from the inside out to support Web technologies pioneered by Netscape and others, so it would be foolish to suppose that Microsoft will always pursue a pure BizTalk-or-die strategy on the B2B front.

We anticipate that Microsoft will, over the next several years, support several other B2B interoperability specifications in its BizTalk products and services. Table 2-11 maps the likely avenues of the BizTalk Framework's evolution into the B2B functional reference model. The table consists purely of speculations by the author and does not in any way constitute commitments by Microsoft.

Don't expect Microsoft to dominate the e-commerce world absolutely with its BizTalk initiative and in the process "cut off the oxygen supply" from other B2B frameworks. That scenario is extremely unlikely. BizTalk is just one of many interoperability frameworks you will have to understand to configure an end-to-end e-commerce environment.

What Are The Fundamental Technologies Behind BizTalk?

Companies stay healthy by building strong but flexible trading environments around—and within—themselves.

The fundamental technologies behind BizTalk and other B2B interoperability frameworks are the ones that are necessary to sustain external and internal trading environments. These basic technologies are EDI and workflow, to which we alluded in previous chapters but have not yet examined in great depth. That is the task for this chapter. We will save for Part Four our discussion of other critical BizTalk Server technologies such as XML, COM, MTS, and MSMQ.

EDI and workflow are more than network and computing technologies. They are organizational paradigms that are converging under modern B2B e-commerce. What they share is a focus on business "value chains," which are interrelated series of activities that each add value, directly or indirectly, to finished goods and services. Historically, these technologies have been separated by their divergent spheres of application: EDI for structured document routing between companies, workflow for structured routing within each organization.

EDI and workflow converge as the boundaries between external and internal business processes dissolve. What's bringing these technologies together is the new paradigm of "virtual business." A virtual business is an amorphous organization with evolving external boundaries, role definitions, and procedures. The virtual business is constantly repositioning itself through dynamic alliances with an ever-changing set of trading partners. Indeed, every internal business function becomes a trading partner to every other function, ever searching for new allies, internal and external, to help it succeed. The virtual business's adaptability helps it rise to new business challenges and reform itself quickly into whatever new business model suits the task at hand.

Increasingly, the virtual business is indistinguishable from the e-marketplace in which it participates. Each entity—business and marketplace—is a value chain that links its varied participants and tasks through structured, online transactions. Each is a set of trading partners in shifting relationships with one another. A new business model gets crystallized in a new set of rules governing the e-marketplace. Each specialized e-marketplace imposes a master business model on the organizations that buy and sell in that environment. The e-marketplace becomes the controlling "virtual business" for a sector of the economy.

The B2B functional reference model crystallizes our understanding of the principal elements that define this new business environment: documents, messages, workflows, and marketplaces. The following discussion places EDI and workflow into the context of the B2B reference model. We provide a primer on each discipline and illustrate their complementary emphases on business content (EDI) and business process (workflow).

3.1 Electronic Data Interchange

EDI structures the content that businesses exchange formally among themselves. It refers to the automated transmission of predefined, standardized, structured business documents between information systems of two or more organizations. It is application-to-application messaging involving documents whose internal data structures are standardized according to explicit agreements among trading partners.

EDI is traditionally interorganizational in scope. It requires organizations to cooperate. Companies must agree on the structure of electronic documents and modify their internal business applications, network services, and computing infrastructures in order to support automated data exchange and processing. EDI transactions take place between companies that already have stable trading relationships. Larger organizations often pressure their smaller suppliers, distributors, and customers into implementing EDI. Generally, the greater the number of trading partners who implement EDI, the more B2B traffic flows over this channel and the lower the transaction costs are for all involved.

Indeed, it is just such a dynamic that has caused the spread of EDI throughout government, heavy manufacturing, and other mature industries over the past generation. EDI is far and away the dominant B2B interoperability framework, thanks to widespread, worldwide implementation of ANSI's X12 standards and the United Nations' EDI for Administration,

Commerce, and Transport (EDIFACT) standards. You could say that BizTalk and the other B2B frameworks are defining the EDI infrastructure for the Internet age.

To engage in EDI, an organization must first establish a formal "trading partner agreement" (TPA) with each trading partner with which it intends to exchange electronic business documents. The TPA is a legal contract that defines the roles and responsibilities of trading partners, the scope and procedures of EDI interchanges, various technical terms and conditions, and the particular "transaction sets" (i.e., electronic business documents) to be exchanged. TPAs may be stand-alone agreements or may be incorporated as special provisions in other contracts between trading partners.

TPAs can include whatever mix of business and technical details the trading partners deem appropriate. They might include agreements on message formatting and encoding, addressing and file-naming conventions, key exchange and management, digital signature and encryption protocols, compression schemes, and login IDs and passwords to be used by the partners' message hosts and applications to establish peer-to-peer connections over the Internet, extranet, or VAN. Or the TPA may defer these technical matters to informal implementation agreements between the trading partners' IT organizations. Once TPAs are established, trading partners mutually register one another in their respective networking and information systems as authorized recipients or senders of EDI messages and documents.

TPAs bond organizations legally, at the technical level, and also at the business level, in terms of enabling mutual data exchange between different companies' line-of-business applications and databases. EDI implies a sequence of messages between functional business groups within the trading partner organizations, any of which may serve as a message originator or recipient. Figure 3-1 shows a typical end-to-end EDI transaction, in which a structured document originates in one company's internal application, gets submitted to a trading partner and transmitted over a wide-area network (such as the Internet or a VAN), and gets routed to the trading partner's destination application.

Exchange of EDI documents is usually via telecommunications services, though some organizations exchange data through transfer of physical storage media such as high-capacity digital tapes. Processing of received EDI documents is by computer only. Human intervention takes place only on error conditions, quality reviews, and special situations, such as review of binary or other data external to the structured EDI transaction documents.

EDI transmissions usually involve routine business documents—such as purchase orders and invoices—but not monetary instruments, which are transmitted in a separate but related service called electronic funds transfer (EFT). Commercial and government organizations have been engaging in EDI and EFT since the 1970s and their bottom-line benefits are well documented. These benefits include reductions in cost, processing time, fulfillment times, and errors per transaction, plus improvements in the breadth and

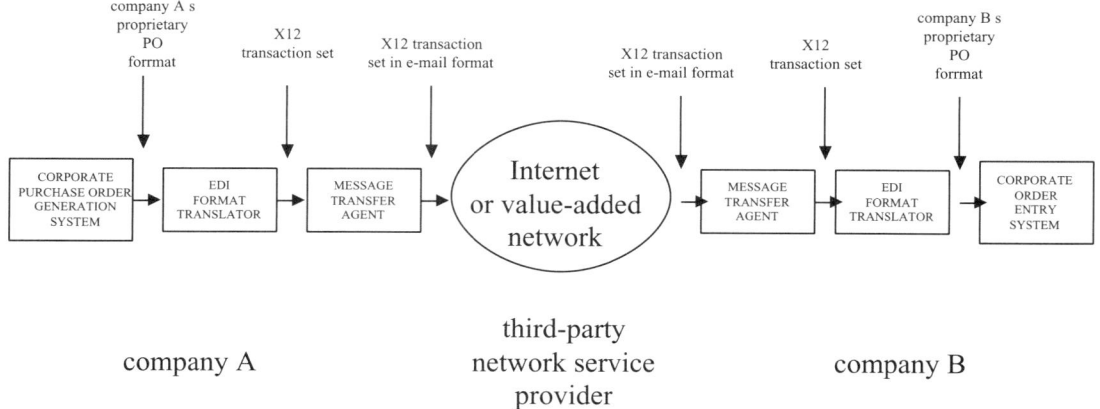

Figure 3-1   *EDI involves transmission of structured, standarized electronic business documents between companies over value-added networks or the Internet.*

depth of management information on administrative processes. Of course, companies can realize these benefits only if they eliminate paper processing and manual rekeying upon implementing electronic data transfers.

EDI often automates routine buying and selling transactions. EDI messages from a buyer to a seller often include standard "transaction sets" for such procurement documents as requests for quotation (RFQs), purchase orders (PO), receiving advice, and payment advice. EDI transaction sets from a seller to a buyer often include bids in response to RFQs, purchase order acknowledgments, shipping notices, and invoices. EDI transaction sets are often defined as legally obligations under TPAs.

In limited EDI implementations, trading partners can agree on a limited range of transaction sets that echo their existing paper-based transactions. However, larger EDI-based e-marketplaces require more generalized data definitions that can be implemented by a broader range of potential trading partners and mapped to their internal data formats. The scope of the data model implemented in the transaction sets determines the breadth of the e-marketplace and the range of organizations that can participate in it. In EDI circles, there is always a tension between organizations that want stable transaction sets and others that want new transaction sets to support new requirements, business processes, and trading communities.

In order to generate, transmit, receive, and process EDI transaction sets, trading partners establish standards for their respective network and computing infrastructures. EDI implementation agreements usually cover the following important points: transaction sets; transmission, storaging, and forwarding; message addressing; mapping and translation; security; directory; archiving; and auditing.

3.1.1 Transaction Sets

Trading partners agree on a standardized approach for expressing and conveying business data in EDI transactions. Standard EDI transaction sets usually correspond to routine business documents such as purchase orders, quotations, invoices, as well as logistical and payment-related documentation. Typically, the business data is in standard transaction set formats defined by ANSI's Accredited Standards Committee X12 or the United Nations EDIFACT.

X12 and EDIFACT transaction sets use a standard syntax to describe sequences of standardized data and control elements (expressed through specific header/trailer markup conventions, in a manner analogous, though not identical, to XML). Consequently, we may think of X12 and EDIFACT as defining standard "data dictionaries" of elements to which organizations can semantically map their internal business documents' information models for the purpose of interchanging data with trading partners.

Note that we are using the X12 term *transaction set*, rather than the equivalent EDIFACT term *message*, to refer generically to the basic electronic business document exchanged via EDI. The two standards structure EDI transmissions hierarchically in similar ways. Table 3-1 presents the levels from top to bottom (these are also depicted graphically in Figure 3-2).

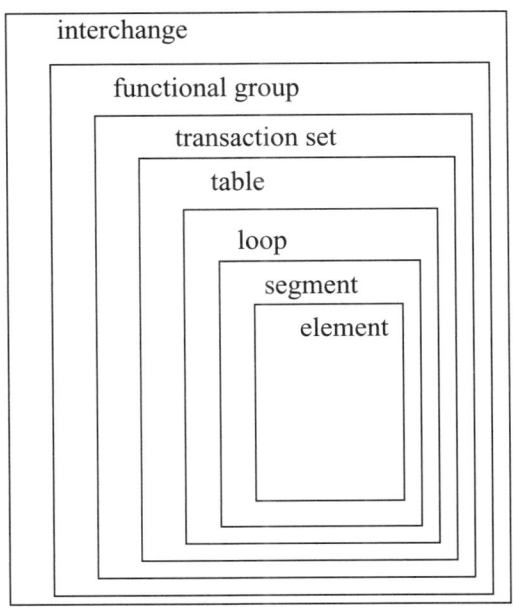

| **Figure 3-2** | *An electronic data interchange nests data hierarchically within logical groupings.* |

Table 3-1	*Hierarchical Structure of EDI Transmissions*

Level	Description
Interchange	The interchange (under X12 or EDIFACT) is the outer data envelope of an EDI transmission, nesting inside the protocol envelope associated with a particular transport technology. The interchange contains a set of one or more functional groups.
Functional group	Each functional group (under X12 or EDIFACT) contains a group of transaction sets of a particular type.
Transaction set	Each X12 transaction set (or EDIFACT "message") defines the information model for a standard business document. Under X12, each transaction set contains, in descending hierarchical order, constructs known as "tables," "loops," "segments," and "elements." (These terms refer to related groups of items in the information model of a business document, and can be explained only with reference to the particular information model instantiated in a particular transaction set.) For example, X12 defines such standard transaction sets as 850 (Purchase Order), 851 (Asset Schedule), 852 (Product Activity Data), 853 (Routing and Carrier Instruction), 854 (Shipment Delivery Discrepancy Information), and 855 (Purchase Order Acknowledgment). By contrast, EDIFACT messages order subordinate content by "segment groups" (analogous to X12 "tables" and "loops") and "segments" (logically equivalent to the X12 construct of the same name).
Table	A table (under X12) is a set of loops within a transaction set. For example, X12 850 (Purchase Order) contains three tables. The first table consists of 10 loops, each of which is identified by the code that designates the first segment in the loop: SAC (Service Promotion, Allowance, or Charge), AMT (Monetary Amount), FA1 (Type of Financial Accounting Data), N9 (Reference Identification), N1 (Name), LM (Source Code Information), SPI (Specification Identifier), N1 (Name), CB1 (Contract and Cost Accounting Standards), and ADV (Advertising Demographic Information).
Loop	A loop (under X12) is a set of mandatory and optional segments within a table. For example, the AMT loop in the X12 850 consists of four segments: AMT (Monetary Amount), REF (Reference Identification), DTM (Date/Time Reference), and PCT (Percent Amounts). All of these segments are optional.
Segment	A segment (under X12 or EDIFACT) is a set of mandatory and optional elements within a loop. Any given segment may be referenced in multiple loops in the same transaction set, or different transaction sets. For example, the AMT segment consists of three elements (the first two of which are mandatory): 522 (Amount Qualifier Code), 782 (Monetary Amount), and 478 (Credit/Debit Flag Code).
Element	An element (under X12 or EDIFACT) is a set of permissible values pertaining to a particular field in a business document. Any given element may be referenced in multiple segments in the same transaction set, or different transaction sets. For example, the 522 (Amount Qualifier Code) element may contain any of hundreds of permissible values, as defined under X12. These permissible values include 1 (Line Item Total), 2 (Batch Total), 3 (Deposit Total), 4 (Lock Box Total), 5 (Total Invoice Amount), 6 (Amount Subject to Total Monetary Discount), 7 (Discount Amount Due), 8 (Total Monetary Discount Amount), and 9 (Total Operational Statement Amount).

Rigid, hierarchical structuring of document data elements enables EDI transactions to be automatically assembled, disassembled, and processed by sending and receiving applications. As shown above, the standards describe formats for encapsulating more than one transaction set in a single EDI transmission. In addition, the standards describe syntaxes for specifying integrity, confidentiality, and authentication features associated with transmitted transaction sets.

3.1.2 Transmission, Storage, and Forwarding

Trading partners agree on a common network environment, service, and/or protocol linking their EDI systems to one another. EDI transmission may be carried over the Internet, extranets, specialized EDI VANs implementing X.25 and frame-relay services, or dial-up connections between trading partners. Trading partners may use batch transmissions, FTP, SMTP, HTTP, and other application-level protocols to send EDI messages.

As noted above, trading partners encapsulate one or more transaction sets in larger data structures called "functional groups" and "interchanges," which are in turn wrapped in envelopes specific to various transport protocols. A trading partner's system sends this message to the recipient's application over the appropriate transport to the appropriate address, where the EDI message (with enclosed functional interchanges and transaction sets) is deposited in the recipient's designated electronic mailbox. VANs generally provide EDI routing, storage, and forwarding services, and may even host mailboxes for smaller customers.

3.1.3 Message Addressing

Internet-based EDI environments may use Internet addresses, such as those associated with SMTP or FTP, to route messages to recipient applications. However, EDI VANs often use "trading partner IDs" in transaction set headers to identify sending and receiving organizations so that messages can be routed appropriately. In such environments, trading partners' EDI translator software inserts these IDs in outbound transactions and reads them on inbound transactions.

For example, a vendor that wishes to bid on a particular request for quotation (RFQ) might prepare an X12-843 transaction set (a bid) and insert the recipient organization's trading partner ID in the transaction set's interchange control and functional group headers (in the "ISA" segment). The sender's VAN will interpret this addressing information and forward the transaction set to the recipient organization via the recipient's VAN. Another addressing option is to use the X12 message's "GS03" header segment to specify the particular application within the recipient's organization to which you wish to route a particular transaction set.

3.1.4 Mapping and Translation

Trading partners must be able to map and translate internal data formats to agreed-upon EDI transaction sets. One approach is for trading partners to install mapping and translation software on their internal data systems that converts between internal formats and EDI transaction sets. Mapping is the process of identifying the relationship between EDI standard data elements and application database fields. Translation is manipulation of source data and creation of target data, based on the map.

For example, companies might configure their existing applications to feed data in "flat file" formats to a commercial off-the-shelf software package that supports creation of data maps and generation of ASC X12 transaction sets based on these maps. Another approach is to subscribe to EDI VAN services to automatically translate between formats prior to forwarding EDI messages to trading partners.

3.1.5 Security

Trading partners agree on common security technologies, such as X.509-based public key infrastructures, to support mutual authentication, digital signatures, encryption, integrity checking, and nonrepudiation on EDI exchanges. If they use a transport such as SMTP with MIME body parts, they might standardize on the S/MIME security protocol, which supports use of X.509 certificates. In such cases, trading partners will be able to translate inbound EDI transaction to internal formats only after the receiving mail client has decrypted the body part and checked its digital signature.

3.1.6 Directory

Trading partners maintain directories of registered trading partners, which enable them to screen and validate inbound EDI transactions as well as address outbound transactions appropriately.

3.1.7 Archiving

Trading partners maintain offline archives of all inbound and outbound EDI messages, before and/or after application of digital signatures and encryption. The archive should include any digital certificates and decryption keys associated with these items, so that they can be authenticated and read long after the original keys have expired.

3.1.8 Auditing

EDI enables trading partners to establish an automated, time-stamped audit trail of every transaction, which can prove very useful for legal and contractual reasons.

3.1.9 EDI and the B2B Reference Model

Summarizing the foregoing discussion in terms of the B2B reference model, we may characterize EDI as follows, in Table 3-2.

As we've shown, EDI focuses on transmitting business content between different companies or organizations. For a paradigm that focuses on business processes over content, we now turn to workflow management technology.

Table 3-2	EDI per the B2B Reference Model
Layer	**Description**
Document	EDI primarily addresses the document layer through its focus on industry-standard transaction sets that encode the content and semantics of B2B exchanges. Contrast this with the BizTalk Framework, which is agnostic to the content of business documents that get wrapped in BizTags.
Message	EDI addresses messaging through its inclusion of trading partner and application identifiers in transaction set headers. These identifiers are essentially addresses used by VANs to route transaction sets on an organization-to-organization or application-to-application basis. However, most EDI transmissions wrap transaction sets in an outer envelope appropriate to the transport protocol—SMTP, FTP, or something else—being used. Compare this with the BizTalk Framework, which defines a richer BizTalk Message than do the EDI standards. However, BizTalk also relies on an outer, transport-specific routing envelope.
Workflow	EDI is a strictly point-to-point B2B phenomenon. It is sometimes one way but more often two way, involving submission of request documents and return of functional acknowledgments. EDI transaction sets do not describe complex routing and handling procedures within the trading partners' systems. Rather, it's up to trading partners to implement the appropriate workflow models in their respective back-end applications. Any such back-end routing and processing workflows are often described in TPAs. Note that BizTalk's simple request/response workflow is not much different from traditional EDI workflow models.
Store	EDI does not specify the back-end data stores and applications needed to support an end-to-end B2B transaction. It leaves these details up to the respective trading partners, just as the BizTalk Framework does not define the back-end stores and applications that engage in B2B transactions.
Marketplace	EDI-enabled "marketplaces" are implicitly defined in trading partner agreements and associated technical implementation plans. Every bilateral or multilateral EDI implementation defines its own B2B value chain, supply chain, or marketplace. However, EDI technical frameworks do not define the roles and responsibilities of business and/or automated agents in these value chains. Contrast this with the BizTalk Framework, which, though it too avoids defining e-marketplace organizational roles, does in fact specify a logical layer of rule-based workflow engines, the BizTalk servers. EDI standards do not assume a rule-based technical infrastructure any more elaborate than a layer of mapping and translation functionality on the sending and receiving ends.

3.2 Workflow

Workflow—as an overall paradigm, as opposed to a discrete set of technologies—is central to many modern management philosophies. The term is often used in the same breath with such related topics as business-process reengineering, value-chain analysis, and just-in-time management.

However, workflow has a precise technical definition that we will use in this book.[1] Workflow applications structure the "store-and-forward" or "asynchronous" organizational processes under which businesses route content. Workflow applications depend on computerized "process definitions" that spell out the precise set of routing and processing steps governing the flow of content. A back-end "workflow enactment service" executes workflows in accordance with computerized process definitions. Workflow applications are traditionally intra-organizational in focus, which obviates the need for EDI-style trading partner agreements and the associated bilateral or multilateral integration projects.

The relevance of workflow to the BizTalk Framework is clearcut. Microsoft has embedded a workflow enactment service, or (in Microsoft's term) "orchestration" service, in its BizTalk Server 2000 product. The vendor also provides a BizTalk workflow/orchestration process definition tool using technology from Visio, a flowcharting tool vendor it acquired in 1999. Microsoft has decisively converged EDI and workflow within its BizTalk product and service strategy, and we can expect to see other BizTalk partners follow suit. Consequently, IT professionals must have a strong understanding of basic workflow concepts and terms in order to deploy BizTalk solutions effectively.

First and foremost, you need to understand how to develop workflow process definitions (or "process models," as they're also called). Process definitions bond the various participants in a workflow to one another as links in a routing chain.

Workflow developers often use graphical process definition tools that allow them to specify tasks, dependencies, and routing and processing steps with flowchart icons on a computer screen. Workflow product vendors often supply their own flowcharting tools that implement a particular paradigm, or conceptual framework, for business process design (though some workflow systems can import process models developed with other third-party design tools). Workflow process models are executed over workflow enactment services, running on one or more servers.

You might model the same workflow in very different ways, depending on the conceptual framework (or flowcharting tool) you employ. In Table 3-3, we distinguish several alternative process-modeling paradigms in today's workflow, business process reengineering, and simulation tools.

[1] The workflow technical discussion in this chapter draws from sections of my book *Workflow Strategies* (Foster City, CA: IDG Books Worldwide, 1997), pp. 45-80.

Table 3-3	*Alternative Workflow Process-Modeling Paradigms*

Paradigm	Description
Address-driven modeling	Models a process as a routing path between predefined users, positions, or groups in the organization structure (see Figure 3-3).
Decision-chain modeling	Models a process as a chain of milestones and associated manual decision points, such a "review resume" (milestone) and "interview/do not interview" (associated decision point).
Event-flow modeling	Describes a process as a chain of manual events, such as human decisions, and automated events, such as routing, collecting, printing, faxing, and archiving documents.
Milestone-document modeling	Shows milestones, documents, roles, and dependencies in a single process map.
Resource-utilization modeling	Explicitly models processes within the context of the organizational structure and provides a strong basis for resource estimation.
Throughput modeling	Focuses on processes as activities that involve flows, accumulations, and rules for transforming inputs into outputs.

However, workflow process design need not be rocket science or a complex engineering project. Some workflow products support end-user development of "ad hoc" workflows that route a single document on a single occasion. Typically, you might employ an e-mail-like "routing slip" interface to define a serial route for a particular document or electronic format that you've just created.

The practical distinction between workflow and e-mail is a fine one. Workflow management systems usually support an "n-hop" addressing model, in contrast to the "next-hop-only" addressing model associated with traditional asynchronous applications such as EDI or e-mail. In workflow environments, you can often specify an arbitrary number of recipients for a particular item, define a rigid routing sequence, and restrict recipients' ability to re-route items in their possession.

Another traditional distinction between workflow and e-mail applications is whether they support application-to-application and/or person-to-person routing. High-powered workflow products often support routing between functional roles or between server or host applications, in a manner

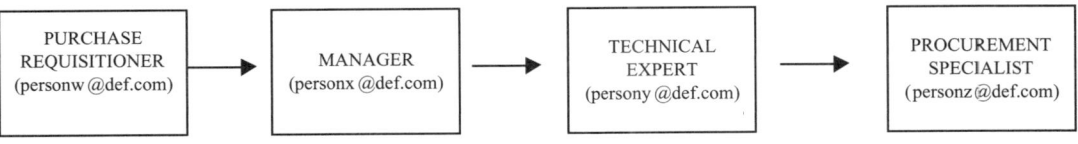

Figure 3-3	*Address-driven modeling defines routing paths between users, positions, or groups.*

similar to traditional EDI. By contrast, e-mail systems usually route items only to individual people or groups of people, placing the items in the recipient's personal e-mail inbox (however, most workflow systems also support person-to-person routing).

Beneath the complexity of different process-modeling approaches, workflow developers draw on a core "vocabulary" of basic process types to specify ever more complex routing chains (listed in Table 3-4 and depicted in Figure 3-4).

Table 3-4	Basic Workflow Process Types
Process Type	**Description**
Sequential routing	There are no parallel paths and predecessor activities must be completed prior to initiation of their successors.
Conditional routing	Alternate paths can be taken, depending on the character of a triggering event.
Parallel routing	Duplicate copies of a workflow item are sent over two or more paths at the same time.
Concurrent routing	Activities share common predecessor tasks, and successor tasks and predecessor tasks must end at the same time.

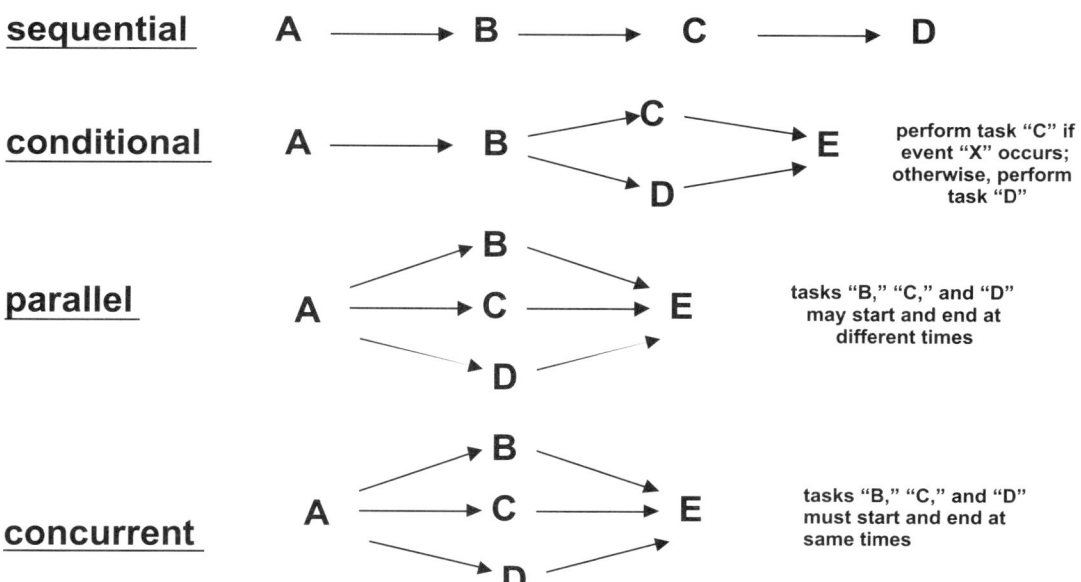

Figure 3-4	Basic workflow process types include sequential, conditional, parallel, and concurrent routing.

However, workflow process models are much more than just arrows connecting tasks or people on a computer screen. Taking a broader perspective, we can see that these models define the three types of organizational controls that give a workflow substance and structure: routes, roles, and rules (as described in Table 3-5).

Workflow can be an environment for fine-grained management control. Organizational controls reside in chains of command, policies, operating procedures, project plans, schedules, budgets, and standard practices. In most modern organizations, management controls are implemented in the sum total of automated information systems that codify and enforce policies and procedures. Workflow applications may span many such information systems, playing the role of a master "policy enforcer," a thread of control that links existing computer networks, shared databases, desktop productivity tools, and other applications. Figure 3-5 depicts the logical layering of individual workflow runs within a process model; the process model executes on a workflow management that integrates with a corporate network and computing infrastructure.

Workflow applications structure the routing process, but not necessarily the content that gets routed. Workflow content may consist of unstructured items such as scanned document images; semistructured documents, such as electronic forms; and/or structured text documents, such as EDI transaction sets. Sophisticated workflow systems allow application developers to define routable "folders" that include text, scanned images, computer-aided design

Table 3-5	Basic Organizational Controls Defining a Workflow
Control	**Description**
Routes	Every organization has a dominant routing path, sometimes hierarchical, sometimes peer-to-peer, but usually a company-specific blend of both models. Workflow depends on prespecified routing paths, in which recipients have limited ability to stop workflows or modify routing paths. As we noted, this distinguishes workflow from traditional e-mail, which lets recipients forward messages to whomever they wish.
Roles	Process models may specify individuals' roles and privileges in the routing process. Such roles might include document originator, reviewer, editor, and approval authority. A workflow application may allocate read/write privileges based on the recipient's workgroup or position in the organization. Recipients may have different views of the same document and be allowed to input or modify different fields.
Rules	Process models may describe document routing and handling procedures to various levels of detail. One rule may limit the range of values that can be input into a particular document field. Another might invoke a spreadsheet application to facilitate complex calculations within a particular document section. Yet another could generate an e-mail notification to the document originator when all necessary management approvals have been secured.

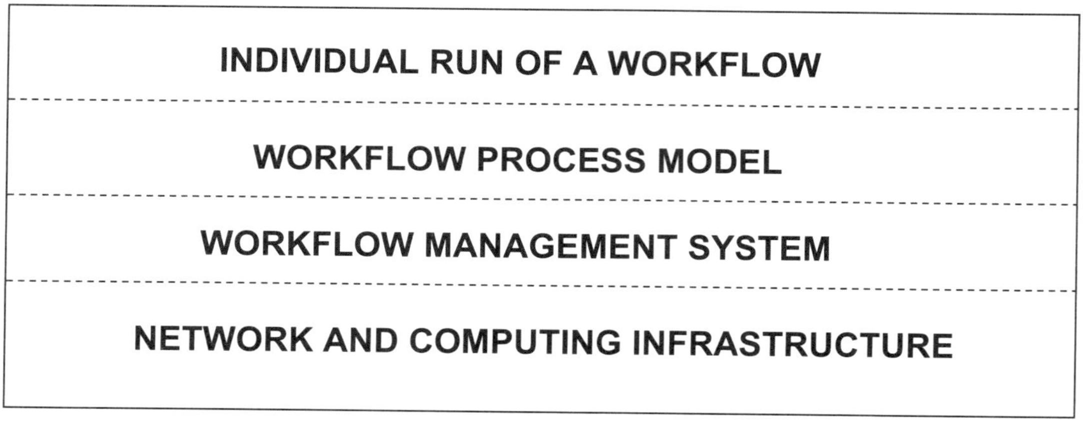

INDIVIDUAL RUN OF A WORKFLOW
WORKFLOW PROCESS MODEL
WORKFLOW MANAGEMENT SYSTEM
NETWORK AND COMPUTING INFRASTRUCTURE

Figure 3-5   *An individual run or instance of a workflow depends on a workflow process model, which operates within a workflow management system, which executes within a network and computing infrastructure.*

drawings, and other multimedia content, such as may be required for coordinating complex engineering project teams. Obviously, organizations may have to invest a lot of money and staff-hours to develop complex multimedia workflow applications that tap into diverse data and document stores.

In terms of real-world implementations, workflow management architectures come in many varieties. They may span a combination of local and wide-area networks and run over a broad range of client and server operating environments. At a high level, one way to distinguish workflow implementations is by their core transport approach: logical or physical routing (as described in Table 3-6).

One useful workflow implementation reference model, from the Brussels-based Workflow Management Coalition (WfMC), organizes these environments into the five high-level functional subsystems (which may be implemented diversely in real-world products), as presented in Table 3-7.

Table 3-6   *Basic Workflow Transport Approaches*

Transport Approaches	Description
Logical routing	A "filestore-based" workflow system transfers logical access privileges pertaining to objects that stay put, physically, in shared, server-based stores, such as those belonging to Web sites or to LAN/WAN-based image, document, or database management systems.
Physical routing	A "messaging-based" workflow system routes objects physically as body parts or file attachments over e-mail or other store-and-forward transport technologies.

Table 3-7	*Workflow Functional Subsystems*
Subsystem	**Description**
Process definition tools	Support development of computerized process representations, including both the automated and manual process components.
Workflow enactment services	Provide run-time environments for initiating, executing, sequencing, and controlling instances of a process definition, adding work items to user worklists and invoking application tools as necessary.
Workflow client applications	Allow workflow participants to interact with workflow enactment services for the purpose of signing on and off the service, initiating processes, displaying worklists, invoking applications, and accessing workflow relevant, application, and control data.
Invoked applications	Launched by the workflow enactment service, per the process definition, for the purpose of initiating or executing an activity.
Administration and monitoring tools	Support real-time surveillance, control, configuration, and optimization of workflow execution.

We now discuss each of these functional subsystems in detail.

3.2.1 Process Definition Tools

Process definition tools allow application developers to specify the organizational policy context implemented within the structure of a workflow. In other words, these tools provide the means to specify the prescribed routes, roles, and rules governing an online business process.

Process architects usually define workflows visually, connecting boxes, arrows, and other on-screen icons and inputting various process parameters into dialog boxes. Flowcharting tools usually support definition of automated workflow activities, such as application auto-launching and event notification, and human-driven activities, such as conditional routing of a document based on inputs into an on-screen e-form field. The tool translates the process architect's model into a format that can be read by the workflow enactment service, which executes the process definition at run time. The workflow enactment service, running over one or more linked servers, functions as a master coordinator and enforcer of the workflow as defined.

As we've noted, developers may choose from a broad range of conceptual frameworks for developing workflow process models. However, these frameworks are just different dialects of a core meta-model that is applicable to all workflows. The process definition "meta-model" consists of the following core workflow elements:

- Types
- Activities
- Roles
- Data

We now discuss each of these workflow elements in detail.

WORKFLOW TYPES

Each workflow is a reusable process, represented in the process design tool and workflow enactment service by a specific "workflow type." The process architect gives each workflow type a unique name and version number. Defining the workflow type involves specifying the conditions that govern the workflow's initiation, termination, security mechanisms, and auditing procedures. These are attributes applicable to the entire workflow, and are not reducible to attributes of particular activities within that workflow.

A unique workflow name and version number identify each process definition to the workflow enactment service. If the workflow is a subprocess or special case of a larger workflow process definition, it will probably inherit features of the master workflow. Under these circumstances, the subsidiary workflow should be given a name that indicates its relationship to the larger process. For example, you could define "purchasing process—pig iron ingots, christmas season 2001" as a special case of "purchasing process—pig iron ingots," which is itself a special case of "purchasing process—iron products." An actual live workflow will use this nomenclature plus other indicators, specific to each workflow enactment service, that define a particular run of the workflow type.

Initiation conditions describe the events under which the workflow enactment service will run a specific workflow type and launch into its first activity. Initiation conditions can be whatever the workflow designer wishes them to be, but generally they fall into several categories. A workflow may start upon a user's login into a particular application. Or it may start when the user creates, submits, or receives a particular document type within an application. Or it might be triggered by an event in a particular database, such as when a particular record gets updated or a particular field value crosses a prespecified threshold. Or it might come to life when the system clock arrives at a prespecified time.

However it comes into being, the workflow application typically causes any number of automatic actions to be taken on networked computers. For example, a document or case folder is automatically originated on the user's screen, given a unique reference number, populated with information from various server or host databases, addressed to the appropriate routing list, and, after the first user finishes with it, transmitted to the next person in the chain.

Throughout its run, the workflow is subject to security conditions defined in its process model. Security conditions specify the following:

- How users authenticate themselves to the workflow enactment service (through such techniques as plaintext passwords, smart cards, digital signatures, and biometrics)
- Who can originate, modify, or delete workflow process definitions
- Who can initiate, terminate, or suspend running workflows
- Who can view the status of current or past workflow runs
- Who can access, read, modify, and delete what application and system data
- What process and application data may be backed up and archived
- What workflow application and system events may be logged and audited

Termination conditions describe the events under which the enactment service will terminate a workflow, notify the appropriate personnel, and archive process data to the appropriate storage systems. Workflows often terminate when the final person in the routing cycle explicitly approves or rejects the routed item, often an electronic form, or when the item is routed back to its originator, or when it simply reaches the last person in the chain and has nowhere else to go. In cases where the final recipient has the authority to approve the content of an electronic form, his or her approval might result in updates being made to corporate databases, notifications being sent to appropriate personnel, and authorization of some corporate action.

WORKFLOW ACTIVITIES

Workflows consist of two or more linked activities, which we may also call "tasks" or "steps." Defining a workflow activity involves specifying its name, type, preconditions, execution conditions, and postconditions. In specifying these attributes for all activities in a workflow, we have effectively defined the full routing chain and rule-set applicable to that business process.

Just as every workflow type should have a unique name, so should every workflow activity. It should be possible to reuse an activity definition many times in a single process definition, as well as in many distinct workflows. An activity's name and definition should indicate whether it's a special case or subset of a more general activity, from which it might inherit various attributes and conditions. In addition, the activity definition should indicate whether it is a single work item or is a proxy for a subprocess, which is a group of interdependent activities with a common process entry point and exit point.

Preconditions specify when the enactment service launches into a particular activity. If it's the first activity in the workflow, the conditions may be that the process as a whole be instantiated and the appropriate user log onto the system. Otherwise, the activity may start when a predecessor activity finishes (in serial workflows), when another activity starts (in parallel or concurrent workflows), or when a specific event occurs or fails to occur (in conditional workflows).

Execution conditions define how a work item is to be processed manually within a particular activity. Table 3-8 describes the categories of workflow execution conditions.

Table 3-8	Workflow Execution Conditions
Condition	**Description**
Application tools to be launched	In accepting a new work item, the user automatically launches the appropriate applications, such as a spreadsheet or computer-aided design (CAD) package, needed to complete that activity. The process definition specifies the name, type, path, and execution parameters of the applications to be invoked in each activity. Execution parameters specify the conditions that will cause applications to be invoked and de-invoked in an activity. An application can be invoked at the start of an activity, in mid-activity (in response, for example, to user inputs), or at its conclusion. Factors that determine which application is invoked would include the nature of the activity and preference of the participant.
Information objects to be presented	In launching an application, the user automatically retrieves and displays the directory, folder, file, or other information object to be processed. The file may be converted from a format understood by the prior activity's application to one compatible with the application currently invoked.
File access, input, and manipulation controls to be applied	Users may be prevented from retrieving information not needed to complete the task. Input controls—such as auto field entry, mandatory field entry, and pick-list selection—would be applied to maintain data integrity and validity. System controls would prevent unauthorized modification and deletion of workflow-relevant information.
Scheduling constraints	Scheduling constraints define the required maximum or minimum timing of an activity. These constraints include in-queue time (the time that a particular item may remain in a user's inbox before being retrieved for active processing), processing time (the time that an item may remain active on a user's "virtual desktop" prior to completion), and out-queue time (the time that a completed work item may remain in a user's workflow outbox prior to forwarding to the next user). Most workflow applications route items automatically upon completion, but some allow users to hold onto completed items temporarily to double-check work or avoid overloading the next recipient.
Automatic notifications to be generated	Some workflow events may be set up to automatically trigger notifications to various users. Figure 3-6 depicts the sequence of automated notifications that might be triggered by various activities within a hypothetical workflow. Process administrators and document originators are the usual recipients of notifications. Any event can be set up to trigger notifications. However, notifications are usually generated to acknowledge delivery, receipt, forwarding, and final approval of routed work items.

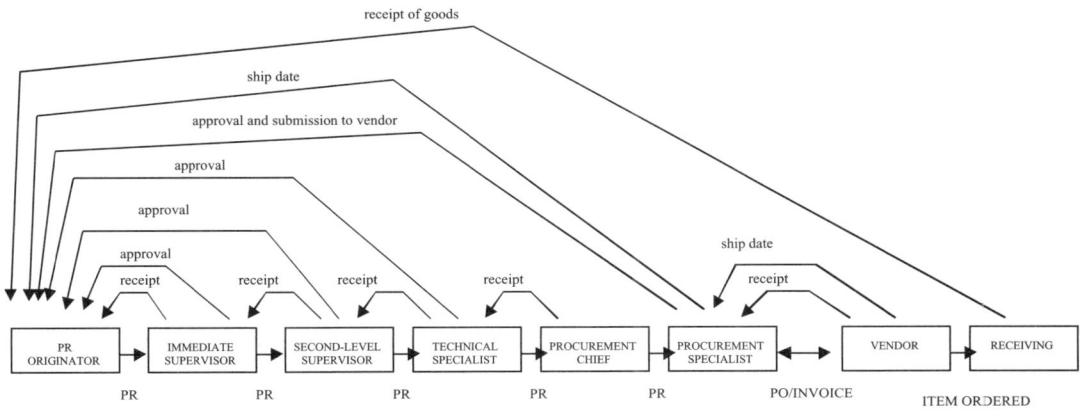

Figure 3-6 *Typical sequence of automated, e-mail-based notifications within an automated procurement workflow.*

Postconditions specify the triggering events that cause an activity to terminate, and also specify what happens next. If the activity is the last in the workflow, the triggering condition may be approval of a particular document and subsequent actions would be termination of the process and archiving of process-relevant data. If it's any other activity, the subsequent action might be startup of another activity (in a serial or conditional workflow) or completion of another activity (in parallel or concurrent workflows).

WORKFLOW ROLES

Workflow roles define participants and their various privileges. A role consists of the following attributes: name, authentication field, organizational entity, and capabilities.

The process definition must specify each workflow role/participant by a unique name, which may be a personal name, job title, or description of responsibilities within the context of a workflow-enabled process. The name may also serve as the participant's login ID to the workflow application.

The authentication field would contain or point to the role/participant's password, public-key certificate, voiceprint, or othe digital tokens associated with the applicable authentication scheme.

The organizational entity would describe the relevant project, workgroup, location, department, or company associated with a participant's role in the workflow. An X.500-like "relative distinguished name" may be used in this regard.

The capabilities definition would indicate whether the user is authorized to do any of the following:

- Originate, review, revise, approve, disapprove, or delete process definitions or segments thereof
- Originate, review, revise, approve, disapprove, or delete work items or components thereof
- Monitor the location and status of workflows in process and/or those already complete
- Suspend workflows in process

WORKFLOW DATA

Workflow data is the content routed in an online business process. Workflow data is user-input information that is read directly by the workflow enactment service for the purpose of triggering routing and execution rules. For example, user inputs into purchase-requisition form fields are used to determine which technical and purchasing specialists need to review the document. The attributes that apply to workflow data are its name, type, and path.

3.2.2 Workflow Enactment Services

Workflow enactment services bring process definitions to life. Figure 3-7 shows a hypothetical workflow executing within a single-server workflow enactment service environment.

A workflow enactment service consists of one or more "workflow engines," which reside on network servers and may be embedded as components in large application environments (such as the BizTalk Server, a mail server such as Exchange 2000, or a database server such as SQL Server). Collectively, these servers are the master controllers, transfer agents, and application-logic repositories for distributed workflow applications. Figure 3-8 graphically depicts workflow enactment services as the centerpiece of a workflow infrastructure.

The core functions of a workflow enactment service are as follows:

- Initiate, execute, schedule, and control actual workflows in accordance with process definitions
- Sign users on and off the system
- Authenticate users
- Add, modify, and delete items in users' workflow inboxes (also known as "worklists")
- Invoke external applications
- Retrieve application files
- Maintain run-time workflow control status data
- Facilitate workflow control, administration, and audit
- Archive process definition, workflow control, workflow relevant, and workflow application data

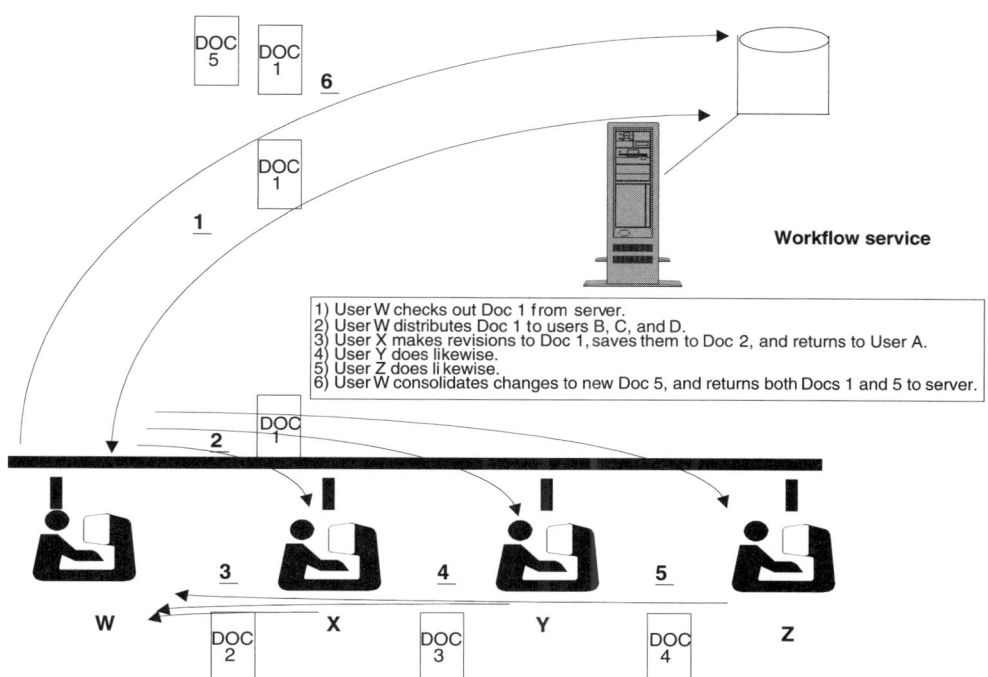

1) User W checks out Doc 1 from server.
2) User W distributes Doc 1 to users B, C, and D.
3) User X makes revisions to Doc 1, saves them to Doc 2, and returns to User A.
4) User Y does likewise.
5) User Z does likewise.
6) User W consolidates changes to new Doc 5, and returns both Docs 1 and 5 to server.

Figure 3-7   *Typical intra-organizational workflow process within a single-server environment.*

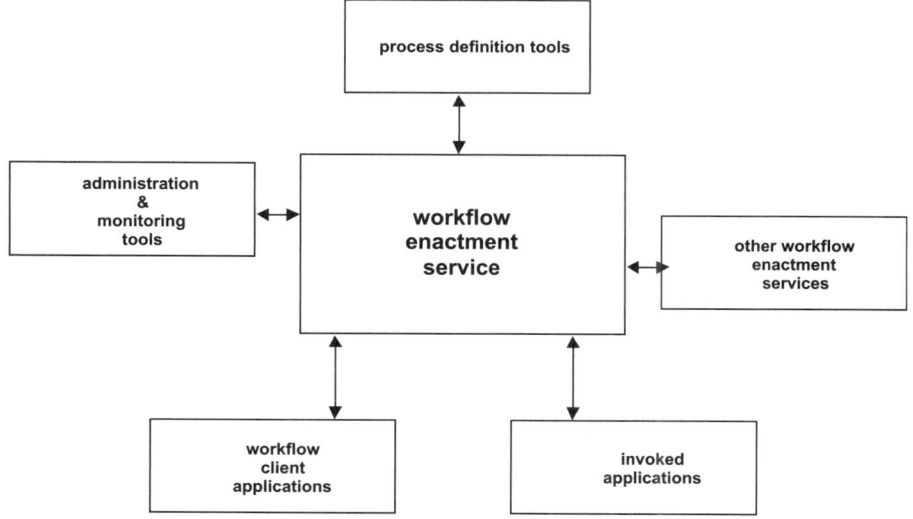

Figure 3-8   *A workflow management systems includes five functional subsystems.*

Workflows may execute on different workflow engines within a single vendor's environment, or across two or more vendors' environments (if the vendors have established interoperability at the server-to-server level). These
alternative configurations of the enactment service—centralized and decentralized—are depicted in Figure 3-9. The WfMC has defined standards for
server-to-server workflow interoperability (as it has for many interfaces in the
workflow reference model), but these standards are largely unimplemented
by workflow vendors. Most real-life workflow environments are largely vendor-proprietary, monolithic implementations, and BizTalk Server is no excep-
tion to the rule.

3.2.3 Workflow Client Applications

Workflow clients, just like e-mail clients, usually present an inbox—or "worklist"—to end users. Indeed, as we've noted above, many workflow environments are integrated with users' e-mail systems and route work items to
users' e-mail inboxes. Figure 3-10 shows users downloading updated worklists from a workflow enactment service, much the same way they routinely
retrieve new e-mail from a mail server (indeed, the worklists may consist of
e-mail that includes workflow-enabled e-forms processed at the workflow
engine).

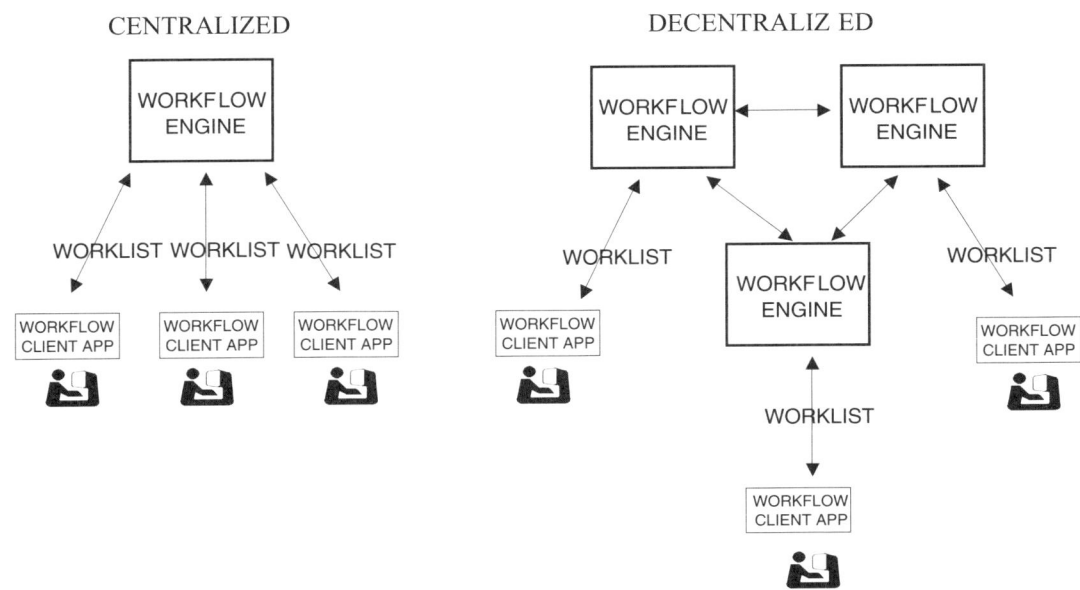

Figure 3-9   *Workflow management systems may be centralized or decentralized in configuration.*

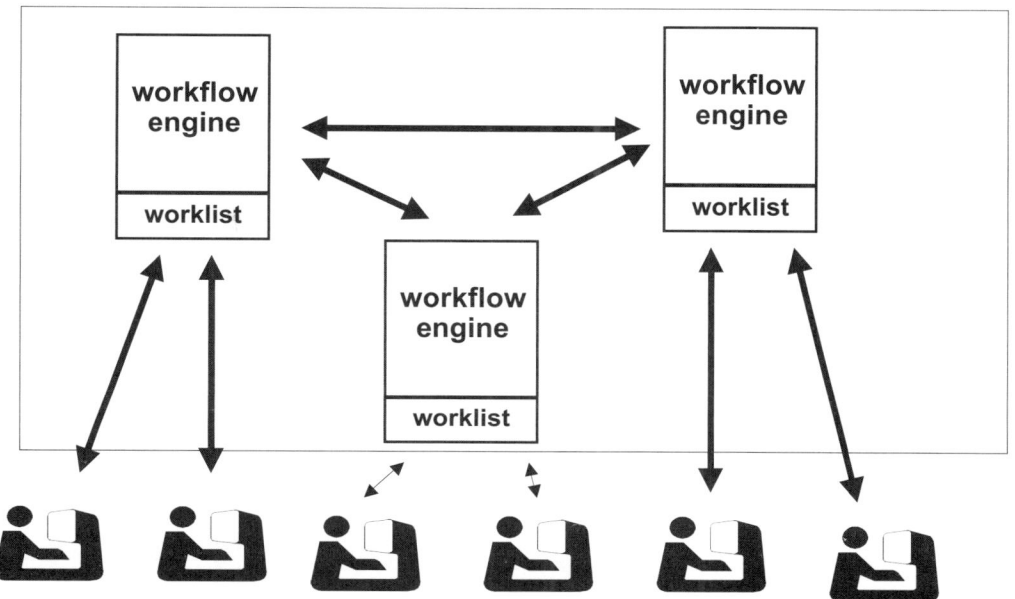

Figure 3-10   *Workflow clients regularly retrieve updated worklists from the workflow enactment service.*

Workflow client applications control the look, feel, and content of users' interaction with the workflow enactment service. The core functions of a workflow client application are:

- Provide user access to a workflow inbox, which incorporates a "worklist handler" that displays worklist items retrieved from the enactment service
- Support login to the enactment service
- Support initiation of process instances
- Support invocation of the appropriate application(s) when a work item is opened
- Provide access to workflow functions and data
- Organize workflow data into on-screen cases, folders, and documents

Depending on the application, worklists typically display the following information:

- List of work items sorted by time of arrival, priority, process type, process instance, or some other criteria
- Name, type, status, creation date, and originator of each work item

- Role and privileges of the current user with respect to the item
- Required completion or due date

Depending on the controlling process definition, users may have a great deal or precious little latitude in worklist manipulation. Users may be allowed to select which of many presented items they will work on, which they will defer, and which they will forward or refuse. Alternately, the workflow enactment service may present only one item at a time to each user, requiring activity completion before the next item is presented. The enactment service may be set up to withdraw and reassign items that have sat unopened in a user's inbox beyond a prespecified time interval. Or the enactment service may have the ability to distribute items among users in order to balance workloads across a workgroup.

3.2.4 Invoked Applications

As discussed above, invoked applications provide tools for users to work with cases, folders, documents, data, images, and other information routed to them by the workflow enactment service.

Ideally, the user should be able to launch the appropriate application and data files (from their client or a server) when accepting or opening a routed work item. If the item is MIME content and the user has the appropriate "helper" application installed on his or her client, this application will launch automatically. Alternately, the client may invoke a remote application automatically using remote procedure calls, CORBA, DCOM, or some other remote invocation object technology.

3.2.5 Administration and Monitoring Tools

Finally, workflow administration and monitoring tools keep workflow systems and applications running smoothly. They enable process administrators to:

- Set up, configure, and optimize the many software components that make up a workflow application
- Activate process definitions or segments thereof
- Assign particular individuals to functional roles per the process definition
- Allocate run-time processes, activities, applications, and data to various workflow engines
- Initiate, suspend, resume, redirect, and terminate process instances
- Monitor executing processes and analyze historical data on completed and terminated processes

3.2.6 Workflow and the B2B Reference Model

Summarizing the foregoing discussion, Table 3-9 characterizes workflow in terms of the B2B reference model.

Table 3-9	Workflow per the B2B Reference Model
Layer	**Description**
Document	Most workflow applications route documents of various sorts, including desktop application files, electronic forms, scanned document images, database extracts, and CAD drawings. Workflow applications often base their processing and routing logic on events that involve documents, such as creation, receipt, field input, field revision, deletion, and approval. However, workflow applications, being primarily intra-organizational (not B2B) in focus, rarely specify content structured on the basis of industry standard EDI transaction sets.
Message	Workflow applications use messaging systems either as their primary transport medium, as a channel for transmitting process-related notifications and alerts, or both. Workflow applications invariably wrap content in the message envelope associated with mail transport, and do not (in contrast to EDI, BizTalk, or other B2B framework) define an inner data "message" envelope (otherwise known as an "interchange" and "functional group").
Workflow	This is, of course, the raison d'etre of workflow systems. They support definition of computerized process models ranging according to various conceptual paradigms and to various degrees of complexity. They support automated execution of these models under single- or multiserver workflow enactment services.
Store	Workflow systems often integrate tightly with back-end document, image, data, and Web stores. In fact, e-forms-oriented workflow applications are often sophisticated front ends to relational databases, with the e-form serving as the data input and query mechanism, with updates to the database contingent on approval of the completed form at the end of the workflow. Figure 3-11 shows the central role of databases in many workflow environments: containers of workflow application data, status information, and process definitions.
Marketplace	Workflow applications are usually intra-organizational and administrative in nature, so they do not define marketplaces under any sense of that term. However, they often cooordinate the internal processes—such as routing and approving purchase requisitions—necessary for companies to participate in an external marketplace. As such, traditional workflow applications complement the B2B focus on EDI, BizTalk, and other e-commerce interoperability frameworks.

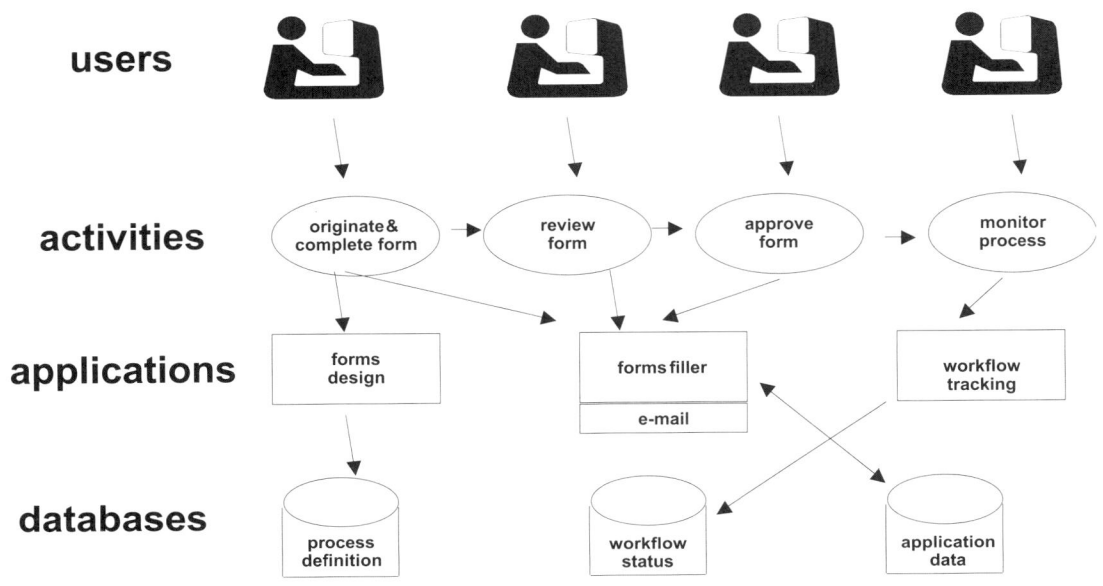

Figure 3-11   *Databases play many important roles in a workflow environment.*

3.3 Where EDI and Workflow Converge

As we have shown, EDI and workflow are complementary technologies, on several levels. EDI structures the content of business transactions, while workflow structures the routing chain that binds one business process to another. EDI is inherently B2B in focus, while workflow has historically been largely intra-organizational. And EDI has a predominantly point-to-point routing model, while workflow supports definition of process models of considerable complexity and sophistication.

E-marketplaces are where EDI and workflow converge. An Internet-based trading community can thrive only where all participants share a common process model—in other words, an agreed-upon set of business rules that govern structured transactions among all comers. Just as important, all participants will have to implement a common B2B interoperability framework that allows them to enter easily into new trading relationships without the need for costly, time-consuming, multilateral coordination of legal agreements and technical interfaces.

E-marketplaces are where different companies' internal data models and process models converge. For that to happen, you need EDI standards and workflow standards. BizTalk is Microsoft's attempt to bring these worlds together into a new standards framework. Other frameworks are driving toward the same bright spot on the B2B horizon.

REFERENCE

Kobielus, James G., *Workflow Strategies*, Foster City, CA: IDG Books Worldwide, Inc., 1997, pp. 47-80.

Who's Supporting and Implementing BizTalk?

The true test of any standard is how many companies, other than the standard's author, use it to develop interoperable products and services.

BizTalk is a young interoperability framework, and BizTalk-compliant products and services are just now hitting the market. However, Microsoft has recruited such a broad swath of the B2B industry around the framework that we can declare its BizTalk initiative a qualified success. BizTalk is the horizontal framework to beat in today's fast-evolving B2B market. It is considerably more flexible than Open Buying on the Internet (OBI), has more industry momentum than cXML, and has produced more detailed technical specifications than XML/EDI. And, of course, BizTalk has the full backing and support of the mothership of modern enterprise computing, Microsoft. The software giant has never shied from using its influence to bend new markets around its core business strategies.

Politics—the art of building industry alliances—often separates the winning standard from a field of well-intentioned technical specifications. From the start, Microsoft has positioned the BizTalk Framework as a scaffolding for its B2B industry alliances, defining an industry migration path from traditional EDI to Internet-centric e-marketplaces. The vendor has been an important catalyst for bringing various e-commerce industry players together to discuss common application and schema architectures. As time goes by, we will be able to gauge industry support for Microsoft's BizTalk initiative through several indicators (in no particular order of importance):

- Degree to which the general public begins to regard the terms *BizTalk, B2B, EDI, e-business,* and *e-commerce* as near-synonyms

- Sales, installed base, and usage of Microsoft's BizTalk Server product and BizTalk-based MSN marketplace services
- Sales, installed base, and usage of third-party products and services implementing the BizTalk Framework
- Number, range, and importance of vendors that have developed or announced products and services implementing the BizTalk Framework (to the possible exclusion of other standards frameworks)
- Number, range, and importance of vendors represented in the BizTalk Steering Committee
- Number, range, and importance of vendors that have simply announced their token support for the framework
- Number, range, and importance of business document schemas posted to the BizTalk.org repository
- Volume of Internet and VAN traffic wrapped in BizTalk envelopes
- Number and range of organizations evaluating and implementing BizTalk-compliant products and services
- Number, range, and monetary value of technical requests for proposal that specify BizTalk-compliant products and services
- Number of help wanted ads for IT professionals that require BizTalk experience, skills, and knowledge
- Volume of postings to BizTalk discussions at BizTalk.org, on Usenet groups, and on other Internet sites and communities serving e-business application developers
- Number of trade books, magazine articles, and training materials focusing on BizTalk
- Degree to which you can assume general familiarity with BizTalk and don't have to take the time to explain it at cocktail parties (if the subject ever comes up)

Obviously, BizTalk—as a standards framework, initiative, or set of products and services—has a long way to go before it achieves broad industry support to the degree enjoyed by, say, Windows, Java, or HTML. And it may have to share industry mindshare indefinitely with one or more alternative B2B frameworks.

Many of these "industry support indicators" will become more important as BizTalk-compliant solutions penetrate the B2B market, and as the market sorts out the essential B2B frameworks from the also-rans. At this early stage in BizTalk's development, we can best judge its industry support in the following ways:

- Who's on the BizTalk Steering Committee
- Who's announced general support for the BizTalk initative
- Who's posting schemas to BizTalk.org
- Who's announced BizTalk-compliant solutions and
- Which users are candidates for migration to BizTalk Server

4.1 Who's on the BizTalk Steering Committee?

The BizTalk Steering Committee is more symbolic than functional in its contribution to Microsoft's BizTalk initiative. It unites software vendors, service providers, industry consortia, standards groups, a trade association, and end-user organizations in the cause of B2B interoperability. And it validates Microsoft's BizTalk philosophy without endorsing it as the one and only valid approach.

Microsoft won considerable credibility for BizTalk in the EDI arena when it brought the Data Interchange Standards Association, the standards group that manages X12 standards, onto the BizTalk Steering Committee. And enlisting Ariba, cXML's proponent, into the group indicated that Microsoft might not take the adversarial posture that damaged its credibility in the Java and Web communities. Likewise, Commerce One's participation in the committee adds another high-visibility e-marketplace service provider, software vendor, and XML proponent to the cause.

Just as important a symbol is Microsoft's ongoing participation in groups developing other B2B frameworks—OBI, OAGIS, and RosettaNet—and in the OASIS group that has deployed another XML e-commerce schema repository. Microsoft is clearly committed to BizTalk as the overriding B2B framework for its own products and services, but is not implementing the BizTalk Server product as a closed environment. Indeed, one of the BizTalk Server's core features is "any to any" mapping, translation, and routing of business documents between diverse applications, networks, and computing environments, such as various third-party ERP products.

It would be no great stretch for Microsoft to include native "connectors" in BizTalk Server for cXML, OBI, OAGIS, and heretofore unborn B2B standards (though Microsoft has not committed to that course of action). Customer demands to integrate BizTalk Server fully with trading partners and internal business processes may in fact compel Microsoft to support interfaces to many other B2B frameworks.

4.2 Who's Announced General Support for the BizTalk Initiative?

Microsoft's initial announcement of the BizTalk initiative also included the obligatory list of other companies—vendors and corporate users—who express general support for its philosophy and goals.

A company expresses "general support" when it does not commit publicly to committing resources or pursuing a particular course of action (or does not even commit to not implementing rival frameworks or solutions).

The companies expressing general support for the BizTalk initiative fall into the following categories:

- E-commerce and XML software vendors: Active Software Inc., DataChannel Inc., Datastream, Emercis Corp., Intelisys Electronic Commerce, Level 8 Systems Inc., MarketSoft Corporation, Motiva, Oberon Software, SAQQARA Systems Inc., Vitria Technology Inc., and webMethods
- EDI service providers: Harbinger Corp. and Sterling Commerce Inc.
- E-commerce merchant sites: 1-800-FLOWERS, barnesandnoble.com, Best Buy Company Inc., Dell Computer Corp., Eddie Bauer Inc., and Sharp Electronics Corp.

One might argue that these companies generally lack the symbolic importance that would rate them inclusion on the high-profile BizTalk Steering Committee. But that's pure conjecture on our part. We can reasonably assume that the vendors and service providers will soon begin to support the BizTalk Framework in their commercial offerings, and the merchants will eventually migrate toward running their e-storefronts on BizTalk Server, Commerce Server, Windows 2000, SQL Server, and the full range of Microsoft Server products. Putting themselves on this list is tantamount to declaring themselves all-Microsoft shops, where e-business is concerned.

4.3 Who's Posting Schemas to BizTalk.org?

The BizTalk Framework enjoys general support across many sectors of the economy. Evidence for this is the fact that, as of January 2000, over 50 organizations had posted over 150 vertical-market XML schemas to BizTalk.org's schema library. The posted schemas fall into the following industry categories:

- Agriculture, forestry, and fishing
- Construction
- Educational services
- Finance and insurance
- Health care and social assistance
- Information
- Manufacturing
- Professional, scientific, and technical services
- Real estate, rental, and leasing
- Retail trade
- Wholesale trade

Some of these schemas come from companies on the BizTalk Steering Committee and some from firms that had declared their general support for the framework. But many come from lesser-known vendors developing vertical market B2B software and services.

4.4 Who's Announced BizTalk-Compliant Solutions?

A good source of detailed information on BizTalk's industry support is the "news" tab at http://www.biztalk.org/News/news.asp. Here you can learn who has posted a vertical market or specialized business document schema to BizTalk.org's library/repository. You can also learn how the schema publisher plans to implement that schema in its own commercial B2B products and/or services.

As of January 2000, more than 20 of the companies that posted schemas to BizTalk.org had also issued press releases announcing how they plan to integrate these schemas into their commercial offerings. The range of BizTalk-enabled solutions includes:

- Accounting and financial data interchange
- Business document mapping and translation
- Channel partner profiling and relationship management
- Comparison shopping
- Dealer distribution hub management
- EDI
- Electronic storefront development
- Engineering change management
- Enterprise application integration
- ERP integration
- Human resources (HR) self-service
- Inventory control
- Invoicing
- Knowledge management
- Operational resource management
- Order entry and processing
- Procurement
- Proposal life-cycle management
- Recruitment
- Supply chain management
- Travel and entertainment expense management
- Workflow management

These applications represent the mainstream of B2B data and process integration requirements, which indicates that the BizTalk Framework has struck a responsive chord in the industry and provides a foundation to which many vendors feel they can craft commercially viable solutions (even well in advance of Microsoft's delivery of the BizTalk Server product that many proposed solutions depend on).

The following is not an exhaustive listing of BizTalk-compliant solutions that have been released or announced. However, it captures the range of different products, services, and vertical markets that are being BizTalk-enabled. We provide summaries of each announcement, organized alphabetically by vendor.

BUSINESS AND ACCOUNTING SOFTWARE DEVELOPERS' ASSOCIATION • BASDA has published BizTalk Framework–compatible schemas describing XML messages for direct exchange of purchase orders and invoices between different accounting software packages. BASDA's "eBIS-XML" schemas define a uniform financial language that promotes information exchange between ERP and accounting software packages. Many of the world's leading accounting software developers assisted in development of BASDA's eBIS-XML message standards. Unlike a traditional EDI message, an eBIS-XML message can be displayed as a document and printed out as an order or invoice upon receipt. A company does not need to have eBIS-XML-enabled applications to receive and read the electronic message.

CHANNELWAVE SOFTWARE INC. • ChannelWave provides distribution channel-partner relationship management applications. The company has published a BizTalk Framework–compatible schema for exchange of distribution-channel partner profiles. In conjunction with ChannelWave's products, the schema supports B2B communication and transactions between companies and their channel partners. ChannelWave provides a comprehensive "partner profiling" database, which supports partner relationship management applications such as lead distribution and management, forecasting, order/quote configuration, pricing and news distribution.

CLARUS CORPORATION • Clarus, a member of the BizTalk Steering Committee, provides B2B online procurement and operational resource management applications. The company has published 11 BizTalk Framework–compatible schemas for interchange of electronic procurement information. The schemas address the electronic exchange of purchase orders, supplier information, receipt acknowledgments, and accounting data. They also support document routing between applications. The schemas are compatible with OAGIS standards for integrating with back-office applications, such as ERP systems.

COLLATECH INC. • CollaTech provides application software that facilitates configuration and setup of Web-based dealer distribution hub networks, connecting distributors to dealers and their customers. The company has published BizTalk Framework–compatible schemas for definition of e-commerce distribution hubs. The schemas will support dealer submission of XML-based purchase orders and receipt of real-time pricing, updates, inventory, and order status reports through CollaTech's CyberVendor software.

CONCUR TECHNOLOGIES • Concur, a member of the BizTalk Steering Committee, provides B2B procurement, human resources self-service, and travel and entertainment expense management software. Concur's flagship product, EmployeeDesktop, provides a common user interface for accessing its suite of workplace e-commerce solutions, including B2B procurement, HR self-service, and travel and entertainment expense management. It also provides a business portal through which employees can access critical information and services. Concur submitted BizTalk Framework–compatible schemas that support order entry, invoicing, cataloging, trading relationships management, and expense reporting from EmployeeDesktop.

HR-XML CONSORTIUM • The HR-XML Consortium is a newly formed nonprofit group dedicated to the development and promotion of standardized HR-related XML vocabularies for use in B2B HR management systems. The HR-XML Consortium has published three BizTalk Framework–compatible schemas supporting B2B HR data exchange, workflow management, and "talent acquisition" over the Web. One of the consortium's founding members is Icarian, Inc., a Sunnyvale, California-based provider of eWorkforce Management solutions. Icarian provides the Icarian eWorkforce application suite, a Web-based offering for planning, hiring, deployment, and retention of employees in global organizations.

The consortium has designed its BizTalk-compatible HR schemas to support interchange of job postings between employers' HR management systems and online recruiting systems and job boards, search and qualification of employment candidates in job databases before having to commit to purchasing resume or candidate data, and descriptive XML tagging of entries in employee skills and knowledge bases.

KEYFILE CORP. • Keyfile provides workflow management, process automation, enterprise application integration, and e-commerce software. Keyfile has published a BizTalk Framework–compatible workflow schema for embedding within online forms, transactions, and other XML documents. The schema defines the business logic for receiving, handling, and processing XML documents as part of an e-commerce transaction. The schema works with the next release of Keyfile's Keyflow Commerce and XML Forms Designer products, which will provide developers with the ability to:

- Visually author XML-based e-commerce user interfaces and Web pages directly from BizTalk schemas
- Create interactive Web pages and forms that let the users interact directly with the BizTalk Server
- Integrate Keyflow Commerce directly with any application or system that provides BizTalk-compliant XML documents
- Extend the capabilities of the XML forms-based interface by adding structured business logic and transaction tracking and archiving

Lexica LLC • Lexica provides B2B supply-chain management software and services for the insurance industry. It has published BizTalk Framework–compatible XML schemas—called iLingo—both to the BizTalk.org online library and to its own iLingo.org Web site. These schemas facilitate end-to-end automation of insurance selling and transaction processing. The schemas are fundamental to the operation of the company's Lexica Online software product and its consumer-oriented www.insurezone.com e-marketplace service.

Lexica Online is an XML-based software environment that enables an automated supply chain involving insurance companies and their trading partners. Insurezone.com provides a consumer-oriented e-marketplace. It supports instant comparison shopping for insurance policies and the ability to obtain a quote and buy a policy online.

Litefoot Inc. • Litefoot provides knowledge management software. It has published BizTalk Framework–compatible schemas for Personal Information Management and Customer Service. These schemas suppport integration of BizTalk messages with corporate knowledge databases and automation of BizTalk message processing via user-defined software agents and business rules, in conjunction with the company's Knowledge Automation System (KAS) software product. Litefoot's schemas define an open standard for natural-language business rules, allowing corporate domain experts to define and implement BizTalk automation processes. KAS provides a simple, declarative approach to fully automating BizTalk request/reply message routing and content processing.

Motiva Software Corporation • Motiva provides a B2B engineering change management software and workflow product, Motiva DesignGroup. Motiva has published a BizTalk Framework–compatible schema for data and workflow process exchange between Motiva DesignGroup servers and other enterprise business applications, including third-party ERP products and other BizTalk-enabled systems. The schema will enable companies to implement end-to-end change management processes that drive engineering changes throughout the supply chain, regardless of each participant's information technology infrastructure. It supports exchange of product designs, network components and configurations, plant and facility designs and layouts, and project definition data.

Netfish Technologies • Netfish provides B2B EDI and e-commerce software. It has published BizTalk Framework–compatible schemas for ANSI X12 EDI invoices and purchase orders for implementation within its XDI suite of products. These schemas apply to the most recent ANSI X12 EDI standard document formats, which support the four-digit date fields required for Y2K-compliant applications. Netfish plans to contribute additional XML schemas for nearly 300 specific X12 transaction sets.

PROPHET 21, INC. • Prophet 21, Inc. provides business software for wholesale distributors, supporting finance, order management, inventory management, purchasing, and electronic commerce applications within an integrated supply chain. The company has published BizTalk Framework–compatible schemas for wholesale distribution industry-specific data interchanges. These schemas are fundamental to Prophet 21's software products, including Prophet 21 Wholesale and Prophet 21 Acclaim. The schemas define a standard sales order process for wholesale distributors.

SOFTSHARE • Softshare provides server and desktop applications for e-commerce. Its Softshare Delta product supports mapping and translation of data between BizTalk Framework–compatible schemas and other XML, EDI, flat file, text, and other formats, enabling the product's users to integrate BizTalk documents into their business environment. Softshare Delta can generate and automatically address BizTalk documents using the framework's approved set of XML tags. In addition to creating BizTalk documents, Softshare Delta users can author BizTalk-compatible XML schemas for exchange with trading partners.

TECHNOMATION SYSTEMS INC. • Technomation combines personalized portals with enterprise application integration to support enterprise development of B2B services. It has published a BizTalk Framework–compatible schema for "eProposals," a foundation for the vendor's BizOffice Portal for eProposals service, which supports an integrated value chain of proposal creation, quote generation, order entry, inventory control, invoicing, and postsales customer support. The portal-based service and schema support B2B transfer of descriptions of products or services, including specifications, capabilities, and costs, between potential customers, vendors, and other trading partners.

The service also supports standardized representations of business functions in the proposal/quote workflow. BizTalk provides a framework for describing data-handling rules within the eProposals environment. Technomation's eProposal schema assembles, categorizes, and standardizes data and rules for eProposal generation, routing, and handling. It also integrates Technomation's portal-based proposal-creation and quote-generation features with companies' document management applications, back-office systems, and data warehouses. Technomation has based the service on Microsoft's Distributed interNetworking Architecture as well as the BizTalk Framework.

4.5 Which Users Are Candidates for Migration to BizTalk Server?

Microsoft boasts a substantial installed base of e-commerce customers that have built their e-storefronts on Site Server Commerce Edition (SSCE). Many of them have built their dotcom businesses in a predominantly Microsoft server environment, and we can reasonably suppose that many of them are strong candidates for migration to BizTalk Server, Commerce Server, Windows 2000, and the rest of the Microsoft Server suite.

The largest BizTalk deployments are very likely to be application service providers (ASPs) setting themselves up as vertical market trading hubs. As the popularity of BizTalk-based e-marketplace and supply-chain management solutions grows, we might see a "network effect" in Microsoft's favor: large enterprises and trading hubs compelling more firms to commit to implementing BizTalk Server internally. Still, the presence of published BizTalk interoperability specifications could spur the development of third-party BizTalk server products, potentially competing with Microsoft and dampening growth in its share of the "interchange server" or "integration broker" market.

Cynics might describe the BizTalk initiative as yet another Microsoft foray into prematurely announced vaporware that took much longer to bring to market than the vendor initially promised. Microsoft's prominence and influence make this a tempting strategy, since it can cause a new market—such as B2B e-commerce—to hold its collective breath waiting for the big vendor to deliver its long-awaited powerhouse product.

Nevertheless, you have to admit that Microsoft knows how to play this game. It has won an impressive degree of industry support for the BizTalk initiative where it really counts: third parties committing to the BizTalk Framework, developing BizTalk-compliant products and services, and helping to stoke popular expectations in Microsoft's favor. The BizTalk Framework's level of industry support is doubly impressive if you consider that the vendors we've just discussed committed to the framework long before Microsoft shipped a commercial BizTalk Server product, much less a working beta model.

Apparently, many vendors and users are eagerly searching for an Internet-facing alternative to "EDI as usual." Industries are converging on BizTalk because it is a serviceable, extensible framework for B2B e-commerce and supply-chain integration. It's not the only framework, but it's the closest we have so far to a common environment for interoperable B2B applications.

How Open Is the BizTalk Framework?

Microsoft is, as most everyone knows, a near monopoly in its core business—desktop operating systems—and has used its monopoly profits and market power to dominate many other niches of distributed computing.

Microsoft is the predominant champion of "closed-source" programming in an Internet community that has embraced the "open-source" movement with messianic fervor. It has developed an all-encompassing, closed-source systems architecture to match its diverse product groups and ambitions.

Microsoft is also a world-class purveyor of marketecture frameworks for computing and networking. These frameworks either repackage existing Windows-based technologies, products, and standards in a new conceptual scheme (a la Windows Open System Architecture) or illustrate how Windows can play in a world not entirely created by Microsoft (a la its Distributed interNetworking Architecture).

5.1 Microsoft's Familiar Approach to Implementing Open Standards

The company's business model revolves around implementing whatever blend of proprietary and open standards can secure market share most quickly in whatever product niche it targets. The company has always been quick to leverage its predominance in desktop operating systems, and now in server operating systems. Microsoft has been known to take any or all of the following tacks in playing the standards game to its advantage, as presented in Table 5-1.

The BizTalk initiative belongs in the third category presented in Table 5-1. BizTalk is yet another Microsoft attempt to weave open standards into an overarching framework that the company controls. However, the BizTalk Framework includes no Microsoft-proprietary twists to XML, the core World Wide Web Consortium standard on which it is based. Indeed, Microsoft has positioned its internally developed XDR schema specification as simply an interim requirement for BizTalk and will support the W3C's proposed XML Schemas standard whenever this is ratified.

BizTalk is also an aggressive campaign to line up the early support necessary to transform Microsoft's B2B interoperability framework into a de facto industry standard. To win industry support, Microsoft knows it must adopt the rhetorical line that the BizTalk Framework is "open." The company recognizes that the industry's ideological climate in the early years of the 21st century demands such an approach. Several facets of the industry's zeitgeist have curtailed Microsoft's room to maneuver publicly in proposing initiatives such as BizTalk.

First among these prevailing conditions is the universal suspicion (mixed with grudging admiration) that surrounds Microsoft's every move. The company's bold business ventures and aggressive, recalcitrant public posture only fuel these suspicions. Every two-bit conspiracy theorist imagines that Microsoft seeks to extend its distributed-computing hegemony into world economic domination.

Table 5-1	*Microsoft's Approaches to Implementing Industry Standards*
Approach	**Examples**
Develop Windows-centric proprietary standards that are functionally equivalent to rival industry standards.	Messaging Application Programming Interface API (MAPI) over Vendor-Independent Messaging (VIM); ActiveX over Java; Distributed Component Object Model (DCOM) over Common Object Request Broker Architecture (CORBA); Internet Server Application Programming Interface (ISAPI) over Common Gateway Interface (CGI)
Put its own proprietary Windows-centric twist on open technology standards developed elsewhere	Windows-specific Java classes and methods over strict Sun Java Development Kit 1.1 compliance; Microsoft-developed Jscript over Sun and Netscape's JavaScript
Subsume industry standards in a larger, Microsoft-dominated standards framework	Active Directory Services Interface over Lightweight Directory Access Protocol (LDAP); Open Database Connectivity (ODBC) over Structured Query Language (SQL); CryptoAPI over Public Key Cryptography Standards (PKCS).

Then there is the aftermath of the U.S. government's successful court case against Microsoft. This has triggered a landslide of litigation against the firm by competitors, current and deceased, who claim to have suffered financial damage from Microsoft's monopolistic behavior. The court's finding against Microsoft may also lead to partitioning of the firm's operating system business from the rest of the company (though it's not clear where the BizTalk product development group would land in any such reorganization).

We shouldn't underestimate the extent to which Microsoft has abused its market power in crushing competitors, but the firm is obviously a whipping boy for many companies that didn't have the vision, nimbleness, or good fortune to succeed in the fast-moving high-tech industry of the 1980s and 1990s.

5.2 What Does "Open" Mean Anyway?

Microsoft also finds itself in a defensive posture with respect to the vocal, activist open-source community, which has propelled Linux, Apache, Perl, and other community projects into widespread implementation. Open-source zealots regard themselves as the democratic "bazaar" that will someday subvert the monolithic "cathedral" that Microsoft represents. In the face of this ideological challenge, Microsoft has stubbornly defended its core intellectual property—the Windows code base and APIs—against those who call for it to be surrendered to the open-source community.

The computing industry had a field day in late 1998 when open-source advocates unearthed a Microsoft internal strategy memorandum—dubbed the "Halloween Document"—that showed the company considers Linux and other open-source projects a threat to its core business. In the memorandum, Microsoft showed that it understands the alternative software development model advocated by the open-source community, but seriously doubts whether this development model can be transformed into a profitable business model. The core features of the open-source software development model are as follows:

- A core group of enthusiasts coalesces, often via e-mail and Usenet, into a project dedicated to developing open-source code and binaries.
- The core team distributes open-source code and binaries under a royalty-free general public license to all comers.
- External parties are encouraged to modify and extend the open-source code.
- External parties may or may not be required to send their modifications and extensions back to the core team, which may or may not include them in updates to the core open-source code base.

- External parties can apply their own license terms to the original and/or modified source code and binaries, as long as they also make their source code available under royalty-free general public licenses to all comers (and on and on, with no party ever having the right to deny others access to any source code that it develops).

Microsoft made it quite clear in the memorandum that it had no intention of following Netscape's lead when that firm delivered its browser code to the open-source "Mozilla" community. Microsoft indicated that it has no plans to relinquish the three fundamental components of its closed-source business model:

- Corporate ownership of proprietary source code
- Corporate control of access and modifications to proprietary source code
- Corporate revenues derived primarily from license royalties on products that incorporate software binaries

Microsoft has rejected the open-source development model without rejecting the need for "openness" in other facets of its product architecture and business model. Ever the smart political animal, it has made "openness" the philosophical centerpiece of the BizTalk Framework and initiative. To understand how far Microsoft is prepared to take this philosophy, we must first understand the many senses in which the computer and networking industry use the term *openness*. Generally, openness refers to standards, interfaces, and/or technologies that satisfy any and all of the following criteria:

- Described fully in publicly available documents
- Flexible and extensible to support new requirements and features within the general functional scope of the original initiative
- Not bound to any one operating environment, network protocol, database, or programming language
- Available as open-source royalty-free distributions to all interested parties
- Defined, developed, and/or implemented by industry groups that are not dominated or unduly influenced by one vendor; do not impose unreasonable or unfair restrictions on membership; do not conduct business or develop specifications in closed working environments; and publish full, regular updates on their activities

5.3 How Does the BizTalk Initiative Measure Against These Criteria of "Openness"?

Let's examine how well the BizTalk initiative measures up to these criteria.

5.3.1 Is It Described Fully in Publicly Available Documents?

The answer here is "yes, but not fully." As discussed in Chapter 1, Microsoft has left many important features and interfaces unaddressed in the current BizTalk Framework specification, including the following:

- BizTalk Message transport envelope
- BizTalk server functionality
- Software interfaces
- Security mechanisms
- Application state information
- Workflow process definition and execution
- Event model and error messages
- Trading partner agreement formats

5.3.2 Is It Flexible and Extensible?

The answer here is "yes, but by whom?" Microsoft and its hand-picked BizTalk Steering Committee control the framework's evolution. Fortunately, Microsoft has indicated it plans to extend the BizTalk Framework to address many of the gaps noted above. Extending the framework will involve adding new elements to the headers of BizTalk messages and documents. It will also involve elaborating the BizTalk application model to define new functions for the BizTalk server and application-adapter layers and new interactions and interfaces among these layers.

5.3.3 Is It Independent of Any One Operating Environment, Network Protocol, Database, or Programming Language?

The answer here is "yes, on an abstract level, but no on a practical level."

As noted previously, the BizTalk Framework does not specify the operating environments or protocols on which line-of-business applications, BizTalk application adapters, and BizTalk servers run. And it does not specify the specific data stores used to manage BizTalk application data or the programmatic interfaces used to access the functionality of the BizTalk server layer.

However, the BizTalk envelope specification leaves large loopholes for platform-specific end-to-end implementations. The framework strongly implies that BizTalk implementers will develop or optimize their applications to run on Windows 2000 and associated Microsoft Server software, especially Internet Information Server (IIS), Commerce Server, SQL Server, Microsoft Transaction Server (MTS), and MSMQ. Microsoft has defined a specific operating platform—its BizTalk Server 2000, running on Windows 2000—as essential to a fully realized BizTalk-enabled e-commerce environment. As such, the BizTalk Framework is not truly platform independent. Microsoft itself admitted that the BizTalk Framework "creates a vacuum for some technology, product, or capability to administratively manage" such programming issues as transport selection, parameter passing, calling conventions, and data transformation. Clearly, BizTalk Server 2000 fills the void that the framework leaves wide open (and it will likely fill this void alone until the day that open-source BizTalk server products find their way into the marketplace).

Microsoft has wisely adopted XML as a standard format for applications on many platforms to publish and share information schemas in common. However, the company provides developers with access to BizTalk XML schemas only through APIs under its proprietary COM, which is the core object-oriented programming environment of Microsoft's Windows OSs. These APIs allow other companies to write software that can interact with the BizTalk Server 2000 by manipulating the routing, security, and other message tags that are part of the BizTalk Framework Specification. Indeed, Microsoft sees the BizTalk Framework as a component of its proprietary DNA for integrating applications on distributed Windows platforms.

None of the foregoing discussion questions the validity of the expressed aims of the BizTalk philosophy. However, it is clear that the BizTalk Framework, which gives technical substance to this philosophy, still lacks one critical feature. It lacks a rich, flexible, open, and universal language for specifying, packaging, publishing, invoking, and executing transformation rules for information that crosses application, system, and business boundaries. BizTalk's object model is still bound up in the world of COM and presupposes a universal deployment of Windows 2000.

Microsoft states that BizTalk eliminates the need for applications to agree on a particular transport protocol in order to exchange BizTalk message envelopes, since the framework is protocol independent. Nevertheless, Microsoft strongly encourages the use of message-oriented middleware protocols, such as its own MSMQ protocol.

Microsoft claims that BizTalk doesn't require applications to agree on or be aware of one another's calling conventions in order to exchange BizTalk message envelopes and process them successfully. However, the company has left undefined several state variables that require some knowledge of platform-specific application contexts, such as those under its Windows 2000 operating system.

Microsoft claims that BizTalk eliminates the need for special-purpose adapter software layers to support object and data mapping and interchange among multiple applications. However, the BizTalk Framework strongly suggests the need for a general-purpose e-commerce adapter layer such as that provided by its BizTalk Server 2000 product.

5.3.4 Is It Available as Open-Source Royalty-Free Distributions to All Interested Parties?

The answer here is "most certainly not," for reasons stated above.

5.3.5 Is It Dominated or Unduly Influenced by One Vendor?

The answer here is "duh."

5.3.6 Is It Managed by an Industry Group that Does Not Impose Unreasonable or Unfair Restrictions on Membership?

The answer here is "are Microsoft's criteria for hand-picking members of the BizTalk Steering Committee reasonable and fair and, if not, what is the court of appeals?"

5.3.7 Is It Managed by a Group that Does Not Conduct Business or Develop Specifications in Closed Working Environments?

The answer here is "when will the BizTalk Steering Committee begin to operate like a real working group, hold regular meetings, and publish a direction statement and agenda?"

5.3.8 Is It Managed by a Group that Publishes Full, Regular Updates on Their Activities?

The answer here is "that depends on whether the BizTalk Steering Committee addresses the previous question satisfactorily."

5.4 Summary

Fundamentally, then, the BizTalk initiative is not entirely open. With Microsoft at the helm, no one truly expects it to be.

So, on one level, we might regard BizTalk as a clever new twist on Microsoft's long-running "Windows Everywhere" campaign. Perhaps we can forgive Microsoft for its attempt to tie the BizTalk Framework to its own operating and development environments. The best way to roll out a new type of universal e-commerce infrastructure may be to follow the lead of a dominant vendor, one that is attempting to squirt a new type of universal glue into the technical crevices between old-style EDI and workflow.

Only time will tell how well it all hangs together.

PART TWO

BIZTALK APPLICATIONS

This part provides a comprehensive overview of BizTalk applications in B2B e-commerce. Much of the discussion addresses potential applications, since Microsoft had not yet released the commercial BizTalk Server 2000 product at the time this book was written. We describe three B2B integration scenarios into which enterprise and service providers will deploy BizTalk Server 2000: hubbed marketplace integration, extranet supply-chain integration, and enterprise application integration.

Hubbed Marketplace Integration

M̄iddlemen are driving this new world of B2B and B2C e-com-merce, contrary to premature predictions of their demise through "disintermediation."

Buyers and sellers need middlemen to find each other and do business, a process that might otherwise require a painstaking search in an environment as vast as the Internet. At the core of each new e-marketplace is a central "marketmaker" whose primary roles are to match buyers and sellers, broker deals, and facilitate transactions. Today's dominant "e-marketecture" is the hubbed marketplace, a central Web site at which buyers and sellers converge to transact business. Each "hubsite" revolves around a central catalog, directory, or other listing that aggregates items being offered by one or more sellers, and/or being sought by one or more buyers. The hubsite may be hosted and managed by a dominant seller or buyer, or by an independent commerce-brokering organization. Hubsites may be linked into a "federated" marketplace that supports transactions among buyers and sellers in different industries, regions, and nations.

Figure 6-1 shows a single hubbed e-marketplace. Figure 6-2 shows a federated group of linked e-marketplaces.

Hubbed e-marketectures go by many names, which often reflect the nuances of the business models developed by particular marketmakers. Some of the most common names for hubbed marketectures are as follows:

- Aggregator
- Auction
- Bot
- Broker

Figure 6-1
A hubbed e-marketplace matches buyers and sellers, brokers deals, and facilitates transactions.

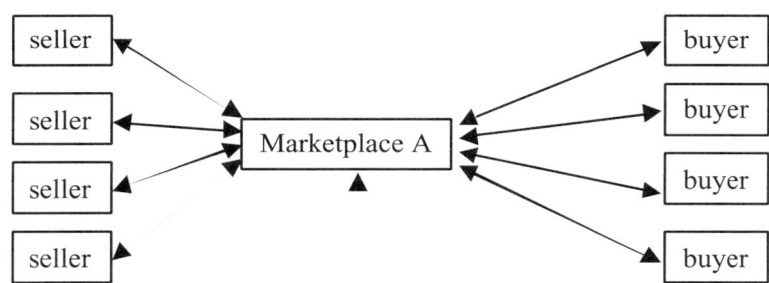

view other marketplace s aggregated catalog content
match buyers and sellers in different marketplaces
broker deals between buyers and sellers in different m
facilitate transactions between marketplaces

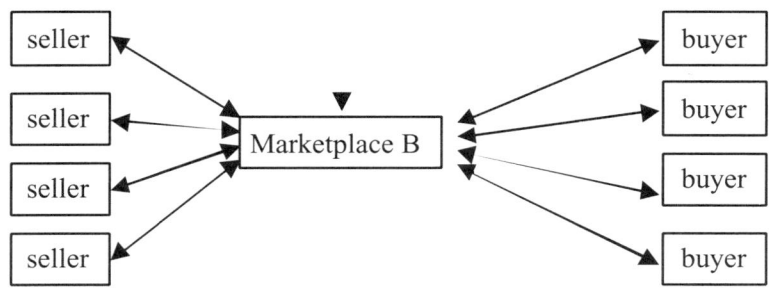

Figure 6-2 *A federated group of linked e-marketplaces supports transactions among buyers and sellers in different trading communities.*

- Community
- Exchange
- Hub
- Listing
- Mall
- Marketplace
- Matchmaker
- Portal

Figure 6-3 shows what they all have in common: reliance on an aggregated catalog, directory, or listing of offers to sell and/or buy.

There's nothing sacrosanct or precise about any of these labels, and many marketmakers use them interchangeably. Indeed, any given marketmaker may combine elements of several business models into its hub-based service. So don't expect the real world to shake down into clean marketplace models. Hubbed e-marketplaces are evolving too fast to put them into any but the most flexible of taxonomies.

In this chapter, we discuss the architectures of hubbed e-marketplaces, describing the functional subsystems necessary to integrate them into unified trading environments. We highlight the practical distinctions between these

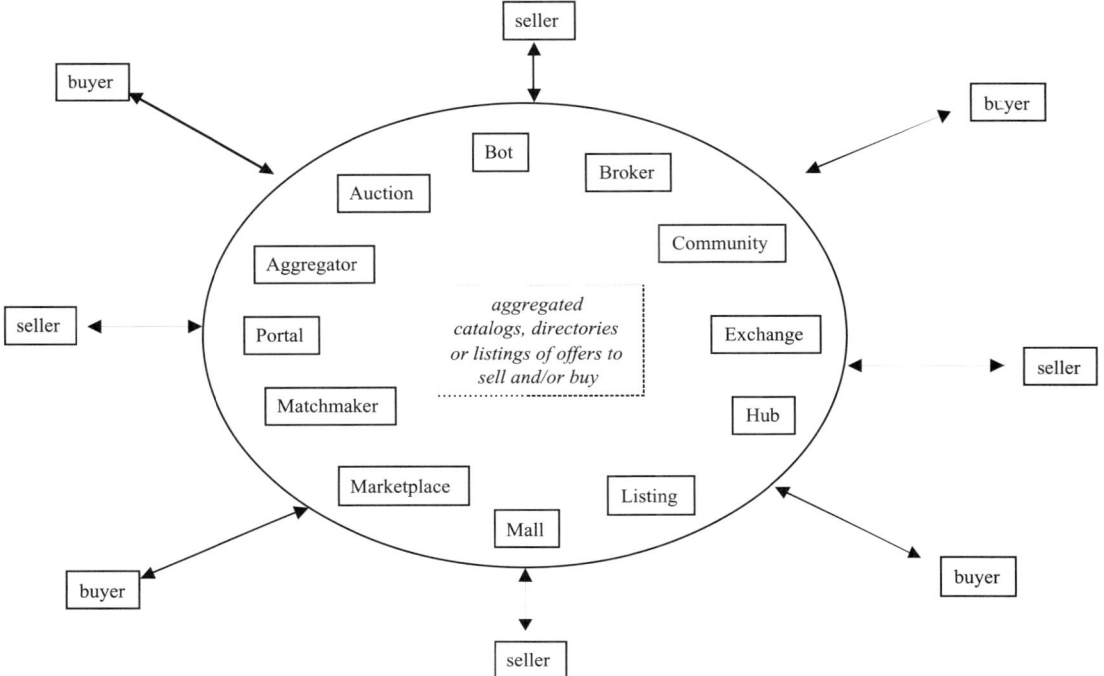

Figure 6-3   *All marketmakers aggregate seller and/or buyer offers in a catalog, directory, or listing.*

various marketmaker models, using a broad "e-marketecture reference model" that defines the fundamental attributes of the various hubbed marketplaces.

6.1 Potential BizTalk Role in Hubbed E-Marketplaces

Before we launch into the e-marketecture reference model, we must address the potential role of BizTalk—the interoperability framework and/or the Microsoft server product—in the world of hubbed e-marketplaces. Where does BizTalk fit in? This question demands a multipart answer.

The first part of the answer is that BizTalk—the framework—is broadly applicable to all e-marketplaces, since it defines a message envelope that does not presume a particular type of business document, catalog, or workflow. As we noted in Part 1, BizTalk is a horizontal-market B2B interoperability specification, so in principle it can be applied to any marketecture.

The second part of the answer is that BizTalk—the server—could allow trading partners (TPs) to integrate their commerce sites with their internal applications, with the marketplace hub, and, via the hub, with trade facilitators and with each other. Consequently, BizTalk Servers could be the common, distributed platform that binds all participants into a common hubbed (or, indeed, nonhubbed) trading environment. Integration would be through exchange of BizTag-enclosed Business Documents over message-brokering backbones between loosely coupled applications. Figure 6-4 shows the potential roles of BizTalk Server in a hubbed e-marketplace: integrating applications within each companies and between separate companies through a trading hub.

That defines the potential applicability of the BizTalk framework and server in real-world hubbed e-marketplaces. However, the third part of the answer addresses those situations where there BizTalk framework and server may not be the best fit for an e-marketplace's requirements.

Microsoft designed the BizTalk Server primarily as a "front end" for some TPs' commerce sites and applications, especially those built with Microsoft's Commerce Server, SQL Server, Windows 2000, and other Microsoft Server products. The company appears to be positioning BizTalk Server as a platform for TP integration into a hubbed e-marketplace or traditional EDI supply-chain scenario. Consequently, BizTalk Server's feature set consists of core EDI functionality: reliable document interchange, mapping, translation, and routing. This feature set does not address the core e-commerce requirements of marketmakers, who must support complex relationships, transaction models, and workflows among buyers, sellers, and other marketplace participants.

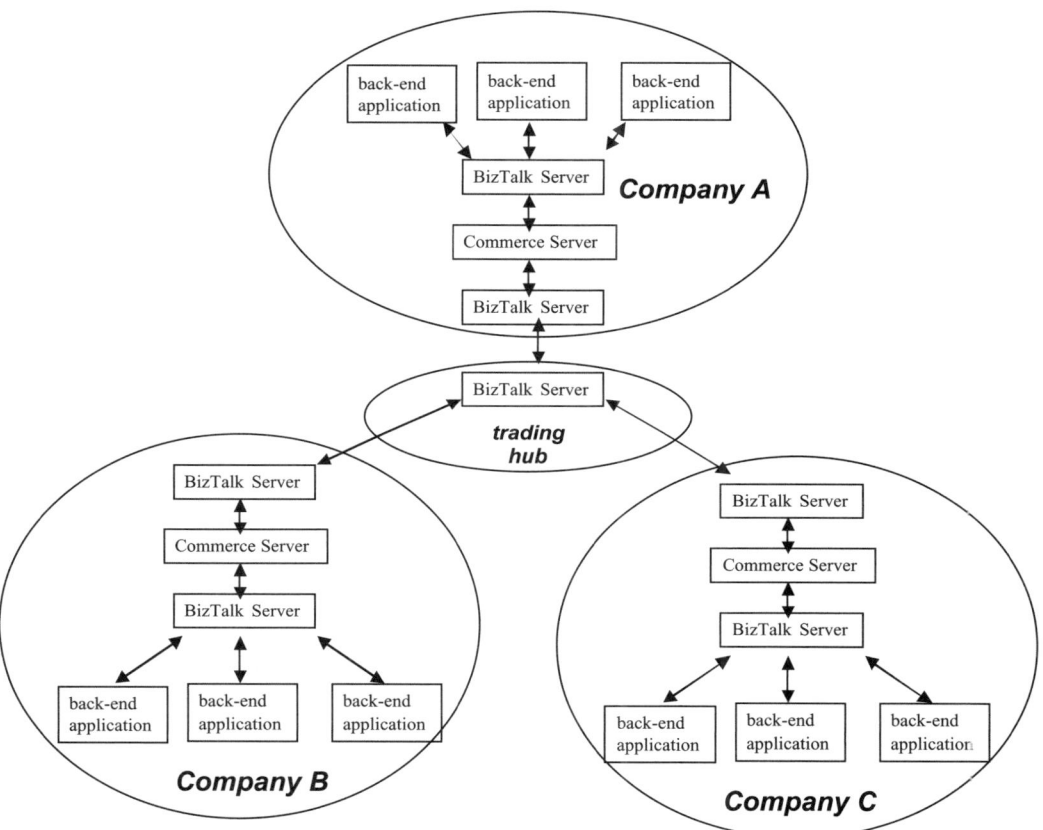

| **Figure 6-4** | *BizTalk Server supports trading partner integration and enterprise application integration.* |

Another BizTalk Server limitation is the implementation-specific features that constrain it to interoperating primarily with other BizTalk Servers within Windows 2000 environments. As a result, the BizTalk Framework might not be applicable to trading environments in which marketmakers and trading partners deploy competing operating systems, such as AS/400, AIX, Solaris, and Linux. If third parties were to develop BizTalk servers for other operating systems, BizTalk would then be able to play in truly multivendor trading environments.

Yet another reason why marketmakers might favor another framework is functional specialization. In some cases, however, marketmakers may find competing frameworks better suited to the type of transactions they plan to broker within their hubsites. For example, e-marketplaces that directly integrate trading partners' enterprise resource planning (ERP) applications may find OAGIS a better choice, since these specifications are geared to interfacing the data and process models of multiple vendors' ERP applications.

6.2 E-Marketecture Reference Model

Now we present the e-marketecture reference model. Think of this as your roadmap through a fascinating new continent where the terrain is unfamiliar, the species are evolving rapidly, and fixed landmarks are hard to make out.

In this chapter, we describe how various real-world hubbed e-marketplaces fit into this reference model. For each type of e-marketplace, we discuss the potential applicability of the BizTalk Server and other Microsoft products, technologies, and tools. (However, we save our in-depth discussion of the BizTalk Server and other Microsoft offerings for Parts 3 and 4.) You should emerge from this chapter with a new appreciation for trading hubs as configurable, adaptable environments that address various economic and business models.

The basic features of any e-marketplace fall into the following functional categories in Table 6-1.

Table 6-1	E-Marketecture Reference Model	
Layer	**Definition**	**Criteria**
Hosting	Structure of marketplace ownership, sponsorship, control, and management	Who is the marketmaker—who owns, sponsors, controls, and manages the trading environment?
		Is the marketmaker a buyer, a seller, a consortium of buyers or sellers, or an independent brokering organization in the marketplace it hosts?
		How does the marketmaker generate the cash flow to sustain marketplace operations and further develop the trading environment?
Membership	Policies determining eligibility, terms, and conditions for participating in the marketplace	What range of buyers and sellers—trading partners—may participate in the marketplace?
		What criteria determine which TPs may participate in a marketplace?
		Are TPs required to do business with each other within that particular e-marketplace, or may they still engage in transactions with each other outside that environment?

	Table 6-1	E-Marketecture Reference Model (cont.)
Layer	**Definition**	**Criteria**
Aggregation	Approaches for organizing buy and sell offers in the marketplace	What types of offers—to sell, to buy, or both—are aggregated in the marketplace?
		Where and how are these offers aggregated?
		Which TPs may post offers to the marketplace?
		How are offers classified, categorized, sorted, searched, compared, and bundled within the marketplace?
		What other types of information and services are aggregated with offers in the marketplace?
Transaction	Procedures for establishing commercial contracts, bargaining, and processing transactions in the marketplace	Which participants, stores, workflows, messages, and documents are involved in end-to-end marketplace transactions?
		What types of offers drive marketplace transactions?
		What types of contracts apply to marketplace transactions or may be negotiated in the marketplace?
		Are marketplace transactions constrained by the terms of preexisting, prenegotiated contracts between TPs?
		Are marketplace transactions bilateral, or may they also involve linked deals with other TPs and/or transaction facilitators?
		Are marketplace transactions one-off deals, or do they figure into long-term purchase commitments between specific TPs?
Pricing	Procedures for determining prices in the marketplace	Are pricing and other transaction terms determined by dynamic bargaining mechanisms in the marketplace?
		If transactions rely on dynamic pricing, which bargaining mechanisms are employed?
		If transactions rely on auction mechanisms, which type of auction?

Table 6-1	E-Marketecture Reference Model (cont.)	
Layer	**Definition**	**Criteria**
Payment	Procedures for submitting, processing, and settling payments in the marketplace	How is payment tendered, accepted, and processed in the marketplace? What intermediaries process, convert, and settle payments?
Facilitation	Organization of third-party responsibilities for assisting buyers, sellers, and/or marketmakers in setting up, executing, and consummating transactions	What range of transaction facilitation services—such as financing, fulfillment, shipping, insurance, escrow, and logistics—are provided in the marketplace? What intermediaries provide these services?

The details of these functional categories are the primary substance of this chapter. In the following discussion, we refer to each of these functional layers as a "model" with respect to the architecture of a particular e-marketplace. As we will show, you can describe any e-marketplace as a "stack" of these seven functional models: hosting, membership, aggregation, transaction, pricing, payment, and facilitation. Figure 6-5 presents the hubbed e-marketplace's layered architecture graphically.

Note that most of the components of the B2B functional reference model, presented in Part 1, map into the "transaction" model of this more all-encompassing interpretive framework. This is because the BizTalk Framework and other B2B interoperability specifications primarily address the core EDI and workflow requirements of e-marketplaces, but not the broader business context of the e-marketplaces they support.

By contrast, the e-marketecture reference model places B2B interoperability frameworks in their full economic context: as nitty-gritty technical specifications that support online environments where buyers and sellers meet to do business. What distinguishes one e-marketplace from another is not so much that it uses is the BizTalk Framework, cXML, XML/EDI, or some other set of technical interfaces. What distinguishes it is the business rules—the process model—that drive the transactional workflows that these e-marketplaces were set up to host. As we pointed out in Chapter 3, B2B converges EDI and workflow, and you can host these applications on any number of network protocols and computing platforms.

From a technical standpoint, this new world of hubbed trading environments depends on the very "glue layer" that Microsoft disparaged in the BizTalk Philosophy document. The glue layer resides in the marketmaker and its hubsite (or, what will over time become the more scenario, in a con-

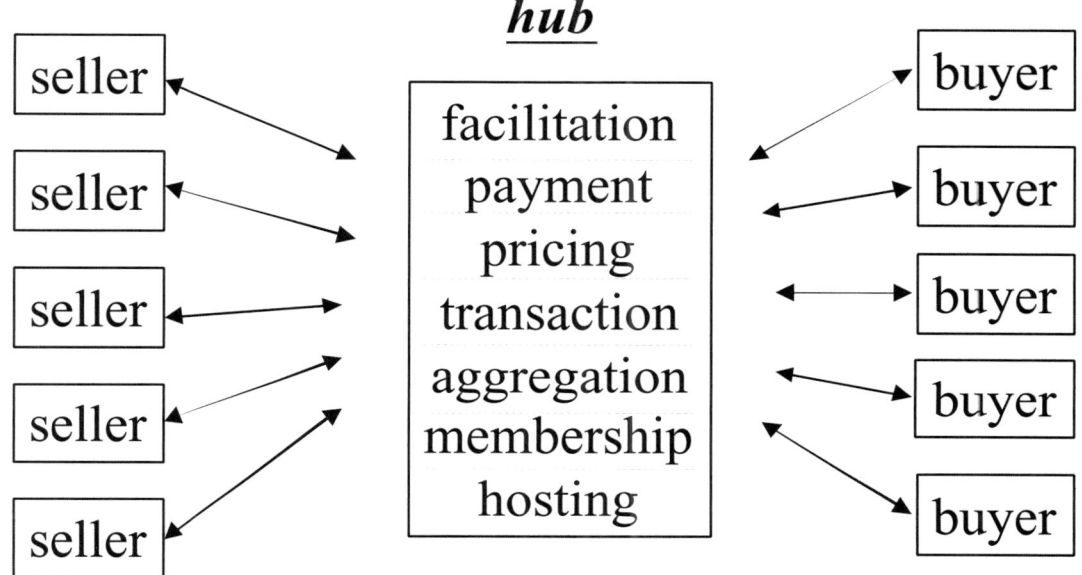

Figure 6-5 *Hubbed e-marketplaces consist of seven functional service layers: hosting, membership, aggregation, transaction, pricing, payment, and facilitation.*

stellation of federated, communicating hubsites). The glue resides in the marketplace's core workflow process model, which is at heart a set of rules for transforming one TP's outputs into another's inputs. A full-featured e-marketplace hubsite meets the criteria, outlined in Chapter 1, for an e-commerce glue layer:

- Implements an intermediate layer of software adapters between communicating TP applications
- Exposes the functionality of possibly incompatible TP applications to each other
- Translates data exchanged between TP applications
- Manages the transfer of data between TP applications over appropriate protocols (such as those defined in the BizTalk Framework)
- Enforces appropriate business rules in interactions between TP applications

So, in e-commerce, there's glue, but there's also "superglue." The BizTalk Server is basic glue for interoperable e-commerce, but so are a host of other new-generation B2B "interchange servers" or "message switches," such as Mercator Software's E-Business Broker Suite, which manages document mapping, translation, and message-based routing between dissimilar applications. As we noted above, the BizTalk Server fits in primarily at the TP level but is not, in its first iteration, designed to support the complex development and operational requirements of trading hubs.

The superglue in the e-commerce equation is the trading hub. This is a niche where software products such as Ariba Technologies' TradingDynamics Market Suite are more appropriate solutions. Products such as these enable marketmakers to configure the hosting, membership, aggregation, transaction, pricing, payment, and facilitation options appropriate to their trading environments. So you can interpret the e-marketecture reference model as a framework for defining e-commerce superglue (Ironically, though, e-marketplaces are very fluid creations, which continually evolve their process models, so we should not interpret the "superglue" metaphor as implying any adhesive rigidity in the composition of a hubbed trading environment.)

The bottom line on all this is that glue is power in our new networked economy. Economists spend their lives contributing to the formulation of macro- and micro-economic policies, but marketmakers can effect policy changes with the click of a mouse. When marketmakers modify the business rules underlying hubbed trading environments, they change the ground rules for sectors of the economy: determining who can trade with whom, what they can trade, how they can bargain, and how they can come to terms. Change the business rules at the marketplace hub and you reengineer supply chains far and wide.

With all that as context, we now proceed to an in-depth discussion of functional models in the architecture of a hubbed e-marketplace.

6.3 Hosting Model

A marketplace is a business like any other, but unlike any other.

Throughout human history, stable marketplaces have sprung up in locations where people regularly crossed paths, each bearing something that others desire. Many of the urban settlements we inhabit got their starts as simple crossroads, places to set up stalls, pull out pocketbooks, and haggle.

Think of the city you live in. Its local economy is just a crossroads marketplace on a larger scale, seemingly running under its own power, automatically regulating itself through classical economist Adam Smith's "invisible hand," but we all know that's an illusion. As citizens, we assemble government institutions to tend to the needs of the local economy and the state, national, and international economies of which it's a component. We grant these institutions revenue-raising powers and assign them duties essential to any functioning economy, such as minting the currency, preserving the peace, enforcing contracts, maintaining roads, and transporting mail. We may disagree violently on the best way to organize, run, and fund these institutions. We disagree on what mix of services various governments should provide. But we all know that stable governance is essential to a prosperous marketplace.

Hosting an economy is not a simple responsibility, and there's plenty of opportunity for governments to commit grievous errors. Managing an economy is like managing a business—a vast, unwieldy business, but a business nonetheless. Governments govern best when they recognize their core responsibility: hosting stable, prosperous, dynamic trading environments. They govern best when they create basic conditions for free markets to foster innovation, employment, and productivity. They govern worst when they micro-manage the economy, stifle private initiative with counterproductive regulations, and take more than their fair share of the fruits of commerce.

Hosting a privately managed marketplace is a bit like running an economy, but on a narrower scale. We're perhaps most familiar with private marketplaces in the financial industry, such as the New York Stock Exchange (NYSE) and Lloyd's of London. These are not government agencies—they're really just closed trading communities—but that hasn't stopped them from developing over the past few centuries into economic institutions of considerable clout. As private marketplaces, they have become central players in the very public global economy. They tread that fine line between being private concerns and public utilities.

Hosting an e-marketplace is something you or I could do this minute by paving our very own crossroads on the World Wide Web. After all, Lloyd's began inauspiciously, as an informal meeting of mercantile underwriters in a coffee shop, so there's no reason to think you need an official government license to set up your own private marketplace. To get things started, all you need are postings on your Web site by people who want to sell or buy something—anything, even something as ordinary as old, mint-condition Superman comic books. If people begin to trade on information they find at your site, and come back repeatedly for more of the same, you have yourself an e-marketplace. Charge them for the privilege of trading through your site, and you have yourself a business.

Of course, hosting a B2B hubbed e-marketplace is an altogether more complicated and costly undertaking. You probably need to have some preexisting occupation, recognition, or connections in the industry in which you're trying to set up a trading hub, whether that industry be aluminum siding or aerospace engineering. If you're a commodities broker, trade association, general contractor, or venture capitalist, you may already have amassed the business connections you need to set up yourself as a e-marketmaker. If you're a dominant buyer in the market, you can turn your existing supply chain into an e-marketplace. If you're a dominant seller, you can use your existing distribution channels as the launchpad for an e-marketplace. In other words, your existing business model may already place you at the crossroads of a substantial marketplace just itching to go online.

A marketplace's hosting model defines who owns, sponsors, controls, and manages the trading environment. We group B2B e-marketplaces into four basic hosting models (per Figure 6-6 and Table 6-2):

- Broker-hosted marketplaces: These are environments managed by an entity that is neither a buyer or seller of the traded good or service—instead, the marketmaker simply brokers deals between others who bear the associated financial risks and rewards.
- Seller-hosted marketplaces: These are environments managed by one of the sellers in the marketplace, often a dominant seller, or by a consortium of sellers.
- Buyer-hosted marketplaces: These are environments managed by one of the buyers in the marketplace, often a dominant buyer, or by consortium of buyers.
- Industry-hosted marketplaces: These are environments managed by an organization owned and/or controlled by a broad range of buyers and sellers in an industry.

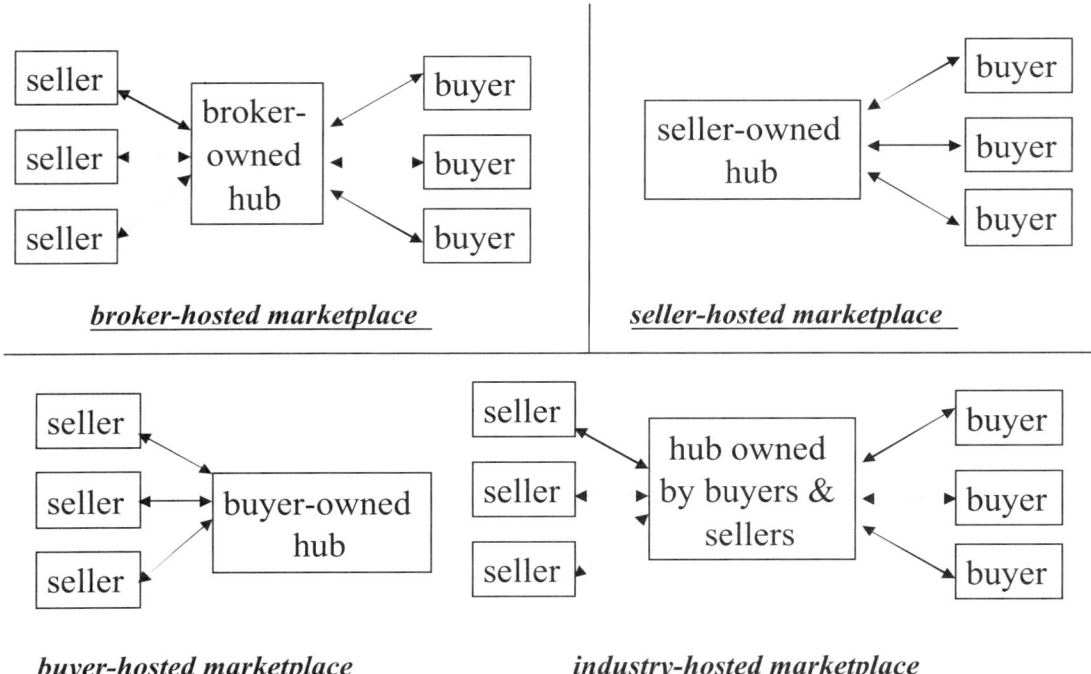

Figure 6-6   *E-marketplace hosting models include broker-hosted, seller-hosted, buyer-hosted, and industry-hosted.*

Table 6-2	Hosting Models

E-Commerce Business Models	Management	Tenants	Postings	Inventories
Broker-hosted e-marketplace	Managed by entity that is neither buyer nor seller of traded good or service	No buyer or seller need be permanent, long-term, or exclusive tenant in marketplace, or an established trading partner	Buy offers and sell offers from multiple parties	Site owner brokers transactions between others who maintain the inventories being traded
Seller-hosted e-marketplace	Managed by one or more entities that are sellers of the traded good or service	Site owner(s) are permanent, exclusive anchor tenants	Sell offers from site owner(s)	Site owner(s) maintain inventories being traded
Buyer-hosted e-marketplace	Managed by one or more entities that are buyers of the traded good or service	Site owner(s) are permanent, exclusive anchor tenants; also include owners' established trading partners, who may or may not be permanent or exclusive to marketplace	Buy and sell offers, with site owner(s) primarily extending buy offers	Site owner(s) and trading partners maintain inventories being traded
Industry-hosted e-marketplace	Managed by entity that is owned by buyers, sellers, and independent brokers of the traded goods and services	Site owners are permanent, long-term tenants; trading partners may be established or ad hoc, long-term or short-term marketplace participants	Buy and sell offers from site owners and their trading partners	Site owners and trading partners maintain inventories being traded

We find ample evidence in recent news for development of e-marketplaces conforming to all four hosting models.

6.3.1 Broker-Hosted E-Marketplaces

Broker-hosted e-marketplaces are becoming so common that, before long, almost every industry will have not just one of them, but several competing hubs. These brokering hubs will either compete for the same postings—in other words, buy and sell offers for a common set of goods and services—or specialize by niche, region, service offerings, and other features.

In fact, we can already see this multi-hub-per-industry trend in full swing. We'll simply list some of the new broker-hosted e-marketplaces. This is certainly not an exhaustive list of all broker-hosted marketplaces in existence at the time this book was written (January-June 2000). We don't even pretend to enumerate all the hubs in each industry. The following list is simply for illustration purposes:

- Advertising: www.adauction.com, www.adoutlet.com, www.buy-media.com
- Antiques: www.circline.com
- Automobile aftermarket: www.autopartsbin.com, www.autovia.com, www.dega.com
- Automobile dealer-to-dealer exchanges: www.motorplace.com
- Architecture, engineering, and construction: www.bidcom.com, www.buzzsaw.com
- Building materials: www.buyinsulation.com, www.buymaterial.com, www.buydrywall.com, www.buyceilings.com, www.buywalls.com, www.buyplaster.com, www.buyacoustical.com, www.buyfireproofing.com, www.buyfirestopping.com
- Chemicals: www.chematch.com, www.chemdex.com, www.chemconnect.com, www.e-chemicals.com
- Contract programmers: www.itsquare.com
- Electronic components: www.necx.com, www.electronicsbin.com, www.netbuy.com, www.partminer.com, www.questlink.com, www.ecnet.com, www.chipcenter.com
- Energy: www.altranet.com
- Expertise: www.infomarco.com, www.hellobrain.com, www.high-techmatrix.com
- Freelance services: www.elance.com
- Internet domain names: www.afternic.com, www.greatdomains.com
- Life sciences laboratory equipment and supplies: www.sciquest.com
- Maintenance, repair, and operations supplies: www.fastxchange.com
- Medical products, supplies, and equipment: www.neoforma.com, www.promedix.com
- Metals: www.metalsite.com, www.e-steel.com
- Mortgages: www.realestate.com
- Paper: www.paperexchange.com
- Pharmaceuticals: www.pharmabid.com

- Plastics: www.plasticsnet.com, www.plasticsbin.com
- Pleasure boats, gears, and accessories: www.boatscape.com
- R&D intellectual capital: www.yet2.com
- Surplus business assets: www.tradeout.com, www.imark.com
- Veterinarian equipment and supplies: www.vetmall.com
- Wholesale used automobiles: www.autodaq.com

In a few years' time, many of these early broker-hosted hubs will seem almost quaint, much the way a corporate Web-site design from 1995 looks painfully amateurish by year 2000 standards. Before long, the "superbrokers" will dominate the B2B e-commerce marketscape. In fact, many of them have already arrived and have established themselves as operators of several, in some cases dozens of, vertical e-marketplaces. Some B2B e-commerce superbrokers come from the traditional EDI world—for example, Harbinger and Sterling Commerce. Some, such as EDS, come from systems integration and facilities management backgrounds. Still others are primarily ERP software vendors, such as SAP, Oracle, and i2. In addition, telecommunications companies around the world have launched themselves into the world of broker-hosted e-commerce, including such well-known carriers as British Telecom, Swisscom, Cable and Wireless, and NTT. There's even a global financial services firm—American Express—in the B2B e-commerce superbroker arena.

And then we have what Wall Street refers to as the "pure plays" in the superbroker space: B2B e-marketplace service providers such as Ariba Technologies, Commerce One, Vertical Net, Purchase Pro, and Freemarkets. They are making their mark not only as operators of multiple vertical e-marketplaces, but as development, integration, and equity partners with large companies—including many of those listed above—that are trying to set up their own private e-marketplaces.

Broker-hosted e-marketplaces will be one of the chief magnets for venture capital, initial public offerings (IPOs), mergers, and acquisitions throughout the next several years. These online marketplaces will rapidly become ubiquitous. And as they do, they will blend into the background of a Web already populated by such similar creatures as online malls and portals.

It's easy to confuse broker-hosted e-marketplaces with these other e-commerce business models, but you'll know a broker hub when you see one. Generally, broker-hosted e-marketplaces fit the following criteria:

- Managed by an entity that is neither a buyer or seller of the traded good or service
- Feature two types of commercial postings: buy offers and sell offers
- Present offers posted by multiple sellers and multiple buyers, none of which need be permanent, long-term, or exclusive "tenants" in the marketplace, and none of which need be established trading partners with each other
- Broker deals between others who maintain the inventories being traded

The broker-hosted e-marketplace is a dynamic trading environment, hosting an ever-changing mix of buyers and sellers who may never fall into routine trading-partner patterns. An online mall, by contrast, generally hosts a stable set of sellers. The online mall fits the following criteria:

- Managed by an entity that is neither a buyer or seller of the traded good or service
- Features one type of commercial posting: sell offers
- Presents offers posted by multiple sellers, many or most of which are long-term or permanent, but not necessarily exclusive, "tenants" of the site
- Refers or forwards transactions to long-term site tenants, who maintain the inventories on the items being traded

A portal is similar to an online mall but usually counts e-commerce as just one of its many services, not its sole reason for being. Portals generally fit the following criteria:

- Managed by an entity that is neither a buyer or seller of the traded good or service
- Features one type of commercial posting—sell offers—but also presents a broad array of noncommerce content and services, such as search engines, news services, and collaboration services
- Presents offers posted by multiple sellers, many or most of which are long-term or permanent, but usually not exclusive, "tenants" of the site
- Captures, refers, or forwards transactions for long-term site tenants, who maintain the inventories on the items being traded

To round off the discussion, we should note that the typical online e-commerce storefront is neither a marketplace, mall, or portal. It is an open order point maintained by a single merchant. Online storefronts generally fit the following criteria:

- Managed by an entity that is primarily a seller of the traded good or service
- Features one type of commercial posting: sell offers
- Presents offers posted primarily by one seller—the site's owner—who is the permanent and exclusive "anchor tenant"
- Processes transactions in which the site's owner maintains the inventories being traded

All of these e-commerce business models will undoubtedly thrive in the early years of the 21st century. However, broker-hosted e-marketplaces will come to predominate, since they host the freewheeling trading paradigm favored by the most dynamic sectors of the economy.

Before we develop this topic further, we should point out that the term *hosting*—as we use it in this book—does not refer to the computer operating system, application software, or data-processing facility on which the online marketplace runs. Physical hosting is obviously a critical issue, but we use the term to describe the manner in which a central marketmaker organizes a trading environment structurally.

Where physical hosting is concerned, every marketmaker must decide whether they will operate the technical infrastructure for their trading environment themselves or rely on a contractor, application service provider (ASP), or Web-site hosting company to keep it all plugged in and turned on. We expect that, within the next few years, most e-marketmakers will contract with third parties for physical hosting services. Broker-hosted e-marketplaces should be at the forefront of this trend, since they are geared to facilitate business deals in a dynamic environment and tend to avoid the "mortar" side of the "click and mortar" dichotomy.

The economic movers and shakers who create trading hubs will, more often than not, be oblivious to the advantages of implementing their environments on BizTalk-based products versus those of Microsoft's competitors. They'll delegate such details.

6.3.2 Seller-Hosted E-Marketplaces

Seller-hosted e-marketplaces will be the distribution channels of the future for today's business titans, or so their sponsors fondly hope.

As we noted above, these hubs are managed either by one of the sellers in a particular marketplace or by a consortium of sellers. We may characterize seller-hosted marketplaces as follows:

- Managed by one or more entities that are sellers of the traded good or service
- Feature one type of commercial posting: sell offers
- Present offers posted primarily by the site's sponsors, who are permanent, perhaps exclusive, anchor tenants
- Process transactions in which the site's owners and sponsors maintain the inventories being traded

At the time this book was written, only a few seller-hosted e-marketplaces of any magnitude had been announced, and all were in the planning and implementation stage. Nevertheless, the sponsors have released some tantalizing details that give us a glimpse of what they have in mind.

One noteworthy initiative is an international airline-industry e-marketplace planned by 27 large carriers, including American Airlines, United Airlines, Northwest Airlines, Continental Airlines, Delta Airlines, KLM Royal Dutch Airlines, Singapore Airlines, Air Canada, Alitalia, Varig, Singapore Airlines, and US Airways. Announced in late 1999, this initiative brings the airlines together to form a travel Web-site offering discounted bookings on fares, hotel rooms, car rentals, cruises, and vacation packages. The as yet unnamed site will compete with independent travel agents and such online travel-related sites as Travelocity and Expedia.

What motivates the sponsoring airlines is obviously the possibility of saving anywhere between $5 and $10 per passenger in commission fees they pay to independent online brokers, as well as in fees paid to online database companies that link airlines to travel agencies and other hospitality-related businesses. This project is the airlines' effort to control the end-to-end travel process, from booking tickets to assigning seats, managing customer profiles and frequent-flier miles, and conducting flight operations.

This is clearly one industry's attempt to "disintermediate" the middleman by creating its own pet middleman. There will undoubtedly be more. The leading sellers in each industry will increasingly come together to create shared hubs aimed at preserving their control over pricing and distribution of their goods and services. Industries will either reengineer their distribution channels around the hubbed marketplace model or cede control—and increasingly lucrative online transaction fees—to the upstart broker-hosted hubs.

6.3.3 Buyer-Hosted E-Marketplaces

Buyer-hosted e-marketplaces are the supply chains of the future, replacing today's extranet architectures with Web-based trading environments.

As we noted above, these hubs are managed either by one of the buyers in a particular marketplace or by a consortium of buyers. We may characterize buyer-hosted e-marketplaces as follows:

- Managed by one or more entities that are buyers of the traded good or service
- Feature both buy and sell offers, with the dominant partners primarily extending buy offers
- Present offers posted by the site's sponsors, who are permanent, perhaps exclusive, anchor tenants, and their established trading partners, who may or may not be permanent participants and who may or may not participate exclusively in this particular trading hub
- Process transactions in which the site's sponsors and established trading partners maintain the inventories being traded

Sponsoring companies design their buyer-hosted e-marketplaces to foster competition down in their supply chains. That's because competition's benefits will, in principle, flow back up the supply chain in the form of lower prices, greater choice, and better quality for the dominant buyers who set the marketplace in motion.

At the time this book was written, just a few high-profile buyer-hosted e-marketplaces had been announced and were preparing to come online in early 2000. The most noteworthy are sponsored by the two leading U.S. automakers: General Motors and Ford. In February 2000, both automakers announced that they will merge their respective e-marketplaces into a larger auto industry supply-chain portal—covisint— in which Daimler-Chrysler will also participate. This hub, when implemented, will create an even larger buyer-hosted e-marketplace in the worldwide auto industry.

We now profile GM and Ford's separate initiatives, which provide a glimpse at both the potential and pitfalls of buyer-hosted e-marketplaces.

In November 1999, GM teamed up with Commerce One to establish the TradeXchange B2B e-marketplace and Supply Power B2B portal. TradeXchange is a hubbed e-marketplace for GM's supply chain, operating on Commerce One's MarketSite e-commerce hub software. A high-level profile of TradeExchange is as follows:

- Managed jointly by GM, the world's largest industrial company and vehicle manufacturer, and Commerce One
- Features both types of commercial postings—buy and sell offers— for automotive products, raw materials, parts, and services
- Presents offers posted by GM, which is the permanent, exclusive anchor tenant, and by GM's 30,000 established suppliers (direct, indirect, and aftermarket) and dealers
- Processes transactions in which GM and its established trading partners maintain the inventories being traded, supporting purchase authorization, execution, tracking, accounting, and contractual procedures.

GM does not dictate prices of goods traded on TradeXchange, which supports three transaction models:

- Catalog-based order point
- Bid-ask trading
- Online auctions

GM will move its entire $80 billion annual purchasing budget online to TradeXchange and will use the exchange to auction off surplus and used equipment. GM will primarily buy, but not resell, products and services through the exchange. GM suppliers must use the exchange to sell to the manufacturer. GM dealers may optionally use the exchange to purchase parts from GM and suppliers.

GM charges suppliers transaction fees on sales to the industrial giant through TradeXchange, as well as fees on transactions between trading partners to which GM is not a party. Options include GM charging a flat transaction fee or a small percentage fee on each transaction through the site. GM also stands to make money providing buyers with financing services through General Motors Acceptance Corporation (GMAC). These fees could prove quite lucrative to the manufacturer, since its supply chain has the potential of conducting as much as $500 billion in purchasing annually over TradeXchange.

TradeXchange will interoperate with GM's SupplyPower B2B portal, which will support a broad range of supply-chain collaboration applications in conjunction with e-commerce. GM SupplyPower will allow suppliers to engage in self-service transactions and real-time interaction over the Web with multiple GM organizations, including the following:

- Purchasing: Suppliers will be able to receive bid packages, submit quotes, receive purchase contracts, share quality and warranty information, share supplier performance metrics, and participate in a suggestion program.
- Finance: Suppliers will be able to query invoice payment status and share information on new vehicle sales and trade discounts programs.
- Engineering: Suppliers will be able to collaborate on vehicle designs by sharing math-based design data. They will also be able to collaborate on vehicle testing and receive vehicle program management information.
- Production control and logistics: Suppliers will be able to collaborate on production capacity planning and production schedules and share inventory and production information.

GM SupplyPower will be GM departments' primary means to communicate with suppliers, using such online services as e-mail, bulletin boards, suggestion boxes, and real-time news feeds. Suppliers will be able to define individual profiles to personalize their interface to GM SupplyPower services.

It's significant that GM has established both a seller-hosted marketplace and an online B2B portal. The former hub is for commerce and the latter primarily for collaboration, and the two will form an integrated web of services for GM's supply chain and dealers. The two online business models are complementary.

Around the same time that GM announced these initiatives, Ford teamed up with Oracle to announce AutoExchange, its seller-hosted supply-chain e-marketplace. AutoExchange, is similar in functional scope to GM TradeXchange, in the following ways:

- Managed jointly by Ford, the second-largest automaker, and Oracle, which will also physical host and manage the site
- Features both types of commercial postings—buy and sell offers—for automotive products, raw materials, parts, and services.
- Presents offers posted by Ford, which is the permanent, exclusive, anchor tenant, and by Ford's 30,000 established suppliers (direct, indirect, and aftermarket) and dealers
- Processes transactions in which Ford and its established trading partners maintain the inventories being traded; supports purchase authorization, accounting and contractual procedures

AutoExchange has the potential of hosting as much as $300 billion in annual transactions in Ford's supply chain. Ford and Oracle could recoup as much perhaps $1 billion annually in transaction fees and other charges in AutoExchange's first year, rising to $5 billion annually by the fifth year.

It's not clear yet whether auto industry suppliers will choose to run their online procurement operations exclusively over the GM or Ford e-marketplace, or over the merged e-marketplace that also includes Daimler-Chrysler. More likely, suppliers will build layers of mapping/translation software to link their internal procurement systems to the separate, proprietary interfaces exposed by TradeXchange and AutoExchange, respectively, as well as to separate interfaces associated with other auto manufacturers. We expect that suppliers will increasingly demand that all auto-industry exchanges implement a common set of interfaces—EDI, workflow, transactions, auctions, catalogs, and the like—so that the auto industry can operate as one large, open, online trading environment, rather than as separate, noninteroperable, supply-chain hubs managed by leading manufacturers.

The chief problem with buyer-hosted e-marketplaces is that they aim to lock suppliers into a sponsoring company's procurement system, as if the sponsor were the sole buyer of all goods and services in the industry (or at least the sole buyer of goods and services from each supplier). That is clearly not the case in the global auto manufacturing business. Many suppliers sell to GM, Ford, and Daimler-Chrysler, as well as to Toyota, Nissan, Mazda, Fiat, and other manufacturers, which, no doubt, are also considering establishing their own online purchasing hubs.

In one respect, these buyer-hosted e-marketplaces are a step backward for the auto industry. The industry has long had a common, standardized, interoperable EDI environment—managed under the Automotive Network Exchange (ANX) program—that supports a baseline level of B2B document and data interchange. Over the next several years, we expect to see the automakers' hubbed e-marketplaces evolve into a common, next-generation, loosely coupled EDI infrastructure. However, it's too early to say whether the auto industry will base this infrastructure on BizTalk, cXML, or XML/EDI, or on some yet to be defined set of e-commerce standards.

The GM/Ford/Daimler-Chrysler e-marketplace—Covisint— may not turn out to be the fat cash cows that its sponsors expect. The manufacturers are basing their e-marketplace revenue forecasts on the prospect of supporting not just their own online procurement processes, but also those of their suppliers, and their suppliers' suppliers. However, the big automakers cannot mandate that suppliers sell to one another other over the converged e-marketplace. Consequently, if transaction fees in these e-marketplaces prove too high, nothing's stopping suppliers from trading with one another in rival e-marketplaces hosted by brokering organizations.

This is no idle threat to GM, Ford, and Daimler-Chrysler's e-marketplace strategies. As we showed previously, there are already a few brokered e-marketplaces that focus on automotive-related products. We will certainly see more of these in the next few years, many of them basing their business models on hosting deals that would have been inconvenient or unprofitable to transact on the automakers' hubs.

6.3.4 Industry-Hosted E-Marketplaces

Industry-hosted e-marketplaces provide trading environments that are not controlled by any one buyer or seller in a vertical market. One or more buyers or sellers may take the initiative to set them up, but a broad-based industry consortium or coalition defines the policies that govern the marketplace and monitors its operations.

One early example of an industry-hosted e-marketplace is the Petrocosm Marketplace, announced in January 2000 by Chevron and Ariba. These firms are organizing an independent marketplace that (they hope) will be owned by a broad range of buyers and sellers in the oil and gas industry.

The Petrocosm Marketplace will allow companies of all sizes to buy and sell drilling, electrical, and other equipment required throughout the oil and gas industry supply chain. The marketplace will also support acquisition of professional, engineering, and construction services for the energy industry. Organizers anticipate that the Petrocosm Marketplace will help energy companies save billions of dollars annually through aggregated purchasing, lower transaction costs, and access to larger global markets.

Petrocosm is a venture-backed company in which Ariba, Chevron, and Crosspoint Venture Partners each hold minority stakes. The sponsors expect that majority equity ownership in Petrocosm will be held by energy industry participants of all sizes. The equity stake for each participant is expected to be based on the amount of business that each firm commits to conducting through the Petrocosm hub.

Using the framework we introduced earlier, the Petrocosm Marketplace may be described thusly:

- Managed by an entity that is owned by buyers, sellers, and independent brokers of the traded goods and services
- Features two types of commercial postings—buy offers and sell offers—for energy-related products and services
- Presents offers posted by multiple sellers and multiple buyers, some of which are stakeholders—hence, permanent or long-term tenants—in the marketplace, as well as offers posted by established trading partners of stakeholders, but no such restrictions will exclude participation by others in the marketplace
- Processes transactions in which stakeholders, their established trading partners, and other sellers maintain the inventories being traded,

but also brokers deals between others—not necessarily marketplace stakeholders or tenants—who maintain the inventories being traded

Chevron will target a substantial portion of its annual $10 billion procurement budget for the Petrocosm Marketplace to give the hub a necessary shot of upfront transaction liquidity.

Ariba, one of the leading B2B "superbrokers," will physically host and manage Petrocosm and receive revenues based on a percentage of transaction-based network revenue streams. The marketplace will run on top of Ariba's B2B hosting, transaction, and supply-chain automation products and services.

Petrocosm will host a broad range of energy industry-specific catalogs containing millions of items. It will integrate with buyer and seller organizations' existing procurement and ERP systems. It will support electronic payments and provide logistical services for buyers and sellers. It will support several transactions and pricing models, including auctions, reverse auctions, bid/ask trading, strategic sourcing, spot buying, and customer-specific pricing. And it will host online community forums for buyers and sellers in the marketplace.

However, just as in the auto industry, there will be a rival energy-industry trading hub, this one a buyer-hosted marketplace run by the Royal Dutch/Shell Group and Commerce One. This marketplace, which did not have a name at the time this book was written, was also scheduled to go online in the second quarter of 2000. So far, there's no indication which if either initiative—Chevron's or Shell's—is gaining the necessary support from rivals, suppliers, distributors, and others in the global energy industry. Chevron is using the ostensible "neutrality" of its approach in marketing pitches, but it's not at all certain that hard-boiled commodities traders will care about anything other than dollars and cents. The bottom-line concern for the average trader is always: Where can we execute an order at the most advantageous price and with the lowest transaction charges?

All of which goes to show that anybody who expects one trading hub to someday dominate the entire world economy, or even one substantial sector of one regional economy, will probably be disappointed. We will see marketplaces proliferate and compete amongst themselves at all levels of the global economy. We're likely to see "hub wars" become a dominant theme of the international economic and political system in this new century.

It's important to note that the NYSE—the vaunted "Big Board"—has not pushed other stock exchanges into oblivion. Indeed, the NYSE has had to come to terms with thriving stock exchanges in other countries and other North American cities. And, of course, the NYSE has had the fight of its life recently against the original equities e-marketplace: the National Association of Securities Dealers Automated Quotation (NASDAQ) system. From its inception more than 30 years ago, NASDAQ has always been a broker-hosted e-marketplace par excellence.

Will one e-marketplace hosting model—broker, seller, buyer, or industry—someday drive all others into extinction? Maybe, but it's not likely. Different marketplaces will adopt different hosting models, depending on the structure and competitive dynamics of each industry—or perhaps based on the "first mover" advantage of an early marketplace that succeeded simply because it worked well, thereby enshrining the host's initial business model in the long-term structure of that market.

We're likely to see increasingly hybridization of these e-marketplace hosting models. Marketmakers will experiment with models that help them assemble marketplaces with greater visibility, more participants, deeper catalogs, higher trading volumes, and higher transactions fees.

On this latter point, marketmakers will find ever more creative approaches to extracting additional fees and other revenues from their trading environments. No marketplace can survive for long if the marketmaker is going broke, just as no economy can prosper for long if the hosting government has trouble collecting taxes. E-marketmakers will rely on the following revenue-raising approaches to sustain their business models:

- Fees, such as those associated with marketmaker-provided membership, registration, listing, transaction, finder, referral, and advertising services
- Sales or license revenues, if the marketmaker is also a seller or reseller in the marketplace
- Contract revenues, if the marketmaker provides consulting, systems integration, physical hosting, operations, administration, and other services in the marketplace

Marketmakers who attempt to extract more than their fair share of the liquidity passing through their hubs will see a sort of "tax revolt." Traders will vote with their orders, taking their business to the next hub down the pike, which, after all, is just an URL away.

6.4 Membership Model

Membership has its privileges, and in B2B trading communities it can mean the difference between prosperity and bankruptcy.

Cynics might claim that the almighty dollar—especially piles of it—will secure your membership in any community you might wish to join. But that's not always true. You can't, for example, just bribe your way into a seat on the NYSE: The number of seats is fixed and eligibility criteria are rigorous. Lacking such a seat, you're at a distinct competitive disadvantage in buying and selling stocks listed on the exchange. You'll have to establish a business relationship with an NYSE member firm, which, unlike you, is authorized to place a specialist or broker on the trading floor. Add the trader's transaction fees to those you charge your customers, and you'll realize the competitive burden you're under. You're essentially and inherently a high-cost reseller of the item being traded.

Many e-marketplaces have nontrivial membership criteria, and quite often you have to be an active, registered industry player in order to qualify. At the very least, you will have to fill out an online registration form and accept a membership agreement, user agreement, and/or terms and conditions posted on the site. Even then, you're not usually a member until you receive a formal acceptance by the marketmaker—via e-mail, fax, or phone call—perhaps within 24 hours if everything checks out all right. Once you're in, you can begin to transact business, but always according to the terms and conditions of membership, which marketmakers can usually change as they see fit.

A marketplace's membership model defines who can participate in the marketplace and under what general terms and conditions. A marketmaker would usually maintain membership profiles under a directory service. In the BizTalk Server environment, the likely directory service would be Active Directory, a core component of Windows 2000. Members would normally be required to authenticate themselves by inputting a login ID and password at an opening screen, such as a Web e-form presented by Microsoft Internet Information Server. Members might be required to present strong authentication at login, such as an X.509 public-key certificate issued by Microsoft Certificate Server.

In terms of their membership models, we group e-marketplaces into three broad categories: private, vertical, and horizontal. Figure 6-7 shows these membership models.

6.4.1 Private Marketplaces

This is the membership model behind what we have traditionally referred to as EDI trading communities or extranets. In addition, seller- and buyer-hosted e-marketplaces usually adopt this model.

Under the private marketplace model, you must have some preexisting business relationship with the marketmaker or another market member in order to participate. Essentially, you qualify for membership if you already belong to an existing member's distribution channel, supply chain, or both.

When you participate in a private marketplace, you often enter into a complex "trading partner agreement (TPA)" with the marketmaker and/or other TPs. We discussed TPAs in detail in Chapter 3. TPAs are legal documents that specify the rights and responsibilities of TPs with respect to one another. TPAs often figure into a broader business relationship that may, for example, stipulate exclusivity arrangements that require one TP to acquire a particular good or service from the other TP for a particular period of time.

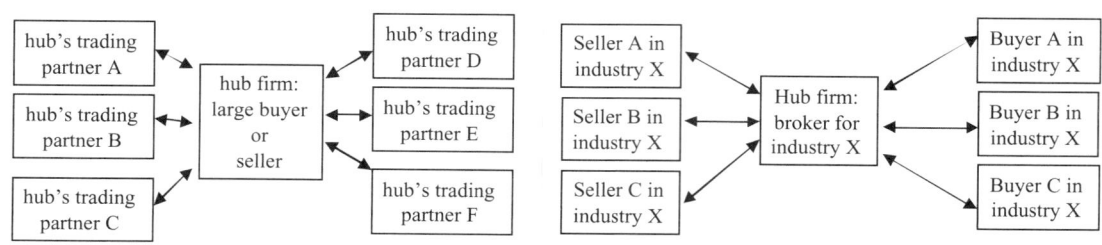

private marketplace   *vertical marketplace*

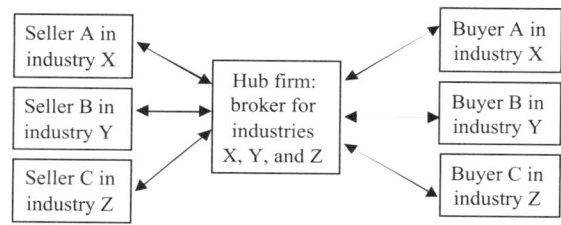

horizontal marketplace

Figure 6-7   *E-marketplace membership models include private, vertical, and horizontal trading communities.*

In other words, the overall business relationship often sets the bounds for the types of items traded within a private marketplace.

Once TPAs are established, TPs mutually register one another in their respective networking and information systems as authorized recipients or senders of EDI messages and documents. TPs also must configure their respective network and data-processing systems to interoperate. Among other things, TPs usually enter each into their respective directory services, assign one another user IDs and passwords, define access controls and other privileges specific to each TP, and perhaps also issue TPs public-key certificates for strong authentication into one another's applications and databases. In many cases, TPs grant one another several accounts on one another's applications, supporting the coordination requirements of various functional groups.

One interesting twist on the private marketplace model is the "invitation" mechanism built into the Ariba Network service. If you're a supplier, a buyer who uses Ariba's ORMS e-procurement software can send you an e-mail invitation to join the service and post your catalog online. You receive the e-mail and follow an URL hyperlink contained within it to an Ariba Network registration screen. At this screen, you enter the personal identification number (PIN) contained in the invitation message, as well as your company's Data Universal Numbering System (DUNS) number and profile information. Once you click the "submit" button, you are registered and receive an Ariba Network account name and password. However, your account is inactive until the buyer who "sponsored" you responds to an automated e-mail that requests confirmation of your registration. Once you are confirmed, you can begin to trade on Ariba Network. If you attempt to register without a prior invitation, Ariba itself—the marketmaker—will review your application, which will probably take longer than if you had a buyer-sponsor in the first place.

Increasingly, Web-based B2B e-marketplaces are supporting extranet-like integration between established TPs. Some trading-hub software products allow particular TPs to set up customized workflows, transactions, and other services among themselves within the shared e-marketplace, in accordance with TPAs, policies, and procedures. As B2B trading hubs mature and absorb more traditional extranet and EDI functions, we can expect to see further development of "virtual private marketplaces." These are environments that apply private membership models, with appropriate policies and access controls, to public trading environments.

6.4.2 Vertical Marketplaces

This is the membership model behind many broker-hosted e-marketplaces, and, we expect, industry-hosted marketplaces as well.

Under the vertical marketplace model, you need not have a preexisting business relationship with the marketmaker, but you must meet the criteria specific to a particular segment of industry, business, or commerce. For example, if you're involved in the buying or selling of industrial-grade paper products, you can join PaperExchange.com. If you're a qualified buyer or seller of biological and chemical reagents, you can join Chemdex.com. The marketmakers may not have a preset list of organizations they'll admit, but they'll probably do a quick background check before they approve your application.

Depending on the vertical marketmaker, TP eligibility criteria will range between stringent and laughable. They may ask you for upfront registration fees, detailed corporate background information, and credit and customer references—and then make you wait for weeks while they check you out. Or they may simply take your name and e-mail address and open wide the virtual door to online trading. Much of this depends on how desperate the marketmaker is for your business, and on the dollar value of the items traded on their exchange.

Name an industry, product, component, service, or professional category, and you can expect to see at least one vertical e-marketplace—perhaps several—emerge to service it over the next few years. Employment agencies, commodities brokers, trade associations, consultants, technical publishers—the list of organizations and individuals who might organize vertical marketplaces is almost endless. All you need is a vertical market concept, a site, a registration screen, and the commercial postings to set it all in motion. If others begin to accept you as a legitimate registration authority and your site as a worthwhile trading environment, you've jumped the first and most important hurdle.

Membership models will rest on growing repositories of background and transactional profiles of buyers and sellers. As vertical marketplaces evolve, we expect to see ever greater subdivision and specialization within each trading environment. Marketmakers will reorganize online catalogs and offers into more specialized categories so as to target opportunities at more narrowly focused market niches. Any given product segment will split into national, regional, and local marketplaces. Any given marketplace will spawn different bargaining and pricing models, such as various auction and haggling rules, to facilitate bidding under time-sensitive and exceptional circumstances. Any given bidding mechanism will spawn competed and noncompeted variants, which would allow any offer to be presented either to a group of rival buyers or sellers, or to a single party who perceives it as a "for my eyes only" offer.

The final frontier, of course, will be vertical e-marketplaces targeted at precisely one member, presenting customized offers in perfect sync with its requirements. Membership in a powerful e-marketplace means you may never have to search for the best deals. Instead, deals will seek you out, connecting you to the right TPs at the right time and terms.

6.4.3 Horizontal Marketplaces

This is the membership model underlying most portals and online malls, which are principally B2C-oriented trading environments. It is also the model for B2C auction sites such as eBay.

Under the horizontal marketplace model, membership is essentially open to anyone who registers online, fills out a quick form, and (optionally) provides a credit card number. The owner of the portal, mall, or auction site collects personal profile information on the customer and uses this to target commercial offers at individuals (or what amounts to the same thing, target banner ads, which are "monetizable" content that may contribute more to the site owner's bottom line than offers for items that no one wants to buy).

As the number and variety of B2B vertical e-marketplaces grow, we will see verticals begin to amalgamate into increasingly horizontal trading environments, addressing a broad range of markets and serving a broad range of members. When each of us belongs to many vertical e-marketplaces, including several in the same industry, the importance of affiliation with any one specialized trading environment will decline. When online identity-management services such as X.509 public-key certificates and MSN Passport progress to the point where they support authenticated single sign-on to a broad range of B2B and B2C sites, we won't have to fill out separate online registration forms and enter duplicate profile and payment information just to order goods from a new online hub or merchant. When that day comes, and it's not unreasonable to expect it before the year 2010, we will all enjoy universal access to one common horizontal e-marketplace.

And that marketplace will be the public Internet.

6.5 Aggregation Model

The ideal market is a place where you can find whatever you're looking for, or sell whatever you have on hand, at the right price.

E-marketplaces promise commercial cornucopias undreamt of in ages past. At their cores, trading hubs manage central catalogs, directories, or other listings that aggregate items being offered by one or more sellers, and/or being sought by one or more buyers. As vertical hubs link into broader trading environments, the collective catalog expands and the probability of finding what you want also grows.

Actually, it's a jungle out there and getting worse every day. Your chances of finding what you want can improve only if marketmakers help you with your commercial quest. Nothing's worse than a Web site that connects to the whole world but crams hyperlinks helter-skelter into long, busy, bewildering pages. A marketplace's aggregation model—its approach to organizing buy and sell offers—can be what separates an efficient trading environment from a colossal waste of people's time. A poorly designed marketplace is more of an aggravation model for the time-stressed trader.

6.5.1 Content-Aggregation Paradigms

Hubs are crossroads, and like any permanent human settlement, they can evolve into a sprawling metropolis of commercial content, not all of which pleases the eye or makes perfect sense to the casual observer. As we expand the membership models of our e-marketplaces, we open trading environments to greater clutter in the form of new postings from new buyers and sellers.

Content aggregation has been a central feature of both e-commerce software tools and hubbed online marketplaces. In a BizTalk Server environment, the marketplace's aggregated catalogs might be maintained under

Microsoft Commerce Server and SQL Server, or under third-party hub, commerce, or merchant server software and databases.

One way to categorize e-commerce environments is by the node at which they aggregate catalog content (shown in Figure 6-8):

- Buyer-aggregated catalogs: Most e-procurement software packages require buyers to aggregate catalog content from one or more merchants. The e-procurement application makes this catalog content available to internal purchase requisitioners. The application uses workflow functionality to manage the internal requisitioning and ordering process. Typically, these applications generate purchase orders in document formats that suppliers accept, such as ANSI X12, and wrap them in message formats such as OBI for online submission.

- Seller-aggregated catalogs: Seller-aggregated catalogs are the focus of many merchants' e-commerce implementations. Merchants aggregate catalogs for their own wares only and make this available to buyers over the Internet. It's usually up to buyers to figure out how to integrate each vendor's proprietary interface with their internal e-procurement applications.

- Hub-aggregated catalogs: This is the e-marketmaker's approach. The marketmaker assumes the burden of integrating seller catalogs and/or buyer offers. This is the core business model for online portals and malls as well. Sellers and buyers who are members of hubbed e-marketplaces are usually responsible for feeding or posting new content to the hub continually.

As a sell-side server, Microsoft's Commerce Server 2000 will support seller-aggregated and hub-aggregated catalog content. On a per-server basis, its predecessor, Site Server Commerce Edition, already supports millions of catalog entries, hundreds of thousands of shoppers per day, and tens of thousands of user accounts. We expect Commerce Server to scale even higher, in keeping with the requirements of the trading hubs where it will be deployed. It will aggregate catalog entries, advertisements, and other content in scalable data warehouses integrated with SQL Server and Windows 2000.

At the hub level, we see marketmakers adopting a vertical focus and aggregating the following content types: member postings, community services, and information and productivity resources, as illustrated in Figure 6-9.

VERTICAL FOCUS • Usually, your aggregation model is implicit in the concept for your vertical or private e-marketplace. If buyers and sellers refer to your site as, for example, the "used bulldozer market," this indicates they have clear expectations of what to find and not find there. Similarly, if they know it as, for example, the "propane industry's online distribution hub," they won't come there to order non-propane-related products and accessories.

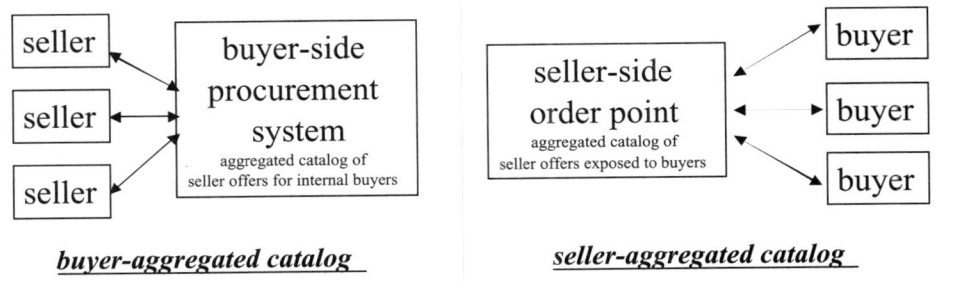

buyer-aggregated catalog   *seller-aggregated catalog*

hub-aggregated catalog

Figure 6-8   *E-marketplace content may be aggregated at the buyer, seller, and/or hub site.*

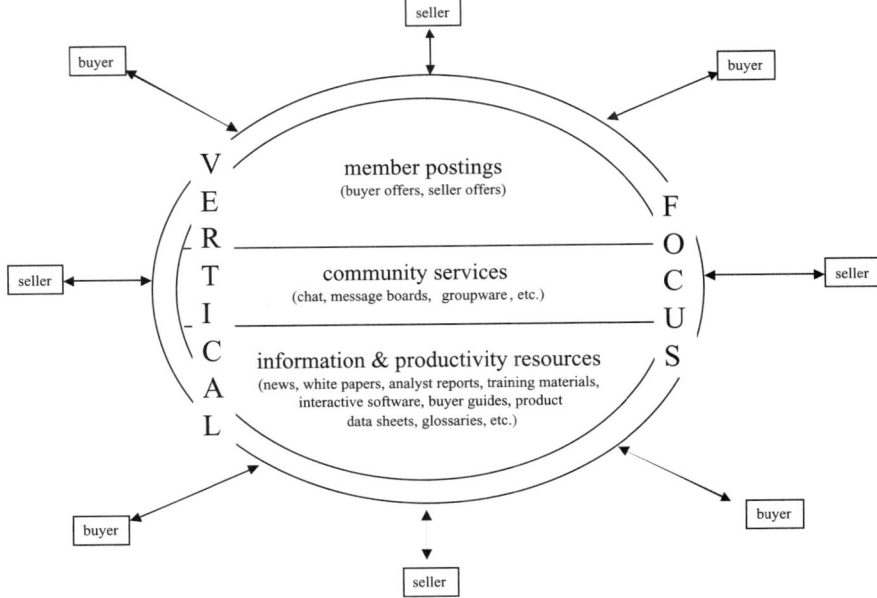

Figure 6-9   *E-marketplace content consists of member posting, community services, and information and productivity resources addressing the vertical market focus of the trading community.*

Nothing beats this sort of conceptual clarity when you're trying to target your service to potential buyers and sellers. If you go off focus, you may dilute the market's conceptual grasp and cause glazed-over eyeballs to shun your site. Likewise, if you define a new vertical niche that takes more than 25 words to explain to a total stranger in an elevator, you should seriously reconsider your business strategy.

MEMBER POSTINGS • An e-marketplace's aggregation model is also implicit in its membership model. In other words, an e-marketplace's members are also its prime content providers. Generally, the more members your marketplace has, the more content—buy and sell offers—you have as well. You expect a preponderance of offers to buy in a buyer-hosted e-marketplace, offers to sell in a seller-run marketplace, and offers of both types in a broker- or industry-hosted marketplace.

You can tell a strong local economy by looking at the thickness of the Sunday newspaper's classified section. In the same way, you can tell a vibrant e-marketplace by the sheer volume of postings it attracts. Consider the number and variety of postings, the range of buyers and sellers posting them, and the speed at which postings lead to trades.

COMMUNITY SERVICES • Your aggregation model should also include services for allowing members to bond into a community, as well as a marketplace. Community services allow marketplace members to locate one another, exchange e-mails, engage in online chats, post to topic-oriented message boards and newsgroups, maintain customized Web pages, and publish events calendars.

Essentially, these are Web-based collaboration tools that supplement the buy and sell activity that is the core function of e-marketplaces. Many vertical e-marketplaces provide access to community services through links from their homepages. For example, a vertical market may offer all its members free Web mail services and Web homepages. Or it may charge for these services, figuring that most established companies already maintain their own e-mail and Web operations. In either case, marketmakers are likely to outsource these services to such vendors as Critical Path and USA.Net, which provide low-cost, scalable collaboration services to many dotcom firms.

As we noted previously, GM will provide B2B collaboration services through a Web site and namespace (www.supplypower.com) that is separate from its B2B trading environments (www.gmtradexchange.com). Each e-marketmaker must decide which collaboration services are best provided on a community basis, and which are the responsibility of each member to provide on its own. For message boards and newsgroups, the marketmaker may want to assign a staff member to moderate discussions, prevent posting of objectionable materials, and monitor issues surfaced by members. Moderated discussions are also a good mechanism for identifying operational issues that should be brought to the attention of the hub's help desk.

INFORMATION AND PRODUCTIVITY RESOURCES • Markets run on fresh news, and that should be a major component of any e-marketplace's content-aggregation model. Many marketmakers post fresh editorial content to their hubs daily, much of it syndicated material sourced from general and business news sites. Many e-marketplaces also post interactive software, buyer guides, product data sheets, industry directories, analyst reports, white papers, training materials, job listings, industry links, and glossaries. As with community services, this is another type of content that makes trading hubs resemble portals.

6.5.2 Content-Disaggregation Paradigms

Hub user interfaces are sometimes too cluttered and impersonal for their own good.

Efficient markets should allow buyers to filter out irrelevant options and allow sellers to target the most promising prospects. Consequently, we also see marketmakers, buyers, and sellers use various techniques to disaggregate and target hub-based commercial content. These techniques include partitioned namespaces, hierarchical categories, classified ads, personalization, localization, search engines, comparison shopping bots, affiliate placements, banner ads, and targeted e-mail.

PARTITIONED NAMESPACES • You may not manage just one e-marketplace but several that offer different goods and cater to different groups of buyers and sellers. You might want to host these trading environments on separate Web sites but at the same time give them URLs that suggest they are all part of a larger group of affiliated marketplaces under common management. One approach to this is to assign them different URLs that share a common template structure but differ in that each URL specifies a particular product.

For example, Comput-Ability Inc. brokers various types of building materials through a set of affiliated sites bearing URLs that are both plain-spoken and easy to remember: www.buyinsulation.com, www.buymaterial. com, www.buydrywall.com, www.buyceilings.com, www.buywalls.com, www.buyplaster.com, www.buyacoustical.com, www.buyfireproofing.com, and www.buyfirestopping.com. Another example is "superbroker" VerticalNet.com, which, organizes trading communities with such URLs as www.poweronline.com, www.publicworksonline.com, www.solidwaste.com, and www.wateronline.com—all of which are accessible through navigation links within the marketmaker's www.verticalnet.com homepage.

HIERARCHICAL CATEGORIES • Within each e-marketplace, you will want to classify and organize items in ways that make sense to your target buyers and sellers. Wherever feasible, you want them to find the right listings right away by navigating through logical categories, though if they have to slog through endless subcategories you'll probably lose them. A good site design places the information and services in greatest demand on the homepage or, at most, one or two clicks away.

Hierarchical categorization is the hallmark of the portal model of e-marketplaces, as exemplied in the B2C space by Yahoo, Excite, and the like, but it is widely implemented in B2B markets as well. As you subdivide your marketplace, you may want to partition your namespace internally, so that buyers and sellers can return quickly to a page by specifying the unique, mnemonic URL associated with it. A familiar example from the B2C world drives this point home. You might start your Yahoo shopping session at "shopping.yahoo.com/," and then drill deeper into "shopping.yahoo.com/Arts_and_Collectibles/."

In this particular example, you could navigate even more deeply by inputting long, complex, mnemonic search strings from the keyboard. However, you'd have to be a glutton for punishment to want to do this. Scripts at Yahoo's Web site automatically enter the appropriate, non-mnemonic URL when you click on the associated hyperlink. That's a good design feature. You want to conceal as much complexity as possible from browsers.

As a rule of thumb, e-marketmakers should want to minimize the number of clicks and keystrokes that stand between buyers, sellers, and successful trades.

CLASSIFIED ADS • Classified ads are flat, nonhierarchical aggregations of buy and sell offers. Think of the classified ads in your local newspaper, or even the yellow pages distributed by your local phone company. The organizing principle is usually not some "semantic map" or some "attribute-based taxonomy" of wares in the marketplace. Rather, it's usually an alphabetical listing of entries by name or, at the most, alphabetical listings within categories that are themselves listed alphabetically. In many classified ads the categories are usually static. A good example of classified ads are job listings such as those maintained at www.monster.com.

PERSONALIZATION • Personalization is a core feature of many e-marketplaces and merchant sites. It allows users to define a default view of the marketplace that suits their personal needs. Users can go right to the marketplace pages they care about, either when they navigate to the hub's URL (through the magic of cookies) or when they enter their member username and password at the hub homepage.

Generally, personalized start-up pages allow market participants to view the status of their accounts, including all trades they've executed, outstanding offers they've posted, and bids they've placed. These pages also allow participants to track "watch lists" of companies, products, and other participants in which they are most interested.

LOCALIZATION • Localization allows e-marketmakers to segment their catalogs into subsets appropriate for various local, regional, and national markets. Locality can be one of the personalization attributes that marketplace members define for themselves.

A good example of localization in the B2C space is CitiQuest's recent agreement with eBay that provides CitiQuest's city-specific portal users with direct access to eBay listings in specific geographic locations. CitiQuest.com users will have direct access via an eBay icon to any one of eBay's dozens of regional homepages or to the eBay homepage. eBay's local sites allow community members to find items located near them and browse through items of local interest. The sites also provide a more convenient venue for trading items that are difficult to ship long distances, such as cars and furniture.

SEARCH ENGINES • Search engines are a critical component of e-marketplaces. Search engines are absolutely necessary when hubs have added more content than can easily fit into a single Web page or human mind. Search features can help users cut through e-marketplace clutter to find items by categories, attributes, keywords, and full-text indexes. However, search engines can also be a Web merchant's tacit admission of failure to aggregate content in an intuitive way.

One important search feature is the ability to save predefined queries as "agents" that execute continuously in the background and notify their "owners" when new content meeting specified criteria hits the e-marketplace. Another important feature is the ability to expose e-marketplace content, such as merchant catalogs, to one or more external search engines, such as Yahoo and Alta Vista, and thereby drive new traffic and membership into the marketplace.

COMPARISON SHOPPING BOTS • Comparison shopping bots are critical components in improving the global efficiency of both B2B and B2C e-marketplaces, highlighting and thereby eliminating price discrepancies between separate marketplaces. It's for this very reason that some e-marketmakers and merchants fear broker-hosted shopping bots.

Bots present targeted sets of offers to sell on the fly, usually in response to buyer inquiries that specify such criteria as manufacturer, model, features, and price. Bots allow you to compare different items feature by feature prior to purchasing. Once you select the product you wish to buy, the bot forwards you to the appropriate merchant.

Bots are essentially broker-hosted e-marketplaces in their own right, since they put potential buyers in touch with potential sellers. Bot site operators typically collect finders and referral fees from merchants. The following bots were in the B2C marketplace at the time this book was written, and it was too early to tell which would succeed in that space and possibly branch into the B2B space:

- www.mysimon.com
- www.dealpilot.com
- www.netsage.com
- www.bottomdollar.com
- www.bizrate.com
- www.shopnow.com
- www.ichoose.com
- www.quotesmith.com
- www.nextag.com
- www.respond.com
- www.mygeek.com
- www.rusure.com
- www.frictionless.com
- www.brandwise.com
- www.pricegrabber.com

We expect that many of today's broker-hosted B2B hubs will develop, license, or acquire bot technology outright over the next several years, since it is so obviously complementary to their core business models. Bot technology is already in evidence in B2B hubs such as www.necx.com, an electronic components marketplace that allows you, for example, to compare several bar-code printers feature by feature prior to purchasing.

AFFILIATE PLACEMENTS • Affiliate placements are hyperlinks on related sites that promote offers and drive traffic to an e-marketplace or merchant site. For example, a healthcare industry e-marketplace might pay the proprietors of health, medicine, and pharmaceutical-related Web sites to place "buy button" icons on their pages. These buttons would send the user to the marketplace to purchase products mentioned in articles on affiliate sites. Typically, the affiliates, like shopping bots, receive referrals fees for directing "clickthrough" traffic to the marketplace.

Another logical group of e-marketplace affiliates includes its member buyers and sellers. One benefit of membership in a marketplace could be affiliate revenues based on hyperlink clickthroughs to the hub.

BANNER ADS • Banner ads on external sites are another means of promoting offers and driving traffic to an e-marketplace or merchant site. Unlike affiliate placements, which are usually static hyperlinks, banner ads usually rotate on the hosting Web sites, such as mass-market portals. Rotation means that ads might, for example, be seen once every five minutes or in response to users' entering a particular keyword in a search box. External banner ad placements usually rely on ad-brokering services such as DoubleClick. The banner-hosting Web site usually receives payments from advertisers based on page impressions and clickthroughs.

Internal banner ad placements can be even more powerful than external banners. Internal banner ads highlight special sales, deals, or time-limited offers in the e-marketplace. One great advantage of internal banner ads is that they eliminate the need to pay referral fees to others. Another advantage is that internal banners can be displayed to the users most likely to be interested in the goods they're promoting, based on transactional data at the marketmaker's disposal.

TARGETED E-MAILS • Many e-marketplaces, merchant sites, and online publishers allow visitors to sign up for free e-mailed newsletters and commercial promotions. This is the "opt-in" or "permission-based" approach to broadcasting commercial messages to users' inboxes. It is the Internet community's preferred direct-mail technique. Users ostensibly accept it as an integral part of their existing relationship with an online merchant.

Merchants are often quick to distinguish permission-based e-mail marketing from what many regard as its evil, illegitimate step-cousin: spam. Also known as unsolicited bulk mail, spam trickles into the inbox of anyone on the Internet, sort of like cosmic background radiation. Spam is the most disaggregated, impersonal, and pushy of all commercial content. It comes out of nowhere, laden with deals screaming for your attention, but it knows nothing of you or your interests. It attempts to direct you to URLs swarming with naked bodies, easy cash, and swampy real estate. But you have to figure that someone somewhere must be making some money from spam, or there wouldn't be so much of it.

After all, spam too is an offer hosted somewhere in the global e-marketplace. Like online catalog entries and banner ads, it too is a piece of monetizable content awaiting consummation. It seeks buyers and won't rest till it has them.

6.6 Transaction Model

Every marketplace is an arena that depends on a particular structured way of doing business.

Transactions in e-marketplaces are virtual, instantaneous, and configured in almost any way the human mind can conceive and program into existence. In an e-marketplace, you do business by exchanging bits with other human beings sitting at their computers somewhere in the world, by letting your information systems talk to their information systems while you all go about your lives, or by you interacting directly with their information systems as the need arises or by them interacting with yours.

In spite of their superhuman power and speed, e-marketplaces are fundamentally no different from their offline counterparts. Just as in the traditional commercial world, every online transaction begins with an order, offer, quote, request, or inquiry of some sort. If conditions are right, orders get executed, offers accepted, quotes presented, requests fulfilled, and inquiries satisfied. Currency gets transferred between the appropriate accounts. Goods and services get delivered. All of these activities follow structured procedures laid down by marketmakers, buyers, sellers, and the other organizations that facilitate transactions.

What binds transactions together is documentation, in both the online and offline worlds. Within almost any business relationship, there is documentation flowing both ways, creating an information chain that some call "red tape," and others defend as a necessary audit trail. In the offline world, you often fill out forms to buy and sell things, and you do the same in e-marketplaces. When you want to do business, you usually have to fill out an electronic form of some sort. If you're a buyer, the e-form is usually a purchase order, request for quotation (RFQ), request for proposal (RFP), bid, or something similar. If you're a seller, it's a quote, proposal, or sales offer.

Whether you're a buyer or seller, once you've completed and submitted the e-form, it starts up a transactional workflow. The form's contents may be processed entirely by automated systems, as is the case with POs submitted to open order points on an e-marketplace or merchant site. Or the data may be seen by other marketplace participants, who respond by submitting forms of their own, as is the case with bid/counterbid procedures in online auctions.

Every trading community is a culture with its own specific formats, rules, and procedures for doing business. An e-marketplace's transaction model defines how traders are introduced, offers floated, contracts negotiated, orders submitted, and deals executed in that community. We can describe e-marketplaces' transaction models in terms of their commercial contracts, bargaining mechanisms, and transactional workflows.

6.6.1 Commercial Contracts

Contracts are commercial relationships codified in documentation.

Contracts come in many varieties because commercial relationships differ greatly. Relationships of all sorts drive transactions in the average marketplace—e or otherwise. Some relationships are shallow and transient, lasting for a single transaction between complete strangers. Others endure for years, serving as the basis for a broad range of transactions between TPs that interact on so many levels that they begin to behave like a single, integrated business enterprise.

There are two basic types of e-marketplace relationships: the contract between an e-marketmaker and a marketplace member, and the contract between one participant and another, such as between a buyer and seller. We show these in Figure 6-10.

MEMBERSHIP AGREEMENTS • The first contract type—the membership agreement—signifies that a company intends to be a steady participant in an e-marketplace, doing business with one or more members of that marketplace on an ongoing basis. A membership agreement structures all activities in the

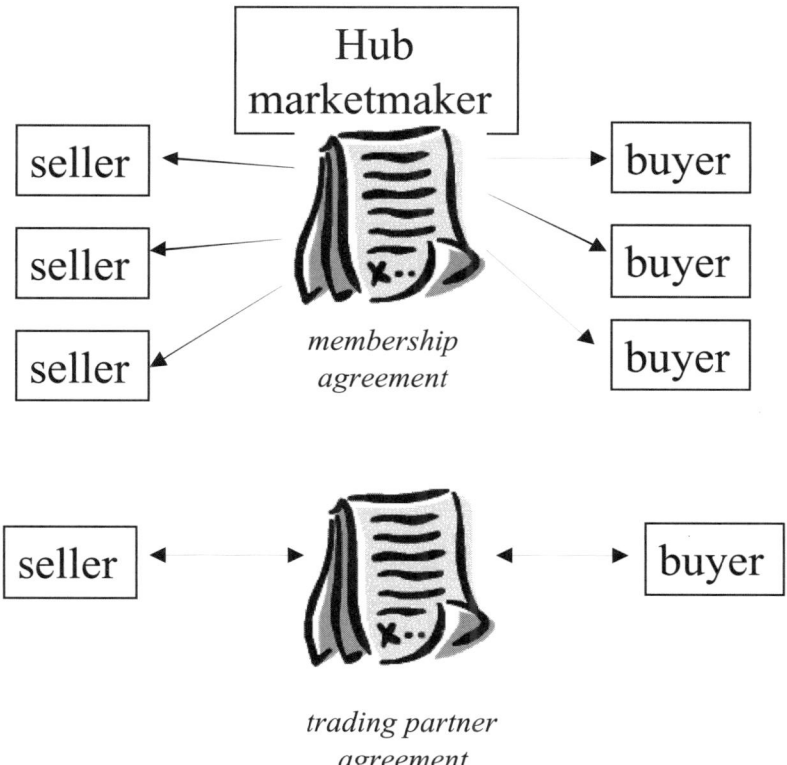

Figure 6-10 *E-marketplace commercial contracts include membership agreements and trading partner agreements.*

e-marketplace. Membership agreements are a standard feature of participating in any capacity in an e-marketplace. They typically address the following basic points:

- Define the scope of transactions supported and services provided in the marketplace
- Define formats, procedures, policies, and workflows associated with transactions
- Describe participant responsibilities, risks, liabilities, and fees associated with transactions
- Declare that the marketmaker is not a party to those transactions
- Limit the marketmaker's legal liability from consequences of those transactions
- List acceptable and unacceptable forms of conduct for marketplace members

- State that the marketmaker alone formulates membership eligibility criteria and decides who may participate in the marketplace and access various features of the service
- Make it known that the marketmaker may at any time change the terms of the membership agreement and discontinue, suspend, or modify marketplace services

TRADING PARTNER AGREEMENTS • The second type of e-marketplace contract—the trading partner agreement—signifies that you intend to conduct a high volume and frequency of business online with one particular company. The two types of contracts are not mutually exclusive: You can enter into a membership agreement in a vertical e-marketplace and one or more TPAs with regular TPs you do business with in that environment. The TPA is much broader than a particular sales or service contract between two companies. The TPA addresses legal and technical issues that apply to ongoing supply-chain relationships.

The TPA usually specifies the parameters that shape EDI transactions between TPs, such as:

- Scope of the relationship
- Roles, responsibilities, risks, and liabilities of the TPs
- Sequence of messages, documents, data types, and acknowledgments to be exchanged between TPs
- Processing performed on messages, documents, and data by each TP
- Networks, addressing, encoding, transaction sets, file-naming, digital signatures, encryption, key exchange, compression, passwords, and other procedures pertaining to B2B document interchanges
- Financial terms, conditions, and obligations applying to TPs within the relationship

BizTalk Server provides tools for tracking TPAs, keeping tabs on the documents and messages interchanged with each TP. TPAs are most appropriate for B2B relationships that involve open-ended, multiyear contracts, such as indefinite delivery/indefinite quantity (ID/IQ) contracts, purchase order agreements, and requirements-type service contracts. When companies engage in transient, short-term, one-off transactions, the typical sales or service contract is more appropriate.

6.6.2 Bargaining Mechanisms

Bargaining is what converges buyers and sellers on mutually agreeable terms of trade.

The structure of a marketplace's bargaining mechanisms may give buyers an advantage in negotiating terms of trade, or sellers may have the advantage. Think of heavy manufacturing before the rise of labor unions, and you'll realize that the sellers of skilled and semiskilled labor-power benefited greatly from the development of organized bargaining blocs.

More often, though, the bargaining advantage is not clear-cut, and may in fact swing back and forth in the development of economic institutions. One generation's underdog is the next generation's fat cat waiting for its comeuppance. How you fare in the marketplace usually depends on how wisely you play the hand you were dealt.

We won't focus here on the balance of bargaining power in e-marketplaces. That could (and probably will) be the subject of many a 21st-century doctoral dissertation. Instead, we identify two broad bargaining paradigms, based on whether buyers or sellers drive the transactions. We show these two bargaining paradigms—buyer-driven and seller driven—in Figure 6-11.

BUYER-DRIVEN TRANSACTIONS • Buyer-driven transactions kick into action when a potential buyer posts an offer to buy, which comes in many varieties and goes by many names, the most common being bid, order, PO, RFQ, and RFP. These documents may express a definite intent to buy from a particular seller at a particular price, or simply indicate a tentative foray into the market.

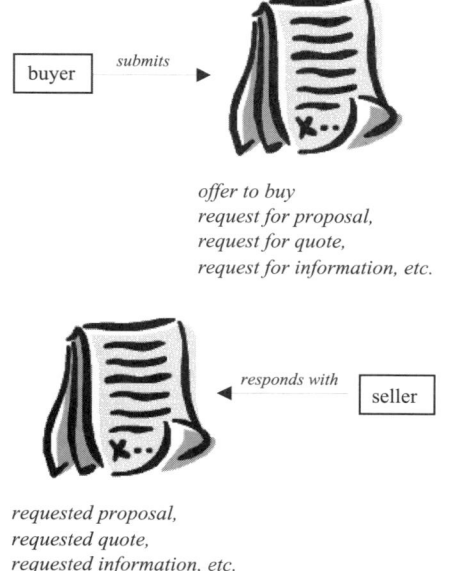

offer to buy
request for proposal,
request for quote,
request for information, etc.

requested proposal,
requested quote,
requested information, etc.

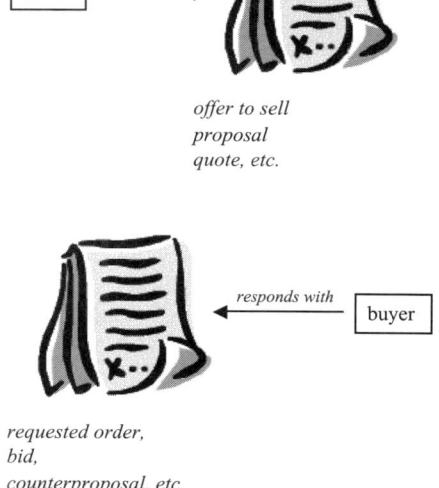

offer to sell
proposal
quote, etc.

requested order,
bid,
counterproposal, etc.

__buyer-driven transactions__   *__seller-driven transactions__*

Figure 6-11   *E-marketplace bargaining paradigms include buyer-driven and seller-driven transactions.*

In daily commerce, buyer-driven transactions are perhaps the most common and familiar. Most of the time we navigate the commercial world with either a definite "shopping list" in hand or a "just browsing" expression on our face. Merchants arrange their wares in attractive packages, floor displays, and shopping environments and wait for our orders. This is in fact the way most online merchants conduct business as well, configuring their online catalogs as open order points exposed to a passing parade of potential browsers. The workflows for these transactions usually conform to a simple back-and-forth model: an order followed by an order confirmation or receipt. Bargaining is often a "take it or leave it" proposition, though some merchants—most notably, automobile dealers—encourage customers to haggle over terms.

Several new buyer-driven transaction models have arisen on the Web, and we increasingly find them in B2B vertical e-marketplaces. We see more e-commerce sites implementing such buyer-driven transaction environments as shopping bots, name-your-terms inquiries, wait-for-best-offer postings, reverse auctions, and haggling. These tools provide more efficient media for what economists refer to as "preference revelation," often through structured e-forms that guide buyers through a set of options until they assemble a profile of their requirements, often in excruciating detail.

The principal differences between these buyer-driven transaction environments are as follows:

- Shopping bots: Buyers post their specific requirements in a query that gets sent concurrently to many sellers' sites, with query processing and results compilation under the control of a specialized search engine. Buyers evaluate different sellers' standing offers against documented requirements and perhaps make a purchase decision immediately, though sellers may not be aware that the user is evaluating them. Sellers do not have an opportunity to compete overtly in improving their chances of winning the buyer's business through shopping bots, though sellers may in fact monitor the bots and adjust their pricing and other terms behind the scenes to give themselves an advantage. As we noted previously, shopping bots abound in the B2C space and are coming on strong in the B2B space as well.

- Name-your-terms transactions: Buyers post their specific, detailed requirements as bids in messages that are transmitted automatically to many sellers. Sellers are aware that they are being evaluated. Sellers' information systems generate immediate responses to the buyer's bid and requirements profile, addressing the buyer's specific requirements with a custom offer, proposal, or quote. The best-known example of a name-your-terms transaction site in the B2C world is www.priceline.com.

- Wait-for-best offer transactions: Buyers post their general or specific requirements as RFPs either in messages to candidate sellers or in postings to a shared board. Sellers need not respond immediately, though the first acceptable offer will probably win the sale. B2C sites that specialize in wait-for-best-offer transactions include www.imandi.com, www.respond.com, www.iwant.com, and www.ewanted.com.

- Reverse auctions: Buyers post their specific requirements as bids to a shared board. Sellers may respond, either automatically or manually, with custom offers that address the buyer's requirements, which usually focus on achieving the lowest purchase price for a particular product or service. Sellers may also compete among themselves, underbidding one another until the buyer selects one of them or the auction deadline arrives. Examples of reverse auctions in the B2C world include www.bidtheworld.com, www.nextag.com, www.liquidprice.com, and www.buyersedge.com.

- Haggle sites: Buyers post their specific requirements as bids in messages to one or more candidate sellers. The candidate sellers respond with counteroffers. Buyers can respond to these counteroffers with their own counteroffers, and this back-and-forth process can last for an indefinite number of rounds. Buyers can accept an offer at any time, or withdraw from haggling. Examples of haggle sites include www.hagglezone.com and www.makeusanoffer.com.

SELLER-DRIVEN TRANSACTIONS • Seller-driven transactions are what we normally associate with "hard-sell" tactics, public relations, telemarketing, direct mail, and spam. However, they are a legitimate and important type of transaction in a healthy marketplace. For example, we would have nowhere near as vibrant a high-tech sector if vendors were shy about proposing new concepts to a puzzled, reluctant marketplace.

Seller-driven transactions start with someone posting an offer to sell, which can take such forms as advertisements, promotions, proposals, and quotes. Indeed, aggregating merchandise descriptions into a catalog and publishing the catalog are often the most powerful offer to sell. After posting the offer, the seller often follows up to make sure the target customer has seen it. During follow-up, sellers often elaborate on their sales pitches, field inquiries, overcome objections, qualify prospects further, and, if all goes well, perhaps even take the order.

The dominant paradigm in today's seller-driven e-marketplaces is the forward auction, otherwise known simply as the "auction." A seller offers an item for buyers to bid on. Buyers compete against each other in rounds, raising the price until the prespecified time limit, at which point the high bidder wins and gets the item. There are many models of forward and reverse auctions, which we will discuss later in this chapter.

6.6.3 Transactional Workflows

Commercial transactions cut a swath within and between two or more organizations, involving a broad range of participants, processing steps, business documents, databases, and coordination and decision points.

When a business process crosses corporate boundaries, the corresponding workflow does as well. A B2B workflow usually involves transmission of several standard business documents in a predetermined sequence between various functional groups within participating companies. Focusing on the immediate players in a sales transaction grossly underestimates the range of companies that will need to swing into action to ensure successful completion of the end-to-end transaction.

As we've noted, the core workflow of many buy-sell transactions is often, on the surface, a simple one: an order followed by a confirmation. However, marketplace transactional workflows can become exceedingly complex (if we're not careful). The surfeit of connectivity, computing power, and reusable software code in e-marketplaces can tempt us to make online workflows more complex than they need be. Before long, the simple point-to-point workflows of traditional EDI applications will seem quaint by comparison with the cast of thousands that might facilitate a complex e-marketplace transaction.

We'll discuss this issue further under "Facilitation Model." However, we'll just call attention to a few of the facilitators that often play roles in complex business transactions in the offline world (if such a world can still be said to exist). There are the buyer and seller organizations, of course, and the various groups within the buyer and seller organizations that played a part in the deal, such as sales, marketing, purchasing, finance, legal, and accounting. The buyers and sellers may have also depended on assent and assistance from their external consultants, banks, appraisers, and insurance companies. The buyer and seller come to terms, the order is placed, and ultimately the deal is closed and settled. Then the order must go to a fulfillment house for processing and handling. An escrow service may get involved to make sure that the buyer renders payment before the item is released for shipping. Once released, the item goes to a shipping company, which may deliver it to the buyer's receiving department or to a temporary warehousing facility. All the while, banks effect the transfer of funds between buyer and seller accounts. Depending on the nature of the transaction, the buyer and seller may also need submit forms and documentation to various government agencies at the local, state, and federal levels. The taxman, for example, is an indirect party to many if not most commercial transactions.

These B2B workflow participants need standards for interfacing their different systems, and the BizTalk Framework provides just such a standards framework. However, as we've noted elsewhere in this book, BizTalk is just one of several candidate frameworks, and it remains tied, in practical terms, to one operating environment: Windows 2000. No robust standards have yet emerged to support interoperable, cross-platform e-business. The industry is nowhere near delivering anything resembling plug-and-play technical integration at the B2B level. For that to happen, you need an interoperability framework that seamlessly integrates EDI and workflow. The various proposed frameworks—most notably, BizTalk and the XML/EDI Group's initiative—show promise in this regard. They encapsulate EDI transaction sets in message envelopes that specify some, but not all, workflow parameters and transaction state variables. It remains to be seen which of them, if any, will gain the necessary multivendor support. It might be 5 to 10 years before a dominant, universally implemented B2B interoperability framework emerges from today's frantic activity.

All of which shows how devilishly complex a B2B transaction workflow can become, from a business or technical standpoint. As e-marketplaces gear up to support a broader range of online transactions, you'll see transactional workflows become more convoluted. Everybody who has a piece of the transaction will be online and connected to one another through the e-marketmaker. You'll need a graphical flowchart with circles, arrows, and flashing icons to tell the players apart.

6.7 Pricing Model

Pricing is the golden thread that runs through most commercial transactions.

Price is often the primary factor that clinches deals and sustains ongoing business relationships. Marketplaces are essentially machines that calculate, recalculate, and calibrate prices, based on transactions that involve many buyers and sellers. Economists teach that the market price is the intersection of the supply and demand curves, but these high-level models almost never drill down to the transaction level, where the asking and bid prices may be miles apart. Bargaining is what brings a seller's asking price and a customer's bid price together, or shows that a hoped-for transaction was never meant to be.

E-marketplaces are pricing machines par excellence, blending "static" and "dynamic" pricing models in creative ways. We increasingly hear this distinction between static and dynamic pricing, but, down deep, it is a misleading dichotomy. From an economic standpoint, most prices are fundamentally dynamic. They vary with general market conditions, with the time of the season or month, and with the intensity of a buyer's demand or a seller's eagerness to unload surplus inventory. Indeed, many shopping bots allow you to track how a particular merchant's price for a particular good has varied on a daily, weekly, or monthly basis.

E-marketplace transactions, like their offline counterparts, rely primarily on fixed asking prices, as quoted in online catalogs. This is a "take it or leave it" bargaining model. In the context of a particular transaction, the seller won't budge on its initial asking price and the buyer either accepts it or passes on the deal. And the buyer often does not even consider the possibility of haggling over price, knowing that the seller would not welcome it.

The take-it-or-leave-it approach is the primary bargaining model for many mundane consumer and business transactions in the industrialized world. In fact, it's so common that we rarely recognize it as a type of bargaining, preferring the illusion that this is how business is transacted everywhere. However, back-and-forth negotiation is the standard operating procedure for many upper-echelon, high-value corporate transactions. And many developing countries still rely on haggling for everyday marketplace transactions. Indeed, many people in other societies enjoy the give and take of street bargaining, which is as much a social as an economic activity.

When we speak of dynamic pricing, what we mean is that the final price on a transaction is not known in advance by the seller or buyer. Dynamic pricing depends on the seller and buyer being willing to consider prices other than those they initially had in mind. It's typically a game of offer and counteroffer, going on until one party accepts the other's offer and the deal is done.

The e-commerce world has eagerly adopted dynamic pricing models for both business and consumer transactions, as exemplified by the rapid rise of eBay and its imitators. The auction is the main dynamic pricing paradigm in the B2B and B2C spheres. The range of e-marketplace auction models is truly astounding (though they generally lack the fast-talking auctioneers and throat-clearing fat cats that make auctions so entertaining on the silver screen).

An auction is a structured competitive bidding process. There are many auction models. It's easy to get confused by the diversity of auction models and the complexity of their rules. However, we can distinguish the principal models by several factors:

- Who conducts the auction?
- Who may extend and bid on offers?
- What's the duration of the bidding process?
- What's included in a bid?
- What items are being bid?
- What information is published to and/or concealed from bidders?
- How often and in what order can participants bid?
- What event starts the bidding?
- What's the starting price, if any?
- What's the direction in which prices move during bidding?
- What's the minimum price increment during bidding?

- What's the maximum amount of time a bidder may take to post a bid?
- What's the bidder's maximum or minimum price limit?
- What determines the winning bid?
- What determines the price charged to the winning bidder?
- What factors break a tie and win the auction?
- How many participants can win?

We now proceed to briefly explain the differences between the leading auction models—forward, reverse, and double auctions—as well as the nuances among variants in these categories. Figure 6-12 provides a high-level overview of these three competitive-bidding models.

6.7.1 Forward Auctions

A forward auction is what most people think of when you say the word *auction*. What defines the forward auction is simply this: A seller extends an offer to sell, and buyers bid on it. It is a seller-driven transaction.

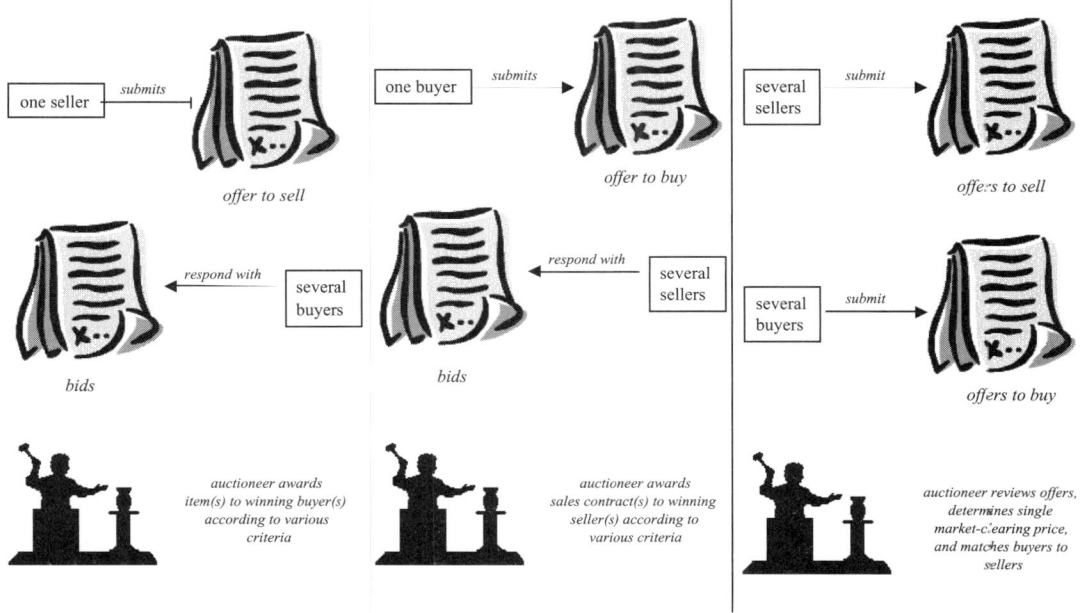

forward auction   **reverse auction**   **double auction**

Figure 6-12   E-marketplace auction models include forward, reverse, and double auctions.

Beyond those simple criteria, forward auctions allow many options:

- An auctioneer may conduct the auction on behalf of the seller, or the seller may conduct the auction on its own behalf.
- The seller may select the specific buyers who may bid, may define bidder eligibility criteria, or may allow anyone to bid.
- The seller may offer multiple items for bid, or just one item.
- The seller may have a minimum acceptable sales price—a "reserve price"—that it keeps secret, or may accept any price.
- The seller may post the offer at a particular asking price, minimum or maximum, or may allow bidders to start at any price.
- Bidding may rise from a low initial asking price, or fall from a high initial asking price.
- Bidding may rise or fall in fixed increments, or in any increments that buyers wish.
- Bidding may start when the seller posts the offer, or at a different start time specified by the auctioneer or seller.
- Bidding may last for a fixed amount of time, or may end at any time the seller or auctioneer wishes.
- Buyer bids may include just a requested price, or may include both a requested price and quantity.
- Buyers may bid just once each, or as often as they like in a counter-bidding sequence.
- Buyers may take as long as they wish to prepare bids, up to the maximum duration of the auction, or may be required to bid within a maximum time interval
- Bidders may be aware of one another's identities, dollar amounts, and quantities during bidding, or they may not.
- Winning bidders' identities, dollar amounts, and quantities may be revealed after the auction, or they may not.
- The winning price may be the highest bid, the second highest bid, the lowest bid equal to or greater than the reserve price, the highest losing bid plus the bid increment, or the first bid.
- There may be a single winner who "takes all," or multiple winners among whom the offered items are allocated.
- Multiple winners may pay the different dollar amounts they bid respectively, or they may pay the same dollar amount (usually the lowest winning bid).
- Tie-breaking criteria may be one of the following: highest bid price, highest quantity requested, or date/time of the earliest bid posted.

Well-known forward-auction sites in B2C space include eBay, Yahoo! Auctions, Ubid.com, Auction Universe, HomeAuctioneer, AuctionWatch.com, FairMarket, FreeMarkets, CommerceBid, OutletZoo, FirstAuction, and AuctionRover. A selected sample of B2B auction sites include Afternic

(Internet domain names), Autodaq (auto dealer used car inventories), Band-X (long distance telecommunications bandwidth), IronMall (pre-owned construction equipment), TradeOut (surplus inventories), and Yahoo! Merchant Auctions (many product and service categories). These sites support various forward-auction models. Essentially, each forward-auction model specifies a particular bargaining protocol that buyers and sellers follow to arrive at a winning bid. We can tell one model from another by how each combines the features just discussed into unique configurations.

One way to classify forward auctions is by degrees of openness, in terms of who may bid and whether bidders' identities and bids may be concealed. We arrange forward auctions along a spectrum from private to public. A private auction is one that follows any or all of the following approaches:

- Limits participation to seller-specified bidders
- Conceals bidders' identities and bids from one another and from the general public
- Conceals winners' identities and bids from everyone except the winner, seller, and auctioneer

The most familiar form of private auction is the sealed-bid auction. Typically, there is no seller-specified minimum price. Bidders are not aware of one another's bids or identities. They may have won the privilege to bid by meeting various eligibility criteria. However, sealed-bid auctions are not entirely private, since they often reveal the winner's bid amounts after the auction closes.

In addition, sealed-bid auctions often limit each bidder to a single bid each, with no opportunity for counterbidding. There may be a time limit for bidders to prepare and post bids. Bids are opened and published at a certain point in time. In most cases, the highest bidder wins. If there are multiple bids at the highest price, the bid that was submitted first wins. The winning bidder pays a purchase price equal to his bid.

Public auctions, by contrast, open participation to everyone and reveal bidder and winner identities and bids throughout the whole process. The most familiar form of public auction is the open-cry auction. In an open-cry environment, bidders are aware of one another's identities and bids. Typically, bidding begins at a seller-specified minimum price. Bidders may counterbid one another repeatedly, raising the price ever upward until the auction's fixed end time. The highest bid wins and purchases the item.

Another way to classify forward auctions, apart from openness, is according to the method by which they determine the winning bid and the purchase prices they charge winners. In this regard, the chief alternative models are English, Vickrey, Japanese, reserve price, clear price, winning bid, second price, and Dutch. We now describe each winner-determination model in turn.

English auctions are the most traditional and common auction type. They assume a "winner-take-all" scenario and use an open-cry bidding technique. The highest bid wins, and the high bidder pays that purchase price. Bidders may counterbid and successively raise bids for the item until a single bidder remains and no other bidders opt to post higher bids.

Vickrey auctions are also won by the high bidder. However, the winner of a Vickrey auction pays a purchase price equal to the second-highest bid (or, another way of putting it, the highest losing bid). Vickrey auctions also assume a winner-take-all scenario. They are a species of private auction with a definite deadline. Each bidder submits a single sealed bid before deadline.

Japanese auctions are also winner-take-all contests won by the high bidder, which pays a purchase price equal to the high bid. Like English auctions, counterbidding is allowed and takes place in an open-cry setting. Unlike English auctions, Japanese auctions have time limits. However, the time limits are not fixed, as they are in Vickrey auctions. Instead, the auctioneer may accelerate deadlines and declare bidding over if he receives the specific bid he is seeking or does not think a current bid will be exceeded.

Reserve-price auctions are won by the buyer who submits the highest bid that equals or exceeds the seller's reserve price (in other words, the seller's minimum acceptable sales price). The high bidder pays a price equal to the high bid, which can never be lower than the seller's reserve price. The seller sets a reserve price if he absolutely refuses to sell below a certain price. Bidders know there's a reserve price, but they don't know what it is. If no bidders meet the reserve price, neither the seller nor the high bidder is under any obligation. Reserve-price auctions are winner-take-all, open-cry bargaining environments.

Clear-price auctions put multiple items up for bid. There may be several winning bidders. The winning bids are the highest bids that, taken altogether, collectively clear out the seller's inventory. Each winning bidder pays the amount of the lowest winning bid and receives one of the items being auctioned. Consequently, these are not winner-take-all contests. Rather, they allocate the inventory equally among all winning bidders, and charge all winners the same amount.

Winning-bid auctions are like clear-price auctions in several respects. Both auction models put multiple items up for bid, award items to the bidders who collectively clear the seller's inventory, and may allocate inventory among several winning bidders. However, unlike clear-price auctions, winning-bid auctions charge winners the prices they individually bid and allocate them the number of items they individually requested. One caveat is that winning buyers who bid higher prices are assured of receiving the quantities they requested. Winners who bid lower prices may receive fewer than they requested, depending on the quantity left after the higher bidders receive their allocations.

Second-price auctions combine aspects of clear-price and reserve-price auctions. If multiple items are being auctioned, second-price auctions resemble clear-price auctions in two respects: awarding items to the bidders who collectively clear the seller's inventory and allocating inventory among several winning bidders. As with reserve-price auctions, the seller sets a minimum acceptable sales price (reserve price), which is kept secret from bidders. However, second-price auctions introduce the concept of a bidder's maximum acceptable purchase price, which the bidder keeps secret from the seller and other bidders. At any point during the bidding process, a buyer may submit a bid equal to the latest market bid plus a fixed bid increment. A buyer will withdraw from further bidding if the current market bid exceeds his maximum acceptable purchase price. However, if the buyer's last bid is one of the top outstanding bids, the buyer will be one of the winners. In that case, he and all other winners will pay a purchase price equal to the lowest of the following: the second-highest bid (plus the bid increment), the lowest winning bid, or the reserve price.

Dutch auctions have "descending price" bidding processes, as opposed to the "ascending price" bidding of other forward auctions. In Dutch auctions, the seller starts with a high asking price, which falls progressively lower as the auction continues. If only one item is up for bid, the winner is the first buyer to call out a bid at the current asking price. The winner pays a purchase price equal to his bid. If multiple items are up for bid, bidders specify their desired prices and quantities, and the winners are the earliest bidders who collectively cleared the seller's inventory. All winning bidders pay the same purchase price, which is equal to the lowest successful bid. As with other multi-item auctions, higher-price bidders are more likely to receive the quantities they've requested. Lower bidders, if they're among the winning group, can refuse quantities that are less than they requested.

6.7.2 Reverse Auctions

Reverse auctions are buyer-driven transactions. A buyer extends an offer to buy, and sellers bid on it. The buyer defines a high price to start the bidding. Prices usually fall during bidding. Prices may drop in fixed increments, or according to the intensity of competition. Counterbidding among rival sellers may or may not take place. Sellers may or may not be aware of one another or their respective bids. The low bidder usually wins and sells at the price.

Like forward auctions, reverse auctions can be private or public, sealed bid or open cry, deadline bound or open ended, single item or multi-item, single winner or multiwinner. Buyers often come into reverse auctions with maximum acceptable purchase prices in mind, and sellers likewise have their minimum acceptable sales prices.

Well-known examples of reverse auctions in the B2C space include BidTheWorld, NexTag, LiquidPrice, and BuyersEdge. Quite naturally, we are finding reverse auctions popping up in e-commerce hubs that revolve around shopping bots. It's a short step from comparing multiple merchant offers to getting those same merchants to compete against one another online for your business.

Many of today's e-commerce business models are essential reverse auctions with various degrees of support for competition and counterbidding among sellers.

For example, "name-your-terms" sites such as Priceline.com generally support a single round of online bidding among multiple merchants in response to a buyer-defined RFQ for a specific type of good or service. Seller bids come immediately in response to a buyer RFQ, usually through Priceline connections with remote merchant commerce applications. The buyer is not obligated to purchase at quoted prices.

Haggling sites such as HaggleZone.com and MakeUsAnOffer.com start with a buyer-submitted RFQ and may involve multiple rounds of counterbidding involving one or more online merchants. As with Priceline, merchant offers come immediately in response to buyer requests and the buyer is not obligated to purchase at quoted prices.

Wait-for-best-offer sites such as Imandi.com, Respond.com, Iwant.com, and eWanted.com let buyers submit RFPs to one or more online merchants. Due to the complexity of the requirements, sellers may not be able to produce immediate, automated sales offers. Instead, sellers may take the time necessary to develop proposals and quotes that directly address the buyer's requirements. These services do not involve intensive counterbidding among buyers and sellers. Buyers are not obligated to buy at quoted prices.

6.7.3 Double Auctions

Double auctions combine concurrent seller- and buyer-driven transactions. Sellers make offers to sell and buyers make offers to buy. Each party, seller or buyer, posts a single offer to an auctioneer. The auctioneer reviews all sell and buy offers, determines a single market-clearing price, and matches sellers to buyers.

The double auction is essentially the marketplace bargaining model that Adam Smith assumed in his classic 1776 publication *The Wealth of Nations*. Instead of an auctioneer, Smith posited a metaphorical "invisible hand" that matched supply to demand and determined a market-clearing price.

Double-auction mechanisms have not yet penetrated the new B2B e-marketplaces in great number. However, it's important to note that the nerve centers of the world economy—stock and commodity exchanges—implement double auctions in their core operations. And most of these exchanges have placed their operations online or are preparing to over the next several years.

It's only a matter of time before we see double auctions alongside forward and reverse auctions in B2B hubbed e-marketplaces. As online trading environments become more important to the macro-economy, online auctioneers will increasingly take on responsibility for maintaining orderly markets, just as stock exchanges are expected to do. Maintaining equilibrium in chaotic markets sometimes requires speedy intervention by a central market-maker to rebalance supply and demand around a market-clearing price. That's a role for which double-auction mechanisms are well suited.

Before we leave this discussion on pricing models, we need to discuss an increasingly common dynamic pricing mechanism that is not, technically, a type of auction. Purchase aggregation, also known as group buying or buyer pooling, is the business model for B2C sites such as Mercata.com, VolumeBuy.com, Accompany.com, actBIG.com, and Zwirl.com. What these hubs do is progressively reduce the price for a given product as the number of orders for that item grows, up to a prespecified deadline, at which time a price is locked in and buyers are obligated to buy. This is not an auction, because it does not involve competitive bidding or counterbidding among sellers or buyers. The net result of these aggregated-purchasing blocs is usually that a merchant has moved a substantial portion of its inventory at a price that may be lower than the initial asking price but is comfortably above its minimum acceptable sales price.

In other words, purchase aggregation allows customers to buy at wholesale prices, while merchants compensate for low margins with high sales volumes. This is a win-win scenario for both the buyer and seller. All of which shows that the most important feature of prices is not whether they are static or dynamic within the context of a particular transaction. What matters is not how vigorously trading partners haggle over terms. What matters is whether buyer and seller have settled on the right price at the right time to clinch the deal.

6.8 Payment Model

Payments keep commercial relationships in good working order, especially when the buyer renders payment promptly, fully, and with minimum fuss.

Liquidity is the key to efficient markets. Trading environments can be only as strong as the velocity of payments that circulate within them. The more quickly currency recirculates into new spending and investment, the more vigorous the marketplace. Buy and sell offers come more quickly, and in greater volume, when all parties have the funds and credit to support ongoing transactions. By contrast, economies stall when liquidity dries up, currencies grow unstable, and payments are slow in coming. One danger sign is when the process of transferring monies between buyer and seller accounts becomes more risky and time-consuming than the purchase transactions that set it all in motion. Chronic inflation and foreign-exchange fluctuations are particularly damaging for commerce, since they increase risks for buyers and sellers alike and also undermine confidence in the value of the common medium of exchange.

Electronic payment and funds transfer technologies are linchpins of modern marketplaces. In fact, these technologies have achieved such ubiquity that most of us—even the technologically unsavvy—use them regularly. We do our banking through automated teller machines (ATMs), have our paychecks deposited electronically in our bank accounts, have our mortgage and insurance payments deducted automatically every month, and may even pay other bills online. We use our PCs to transfer funds between our bank and brokerage accounts via the Internet. We hand our credit cards to store clerks who use them to authorize our purchases through connections to financial networks. So you don't need to look to purely electronic marketplaces for evidence of electronic payment and funds transfer. It's everywhere.

E-marketplaces are almost inconceivable without electronic payments and funds transfer. Electronic transaction and payment models sync up very well, providing the speed and liquidity needed by free-wheeling modern businesses. Electronic payment technologies enable frictionless liquidity, in which monies transfer instantaneously and automatically upon deal confirmation or product delivery. It's no surprise that e-marketplaces rely heavily on the preexisting global infrastructure of credit cards, online funds transfer, and automated clearinghouses. Only an electronic payment infrastructure can keep pace with an e-marketplace's instantaneous buy-sell transactions. And electronic payment technologies have been around long enough to inspire the universal confidence that spurs merchants and consumers to rely on them extensively.

In the past five years, we have seen plenty of innovation in the electronic payment world. Much of this innovation stems from and supports the growth of global e-marketplaces. The most noteworthy trends are the development of Internet-based account consolidation services, Internet-based payment-processing services, Internet-based financial institutions, and Internet-based proxy currencies. Taken together, these developments show that the world economy's end-to-end payment model is, like its B2C and B2B transaction models, beginning to migrate more completely online.

6.8.1 Internet-Based Account-Consolidation Services

Online buyers often suffer from "account overload" when surfing the Web to shop and partake of other services. In other words, each new site usually requires that we create a new account, submit to a new registration procedure, create a new username and password, and enter our personal profile, credit card information, and delivery address yet again. It's getting to the point where you need to be a memory artist—or a conscientious note-taker—to keep track of all the accounts that you've personally created.

Anybody who's ever surfed the Web recognizes this as a sorry state of affairs. We could eliminate it if online buyers were somehow able to present to every new site, transparently and automatically, a set of digital credentials that speed them through the registration, login, and purchasing process. After all, it's in online merchants' best interest to cut straight to the purchase trans-action.

Some Internet-based payment processors—such as CyberCash, eCharge, iPIN, and TransPoint—provide account consolidation and management ser-vices for online buyers. Essentially, buyers create secure, personal, online "wallets" that contain one or more credit card numbers to be used in pur-chasing from online merchants that agree to use a particular company's cred-it card capture, authorization, and processing services. Typically, the buyer clicks on a "buy" button on a merchant site that is affiliated with the payment processor in order to purchase an item posted on that site. Usually, buyers can review participating merchants' bills online and authorize payment—electronically or via drafted paper check—to merchants from linked bank accounts. In most cases, payment processors safeguard the privacy user account, profile, and transaction information.

Some companies provide Internet account consolidation services that do not support online bill review and payment, but do automate registering, logging in, and purchasing from affiliated merchant sites. Examples of such services include Ezlogin, Gator, Jotter, Lumeria, MSN Passport, Novell digi-talme, PassLogix, VerticalOne, and Yodlee. Increasingly, these services use the Electronic Commerce Markup Language (ECML), a dialect of XML, as a standard syntax for exchanging user profile information with merchant sites.

6.8.2 Internet-Based Payment-Processing Services

Most B2C and B2B e-commerce transactions rely on buyers providing credit card information to sellers over encrypted Secure Sockets Layer (SSL) ses-sions. To make this possible, most online merchants—like their offline coun-terparts—rely on existing payment-processing industry services.

Before we discuss the emerging market for Internet-based payment-processing services, we will briefly review the standard procedures for credit card authorization, processing, and settlement. Payment-processing services include authorization, capture, conveyance, and settlement of payments sub-mitted through any of the following means: bank credit cards, private-label merchant credit cards, travel and entertainment cards, corporate cards, bank debit cards, electronic checks, recurring debits, and prepayments. It's a com-plex online B2B workflow in its own right, involving many companies and processes.

In the click or mortar worlds, the typical credit card payment cycle involves authorizing card transactions at the point of sale, capturing data related to transactions, settling transactions with card associations on behalf of the merchant, and producing transaction reports for the merchant. In the course of processing a credit card transaction, various organizations interoperate to capture and authorize the transaction, usually within 8 to 15 seconds. The authorization process involves obtaining approval from the card-issuing bank for the cardholder's purchase at the merchant site. Authorization procedures confirm that the cardholder has the available credit to cover the purchase and verify that the card has not been reported lost or stolen. During transaction authorization, transaction data, such as dollar amount and card number, are captured in the payment-processing network. Payment processors use this data to settle the transaction and prepare reports for the merchant. Payment processors also provide services to help merchants control the risks associated with credit card fraud and bad credit risks.

Payment settlement involves managing a record of each merchant's transactions and transferring funds from the card issuer to the merchant. The payment processor transmits transaction information to the card-issuing bank through the card associations, such as Visa and MasterCard. The payment processor arranges for funds to be transferred to the merchant's bank account via automated clearinghouse or Fedwire transfer (for transactions between U.S.-based buyers and sellers). The card-issuing bank then bills the cardholder directly. Settlement payments made to merchant accounts often reflect a discount from the full transaction price, which generally includes the payment processor's fee and any card association interchange fees. Settlement procedures usually result in the merchant's account being credited within 24 to 72 hours from the time of closing a batch of transactions.

In the United States, the dominant payment-processing and settlement service providers are Citibank, First Data, and Paymentech. In addition, there are many companies that specialize in capturing and authorizing card transactions for merchants and in conveying transactions to the large settlement service organizations.

Among the niche payment processors are a new breed of firms that specialize in capturing, authorizing, and processing transactions for Internet-based merchants (and for individuals who sell things over the Internet). Some Internet-based specialist payment processors include BillPoint, CyberCash, CyberSource, eCharge, iPIN, PayPal, TransPoint, and WorldPay. As with traditional payment processors, all of these specialist processors make money from a combination of transaction fees on merchants and/or the float between buyer payment and transfer to merchant accounts. We will briefly discuss each of their offerings.

BillPoint, a wholly owned eBay subsidiary, facilitates secure person-to-person (rather than person-to-merchant) credit card payments over the Internet (you might even label BillPoint, like its corporate parent a pioneer in

"C2C" e-commerce). BillPoint addresses the payment needs of online auction sites where the "merchants" are in fact ordinary individuals who have posted sales offers. BillPoint eliminates the trouble, delays, and risks associated with postal mailing checks and money orders (which is how most auction customers currently arrange payment).

CyberCash provides secure B2C and B2B transaction services for Internet-based merchants. CyberSource provides online merchants with credit card, electronic check, and "micropayment" processing services. Micropayments refer to charges, as low as one cent, that are normally too small for cost-effective processing by Visa or MasterCard. Buyers can subscribe to CyberCash's InstaBuy service, which creates a secure, personal, online wallet containing one or more credit card numbers to be used in purchasing from InstaBuy-affiliated online merchants.

CyberSource provides a wide range of secure B2C and B2B transaction services for Internet-based merchants. CyberSource provides online merchants with credit card and electronic check processing, tax calculation, fraud screening, export compliance, distribution control, delivery address verification, fulfillment messaging, digital product registration, digital delivery, digital warehousing, and gift certificate services.

eCharge positions its service as an alternative to Visa and MasterCard for online, credit-based B2C and B2B purchases. An eCharge account provides customers with revolving credit and prepayments for use in purchasing from participating online merchants. Customers can sign up for their eCharge accounts online, get real-time account approvals, and buy immediately. Businesses and families with eCharge accounts can set up subaccounts with individual spending limits and restrictions on merchant sites from which they can purchase. eCharge account holders need to enter their personal and shipping information only once, when they establish the account. Purchases involve clicking on an eCharge logo on a participating merchant's Web site. eCharge does not divulge customers' personal information to participating merchants. The service adds charges to a customer's ISP or telco bill and allows customers to review their eCharge statements and pay for purchases online. eCharge is attempting to recruit merchants by offering them the opportunity to save up to 100 basis points on transaction fees over traditional credit card fees. Like CyberSource, eCharge provides merchants with online settlement and accounting services. eCharge can also process micropayments for purchases as small as one cent, which could not be processed cost-effectively with traditional credit cards. Merchants using eCharge's services include Microsoft, AT&T, ReleaseNow, and Intershop Communications.

iPin's service is similar to eCharge in many respects. iPIN is an alternative to traditional credit cards for B2C transactions. It tallies micropayment purchases that customers make throughout the month at iPIN-affiliated online merchants and adds the charges to the customer's ISP bill (if the ISP has an agreement with iPIN). The customer does not need to prepay or prefund her iPIN account with a credit card before making a purchase. There is no charge to the customer for using the service and no client-side installation requirements.

PayPal seems to regard itself as the Western Union of the Internet: a service for wiring (or, in PayPal's term, "beaming") money electronically to friends and family members. However, unlike Western Union, PayPal is a C2C funds transfer service that is free of charge to senders (PayPal's provider, Confinity, Inc., proposes to make money off the float on subscribers' deposited funds). And unlike the C2C-oriented BillPoint, PayPal does not associate these funds transfers with auction buy-sell transactions, though senders and receivers may in fact be using the service for this very purpose. Instead, users prepay their PayPal accounts with charges on their traditional credit card accounts or direct deposits from their bank accounts. A PayPal account holder then accesses the PayPal application software on his computer (or PalmPilot or cell phone) to send an e-mail to the payee announcing that there's money waiting for him or her. Mail recipients can receive funds only if they have a PayPal account; fortunately, the funds-waiting message provides an URL that the payee can follow to sign up (for free) to PayPal and see their new funds in their own PayPal account. PayPal account holders can withdraw funds by requesting a paper check or direct deposit to their bank account.

TransPoint—a joint venture of First Data, Microsoft, and Citibank—is an online billing and payment service for B2C, B2B, and C2C applications. TransPoint users link their TransPoint accounts to their bank accounts. They access their TransPoint accounts securely from the TransPoint Web site or the site of any participating portal, hub, or financial institution. Within the TransPoint environment, users maintain personal lists of companies and individuals to pay and can transmit payments to any business or individual, either electronically or through requests to draft paper checks. Customers may review bills online for merchants that post bills electronically. They can also schedule payments online and receive confirmation that payments were made. Financial portals and online billers can cobrand and customize TransPoint services alongside those third parties' related services, such as providing account balances and financial advice.

WorldPay provides a wide range of B2C and B2B transaction services for Internet-based merchants in many countries. As with the other online payment specialists, WorldPay allows online merchants to place buy buttons on their Websites that connect transparently to these payment services. WorldPay securely processes credit card, debit card, travel-entertainment card, electronic check, and micropayment transactions in over 160 currencies. The company processes multicurrency transactions, and allows customers to avoid currency fluctuations. Merchants that use WorldPay services can track their transactions via their own personalized online account management system.

WorldPay, CyberCash, CyberSource, eCharge, and iPIN provide international payment-gateway services. Other payment-gateway providers include Anacom, Authorize.net, Cardservice International, Coral Capital, DataCash, Digital Courier Technologies, First Atlantic Commerce, iMall, NetBanx, Planet Group, Signio, and Trintech. These firms specialize in conveying, converting, and settling multicurrency credit card transactions that involve buyers and sellers in the United States and other countries. Buyers present payment in one currency and the gateway takes care of converting and settling it in the merchant's preferred currency.

International commerce introduces additional processing delays, processing and interchange fees, taxes, duties, freight-insurance premiums, shipping and handling charges, customs clearance fees, import/export regulations, and currency exchange risks into the equation. Merchants who export often use software that computes the "delivered cost" or "landed price" of goods in the currency of the buyer, taking into consideration a wide variety of fees as well as exchange-rate fluctuations. Increasingly, we see online merchants and trading hubs integrating their services with third-party translation services, enabling prices to be translated in real-time, via the appropriate exchange rate, into the customer's currency. Many international payment processors are also providing services that facilitate the full range of "delivered cost" calculations, manage export/import restrictions and logistics, and help identify the most cost-effective transport carrier.

6.8.3 Internet-Based Financial Institutions

If we buy and pay online, it makes sense that our checking, savings, credit, brokerage, and other accounts—and the institutions that maintain them—should also migrate to this new environment. That is happening all around us. Millions of us have online brokerage accounts with Schwab, E*Trade, and other institutions. And, increasingly, we are seeing online banks, such as WingspanBank.com, Telebank, B2Bank.com, and USABancShares.com. In these banks, the only teller window is the browser and banker's hours are 24x7x365. And of course, they, like their offline counterparts in the United States, are insured by the Federal Deposit Insurance Corporation.

WingspanBank, for example, provides most of the services of traditional brick-and-mortar banks: checking accounts (with printed checks), credit cards, certificates of deposit, consumer loans, mortgage loans, home equity loans, and participation in nationwide ATM networks. You can also use WingspanBank to pay bills online, research investments, plan your finances, and receive quotes from third parties on stocks, mutual funds, and auto, life, homeowners, and other types of insurance.

The range of Internet-based banks is still small, but we expect that most brick-and-mortar banks will begin hosting their own online doppelgangers within the next 5–10 years. The banking industry, which has reengineered its stodgy business model around ATMs over the past generation, will have no choice but to migrate to this new environment. They will have to follow our money to where it now lives: the Internet.

6.8.4 Internet-Based Proxy Currencies

Perhaps the most striking development in the online economy is the development of Internet-based proxy currencies. Fundamentally, proxy currencies are scrips that e-marketmakers issue for either of two purposes:

- Denominate exchange values on barter transactions that are conducted within their e-marketplaces
- Serve as promotional tokens—similar to gift certificates or frequent-flier miles—to encourage continued patronage of sellers in their e-marketplaces

Proxy currencies may or may not be transferrable to other parties. By contrast "real" currencies, such as the U.S. dollar and the Euro, are usually transferable to others (or, in international transactions, "convertible"). We should note that the Euro is starting out as a proxy, with a defined exchange rate, for the "real" currencies that it is legislated to replace.

The primary circulators of Internet-based proxy currencies fall into two categories: B2B and B2C e-marketmakers.

First, there are the online B2B barter hubs: BarterTrust.com, Ubarter.com, and BigVine.com. Each of them issues a noncash electronic currency, with a specified exchange rate to the U.S. dollar, that members of their barter marketplaces use to buy and sell products and services from one another. Typically, businesses enter into these barter exchanges when they wish to offload surplus inventory, decrease cash expenditures, and preserve their cash balances. Exchange members post buy and sell orders, just as they would in any hubbed e-marketplace, but they quote prices in the marketmaker's own proxy currency, not in the U.S. dollar. The marketmaker charges a fee (in U.S. dollars) for all transactions. Obviously, one limitation of these environments is that the proxy currency does not have anything approaching the liquidity of "real" currencies, since it can be used only on items posted in the exchange run by the currency's issuer.

Second, we are also seeing Internet-based proxy currencies in the B2C sphere. Examples include Flooz.com and Beenz.com. They are both interesting alternative business models.

You pay for "flooz" currency with "real" currency (as opposed to in-kind transfers or barter exchanges). However, flooz is transferable and you can send it, like a gift certificate, to anyone with an e-mail account. The recipient can then use the flooz to purchase items from any participating online merchant. Flooz.com makes money on the float between the time that a user deposits "real" currency in his or her flooz account and the time when a flooz-accepting merchant requests payment in "real" currency for a flooz-denominated purchase.

You pay for "beenz" currency simply by being active on the Internet (no in-kind or real-currency transfers are necessary). You accrue beenz by doing any of the following: surfing to the Web site of any Beenz-affiliated merchant, filling out merchants' online surveys, and/or purchasing items (with "real" currency) from those merchants. You can then use your beenz to buy more merchandise from online merchants.

It's still too early to tell which if any of these proxy currency schemes will succeed. It's also not clear whether this form of payment is better suited to vertical B2B or horizontal B2C marketplaces. For any of them to stand a chance, their issuers need to build large, stable, and attractive e-marketplaces of buyers and sellers that transact business with one another regularly. These marketplaces need to be very attractive trading environments in order for buyers to overlook the inevitable loss of liquidity that comes with using scrip in place of "real" currency.

E-marketmakers also need to build widespread recognition of and trust in their role as issuers of what the less charitable might regard as "funny money." The concept of proxy currencies doesn't seem so strange when you take a historical perspective on it. Every new payment instrument has had its fervent, indeed hysterical, detractors. Throughout the course of history, we have seen such innovations as paper currency, personal checks, credit cards, and electronic funds transfer enter the world under a cloud of suspicion and eventually emerge triumphant in daily commerce. Until just recently in historical time, only gold and silver were regarded as "real," legitimate legal tender. Die-hard bullion fetishists still pine for the good old days when everyone accepted the dubious notion that Fort Knox, Spanish dubloons, and the like held all the world's exchange value.

Maybe all of today's national currencies will someday merge into a supranational proxy currency that gets its start in a successful hubbed e-marketplace. That scenario represents the fondest dream of some people, and the direst nightmare of others. Will the inconvenience, costs, and delays associated with multicurrency international commerce make a global proxy currency the path of least resistance? Will the need to maximize global liquidity drive the current government-hubbed international monetary system into extinction? What happens to national political sovereignty when the marketmakers-in-chief—central governments—cannot control their internal medium of exchange to favor domestic buyers and sellers?

Whether today's monetary system survives in its current form depends partly on whether we design e-marketplaces to shield buyers and sellers from the sordid details of currency exchanges and cross-border logistics. We don't need to converge all national currencies on a common scrip if we can translate effortlessly and transparently among them. Under that optimistic scenario, we would be able to submerge today's awkward international payments model—as if it were a piece of convoluted, legacy programming code—under the user-friendly graphical interfaces of online marketplaces.

6.9 Facilitation Model

Facilitators are the icons that rim an e-marketplace's homepage, or that clamor for your attention when you get to the point of buying something, or that led you to that marketplace in the first place.

More to the point, a facilitator provides services to buyers, sellers, and/or marketmakers to assist in setting up, executing, and consummating transactions. Almost any economic transaction—apart from the simple, street-level "cash and carry" purchases—relies on a suite of facilitators that pocket many of the more lucrative fees. No doubt you're familiar with the following types of facilitators, which play important roles in both online and offline transactions:

- Advertising services
- Affiliate led-referral services
- Appraisal services
- Arbitration services
- Banking services
- Billing and collection services
- Certification and registration services
- Complaint-reporting and investigation services
- Consulting services
- Credit-check services
- Currency-exchange services
- Customer relationship management services
- Customs brokerage services
- Escrow services
- Financing and leasing services
- Fulfillment services
- Insurance services
- Legal services
- Market research services
- News and information services
- Notary services
- Payment processing services
- Product analysis and review services
- Public relations services
- Quality assurance and testing services
- Relocation services

- Settlement and clearing services
- Shipping and handling services
- Title search services
- Warehousing services
- Warranty and extended-support services

Figure 6-13 shows how these and other facilitators form part of the core service model of many an e-marketplace. All of these types of facilitators have taken up residence on the Internet, and many are seeking out long-term relationships with portals, online merchants, and e-marketmakers. We have just reviewed a very important class of transaction facilitators: payment processing firms. In the remainder of this chapter, we discuss some of the new breed of facilitators that run their operations primarily online and serve e-marketplaces.

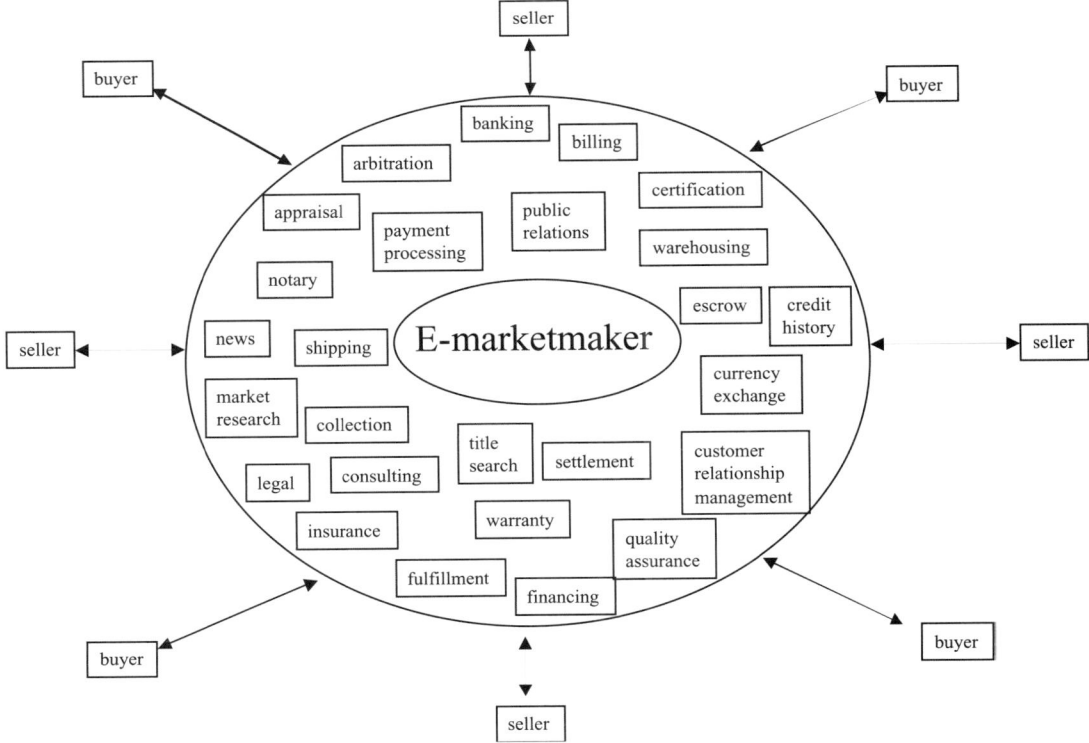

Figure 6-13   *E-marketplace facilitation models include sundry third parties that provide services to buyers, sellers, and/or marketmakers to assist in setting up, executing, and consummating transactions.*

Third-party facilitators are integral components of e-marketplaces. For example, let's examine some facilitators that have established relationships with one real-world e-marketplace: www.chemicalonline.com. All of the following companies provide their services, at a fee, to buyers and sellers in the ChemicalOnline vertical marketplace, which is one of dozens hosted by VerticalNet.

If you're interested in getting a loan to pay for chemicals you purchase online, the site's homepage includes an icon that links you to a page that promotes one financing firm: SierraCities.com (http://www.chemicalonline.com/content/firstsierra/home.asp). From there, you can click on buttons to take you to more information on business loans and equipment leases, to a tool that helps you calculate your payments, and to a profile of SierraCities.com. Of course, there is a prominent button that lets you "Apply Now!"

If you'd rather finance a buy through revolving credit, you can click on an icon in the upper-right corner of that page, which takes you to Bank One's Web site to apply for a Business Visa credit card.

If you want to research a prospective buyer or seller further, you can click on the link for Powerize.com and download reports, journal articles, and other background pieces.

If you are selling something and want to know whether a potential buyer is a good credit risk, you can click on an icon for CreditFYI, a service that does an immediate online credit check on the prospect. For a fee, you can get a credit report and a rating of the buyer's likelihood of paying its bills on time.

If buyers and sellers are not sure of each others' trustworthiness, they can click on the Tradesafe icon to use that online escrow service. Another online escrow service, not integrated with ChemicalOnline, is iEscrow, which provides escrow services for such leading B2C marketplaces as eBay, Amazon, Go Networks, Looksmart, and Fairmarket.

Escrow services give buyers that assurance that they are getting the product they purchased and give sellers confidence that they will receive payments, no matter where in the world these parties are located. In this example, the way it works is that either party, buyer or seller, can start a transaction on ChemicalOnline. Tradesafe then invites the other party to participate. When both parties agree to the transaction, the buyer pays Tradesafe. When Tradesafe secures the payment, Tradesafe instructs the seller to ship the items. Once the seller ships, it immediately notifies Tradesafe of shipping details and a tracking number. When the buyer receives the items, the buyer has an inspection period (mutually agreed upon by the buyer and the seller) to approve the item. The buyer accepts the items by visiting Tradesafe's Website or by allowing the inspection period to expire. Tradesafe then mails a check to the seller and the transaction is complete. If the buyer rejects the merchandise, she can return it to the seller in its original condition and receives a refund from Tradesafe.

These are just a handful of the services that an e-marketmaker might conceivably host in its environment. As e-marketplaces develop, marketmakers will integrate a broader range of third-party facilitators into their services. This is in fact one more important component of an e-marketmaker's aggregation model: the ability to congregate a range of facilitation services that support the end-to-end transaction cycle. The average buyer increasingly uses third-party services—integrated into merchant sites and e-marketplaces—to obtain financing, research merchants, evaluate competing solutions, review industry news, request appraisals, submit escrow payments, specify a shipping carrier, obtain title insurance, sign up for an extended service plan, and locate temporary storage for an item she is purchasing through an e-marketplace. Sellers access third parties online to check customer creditworthiness, detect credit fraud, calculate delivered costs, prepare documentation for export compliance, and request order-fulfillment services.

Brick-and-mortar companies are actively evolving their services into the Internet economy, so you can, for example, request Fedex, UPS, or Airborne Express shipping on your next online purchase. In this example, existing transportation companies are competing with a new crop of Internet-based shipping services, such as Iconomy.com and Iship.com.

Likewise, the traditional fulfillment services industry finds itself competing with Internet-based upstarts such as SubmitOrder.com. Consumer Reports and the Better Business Bureau face competition from product review and complaint sites such as Epinions.com, Ugripe.com, Productopia.com, and Deja.com.

E-marketmakers have every incentive to outsource every function other than their core services: service development, membership management, and content aggregation. The e-marketmaker's core responsibility is defining the scope and policies of the online trading community, providing an orderly, stable, and efficient environment for transacting business, and maintaining the appropriate mix of facilitation partners. Physical hosting, transaction processing, and payment services will be best outsourced to others who have the network and computing infrastructure to provide these services more cheaply and reliably. Rapid scalability of online trading communities will require an aggressive program of outsourcing as many functions as possible to the right business partners.

Over time, we will see trading hubs evolve into distributed transactions environments that depend on interoperability among multiple facilitators (many of whom derive their revenues primarily from transaction fees):

- Hosting partners: These firms will host the network and computing resources needed to ensure scalable, reliable, round-the-clock operations for the e-marketplace.

- Point-of-sale partners: These firms will recruit affiliated Web sites and help them integrate buy buttons on their sites that plug into the e-marketplace supporting remote catalog lookup and order placement.
- Merchant partners: These firms will maintain catalogs, capture orders, and link to transaction processors to validate and transmit orders.
- Transaction-processing partners: These firms will process transactions and submit them to payment networks and fulfillment partners.
- Fulfillment partners: These firms will maintain inventories, receive orders, and ship requested items to buyers.
- Customer relationship management partners: These firms will run the customer service, help desk, message board, collaboration services, and online training operations.

Over time, it will become difficult to tell the e-marketmaker from the suite of facilitators that it has enlisted to run its trading community. That will be a natural progression in the development of hubbed e-marketplaces. Ultimately, the entire world economy will become a constellation of interconnected e-marketplaces that connect buyers and sellers without regard for the particular trading community that hosted their offer. Confederated e-marketmakers and their legions of facilitators will divvy up shares of transaction and interchange fees.

As long as the trade goes through as expected, buyer and seller will not care who the middlemen were or how they work together across the big, broad Internet.

Extranet Supply-Chain Integration

Established trading partners (TPs) will continue to link directly to each other when their relationship demands an extra measure of security, performance, and process integration.

When TPs link directly to each other, we call this arrangement an "extranet." Extranets have been with us for quite some time, though the term itself is a recent coinage. Extranets are closed, secure trading environments between companies and their TPs, including customers, dealers, distributors, suppliers, and contractors. These environments integrate different TPs' internal business processes through data sharing, application-to-application interfaces, and/or workflow integration. They also provide one TP's employees with authorized access to other TPs' internal applications and data, subject to access controls enforced within extranet policy-administration systems.

Extranets are where corporate intranets intersect, often through secure "tunnels," document interchanges, or virtual circuits. In effect, many EDI implementations are extranets: private networks that support supply-chain integration among businesses that do a high volume of regular business with each other. Traditionally, companies have used leased lines and value-added networks (VANs) for their extranets. Alternately, companies may use secure, encrypted Internet Protocol (IP) connections to establish virtual private networks (VPNs) over the public Internet. Figure 7-1 shows an extranet between two trading parnters, by means of a "tunnel"—in other words, a secure channel—over the Internet between the trading partners' protected subnets.

What's new is the trend toward direct B2B integration over the Internet and World Wide Web. This trend, barely five years old, reflects the Internet's maturation into a "production network" for secure business-to-business com-

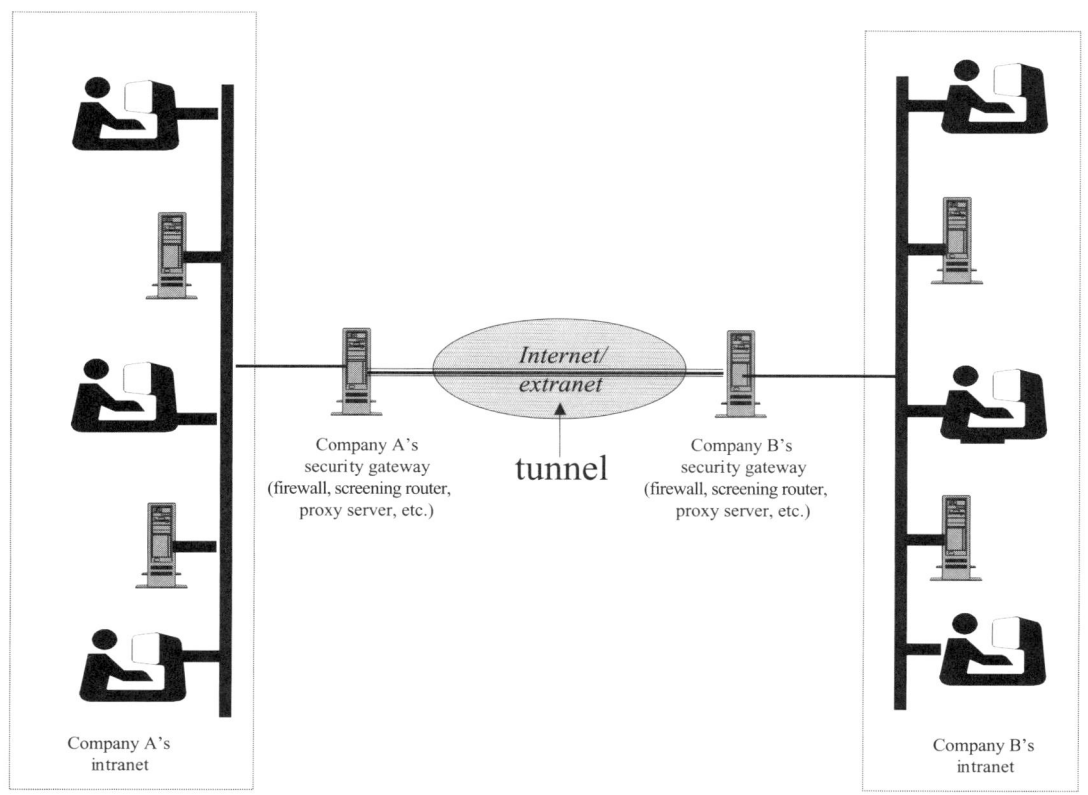

Internet/
extranet

Company A's
security gateway
(firewall, screening router,
proxy server, etc.)

tunnel

Company B's
security gateway
(firewall, screening router,
proxy server, etc.)

Company A's
intranet

Company B's
intranet

Figure 7-1   *Implementing an extranet involves establishing a tunnel or secure channel over the Internet between trading partners' intranets.*

munications and transactions. The new order of extranets is built heavily on Web standards, such as Java, HyperText Transfer Protocol (HTTP), HyperText Markup Language (HTML), and, of course, trusty old Transmission Control Protocol/Internet Protocol (TCP/IP). This network infrastructure has become so widespread that we can almost take it for granted. If you have even one Web server, you have the basis for your extranet. Alternately, you can choose to host your extranet applications in whole or part on a VAN or ISP's Web sites.

Enterprises everywhere are making the Internet a safer place to do business by implementing such network security technologies as encrypting routers, firewalls, proxy servers, protocol tunneling, public-key certificates, and authentication tokens. As a result, network managers are having to educate themselves on a new crop of extranet-relevant security standards, such as IPsec (the security architecture of IP version 6) and the Microsoft-developed Point-to-Point Tunneling Protocol (PPTP). Leading router and firewall vendors support industry-standard tunneling—in other words, packet encryption and encapsulation—technologies in their products, making it possible for two or more companies to establish secure VPNs over the Internet.

Today's business environment is gradually, perhaps inexorably, transforming corporate intranets into partial or total extranets. As your company outsources more functions to contractors, you will need to provide these new business partners with access to proprietary business data residing on your intranet. You will need to establish and reconfigure extranet connections quickly in order to integrate new outsourcers fully into existing business processes.

7.1 Potential BizTalk Role in Extranet Supply Chains

Microsoft has designed BizTalk Server primarily as a platform for extranet supply-chain integration—in particular, for EDI-style data sharing and workflow.

BizTalk Server is Microsoft's B2B mapping, translation, workflow, and interchange server, not a full-fledged e-marketplace hub development and management platform. Figure 7-2 shows how enterprises would deploy BizTalk Server behind their extranet security gateways, such as firewalls.

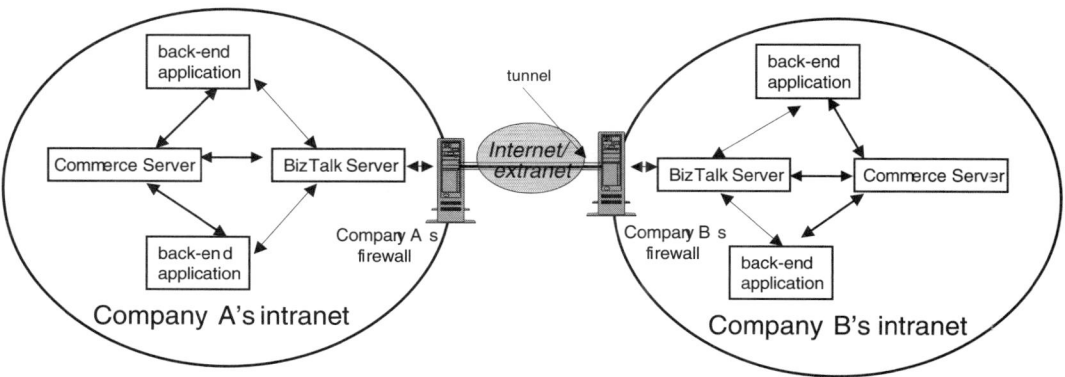

Figure 7-2   *Enterprises can deploy BizTalk Server in their extranets behind security gateways, such as firewalls.*

The core BizTalk Server features address traditional EDI requirements:

- Streamline enterprise management of TP agreements, profiles, identities, roles, and privileges
- Map internal data structures into standard EDI structures
- Translate internal data into standard document formats for submission to TPs
- Enable reliable EDI document and message interchange over various transport protocols
- Enable two or more TPs to integrate their internal applications through structured B2B workflows in support of supply-chain management (SCM), customer relationship management (CRM), and bill presentment and payment (BPP)
- Enable each individual TP to integrate its extranet applications with its internal applications and databases, such as procurement, enterprise resource planning (ERP), operational resource management (ORM), and integrated logistics support (ILS).

Extranet supply-chain integration depends on all this B2B functionality, which we will discuss in this chapter. Consequently, BizTalk's potential role in extranets is to provide an operating platform and interoperability framework for TPs to integrate tightly with each other for EDI-style structured B2B workflows. The latter bullet point—sometimes referred to as enterprise application integration (EAI)—is intra-organizational, not B2B in focus. We will discuss EAI more fully in the following chapter.

For detailed discussions of specific Microsoft support for all of this functionality—in BizTalk Server 2000 and other products—we refer the reader to Part 3. BizTalk Server 2000 is just one component in Microsoft's broader extranet-enabling architecture, which includes Commerce Server 2000, SQL Server 2000, Windows 2000, Active Directory, Internet Information Server, Microsoft Certificate Server, Microsoft Message Queue Server, and Microsoft Transaction Server.

7.2 Extranets and the E-Marketecture Reference Model

When you examine an extranet, it starts to resemble the hubbed e-marketplaces we discussed in Chapter 6. An extranet's dominant TP is in effect the hub that anchors the trading community. The dominant firm in an industry often organizes an extranet to link it securely with TPs. For example, an automotive manufacturer might establish secure channels for communicating with suppliers, or a government agency may link directly to important contractors' intranets.

Extranets are essentially private e-marketplaces, exclusive trading communities that directly connect established TPs in support of business process integration. Depending on their membership and management models, extranets often fall into a gray area between buyer- and seller-hosted e-marketplaces. How you classify an extranet depends on the strategic role of the dominant TP. Do the other TPs constitute its supply chain or distribution channel?

One way to distinguish extranets from the new generation of hubbed e-marketplaces is their membership model. Extranets are closed supply chains or distribution channels and do not generally support vertical industry membership models (unless the dominant TP is a monopoly seller or monopsony buyer in a particular marketplace). Another way to tell them apart from broker-hosted e-marketplaces is that the dominant TPs in extranets do not broker deals among third parties. Furthermore, extranets rarely host the dynamic pricing, online payment, and third-party facilitation services of brokered e-marketplaces.

We describe extranets as trading communities that fit the following criteria:

- Hosted and managed by one or more entities that are buyers and/or sellers of the traded good or service
- Host buy and/or sell offers, with participants often extending both types of offers
- Present offers in aggregated catalogs or in disaggregated request-response document interchanges
- Present offers posted by the site's sponsors, which are permanent, exclusive anchor tenants, and their established trading partners, which are often long-term participants but which may or may not participate exclusively in this particular trading community
- Process transactions in which established trading partners maintain the inventories being traded, but involve no TP brokering of deals between third parties

As we noted in the previous chapter, we will see increasing support for extranet-like TP-to-TP integration in broker-hubbed e-marketplaces. Some trading-hub software products allow particular TPs to set up customized workflows, transactions, and other services among themselves within the shared e-marketplace, in accordance with trading partner agreements (TPAs), policies, and procedures. As B2B trading hubs mature and absorb more traditional extranet and EDI functions, we can expect to see further development of "virtual private marketplaces." These are environments that apply private membership models, with appropriate policies and access controls, to public trading environments.

We can use the e-marketecture reference model to define extranets and compare them to broker-hubbed e-marketplaces. Extranets consist of the same seven layers as any other online trading environment: hosting, membership, aggregation, transaction, pricing, payment, and facilitation.

7.3 Extranet Hosting Model

Extranets are secure networks among established TPs that cooperate in hosting the connections and linked applications.

Typically, one or more TPs host on their own computers the principal applications, databases, and documents required by other partners. Many network managers still rely on the traditional alternatives for business-to-business communication: leased telecommunications circuits or VPNs run by specialized EDI VAN service providers. These traditional approaches limit remote network access to a narrow group of trusted TPs. However, neither can offer anywhere near the flexibility, cost-effectiveness, or ubiquity of Internet-based B2B communications, which can often be enabled through simple routing-table updates and policy changes on gateway devices.

Firewalls, encrypting routers, screening routers, proxy servers, and dial-up modems collectively define the "gateway" into your corporate network. You may deploy them at the boundary of your intranet to control the interface with your extranet partners, or protect your company against all manner of threats from the Internet at large. In addition, you may deploy them internally in cases where some business units need to shield information from other parts of the company.

Firewalls are the principal extranet gateways. If you have an intranet, chances are that you have already implemented at least one firewall—probably several—to protect your network and systems from actual and potential Internet marauders. You may also have some remote access servers for dial-up public-switched-telephone-network (PSTN) connections, though TCP/IP-based Internet firewalls are the preferred solution for extranet security. Typically installed at the intranet's perimeter, firewalls and their close cousins—encrypting routers—usually serve as a company's sentinel or secure gateway to extranets and the Internet. Firewalls often perform application-level proxy services, in addition to such core functionality as filtering and blocking packets at the network layer.

Firewalls have many functions, not all of which are supported in all vendors' products. First and foremost, they look at inbound and outbound packets' source and destination addresses, as well as at the services being requested, and grant or deny access accordingly. Firewalls may also perform related functions such as preventing internal network addresses from being disclosed to remote users, preventing packets from spoofed external IP addresses from entering the intranet, maintaining audit logs of inbound and outbound traffic, examining packet contents for viruses, and requiring inbound users to enter login names and passwords. Firewalls keep casual Internet/extranet users away from precious company data, limit legitimate users to selected applications and databases, allow network administrators to monitor outbound communications, and produce a detailed audit trail of all successful and attempted logins.

Today's extranets often rely on a "dueling firewalls" topology, in which companies provide one another with secure, "tunneled" access to their respective intranets over the public Internet. Tunnels are secure server-to-server or client-to-server associations involving network-level packet encryption. TPs may host applications and data on Web servers either outside or inside their perimeter firewalls. This extranet design is analogous to the traditional leased-line topology, but uses routing tables and packet-level encryption instead of dedicated copper or fiber circuits. We might regard this configuration as an "internally hosted extranet," since the hardware and software infrastructure for connecting and integrating TPs is hosted within each TP's intranet.

In terms of their topology, internally hosted extranets come in three basic configurations. Hub-and-spoke configurations involve tunneled connections radiating to many organizations from a dominant TP. Mesh configurations involve direct connections between all or most TPs. Point-to-point configurations involve direct connections between two TPs. Combining these configuration models allows you to construct real-world extranets of arbitrary complexity. We show these configurations in Figure 7-3.

You might also subscribe to an ISP's extranet services, in which case the carrier often installs firewalls on your premises (under this scenario, the service provider usually continues to own the firewalls and manage them remotely). Or you might contract for a third-party service provider to host your extranet as a virtual private marketplace on their hub, as we discussed in Chapter 6. We might refer to either of these configurations as an "externally hosted extranet," and note that it usually entails a hub-and-spoke configuration (the same logical configuration we associate with hubbed e-marketplaces).

Under the virtual private marketplace scenario, TPs rely on a third-party Internet-based service provider to host such TP applications as online procurement, catalog aggregation, EDI, transaction processing, and electronic funds transfer. Typically, the service provider's computers remain entirely outside the firewalls of the respective TPs, minimizing partners' exposure to unauthorized data access, tampering, and theft. This approach is analogous to the traditional EDI VAN topology, but uses today's ubiquitous Internet infrastructure in lieu of VAN-specific X.25 or frame-relay networks. It is not a broker-hosted e-marketplace for one simple reason: The service provider does not match buyers to sellers or collect fees for transactions processed over its systems.

Whichever extranet approach is selected, internally or externally hosted, your company may already have most if not all of the basic ingredients needed to make it happen. Extranet ingredients include legacy corporate applications, Web servers, commerce servers, proxy servers, firewalls, and Internet service providers (ISPs). ISPs are ramping up to provide extranet customers with end-to-end security through a combination of encrypting and tunneling routers, firewalls, and public key infrastructures.

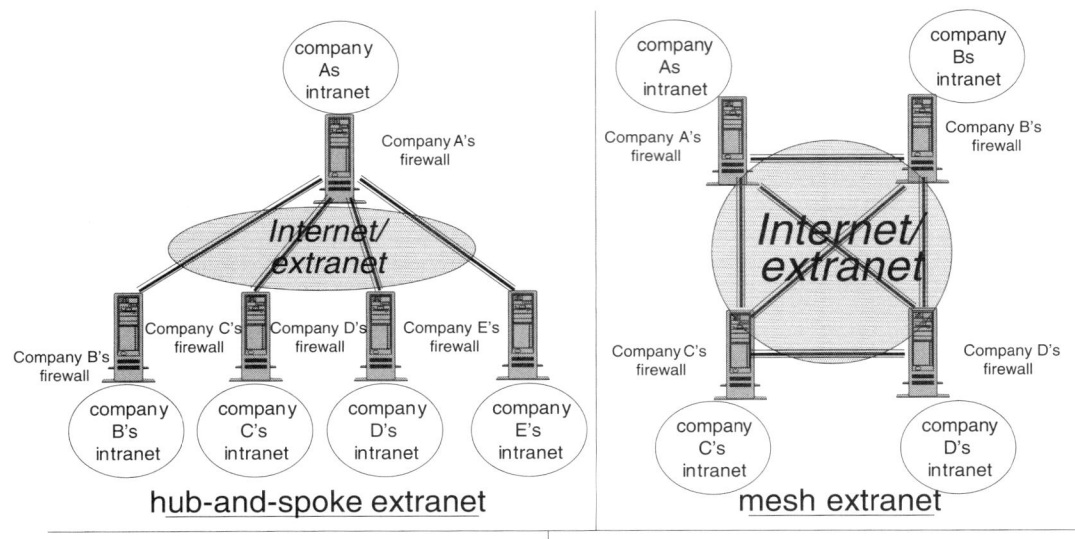

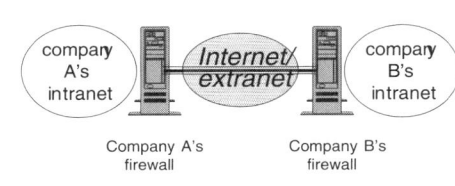

Figure 7-3 *Extranet configuration options include hub-and-spoke, mesh, and point-to-point.*

Another important set of ingredients in your extranet are the "middleware" services supported in your computer and network environments. Middleware services bind different companies' applications together into a unified data-sharing and/or object-passing environment. The principal middleware technologies include message brokers, object request brokers, transaction processing monitors, and remote procedure calls. We will discuss these technologies in greater detail in Part 4 as enabling technologies for BizTalk Server 2000 and BizTalk-enabled applications.

7.4 Extranet Membership Model

Extranets usually have stringent membership requirements—you can connect only if you're the established long-term TP of an existing member.

Extranet membership has its privileges but also its costs. If you satisfy eligibility requirements, then you'll need to clear the next several hurdles before you're an extranet participant in good working order. First, you'll need to establish TPAs with one or more current extranet members. Next, you'll need to work out the technical details of implementing secure firewalls, proxies, encrypting routers, and tunneled connections with each of your TPs. You will also need to define authentication schemes, access controls, encryption mechanisms, and other security features governing your interactions with TPs, both within your intranet and theirs. This will require painstaking attention to directories, public key infrastructures, and policy management tools on each end of the connection.

Setting up an extranet usually involves considerable management- and technical-level coordination with TPs, due to the risks associated with providing other firms' personnel with access to your business data. An extranet is essentially an extension of a company's intranet to its partners in a secure way. It differs from electronic commerce in that the partner is a known entity, not just anyone willing to type in a credit card number over an SSL session. Many extranet transactions involve exchange of money, intellectual property, and other items of commercial value. Consequently, they must be electronically signed, sealed, delivered, and tracked in a manner that can stand up in a court of law.

One could argue that extranets are based both on trust and on its absence. Companies enter into extranets only when they trust that TPs' networks live up to basic security levels. Before opening strategic systems to an external partner, you must have confidence that their security is at least as strong as your own and that it will stay at that level, or at least that the TP's users present digitally signed and encrypted objects that can be verified, via valid X.509 public key certificates and trusted certificate authorities (CAs), as coming from those users. If you can at least trust the credentials that TPs present online, you can apply the appropriate access controls.

CAs are essentially "trust brokers" in network environments. Secure network applications increasingly depend on the ability to retrieve other users' X.509 public key certificates online from a trusted commercial CA (such as Verisign) or government CAs. The certificate would contain the person's name, public key, other descriptive information, and the CA's authenticating digital signature. You can use someone's public key, retrieved from the certificate, to verify the authenticity and integrity of an electronic document he or she sent you. You can also access decryption keys that allow you to open and read it. The dominant standards for public key certificates are X.509, an International Telecommunications Union (ITU) Telecommunications Standardization Sector (TSS) specification, and PKCS-6, developed by RSA Data Security. These standards define formats for certificates that bind user identifiers to public keys.

Absence of trust is also a foundation for extranets. Extending your corporate jewels to third parties is a risky proposition, no matter how you look at it. You take a calculated risk when opening your network to third parties. Enterprises implement firewalls, tunnels, and public key infrastructures on the general assumption that trust is naive and that they need protection against all potential threats from the Internet. Essentially, extranet security assumes that trust is irrelevant and that, all other things held equal, you should trust no one because knee-jerk trust implies or encourages an absence of controls. Judicious technical and management controls, enforced through network and system security mechanisms, delineate the boundaries that are the foundation for well-managed organizations, markets, and economies.

Controls are boundary and risk management tools that operate both within and between businesses. Controls define "who may do what with what," within the context of business and commercial relationships. In other words, they define the policy infrastructure for business. At the core of this policy infrastructure are identity management services, which enable companies to establish virtual rather than physical boundaries around their applications and other resources.

Identity management services often go by the name of "directory services." Directories include information on the identities of users, the groups to which they belong, and the resources (such as printers, servers, and routers) to which they may require access. Generally, directory services support naming, addressing, search, control, and management of users, groups, and resources.

Every network application has some sort of directory that determines who may access the application and what privileges they enjoy within the application. As such, directories are a critical component for defining and enforcing policies in networked applications, including those deployed on extranets, intranets, and the Internet. Applications may have their own special-purpose directory services, or they may rely on general-purpose directory services, which provide a shared resource for naming, finding, accessing, and protecting resources across a network.

Extranets' membership models usually rely on general-purpose directory and security services to define and enforce the ground rules for participation. Directories give companies the tools to define the identities, roles, and privileges associated with both internal and external users, including employees of suppliers, contractors, distributors, and customers. Figure 7-4 shows how extranet membership depends on the "virtual boundaries" defined within directories in front of and behind firewalls. Figure 7-5 shows how CAs and public key-enabled applications interoperate with directory services.

directories, in front of and behind firewall,
store identity, role, and privilege
information for external and internal personnel

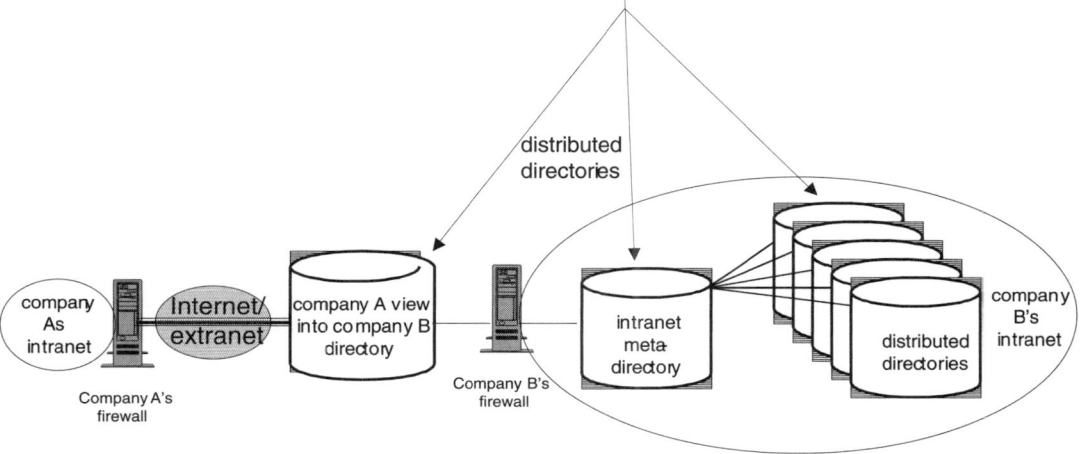

Figure 7-4 *Directory services store identity, role, and privilege information to use in defining virtual boundaries among trading partners in an extranet.*

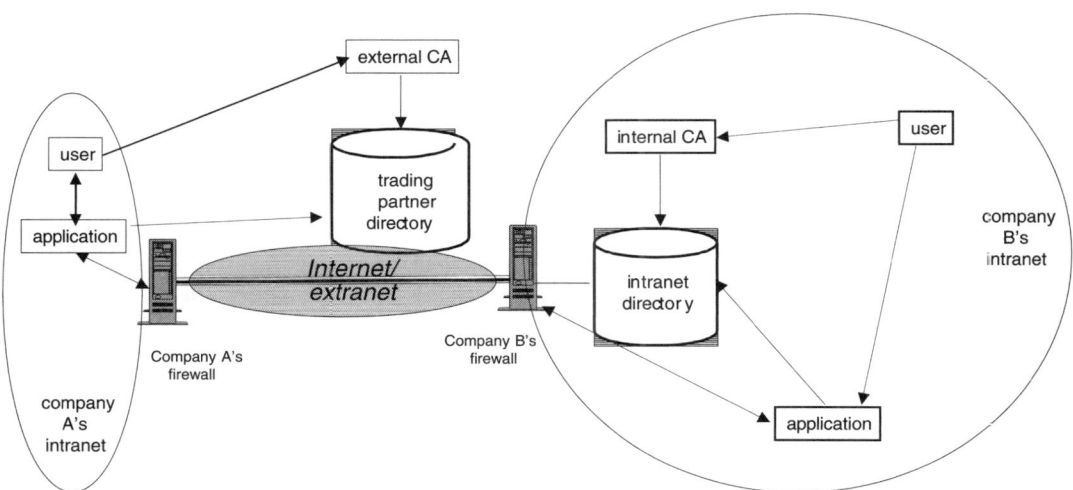

¥Users apply for public-key certificates from internal or external certificate authority (CA)
¥CA issues certificates and publishes certifcates to directories
¥Applications retrieve certificates from directory for security operations such as user authentication, digital signature,
¥encryption, integrity-checking, and nonrepudiation

Figure 7-5 *Certificate authorities manage extranet trading partners' public key certificates in directory services.*

Hierarchical namespaces, such as those implemented in X.500-compliant directories, allow companies to structure logical links among users, groups, and resources in complex ways that mirror external and internal business relationships. Inclusion in the shared directory essentially defines who's a member of the extranet and who's not—in other words, whose login ID and password will work the next time they log in to a TP's systems over a secure channel. Some directory services allow users to modify various attributes on themselves, such as their postal addresses, phone numbers, and interest profiles.

In terms of physical hosting, directories define attributes of users, groups, and resources but don't necessarily store all the data related to those resources in the directory database. In many cases, the directory merely contains pointers that refer the client or application to the location of the desired network resource. In addition, directories may extend over multiserver and geographically dispersed environments, a configuration that often requires high reliability, scalability, and availability. Furthermore, enterprise-ready directories often support multimaster replication, distributed databases, and the ability to work across various local and wide-area networks. A complete enterprise directory must include meta-directory functionality, particularly the ability to combine or "join" information from several special-purpose directories.

Directory services support several security services that are fundamental to secure extranets: authentication, authorization, content confidentiality, content integrity, and nonrepudiation. These security services define the virtual boundaries governing interactions among extranet member TPs. These services specify who can do what with what. They also provide mechanisms for TPs to monitor and enforce mutual compliance with shared policies and procedures.

We now discuss each of these security services in turn.

7.4.1 Authentication

Authentication defines the "who" in "who may do what with what." Is the person attempting to access your database truly who they purport to be? When you provide a trusted TP with access to your intranet, you need to be able to authenticate their every network transaction, including logins, communications sessions, resource requests, and e-mail messages—even down to the packet level.

Today's network authentication products allow companies to add login security features above and beyond mere passwords. Authentication products allow network managers to spoof-proof their networks inside and out, verifying the origin and integrity of resource requests, files, messages, packets, sessions, software modules, and network nodes. Secure tokens, digital signatures, certificate authorities, credentials servers, biometrics, and other advanced authentication technologies make it possible to secure access to the intranet and all networked information resources.

More and more authentication vendors are incorporating open standards into their products, enabling them to work with a growing range of third-party firewalls, communications gateways, applications, and e-mail systems. Many authentication products use a mixture of public key cryptographic techniques—such as RSA Data Security's Public Key Cryptography Standards (PKCS)—and secret-key technologies, such as Data Encryption Standard (DES) ciphers, to support user authentication along with secure key exchange and encryption, tamper-proofing, and nonrepudiation services.

The most widely adopted authentication standards include the following:

- X.509 Public Key Certificates: An ITU standard that specifies a syntax for public key certificates
- Secure Sockets Layer (SSL): An Internet Engineering Task Force (IETF) standard, also known as Transport Layer Security (TLS), that supports authentication and confidentiality on Web browsing sessions over the HTTP, FTP, and Telnet protocols
- Challenge-Handshake Authentication Protocol (CHAP): An authentication technique defined in RFC 1334, supporting dial-up, remote, authenticated user access to intranet/extranets over the Point-to-Point Protocol (PPP)
- Remote Authentication Dial-In User Service (RADIUS): A specification, for authentication, authorization, and accounting of remote user access in client-server environments
- Secure Multipurpose Internet Mail Extensions (S/MIME): A standard, developed by the IETF, that adds digital signature-based authentication (plus encryption) to Internet MIME messages described in RFC 1521, using X.509 public key certificates
- Kerberos: An authentication service, developed at the Massachusetts Institute of Technology and embedded in Windows 2000, which uses secret key ciphers for authentication and encryption, authenticating requests for network resources.
- Secure Electronic Transactions (SET): A specification sponsored by MasterCard International Inc. and Visa USA that supports secure payments involving consumers, merchants, banks, and credit card processors, using authenticated X.509-based electronic certificates in lieu of credit card or debit card numbers

Many authentication products also support mutual authentication, a critical feature for secure intranets and extranets, which enables client and server software modules—or two Web servers communicating over the extranet—to verify each other's authenticity prior to establishing a connection or association.

7.4.2 Authorization

Authorization is the "may do what with what" end of the security equation.

Extranets are usually logical overlays—defined only by access privileges and routing tables—on today's intranet and Internet infrastructure, rather than new physical networks in their own right. One and the same corporate Web site, application, and database may reside on all three networks—Internet, intranet, and extranet—depending on who's accessing them, what they're accessing, and what access controls apply.

The most fundamental component of an extranet application is a pool of business information that you want authenticated, authorized TPs to be able to access. You may, for example, choose to provide customers with access to your online purchasing and inventory systems to track the status of their orders, or allow engineering contractors real-time access to CAD/CAM specs and drawings. Providing TPs with such access may be as simple as adding them to the relevant applications' authorized access control lists. Or, if you rely on an EDI VAN to host the data, the VAN would be responsible for enforcing your corporate access control policies.

What best distinguishes extranets from intranets and the Internet is this issue of who has authorized access to company data. Extranet applications are founded on partner access to business data, while private access from within one's own organization is the basis for intranet applications, and unlimited public access defines a truly Internet application, such as an electronic commerce Web site.

Increasingly, role-based access control is the preferred model, with roles described via additional user attributes in the directory. In extranet environments, you may not care so much whether someone in your company or a supplier organization manages a particular function. More important is the role that person performs, and the same directory may apply the same access controls to internal and external staff.

Once you've authenticated external users to your extranet application, you need to make sure they can access only those resources for which they're authorized. Directories typically support authorization through access control lists (ACLs), which use the directory as a repository for storing, distributing, locating, and retrieving access controls. Access controls define the relationship between authenticated users and various network resources. These controls define what resources people can originate, access, read, modify, copy, manipulate, and manage. Directories may also support auditing features that allow you to determine who has accessed what resource at what time.

Traditionally, individual network operating systems, messaging services, and applications have managed their own authorization schemes, also known as access control or privilege management, in a system-specific fashion. General-purpose authorization mechanisms have yet to emerge that manage access controls across multiple operating environments, applications,

and services. However, as these mechanisms emerge, directories will probably play a pivotal role in defining and enforcing access controls.

7.4.3 Content Confidentiality

Content confidentiality, also known as encryption, ensures that only authenticated, authorized parties can view what you send them. You may trust your
TPs completely but still have cold feet about transmitting sensitive business
information to them over the wide-open Internet. Consequently, encryption
services are absolutely essential for full-bore extranet commerce.

Encryption is supported by several of the security protocols discussed
previously, including SSL, S/MIME, and SET. Extranet users will probably
employ all or most of these techniques, depending on the object being
encrypted. SSL encrypts communications sessions between Web browsers
and servers. S/MIME encrypts e-mail body parts and attachments. SET
encrypts credit card numbers and other sensitive information on electronic-
commerce transactions.

A combination of secret key and public key technologies is usually
required for most high-volume extranet applications. Secret key schemes
have proven to be more efficient for fast, high-volume encryption and
decryption, but are vulnerable to theft or misappropriation of secret keys. In
many commercial applications, a secret key technique such as Digital
Encryption Standard (DES) or Triple-DES is used to encrypt the body of a
message, while public key cryptography is used to encrypt the DES key so
that it may be transmitted along with the DES-encrypted message.

Secret key cryptography is symmetrical in nature. Secret key systems
require the same key to encrypt and decrypt. This technology predates public key cryptography by generations—some might say it's been around since
the dawn of civilization. Symmetrical schemes require that secret keys be
conveyed or transmitted to the recipient prior to exchange of encrypted
materials. Symmetrical schemes have proven to be more efficient than public-key technologies for fast, high-volume encryption and decryption. In
many commercial applications, a symmetrical scheme such as DES and
Triple-DES will be used to encrypt the body of a messages. Public key cryptography will be used to encrypt the DES key so that it may be transmitted
along with the DES-encrypted message.

Public key cryptography has made it possible to deploy mass-market
cryptographic applications on a global basis. Every user on a public key system has two different "asymmetrical" keys for encrypting and decrypting
information; one key is published to the world and the other is held in private. User A's public key may be used by others to encrypt items that may be
read only by User A, who uses his private key to decrypt them. Likewise,
User A may encrypt an item with his private key and make it generally available; others may decrypt it by using his public key, in the process certifying

that he was the one who encrypted the item. This scheme spares users from the logistical difficulties inherent in exchanging and securing secret keys prior to exchanging encrypted items. Most commercial implementations of public key technology license basic mathematical algorithms from RSA Data Security, a firm founded by cryptography pioneers Rivest, Shamir, and Adelman. The world's dominant public key standard is RSA's PKCS. The Internet community has developed a PKCS-based secure messaging standard, S/MIME, which integrates with MIME content exchanged over SMTP mail backbones. S/MIME supports user authentication, message encryption, and content integrity assurances. Another public key algorithm, Pretty Good Privacy (PGP), has also achieved considerable acceptance in the marketplace.

Tunneling is a specialized type of encryption used in extranets. Tunneling allows companies to establish secure B2B VPNs over the public Internet. Tunneling refers to the technique of encrypting packets so that they can be transmitted confidentially over an insecure virtual circuit, such as an Internet TCP/IP connection. Tunneling also enables new protocols to be encapsulated and delivered unmodified to a remote intranet that has been set up to handle them properly, such as when IP version 6 packets are tunneled over legacy IP version 4 wide-area networks, thereby facilitating eventual transition to the new protocol. Tunneled packets are decrypted at the receiving end and then routed in the clear on the recipient's intranet to their ultimate destinations.

The leading tunneling protocols are as follows:

● IPsec: network-level authentication, data integrity, and encryption features built into the emerging IP version 6; defined in RFCs 1826 and 1827
● Point-to-Point Tunneling Protocol: an extension to the Point-to-Point Protocol that was developed by Microsoft and leading manufacturers of firewalls, routers, and remote access servers; supports tunneling of IP, IPX, or NetBEUI protocols inside IP packets
● Layer 2 Tunneling Protocol (L2TP): a proposed Internet standard combining Cisco's Layer 2 Forwarding technology with Microsoft's PPTP
● Proprietary tunneling specifications from various router and firewall vendors, including Cisco Systems and Check Point Software

Lack of widely accepted tunneling standards has heretofore limited TP's ability to establish Internet-based VPNs between their respective firewalls.

7.4.4 Content Integrity

Content integrity assurances are an inherent feature of public-key-based "digital signature" technologies. A digital signature is a string of bits that can be used to mathematically certify that a document was originated by a particular user and has not been altered or tampered with during transmission. To produce a digital signature, a user's application reduces the document's bit sequence to a condensed string known as a "hash," and then encrypts the hash with the user's private key. The digital signature is typically attached to the document for transmission.

At the receiving end, the digital signature is decrypted with the user's public key and compared to the document hash. If the two match, the document is authentic and was not tampered with. The main digital signature standards are PKCS-6 from RSA Data Security and the U.S. government's Digital Signature Algorithm (DSA).

7.4.5 Nonrepudiation

Nonrepudiation services are another inherent feature of digital signatures. Nonrepudiation refers to the ability of a third party to prove that the person who claims to have sent or received something is telling the truth. Depending on what they're applied to, digital signatures provide various levels of nonrepudiation:

- Nonrepudiation of origin: Applied to transmitted content, such as a file attachment, a digital signature proves that the person who claims to have sent it in fact did so. We have this assurance because senders use their private keys—to which only they have access—to generate the digital signature on a document. We verify this claim by using that person's public key to decrypt the digital signature and compare it to a hash of the plaintext of the signed document.
- Nonrepudiation of submission: Applied to an e-mail or EDI message envelope, digital signatures can prove that a particular client or server submitted the message.
- Nonrepudiation of delivery: Applied to an e-mail or EDI delivery report and a hash of message contents (and generated by the receiving mail server), digital signatures can prove that a particular message was delivered to a particular mail server.
- Nonrepudiation of receipt: Applied to an e-mail or EDI receipt acknowledgment and a hash of message contents (and generated by the receiving mail client or intenal business application), digital signatures prove that a particular message was received by a particular client or application.
- Nonrepudiation of forwarding: Applied to an e-mail or EDI forwarding acknowledgment and a hash of message contents (and generated by the forwarder and recipient of the forwarded message), digital signatures prove that a particular message was forwarded to a particular client or application.

Nonrepudiation is an important feature of EDI and workflow environments, where the current location and status of routed items must be tracked.

Participants in intra- and interorganizational workflows must take responsibility for the documents and other items on their virtual desktops, and nonrepudiations provide an unimpeachable audit trail.

7.5 Extranet Aggregation Model

Extranet content aggregation refers to TPs' online catalogs, as in the world of hubbed e-marketplaces. However, it also describes the range of internal services, applications, and data that companies choose to expose to their TPs via extranets.

Extranets connect two or more preexisting corporate intranets, each of which may consist of many internal Web sites. As you and your TPs get deeper into one another's business processes, you will probably want to provide authorized access to these sites as well as a wider range of databases, documents, and other resources on your respective intranets. You may also consider partitioning the namespace of your primary Web server and setting up multiple virtual servers dedicated to various TPs. These shared resources and virtual servers can then serve as the basis for coordination and collaboration between internal and external personnel. For example, you may provide TPs with authenticated, authorized access to your internal order entry, fulfillment, and tracking system.

Enterprise application integration (EAI) is the key to your extranet aggregation model. To prepare your intranet Web sites for extranet-grade applications, you should consider linking those sites' applications to existing databases via various EAI techniques, including scripts, database connectors, object communications protocols, and message-oriented middleware. We will discuss EAI technologies in more detail in Chapter 8.

An extranet's content-aggregation approach includes two principal hosting options:

* Content aggregated and hosted outside the firewall: What new services, applications, and data have companies aggregated and deployed in front of their firewalls for authenticated, authorized access by TPs?
* Content aggregated and hosted behind the firewall: What existing services, applications, and data—which are already aggregated and deployed for internal users—have companies chosen to expose, via firewalls, to authenticated, authorized access by TPs?

If you keep your content behind your firewalls, you may provide access to it through an application-layer gateway on the firewall. An application-layer gateway intercepts the TP's login to the back-end intranet resource they're requesting and then inspects the information that passes both ways. Or you may also dispense altogether with the notion of having external parties log into internal applications (even through proxies) and simply pass messages both ways (the traditional EDI approach). In this case, you're not exposing any internal content to TPs—instead, you're simply providing them with a recipient e-mail or EDI address for transmitting messages and documents.

Obviously, you will need to maintain authentication and access controls appropriate to whatever extranet content aggregation and hosting option you choose. If you host content behind your firewall, you can monitor and control access at the lowest level. If you host data outside your firewall, you will be exposing it to greater risk of hacking, theft, and unauthorized disclosure. Ideally, you would perform a thorough going security and risk analysis, weighing the costs and benefits of hosting and securing sensitive business data in various locations, prior to making hosting decisions.

Your extranet content aggregation approach may have serious performance consequences, such as when your principal Web site becomes a bottleneck preventing speedy data delivery to TPs. As your intranet funnels more traffic to and from extranets, you and your TPs may find it prudent to set up proxy and reverse-proxy services on your respective intranet boundaries. These nodes speed the flow of frequently requested data to internal and external users through the following cache-management functions:

- Proxy servers intercept and consolidate internal users' requests for external Web pages (such as those residing on TPs' Web sites), cache frequently accessed pages, and control outbound access to services at the application level.
- Reverse proxies intercept and consolidate external users' requests for internal Web pages (those residing on your Web sites), caching frequently accessed pages, and controlling inbound access services at the application level.

Proxy and reverse-proxy services can help extranet TPs prevent redundant page or file downloads from bogging down their respective intranets. They also allow each TP to present a single corporate-wide IP address to the outside world, thereby protecting intranet servers from hackers. TPs may choose to configure proxy servers flexibly in keeping with their extranet requirements, either implementing one centralized proxy, one for each service (such as HTTP, SSL, File Transfer Protocol, Telnet, and Network News Transfer Protocol), one for each region, or even one for each TP connected to your intranet.

7.6 Extranet Transaction Model

Extranets usually have a well-defined transaction model, as specified in legal and technical agreements between TPs. Where supply chains are concerned, the transaction model primarily involves submission, processing, and tracking of purchase, engineering, and service orders according to prices, terms, and conditions in preexisting contracts. In this sense, extranets support "hard-wired," continuing B2B purchasing commitments, as opposed to the ad-hoc deal-making that characterizes many hubbed e-marketplaces.

7.6.1 Commercial Contracts

Extranet operations conform to roles and responsibilities defined in trading partner agreements. As discussed in Chapter 6, you enter into TPAs with companies when you intend to conduct a high volume and frequency of online business with them. TPAs are separate from particular sales or service contracts between two companies. These agreements address legal and technical issues that apply to ongoing supply-chain relationships—in other words, they apply to an anticipated future steady stream of orders flowing in one or both directions between TPs.

7.6.2 Bargaining Mechanisms

Extranets are operational environments where established TPs transact business according to fixed roles, responsibilities, terms, and conditions. Typically, they are not online environments for back-and-forth bargaining and negotiation. Any bargaining that may go on between TPs takes place "out of band" from the extranet, when companies are negotiating TPAs and the various sales and service contracts.

7.6.3 Transactional Workflows

Extranet transactional workflows are often highly structured and quite complex. These workflows take place both on a B2B level and within the organizations and intranets of each TP. We usually refer to the B2B component of extranet workflows as EDI, and the internal component as EAI.

EDI, of course, refers to the automated transmission of predefined, standardized, structured business documents between the information systems of two or more organizations. EDI is application-to-application messaging that involves documents whose internal data structures are standardized according to explicit agreements among TPs. Typically, it involves submission of purchase orders that trigger events in the seller's sales, production, engineering, inventory, shipping, service, and other departments. Various organizations in both the selling and buying TPs generate structured business documents, acknowledgments, and notifications at various points in the order-fulfillment workflow. EAI defines how the B2B workflow draws on applications, services, and data deep within each TP's intranet.

Another way of looking at extranet workflows is in terms of the actual applications that they support. We can identify three categories of applications supported by extranet workflows: supply-chain management, enterprise resource planning, and customer relationship management. You can scarcely build a viable extranet without mutual TP support for SCM, ERP, and CRM applications that link partners' business processes. Figure 7-6 shows extranet workflows built from interfacing trading partners' internal SCM, ERP, and CRM applications.

SCM applications support TP-to-TP processes for submitting, tracking, fulfilling, and delivering orders. Consequently, SCM defines the core B2B workflow of most extranets. Most EDI applications are SCM-oriented, since they involve the following request-response scenarios:

- Request: One TP—the buyer—submits a purchase, engineering, or change order (and associated documentation) to the other TP.
- Response: The other TP—the seller—returns a schedule (plus associated documentation) for delivery of the requested items. In addition, the seller often submits an invoice—a payment request, to which the buyer responds by rendering payment through an online automated clearinghouse (ACH) or other means.

ERP applications primarily support a TP's internal management of material flows within a supply chain. ERP applications include those in support of procurement, inventory control, manufacturing, quality assurance, spare parts, distribution, shipping, and receiving. ERP applications also support invoicing and payment for items ordered and delivered.

TPs build an extranet-based supply chain by interfacing their various ERP applications over secure communications channels. For example, a buyer might interface its procurement application to its supplier's order-entry application; its receiving application to its supplier's shipping application; or its accounts payable application to its supplier's accounts receivable applica-

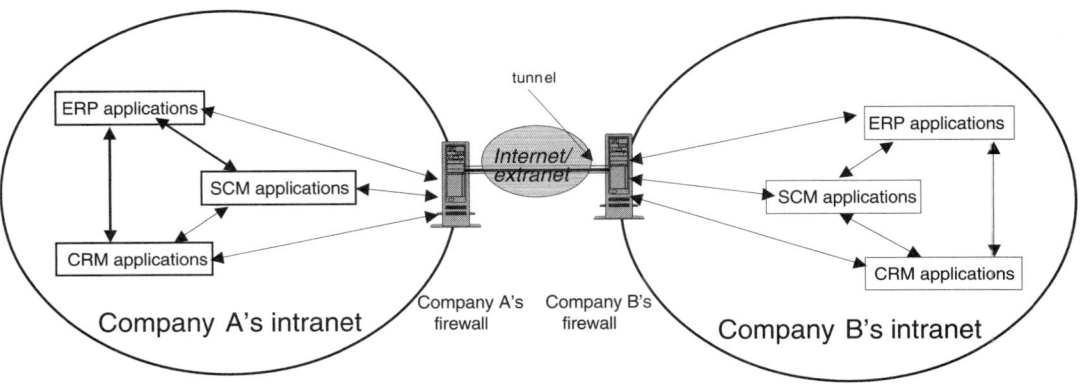

Figure 7-6   *Extranet workflows interface trading partners' internal SCM, ERP, and CRM applications.*

tion. When linked into extranet supply chains, ERP applications usually exchange standard EDI transaction sets with TPs, as defined in TPAs.

However, ERP applications also support tight internal workflow integration through vendor-proprietary program and data interfaces. Companies usually source most of their ERP applications from a single strategic vendor, such as SAP, Baan, J.D. Edwards, PeopleSoft, i2, and Manugistics. A vendor's ERP suite may include any or all of the following linked applications:

- Accounts payable and receivable
- Asset management
- Cash management
- Collections
- Cost analysis and estimation
- Credit management
- Demand forecasting
- Electronic funds transfer
- Equipment management
- Human resource management
- Inventory management and control
- Invoicing
- Just-in-time manufacturing
- Materials forecasting, tracking, management, and replenishment
- Order capture, tracking, management, and fulfillment
- Process control
- Procurement
- Product data management
- Production planning, scheduling, tracking, and control
- Quality assurance and inspection
- Spare parts, supplies, and logistics
- Shipping and receiving
- Transportation scheduling, routing, and optimization
- Travel expense management
- Warehouse management
- Vendor management

CRM applications automate the processes that TPs use to support customers and distributors via extranets. Buyers typically interface their internal ERP and other applications with their suppliers' CRM applications via extranet connections. Principal CRM applications include the following:

- Account management
- Contract management
- Customer profile management
- Customer self-service
- Defect management

- Depot repair management
- Field service scheduling and dispatch
- Help desk management
- Product management
- Service management
- Spare part and logistics management
- Warranty management

Every vertical industry—indeed, every pair of linked TPs—combines various SCM, ERP, and CRM applications in particular configurations. In a very real sense, an extranet is a "captive marketplace" with a custom-tailored workflow binding two or more TPs into an extended enterprise.

7.7 Extranet Pricing Model

Extranet transactions almost always rely on fixed prices that are defined "out of band," in TPAs and sales or service contracts. The TPA defines financial terms, conditions, and obligations applying to TPs within the relationship. TPs submit online purchase orders against predefined sell offers with predefined prices.

Auctions and other dynamic-pricing mechanisms are nowhere to be found in traditional extranets. Consequently, we can regard traditional extranets as relying on the "take it or leave it" bargaining model described in Chapter 6. Extranets are almost always a haggle-free zone.

7.8 Extranet Payment Model

Extranets typically manage electronic funds transfers through TP connections, via their respective banks, to ACH interbank services. When buyer and seller are both in the United States, interbank ACH transactions are carried on the FedWire network. When buyer and seller are in different countries, interbank ACH transactions run over a network operated by the nonprofit Society for Worldwide Interbank Financial Telecommunications (SWIFT).

In extranet transactions, TPs usually transmit invoices to each other online (e.g., in ANSI X12 810 format). Buyers then return "payment orders" (e.g., in ANSI X12 820 format) that initiate the online payment process that ultimately results in monetary transfers to seller accounts. All of these electronic billing and payment transactions are managed through buyers' and sellers' ERP applications. Credit cards are seldom used to render payment in extranet transactions.

7.9 Extranet Facilitation Model

Extranets may or may not connect TPs with the full range of facilitators—such as banks, insurers, escrow services, fulfillment houses, shipping companies, and customs brokers—needed to execute an end-to-end transaction. There's nothing stopping TPs from linking these facilitators into a hub-and-spoke, mesh, or other extranet configurations.

However, we should remember that extranets are not usually full-fledged e-marketplaces such as those we profiled in Chapter 6. An extranet is a secure, exclusive, online supply chain among established TPs, and has been set up primarily to route structured documents to and fro to support a limited range of structured transactions. In support of structured EDI transactions, TPs usually support many if not most of the necessary facilitation services within their respective organizations.

Indeed, companies often go to great expense to integrate extranet transactions with their internal business procedures, applications, and databases. That's where complex EAI implementations enter the B2B equation. And EAI is the focus of the next chapter.

Enterprise Application Integration

Companies must get their internal systems talking to one another before they can interface effectively to external suppliers, customers, and other trading partners (TPs) over extranets or the Internet.

Behind every TP is a constellation of back-end applications, databases, and other resources that must interoperate for that organization to participate in online marketplaces. What we call enterprise application integration (EAI) is the "glue" that enables a single TP's dispersed applications to behave as if they were kindred software modules running on the same machine. EAI is an operational necessity in most intranets where companies have deployed best-of-breed applications and platforms that are incompatible in terms of their ability to share data and interface process logic.

EAI is the internal "plumbing" within your company's distributed computing environment. EAI technologies bind such diverse environments as Web servers, file servers, database servers, enterprise resource planning (ERP) applications, messaging servers, document management systems, certificate servers, and directories into a more seamless whole. Integrating dissimilar applications usually requires that companies implement intermediate layers of software adapters or "middleware" between communicating applications. In practice, middleware goes by various names, including translators, converters, bridges, gateways, object brokers, message brokers, remote procedure calls, transaction monitors, and workflow engines.

There are many important distinctions between these middleware technologies, which we will discuss in this chapter. Understood as a class of technologies, however, middleware solutions support the following core application-to-application communications functions (illustrated in Figure 8-1):

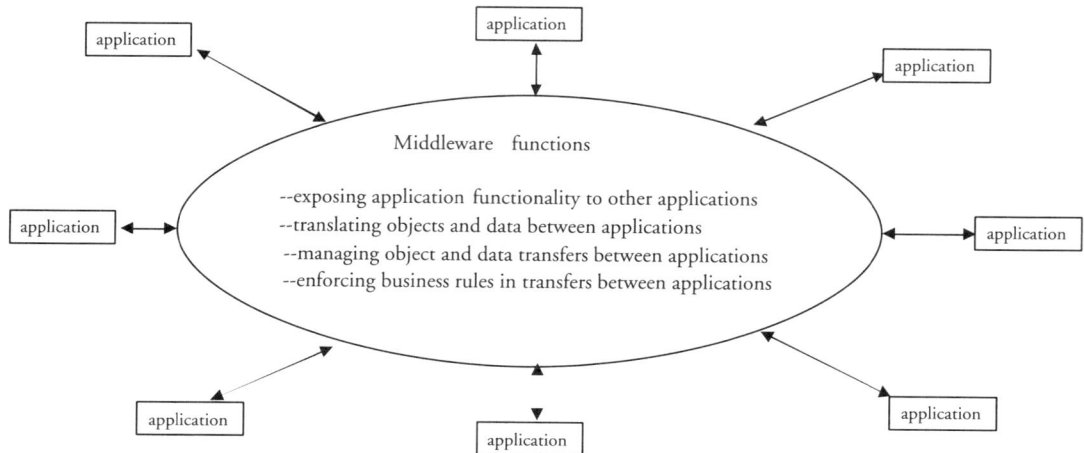

Figure 8-1   *Middleware support application-to-application interoperability.*

- Exposing the functionality of otherwise incompatible applications
- Translating objects and data shared by the applications
- Managing transfer of objects and data between the applications over appropriate protocols
- Enforcing appropriate business rules in interactions between the applications.

The ideal middleware environment would allow otherwise incompatible applications to communicate transparently with one another. Applications would communicate functionality, data, and status without regard for one another's programming interfaces, calling conventions, data types and formats, locations, communications protocols, and object models. A distributed middleware infrastructure would render to each application component the interface parameters and data they expect to see. Middleware would hub diverse components into a logically integrated application environment (much the way an e-marketplace "middleman" joins diverse buyers and sellers into a logically integrated trading environment).

8.1 Potential BizTalk Role in Enterprise Application Integration

BizTalk Server is middleware for "any-to-any" EAI and EDI. It is one part workflow engine, one part format-translation engine, and one part message broker.

BizTalk Server's workflow features make it just as appropriate a solution for integration within companies as between companies. BizTalk Server provides an EAI/EDI software-adaptability layer with translators, adapters, and other components that support transparent communications among otherwise incompatible applications. BizTalk Server's primary middleware functions, which we will explore more deeply in Part 3, are:

- Map and translate between various content formats, including EDI transaction sets, XML documents, and application-specific formats, such as various vendors' ERP and CRM products
- Support integrated modeling, execution, monitoring, and control of document routing and processing workflows between applications and organizations
- Support scriptable, rule-driven, and content-based routing over various asynchronous and synchronous communications protocols
- Support definition, editing, and management of XML schemas, TP profiles, and TPAs
- Support digital signatures, confidentiality, integrity, and nonrepudiation services through integration with public key infrastructures (PKIs)

The BizTalk Server and BizTalk Framework support a particular middleware approach: loosely coupled, asynchronous EAI, in which applications communicate with one another other in store-and-forward fashion. Under this approach immediate communication is not necessary, but reliable end-to-end delivery is essential. Message-brokering technologies such as Microsoft Message Queue Server are the most appropriate transaction environment for asynchronous EAI (though other asynchronous protocols, such as SMTP, and synchronous protocols such as HTTP and FTP, might also support this style of application-to-application communications). BizTalk Server does not provide an appropriate environment for tightly coupled EAI, which requires immediate responses over synchronous application-to-application conversations. Synchronous EAI requires such middleware approaches as remote procedure calls (RPCs), Common Object Request Broker Architecture (CORBA), and Distributed Component Object Model (DCOM).

In a larger sense, XML is the middleware for the new age of loosely coupled network applications, and BizTalk defines just one dialect of that new lingua franca. XML provides a versatile language for decoupling distributed applications from the operating environments across which they sprawl. In the new application paradigm, vendor-dominated operating environments take a subordinate role to cross-platform services, such as directories, Web publishing, and e-commerce. And these cross-platform services increasingly implement XML down to their very cores.

Most fundamentally, XML is helping shift industry momentum away from tightly coupled computing models toward messaging-brokering middleware. XML's emergence is contributing to a broad decline in platforms' reliance on remote procedure calls, CORBA, DCOM, and other interapplication communication schemes that bind distributed objects tightly to each other. XML plays nicely into a world where message brokering, loosely coupled architectures, and scalable application servers make up the predominant computing environment. It shifts the emphasis toward environments in which loosely coupled components operate asynchronously and assemble themselves dynamically into larger services upon demand.

Tightly coupled object technologies such as DCOM and CORBA still have a role in this new order, primarily in support of distributed applications that demand tightly coupled components in relatively homogeneous environments (such as intranets). Even here, XML is proving pivotal, insofar as software vendors will increasingly rely on XML "wrapper" technologies—such as the Simple Object Access Protocol (SOAP)— to integrate otherwise incompatible object technologies across multivendor, multiplatform environments.

All of which indicates that BizTalk Server will become increasingly important as a means for bridging loosely coupled EAI and EDI environments and for enabling a modicum of interoperability between synchronous object specifications, such as Microsoft's DCOM, and other middleware technologies.

8.2 EAI and the E-Marketecture Reference Model

Each TP is essentially a trading community unto itself, a supply chain under single ownership.

As we noted in Part 1, enterprises are not different in kind from B2B supply chains. Today's businesses are dynamic value chains that connect and configure themselves through structured, online transactions. Workflow-oriented middleware environments such as BizTalk Server enforce the business rules for these transactions, both within and among connected TPs. At the heart of BizTalk Server and similar products from other vendors are the following fundamental EAI/EDI services:

- Accept any type of business data, structured in almost any business document format, and wrapped in almost any type of message or communications envelope from any application
- Map and translate that data, document format, and message envelope into any other
- Route the translated data to any target application
- Track the status of the end-to-end workflow in which that interchange plays a part

Supply chains—internal or external—depend on structured workflows, which depend in turn on EAI within and between companies. Within the e-marketecture reference model, workflow resides squarely within the transaction model. Within today's distributed computing environments, the primary repository of workflow logic is the application server.

Application servers are the dominant platforms for the new age of e-commerce. They are also the focus for EAI in support of corporate e-commerce initiatives. They project corporate data to clients under the control of programmable business rules, which specify workflows consisting of tasks, dependencies, and routing and processing steps. What distinguishes application servers from traditional host computing platforms is their fundamental orientation toward browser-based clients, component-based object models, and standards-based protocols and development interfaces.

Most online merchant sites are in fact application servers that access and integrate data and functionality within that merchant's intranet. E-marketplace hubsites also run on specialized application servers that tie into a broad range of back-end systems deployed for this particular purpose. A run-of-the-mill Web site performs application server functions only to the extent that it integrates with back-end databases through Common Gateway Interface (CGI) and other scripting and data access techniques.

We may also regard BizTalk Server as an application server of a higher order—an "application broker" or "integration broker"—since it aims at bridging multiple legacy applications into a seamless, Internet-oriented, any-to-any EAI/EDI environment. Application brokers validate, map, translate, manipulate, and route EDI documents, ERP system outputs, and other objects between dissimilar applications and systems. These brokers map between dissimilar XML formats—such as those specified in BizTalk, cXML, and OAGIS—and connect applications across various synchronous, asynchronous, message-brokering, and object-communications protocols.

Application servers or brokers rely on the following fundamental specifications, interfaces, and technologies (illustrated in Figure 8-2):

- Markup languages tag data and program elements for full-fidelity display, sharing, and semantics interchange across the various tiers, from the database to the application server to the client.
- Development interfaces support specification, configuration, and maintenance of source code and executable program code, as well as access and invocation of program libraries through published programming conventions.
- Object technologies support distribution, interoperability, and portability of modular program code across the various tiers.
- Connector technologies support data access, consolidation, and integration from diverse information stores, including directories, relational databases, and ERP applications.
- Transaction technologies support reliable computing across distributed information stores, enabling administrators to recover quickly from system crashes without corrupting the cross-referential integrity of dispersed databases.

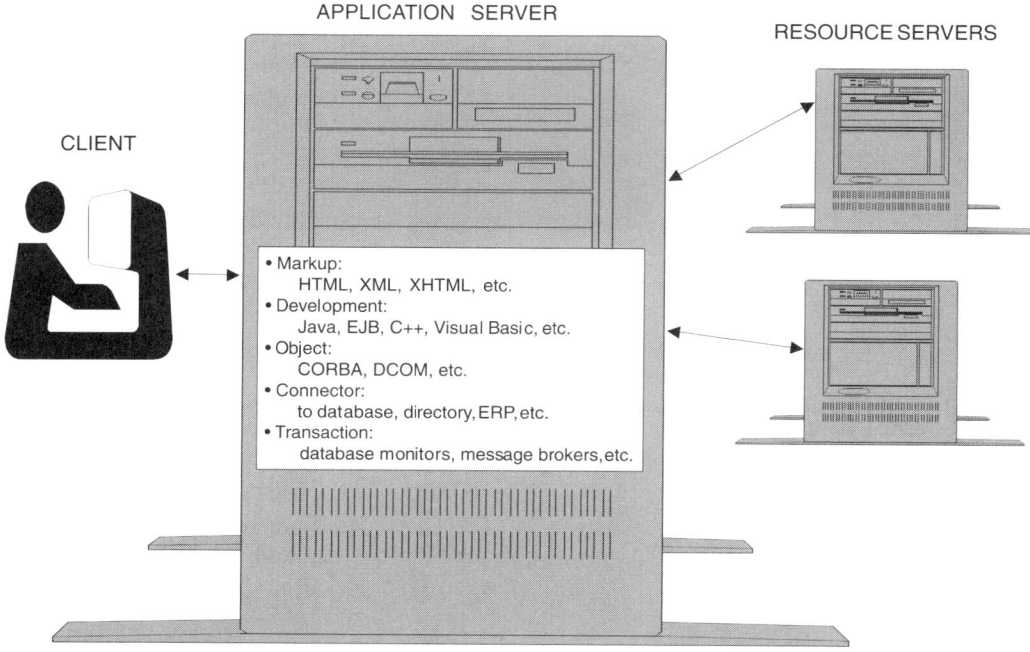

Figure 8-2   *Fundamental EAI and application server technologies include markup languages, development interfaces, object technologies, connector technologies, and transaction technologies.*

We will now describe the high-level role of each technology in EAI generally—and application servers, in particular. We discuss the range of standards supported in today's application servers. In Part 4, we will go into greater depth on BizTalk Server and other Microsoft products' support for various specifications and technologies in these and related areas.

8.3 Markup Languages

Markup technologies tag data and program elements for full-fidelity display, sharing, and semantics interchange across the various tiers of distributed computing, from the database to the application server to the client.

Leading markup standards include XML and HTML. Markup languages provide text-based notational conventions—called "markup"—for embedding within a document to describe the constituent elements of that document. Markup specifies how the document is to be processed by specialized programs known as parsers, which pass content to external applications. The content of a marked-up document may be character data, text in various codings and formats, or references to binary information stored outside the document.

Markup takes the following forms:

- Tags are a type of metadata that attaches descriptive names to constituent content elements in a document, delimiting the beginning and end of each element and attribute within a document.
- Declarations define the logical structure and properties of a document, including the version of the markup language that it supports; what character sets and human languages comprise its content; and what entities, elements, attributes, default values, data types, links, and pointers it contains or references.
- References invoke parameters that were defined previously within declarations.
- Processing instructions contain specific procedures and rules to be invoked by applications that process the marked-up content.
- Comments contain explanations of a marked-up document and its contents for use by human readers.

XML is the driving force behind the evolution of markup languages these days. It has spawned a new generation of markup "dialects" that are taking over many important roles in distributed computing environments. Vendors—most notably, Microsoft—are implementing XML in their core product architectures. Most application server vendors have already implemented XML within their products, as have many leading relational database management system and e-commerce software vendors. Figure 8-3 shows the many roles of XML in an enterprise application architecture.

Defined in early 1998, XML refers to an evolving suite of core specifications for defining content that carries its own application context, including its "namespace," "stylesheet," and "document object model." XML is not a single, stand-alone language so much as a "meta-language" used to define higher-level markup languages for particular application and commerce environments. To that extent, XML's purpose is to evolve into a collection of related markup languages, any of which would be fully comprehensible to any application or device that incorporates a standards-compliant XML parser software component. One important focus of XML-based standardization is in e-commerce "schemas," an area where Microsoft has asserted itself forcefully with its BizTalk Framework.

XML allows application developers to make information objects "self-describing," which means that objects can contain or point to all or most of the context necessary for full-fidelity, automated processing by recipient applications. In addition, XML content is readable and comprehensible by humans, and is thereby readily self-explanatory to the educated eye.

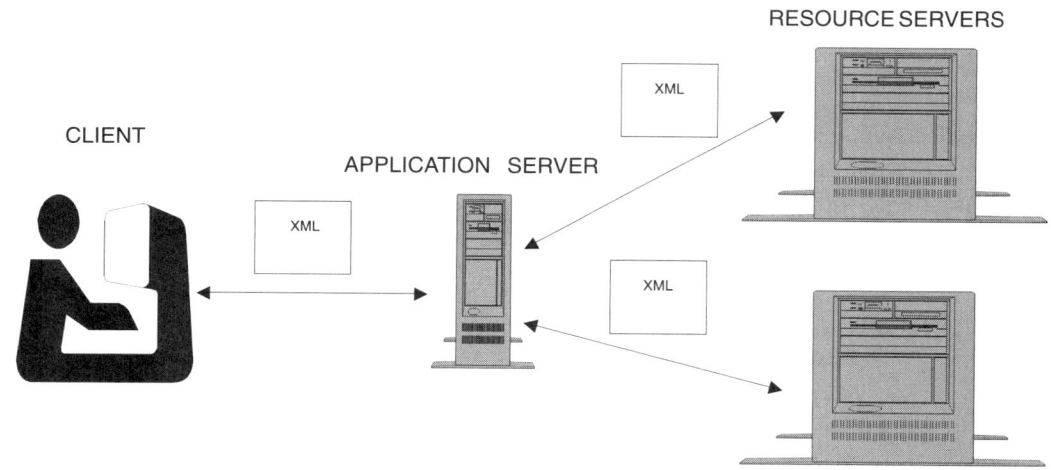

RESOURCE SERVERS

XML

CLIENT

APPLICATION SERVER

XML

XML

application-independent format for
data display, search, and manipulation

application-independent format for
data aggregation, normalization, and processing

application-independent format for
data indexing, storage, and delivery

Figure 8-3   *XML plays many roles in an enterprise application architecture.*

At the application server, XML provides a universal format for data interchange, aggregation, search, and manipulation. XML also represents a universal format for encoding, interchange, and reuse of business logic at this level.

This is the tier where XML will play its primary role in distributed environments, and application server vendors have acknowledged that fact by implementing XML almost universally in their commercial products. Application servers with integrated XML processors can evaluate and handle incoming XML data objects dynamically by examining their self-describing tags. Servers can peer easily into objects' structure through their tags and schema, thereby easing the processing burden associated with handling diverse formats on inbound data. XML tags also facilitate granular access by server-side scripts, Enterprise JavaBeans (JBs), and other application logic modules to data structures.

If data sources already output XML data, the server can use a single XML processor to manage data parsing and consolidation, and need not deploy custom interface code for each data source. More typically, though, an XML-enabled server translates data from legacy databases into XML format and integrates diverse data objects into a unified, logical view. In addition, the server usually transforms XML to HTML for delivery to non-XML-enabled clients through Web servers.

XML is simpler than its parent language, SGML. It is more flexible and data-structure-oriented than its sister specification—HTML (currently in version 4.0)—which primarily defines the presentation and display of Web pages. They will continue to evolve independently under the supervision of the World Wide Web Consortium (W3C).

XML is absorbing HTML through a new standard called Extensible Hyper Text Markup Language (XHTML). XHTML 1.0 is a W3C Recommendation that combines HTML data-presentation with XML data-structuring tags. The W3C has stated that all future enhancements to HTML will be in the context of XHTML—in other words, there will be no HTML 5.0 by that name. XHTML 1.0 preserves all HTML 4.0 tags and allows programmers to add new presentation-oriented tags. XHTML allows developers to include tags from HTML and multiple XML dialects in a single document. Application servers can extract only those XHTML data and presentation elements appropriate to a particular client when transmitting content.

It remains to be seen whether content developers will be any more eager to adopt XHTML 1.0 than HTML 4.0, which has languished in the marketplace. For this new markup language to succeed, it will need to be adopted widely in browsers, application servers, Web servers, databases, and other distributed-computing applications.

8.4 Development Interfaces

Development interfaces support specification, configuration, and maintenance of source code and executable program code, as well as access and invocation of program libraries through programming interfaces. Leading development technologies include C, C++, Visual Basic, Java, and ECMAScript (also known as JavaScript).

Application servers are sophisticated development environments that often combine HTML authoring, EJB libraries, and sophisticated connectors to back-end databases. Developing Web-oriented applications is much more that authoring attractive HTML pages. What's much more challenging—and the province of experienced developers—is designing full-fledged, enterprise-grade Web applications with HTML, Cascading Style Sheets (CSSs), EJBs, complex scripting, streaming real-time video and audio, transaction security, and legacy database integration. There's also the challenge of testing these applications in the various client environments—such as Microsoft Internet Explorer and Netscape Navigator—through which users might access them. And there's the tedious task of maintaining these applications, the sites on which they run, and the fresh content they serve to a waiting world.

It's not simple, but few expected it to be. Several years ago, we all heard and many bought into Java's "write once, run anywhere" philosophy, which promised to ease the development burden for applications designed to run on such diverse platforms as Windows, Unix, and Macintosh.   Up sprang a wealth of commercial Java development tools to make it a reality.

But, ironically, now that Java has established itself as one of the Web's dominant programming languages and component technologies, we don't hear as much emphasis paid to cross-platform development. Ask almost any consultant, programmer, or independent software vendor, and they will laugh off the notion of "write once, run anywhere" as an unattainable ideal. Few can recommend any Web development tools or guidelines for realizing it in practice.

It's not that cross-platform Web applications aren't possible, but that the state of Web development tools and technologies in general—and Java in particular—has gotten much more complex and messy. The fact that no two Java software vendors offer the same set of templates, beans, classes, methods, and other development features means that "write once, run anywhere," if possible at all, must be addressed through painstaking application planning, design, and testing. It cannot be taken for granted.

Another, more fundamental, factor is often overlooked in discussions of cross-platform application development. Java, for all its burgeoning diversity, is only one detail in a complex canvas. Often, the best you can do, given limited time and development resources, is optimize an application for a particular target-client environment and pray that pages display and components execute reasonably well in other environments. Every target-client environment consists of a special blend of operating system, browser, Java virtual machine (JVM), just-in-time (JIT) compiler, plug-ins, and other technologies necessary to execute and display Web pages and components.

And there's a third factor why we've put cross-platform on the back burner of Web application development objectives. The universe of Web application development tools, techniques, and technologies is growing rapidly, and developers want to push the state of the art with interactivity and multimedia features. Users can usually acquire fancy new browsers, or update existing ones, at zero or minimal cost, and seem eager to do so, which means that most will catch up with the state of the art in short order.

Web application developers must pursue a balancing strategy: develop sophisticated, data-rich applications as efficiently as possible without greatly compromising cross-platform portability. Increasingly, developers are attempting this balancing act while pursuing three fundamental development strategies: partitioning, jazzing, and componentizing.

8.4.1 Partitioning

Typically, developers partition Web applications to run across the three distributed tiers of browser, application server, and database server. Under this strategy, the client/browser (tier 1) operates as a container for objects—principally, HTML pages, Graphics Interchange Format (GIF) images, and Java applets—downloaded from the application server or Web server (tier 2). The application server, in turn, links through script programs—such as Common Gateway Interface and Perl—to an external database server (tier 3), which fetches records and fields in response to SQL queries. The results of these queries are formatted by the Web server into HTML pages and tables, which are sent to the browser for display.

This three-tier application partitioning approach is by far the most popular configuration for e-commerce, extranet, intranet, and other dynamic data-driven applications, which typically require scalable access to one or more legacy corporate databases. The application server does the heavy processing. It collects, merges, and formats database query results into HTML/GIF documents for delivery to browsers, sometimes as plain text and sometimes in encrypted form using Web security protocols such as SSL.

This architectural approach facilitates development of a consistent cross-platform look and feel for mainstream corporate database applications ported to the Web. By exercising only the lowest common denominator of functionality in the browser/client tier—the "thin" HTML client—developers have greater assurance that Web applications will display and execute approximately the same everywhere. All or most of the business logic is implemented and executed at the application server, based on database-connector interfaces, and tool-based application templates.

Templates, such as Microsoft's Active Server Page (ASP) and Allaire's ColdFusion, provide a visual tool for implementing the most common server-based database, security, and other application features. For example, an e-commerce application might include such template-driven features as managing electronic catalogs; accessing product, user, pricing, inventory, promotion, and shipping/handling information; and defining order-processing workflows with business rules.

8.4.2 Jazzing

Developers often strive to serve jazzed-up Web pages to clients capable of displaying and executing objects tagged in enhanced markup languages, such as HTML 4.0 and XML, and also capable of handling sophisticated stylesheets, scripting languages, and downloadable executables. Under this development strategy, the browser becomes a more versatile container for objects delivered over the Web. Web pages, when downloaded to a browser-enabled application, provide all-purpose presentation containers for rich text, in-line graphics, animations, streams, scripts, hyperlinks, frames, forms, tables, plug-ins, applets, components, channels, legacy data formats, and other digital objects. Developers can author Web pages as collections of extensible, scriptable, dynamic objects that can be manipulated more intricately from applications.

The application developer leverages sophisticated features of HTML v. 4.0 and/or 3.2. These features include forms, tables, frames, absolute positioning, 3-D overlays, cascading stylesheets, transition effects, drag and drop, data manipulation, data binding, and downloadable run-time fonts.

Likewise, data-driven Web applications use XML to tag data objects within Web pages and facilitate more powerful searching, indexing, and querying of data by XML-enabled clients and browsers. XML allows Web developers to define flexible, object-oriented document metadata formats for diverse applications. Web pages embedded with XML data tags can be browsed, searched, and processed more efficiently than today's flat HTML data structures, which are geared more toward supporting presentation than rigorous data structuring.

In addition, developers exploit the possibilities of various downloadable executables, such as Java applets and ActiveX controls, and animation plug-ins, such as Shockwave. Making all these page elements play together at the browser level is the work of standard-based scripting languages such as ECMAScript and vendor-proprietary scripts such as Microsoft's VBScript. Client-side scripts allow browsers to, among other things, check the validity of user input forms data before the data is submitted to remote servers.

However, jazzing is the strategy under which Web applications most often lose their cross-platform functionality, since it's difficult if not impossible (except in an intranet environment) to guarantee that all browser/clients have the same configuration. For example, Microsoft's ASPs—its developmental template for embedding scripts and ActiveX Controls in HTML pages—display and execute fully only inside Internet Explorer and may be configured to serve equivalent (but possibly less sophisticated) Java applets to other, non-ActiveX-supporting browsers.

Your best hope for cross-platform Web applications is in an intranet environment, where the information technology department can often define and enforce the configuration of every desktop and browser. Otherwise, you will need to shoot at a moving target: developing applications that depend only on those functions, formats, and APIs currently supported in the current versions of the most prevalent browser environments. For the more complex Web applications, your cross-platform browser compatibility checklist can grow to encompass standards and specifications for all of the following items: markup tags, virtual machines, just-in-time compilers, scripting languages, security, stylesheets, multimedia, and objects.

8.4.3 Componentizing

Developers also build up and deploy Web applications as sets of reusable, interlocking, interoperating application components, such as JavaBeans and EJBs, at the client, application server, and/or database server tiers.

The day is soon coming when applications will completely merge and decompose into a spectral palette of capabilities applicable to any object (e.g., text, graphics, images, video, audio) on the user's computerized work surface. This will be truly document-oriented computing—and compound multimedia documents at that—as opposed to the traditional application-oriented paradigm with which most of us are familiar. Under the componentizing approach, developers have the ability to transform any or all three tiers—browser, application server, and data source—into containers for reusable objects, often referred to as "components." You may choose to run components only at the client tier—in the form of downloadable applets—or at the Web server and/or database tiers as well, wherever it is feasible to install the appropriate "virtual machine" software to handle such components. At the application server level, a persistent Java object is called a "servlet," provides the ability to extend the server's core function set, and requires a server-side JVM to run.

As noted previously, JavaBeans has established itself as one of the leading component technologies for Web applications. JavaBeans are reusable Java code modules that can be integrated and compiled into Java applications at any of the three tiers: client, application server, and data source. EJB extends the JavaBeans component model to support server-side applications with security, online transaction processing, database integration, and other scaleable enterprise functionality. Run-time interactions between JavaBeans across all tiers is enabled through Java's Remote Method Invocation (RMI) interface over either of two object-communications "wire protocols": the Java Remote Method Protocol (JRMP) or Internet Inter-ORB Protocol (IIOP).

JavaBeans' ascendancy is all for the best, since it focuses Web developers on a more cohesive set of mainstream component specifications for cross-platform applications. It also has spawned a fast-growing market for third-party JavaBeans that can be integrated with any development tool. In fact, most JavaBeans tools come bundled with Beans from the tool vendor and at least one outside Bean supplier. JavaBeans tools also generally allow users to import new Beans from any source they wish, or build their own Beans from scratch (or through modifications to existing Beans). Most JavaBeans tools provide visual, drag-and-drop palettes and wizards for laying, linking, and customizing Beans and associated business logic. These tools let you build and compile complex, ready-to-run applications with almost no original code.

Still, JavaBeans is not the only game in Web, desktop, and server component technologies. To the extent you already have COM components installed at various tiers in your network, you will have to concern yourself with bridging JavaBeans to those components via various object protocols. We'll continue to have to deal with JavaBeans-to-COM integration issues for the indefinite future, considering that COM is the principal component technology for the world's dominant computing environment, Microsoft Windows.

8.5 Object Technologies

Object technologies support distribution, interoperability, and portability of modular program code across the various networked tiers, including clients, application servers, and database servers. Leading object-computing standards include Common Object Request Broker Architecture, Component Object Model, and Distributed COM.

An object is a discrete unit of functionality that exposes its behaviors through a set of fully described communication interfaces. Object technologies may bind different applications across a network, on a single desktop, or both. Object-oriented computing supports flexible integration of images, documents, databases, executable software, and other digital items into compact, reusable application structures.

Object technologies use declarative interface specifications and separate these interfaces from implementation details on each network and operating environment. In this manner, object implementations can be replaced and updated without requiring changes to existing applications that rely on them.

Fully distributed object-oriented computing requires that identifiers and attributes of all executables and files be registered in a master network directory and maintained in repositories, ensuring that these items can be easily located and invoked when needed. A functional entity known as an object request broker supports the registry, directory, and locator functions in a network environment. Several competing, overlapping object-computing standards have been proposed, each of which defines APIs, ORB mechanisms, and repositories.

8.5.1 CORBA

The Object Management Group (OMG) vendor consortium's CORBA specification has been around since 1990 and has since achieved wider industry support than any other object architecture (though COM/DCOM has achieved greater installed base due to Windows's desktop ubiquity). CORBA provides high-level object "wrappers" that allow one application to locate and invoke data and functions internal to another application. CORBA 2.0 supports distributed objects and supports IIOP as its standard "wire protocol" for linking diverse applications objects.

CORBA's primary orientation is toward networked objects. In CORBA, an object is an independent software component providing a related set of behaviors for any other CORBA-enabled networked component. Most CORBA objects focus on networked interapplication communications with location independence, transport independence, and platform independence. CORBA objects operate across an arbitrarily scalable distributed network.

8.5.2 COM/DCOM

COM is Microsoft's object-computing framework and is an intrinsic component of the Windows operating systems. It allows any component created in a Windows application to be placed into an open document in another Windows application. COM serves as the basis for the object-oriented Windows 2000 file system. As necessary, COM redirects file operations to other object-oriented environments or to legacy file, document, database, and image environments.

COM is primarily for interapplication communications on a single Windows system, while DCOM is an extension to COM for cross-network Windows-to-Windows application interoperability. In COM/DCOM, an object is typically a subcomponent of a Windows application, exposing functionality to other parts of the application or to other applications. Reflecting its roots in Object Linking and Embedding (OLE) technology, COM primarily enables application-to-application interoperability on the same desktop through drag-and-drop, cut-and-paste, and other Windows GUI operations. DCOM is similar to CORBA in its orientation toward networked objects that may not be tied to a visual presentation paradigm.

In many ways, CORBA and COM/DCOM are semantically equivalent in their respective syntaxes, structures, and features. However, they have different ways of describing what an object is, how it is typically used, and how the components of the object model are organized.

8.6 Connector Technologies

Connector technologies support data access, consolidation, and integration from diverse information stores, including directories, relational databases, and ERP applications. Leading connector standards include Structured Query Language (SQL), Open Database Connectivity (ODBC), Java Database Connectivity (JDBC), and OLE DB. They support definition of either general-purpose data-sharing models or schemas or ad hoc information models common to incompatible applications.

To make data-driven three-tier applications practical, you need some way to connect tier 2 (application server) and tier 3 (database server) effectively for online transaction processing, using software that supports both your application server and database interfaces. This software must translate user information requests into queries that can be executed by the database, and return database results in a format that can be processed by the application server and delivered to the browser for display.

The most common Web server software interface specification is CGI, which allows developers to create Web pages that return data based on user input, calling a compiled C program or Perl script to access databases and other data sources. Though supported by all Web servers, CGI is inefficient and unsuitable for scalable Web/database applications. With CGI, a Web server must launch a new process every time it receives a request, a limitation that soon bogs down server processor, memory, and disk utilization when hundreds or thousands of simultaneous database transactions must be served.

A more scalable Web server interfacing approach is to use APIs provided by Web server vendors, an approach that, unfortunately, generally commits you to running the application on the respective vendors' Web server software. The principal Web server integration APIs are Microsoft's Internet Server API (ISAPI) and Netscape Server API (NSAPI), which provide shared executable libraries available to all applications running on the server.

The most common database server API is ODBC, which is supported by software drivers shipped with most commercial relational database management systems (RDBMSs). However, ODBC is increasingly taking a back seat to the upstart JDBC specification, which interfaces applications to databases by means of standard Java programming classes and methods. JDBC is supported in Sun's Java Development Kit, which is included in all commercial Java application development tools. JDBC drivers, written in Java, can be downloaded as part of an applet or installed permanently on a machine to bridge to existing database access libraries.

Your Web server applications and source databases will need to communicate either through matching "software drivers" configurations, such as ODBC-to-ODBC or JDBC-to-JDBC, or through "a software bridge" that converts from one driver standard to another, or to native software driver provided by RDBMS vendors. Most Java development tools support all of these "database connector" options and usually provide a run-time license to a RDBMS to support application development. Some "database connector" software requires that database driver and client software be installed on each client/browser accessing a particular RDBMS.

Depending on the number and variety of external databases accessed by your Web server, you may need to invest in middleware software that translates or "bridges" between any of several database drivers. This database bridging software is usually installed either at the Web server or database server. As more RDBMS vendors provide native JDBC drivers to match the JDBC drivers in Web browsers and servers, the need for this database bridging middleware will disappear.

Once you have this "data connection plumbing" figured out on your three-tier application, you can move into the business of integrating datastores with your Web servers. Most Web application development products provide sophisticated visual tools for importing, defining, dragging, dropping, and customizing data objects in Web applications. Enterprise-grade

Web development tools have rich database integration features on a par with the best in the industry, supporting visual creation of tables, stored procedures, triggers, and business rules, as well as testing, debugging, and tuning of SQL queries.

Developing an application involves determining where external data resides, defining connections to that data, building the applications, and defining real-time actions that the application server takes to request, retrieve, and process the data. Ideally, your application server should present to developers a single "resource model," in which there are resource connectors that support a single declarative and programmatic interface, and bind with multiple programming languages. These connectors would support access to all back-end datastores in a manner that is consistent across different RDBMSs, ERPs, transaction environments, filestores, and directories. They would also support both interactive and batch access to such data. The application server would expose declarative and programmatic interfaces (such as classes, methods, properties, APIs) to C, C++, Java, ECMAScript, Visual Basic, and other leading languages.

Performance is a must in high-volume EAI and EDI applications. Persistent data connections would free the application server from having to connect and disconnect continually when accessing external data stores. The application server should also support improved performance through multitasking, multithreading, and multiprocessing.

8.7 Transaction Technologies

Transaction technologies support reliable computing across distributed information stores, enabling administrators to recover quickly from system crashes without corrupting the cross-referential integrity of dispersed databases.

As you bring more distributed databases into your Web application, another layer of middleware to consider—essentially a fourth tier—is transaction services such as loosely coupled message brokering or distributed database transaction processing. Transaction technologies support processing of high-performance, scalable, secure, multiplatform, distributed enterprise transactions across networked data stores. They use server-based concurrency control, transaction logging, and rollback to safeguard the integrity of distributed databases in case a transaction is aborted and linked datastores need to be rolled back to their previous states.

Leading network-oriented transaction technologies fall into two categories: distributed transaction processing monitors (DTPMs) and message brokers.

8.7.1 Distributed Transaction Processing Monitors

DTPMs ensure that transactions are completed successfully, or that connected systems can be rolled back to their prior state if the end-to-end transaction is unsuccessful. DTPM technologies include Microsoft Transaction Server (MTS), BEA/Tuxedo, Transarc Encina, IBM TxSeries, IBM CICS, and Sun Java Transaction Services.

DTPMs coordinate rollbacks by directing individual applications' "resource manager" components that take part in distributed transactions. In order to participate in a DTPM environment, an application's resource manager must have an interface to the "transaction manager" component of the DTPM environment. The application must also keep records of data updates in a separate log or journal file. An application's transactional log file assigns a unique identifier to each transaction and describes precisely what data was input or modified in the transaction.

The DTPM manages transactions using a process known as "two-phase commit." The first phase in a transaction is when all applications report to the DTPM that they have succeeded in updating their respective databases. The second phase is when the DTPM interrogates each resource manager to see if it is prepared to commit changes from their log files to their persistent databases. If all resource managers report that they are prepared to commit, the DTPM orders all of them to commit changes, at which point that updated data is unlocked and made available to other transactions. If at any point in this process even one application's resource manager indicates that it has not updated its log file or is not prepared to commit, the DTPM orders all applications to cancel the transaction and roll back their databases to their prior states.

8.7.2 Message Brokers

Message brokering services, illustrated in Figure 8-4, enable distributed applications to communicate reliably over networks using messages. One or more sending applications can submit messages to one or more receiving applications, often through broadcast, multicast, or publish/subscribe mechanisms. Leading message-brokering products include Microsoft Message Queue Server (MSMQ), IBM MQ Series, TIBCO TIB/Rendezvous, Momentum X-IPC, BEA MessageQ, PeerLogic PIPES, and TIBCO.

Applications hand off messages to distributed message transaction management services, which route the messages and may or may not reformat or translate them for delivery to other applications. The message transaction management service ensures that messages are delivered in the proper order or priority. The environment also ensures reliable message delivery to intended recipients, by means of confirmations, receipts, or acknowledgments exchanged by applications. Message transaction managers support deferred

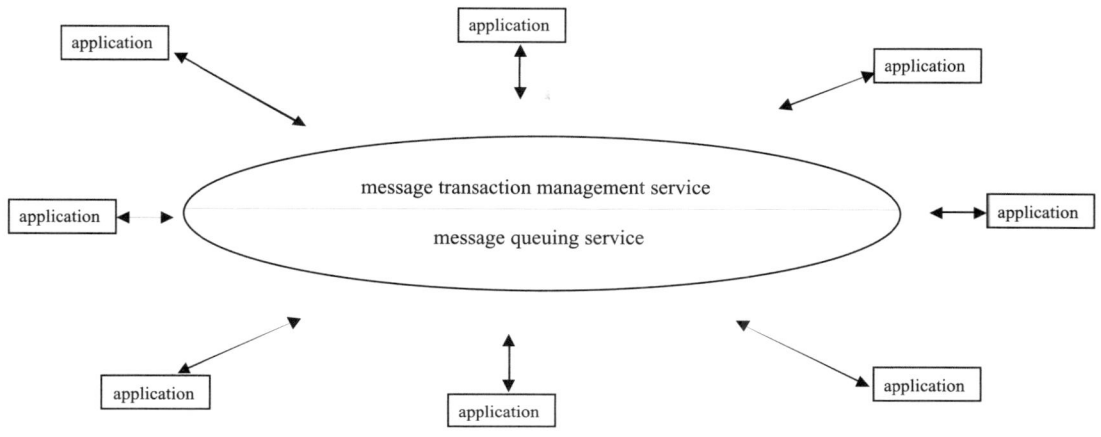

Figure 8-4: *Message-brokering services support message transaction management and queuing between diverse applications.*

message delivery among applications that may not all be online at the same time or continuously available.

Message transaction managers use a distributed queuing service that stores messages in queues at the sending application's end, at intermediate network nodes, and/or at the receiving application's end. Queues may be stored in memory or on disk at various network nodes. Transaction managers maintain message queues, manage relationships between applications and queues, handle network restarts, and move messages across the network. Transaction managers rely on underlying communications protocols, such as HTTP and TCP/IP, to move messages between applications.

As you roll out your BizTalk Server implementation, you will become intimately familiar with message brokering, DTPM, and other transactional technologies, especially Microsoft's MSMQ and MTS. Likewise, you will immerse yourself in Microsoft's Distributed interNetworking Architecture (DNA). We can map DNA standards, specifications, and technologies into the following categories:

- Markup: XML, HTML
- Development: Visual Basic, VBScript, Active Server Pages
- Object: COM, COM+, DCOM, Simple Object Access Protocol (SOAP)
- Connector: ActiveX Data Objects (ADO), OLE DB, ODBC
- Transaction: MTS, MSMQ

These technologies are Microsoft's glue for business process integration, as implemented in the BizTalk Server, Commerce Server, and the company's other products and services. You would use these technologies to craft EAI, extranet, and e-marketplace solutions in Microsoft's product architecture. We now proceed to Part 3, where we discuss the details of Microsoft's e-commerce products and services that implement the BizTalk Framework and the ONA technical architecture.

PART THREE

BIZTALK PRODUCTS AND SERVICES

This part discusses commercial BizTalk-enabled products and services that have been announced for availability in 2000. We focus on Microsoft's two-pronged strategy for rolling out BizTalk-enabled offerings: as server-based software products and as portal-based e-commerce services. We provide an in-depth discussion of Microsoft's BizTalk Server 2000 product and the company's roadmap for further development of this product and integration with Windows 2000, Windows DNA 2000 application server products, and other products and services.

Microsoft BizTalk Server 2000

BizTalk Server 2000 is the EDI and workflow integration center-piece of Microsoft's ambitious e-business architecture.

Microsoft has a two-pronged e-business product strategy, encompassing both server-based software and small-business-oriented online services. Microsoft's e-business software architecture revolves around the notion of "pipelines" or "channels," which are transactional workflows available to developers as Component Object Model (COM) objects from various programming languages. BizTalk Server 2000 is the "commerce interchange pipeline" component of Microsoft's server software strategy. Commerce Server 2000 is the "order processing pipeline" component.

Both of these products descend from a common predecessor—Site Server Commerce Edition version 3 (SSCE3)—which supported both the commerce-interchange and order-processing pipelines but lacked much of the functionality, scalability, and reliability found in the new generation of Windows 2000-based products. Microsoft has also upgraded existing Microsoft Server database, host integration, clustering, development, and administration products to support scalable e-business transactions.

Microsoft's commerce-related software products fall into several categories, as presented in Table 9-1.

In this chapter, we discuss BizTalk Server 2000 in functional and architectural detail and also present various deployment scenarios. We save our detailed discussions of other Microsoft commerce-related products and services for the subsequent chapters of Part 3. We save our discussion of Windows 2000 and its various features, components, and interfaces for Part Four. In that Part, we will discuss Active Directory, Microsoft Management Console (MMC), Distributed File Services, Distributed Security Services,

Table 9-1	*Microsoft Commerce-Related Software Products*
Layer	**Description**
Operating environment	Windows 2000 (as well as its predecessor, Windows NT 4.0)
Application server software	BizTalk Server 2000
	Commerce Server 2000 (as well as its and BizTalk Server 2000's common predecessor, SSCE3)
	SQL Server 2000 (as well as its predecessor, SQL Server 7.0)
	Host Integration Server 2000 (as well as its predecessor, SNA Server 4.0)
Development tools	BizTalk Server Software Development Kit (SDK)
	Visual Studio
	Visio-based visual workflow/"orchestration" design and modeling tool (as yet unnamed when this book was published)
Administration tools	BizTalk Management Desk
	BizTalk Server Administration Console
	Commerce Desk
	Application Center 2000

Distributed Component Object Model (DCOM), Distributed interNetworking Architecture (DNA), Microsoft Transaction Server (MTS), Message Queue Server (MSMQ), COM, COM+, Active Server Pages (ASP), and Simple Object Access Protocol (SOAP).

9.1 BizTalk Server's Role in Microsoft's Application Server Family

BizTalk Server 2000 is the interchange server component of Microsoft's commerce strategy. BizTalk Server 2000's purpose is to integrate applications within the enterprise and between businesses through structured interchange of structured documents. It is, in effect, the functional middleman or middleware in B2B and EAI interchanges (to reintroduce the dominant theme from Chapter 6).

In Figure 9-1, we show BizTalk Server 2000 in the context of Microsoft's core commerce-related products and services. In Figure 9-2, we distinguish its role from those of Microsoft's other commerce-related application server products.

BizTalk Server 2000 provides interchange-processing services to Microsoft applications (such as other Microsoft Server application servers) and non-Microsoft applications (such as ERP and CRM systems). BizTalk Server 2000 provides a rule-driven workflow engine (which Microsoft calls an "orchestration engine") that allows applications to interchange BizTalk Messages, plus their component BizTalk Documents and Business Documents, with one another. It also routes and processes EDI and other file formats that are not wrapped in BizTalk envelopes. The server integrates with other applications through various transport protocols, message brokering services, object brokering services, data access interfaces, and other technologies. It may be deployed within an intranet, extranet, or Internet-based EDI or EAI environment. Developers define BizTalk workflow routes, rules,

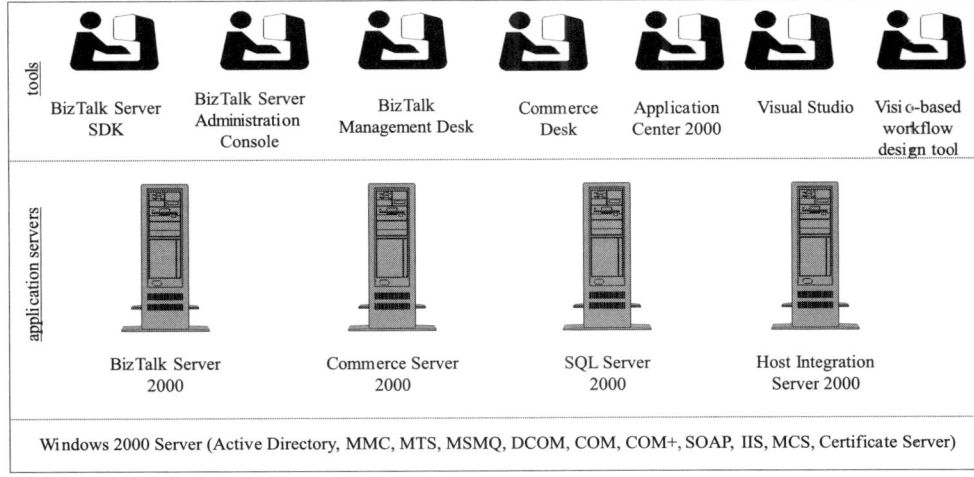

Figure 9-1 *Microsoft's e-commerce-related products and services include BizTalk Server 2000, Commerce Server 2000, other application servers, development tools, administration tools, and MSN commerce services.*

and roles with a combination of tools, including BizTalk Management Desk, the BizTalk SDK, and/or a Visio-based visual flowcharting tool. The visual flowcharting tool outputs process definition files in Microsoft's proprietary "XLANG" schema, which drives execution of workflows within one or more networked BizTalk Servers. Administrators can monitor those workflows with the BizTalk Server Administration Console.

BizTalk Server 2000's core functions fall into three categories: application integration, content processing, and service management. Application integration involves defining the mapping, processing, and routing services to be performed for various data types. It also involves maintaining profiles of trading partners and their associated technical-integration requirements. Content processing involves validating, translating, transforming, encoding, encrypting, signing, routing, storing, forwarding, and delivering messages and documents efficiently and reliably. Service management involves configuring, monitoring, and controlling an end-to-end BizTalk server implementation, including all software and hardware components.

We present BizTalk Server 2000's primary functions in Table 9-2 and Figure 9-3.

Implementing, monitoring, and administering BizTalk Server 2000 requires several Microsoft software tools, presented in Table 9-3 and Figure 9-4.

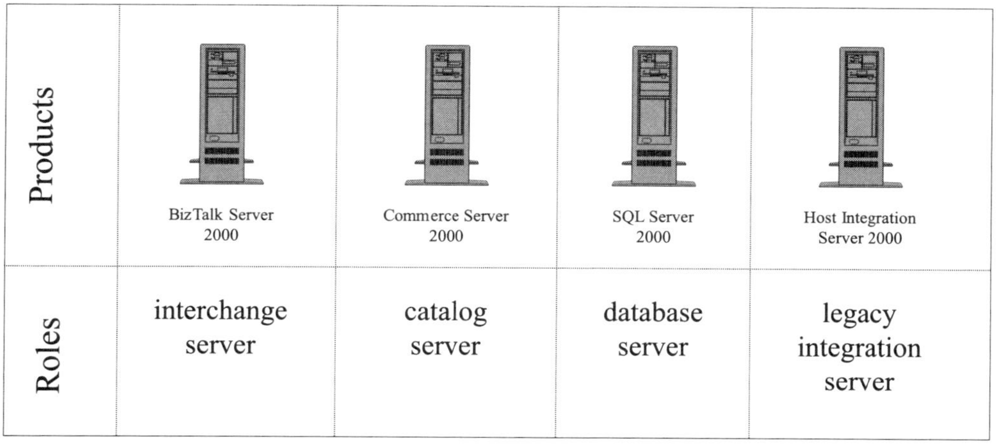

	BizTalk Server 2000	Commerce Server 2000	SQL Server 2000	Host Integration Server 2000
Products				
Roles	interchange server	catalog server	database server	legacy integration server

Figure 9-2   *Microsoft's e-commerce-related application servers support interchange, catalog, database, and legacy connectivity, functionality.*

Table 9-2	*BizTalk Server 2000's Primary Functions*
Category	**Description**
Application integration	Connecting, integrating, mapping, and translating between applications' various EDI formats, XML schemas, transport protocols, object brokers, message brokers, transaction monitors, data query interfaces, ERP and CRM applications, and file formats
	Defining schema mappings between data elements in source and destination documents
	Defining and maintaining trading partner, application, and security profiles
	Defining and maintaining trading partner agreements for data interchange
	Modeling document routing and processing workflows between applications and organizations
Content processing	Receiving incoming data items, parsing them, and validating their structural and semantic integrity
	Transforming data items between source and destination formats according to predefined schema mappings
	Supporting digital signatures, confidentiality, integrity, and nonrepudiation services on data items through integration with public key infrastructure
	Storing data items and tracking information locally
	Queuing inbound and outbound data items, pending further processing and routing
	Routing and delivering outbound data items, reliably to their intended recipients
Service management	Implementing, configuring, administering, and troubleshooting BizTalk Servers, receive and transmit services, shared queues, and document-tracking databases within server groups
	Monitoring and administering document routing and processing pipelines or workflows between applications and organizations
	Tracking and analyzing data on interchanges

We now describe each of BizTalk Server 2000's core functions in greater detail, explaining the role for each of these tools in the context most appropriate to each. We will save our discussion of Application Center 2000 for Chapter 11.

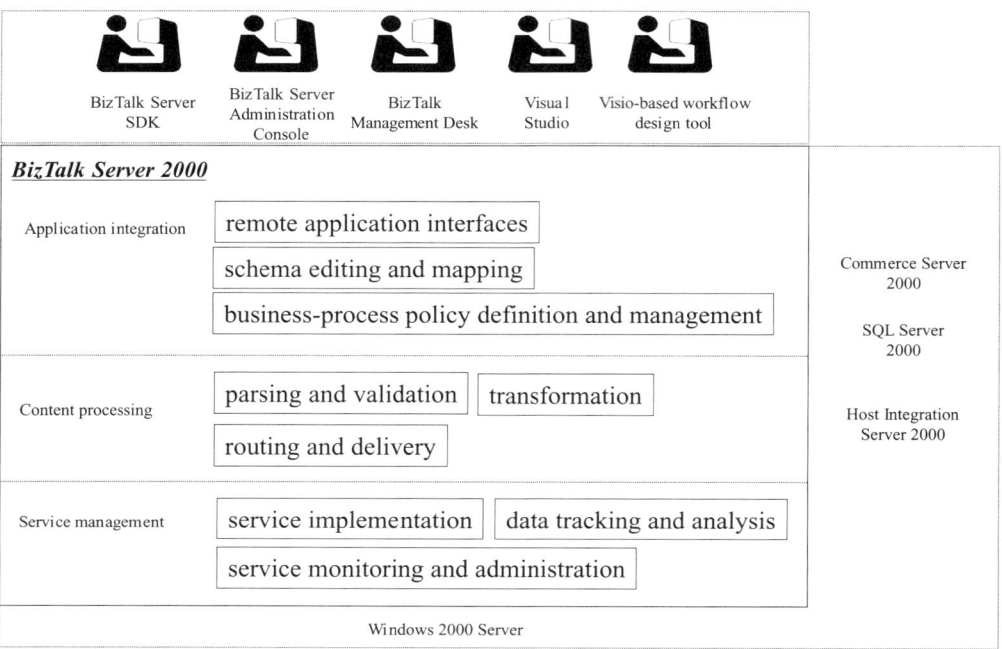

Figure 9-3   *BizTalk Server 2000 supports integration with enterprise and trading partner applications, rule-based content processing and security, and management of B2B and EAI services.*

Table 9-3   *Microsoft's E-commerce-Related Development and Administration Tools*

Tool	Description
BizTalk Server SDK	Provides programmatic access to BizTalk Server 2000 functionality, supports integration of external applications with the server, and supports extension of server functionality.
BizTalk Server Administration Console	Supports configuration, operation, optimization, and administration of BizTalk Server 2000 and associated databases, queues, transmit and receive components, and other features.
BizTalk Management Desk	Supports administration of organizations, agreements, documents, maps, envelopes, and tracking on BizTalk Server 2000. It includes the BizTalk XML schema editing and mapping tools.
Visual Studio	Microsoft's popular development toolkit that supports building of rich COM, COM+, and DNA applications using Visual Basic, C++, and Java.
Visio-based workflow design and modeling tool	Tool (as yet unnamed when this book was published) for defining visual workflow process maps.
Application Center 2000	Tool for integrated management of BizTalk Server 2000 and other Microsoft application servers as components of a scalable Web-farm deployment.

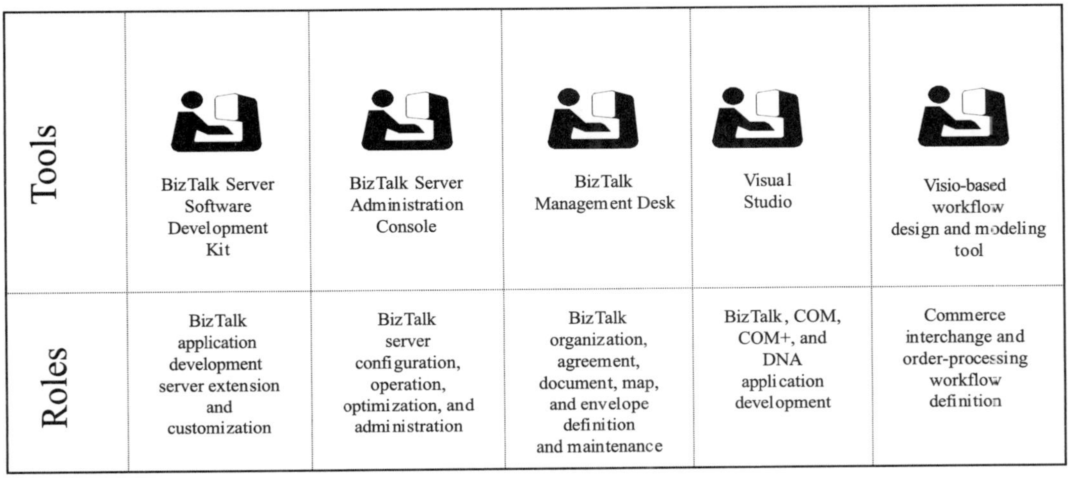

Tools	BizTalk Server Software Development Kit	BizTalk Server Administration Console	BizTalk Management Desk	Visual Studio	Visio-based workflow design and modeling tool
Roles	BizTalk application development server extension and customization	BizTalk server configuration, operation, optimization, and administration	BizTalk organization, agreement, document, map, and envelope definition and maintenance	BizTalk, COM, COM+, and DNA application development	Commerce interchange and order-processing workflow definition

Figure 9-4 *Microsoft provides a range of development and administration tools for BizTalk Server 2000.*

9.2 Application Integration

Application integration involves defining the parsing, mapping, processing, and routing services to be performed for various data types, as well as maintaining profiles of trading partners and their associated technical integration requirements.

Microsoft provides a software developer's kit for integrating third-party applications programmatically with BizTalk Server 2000. This kit enables third-party developers to implement the following levels of application integration:

- Enable applications to exchange business documents with BizTalk Server 2000 via direct programmatic calls and/or application integration connectors
- Allow applications to exchange trading partner agreement information with BizTalk Server 2000 by the same programmatic means
- Develop components to extend BizTalk Server 2000's pipeline features, such as translation, digital signature and verification, encryption/decryption, parsing, and transport functionality
- Develop components to extend BizTalk Server 2000's auditing and tracking features
- Extend the mapping capabilities of BizTalk Management Desk

We can divide application integration into the following broad function sets:

- Remote application interfaces
- Schema editing and mapping
- Business process policy definition and management

9.2.1 Remote Application Interfaces

As we noted in Chapter 8, BizTalk Server 2000 provides an EDI/EAI software-adaptability layer with translators, adapters, and other components that support transparent communications among otherwise incompatible remote applications.

Microsoft overstates its case when it claims that BizTalk Server 2000 interfaces to "any format" and "any protocol," since the product is notable for its lack of support for the Common Object Request Broker Architecture (CORBA) and Internet Inter-ORB Protocol (IIOP), which compete with Microsoft's Distributed COM (DCOM). It also lacks built-in adapters for many vertical-market EDI formats, ERP and CRM file formats, legacy transport protocols, message brokers, transaction monitors, and competing XML-based B2B interoperability formats. Microsoft says it is considering including interfaces for competing B2B standards such as cXML and OAGIS, but, as of the date this book was published, had not yet committed to this course of action.

Nevertheless, BizTalk Server 2000 does interface to a broad range of content formats and middleware environments and parses the data output by these various sources. Microsoft provides a software development kit for building additional transport, parser, and serializer components for BizTalk Server 2000. The server has application interfaces, or "connectors," to the formats and environments shown in Table 9-4 and Figure 9-5.

BizTalk Server 2000's connectors support various receive and transport (or send) services. Supported receive services are described in Table 9-5 and transport services in Table 9-6. Note that BizTalk Server 2000 does not support transport or receive interfaces to traditional X.25 EDI value-added networks (VANs); instead, it relies on IP-based internetworking protocols.

Development of hubbed e-marketplaces, extranets, and EAI depends on tight interfaces with ERP, CRM, sales force automation, and other line-of-business applications. BizTalk Server 2000 includes an Application Integration Connector (AIC) that uses DCOM to communicate with SAP's popular R/3 ERP product. Other ERP software developers have committed to integrating their product with BizTalk Server 2000. These vendors will provide complete packages including AICs, document schemas, and maps.

Each BizTalk Server 2000 deployment is a unique assortment of connectors to a range of Microsoft, third-party, and custom applications. Figure 9-6 shows a hypothetical BizTalk Server 2000 deployment in which the server receives and transmits data in a wide range of formats, including BizTalk

Table 9-4		*BizTalk Server 2000's Interfaces to Remote Applications via Various Content Types and Middleware Protocols*

Category	Subcategory	Connectors
Content types	EDI formats	ANSI X12, EDIFACT
	XML schemas	XML-based document templates, well-formed XML, XML Data Reduced, cXML (considering), OAGIS (considering), OTP (considering), ICE (considering), OBI (considering), RosettaNet (considering)
	Data access	ADO recordsets persisted as XML, OLE DB
	ERP/CRM applications	SAP, Baan, PeopleSoft, JD Edwards, Great Plains Software, Navision, others
	Other file formats	HTML, structured document formats, delimited flat file, positional flat file, fax (outbound only)
Middleware protocols	Transport protocols	HTTP, SMTP, local file system, SNA/LU6.2/APPC (via gateway in Host Integration Server 2000)
	Message brokers	MSMQ, MQ Series (via bridge in Host Integration Server 2000)
	Object brokers	DCOM
	Remote procedure calls	SOAP
	Transaction monitors	MTS, CICS (via COM-TI in Host Integration Server 2000), IMS (via COM-TI Host Integration Server 2000)
	Content security	HTTP/S, SSL, S/MIME

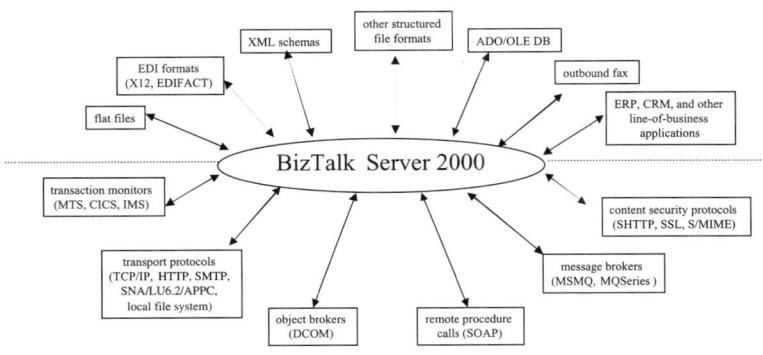

Figure 9-5		*BizTalk Server 2000 includes remote application connectors for various content types and middleware protocols, enabling the server to map, translate, and route items between diverse applications under EDI and EAI scenarios.*

Table 9-5	BizTalk Server 2000's Receive Services
Receive Service	**Description**
File	Polls files based on activity in the source directory. It copies files from this directory and submits them to BizTalk Server 2000.
HTTP	ASP containing scripts that perform two functions: retrieving files posted by source applications and submitting those files to BizTalk Server 2000. Applications may use BizTalk Server 2000's HTTP receive service to submit documents when the application can perform an HTTP POST but cannot use COM to call BizTalk Server.
SMTP	Extracts files from interchanges posted to a predetermined e-mail address and submits them to BizTalk Server 2000.
MSMQ	Extracts files from an MSMQ queue and submits them to BizTalk Server 2000. MSMQ is a communication infrastructure for Windows 2000 that enables applications to communicate across heterogeneous networks and with computers that may be offline. The MSMQ receive service runs continuously and is configured to poll the queue to which the business application saves the file.
DCOM	Receives files from another application that has been configured with a DCOM client.

Table 9-6	BizTalk Server 2000's Transport Services
Transport Service	**Description**
File	Places a file in a path on the Windows 2000 distributed file system from which a target application can retrieve it.
HTTP	ASP that performs two functions: retrieving a file posted by BizTalk Server 2000 and posting the file to an HTTP location at a URL from which the target application or user can download it. Applications may use BizTalk Server 2000's HTTP transport service to retrieve document from BizTalk Server when the application can perform an HTTP GET but cannot use COM to call BizTalk Server.
SMTP	Transmits the file as a body part in an e-mail message over an SMTP backbone to an inbox from which the target application or user can retrieve it.
MSMQ	Posts the file to an MSMQ queue from which the target application can retrieve it.
DCOM	Transmits the file to another application that has been configured with DCOM client software.
Fax	Transmits the file to a fax device from which the target application or user can retrieve it.

Messages/Documents, X12, EDIFACT, flat and hierarchical files, ERP and CRM file formats, ADO recordsets, and well-formed XML. As this graphic shows, BizTalk Server 2000 is able to receive and transmit all these file types over any supported protocol or middleware technology.

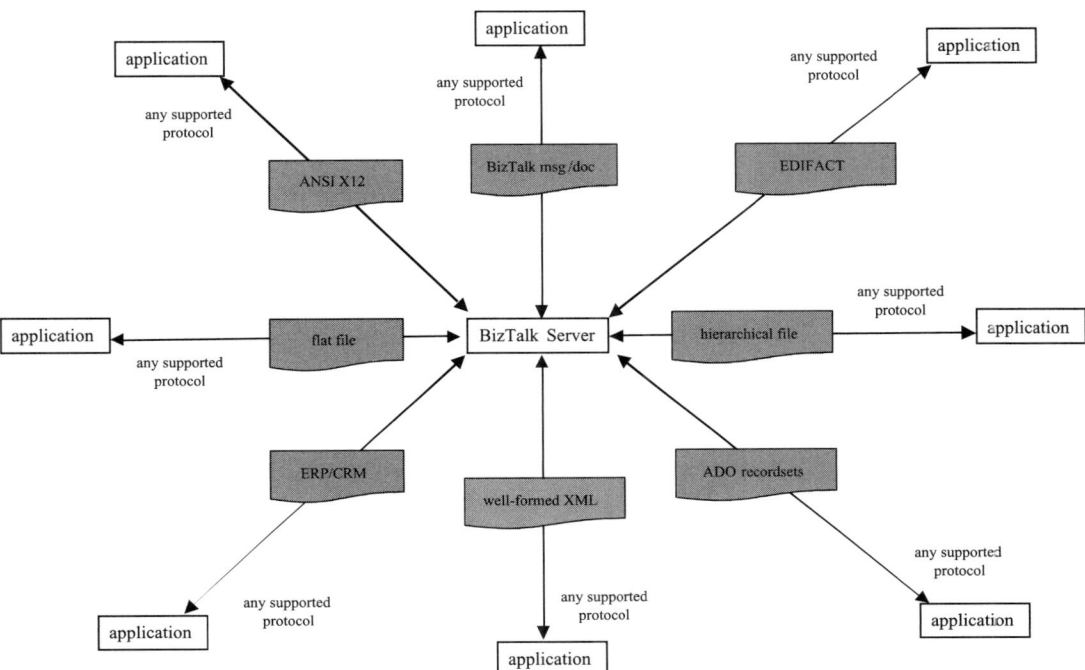

Figure 9-6 *BizTalk Server 2000 supports application-to-application interoperability at the data-sharing level among trading partners and applications that produce and consume various document formats, such as those in this hypothetical deployment scenario.*

Figure 9-7 presents a slightly different take on the same any-to-any flexibility in BizTalk Server 2000. This hypothetical configuration shows the range of transport protocols for which BizTalk Server 2000 provides connectors, including HTTP, SMTP, SNA, and TCP/IP. BizTalk Server can also exchange files with applications over the Windows 2000 distributed file system. Any supported file type can flow over any of these protocols.

Figure 9-8 shows yet another layer of application-to-application interoperability that BizTalk Server 2000 supports, this time on the middleware level. Essentially, BizTalk Server operates as a "superbroker" that (in conjunction with Host Integration Server 2000) enables some level of data-sharing interoperability between applications that implement various approaches to object brokering (DCOM), message brokering (MSMQ, MQSeries), remote procedure calls (SOAP), and distributed transaction processing (MTS, CICS, etc.).

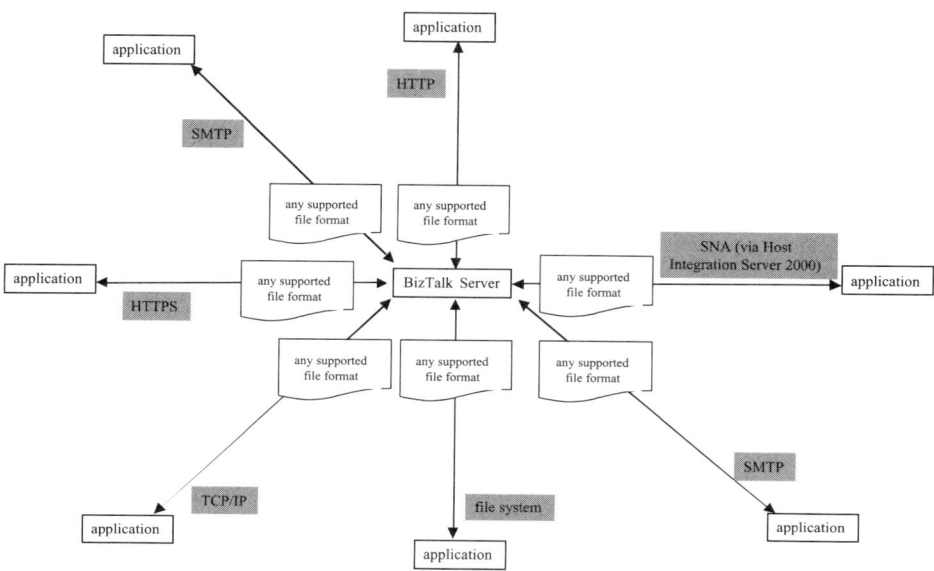

BizTalk Server 2000 supports application-to-application interoperability at the data-sharing level among trading partners and applications that implement various transport protocols, such as those in this hypothetical deployment scenario.

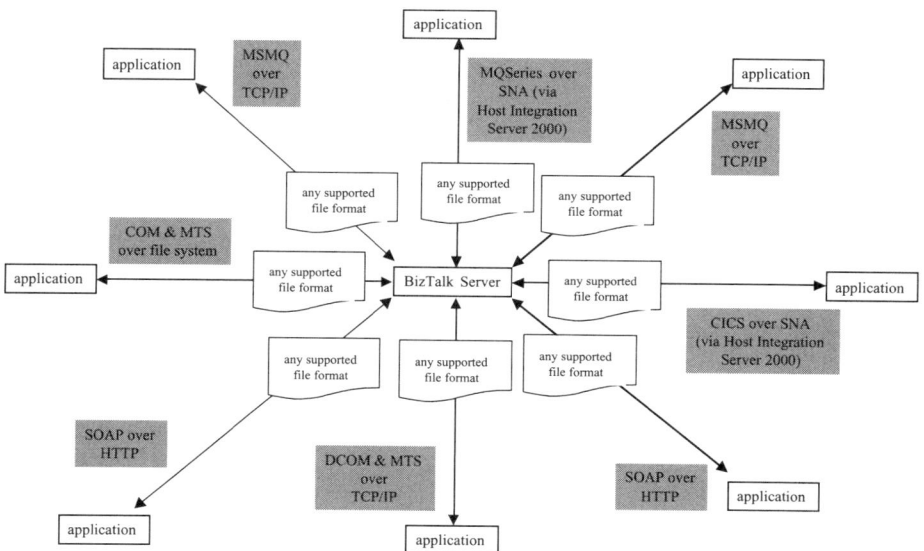

BizTalk Server 2000 supports application-to-application interoperability at the data-sharing level among trading partners and applications that implement various middleware technologies, such as those in this hypothetical deployment scenario.

9.2.2 Schema Editing and Mapping

It's not enough to simply receive, parse, and validate data fed in from multiple applications, though BizTalk Server 2000 supports these functions well. End-to-end EDI and EAI interoperability also depends on flexible mapping, transformation, and translation of data between various document information models—also known as schemas—and between various application file formats.

Content transformation is a core feature of BizTalk Server 2000. When companies interface their ERP and other line-of-business applications through BizTalk Server 2000, they define business documents' logical data structures and specify automated data transformation procedures by means of two Microsoft tools: BizTalk Editor and BizTalk Mapper. These utilities, accessed through the BizTalk Management Desk tool set, allow programmers to define how BizTalk Server 2000 transforms and translates the content of incoming documents prior to routing them to destination applications and trading partners.

BizTalk Editor allows programmers to build, modify, and inspect XML schema specifications, for the purpose of defining element-level schema-to-schema correspondences. The tool interprets a document's structure as a set of records and fields. It presents the document's structure visually under a "tree control" view and provides a detailed property view that allows users to edit all the records and fields contained in a document specification. The tool allows developers to automatically create a BizTalk Framework-compliant XML Data Reduced (XDR) schema that describes the document's structure and contents. It also allows developers to publish the schemas they create to schema repositories on the Web, such as BizTalk.org, and to corporate repositories on intranets or extranets.

Figure 9-9 shows a screen from BizTalk Management Desk's BizTalk Editor.

BizTalk Editor allows developers to build new XML document schema specifications in any of three ways (described in Table 9-7 and illustrated in Figure 9-10).

Table 9-8 lists some of the many EDI transaction sets and XML-based business documents from which developers can automatically build schema specifications in BizTalk Editor.

Once developers have defined XML schema specifications for business documents, they can use the BizTalk Mapper tool to define element-level correspondences between one schema specification and another. Developers can graphically depict structural-transformation relationships—in other words, "maps"—between source-specification data elements and destination-specification data elements. Developers build maps with simple visual links and with on-screen palettes of "functoids" and other programming objects. Consequently, maps provide instructions that define relationships between two different specification formats.

Table 9-7	Approaches to Creating New XML Document Schema Specifications Under BizTalk Editor
Approach	**Description**
From an existing XML schema specification	Developers can use existing XML schema specifications, including those they created with BizTalk Editor, as the basis for building new specifications. Doing so is a straightforward process of three steps. First, duplicate the structure of the existing document, including its root node and all records, fields, and property values. Second, modify the document's structure, as displayed in the BizTalk Editor's document-tree pane, by adding, deleting, moving, copying, or modifying records and fields. Finally, modify or specify new property values for the remaining records and fields. BizTalk Editor allows schemas to be retrieved, via WebDAV, from the BizTalk.org repository.
From an existing well-formed XML document instance	Developers can use some existing well-formed XML document types as the basis for generating XML schema specifications in BizTalk Editor. When BizTalk Editor imports a document instance, the tool infers the document's logical data structure and then creates a BizTalk Framework-compliant schema for it (XML Data Reduced compliant currently, and XML Schema compliant, Microsoft says, as soon as that specification becomes a ratified W3C standard).
From a blank specification that contains no logical data structure	Developers can also build custom XML schema specifications by starting with a template that has only a root node and no records or fields. When using a blank specification to create XML document schemas, BizTalk Editor provides the developer with several template options. These options include X12 and EDI-FACT transaction sets and several common, logical, XML-based document templates, such as purchase orders, invoices, and advance shipping notices. For EDI documents, the developers select the standard (ANSI X12 or UN EDIFACT), version (such as ANSI X12 version 4010), and type of transaction set (such as ANSI X12 4010 Type 850 purchase orders). Alternately, developers can base their schemas on flat files, such as hierarchical, delimited, or positional files. Building the specification usually involves adding new records and fields to the template and specifying their property values, or deleting existing records and fields from the template.

Figure 9-11 shows a screen from BizTalk Management Desk's BizTalk Mapper.

Maps, stored as Extensible Stylesheet Language Transformation (XSLT) files, drive BizTalk Server 2000's transformation engine in transforming document content from one structural form to another for both EDI and EAI applications. Indeed, maps are the pivot upon which trading partners exchange structured data with a common understanding of its business semantics. Figure 9-12 shows how BizTalk Mapper facilitates creation of source-to-destination structural mappings among XML schemas.

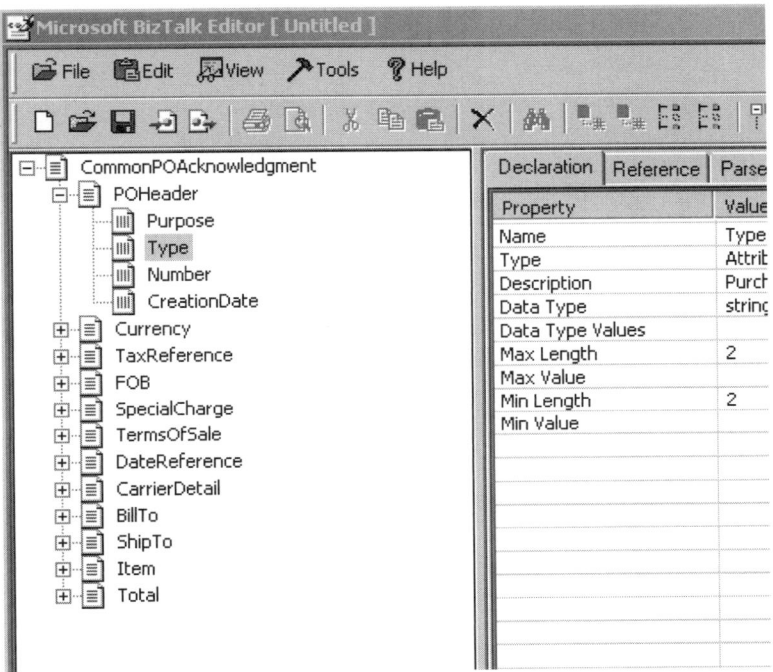

Figure 9-9 *A screen from BizTalk Management Desk's BizTalk Editor.*

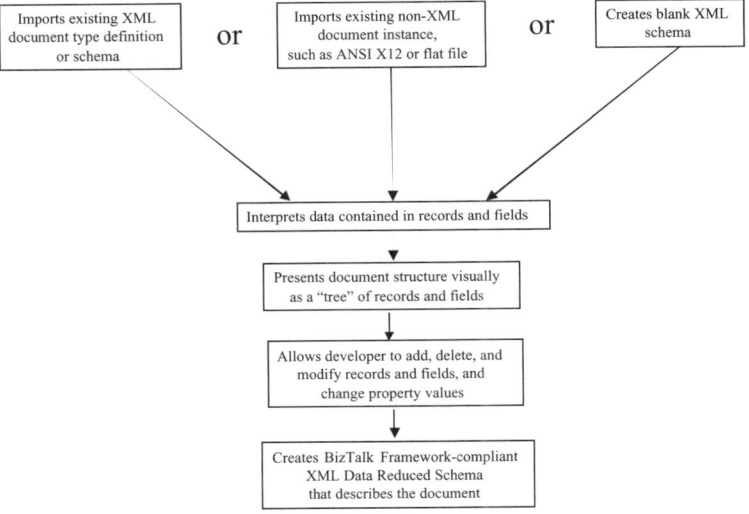

Figure 9-10 *BizTalk Editor supports three approaches for developers to create XML document schema specifications.*

Table 9-8 EDI Transaction Set or Document Templates Available in BizTalk Editor

Standard	Standard Version	Transaction Sets or Documents
X12	2040 3010 3050 4010	214 Shipment Status Message 810 Invoice 813 Tax Return Data 816 Organizational Relationships 824 Application Advice 832 Price/Sales Catalog 838 Trading Partner Profile 846 Inventory Inquiry/Advice 850 Purchase Order 852 Product Activity Data 855 Purchase Order Acknowledgment 856 Advance Ship Notice 861 Receiving Advice 864 Text Message 867 Product Transfer and Resale Report 940 Warehouse Shipping Order 944 Warehouse Stock Transfer Receipt Advice 945 Warehouse Shipping Advice 997 Functional Acknowledgment
UN/EDIFACT	D93 D97	CONTRL DESADV GDMVMT INVOIC INVRPT ORDERS ORDRSP PARTIN PAYEXT SLSRPT
XML	N/A	Purchase Order Purchase Requisition Invoice Advanced Ship Notice Catalog Whole Catalog Update Trading Partner Information Request Trading Partner Information Trading Partner Certificate Request Trading Partner Certificate Product Information Request Product Information Price Request Price Inventory Request Inventory Customs Information Manifest

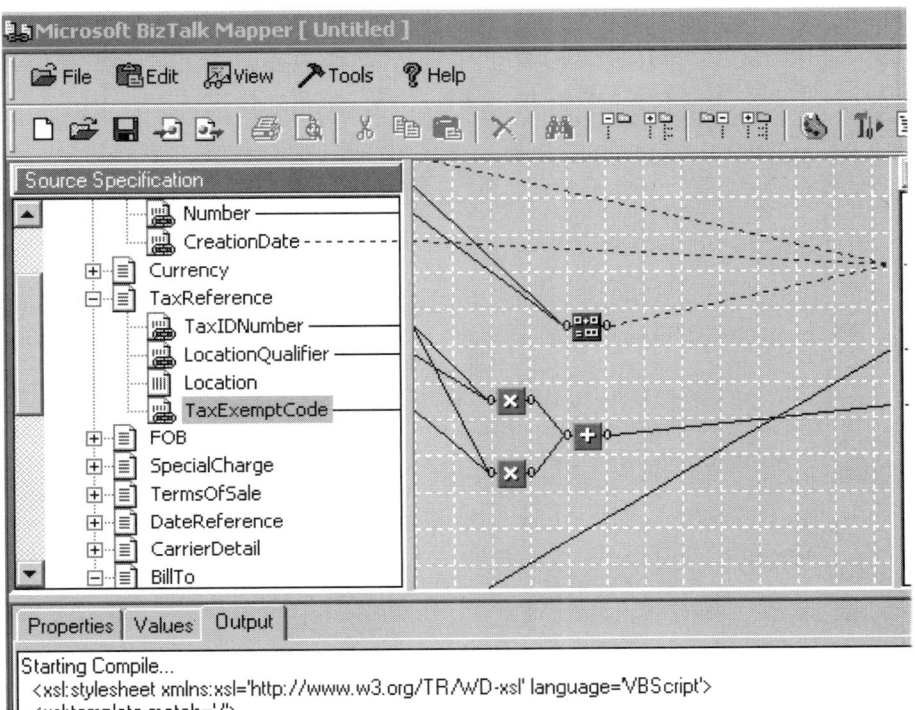

Figure 9-11   *A screen from BizTalk Management Desk's BizTalk Mapper.*

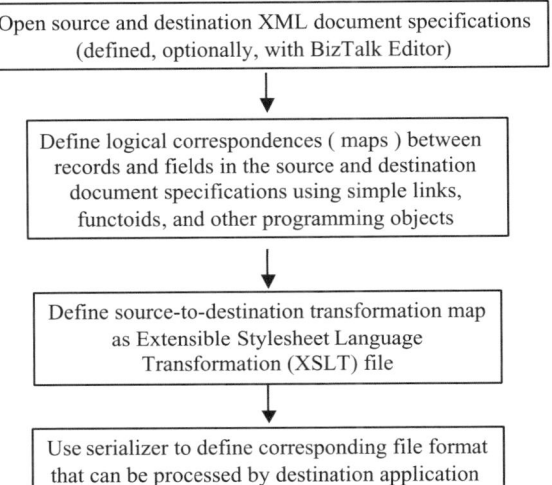

Figure 9-12   *BizTalk Mapper enables developers to map data structures between source and destination XML schemas.*

At run time, BizTalk Server 2000 uses the outputs of the mapper to direct the transformation of incoming and outgoing documents to and from BizTalk-Framework-compliant XML schemas. A "parser" program in BizTalk Server 2000 manages the parallel, but separate task, of translating incoming documents from application-specific file formats into XML syntax so that the server can map the documents to logical data structures required by the destination application. A corresponding "serializer" program in BizTalk Server 2000 manages the equally important task of translating the outgoing, mapped XML document into an application-specific file format understood by the destination application (an important feature, considering that not all applications are XML-enabled—yet).

Structural transformations take place between two XML representations of the same data, distinguishing the transformation process from the closely related process of translating content into and out of XML-based application file formats. By using XML to describe data structures in a general way, BizTalk Server can translate documents to both XML and non-XML business document formats consistently, depending on what formats destination applications can consume. Figure 9-13 shows the map-driven translations and transformations that BizTalk Server 2000 performs on a typical inbound BizTalk Message and the contents of its constituent BizTalk Document.

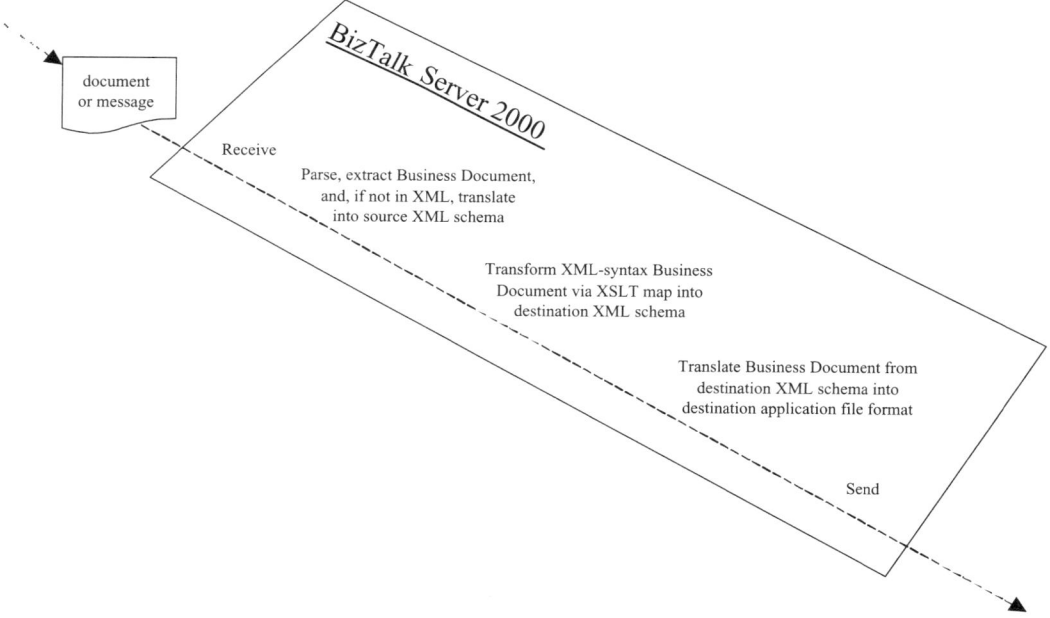

Figure 9-13 *BizTalk Server 2000 performs map-driven translations and transformations on inbound messages and documents.*

9.2.3 Business Process Policy Definition and Management

Trading partners are sources and destinations for structured business documents. Agreements between trading partners define the policies that govern B2B workflows.

BizTalk Management Desk is Microsoft's primary tool for managing definitions of trading partners and the agreements that bind trading partners into supply chains. As such, BizTalk Management Desk is a critical component of the BizTalk Server 2000 product, producing the B2B policy-driven specifications that guide the total BizTalk-enabled EDI and workflow environment. We've already discussed two BizTalk Management Desk components: BizTalk Editor and BizTalk Mapper. We now present these features in the context of BizTalk Management Desk's full business-process policy-management functionality.

We describe BizTalk Management Desk's principal business-process policy management modules in Table 9-9 and Figure 9-14.

DOCUMENTS

Document management, in this context, refers to the ability to define XML document schema specifications, a function that BizTalk Editor supports. Business processes require policies regarding the semantic scope and meaning of various documents, records, fields, and other elements. XML-formatted Business Documents are the basic entities that BizTalk Server 2000 translates, transforms, routes, and processes.

Table 9-9	BizTalk Management Desk Business-Process Policy Definition and Management Modules
Module	**Description**
Documents	Supports definition, modification, and inspection of XML document schema specifications
Maps	Supports definition of element-level correspondences between one XML schema specification and another
Envelopes	Supports definition of the source, destination, workflow, encoding, contents, schemas, maps, transport parameters, and security parameters associated with a business document
Organizations	Supports creation and management of organizations and groups that engage in electronic data interchanges
Agreements (also known as "ports")	Supports definition and management of relationships and methods of electronic data interchanges among two or more organizations
Tracking	Supports tracking of documents that pass through BizTalk Server in batches or singly and records-processing activity against those documents

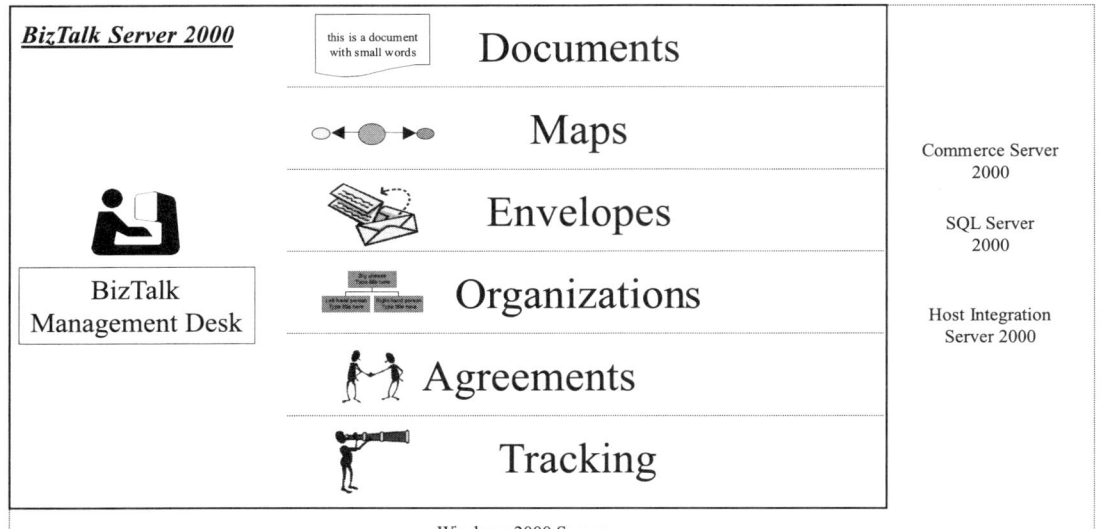

Figure 9-14 *BizTalk Management Desk modules support policy administration on documents, maps, envelopes, organizations, agreements, and tracking under BizTalk Server 2000.*

MAPS

Map management refers to the ability to define element-level correspondences between XML document schema specifications, a function supported by BizTalk Mapper. Business processes require policies that lay out tables of correspondence between data elements used in different documents, forms, applications, functions, and organizations. BizTalk Server 2000 may map one Business Document schema into another in order to interface the otherwise incompatible data models of diverse trading partner and line-of-business applications.

ENVELOPES

Envelope management refers to the ability to define the Business Document payload of a BizTalk Message, as well as define the data in the headers of the BizTalk Message and BizTalk Document. Business processes require policies that spell out the channels through which documents flow. Policies also define the processing and handling of this data at every step in the process. As we saw in Chapter 1, workflow parameters ride in the nested headers of the transport envelope, BizTalk Message envelope, and BizTalk Document envelope that contain a Business Document. Workflow-relevant data also resides in the body of Business Documents. BizTalk Management Desk provides tools for defining envelope parameters and payloads to be processed by BizTalk Server 2000 and BizTalk-enabled applications.

BizTalk Management Desk's Envelopes module enables developers to create and manage electronic envelopes for routing EDI and EAI documents. Defining a BizTalk Message envelope involves specifying the properties presented in Table 9-10.

Table 9-10	*BizTalk Management Desk Envelope Definition Properties*
Property	**Description**
Envelope name	The only required envelope property under BizTalk Management Desk. Creating an envelope involves giving it a unique name. The envelope's name is the only property exposed when selecting a trading partner agreement under BizTalk Management Desk. The name should indicate the properties of the envelope, such as the document being transmitted, the direction of transmission, and the source and/or destination organization. One example of an envelope name would be "X12 4010 850 Outbound to Skeemco." BizTalk Management Desk requires that envelope names not contain such reserved characters as the greater-than, less-than, ampersand, double-quote, and single-quote signs.
Envelope direction	Specifies whether the envelope is inbound to BizTalk Server 2000, outbound, or flowing in both directions. When specifying an envelope direction of inbound or outbound, developers should define that direction with respect to their organization. When importing an envelope created by a trading partner, developers should keep in mind that the indicated direction on the imported envelope will be in relation to the partner organization (and should be reversed to reflect the direction with respect to one's own organization). For envelopes using the industry standard EDI formats of X12 or EDIFACT, developers may specify that they can be sent in both directions.
Envelope format	Specifies the format of the envelope, or, rather, the type of Business Document contained in the envelope. Only one type of Business Document can be contained in a BizTalk Document envelope. BizTalk Management Desk supports the following options for this property: X12 (default), EDIFACT, custom XML, flat file, and custom. If a developer chooses X12, EDIFACT, or custom formats, he or she will need to specify any delimiters to be used. X12 delimiters include component element separator, element separator, and segment terminator. EDIFACT delimiters include component element separator, element separator, release indicator, and segment terminator.
Custom envelope schema	Specifies the schema used for a custom-defined envelope.
Version	Specifies the version of the schema within a custom-defined envelope.
Export in organization	Specifies if the envelope's receive location should be included when exporting one's own organizational definition for use by a trading partner. The options are no (default) and yes.

Table 9-10	BizTalk Management Desk Envelope Definition Properties (cont.)
Property	**Description**
Source organization identifier	Specifies the organization identifier for the organization that is the source of a document. The default setting for this property is the organization identifier that has been set as the default for the source organization.
Destination organization identifier	Specifies the organization identifier for the organization that is the destination of a document. The default setting for this property is the organization identifier that has been set as the default for the destination organization.
Transport mode	Specifies whether and how documents should be transmitted after they have been processed in BizTalk Server 2000. The options are auto, custom, and none. Auto, the default option, specifies that BizTalk Server 2000 will use the transport type associated with the receive location of the destination organization. A value of "custom" indicates that the developer will manually configure a transport component; it also activates the transport service property, which enables developers to choose a transport service component. A value of "none" specifies that BizTalk Server 2000 should process the documents but not transmit them.
Transport service	Specifies which transport service component BizTalk Server 2000 should use to transmit and receive the envelope. The options include "SendFAX," "SendHTTP," "SendHTTPS," "SendLocalFile," "SendMSMQ," "SendSMTP," and "PipeToPipeTransfer." This property is active only when the transport-mode property is set to "custom."
Batch	Specifies whether and how BizTalk Server 2000 should batch documents. The default option, "no," specifies that the BizTalk Server 2000 should not batch documents, and that each document will be transmitted individually when the server has finished processing it. A setting of "yes" specifies that BizTalk Server 2000 should batch documents using default settings set by the system administrator. Preset default batch-mode settings for each transport service are set in the BizTalk Server Administration Console. The transport service used is determined by the transport type that an administrator has selected.
Encoding mode	Specifies how an encoding component should be used with the envelope. The default value, "auto," specifies that the encoding type associated with the receive location of the destination organization should be used. A value of "custom" specifies that the administrator will manually configure an encoding component; it also activates the encoding component property, which enables the system administrator to select and configure an encoding component. A value of "none" specifies that no encoding should be performed on this envelope.

Table 9-10	BizTalk Management Desk Envelope Definition Properties (cont.)

Property	Description
Encoding component	Specifies the type of encoding component that should be used with the envelope. This property is active only if the encoding mode property is specified as "custom." The encoding component options are "AddHeader" and "EncodeMIME." After selecting a component, the system administrator can configure its properties.
Signature mode	Specifies whether and how a signature mode should be selected for the envelope. The default value, "auto," specifies that the signature type selected in the receive location of the destination organization should be used. The "custom" option specifies that the system administrator will manually configure a signature component; this option activates the signature component property, which enables the administrator to select and configure a signature component. The "none" option specifies that no signature will be included for this envelope.
Signature component	Specifies the signature component to be used for the envelope. This property is active only if the signature mode property is set to "custom." The signature options are "DigitalSig" and "EncodeSMIME."
Encryption mode	Specifies whether and how an encryption mode should be selected for the envelope. The default value, "auto," specifies that the encryption type selected in the receive location of the destination organization should be used. The "custom" option specifies that the system administrator will manually configure an encryption component; this option activates the encryption component property, enabling the administrator to select and configure an encryption component. The "none" option specifies that no encryption will be performed for this envelope.
Encryption component	Specifies the encryption component to be used for the envelope. This property is active only if the encryption mode property is specified as "custom." The options include "EncodeSMIME" and "EncryptPKCS."

Developers would specify only the first three properties—envelope name, direction, and format—when creating an envelope from within BizTalk Management Desk's Envelopes module. They would configure the rest of the properties from within the Agreements module (to be discussed shortly), in the process of defining an envelope for use with a particular agreement.

ORGANIZATIONS

Organization management refers to the ability to define the functional groups that engage in interchange of structured business documents. BizTalk Management Desk's Organizations module lets developers or administrators create and manage definitions of organizations and groups.

An organization, as defined in BizTalk Management Desk, can represent an entire company, a division within a company, or any business unit within any company. Any organization can be designated as the source or destination of electronic documents. For example, two divisions within the same company may be defined as separate organizations for the purpose of routing documents through BizTalk Server 2000. A group, as defined in BizTalk Management Desk, is a special type of organization that contains one or more individual organizations. An organization or group consists of a set of properties that define certain key characteristics related to the electronic exchange of documents.

Table 9-11 presents the properties of organizations that may be configured under BizTalk Management Desk.

Administrators may create internal organizations to represent business units within their own company and partner organizations to represent business units and companies that are external to their organization. Administrators can export an organization that they have created. Once exported, that organization can be imported by any other organization. One can also import organizations that have been exported by another company.

AGREEMENTS

Agreement management refers to the ability to define relationships and methods of electronic data interchange among two or more organizations. In other words, it is the ability to link business documents, document-to-document mappings, document routing and processing envelopes, and organizations into a broader policy context that drives BizTalk Server 2000's run-time operations.

Agreements (or "ports"), as defined under BizTalk Management Desk, define the broad parameters for technical integration among trading partners, pursuant to whatever trading partner agreement those two organizations have worked out. BizTalk Management Desk's Agreements module enables application developers and system administrators to define technical-integration agreements.

Figure 9-15 shows a screen from BizTalk Management Desk's Agreement Editor.

A BizTalk Management Desk-defined agreement is very concrete and narrowly scoped. The agreement specifies precisely how BizTalk Server 2000 processes one particular type of document that is encapsulated in one type

Table 9-11	BizTalk Management Desk Organization Definition Properties

Property	Description
Organization identifiers	Specifies the unique identifiers that an organization presents to BizTalk Server 2000 and to other organizations. An organization can have more than one organization identifier, but each must be unique for that organization. Examples include phone number, Web addresses, and Dun & Bradstreet DUNS Number. When BizTalk Server 2000 sends a business document, it includes in the BizTalk Document header the organization identifiers of the destination organization that will receive the document and the source organization that sent it. When BizTalk Server receives a business document, it reads the header to determine the organization identifiers of the source and destination organizations, and then uses that information along with other information about the document to route the document to the correct application.
Receive locations	Specifies addresses or locations to which BizTalk Server 2000 routes documents, as well as what protocol is used to route them there and whether any encoding, encrypting, or signing is applied to the envelope that encapsulates the documents. An organization can have multiple receive locations. In order for BizTalk Server 2000 to process the incoming document at the receive location, the system administrator must set up an associated receive service in the server (e.g., SMTP or HTTP), and also specify a receive location in BizTalk Management Desk.
Documents	Specifies documents that the organization exchanges with other organizations. In Microsoft BizTalk Management Desk, one configures a document definition as a set of properties that specify the characteristics of the underlying Business Document to be sent and/or received through BizTalk Server 2000. Document properties specify the name of the document, the pathname of the XML schema that represents the business document, the direction that the document will travel with respect to BizTalk Server, the document type and version, any EDI characteristics of the document, and whether this document will be included when the organization is exported. Once a document direction has been specified and an organization definition in which it figures has been saved, the administrator may not change the direction property without deleting the document definition and creating a new one.
Applications	Specifies applications belonging to internal organizations and configures components for those applications. When adding an application to an organization, the administrator must select and configure a component for that application. When an application component is set up and properly configured in BizTalk Management Desk, BizTalk Server 2000 may send documents directly to the associated application.
Certificates	Specifies the X.509 public key certificates that BizTalk Server 2000 uses to encrypt and/or sign envelopes for security and authentication. BizTalk Server 2000 integrates fully with Microsoft Certificate Server and relies on it for all public key signature and encryption capabilities. The system administrator must add certificates to the system before they can become available to add to organizations. One can specify a default certificate to be used for signatures.
Group membership	Specifies the groups to which an organization belongs. Groups enable the administrator to better manage many organizations.

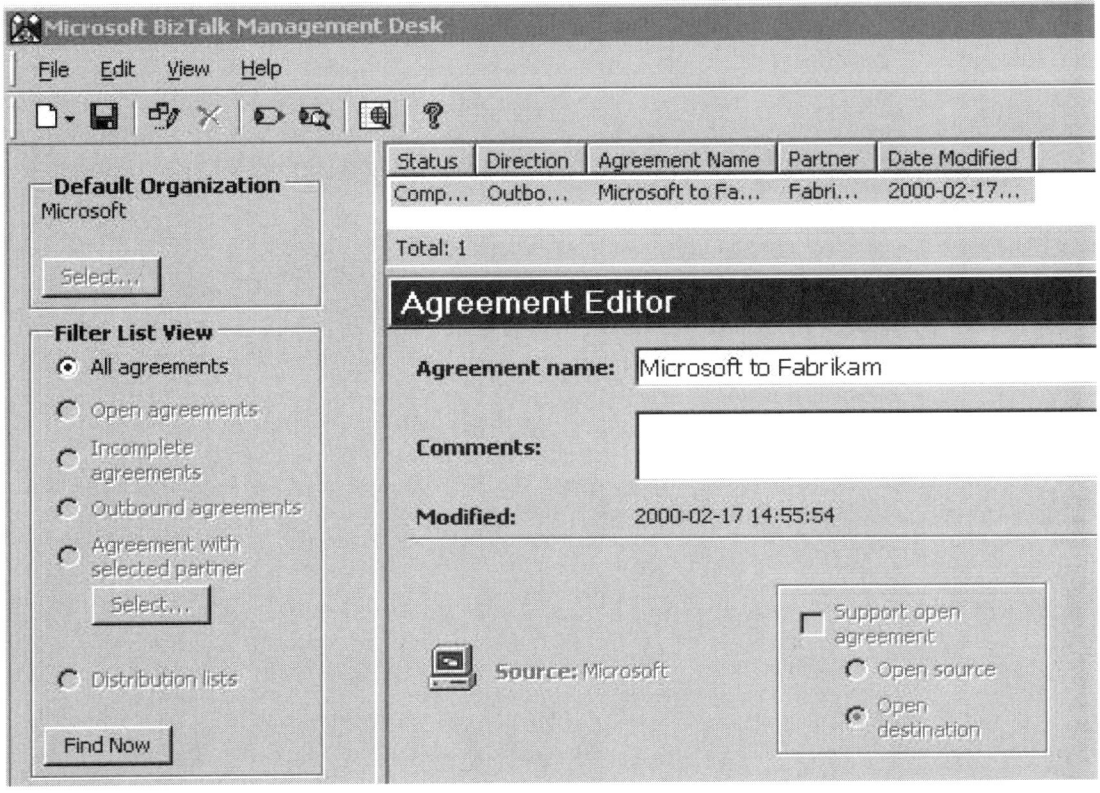

Figure 9-15 *BizTalk Management Desk's Agreement Editor.*

of envelope and that flows in one direction between one pair of trading partners. A complex set of B2B interchange scenarios—as is typical of the real world—would require many separate BizTalk Management Desk–defined agreements. Consequently, agreements are basic process definitions, and they drive BizTalk Server 2000's EDI and EAI workflow functionality.

Envelope configurations can be reused in multiple agreements between the same source and destination organizations. However, new envelopes must be configured if the roles of the two organizations are reversed, in which case the partners trade places as source and destination organizations.

In terms of processing by BizTalk Server 2000, the principal workflow-relevant message/document data consists of the source organization identifier, destination organization identifier, and name of the source document. This data resides in the header of the BizTalk Document, which encapsulates the Business Document being exchanged. BizTalk Server 2000 extracts this data from the incoming message to determine which agreement must be applied to the encapsulated document for purposes of processing and routing.

Other workflow-relevant message/document data available to BizTalk Server 2000 resides in the body of the Business Document. Administrators can define "routing expressions" under BizTalk Management Desk's Agreements module that, in conjunction with scripted rules, determine how particular documents will be processed and routed, depending on the values of particular fields in those documents.

Table 9-12 presents agreement properties that may be configured under BizTalk Management Desk.

Table 9-12	BizTalk Management Desk Agreement Definition Properties
Property	**Description**
Agreement name	Specifies a name that should distinguish the agreement from other agreements, though the name, from a purely technical standpoint, need not be unique. One technical restriction is that agreement names must not contain such reserved characters as the greater-than, less-than, ampersand, double-quote, and single-quote signs.
Source organization	Specifies the organization that sends documents under the agreement. Once an administrator saves an agreement that specifies a particular source organization, the administrator will not be able to select a different source organization without first deleting the agreement and creating a new one.
Destination organization	Specifies the organization that receives documents under the agreement.
Source document	Specifies the document format sent by the source organization under the agreement.
Envelope configuration	Specifies the advanced envelope configuration properties associated with the agreement. Advanced envelope properties include customer envelope schema, version, export in organization, source and destination organization identifiers, transport mode and service, batch, encoding mode and component, signature mode and component, and encryption mode and component. As noted previously, the three basic envelope properties—name, direction, and format—are set under BizTalk Management Desk's Envelopes module. However, the advanced envelope properties are set under the Agreements module. For ease of explication, we presented basic and advanced envelope properties previously under the "envelope" section of this chapter.
Destination document	Specifies the document format required by the destination organization under the agreement, in cases where the destination requires a format different from that of the source document.
Document map	Specifies how BizTalk Server 2000 is to map the source document format to the destination document format, if these two formats happen to differ.

Table 9-12	*BizTalk Management Desk Agreement Definition Properties (cont.)*

Property	Description
Receipts	Specifies what type of receipt, if any, that a source organization's administrator has requested in return for a source document processed by BizTalk Server 2000. One can configure an agreement to return, or require the return of, two different levels of receipts. A "return receipt" (or Level 1 receipt) indicates that documents have been received by the destination organization, but have not been opened and verified. A "functional acknowledgment" (also known as a Level 2 receipt) indicates that documents have been received by the destination organization and have been opened and verified. Administrators can use BizTalk Management Desk to define document formats, maps, envelope configurations, and receive locations for receipts, just as with any business document. Receipts can be sent by the destination organization to the source BizTalk Server and from the source BizTalk Server to the source organization.
Routing expressions	Specifies fields from within the source document schema and uses those fields to create routing condition expressions. When BizTalk Server 2000 receives documents matching the agreement, the server evaluates the expressions and processes the documents only if all of the expressions are found to be true. Routing expressions are central to the BizTalk Server 2000 feature known as "content-based routing."
Receive address	A display-only agreement property that the administrator must set from within BizTalk Management Desk's Organizations module. For the SMTP, HTTP, HTTPS, and MSMQ transport types, it will display either the address that the administrator specified in the receive location of the destination organization or the address that the administrator entered manually in the transport component properties in the Advanced Envelope Configuration dialog box.
Backup envelope configuration	Specifies a backup envelope configuration to be used to transport documents to the destination organization, in case the primary envelope configuration specified in the Agreement properties should fail for any reason.

From within the Agreements module, administrators can override some default organization properties that were specified in the Organization module, in cases where the particulars of an agreement create a special instance that renders the defaults invalid. These overrides are as follows:

- The ability to select organization identifiers for the source or destination organization different from the default selections
- The ability to manually configure transport, encoding, signature, and encryption components different from the ones specified in the receive location for the destination organization

Supplementing BizTalk Management Desk is a visual workflow process definition tool that uses the same GUI and work surface as Microsoft's separate Visio 2000 product. This tool supports development of BizTalk workflow "orchestration" scripts for content-, event-, and time-based routing of business documents and data. The tool enables definition, automation, and integration of complex business processes to be executed across BizTalk Server 2000 and other Microsoft and third-party application servers (linked through the various middleware and content connectors/adapters discussed earlier). Different organizations can define orchestrations for their respective segments of an end-to-end B2B process and then combine these segments into a unified workflow executing across a network of BizTalk Server.

As shown in Figure 9-16, the visual process definition tool allows analysts to map out the business process on one side of the on-screen work surface and the corresponding COM components on the other side. In this way, the tool supports separation of the visual representation of a business process from its software implementation.

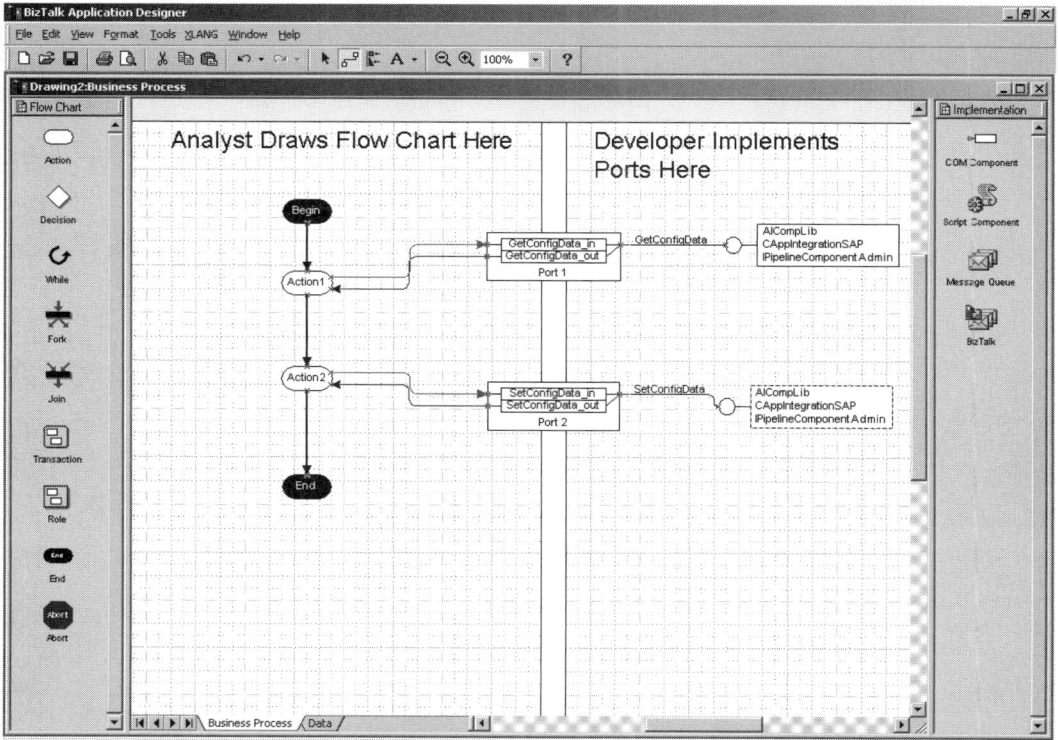

Figure 9-16   *BizTalk Server's visual process definition tool supports separation of a business process's visual representation from its software implementation.*

Process designers can use the visual process flowcharting tool to specify traditional "ACID" (atomic, consistent, independent, durable) transactional handling of two or more synchronous activities. Tightly coupled ACID transactions allow activities to succeed or fail as a linked group within a prespecified timeframe, and to be rolled back jointly if any one of them fails to execute fully. Alternately, process designers can specify "long-running transactions" involving two or more linked activities that may execute at different times and may not have a prespecified completion timeframe. Long-running transactions will become more prevalent in Internet-centric B2B environments, which we can generally characterize as asynchronous, loosely coupled, message-oriented, and multivendor in architecture (an environment where MSMQ and SOAP, supported by BizTalk Server 2000 through adapters, are appropriate middleware technologies).

TRACKING

Tracking management refers to the ability to receive status updates on documents that pass through BizTalk Server and record how those documents were processed. Administrators can specify fields within the source document specification to log into a tracking database for each document processed by an agreement. System administrators can log such activity data as a document's sender and receiver, name and type, time parameters, and user-defined fields. In addition, copies of incoming and outgoing document instances can be saved for future reference. This information can be searched and analyzed to evaluate the traffic loading and performance of a particular deployed BizTalk Server 2000.

Table 9-13 presents the tracking properties that may be configured under BizTalk Management Desk.

In the final analysis, this data enables enterprises to compile an audit log of BizTalk-enabled transactions. The bottom line on all business policies

Table 9-13	*BizTalk Management Desk Tracking Definition Properties*
Property	**Description**
Document fields to log	Specifies the document fields to log.
Unique field	Specifies the fields that identify each document as unique, such as the purchase order number.
Save source document	Specifies that the system administrator wants to save a copy of the source document.
Save destination document	Specifies that the system administrator wants to save a copy of the destination document.
Save functional receipt	Specifies that the system administrator wants to save a copy of the functional receipt (if any).

is that they are meaningless unless administrators have the tools and data to define, enforce, and audit them. BizTalk Management Desk, a central component of BizTalk Server 2000, addresses those critical policy management requirements.

9.3 Content Processing

Content processing involves validating, translating, transforming, encoding, encrypting, signing, routing, storing, forwarding, and delivering messages and documents efficiently and reliably. We can divide content processing into the following broad function sets:

- Parsing and validation: receiving incoming data items and validating their structural integrity
- Transformation: transforming data items between source and destination formats according to predefined schema mappings
- Routing and delivery: routing and delivering outbound data items securely and reliably to their intended recipients; queuing inbound and outbound data items pending further processing and routing; and storing data items and tracking information locally

As we noted above, application developers and system administrators use BizTalk Management Desk to define business rules and parameters in most of these areas.

BizTalk Server 2000 parses incoming messages and documents to validate their structure, extract workflow-relevant data, and execute appropriate agreements previously defined in BizTalk Management Desk. The server transforms data between source and destination formats in accordance with maps defined in BizTalk Management Desk. It builds envelopes from the document formats, addresses, encodings, and security mechanisms specified in BizTalk Management Desk. It applies digital signatures to outbound documents using public keys in trading partner X.509 certificates specified in BizTalk Management Desk. It routes envelopes to trading partners and other applications using transport services set up and managed from within BizTalk Management Desk. Figure 9-17 shows an example of BizTalk Server 2000 performing document transformation and protocol conversions for interchanges between trading partners, in accordance with an agreement between the partners.

9.3.1 Content-Processing Components

What drives these functions in real time are a set of content-processing components in BizTalk Server 2000. BizTalk Server 2000 processes content through several types of functional software modules that system administra-

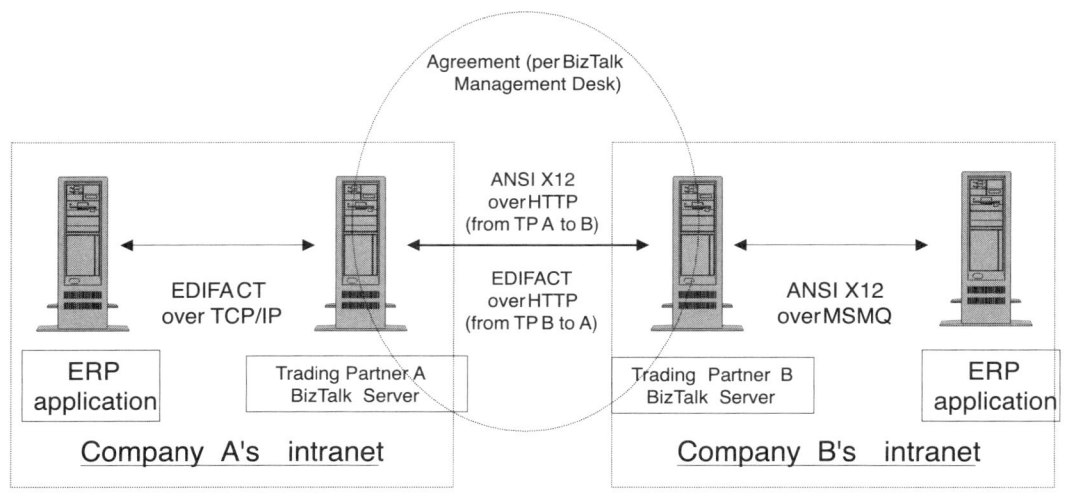

Figure 9-17   *This is a hypothetical case in which BizTalk Server 2000 performs document transformations between X12 and EDIFACT and bridges between the MSMQ message-brokering protocol and TCP/IP transport protocol, in accordance with an agreement between the two trading partners.*

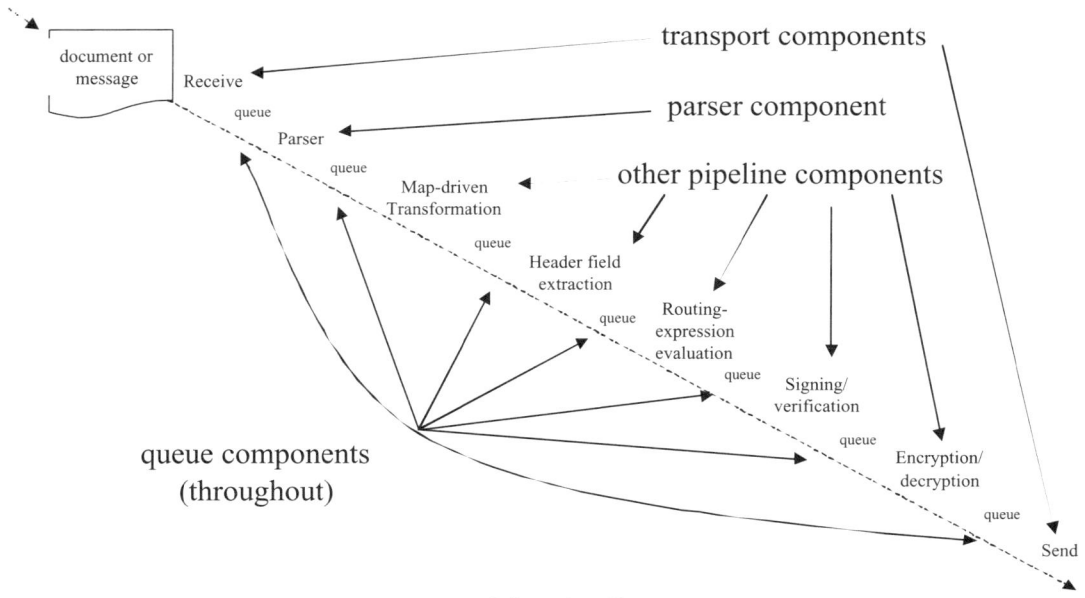

Figure 9-18   *BizTalk Server 2000 includes content-processing components of four types: transport, parser, pipeline, and queue.*

tors manage through the BizTalk Server Administration Console. These components support transport, parser, queue, and pipeline functionality. We describe these components in Table 9-14 and depict their linked roles graphically in Figure 9-18.

BizTalk Server 2000 includes sending and receiving transport components associated with various transport protocols, object brokers, message brokers, and content security protocols discussed earlier. These components support various asynchronous and synchronous transport protocol options. Further detail on BizTalk Server 2000's transport components is presented in Table 9-15.

9.3.2 Content-Processing Steps

Upon receiving inbound documents via various transport services, BizTalk Server 2000 implements the following high-level content-processing steps:

- Decodes, parses, and extracts message and document header information;

Table 9-14	BizTalk Server 2000's Content-Processing Components
Components	**Description**
Transport	Enable the server to exchange BizTalk Messages with remote applications—in other words, with applications that lack a local application's ability to communicate directly with BizTalk Server via Windows 2000's native COM interfaces. As noted above, BizTalk Server supports transport components for such protocols as HTTP, SMTP, HTTPS, DCOM, and MSMQ.
Parser	Extract basic BizTalk Message/Document header information that defines an interchange's specific document format. Parsers can also extract routing information from within a Business Document. BizTalk Server supports parsers for X12 and EDIFACT formats, which allow the server to process EDI interchanges. The server also includes parser components for flat files and well-formed XML. Third-party developers can develop new parser components to work with BizTalk. One of the core features of XML parsers is their ability to validate the schemas of XML documents against schemas and Document Type Definitions (DTDs).
Queue	Stores interchanges in several queues: pending (received but not yet processed), work (currently being processed), sending (queued for transmission), and suspended (attempted transmission but failed). If several BizTalk Servers operate as a cluster, they have a Shared Queue (SQ) database that stores all checkpoint information related to interchanges processed by the individual servers. In the event one BizTalk Server fails, the SQ database can retrieve the interchange checkpoint information and resubmit the interchange to another available server.
Pipeline	Manages an "orchestration" channel (sometimes known as a commerce interchange pipeline) that consists of a set of processing steps necessary to receive, validate, map, transform, and route BizTalk Messages and BizTalk Documents. The server's core workflow functionality rides on these pipeline components.

Table 9-15	BizTalk Server 2000's Transport Components	

Component	Sending	Receiving
HTTP	The SendHTTP component transports documents over HTTP connections.	The ReceiveHTTP/S component uses ASPs to receive documents, which are secured with SSL certificates, and then submits the documents to BizTalk Server.
HTTP/S	The Send HTTP/S component transports documents over HTTP connections that use SSL.	The ReceiveHTTP/S component uses ASPs to receive documents, which are secured with SSL certificates, and then submits the documents to BizTalk Server.
SMTP	The Send SMTP component creates an SMTP-based e-mail message, which includes the document in the message body or as an attachment.	The ReceiveSMTP component uses an e-mail message to receive a document and then submits the document to BizTalk Server.
MSMQ	The Send MSMQ component sends documents over MSMQ 2.0 to a destination queue.	The ReceiveMSMQ component checks the queue on a periodic basis and when a message arrives, passes it to BizTalk Server.
DCOM	The SendDCOM component sends a document from one BizTalk Server to another, or calls a pipeline on a remote Microsoft Commerce Server.	The ReceiveDCOM component receives documents, creates MtsTxPipeline or MtsPipeline objects, and then uses those objects to load and run the specified pipeline.
Fax	The SendFax component translates a BizTalk Message to fax format and transmits it to remote parties, via a fax gateway in Windows 2000. This component supports transmission of document images to businesses that do not run BizTalk Server.	There is no "ReceiveFax" capability in BizTalk Server.
LocalFile	The SendLocalFile component sends the document to a pathname on the Windows 2000 distributed file system.	The ReceiveLocalFile service looks for a file or files on the local server. When it finds a file or files, the service calls BizTalk Server.

- Evaluates parsed fields (especially document types and priorities) against applicable agreements in order to determine appropriate document processing and routing;
- Performs various "pipeline" processing steps, including map-driven transformation, digital signature verification, decryption, and routing-expression evaluation; and
- Sends documents to appropriate trading partners and applications.

BizTalk Server 2000's content-processing options are many. For starters, the server can perform content-based routing. As described previously, this is an approach under which the server selects the appropriate agreements and destination organizations in run time, based on values of any fields in the header or body of an inbound document.

BizTalk Server 2000 can process interchanges that include multiple documents. It can also expedite routing of high-priority documents, enabling near-real-time document processing. It bases routing decisions on data that it extracts from document headers, especially such data as document types and priorities.

Support for near-real-time message delivery enables BizTalk Server 2000 to provide synchronous communication. Under such a scenario, an application submits a document through BizTalk Server 2000 and then, on the same session or call, receives a response document. The response document may be a delivery receipt or any other type of business document.

The server supports reliable delivery of outbound documents. BizTalk Server 2000 can request delivery receipts and/or functional acknowledgments from recipient applications to prove that a document was delivered successfully to its addressee. The server maintains outbound documents in local queues in the event that delivery was not successful and the documents need to be retransmitted. In addition, the server places malformed messages or those missing header information in a "dead letter queue" for manual processing.

An inbound document may have been digitally signed and/or encrypted by its originator. BizTalk Server 2000 can verify a document's digital signature and decrypt the content, per the relevant agreement.

BizTalk Server 2000 defines these various functions as "stages." Stages are COM components exposed to various programming languages, including C++, Visual Basic, and Java. These components operate on commerce data objects—in other words, documents—that pass through the pipeline. A pipeline is essentially a structured workflow of processing steps, and BizTalk Server 2000's workflow is known as an "orchestration" channel or Commerce Interchange Pipeline (CIP). The server organizes stages into two primary workflows: transmit and receive. Figure 9-19 shows the typical stages in transmit and receive workflows. Middleware technologies—such as DCOM and MSMQ—allow BizTalk to interface its workflows to external applications, such as Microsoft's Commerce Server 2000, SQL Server 2000, Host Integration Server 2000, and Application Center 2000. We show transmit and receive workflows in Figure 9-19 and a screen from BizTalk Management Desk's Pipeline Editor in Figure 9-20.

9.3.3 Routing Options

BizTalk Server 2000 supports three methods for routing business documents: self-routing, custom routing, and conditional routing.

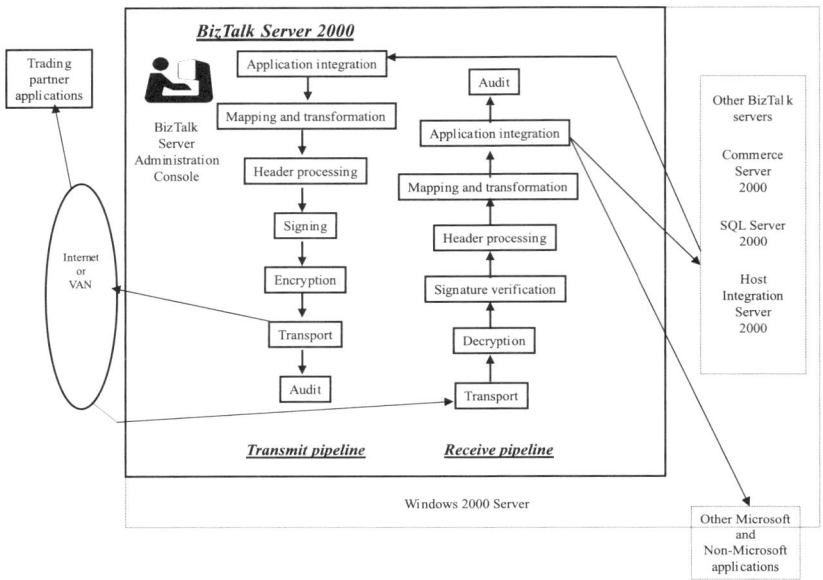

Figure 9-19

BizTalk Server 2000 organizes processing steps, or "stages," into transactional workflows, of which there are two principal types: transmit and receive.

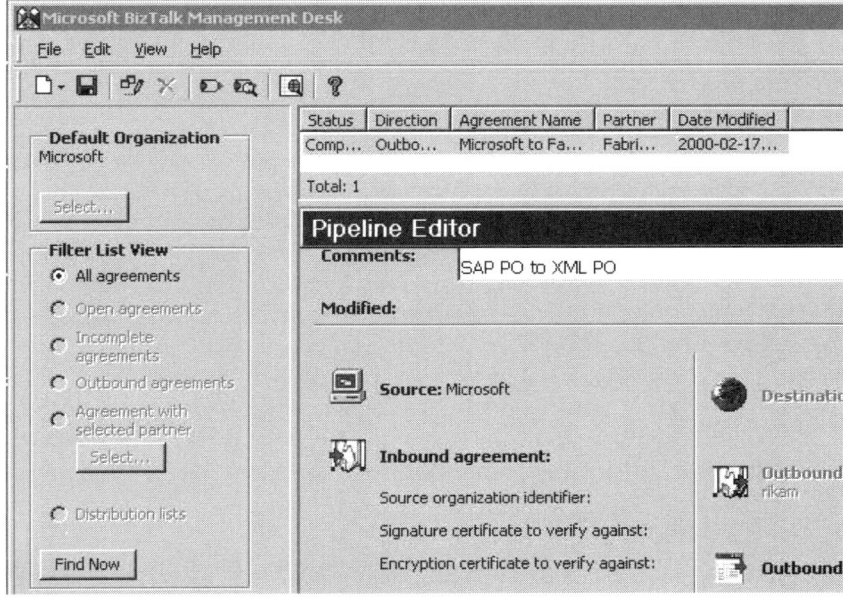

Figure 9-20

A screen from BizTalk Management Desk's Pipeline Editor.

SELF-ROUTING

Self-routing documents are those that contain routing information from which BizTalk Server 2000's parser component can extract the information needed to route the document appropriately. Self-routing works differently for XML, EDI, and flat files.

Self-routing XML files require two things: an XML document schema associated with the document type and routing attributes in the document's header. The required routing attributes, defined through XML markup, consist of the name of the document schema and identifiers for the document's source and destination organization.

Self-routing EDI files require two things: a document schema for each type (X12 or EDIFACT) and routing attributes within the documents. BizTalk Server's EDI parsers can extract routing attributes—source and destination organization qualifiers and IDs—that are contained within X12 or EDIFACT documents.

Self-routing flat files require three things: headers, envelope schemas that describe the contents of the header, and routing attributes in the header. The required attributes, delimited through tabs, commas, or other file-format conventions, include source organization qualifier, source organization ID, destination organization qualifier, destination organization ID, and the name of the document profile. The file path for the flat file's envelope schema must be passed in on the transport dictionary with the file transmission or on a custom receive service as an interchange schema file path.

For EDI and flat files, BizTalk Server 2000's parser identifies the document schema and then converts each document to its intermediary XML equivalent. Once BizTalk Server has a document in XML format, it locates that document's matching agreements and processes the document according to those agreements.

CUSTOM ROUTING

Custom routing requires that the source application provide all necessary routing information to BizTalk Server 2000, so that the document to be routed need not contain the routing attributes.

Custom routing relies on DCOM receive services for the source application to pass routing information to BizTalk Server 2000. Applications can pass custom-routing information as parameters via DCOM Submit or SubmitSync method calls. Routing parameters passed via DCOM include interchange schema file path, document definition name, source entity ID, source entity ID type, destination entity ID, and destination entity ID type.

Alternately, the source application can submit routing information in the transport dictionary it submits to BizTalk Server 2000 under the receive service. If the source does not provide these values in the transport dictionary but passes them in parameters to the DCOM Submit or SubmitSync calls, BizTalk Server 2000 writes the values to the transport dictionary for later processing.

CONDITIONAL ROUTING

Conditional routing may supplement self-routing or custom routing under agreements defined in BizTalk Management Desk, enabling a more flexible, fine-grained, rule-driven workflow functionality.

Conditional routing expressions in agreements enable BizTalk Server 2000 to implement either/or routing, depending on the values of fields in a document. For example, an agreement might specify that an inbound purchase order from a customer be routed to various groups within a sales organization. Routing might depend on the size of the order, the type of items being ordered, and the identity of the individual placing the order (attributes that are typically not in an EDI document's header).

This feature is also known as "content-based routing." It is a fundamental workflow feature in BizTalk Server 2000, enabling it to serve as robust, policy-driven, agreement-driven, map-driven "glue." It supports binding of diverse applications into a unified information service and bonding of diverse trading partners into a unified trading community.

9.4 Service Management

Service management involves deploying, monitoring, administering, and troubleshooting an end-to-end BizTalk server implementation, including all software and hardware components. We can divide service management into the following broad function sets: service implementation, service monitoring and administration, and data tracking and analysis.

We will discuss these responsibilities within the context of three types of BizTalk Server 2000 deployments:

- Single-site single-server deployment: within a machine running BizTalk Server 2000
- Single-site multiserver deployment: within a data center running multiple local instances of BizTalk Server 2000
- Multisite multiserver deployment: within an enterprise running multiple distributed instances of BizTalk Server 2000

These scenarios may apply to EDI-related applications of BizTalk Server 2000, EAI-related applications, or deployments that combine both types of application.

9.4.1 Single-Site Single-Server Deployment

Figure 9-21 shows a typical single-site single-server deployment of BizTalk Server 2000. In this example, a system administrator has dedicated a Windows 2000 machine to running BizTalk Server 2000 and established connectors to several Microsoft application servers (SQL Server 2000, Commerce Server 2000, and Host Integration Server 2000) and various line-of-business applications (such as ERP, CRM, and other application servers). Host mainframe applications interchange data with BizTalk Server 2000 through Host Interchange Server 2000.

BizTalk Server Administration Console is the administrator's primary tool for installing, configuring, and administering BizTalk Server 2000. The console is a Microsoft Management Console (MMC) "snap-in" that integrates BizTalk Server administration under the same graphical user interface through which all other Windows 2000 applications are administered. MMC is a new distributed service under Windows 2000, which we will discuss in greater detail in Part Four.

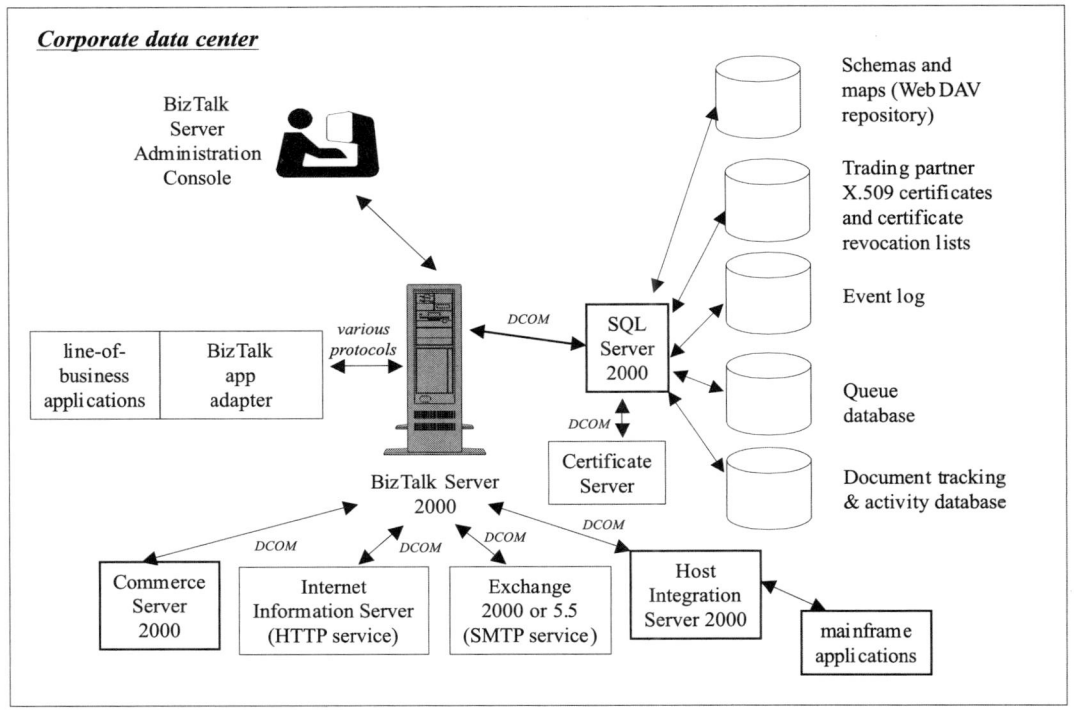

Figure 9-21   *One hypothetical single-server deployment scenario for BizTalk Server 2000, in which the server interfaces to various Microsoft and third-party applications installed in the same data center.*

BizTalk Server Administration Console's left-hand "scope pane" displays a hierarchical, expandable tree view of BizTalk Server objects that an administrator can manage. The console displays the Microsoft BizTalk Server 1.0 folder as a subfolder of the console's root. Typically, MMC would display, just under the root, folders associated with other Microsoft Servers, such as SQL Server, Commerce Server, and Exchange Server (Microsoft's e-mail and groupware product).

Under a single-server BizTalk Server deployment, the BizTalk Server Administration Console would display an administrator-named "server group" that consists of a single machine. Each BizTalk Server group displays as a separate subfolder of the Microsoft BizTalk Server folder. This subfolder, in turn, contains further subfolders for each of the following categories of BizTalk Server components associated with the server group (as discussed previously): queues, pipeline components, parsers, receive services, and transport (i.e., send) services. The console's "discover components" task enables the administrator to automatically determine which components are registered on that server.

Within the console GUI, clicking on the text next to any of the component icons displays additional details about the associated object in the console's right-hand "result pane." Administrators manage an object by right-clicking that object in the console display to access the desired task.

One of the basic tasks for BizTalk Server 2000 administrators is the need to configure receive and transport services. The BizTalk Server Administration Console provides tools to create and configure receive and transport services that are used by agreements in Microsoft BizTalk Management Desk. Some business applications communicate directly with BizTalk Server 2000 via a COM interface. Others send documents to a file receive location through administrator-defined "file receive services" running under BizTalk Server 2000.

When configuring a file receive service, administrators indicate whether the receive service is standard or custom. A standard file-receive service supports submission of interchanges in standard data formats that are supported by BizTalk Server, such as X12, EDIFACT, or XML. A custom file-receive service processes nonstandard file formats.

Defining a custom file-receive service involves specifying pertinent routing information, source entity, destination entity, and document definition name. All of this information enables BizTalk Server 2000 to locate the appropriate agreement for the file type. BizTalk Server Administration Console supports configuration of the file-receive service that can receive a specific type of document from multiple sources, without having to create multiple receive services. This would involve leaving the source fields blank and relying on source information that is specified in the document.

However, the HTTP and SMTP receive services are not configured within the BizTalk Server Administration Console. Configuring the HTTP receive service involves creating an ASP file and copying it to the Internet Information Services (IIS) default folder under MMC (the same management GUI as the BizTalk Server Administration Console but a separate module under that GUI). Configuring the SMTP receive service involves defining, within Exchange Server (5.5 or 2000) and Outlook, a new automated mail recipient agent and a new public folder from which that agent retrieves inbound mail. Consequently, system administrators must make sure they have co-installed BizTalk Server 2000 with both IIS and Exchange Server and either have administrative capabilities on those other servers or have procedures for coordinating with the administrators of those servers.

Defining file-transport services under BizTalk Server 2000 is similar to configuring file-receive services. BizTalk Server 2000 typically transmits data to applications, not to end user, reflecting the traditional EDI orientation toward application-to-application interchanges. However, administrators can set up transport services that transmit data directly to end users, via e-mail or fax.

The console allows administrators to batch outbound interchanges for transport to business applications based on the following criteria: specified time, elapsed time intervals, or document quantities (in other words, batch all interchanges at BizTalk Server 2000 until a certain number of them accumulates, and then send them in batch).

The console provides system administrators with centralized control over document flow prioritization, tracking, analysis, and troubleshooting in BizTalk Server 2000. For example, an administrator can configure the maximum number of times that the server will retry transmission, and the maximum time between retries on failed transmissions for each individual transport service. If transmissions fails after the set maximum number of retries, the server places the document into a "suspended queue."

BizTalk Server 2000's queues are maintained in SQL Server 2000 databases, which means that the former cannot be deployed without at least one instance of the latter. BizTalk Server administrators must set numerous configuration options within SQL Server to enable BizTalk Server SQL databases to read from and write to SQL Server. Among other things, they must install SQL Server Client on BizTalk Server to enable remote management of SQL Server. In addition, the SQL Server Client must use the TCP/IP default instead of the Named Pipes default network library.

BizTalk Server 2000 logs to the queue database all interchanges processed since a prior checkpoint. There is no limit on the size of queues in BizTalk Server. Administrators can view only their local queues, but not those on remote Biztalk Servers. If BizTalk Server crashes or needs to be stopped and then restarted, it can resume processing from the last valid checkpoint. Of course, this feature depends on administrators making regular backups of their SQL Server databases.

BizTalk Server also uses SQL Server to maintain a Document Tracking and Activity (DTA) database. The server lets administrators track documents that it processes, either in batches or singly, and also record processing activity against those documents. DTA captures sender and receiver identifiers, document name and type, user-defined fields, and relevant time parameters. A user can search across documents and interchanges of documents processed by the system. DTA also stores complete copies of the incoming and outgoing document instances for future reference. Logging user-defined document fields enables companies to analyze the types of interchanges processed through BizTalk Server. For example, a system administrator might automatically log dollar amounts and recipients of all outbound purchase orders, thereby facilitating reporting and analysis of procurement actions for each supplier over time.

BizTalk Server uses SQL Server 2000 as a repository for all schemas and maps that it uses to manipulate and transform documents. The database exposes these objects via the Web Distributed Authoring and Versioning (WebDAV) protocol.

The BizTalk Server Administration Console writes all application errors to a local event log and labels them "Commerce Interchange Server" errors. During the beta period, Microsoft identified the application errors in Table 9-16 as common with BizTalk Server 2000. We have organized them into two broad categories: configuration issues and interchange-processing issues. Microsoft includes updates on these and other errors in the Readme file at the root level of the administration console's BizTalk Server folder. By the time this book is published, the vendor may have addressed many or most of these issues, but we discuss them because they are illustrative of error conditions that many system administrators may encounter with BizTalk Server 2000.

Table 9-16	*Categories of BizTalk Server Application Errors Observed During the Beta Period*
Application Errors	**Description**
Configuration issues	BizTalk Server 2000 requires access to SQL Server in order to retrieve information on server groups. If BizTalk Server cannot access SQL Server, the administrator receives the following error message: "Cannot enumerate instances of Microsoft_InterchangeGroup: Getting all Groups from database failed." This error occurs under either of two scenarios. First, the BizTalk Server SQL databases may be offline. Second, SQL Server Client may not be installed correctly on BizTalk Server, such as when the client is not using the TCP/IP default network library.
	BizTalk Server 2000 and MTS report file interchange timeouts differently. BizTalk Server 2000, when transmitting a file that exceeds the default transaction timeout value of 60 seconds, records the transaction as "sent." However, MTS labels the transaction as "aborted."

Table 9-16	*Categories of BizTalk Server Application Errors Observed During the Beta Period (cont.)*

Application Errors	**Description**
Configuration issues (cont.)	BizTalk Server 2000 will not receive DCOM-submitted objects from a client machine if the client machine lacks a DCOM application proxy. Once the system administrator creates a DCOM application proxy on the client, that client can then submit calls to BizTalk Server 2000 and pass dictionary objects only (not Document Object Model or recordset objects).
	BizTalk Server 2000 cannot work with two X.509 certificates that have the same name, and will in fact cause one of the certificates to disappear from the available list of certificates under BizTalk Management Desk.
Interchange-processing issues	BizTalk Server 2000's X12 serializer changes some of the original data after serialization and treats the numeric value of zero as a pad character rather than an actual value. For example, it would change "0.1" to ".1" after serialization and treat the omitted zero value as a pad character. This could cause problems with floating-point units that require the zero to the left of the decimal point.
	BizTalk Server 2000 does not allow DecodeMIME to be used for S/MIME message processing.
	BizTalk Server 2000 cannot reliably decode MIME messages with a content-type header field that contains a content-type and subtype which is anything other than "text." In such cases, BizTalk Server 2000 will decode the message as containing one body part and no attachment. If the message has a content-type set to "application," the data typically represents either uninterpreted binary data or information to be processed by an application. Generally, this data resides in a binary file attachment that cannot be processed by BizTalk Server 2000.
	BizTalk Server's DecodeMIME component will generate a message with a content-type of "application/EDI-content" in cases where content is encoded with the Commerce Interchange Pipeline Manager's (CIPM) EncodeMIME component (in the default configuration). The server will also unexpectedly generate a message with one body part and no attachment. This situation departs from some of the working conventions for current CIPM customers using Microsoft's Site Server Commerce Edition version 3.
	BizTalk Server 2000 cannot successfully parse X12 or flat files with data and delimiters with characters outside the ASCII value range between 0 and 127. Note that the server does not produce a record in the event log describing its failure to parse these files.
	BizTalk Server 2000's local file-receive service cannot decrypt data in files, so it will generate an error message when a file received from a local application contains encrypted data.

Table 9-16	Categories of BizTalk Server Application Errors Observed During the Beta Period (cont.)
Application Errors	**Description**
Interchange-processing issues (cont.)	BizTalk Server 2000's InterchangeService will not start if a user is not logged on to the server under an interactive user account (a requirement for all packages using COM+). If a client application submits documents to BizTalk Server remotely and no user is logged on to the server, the interchange service will not start. The InterchangeService will not start if a user is logged onto BizTalk Server under a local system account.
	BizTalk Server 2000 has a maximum per-interchange size limitation of 20 megabytes. If a file is larger than available memory on the machine running BizTalk Server, the server will not transmit the file.
	BizTalk Server 2000 cannot have multiple threads or servers attempting to batch at the same time. In such scenarios, system administrators may receive the message "Your transaction was deadlocked with another process and has been chosen as the deadlock victim. Rerun your transaction."
	BizTalk Server 2000 fails to stop when requested in situations where the InterchangeSvc Service is running under the system account, rather than, as it should, under a domain user account. System administrators must reboot BizTalk Server to exit this state and then rerun InterchangeSvc under a domain user account.

SINGLE-SITE MULTISERVER DEPLOYMENT

Microsoft has designed BizTalk Server 2000 with multiserver, clustered deployments in mind.

As we noted above, the BizTalk Server Administration Console displays an administrator-named "server group," which may contain one or more instances of BizTalk Server 2000 within a management domain. Each BizTalk Server group folder contains subfolders for each of the individual machines in a server group. Each of these machine-specific subfolders, in turn, contains folders for the various BizTalk Server components on that machine: queues, pipeline components, parsers, receive services, and transport services.

BizTalk Server groups are collections of individual servers that may be managed, configured, and monitored centrally. The console lets administrators configure BizTalk Servers as a group. The following rules apply to BizTalk Server groups:

- Each individual server must belong to a group.
- No server can belong to more than one group.
- All servers within a group must share the same configuration.
- There can be more than one group within a total enterprise-wide BizTalk Server 2000 deployment.

Administrators can exercise the following functions across a group of BizTalk Servers:

* Assign a name to the group as well as to individual servers
* Add servers to the group, remove servers, and configure properties of individual servers without having to take the entire server group offline
* Configure properties, resources, and services shared by all servers in a group
* Monitor and manage interchange queues (input, work, output, and dead-letter) shared by servers in a group

Within a BizTalk Server 2000 group, the separate machines share the following common infrastructure (which we illustrate in Figure 9-22):

* SQ database to monitor interchange activity within the BizTalk Server state engine
* DTA database to log interchange activity and run reports
* Event logs
* Receive and transport service components

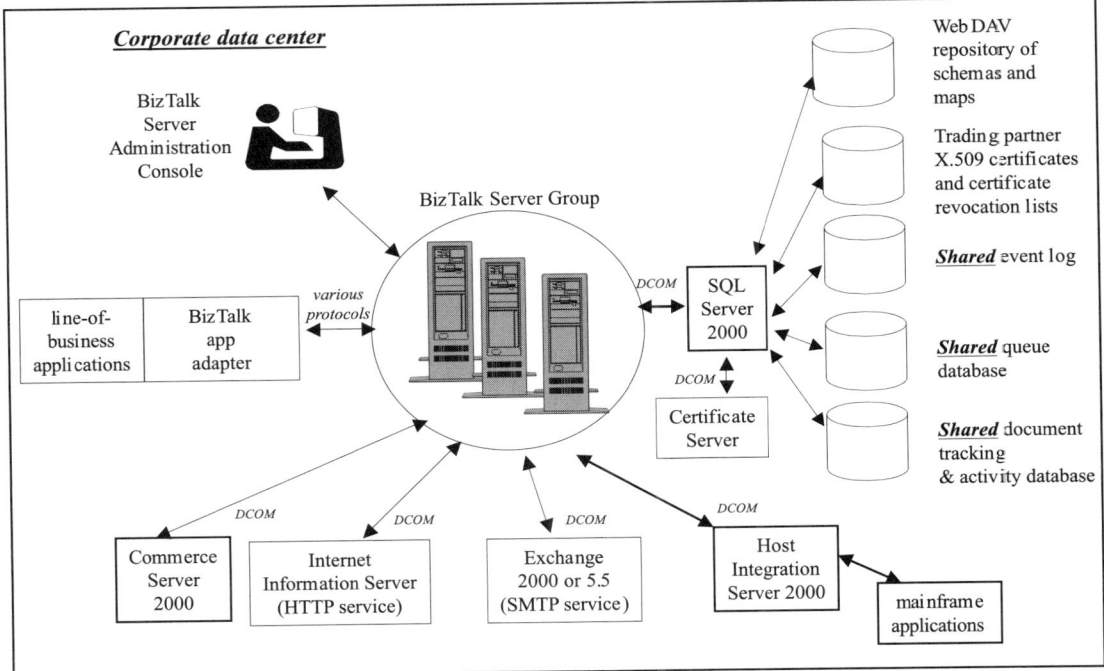

Figure 9-22   *This is one hypothetical single-site, multiserver deployment scenario for BizTalk Server 2000, in which several servers are managed as a group, have identical configurations, and share queue and tracking databases and other components.*

Each machine in a BizTalk Server 2000 group supports the full set of transport, parser, pipeline, and queuing features. As we noted previously, all servers in a group share an identical configuration, with the same set of registered software components. The BizTalk Server Administration Console automatically discovers the components installed on each individual server within a group, querying each machine's registry for its list of registered components. Once it discovers a server's registry, the console adds that machine's current description to its administrative database and flags missing or broken components.

BizTalk Server 2000 routes inbound documents among clustered machines in a server group for near-real-time processing and delivery to applications. By using a priority mechanism for handling documents that it has queued, BizTalk Server is able to process documents on a near-real-time basis while holding others until processing time is available.

Each BizTalk Server that processes an interchange submits the interchange to the SQ database for the group. Individual servers enqueue and dequeue documents against the SQ database, calling the appropriate COM pipeline components to receive, decrypt, verify, translate, transform, sign, encrypt, and transmit documents. The BizTalk Server Administration Console displays the SQ database in a tree view, as a set of queues that represent the processing stages within BizTalk Server's Commerce Interchange Pipeline. At any point in time, any given document may be in the shared pending queue, shared work queue, shared sending queue, or shared suspended queue.

As an architectural feature, the SQ database has several important benefits. First, it centralizes all group document activity in one shared, high-performance database. Second, it ensures continued availability of the server cluster in case one or more nodes fail. Third, it allows individual servers to be added or removed without needing to take the entire server group offline. Fourth, it enables the total group server deployment to scale up in support of growing workloads. Fifth, it enables dynamic load balancing across servers in a group, since any of them can service interchanges in the SQ database.

All processes performed by each server in the group are logged to a centralized DTA database associated with the group. The BizTalk Server Administration Console supports configuration of logging and tracking parameters. Administrators can track and log incoming and outgoing interchange documents, modifications to the suspended queue, and transmission retries. They can also set limits on the size of documents written to the DTA database, up to a maximum 2 gigabytes per document. All documents over this size are stored in the Windows 2000 distributed file system, to which there are pointers in the DTA database. Date/time stamps are applied to documents written to the DTA. Date/time stamps use the local time on the SQL Server that saved the document. However, the date/time stamp is displayed to administrators in the local time of the place from which they are viewing the DTA via BizTalk Server Administration Console.

A BizTalk Server site deployment may include several server groups, each of which has several servers. In these deployments (illustrated in Figure 9-23), each server group has its own dedicated SQ and DTA databases and event log. However, the WebDAV document/schema repository and any X.509 certificate databases (for content security on S/MIME and SSL transactions) are shared across multiple server groups.

Given the importance of shared databases to BizTalk Server groups, it is important to run SQL Server on a dedicated, high-availability machine or cluster. Administrators should protect their SQL Server deployments through use of replicated databases, server clustering, redundant arrays of independent disks, regular backups, disk mirroring and duplexing, and uninterruptible power supplies.

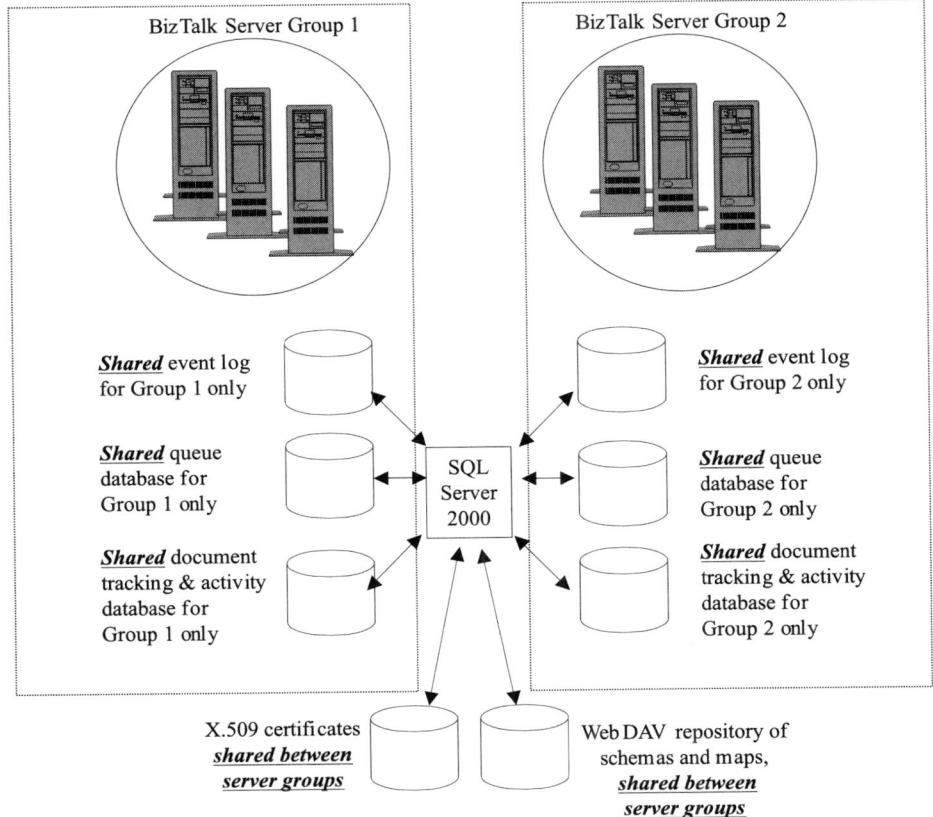

Figure 9-23 *Each BizTalk Server group has its own dedicated SQ and DTA databases, which are not shared with other groups.*

Continuous availability is essential to a BizTalk Server 2000 deployment, considering that an entire business—or industry—may be riding on one or more servers. The BizTalk Server 2000 architecture supports fault tolerance through unified administration, shared queue and tracking databases, and interchangeable server configurations within server groups. Another important fault-tolerance feature is the ability of BizTalk Server 2000 to log to the SQ database all interchange progress through the state engine as of a particular checkpoint in time. If an individual server crashes or needs to be stopped for troubleshooting, interchange processing can resume from the last valid checkpoint.

Never losing an interchange in process is an important reliability feature. BizTalk Server 2000 enables interchanges to be "freed" from a server that is processing them under circumstances in which the server needs to be taken offline or removed from a server group. Administrators can redistribute interchanges to other servers in the group. Any available server within the group can pick up the interchange, check its last valid checkpoint from the SQ, and start processing it.

MULTISITE MULTISERVER DEPLOYMENT

BizTalk Server 2000 can be a hub or spoke in a distributed EAI, extranet, or e-marketplace deployment.

An enterprise can deploy BizTalk Server 2000 at all sites, or just at selected sites, in order to integrate among internal applications and with external trading partners. Companies need not standardize on BizTalk Server 2000 alone, but may deploy it in conjunction with similar interchange servers and middleware products from other vendors. Microsoft has architected BizTalk Server 2000 for heterogeneous application integration, which gives enterprises, service providers, and e-marketmakers the flexibility to roll out the product as broadly or narrowly as they wish.

Figure 9-24 shows a scenario in which a company has standardized on BizTalk Server 2000 as its enterprise-wide interchange server platform. In this scenario, Company A has deployed BizTalk Server 2000 at headquarters and all sites. The headquarters BizTalk Server group functions as a central message switch and workflow engine that routes BizTalk Messages between the various sites over diverse protocols and middleware environments. Each of the sites has deployed BizTalk Server 2000 (individually or in clusters) as well as SQL Server 2000 (or prior versions), other Microsoft applications, and various line-of-business applications (with BizTalk application adapters). Applications at the sites produce documents in various XML schemas, encapsulate them in BizTalk Message and BizTalk Document envelopes, and submit them to the local BizTalk Servers for internal and external routing. Applications rely on BizTalk Server to implement self-routing, custom routing, or conditional routing, depending on the document formats and contents as well as agreements defined under BizTalk Management Desk.

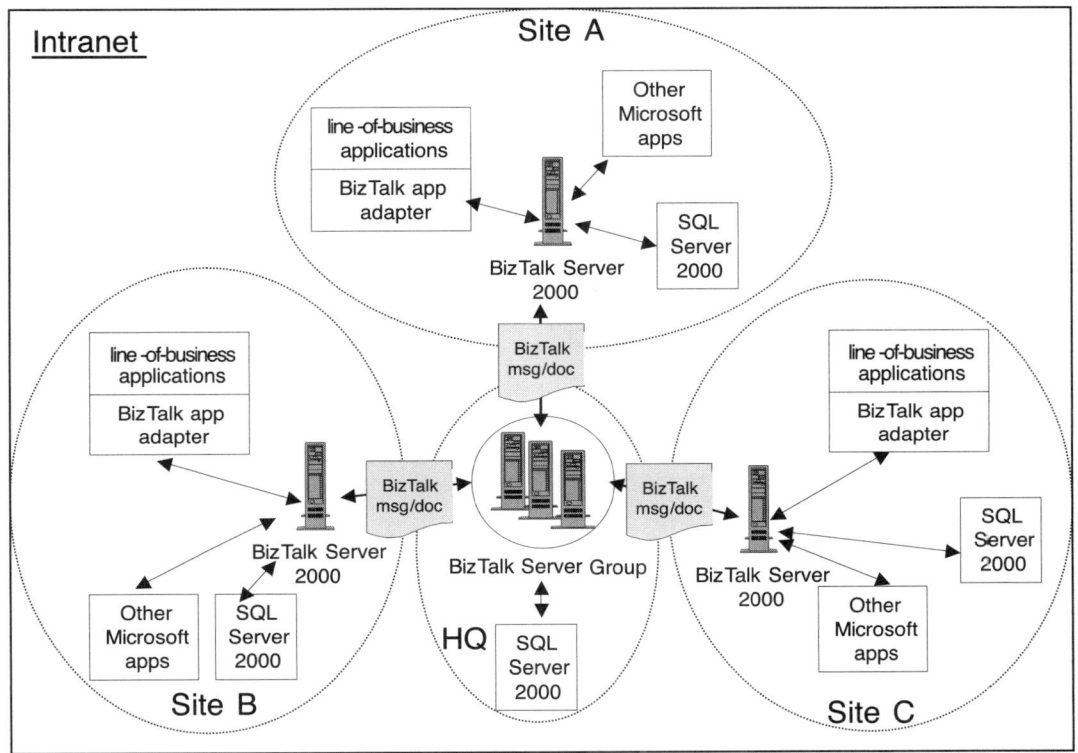

Figure 9-24   *BizTalk Server 2000 may be deployed at each site in an intranet, creating an enterprise-wide application integration environment.*

Figure 9-25 shows an extranet topology among trading partners that have all standardized on BizTalk Server 2000 as their interchange server platform. All the trading partners exchange XML-formatted business documents encapsulated in BizTalk Messages/Documents. Connections are tunneled directly between the trading partners' firewalls.

Figure 9-26 shows a B2B hubbed e-marketplace topology in which the marketmaker and all trading partners have standardized on BizTalk Server 2000 and exchange business documents among themselves in BizTalk Messages.

We are now verging into wishful-thinking territory, where Microsoft is concerned. It is highly unlikely that all participants in an extranet or hubbed e-marketplace will have standardized on one vendor's interchange server, or even one B2B interoperability standards framework. No one seriously expects Microsoft either to monopolize the interchange server market with its BizTalk Server 2000 or to proselytize the BizTalk Framework to the extinction of other industry frameworks (especially not in the current political and regu-

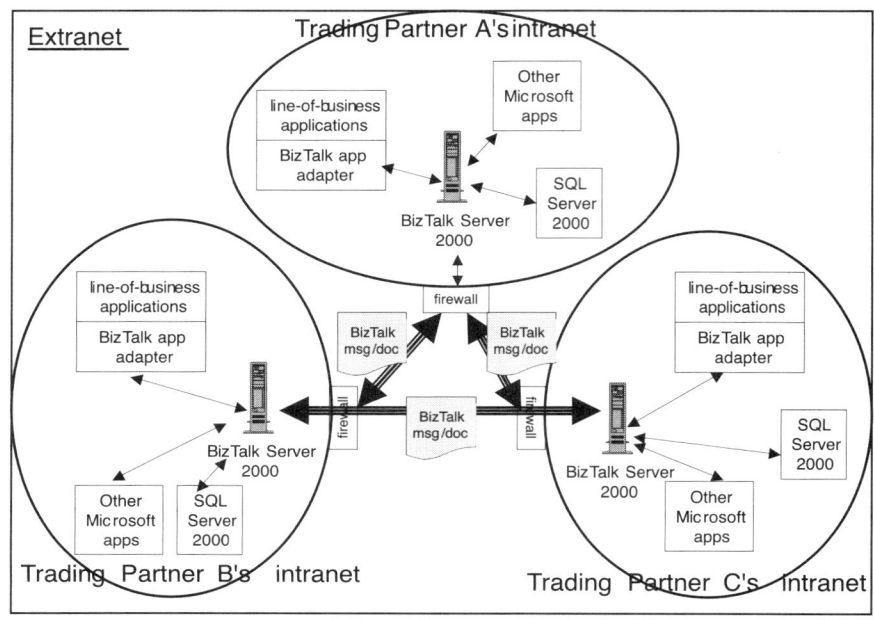

Figure 9-25   *BizTalk Server 2000 may be deployed by each trading partner in an extranet to support B2B interchanges.*

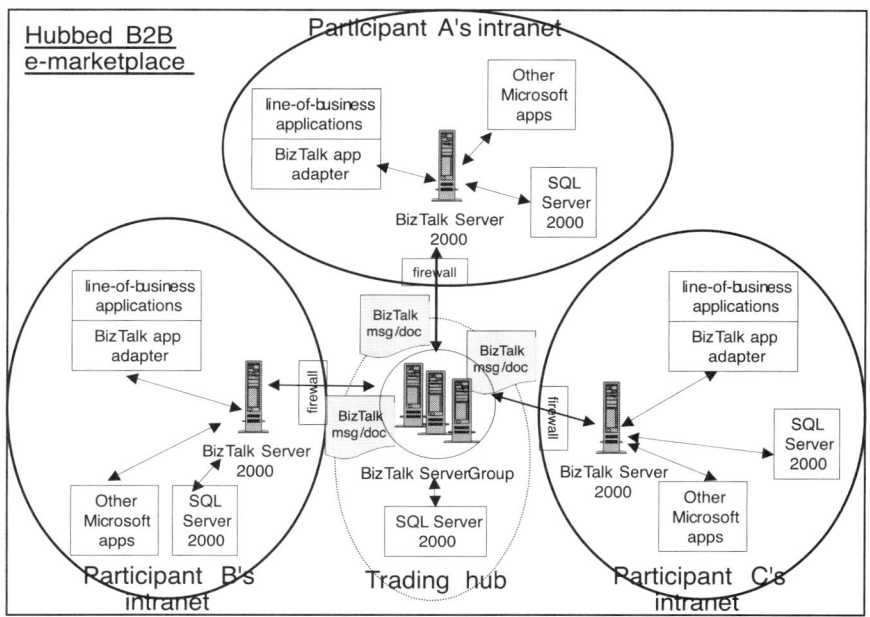

Figure 9-26   *BizTalk Server 2000 may be deployed by each participant in a hubbed e-marketplace to support B2B interchanges with the hub and other participants.*

latory climate). Consequently, Figures 9-25 and 9-26 are useful primarily for pedagogical purposes, to show how interchange servers (such as BizTalk Server 2000) would be deployed for EAI and B2B.

A more realistic deployment scenario is depicted in Figure 9-27. In this example, only one of the trading partners is using BizTalk Server 2000, while the others—and the marketmaker—have standardized on other vendors' interchange servers. Similarly, the trading partners use different message and document formats; different transport protocols and middleware environments; and different vendors' line-of-business applications. But they can interoperate because their various interchange servers—including BizTalk Server 2000—support all or most of the formats, protocols, and middleware technologies common to trading partners.

BizTalk Server 2000 could just as easily sit at the hub as at any of the spokes in an e-marketplace. However, in most real-world trading environments it will be merely one of many interchange nodes that will communicate among themselves as peers in a distributed environment. Consider the diversity of trading partners and facilitators in a typical hubbed e-marketplace, per our discussion in Chapter 6. Then consider the complexity of the

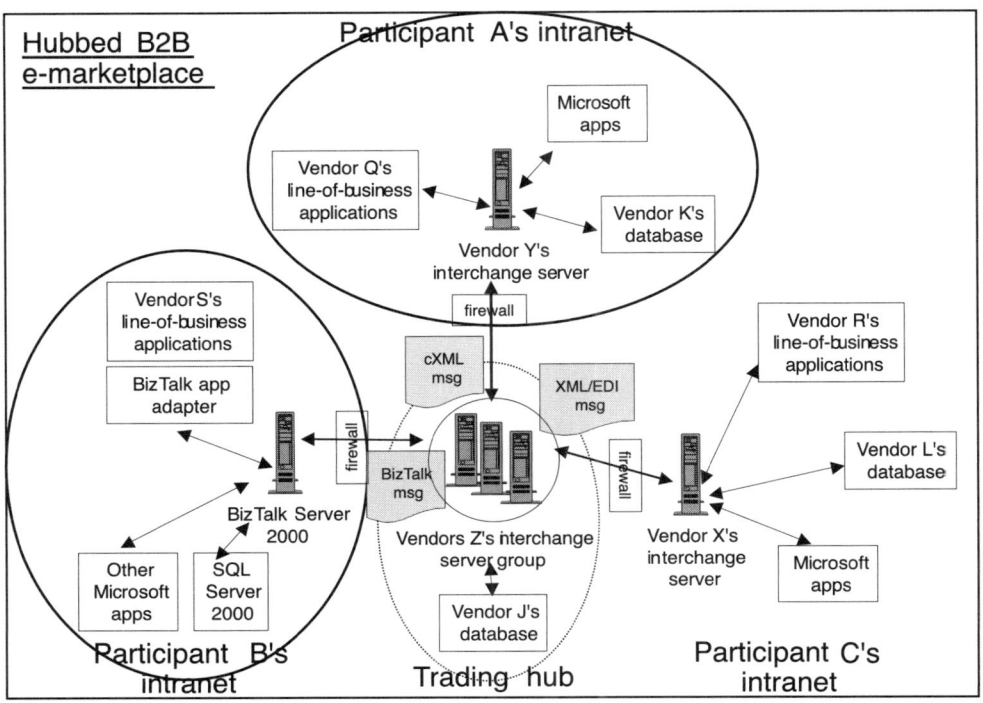

Figure 9-27 *BizTalk Server 2000 is only one of many interchange servers that may be deployed by participants in e-marketplaces to support B2B and EAI interchanges.*

workflows among these participants. What this complexity translates to is a multiplicity of documents, maps, envelopes, organizations, and agreements in a typical interorganizational workflow, or in a typical internal workflow within a complex enterprise.

Figure 9-28 shows, in more of a symbolic than topological view, the any-to-any interchange server connections required among organizations participating in a hubbed e-marketplace. At the core of the market is an e-marketmaker who maintains a central interchange server that connects with the interchange servers that link buyers, sellers, and various trade facilitators (such as payment, finance, insurance, shipping, legal, appraisal, and other service providers) into the trading environment.

In such an environment, which is becoming typical of B2B e-commerce, the end-to-end workflow path is exceedingly complex and not under the control of any one organization or any one interchange server platform. For the typical e-marketplace or extranet, the complete commerce inter-

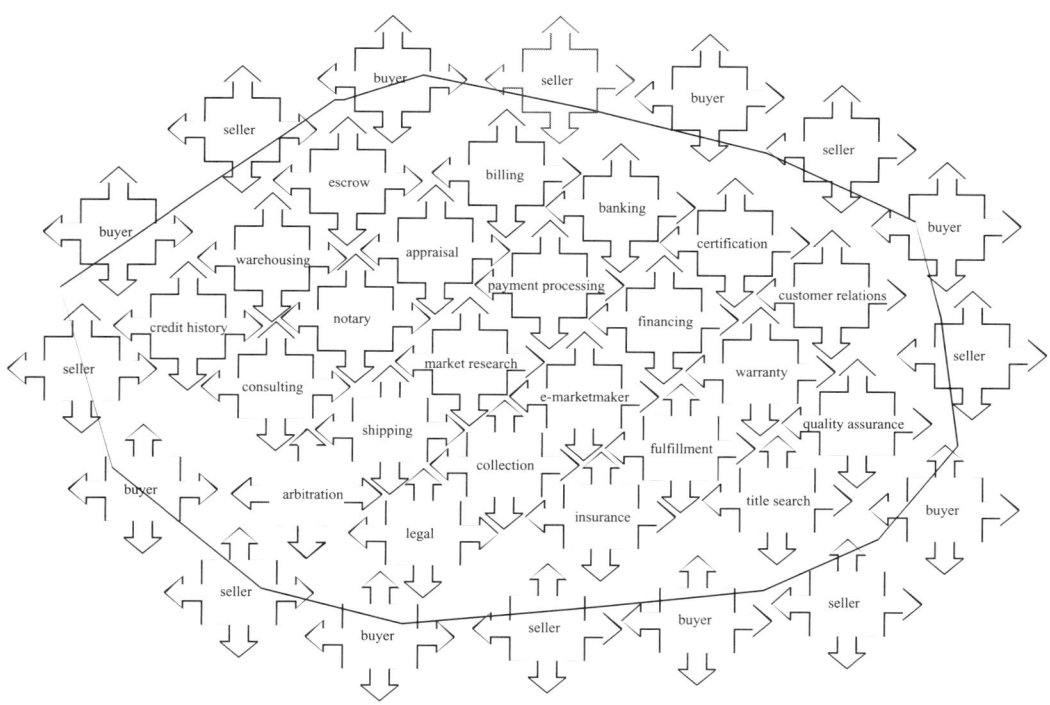

Figure 9-28   *Every participant in an e-marketplace will deploy interchange servers for B2B and EAI interoperability, requiring any-to-any connectivity in order to engage in complex transactional workflows involving many organizations.*

change pipeline is a long and twisty one. It wends its way from application to application, inside and outside any one participant's network, relayed from one interchange server platform to another.

9.5 Summary

Down deep, BizTalk Server 2000 is a sophisticated relay for B2B and EAI traffic, but not really a full-fledged enterprise workflow engine.

Sophisticated as it is, BizTalk Server 2000 can manage workflows only one node at a time, in accordance with agreements that define how a particular node is to process and route a particular document type exchanged between two organizations or applications. BizTalk's orchestration consists only of a chain of processing activities—transformation, decoding, decryption, routing-expression evaluation, etc.—performed within a particular instance of the server. The BizTalk Management Desk does not provide the tools necessary to centrally define and manage an "aggregated" end-to-end transactional workflow involving many BizTalk Servers and BizTalk-enabled applications.

All of which should not detract from the importance of BizTalk Server 2000 in Microsoft's product line or as one of the more prominent interchange servers on the market. This is an increasingly crowded market niche, with Microsoft going up against Bluestone, eXcelon, Extricity, Hewlett-Packard, i2, Manugistics, Mercator Software, Netfish, Vitria, WebMethods, and others. These vendors provide core application integration, content processing, and service management functionality that is comparable—though not identical—to what Microsoft supports in BizTalk Server 2000.

BizTalk Server 2000 and its competitors address the market's need for a new generation of "B2B message switches" that bridge incompatible environments associated with such acronyms as EDI, EAI, ERP, CRM, operational resource management (ORM), and supply-chain management (SCM). Growth of B2B interoperability depends on these interchange servers, just as any-to-any e-mail interoperability once depended on message switches that bridged incompatible messaging environments until SMTP and related e-mail standards became ubiquitous.

Until such time as universal B2B and EAI interoperability standards emerge and are implemented everywhere, interchange servers will need to maintain a wide range of connectors to various protocols, middleware technologies, and content formats. BizTalk Server 2000, like its rivals, is fundamentally a data-passing "switchboard" par excellence.

Microsoft Commerce Server 2000

Commerce Server 2000 is Microsoft's sell-side application server for B2B and B2C e-commerce.

Commerce Server 2000 and BizTalk Server 2000 are twin products. They descend from a common ancestor, Microsoft Site Server Commerce Edition version 3 (SSCE3). They entered the world during approximately the same timeframe: the second half of the year 2000. And they remain attached to a virtual "umbilical cord": the transactional workflow thread that joins Commerce Server 2000's Order Processing Pipeline to BizTalk Server 2000's Commerce Interchange Pipeline within Microsoft's Windows Distributed interNetworking Architecture (DNA) environment (which we will discuss more fully in Part 4 of this book). However, the two application servers are independent siblings. Each is able to function without the other, though they work well together when deployed in the same data center, intranet, or extranet.

10.1 Commerce Server 2000's Role in Microsoft's Application Server Family

Commerce Server 2000 is at heart a catalog server.

The server aggregates monetizable content in the form of product listings with associated descriptions, prices, and order information. It lets browser-based customers select what they want from the online catalog, populate virtual "shopping carts," place orders, enter credit card and shipping information, and track order status. Behind the scenes, Commerce Server 2000 is pulling customer and product data from databases, tailoring the customer's shopping experience to their profiles or preferences, and securing purchase authorizations from third-party payment processors.

At the core of Commerce Server 2000 are two critical architectural features: a data warehouse and a transactional workflow model. Commerce Server 2000's data warehouse is a SQL Server–based repository for aggregated "commerce data objects," which include product information, user profiles, transaction data, advertisements, and promotions. Its transactional workflow is the Order Processing Pipeline, which is a set of software components that process these data objects in a particular structured sequence in order to execute e-commerce transactions.

Taken together, Commerce Server 2000's data warehouse and Order Processing Pipeline support membership, aggregation, transaction, pricing, and payment services for online merchants (per the e-marketplace reference model we introduced in Chapter 6). Put another way, Commerce Server 2000 helps merchants deliver a personalized, content-rich, user-friendly, efficient online shopping experience. It gives online merchants the tools to catch and keep customers, which is always the paramount concern for any business.

Commerce Server 2000 allows merchants to create customized, scalable e-commerce storefronts; drive traffic to those sites through online advertising and promotional campaigns; personalize the shopping experience for each online customer; and analyze the success of those campaigns in real time. Enterprises and independent software vendors can build e-commerce solutions in Commerce Server 2000 quickly with prebuilt business components, out-of-the box solution sites, and a broad range of third-party products. Customized applications on the Commerce Server 2000 can address various horizontal and vertical market requirements. Some of the functional extensions that can be built for Commerce Server 2000 include the ability to integrate with external ERP, EDI, payment, tax, shipping, logistics, procurement, accounting, and customer management applications.

Commerce Server 2000 does not support the functionality that would be necessary to support a full-function trading hub, such as buy-offer aggregation, sophisticated auction mechanisms, and links to vertical market collaboration services. It does support forward auctions, but not reverse or double auctions. Consequently, we may regard Commerce Server 2000 as primarily a dotcom merchant's platform, but not an e-marketmaker platform for hosting complex trading communities.

Microsoft has targeted Commerce Server 2000 at companies building Internet and extranet selling sites. The product supports closed-loop merchandising and real-time marketing to online customers. Improvements over SSCE3 include advanced catalog management features, higher-performance content personalization and targeting, and online analytical processing to gauge site business performance. Typically, companies would deploy Commerce Server 2000 with SQL Server 7 or 2000 for transactional databases, Host Interchange Server 2000 for access to legacy host databases, BizTalk

Server 2000 for interchange processing, and Windows 2000's Active Directory for membership services. Companies might also link Commerce Server 2000 to MSN and other online marketplaces to promote their online sell-sites and interchange commerce-relevant data with customers.

Commerce Server 2000 supports five principal feature sets: user management, campaign management, catalog management, order management, and operational data analysis. The product implements these functions through three layers of software components: Commerce Desk administration tools, run-time services, and commerce data object schemas. We list these components in Table 10-1 and present a graphical overview in Figure 10-1. We will discuss these functional subsystems and components in greater detail later in this chapter.

Table 10-1   *Commerce Server 2000 Functional Layers and Modules*

Layer	Description	Modules
Commerce Desk	Console for daily administration of all merchant site transactional functions	User management
		Campaign management
		Catalog management
		Order management
		Data management
Run-time services	Software components driving operation of all merchant site transactional functions	User profiling service
		Content targeting service (including components for direct mail, advertisements and promotions, real-time recommendations, expression evaluation, and content selection)
		Catalog service
		Order processing pipeline service (including interface to BizTalk Server 2000's Commerce Interchange Pipeline)
		Data analysis service (including components for data import, data warehouse management, and reporting management)
Commerce data object schemas	Information models programmatically exposing structure and functionality of all commerce data objects	User profile schemas (including definitions for profiles, expressions, and terms)
		Advertisement and promotion schemas
		Catalog schemas
		Order form and requisition schemas
		Data warehouse schemas

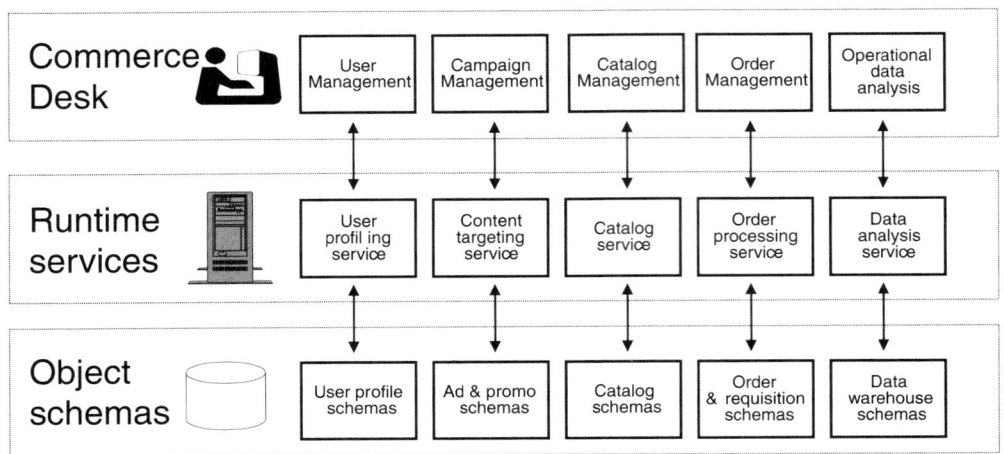

Commerce Desk		User Management	Campaign Management	Catalog Management	Order Management	Operational data analysis

Runtime services		User profil ing service	Content targeting service	Catalog service	Order processing service	Data analysis service

Object schemas		User profile schemas	Ad & promo schemas	Catalog schemas	Order & requisition schemas	Data warehouse schemas

Figure 10-1   *Commerce Server 2000 consists of three principal functional layers: Commerce Desk, runtime services, and commerce data object schemas. These layers' components support the server's core e-commerce functionality: user management, campaign management, catalog management, order management, and data management.*

The site administration tool for Commerce Server 2000 is Commerce Desk, which is comparable to BizTalk Server 2000's BizTalk Management Desk. Commerce Desk is an MMC console for hosting storefront site-administration modules. It also supports remote browser-based access and provides 20 functional modules for common business operations.

Microsoft provides a software development kit for developers to craft new modules for Commerce Desk. The vendor also provides Commerce Server 2000 "solution sites," which are production-quality site designs for quick deployment (in contrast to SSCE3's sample sites, which were more rudimentary and were intended only as simple references for developers to use in crafting more sophisticated commerce sites). Commerce Server 2000's out-of-box solution sites include B2B supplier catalogs and B2C retail storefronts.

Microsoft also provides an MMC-based Packager/UnPackager (PUP) utility, which supports remote staging, distribution, and installation of customized Commerce Server storefronts. PUP packages a Commerce Server site into a single compressed, redistributable unit, including configuration profiles, database schemas, data, folders, and files. At the receiving end, PUP extracts and decompresses the resources of a "pupped" Commerce Server site and installs them. Administrators may package all components of a site or just selected components by calling the "iPUP" COM interface exposed by all site resources. The utility allows administrators to invoke this functionality from MMC or a command line interface.

Microsoft envisions using PUP as an integration layer between its Commerce Server 2000 product and its Web-based Commerce Server 2000 site. The utility will allow Microsoft to distribute new, ready-to-deploy site configurations over the Internet to its customers. It will also allow customers to upload site configurations and contents to Microsoft for aggregation in Microsoft-managed e-marketplaces.

Commerce Server 2000 interfaces with BizTalk Server 2000 for interchanging commerce data objects—such as purchase orders and product catalogs—with remote applications. Figure 10-2 shows two such scenarios.

Scenario A involves interchange of purchase orders. In this scenario, one company captures purchase orders at its Commerce Server 2000 and transfers them, via BizTalk Server 2000, to another company (perhaps an order fulfillment house), which processes them on its back-end commerce applications (perhaps order processing, manufacturing, and shipping applica-

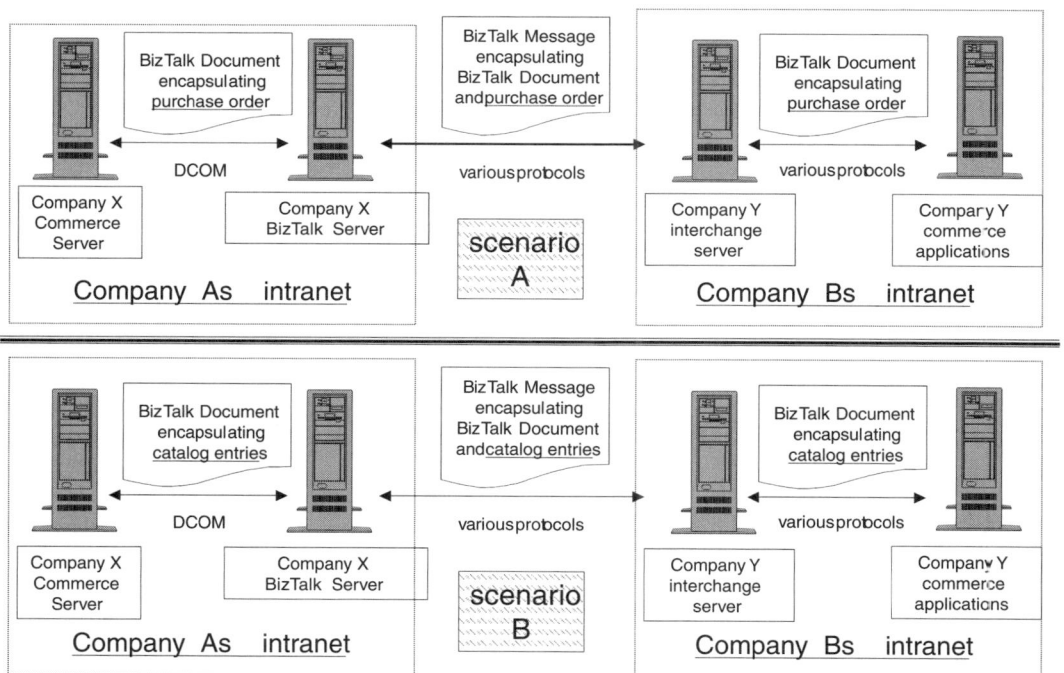

Figure 10-2 *Commerce Server 2000 can submit commerce data objects, such as purchase orders and product catalog entries, to BizTalk Server 2000 for processing and routing to trading partners. Commerce Server 2000 can also receive and process inbound commerce data, such as purchase order confirmations and functional acknowledgments, routed through BizTalk Server 2000.*

tions). Commerce Server 2000 wraps the outbound interchange in a BizTalk Document envelope and then invokes a Microsoft-provided API to submit the document to BizTalk Server 2000. Upon receiving the outbound BizTalk Document that contains the purchase order, BizTalk Server 2000 may translate and transform it into an EDI format that can be processed by the recipient organization's commerce applications, according to an agreement defined under BizTalk Management Desk. Likewise, BizTalk Server 2000 may apply a digital signature to the outbound purchase order and encrypt its contents, per the same agreement. Furthermore, BizTalk Server 2000 may then encapsulate the purchase order in a BizTalk Message envelope, if specified in the agreement. And BizTalk Server 2000 would usually perform the same operations in reverse on inbound purchase order confirmations or functional acknowledgments from the trading partner, per agreements specific to inbound interchanges.

Scenario B involves interchange of product catalogs, or at least subsets of these catalogs. Under this scenario, a company maintains product catalog information on its Commerce Server 2000 and transfers catalog entries, via BizTalk Server 2000, to another company (perhaps an e-marketmaker). Commerce Server 2000 calls a Microsoft-provided catalog API to select entries and submit them to an external application via BizTalk Server. The recipient processes the catalog entries on its back-end commerce application (perhaps a vertical industry trading hub platform that aggregates the entries with catalog data from other merchants). And as in the previous scenario, BizTalk Server 2000 may translate, transform, sign, encrypt, and encapsulate outbound catalog entries according to agreements defined under BizTalk Management Desk.

Under either scenario, BizTalk Server 2000 interfaces locally to Commerce Server 2000 via DCOM, which is Microsoft's object broker technology for program-to-program communications between its application servers. BizTalk Server 2000, in turn, interfaces remotely to the other company's interchange server (which may be another BizTalk Server or a third-party product) via various protocols, such as HTTP, and MSMQ. The recipient organization's interchange server passes the commerce-relevant data to back-end commerce applications (which may run on Microsoft or third-party application servers) via various protocols.

We have assumed under these scenarios that the third-party interchange servers and applications are, like Microsoft's application servers, all "BizTalk-enabled." What this means is that third-party products can wrap outbound commerce data objects in BizTalk envelopes and extract inbound data from BizTalk envelopes. In this real world, however, we cannot take this for granted, considering that Microsoft may never achieve universal deployment of BizTalk Server 2000 or universal support for the BizTalk Framework.

The important thing to remember is that it doesn't matter whether the whole world of e-commerce is BizTalk-enabled (though Microsoft of course wishes you would think otherwise). As we showed in Chapter 9, BizTalk Server 2000 provides a translation layer that interfaces Commerce Server 2000 to many of the e-commerce content standards and network middleware environments in use in the world today. However, Microsoft was still undecided, as of the date this book was written, as to whether it would interface BizTalk Server 2000 to competing e-commerce interoperability specifications such as cXML and OBI.

10.2 User Management

Commerce Server 2000's user management services enable e-commerce sites to identify, profile, authenticate, and authorize browser-based customers. User profiles also allow online merchants to personalize commerce services for each customer.

The basis for Commerce Server 2000's user management functionality is a SQL Server–based repository of user objects with associated schemas. A schema is an information model that specifies the elements and attributes that characterize a logical entity, such as an individual user. Commerce Server 2000 defines user schemas that consist of "profiles," "terms," and "expressions." Table 10-2 describes these elements and the typical attributes of which they are composed.

Table 10-2	Commerce Server 2000 User
Element	**Description**
User profiles	Define logical data objects associated with individual customers or potential customers in Commerce Server 2000. User profiles have mandatory fields, usually user names and passwords. These mandatory fields are those that uniquely identify and authenticate individuals to Commerce Server 2000, thereby serving as the basis for the system to assign globally unique identifiers (GUIDs) for particular instances of user objects. Commerce Server 2000's User Profile Object (UPO) is the successor to SSCE3's Active User Object (AUO).
User terms	Consist of attributes associated with particular user profiles. User terms drive Commerce Server 2000's content targeting and service personalization functionality. Typical user terms include group memberships, addresses, birth dates, income, education, preferences, and transaction history. Commerce Server 2000 maintains a common store of business terms used in profiles and expressions.
User expressions	User expressions consist of conditional rules, using boolean operators, that Commerce Server 2000 evaluates against profile instances in order to target content and personalize service delivery. One natural-language example of a user expression is "if user has purchased more than 10 times from the site, then user is a frequent buyer."

Administrators use Commerce Desk's "meta-schema" definition tool to create schemas for user profiles, terms, and expressions in Commerce Desk (as well as for other entities such as organizations, accounts, requisitions, purchase orders, advertisements, and product catalogs). User-object schemas define the information model for a user profile data repository that Commerce Server 2000 maintains in SQL Server 2000. Microsoft often refers to user profile, term, and expression schemas as "BizData definitions." A sample user profile, including various commerce-relevant terms, would look as follows:

User.Surname = "Kobielus"
User.Firstname = "James"
User.Nickname = "Jim"
User.Email = "james_kobielus@hotmail.com"
User.BirthDate = "November 13, 1958"
User.Gender = "male"
User.BirthCountry = "USA"
User.ResidenceCountry = "USA"
User.FirstLanguage = "English"
User.FamilyStatus = "married with children"
User.Occupation = "analyst"
User.Interests = "technology", "business", "music", "conversation",
               "reader feedback"
User.EducationLevel = "graduate school"

Commerce Server 2000's profiling system provides run-time services for instantiating user "BizData" schemas in support of authentication, authorization, content targeting, and service personalization. The server aggregates user data from multiple back-end directories and other data stores into its Commerce Property Store, which it maintains under SQL Server 7 or 2000. It translates and maps all imported user data into XML syntax for storage and manipulation within its user profile repository.

Commerce Server 2000 can store user profile attributes in any of several external data stores, but aggregates the information logically as a single user-profile object. Commerce Server 2000 provides out-of-box support for Windows 2000 Active Directory, SQL Server 7 and 2000, SSCE3 Membership Directory, and various databases, including DB2 and Oracle. Storing user profile data in Active Directory facilitates integration of this data with other applications running on Windows 2000.

Commerce Server 2000 can use any of the following interfaces to read from and write to external stores of user information:

- Active Directory Services Interface (ADSI) for access to Windows 2000's Active Directory (AD)

- Lightweight Directory Access Protocol (LDAP) for access to third-party directories
- OLE DB to access its Commerce SQL Property Store under SQL Server 2000 or SQL Server 7
- Open Database Connectivity (ODBC) to access third-party databases

Figure 10-3 shows the layered architecture that Commerce Server 2000 uses to aggregate external data into its user profile repository. The server's profile service provides an API for profile objects to access back-end user data. An ActiveX Data Object (ADO) API supports batch selection, insertion,

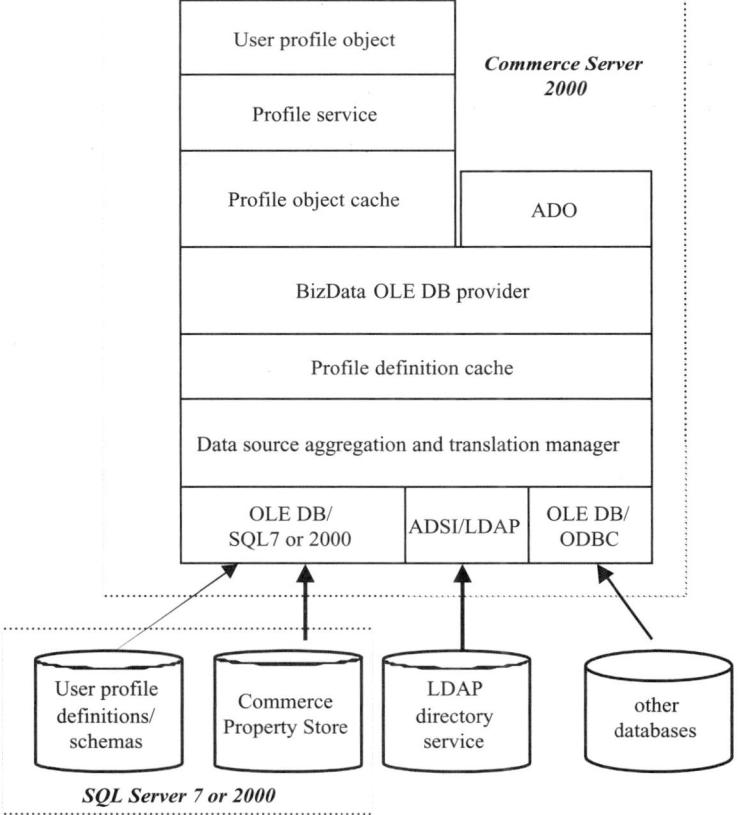

Figure 10-3 *Commerce Server 2000 aggregates external data into its user-profile repository through a server software architecture that relies on a "BizData OLE DB provider," a data source aggregation manager, and optimized data-source plug-ins for directories, SQL Server 7 and 2000, and ODBC sources.*

and updating of user profile object data. Several software layers on Commerce Server 2000 enable user profile objects to access external data sources. These layers include a BizData OLE DB provider, a profile definition cache, a data-source translation and aggregation manager, and optimized data-source provider plug-ins for various directories and databases. Commerce Server 2000 stores user profile definitions/schemas ("BizData" schemas) as well as user-profile properties under SQL Server 7 or 2000.

Figure 10-4 shows how Commerce Desk interfaces to Commerce Server 2000's user-profile schema and data repository. Commerce Desk's User Management Console includes designers for specifying profile, term, and expression schemas and for mapping those schemas to back-end data-source formats. Commerce Desk then submits these schema definitions to a BizData administration object running under Commerce Server 2000. The server stores the schema definitions in SQL Server 7 or 2000 and performs the specified mapping and translation.

Commerce Server 2000 works with various user authentication mechanisms. It supports all authentication schemes used by Microsoft Internet Information Services, Windows 2000 Server, and Windows NT Server. It supports browser-based forms authentication against Windows 2000 Active Directory under a user's existing AD account, as well as browser-based forms

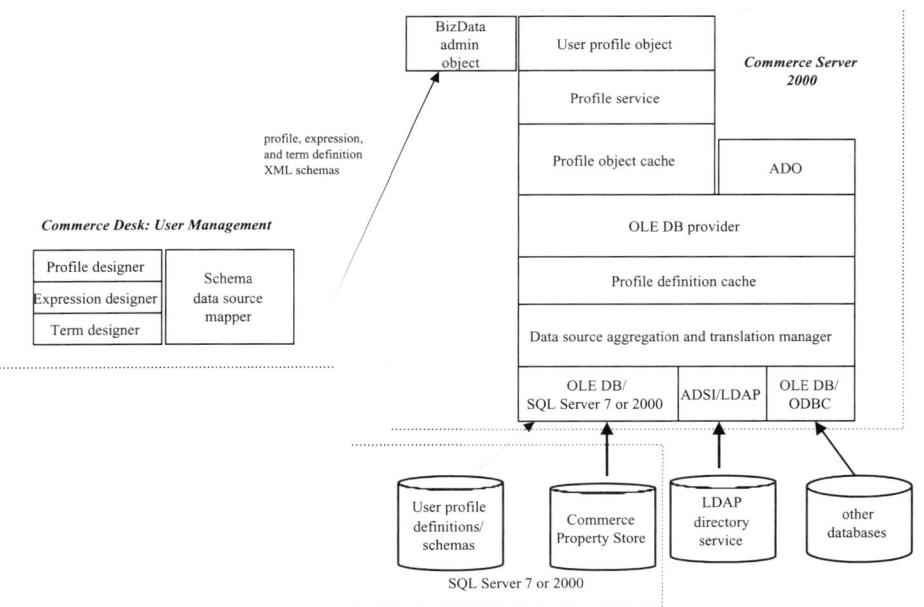

Figure 10-4 *Commerce Desk provides tools for defining schemas for Commerce Server 2000 user profiles, terms, and expressions and for mapping and translating these schemas to the formats supported by various data sources.*

authentication with or without cookies. It supports authentication using encrypted data encrypted on cookies or URLs.

User profiles, terms, and expressions drive all run-time services under Commerce Server 2000. In addition to authentication, user "BizData" determines how the server targets advertisements and promotions, proffers real-time recommendations, populates direct mail lists, personalizes product displays, tailors order-processing transactions to each user's profile, and logs user activities under Commerce Server 2000. Figure 10-5 shows how Commerce Server 2000's various run-time services employ user "BizData" information. In all subsystems the server evaluates user profile properties against expressions, which are business rules, and then passes the results of these "expression evaluations" to COM objects that manage the various server-based functions.

To speed performance on all these profile-driven operations, Commerce Server 2000 provides extensive data caching on profile properties, expressions, and results. Microsoft has designed Commerce Server 2000 as a scalable product capable of supporting more than 100,000 concurrent browser-based users per server engaged in a mix of login, read, and write operations. Commerce Server 2000 integrates tightly with Windows 2000's Internet Information Server, which manages rendering and processing of Active Server Pages (ASPs) for interactions with browser-based clients.

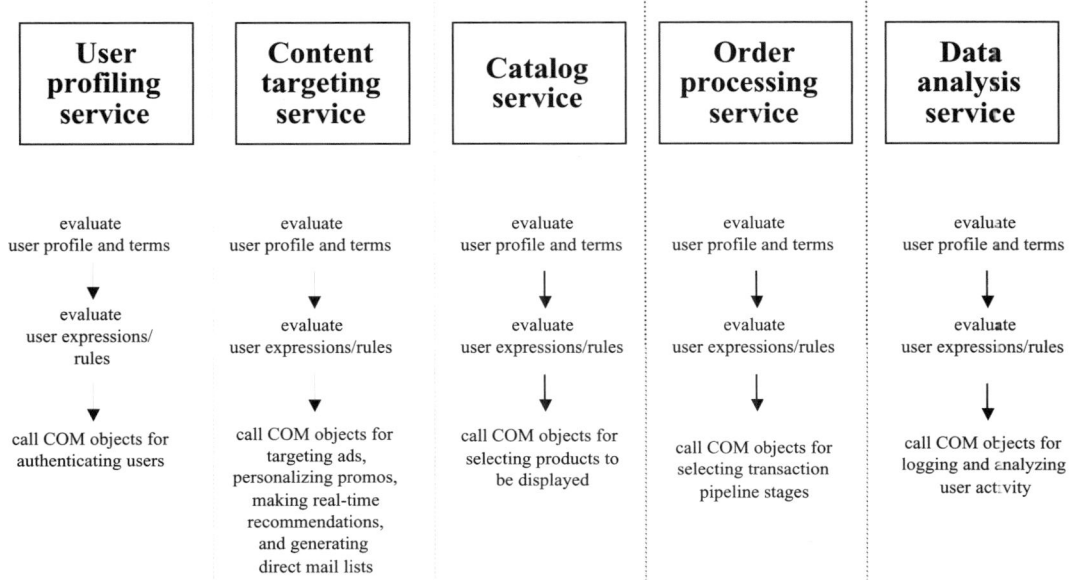

Figure 10-5   *User profiles, terms, and expression drive Commerce Server 2000's authentication, targeting, and personalization functions.*

10.3 Campaign Management

Commerce Server 2000's campaign management services enable e-commerce administrators to mount a coordinated online marketing campaign. The product provides tools for administrators to drive traffic to their sites, target advertisements and promotions to each user's profile, and stimulate, through real-time recommendations, customer purchasing of items relevant to their explicit or implicit preferences. Site administrators can use historical data to design effective advertising and merchandising models, develop future campaign strategies, and personalize e-commerce services.

Commerce Desk's Campaign Manager combines all content delivery vehicles into a coordinated online marketing campaign. Site administrators can target several types of marketing data content to users based on their profiles, buying patterns, and other variables, as presented in Table 10-3.

Making a coordinated online marketing campaign possible are the software platforms and components presented in Table 10-4 and illustrated in

Table 10-3	*Commerce Server 2000 Targeted Marketing Campaign Data Types*
Data Type	**Description**
Direct marketing	Administrators can define expression rules for submitting direct-marketing-related e-mails to targeted lists of users, based on their profiles, buying histories, and other variables. They can define per-user message formats. They can also monitor performance of e-mail-based direct marketing campaigns, including clickthroughs from mail-embedded URLs all the way to the resulting online purchase.
Advertisements	Administrators can define expression rules for presenting onscreen ads in response to user profiles, buying histories, shopping cart contents, and other variables. They can schedule ad presentation and monitor performance of advertising campaigns.
Promotions	Administrators can define expression rules for presenting promotional discounts and special pricing keyed to particular products in their Commerce Server 2000 catalog or items in a customer's online shopping basket during a browsing session. They can also monitor performance of promotional campaigns, tracking all the way to the ultimate purchase.
Real-time recommendations	Administrators can define expression rules for generating real-time recommendations to users of products that they might want, based on user profiles, buying histories, and other variables. These rules allow administrators to target their up-selling, cross-selling, and inventory-selling efforts at those users most likely to respond favorably. The inventory-selling feature suppresses recommendations of popular items in favor of slower-selling items in a merchant's inventory.

Figure 10-6. E-commerce site administrators manage online marketing campaigns with software in Commerce Desk, Commerce Server 2000, SQL Server 7 or 2000, Microsoft Exchange Server 5.5 or 2000, Microsoft Internet Information Server 5.0, and BizTalk Server 2000. Commerce Desk allows administrators to define the business rules that govern these application servers, as well as the schemas that define each of the commerce data objects used in marketing campaigns.

Table 10-4	Commerce Server 2000 Campaign Management Architecture Components	
Platform	**Component**	**Description**
Commerce Desk	Expression builder	Lets administrators define conditional rules to drive content targeting, service personalization, real-time recommendations, direct mailing, and order processing under Commerce Server 2000. It uses boolean operators and profile attributes to build conditional expressions in XML syntax. In addition to keying on user profile information, expressions can incorporate variables related to the contents of a customer's online "shopping basket" as well as other context variables such as the site section, page elements, and time associated with a user interaction through Commerce Server 2000.
	Direct mail editor	Lets administrators define the content of bulk direct mailings to be transmitted from Commerce Server 2000.
	List manager	Supports definition, compilation, and management of lists of e-mail addresses for bulk e-mailings from Commerce Server 2000, as well as opt-out addresses. The list manager is most effective when Commerce Server 2000 administrators use customers' e-mail addresses as their default user IDs. The tool allows administrators or marketing managers to build dynamic and static lists. Lists can be built from SQL Server data warehouse calculations of user profiles and behavior, from imported flat files or data warehouse files, and from SQL queries on back-end databases. Commerce Desk's list manager and Commerce Server 2000's corresponding list server scale to millions of list rows. Lists can also be exported from Commerce Desk to external databases. Microsoft provides a full API supporting programmatic access to list management functions.
Commerce Server 2000	Expression evaluator	Interprets user expressions against user profiles and terms in order to drive targeting, personalization, and order-processing functions across all components of Commerce Server 2000. It supports transformation of expressions into SQL queries for submission of external data sources.

Table 10-4	Commerce Server 2000 Campaign Management Architecture Components (cont.)	
Platform	**Component**	**Description**
	Content selector	Uses expression evaluations and related-sell predictions as inputs in selecting advertisements, promotions, direct mail, product entries, and other content for presentation to users.
	Related-sell predictor	Uses expression evaluations as inputs in predicting what other products should be presented to users from Commerce Server 2000's catalog, based on their likely interest or need for such products. It supports up-selling, cross-selling, and inventory selling. It builds on the "Intelligent Cross-Sell" feature from SSCE3, providing personalized product recommendations. The service allows administrators to tweak the prediction algorithms and adjust the number of recommendations returned.
	List server	Sends bulk direct mailings to users via Exchange Server 5.5/2000 and/or BizTalk Server 2000. It tracks mailings, mail responses, and clickthroughs from URLs embedded in sent messages.
SQL Server 7 or 2000		Maintains databases for user profiles, product catalogs, opt-in and opt-out mailing lists, advertisements and promotions, marketing information, campaign status, and usage analysis.
Internet Information Server 5.0		Delivers ASPs to browser-based clients of Commerce Server 2000, supporting the primary, page-oriented user interface for commerce applications.
Exchange Server 5.5 or 2000		Relays direct marketing messages from Commerce Server 2000's list server to e-mail addresses on mailing lists maintained under Commerce Desk.
BizTalk Server 2000		Relays direct marketing e-mails from Commerce Server 2000's list server to addresses on e-mail systems and line-of-business applications.

Taken together, these platforms and tools let Commerce Server 2000 sites get the right message to the right customer at the right time through various online channels. They allow sites to personalize the shopping experience for each customer. And they provide the means to bind customers ever more closely into a membership environment surrounding each commerce site.

Microsoft has expressed a general intention of supporting online marketing campaign management through its MSN services. The vendor's goal is

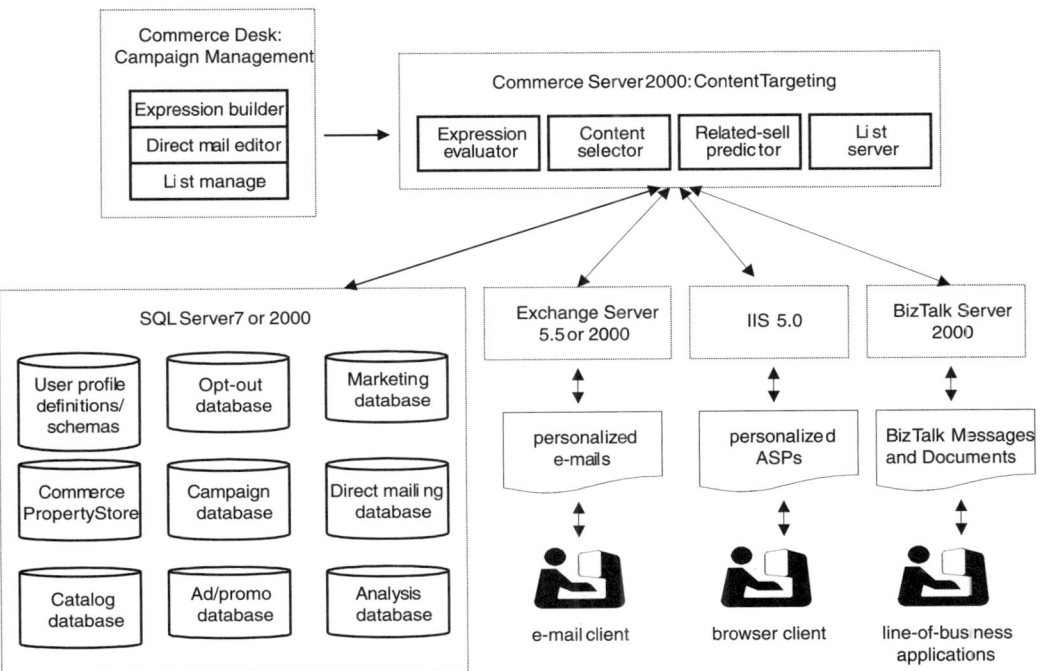

Commerce Desk provides tools for managing online marketing campaigns through Commerce Server 2000, SQL Server 7 or 2000, Exchange Server 5.5 or 2000, Internet Information Server 5.0, and BizTalk Server 2000.

to provide a solution set that lets people build not only storefronts online but also their revenue streams as well by connecting merchants with customers. Commerce Server 2000 customers will be able to list their companies, products, and promotions in MSN e-marketplace directories and catalogs. It's with this background that we can understand why Microsoft has established the following online properties under MSN:

- bCentral: small business site hosting promotion, marketing, and management services
- ClearLead: lead management services
- LinkExchange: banner advertising exchange services
- Passport: account consolidation and single sign-on services
- Transpoint: bill presentment and payment services

Microsoft will no doubt continue to develop online properties that drive business toward its Commerce Server 2000 customers.

10.4 Catalog Management

Commerce Server 2000's catalog management services enable site administrators to define catalog schemas and import, compile, transform, search, target, and export product catalog content. E-commerce site administrators manage online catalogs with software in Commerce Desk, Commerce Server 2000, SQL Server 7 or 2000, and BizTalk Server 2000.

Commerce Server 2000 supports catalog import and exchange through BizTalk Server 2000, which makes it easier to build sophisticated sites that interact with catalogs from various suppliers and partners. It also supports attribute-based, free-text, and stepwise parametric search of catalogs, which facilitate catalog content targeting. Table 10-5 presents Commerce Server 2000's principal catalog management functions and explains the catalog-management role of each of these products. Figure 10-7 presents the interactions among these components graphically.

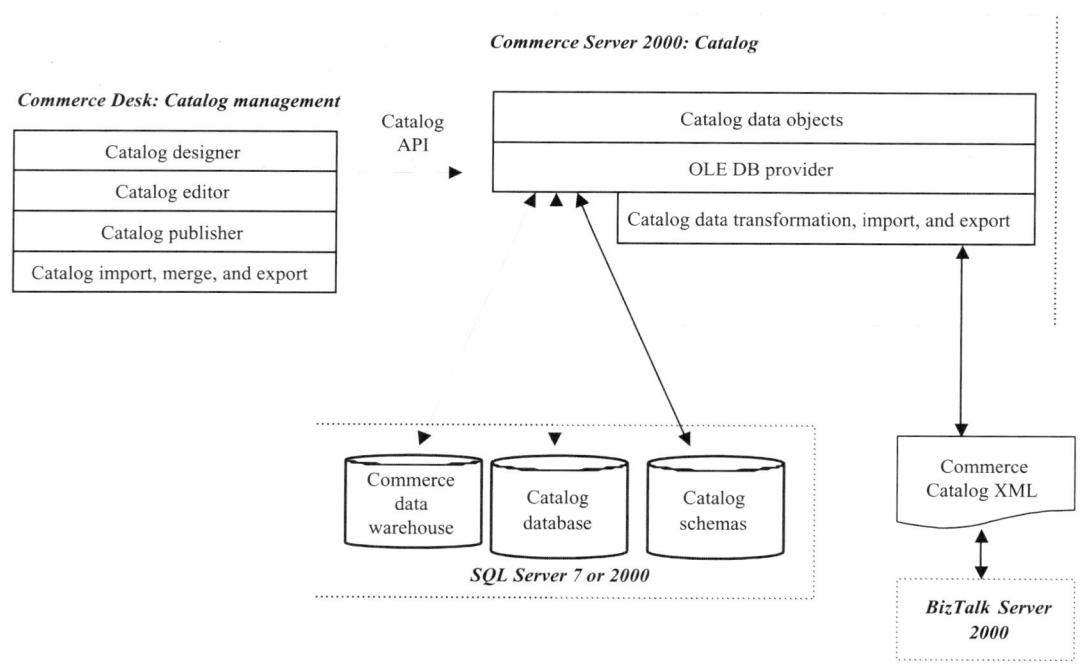

Figure 10-7   *Commerce Desk provides tools for managing product catalogs in Commerce Server 2000, which stores catalog schemas and data in SQL Server 7 or 2000 and exchanges catalogs through BizTalk Server 2000.*

Table 10-5	*Commerce Server 2000 Catalog Management Functions*
Function	**Description**
Define	Includes catalog design, editing, and publishing tools. These allow commerce site administrators to define custom product types and category hierarchies. Administrators can define logical product schemas, categories, products, product attributes, product variants, and custom catalogs. They can define an unlimited number of products and category levels per site; multiple catalogs per site; multiple category hierarchies per catalog; and intricate relationships among products and categories. They can enter and manage product data from within Commerce Desk, both interactively and in bulk. Commerce Server 2000 stores catalog schemas and data in SQL Server 7 or 2000 (via an ADO/OLE DB) interface, and exports product data to a "data warehouse" under SQL Server for reporting and analysis. Commerce Desk includes sample catalogs to get site administrators going with minimal setup.
Import, compile, transform, and export	Provides tools for importing and exporting catalog contents. Commerce Server 2000 supports interchange of catalog contents through BizTalk Server 2000 via a Catalog API (to a COM object) that exports and imports data in the Microsoft-defined Commerce Catalog XML format and in CSV format. The Commerce Catalog XML format is an XML Data Reduced schema that the vendor has published on the BizTalk.org schema repository. Administrators can use the Catalog API to import and export catalog information on individual products, groups of products, and product categories. The Catalog XML format represents both catalog schemas and data. Objects exported via the Catalog XML format may be mapped using the BizTalk Mapper tool in the BizTalk Management Desk. Administrators who deploy BizTalk Server 2000 with Commerce Server 2000 may rely on the former for document transformation, or may use Commerce Server 2000 for this purpose. It can transform outbound and inbound catalog contents through a data transformation service (DTS) in SQL Server 7 or 2000. It can also automatically import catalogs received through BizTalk Server 2000, thereby enabling catalog aggregation within SQL Server 7 or 2000.
Target	Enables administrators to build expressions for targeting display of product catalog content to users by Commerce Server 2000. Catalog content figures into targeting of promotions, advertising, real-time recommendations, and direct mail to users.
Search	Enables administrators to build expressions for queries and reports on product catalog data. The tools supports multiple search mechanisms, including free text, property-based, and progressive refinement. Users can search across multiple catalogs and browse by category.

Commerce Server 2000 can support third-party catalog systems as well. Microsoft provides tools for integrating third-party catalogs with SQL Server's data warehouse.

10.5 Order Management

Commerce Server 2000's order management services process online purchase transactions.

Commerce Server 2000, like BizTalk Server 2000, uses the term *pipeline* to refer to a framework for designing structured transactional workflows. A pipeline describes a list of tasks that occur in a particular order to set up and finalize a purchase transaction. Commerce Desk includes a pipeline development and editing tool for Commerce Server 2000. Commerce Desk allows developers to assemble Order Processing Pipelines that consist of "stages," each of which corresponds to a COM or COM+ component that operates on a commerce data object, such as a purchase order, requisition, catalog, or shopping basket. Pipeline components may be nested to create workflows of arbitrary complexity. Developers can create their own pipeline components. They can also create pipelines that execute either all stages or none at all, using the transactional features in Microsoft Transaction Server (MTS).

Developers craft an Order Processing Pipeline (OPP) in Commerce Desk. Table 10-6 shows some of the stages in the process of a purchase order form, as well as the corresponding COM components.

Stages in an OPP fall into three principal segments, as presented in Table 10-7.

If the customer submits the order to Commerce Server 2000 from a browser, then the OPP receives the order through an ASP on IIS 5.0 and submits the receipt through another ASP back to the customer. If the customer submits the order in a BizTalk Message relayed by BizTalk Server 2000, the OPP returns receipts in BizTalk Messages. In this way, Commerce Server 2000 and BizTalk Server 2000 manage two ends of the same transactional workflow. The former's OPP and the latter's Commerce Interchange Pipeline (CIP)—also known as "BizTalk Orchestration"— manage interorganizational workflows between online merchants and their trading partners. Figure 10-8 shows the high-level interface between Commerce Server 2000 and BizTalk

Table 10-6 *Some Order Processing Pipeline Stages and Corresponding COM Components*

Stage	Components
Product Info	QueryProdInfoADO
Item Price	DefaultItemPrice
Order Subtotal	DefaultOrderSubtotal
Shipping	Overnight; 2-DayGround
Tax	SimpleUSTax
Payment	CreditCardAuth

Table 10-7	*Commerce Server 2000 Order Processing Pipeline Segments*

Segment	Description
Product pipeline	Computes price and discount information for individual products that the customer has selected.
Plan pipeline	Builds the customer's online "shopping basket." It presents the customer with an order total that includes all discounts, taxes, and shipping and handling charges. And it makes sure the order items are in the merchant's inventory.
Purchase pipeline	Finalizes the purchase by performing credit card validation, writing the order to the merchant's SQL Server 7 or 2000 database, and generating a receipt for the customer.

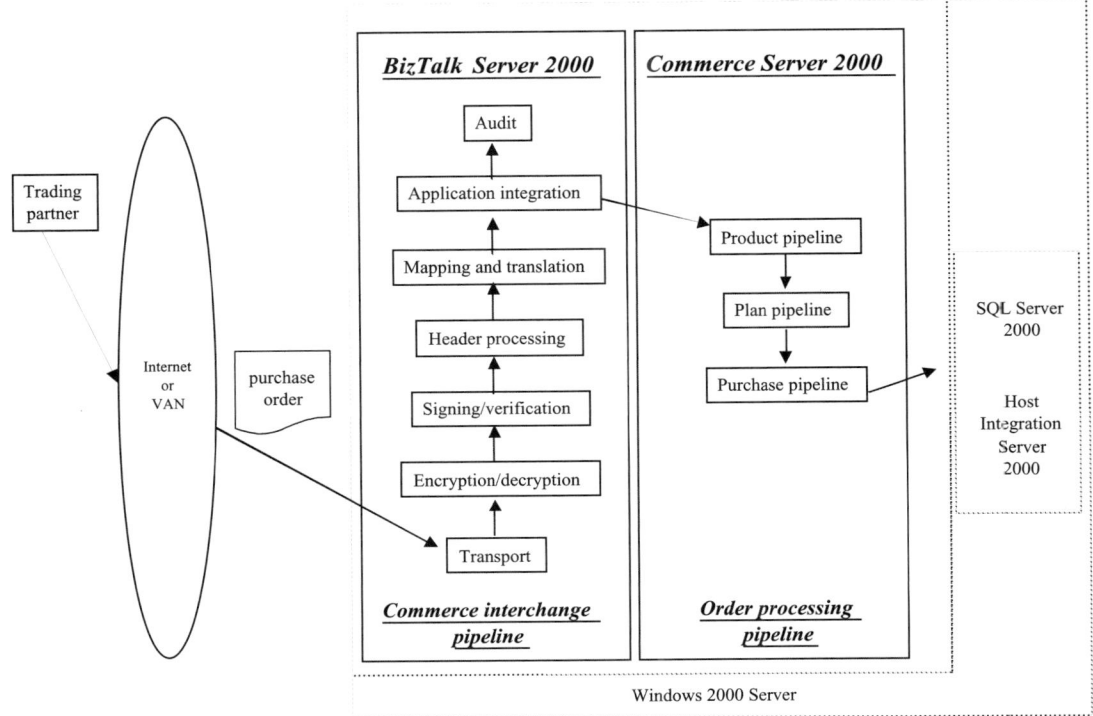

Figure 10-8	*Commerce Server 2000's Order Processing Pipeline links to BizTalk Server 2000's Commerce Interchange Pipeline to process purchase transactions from B2B trading partners over the Internet.*

Server 2000, indicating how the OPP and CIP connect to process an inbound purchase order submitted over the Internet by a B2B trading partner.

Commerce Server 2000 has several new OPP features that were lacking from SSCE3 and were included to address B2B procurement requirements. The new features including support for new currency data types, purchase order approval processes, multiple purchase orders per requisition, multiple shipments per purchase order, and processing of purchase orders submitted in BizTalk Message/Document and Open Buying on the Internet (OBI) envelopes. The new shipments architecture allows purchase orders to be split up by shipment method, shipping addresses, or any other order field.

10.6 Operational Data Analysis

Commerce Server 2000's operational data analysis services enable managers to monitor the business performance of their e-commerce site in real time.

The centerpiece of Commerce Server 2000's operational data analysis functionality is a data warehouse running on SQL Server 7 or 2000 (illustrated in Figure 10-9). Commerce Desk provides administrators with interactive tools for harnessing information in the data warehouse. They can track online sales by product, catalog, user, and other variables fed in by the other functional modules of Commerce Server 2000. They can also determine which pages and sections of the site were visited most and least frequently (through imported IIS 5.0 Web logs). All of this data helps businesses assess the effectiveness of their current site design, marketing campaigns, and product mix. They can determine the effectiveness of all components of their marketing campaign, including direct e-mailings, advertisements, promotions, and real-time recommendations. And they use SQL Server's data online analytical processing (OLAP) features to mine the data for implicit user behaviors, trends, and segmentation.

For example, business managers might access Commerce Desk's analytical tools to to see how a new online product promotion affected sales. They could then revise user expressions to try out a new content targeting approach. For example, campaign analysis results might factor into updates to targeted mailing lists, or be used to adjust real-time recommendations, so as to focus the marketing message more completely on particular user profiles.

For site performance tracking applications, Commerce Desk also provides more than 60 standard report formats out of the box. The tool allows administrators to save custom views of standard reports and to schedule report generation. They can export analytical data both incrementally and in bulk. Third-party analysis and reporting products can tap into Commerce Server 2000 data warehouse through an OLE DB interface.

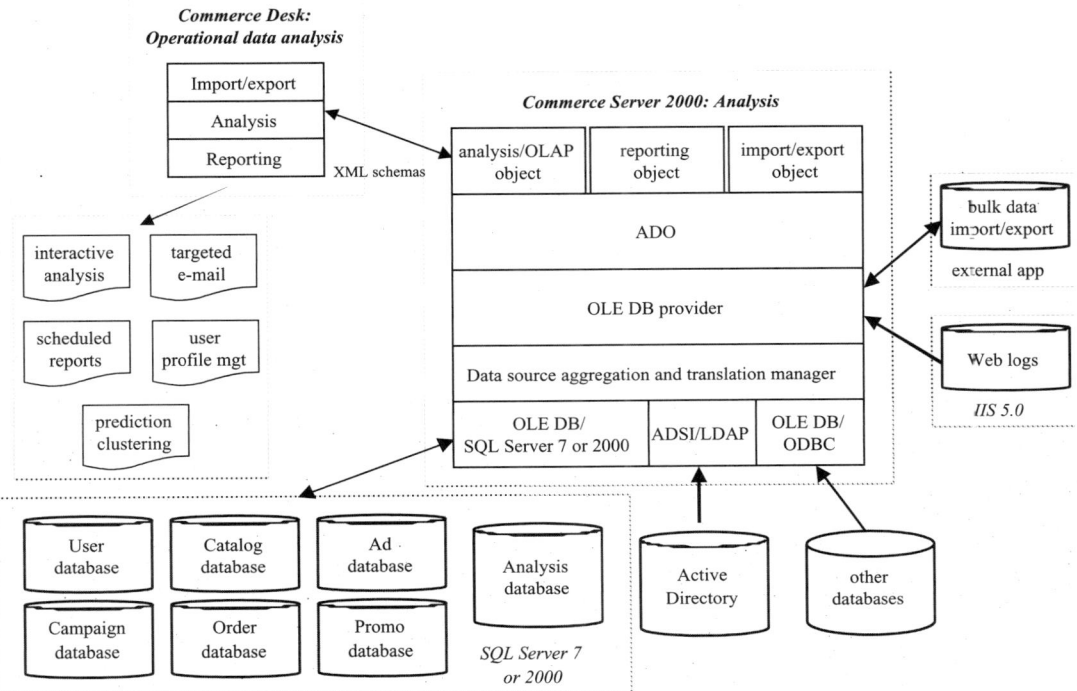

Figure 10-9 A SQL Server-based data warehouse supports Commerce Server 2000's operational data analysis functions.

As we have seen, Commerce Desk manages three types of data critical to the daily operations of an online storefront hosted on Commerce Server 2000. The tool manages user profile information, thereby defining the site's membership model and driving the marketing, authentication, and personalization processes. It manages the sales offers presented in a merchant's catalog, thereby defining the aggregation and pricing models and driving online purchase transactions. And it manages the real-time operational data that determines how well—or poorly—the site is contributing to the merchant's business objectives.

10.7 Summary

Commerce Server 2000's role in Microsoft's e-commerce strategy is clear. It hosts complete online businesses, aggregating commerce-relevant information fed in from many other Microsoft platforms, including Windows 2000's

Active Directory, SQL Server 2000, Host Information Server 2000, and Internet Information Server 5.0. And it participates in distributed trading environments anchored by Microsoft's B2B workflow engine: BizTalk Server 2000.

In the next chapter, we discuss SQL Server 2000 and Host Integration Server 2000. We also discuss a tool—Application Center 2000—for managing these and other Microsoft application servers as part of a clustered Web-farm deployment.

Other Microsoft Commerce-Related Products and Services

SQL Server 2000, Host Integration Server 2000, and Application Center 2000 round out Microsoft's e-commerce application-server family, providing the glue that anchors BizTalk Server 2000 and Commerce Server 2000 solidly in the enterprise data center.

As we've shown in previous chapters, BizTalk Server 2000 and Commerce Server 2000 rely heavily on SQL Server 2000 for core data storage, processing, and management services. In this chapter, we present a consolidated portrait of SQL Server 2000's many roles in Microsoft-based e-commerce applications. We also show how Host Integration Server 2000, heretofore not discussed in much detail, integrates legacy mainframe databases and transaction environments into the world of BizTalk-hubbed e-marketplaces. And we outline Application Center 2000's role in supporting scalable, reliable, continuously available e-commerce data-center operations.

What these servers share is a common operating platform, Microsoft Windows 2000; a common development tool, Microsoft Visual Studio; and a common development framework, the Web-oriented Distributed interNetworking Architecture (DNA). In September 1999, Microsoft announced these servers as components of its Windows DNA 2000 product family, a comprehensive, integrated environment that implements DNA. DNA is Microsoft's attempt to bridge many of its longtime programming interfaces into a new, Internet-oriented application environment. DNA includes interfaces that Microsoft has supported for years in its Windows platforms, plus some new standards developed elsewhere and subsequently embraced by Microsoft.

DNA's fundamentals, which we'll explore in greater detail in Part Four, consist of the following:

- Markup languages: XML, HTML
- Development interfaces: Active Server Pages, Visual Basic, VBScript, ECMAScript
- Object technologies: COM, COM+, DCOM, Simple Object Access Protocol (SOAP)
- Connector technologies: ActiveX Data Objects (ADO), OLE DB, Open Database Connectivity (ODBC)
- Transaction technologies: MTS, MSMQ

In this chapter, we also discuss how Windows DNA 2000 servers—SQL Server 2000, Host Integration Server 2000, Application Center 2000, BizTalk Server 2000, and Commerce Server 2000 (and, of course, Windows 2000)—integrate with the online commerce services in Microsoft's MSN portal environment. MSN e-marketplace services include bCentral for small business services, ClearLead for lead management, LinkExchange for online banner exchange, Passport for account consolidation and single sign-on, and Transpoint for bill presentment and payment. Microsoft has declared a general intention of supporting the BizTalk Framework and implementing BizTalk Server 2000 in its online services, primarily oriented toward an application service provider (ASP) business model. However, the company has not, as of the date this book went to press, presented a concrete roadmap or architecture for accomplishing this. Nonetheless, we discuss these services to show how a complete BizTalk-enabled e-commerce transactional pipeline—tying trading partners' internal systems with applicatoin service provider-based services—might look.

11.1 SQL Server 2000

SQL Server 2000 is the database server component of Microsoft's e-commerce strategy.

SQL Server 2000 is the successor to Microsoft's SQL Server 7.0 database server (which debuted in late 1998). This new generation integrates with Windows 2000 features such as Active Directory, Microsoft Management Console (MMC), Microsoft Cluster Server, Microsoft Certificate Server, Kerberos, native XML support, and multilingual user interfaces. And it adds considerable new functionality to the product, following the same development path that emphasizes improvements in scalability, availability, data warehousing, online analytical processing (OLAP), and manageability.

We discuss these new features in Table 11-1.

We present an overview of SQL Server 2000's total functionality, both new and pre-existing, in Figure 11-1.

As we discussed in Chapters 9 and 10, SQL Server 2000 (and its predecessor, SQL Server 7.0) provides databases and features that are critical to BizTalk Server 2000 and Commerce Server 2000. Consequently, SQL Server

Table 11-1	New Features in SQL Server 2000
Feature	**Description**
Support for multiple Windows versions	Runs on Windows 2000, Windows NT 4.0, and Windows 98. However, its full functionality is available only on Windows 2000 Server, with which it integrates tightly.
Native XML support	Provides native support for XML. It supports BizTalk Framework specifications through its ability to read, write, and store documents in native XML format.
Accessibility enhancements	Supports browser-based access to database applications. And it leverages Windows 2000's ability to tailor the user interface to the language spoken by a particular user. These features are critical to the Windows DNA 2000 family's support for worldwide deployment of e-commerce and other Web-centric applications.
Data-processing feature enhancements	Builds on its predecessor's tightly integrated OLAP, data transformation, data warehousing, and natural-language query capabilities. SQL Server 2000's data transformation services (DTS) supports BizTalk Server 2000's core document translation and transformation functions. SQL Server 2000 adds materialized views to improve the performance of complex queries against very large databases. It also introduces new data-mining functionality designed to automatically discover hidden relationships in large data sets and make predictions from historical data.
Scalability enhancements	Supports enhanced scalability. It takes advantage of Windows 2000's support for faster processors, additional processors, and more system memory. When running on Windows 2000 Data Center, SQL Server 2000 Enterprise Edition can scale up to machines that run 64 gigabyte of random access memory (RAM), up to 32 processors in symmetric multiprocessing (SMP) mode, and four-node failover clustering. It will eventually run on 64-bit hardware platforms when they become available.
Availability enhancements	Provides greater availability through improved clustering support, taking advantage of Windows 2000's four-way clustering and failover capability. This feature reduces the need to restart SQL Server 2000, reduces the number of system errors, and protects the database from applications that would have otherwise caused it to fail. Individual SQL Servers in a four-node clustered configuration can be upgraded without impacting applications running in the cluster, since one server can automatically failover to others.
Manageability enhancements	SQL Server 2000 performance can be monitored alongside that of other applications in Windows 2000's MMC. SQL Server 2000 also include various improvements to existing management tools and utilities, enabling more self-tuning and self-management of the database server. Furthermore, SQL Server 2000 uses Active Directory as a single, unified repository of configuration, location, and maintenance information. Active Directory, a core feature of Windows 2000, enables a distributed SQL Server deployment to be self-describing. The directory supports location-independent administration and allows administrators to find, manage, and share data assets more efficiently. SQL Server 2000 automatically registers itself in Active Directory upon installation and reports changes in its environment to the directory service during operations. Active

Table 11-1	*New Features in SQL Server 2000 (cont.)*

Feature	Description
Manageability enhancements	Directory stores properties about each SQL Server 2000 machine and database, including a description, alias, version, database size, and the date of the last database backup. Applications may connect to a SQL Server 2000 database by looking up that database's registration information in Active Directory. This feature allows administrators to change the name or location of a database without having to update the applications that use the database. Database administrators can use Active Directory to determine when new SQL Servers have been installed in the corporate network. They can also access the directory to determine when SQL Server 2000 has been upgraded, when users have created new databases or OLAP "cubes," when data is available for replication, and when it has been backed up. All of these directory-enabled functions allow administrators to manage a network of SQL Servers without knowing the names and locations of any of the servers. Instead, administrators can search for servers and databases by alias.
Security enhancements	SQL Server 2000 can use Windows 2000's Kerberos-based authentication services to pass client credentials to remote servers.

Visual Studio   Microsoft Management Console

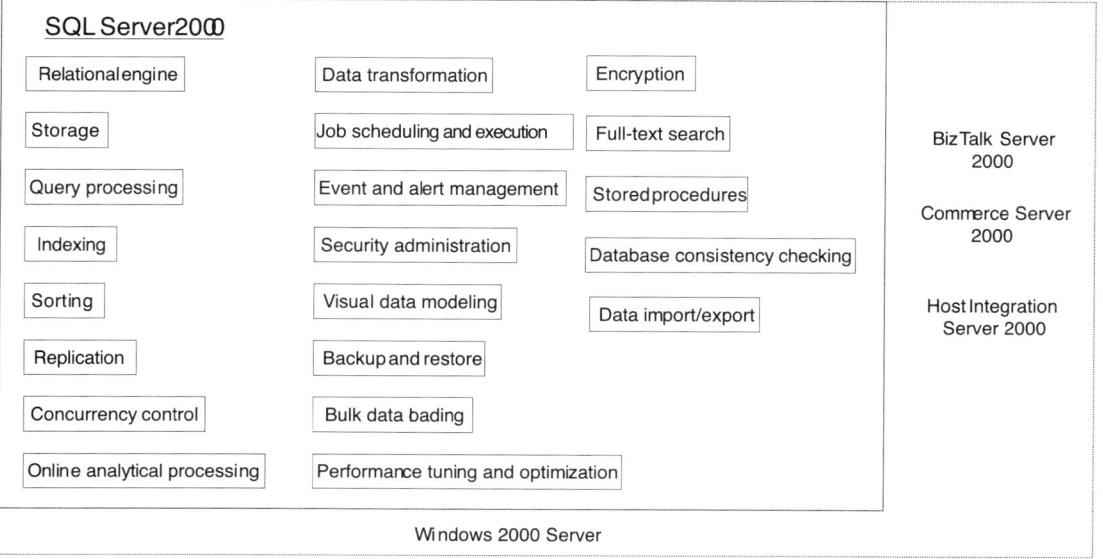

Figure 11-1	*SQL Server 2000 is an enterprise-grade relational database management server that integrates tightly with Windows 2000.*

(2000 or 7.0) must always be present in any deployment of BizTalk Server 2000 or Commerce Server 2000. Figure 11-2 provides a graphical overview of SQL Server's role in a Windows DNA 2000 data-center deployment.

SQL Server 2000 integrates with other Windows DNA 2000 servers through OLE DB, ADO, COM, COM+, DCOM, MTS, and MSMQ. It uses IIS 5.0, a component of Windows 2000, to interface to Web browsers. It uses Windows 2000's embedded SMTP message router, or Exchange 2000, to support inbound and outbound messaging. It relies on BizTalk Server 2000 and Commerce Server 2000 to interface with B2B and B2C applications. And it integrates with Host Integration Server 2000, to be discussed shortly, to connect to mainframe applications and databases, as well as to other relational database management servers.

11.2 Host Integration Server 2000

Host Integration Server (HIS) 2000 is the legacy integration server component of Microsoft's commerce strategy, providing an infrastructure that interfaces Windows DNA 2000 to non-Microsoft platforms and technologies.

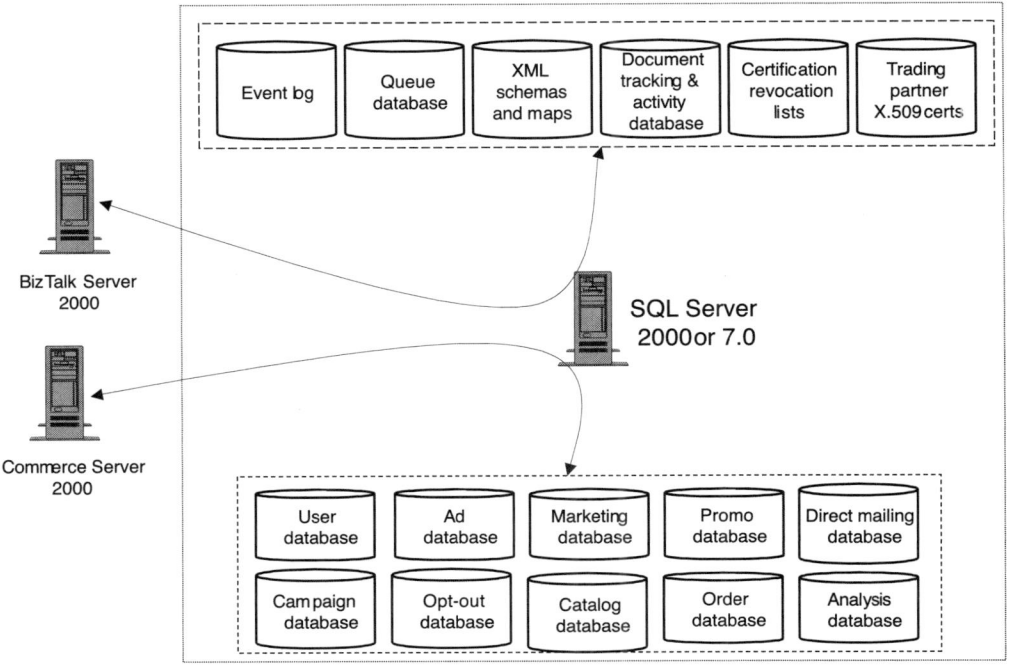

Figure 11-2   *SQL Server 2000 provides critical software infrastructure for other Windows DNA 2000 application servers, including BizTalk Server 2000 and Commerce Server 2000.*

HIS 2000, the successor to Microsoft's SNA Server 4.0 product, supports bidirectional network, security, data, and transaction integration between Windows DNA 2000 servers—such as BizTalk Server 2000 and SQL Server 2000—and other vendors' databases on many host computing platforms. HIS 2000 primarily integrates with IBM hosts via IBM's Systems Network Architecture (SNA) protocols and transaction services. HIS 2000 also supports bidirectional replication with Oracle's market-leading relational databases via TCP/IP. Figure 11-3 shows how HIS 2000 integrates with BizTalk Server 2000, other Windows DNA 2000 servers, various IBM host computers, and other computing environments.

HIS 2000 supports either of two integration strategies: coexistence between DNA 2000 products and host computing environments or migration from host computing to DNA 2000. The server enables tightly coupled transaction integration or loosely coupled data integration between Microsoft and non-Microsoft environments.

Tightly coupled integration involves bridging between Microsoft's object-computing transaction technologies—MTS, COM, COM+, and DCOM—and IBM's transaction services: Customer Information Control System (CICS) and Information Management Service (IMS). HIS 2000 pro-

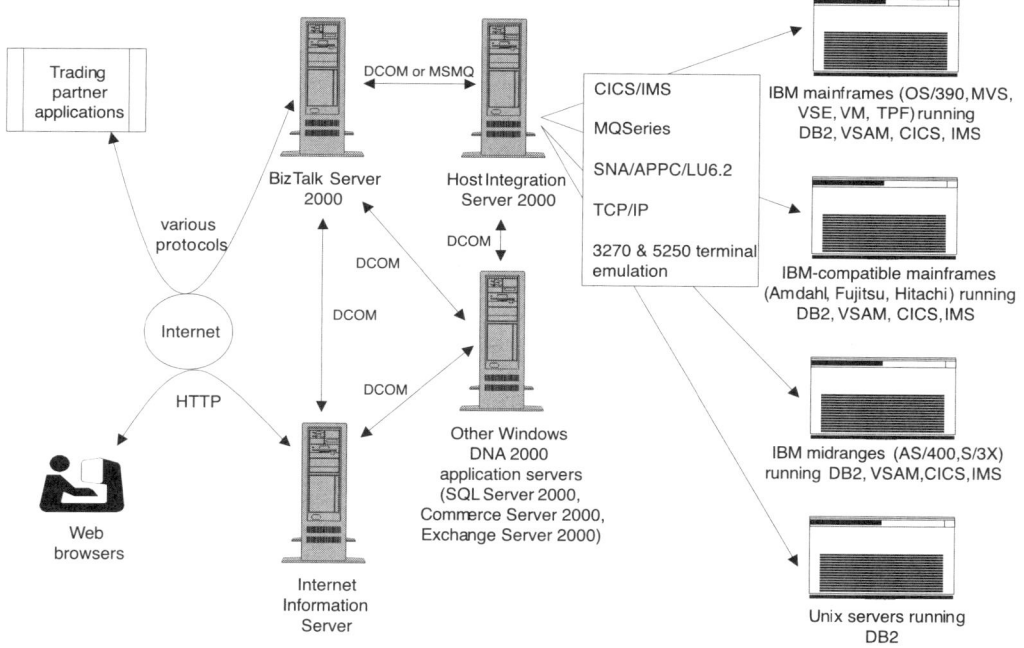

Figure 11-3   *Host Integration Server 2000 is the legacy integration server component of Microsoft's commerce strategy, providing an infrastructure that interfaces Windows DNA 2000 application servers, including BizTalk Server 2000, to non-Microsoft host computing platforms.*

Table 11-2	Host Integration Server 2000 Functionality
Feature	**Description**
Network integration services	Integration with various host computing platforms
	Integration via various physical connectivity facilities
	Integration via various protocols
	Emulation of 3270 and 5250 terminals, scalable up to 30,000 concurrent terminal-emulation sessions with load balancing and hot backup across sessions
	Enable LU 1, 3, and 6.2 (APPC) devices to print to Windows 2000 or NT 4.0 printers
Security integration services	Password synchronization
	Single sign-on
Data integration services	Direct data access
	Distributed data query
	Bidirectional data replication
	Distributed data transformation
	Bulk data transfer
	External access to stored procedures
Transaction integration services	Interfaces between MSMQ 2.0 and MQ Series 5.1 asynchronous message-brokering transaction services
	Interfaces between Microsoft MTS/COM/DCOM and IBM CICS/IMS synchronous object transaction services

vides this level of integration through its COM Transaction Integrator (TI) facility. As we'll discuss below, BizTalk Server 2000, in conjunction with HIS 2000, can integrate tightly with IBM transactions by calling COM objects that encapsulate CICS and IMS services.

Loosely coupled integration involves either of two approaches: message brokering or direct data access. HIS 2000 bridges between Microsoft's message-brokering technology—MSMQ 2.0, running under Windows 2000—and IBM's MQ Series. BizTalk Server 2000, in conjunction with HIS 2000, can interface MSMQ to MQ Series transactions, enabling Windows DNA 2000 applications to exchange messages directly with applications running IBM's MQ Series on dozens of platforms. We will discuss this "bridging" technology in greater detail later in this chapter.

HIS 2000 also supports loosely coupled integration through direct data access between Windows DNA 2000 servers and host databases. This integration relies on database drivers in HIS 2000 that integrate DNA 2000 servers with host databases through Microsoft's ADO, OLE DB, and ODBC interfaces.

Table 11-2 shows HIS 2000's principal functionality.

HIS 2000 integrates tightly with Windows 2000 but also runs on Windows NT 4.0. All HIS 2000 functions run on Windows 2000 or NT 4.0, and there is no code to install on host computers to support network, security, data, or transaction integration with the Windows DNA 2000 world. Microsoft has committed to providing a software development kit (SDK) for HIS 2000 sometime soon after the server's initial commercial availability. The SDK will enable independent software vendors and enterprises to build their own customized integration components.

On Windows 2000, HIS 2000 stores all user, resource, and administrative information in Active Directory. Administrators manage one or more HIS 2000 installations remotely via MMC snap-ins that are created automatically upon installation. Configuration and management snap-ins for HIS 2000's SNA gateway and MSMQ-MQ Series bridge use Windows 2000's Windows Management Instrumentation (WMI) interface.

The Windows NT 4.0 version of HIS 2000 lacks access to Windows 2000-specific features such as Active Directory, MMC, COM+, and WMI. On NT 4, HIS 2000 includes all bug fixes shipped in SNA Server 4.0 service packs 1, 2, and 3.

11.2.1 Network Integration Services

HIS 2000 is similar to BizTalk Server 2000 in its core function: providing a central gateway and integration point between dissimilar information-processing environments. Both gateways support protocol conversion, data transfer and transformation, transaction integration, and security services.

The critical difference between them is that HIS 2000 integrates Windows DNA 2000 into the IBM-centric computing world of yesteryear, while BizTalk Server 2000 integrates Windows DNA 2000 into the Web-centric environment of the new millennium. Unlike HIS 2000, BizTalk Server 2000 processes XML-based documents and message envelopes, which are fast becoming the common currency of B2B application integration. So, taken together, HIS 2000 and BizTalk Server 2000 position Windows DNA 2000 as a "bridge" between the past and the future of distributed computing.

HIS 2000 includes a broad range of connection interfaces into IBM, Microsoft, and Web environments, as well as into the other network operating environments that populate the crowded universe of modern computing. HIS 2000 provides a gateway for integrating Windows DNA 2000 platforms with the host computing platforms, physical connectivity facilities, and protocols listed in Table 11-3 (which is identical to the list of network environments integrated in SNA Server 4.0).

HIS 2000 introduces several enhancements in Microsoft's SNA gateway functionality, including the following features:

- Support for multiple 3270 terminal sessions

Table 11-3	*Host Integration Server 2000 Connectivity*
Type of Integration	**Description**
Host computing platforms	IBM mainframes: OS/390, MVS, VSE, VM, TPF
	IBM-compatible mainframes: Amdahl, Fujitsu, Hitachi
	IBM midrange computers: AS/400, S/3X
	DB2 databases running on Unix servers
Physical connectivity	802.2 over Ethernet, token ring, frame relay, and asynchronous transfer model
	Synchronous Data Link Control over leased or switched telephone circuits
	X.25/QLLC over private or packet switched networks
	ESCON channel
	Bus&Tag channel
	DFT over coax cabling
	Twinax over twisted pair cabling
Protocols	SNA: APPC, LU6.2, LU2, LU0
	TCP/IP
	IPX/SPX
	NetBEUI
	Banyan VINES
	AppleTalk
	DLC
	DecNet

- Downloadable applets to support Telnet on 3270 and 5250 terminal-emulation sessions from Web browsers
- Support for more concurrent host printer-emulation sessions
- Load balancing and hot backup for LU6.2 applications that use two-phase commit
- Physical unit (PU) passthrough
- SNA session-level and distributed link-service compression

11.2.2 Security Integration Services

HIS 2000 supports synchronization of host account information with Windows 2000/NT domains, enabling single sign-on, which allows users to maintain a single account and password to log on to Windows 2000/NT and host computers. HIS 2000 supports one-way synchronization from host RACF, ACF/2, and Top Secret security systems to Windows 2000/NT domains.

11.2.3 Data Integration Services

We group HIS 2000's data integration services into the following categories: direct data access, distributed data query, bidirectional data replication, bulk data transfer, distributed data transformation, and external access to stored procedures. We now discuss each of these features.

DIRECT DATA ACCESS

HIS 2000 includes OLE DB providers and ODBC drivers that enable direct access from Windows DNA 2000 platforms to host-based relational and non-relational databases and file systems.

HIS 2000 provides drivers for direct access to data in DB2 (on several platforms), Virtual Storage Access Method (VSAM), the AS/400 file system and queues, and Oracle databases. Within HIS 2000, Microsoft's object-based OLE DB data access technology supports access to individual records, queries and joins of heterogeneous records, and bidirectional, scheduled replication of partial or entire databases.

HIS 2000's OLE DB providers for DB2, VSAM, and the AS/400 file system use IBM's Distributed Data Management (DDM) Record-Level Input/Output protocol. Microsoft's DDM client uses its own WinAPPC API and IBM's SNA LU6.2 network protocol to communicate with IBM hosts that support IBM DDM server components. HIS 2000's OLE DB providers offer both sequential and index access methods, depending on the target mainframe data-set type or AS/400 file type.

Microsoft has introduced several enhancements in direct DB2 data access in HIS 2000:

- Implemented "free threaded objects," which increase data-access scalability and performance by allowing multiple applications to access a single instance of HIS 2000's OLE DB provider for DB2
- Upgraded the OLE DB provider and ODBC driver for DB2 (OS/390 and AS/400) to support two-phase commit protocols over LU6.2, implementing the two-phase commit protocol defined under the Open Group's Distributed Relational Database Architecture (DRDA) specification
- Included a new performance monitor tool that enables administrators to conduct predeployment testing and planning
- Simplified configuration of DB2 access
- Provided customers with tools for migrating data from DB2 to SQL Server

DISTRIBUTED DATA QUERY

HIS 2000 extends SQL Server's Distributed Query Processor (DQP) feature to heterogeneous databases.

HIS 2000 supports client-initiated queries of heterogeneous relational and non-relational data sources, and joins of the results of these queries. HIS 2000 accesses heterogeneous data using its various OLE DB providers, as described above. However, it does not support host-initiated queries, a feature that is under Microsoft evaluation for future releases.

HIS 2000 supports distributed queries to multiple DB2 databases via DRDA interfaces. Microsoft has developed OLE DB providers and ODBC drives for all DRDA-compliant DB2 systems. It has implemented the DB2 OLE DB providers and ODBC drivers as DRDA application requestors (ARs), supporting DRDA Level 3. Microsoft ODBC drivers for DB2 support ODBC 3.x interfaces and provide the ability to issue dynamic SQL calls.

BIDIRECTIONAL DATA REPLICATION

HIS 2000 supports data replication between Microsoft SQL Server and other databases, including IBM DB2, IBM VSAM, and Oracle.

Replication distributes data and stored procedures across an enterprise. Replication can be implemented between databases on the same server or different servers connected through networks.

SQL Servers can replicate among themselves in unidirectional or bidirectional mode. Replication technology in SQL Server allows enterprises to make duplicate copies of their data, move those copies to different locations, and synchronize the data automatically across all copies. SQL Server uses an internal facility known as the Distributed Transaction Coordinator (DTC) to manage transactional "all-or-nothing" replication with other SQL Servers.

SNA Server 4.0 could replicate between SQL Server and heterogeneous databases only in unidirectional mode: from SQL Server to external databases but not in the opposite direction. However, HIS 2000 also supports bidirectional replication from some external databases (DB2/400 and Oracle) back to SQL Server. Bidirectional replication enables SQL Server to capture changes from heterogeneous sources and synchronize those changes in its own databases. This feature allows enterprises to aggregate data from back-end hosts into SQL Server and thereby serve browser clients from SQL Server without the need to provide direct access to legacy hosts from the Web. When replicating to and from external databases, SQL Server does not use DTC, which means that inconsistencies may result in distributed databases if the replication procedure is interrupted at any stage. However, HIS 2000 guarantees delivery of replicated data to and from external databases.

HIS 2000 supports three types of bidirectional replication: snapshot, incremental, and merge, as discussed in Table 11-4.

Table 11-4	Bidirectional Replication Options in Host Integration Server 2000
Type of Replication	**Description**
Snapshot	Takes a "snapshot" of all current data in a source database and replaces the entire replica at a target database on a periodic basis, in contrast to pushing changes when they occur. HIS 2000 supports bidirectional snapshot replication between SQL Server and Oracle and between SQL Server and DB2/400.
Incremental	Writes into a change log selected updates from the source database, then distributes these updates asynchronously to target databases as incremental changes. HIS 2000 supports bidirectional incremental replication between SQL Server and Oracle and between SQL Server and DB2/400.
Merge	Allows sites to make autonomous changes to replicated data and then, at a later time, merge changes made at all sites (without guaranteeing transactional consistency). HIS 2000 supports bidirectional merge replication between SQL Server and Oracle.

BULK DATA TRANSFER

HIS 2000 provides enhancements to SNA Server's bulk data transfer functionality. Key new features include fast, unidirectional transfer of native AS/400, AS/36, and VSAM files to SQL Server. This feature relies on COM automation control access to HIS 2000 and SQL Server's Distributed Transformation Services (DTS).

2000 also enables SQL Server and other applications to access AS/400 data queues via COM automation controls. These data queues are system objects that AS/400 uses for interprocess communications between multiple programs or jobs. Data queues allow multiple programs to send and receive shared messages via a central repository without first writing the message data to a physical database file, thereby improving performance of AS/400-based applications.

DISTRIBUTED DATA TRANSFORMATION

HIS 2000 extends SQL Server's Distributed Transformation Services feature to integrate with heterogeneous databases.

HIS DTS enables companies to transform data between various formats as it moves between SQL Server and heterogeneous databases. This feature supports development and update of data warehouses through data transformations tied to query, replication, and bulk data transfer operations.

EXTERNAL ACCESS TO STORED PROCEDURES

2000 carries forward SNA Server 4.0's support for SQL Server access to stored procedures on DB2 databases on various platforms. HIS 2000 can call DB2 stored procedures, thereby returning parameters values (but not result sets). It also supports pooling of OLE DB sessions.

11.2.4 Transaction Integration Services

HIS 2000 carries forward two transaction integration services from SNA Server 4.0: COM Transaction Integrator (COMTI) and MSMQ-MQ Series bridging. These services operate over SNA or TCP/IP and don't require any changes to host or host code.

Transaction integration is essential to multiplatform online transaction processing (OLTP). This functionality in HIS 2000 allows developers to integrate Windows DNA 2000 and host-based business logic into a distributed transaction environment in which all nodes cooperate to manage a single "distributed unit of work." Consequently, developers can build applications that span platform boundaries while guaranteeing transaction integrity, eliminating the need to rewrite existing host-based applications, and preserving investments in legacy, best-of-breed, and in-house-developed applications.

Developers can use synchronous or asynchronous middleware for these solutions, depending on which approach makes most sense for the applications being integrated and the business problems being addressed. Synchronous approaches are most feasible in homogeneous computing environments—such as corporate intranets—where server platforms are continuously available and transmission facilities are fast and reliable. Asynchronous approaches, by contrast, are appropriate to environments—such as the Internet or extranets—that have heterogeneous computing platforms that may not always be available and are connected through unreliable, narrowband transmission facilities. Of course, applications on either side must be written to support messaging and also agree on a common message format.

HIS 2000 supports synchronous and asynchronous program integration in heterogeneous environments by means of interfaces between Microsoft and third-party middleware technologies. Synchronous middleware—such as COM—invokes external functions through a request-response model in which the requesting program opens a "channel" (i.e., set of application input/output buffers and queues) and does not engage in other transactions until it receives acknowledgments and confirmations from the serving program. Asynchronous middleware—such as MSMQ—invokes external functions by sending structured messages, but keeps on processing other transactions while waiting for acknowledgments and confirmations in response to outbound messages.

COM Transaction Integrator

COMTI enables bidirectional integration between Windows DNA 2000 transactions (using COM, COM+, and MTS technologies) and IBM host-based transactions (using CICS or IMS).

COMTI technology enables "wrapping" of CICS and IMS transactional services in MTS/COM/COM+ components. COMTI objects expose CICS and IMS functionality for access from within COM-compliant tools. Developers use HIS 2000's visually oriented Component Builder utility to encapsulate existing CICS/IMS business logic in COMTI objects. The utility automatically generates the appropriate COM interfaces based on a COBOL description of the host-based transaction program's input/output buffers. No modifications are required to CICS/IMS host-based code; in fact, COMTI developers need not learn how to program host computers in order to access host transactional services.

A COMTI object supports an end-to-end transactional "distributed unit of work" involving Windows DNA 2000 and host platforms. COMTI extends the scope of MTS/COM+ distributed two-phase-commit transactions to CICS and IMS via IBM's Sync Level 2 protocol. As COM+ components, COMTI objects may be reused within many Microsoft and third-party COM-compliant development tools.

COMTI objects drive distributed transactions from Windows DNA 2000 via COM automation. They also allow host-based CICS transactions to initiate MTS transactions running on Windows DNA 2000 platforms.

HIS 2000, in conjunction with BizTalk Server 2000, enables external applications to drive CICS and IMS transactions via a loosely coupled, message-oriented COMTI interface. BizTalk Server 2000 can consume and parse XML documents and messages and, per "agreements" defined under BizTalk Management Desk, invoke COMTI objects on HIS 2000 via the COM+/COMTI "Ipipeline" interface. Figure 11-4 shows a high-level configuration of HIS 2000's support for synchronous transaction integration through COMTI technology.

MSMQ-MQ SERIES BRIDGING

HIS 2000 bridges between MSMQ 2.0 and IBM's MQ Series 5.1 to facilitate bidirectional routing of structured messages between Windows DNA 2000 platforms and the many operating environments that support IBM's message-brokering technology. New features in HIS 2000's MSMQ-MQ Series Bridge (over and above SNA Server 4.0) include integrated setup of the bridge with the rest of HIS 2000, encryption between MSMQ clients and the bridge, and a configuration wizard for easier installation. Microsoft has also upgraded the software driver that enables communications between MSMQ and MQ Series.

HIS 2000, in conjunction with BizTalk Server 2000, enables external applications to drive MQ Series transactions via a loosely coupled, message-

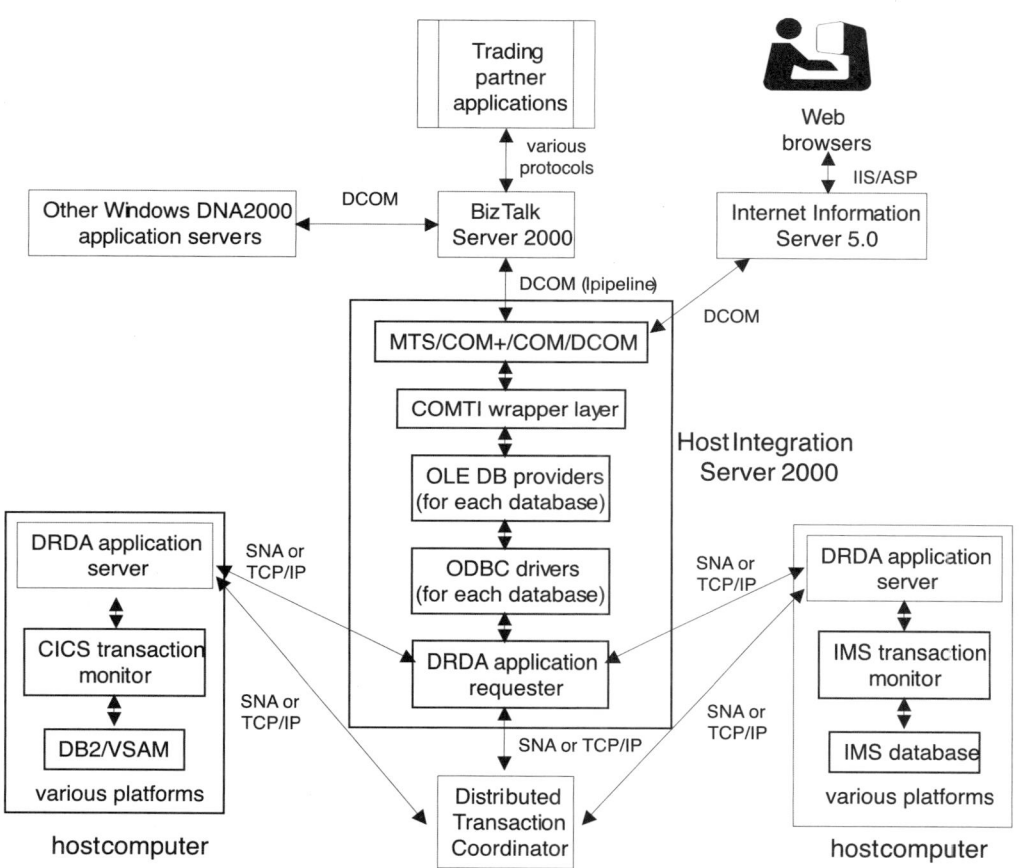

Figure 11-4   *Host Integration Server 2000 supports synchronous transaction integration through COMTI, which wraps CICS and IMS transaction services as MTS/COM/COM+ objects and thereby exposes them to Windows DNA 2000 applications.*

oriented COM interface (not COMTI). Microsoft reports that a majority of its customers are considering deployment of the MSMQ-to-MQ Series Bridge as their primary means for transaction integration, especially for B2B supply-chain integration.

Note that HIS 2000 will not initially support the COM+ Queued Components feature of Windows 2000. This feature allows COM+ invocation calls to be recorded and sent asynchronously to a server-based COM object. At the destination COM object, the COM+ invocations are "played back" at a later time, and the response uses the same asynchronous process for responding to the invoking application.

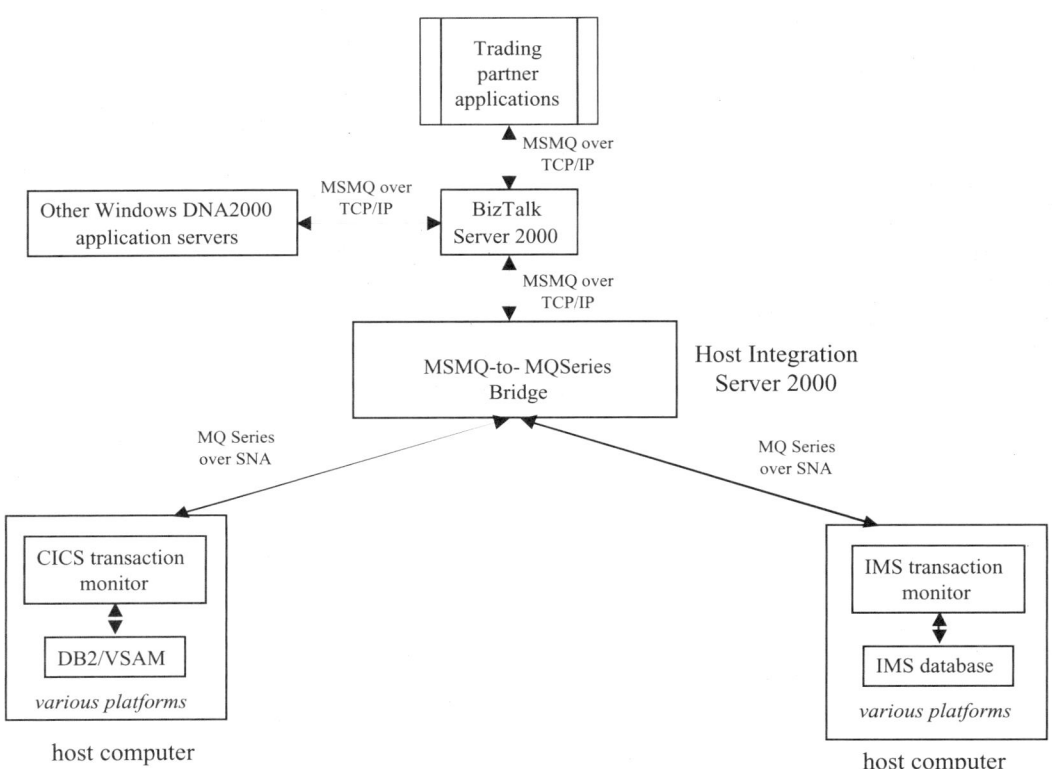

Figure 11-5   *Host Integration Server 2000 supports asynchronous transaction integration through its MSMQ-to-MQ Series bridging functionality.*

11.3 Application Center 2000

Application Center 2000 is the Web-farm management tool in Microsoft's Windows DNA 2000 e-commerce strategy.

   Application Center 2000 is a new product that supports unified management of Windows 2000–based applications running on high-availability server farms. Application Center provides MMC-based tools to configure and manage clustered arrays of computers running Windows 2000 Server, BizTalk Server 2000, Commerce Server 2000, SQL Server 2000, Host Integration Server 2000, Exchange Server 2000, and other Windows DNA 2000 and Microsoft Server products. The tool supports isolation of a failed server in a cluster, and works in conjunction with the Windows Clustering services in Windows 2000 Server.

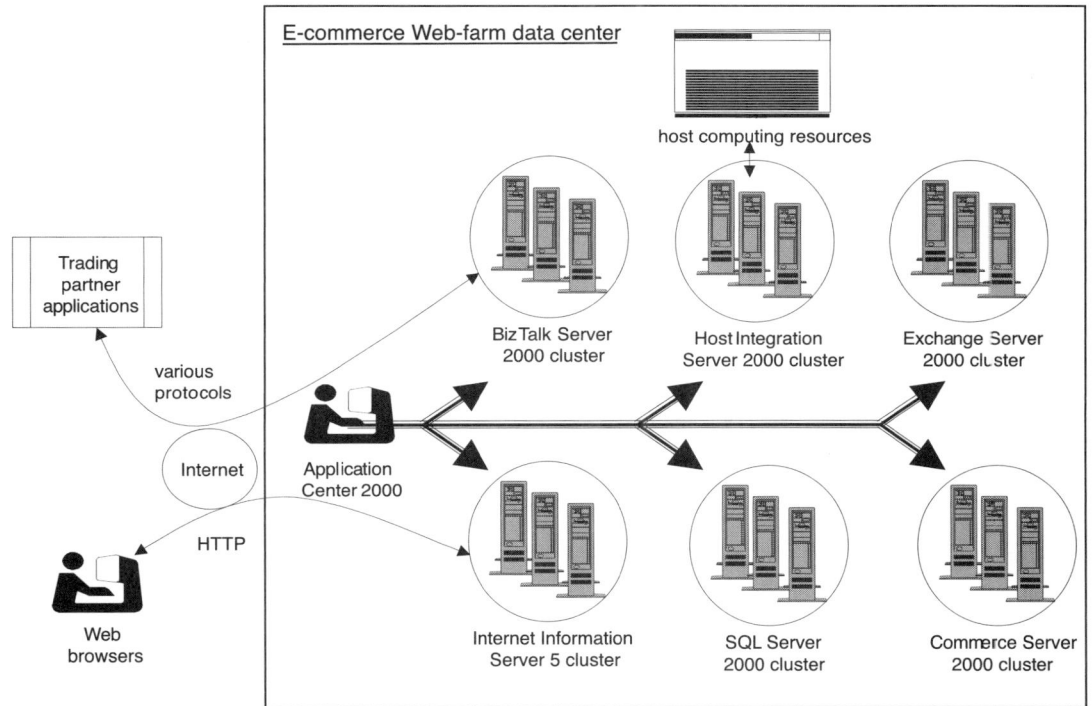

E-commerce Web-farm data center

host computing resources

Trading partner applications

various protocols

Internet

Application Center 2000

HTTP

Web browsers

BizTalk Server 2000 cluster

Host Integration Server 2000 cluster

Exchange Server 2000 cluster

Internet Information Server 5 cluster

SQL Server 2000 cluster

Commerce Server 2000 cluster

Figure 11-6 *Application Center 2000 administers clustered Windows DNA 2000 application servers, such as BizTalk Server 2000 and Commerce Server 2000, supporting high-volume, high-availability data processing services.*

Application Center 2000 includes a centralized, MMC-based management console that enables administrators to manage and monitor Web applications running in multiserver farms. It provides administrators with a unified view of all data-center server resources. It provides tools for application and component load balancing, fault tolerance, configuration management, performance and health monitoring, and content replication and synchronization across all Windows DNA 2000 servers. These functions enable data-center administrators to scale up Web farms of Windows DNA 2000 servers to support high-volume e-commerce, extranet, and intranet applications with 7x24 availability. Application Center 2000 can automatically load balance among Web servers, application servers, and database servers to maximize system performance.

Figure 11-6 provides a graphical depiction of Application Center 2000's role as a management tool in an e-commerce Web-farm data center that uses clustered Windows DNA 2000 application servers, including BizTalk Server 2000. Online merchants are one type of company that might benefit from use of Application Center 2000 to manage high-volume Windows DNA 2000 deployments. Operators of hubbed e-marketplaces are another.

11.4 MSN E-Marketplace Services

Microsoft has committed to supporting the BizTalk Framework and implementing BizTalk Server 2000 in its MSN small-business commerce services.

However, the company has, as of the date this book was written, provided few specifics on its plans for integrating BizTalk standards and technologies into MSN's online services. Still, we have little reason to doubt that Microsoft will rapidly integrate its Windows DNA 2000 products into its online properties.

As of mid 2000, Microsoft had only made a tentative foray into the new world of application service providers and online e-marketmakers. It has branded its online commerce services under the name "MSN bCentral" (www.bcentral.com). MSN bCentral is a horizontal e-marketplace for small businesses to obtain most of what they need to launch and sustain their dot-com operations. The portal organizes its offerings in categories that address the life-cycle dotcom requirements of small businesses: "start on the Web," "market your business online," and "manage more effectively."

Microsoft's strategy in building bCentral has been to sell both its own products and services as well as those from selected strategic partners. The site does not maintain a single aggregated product/service catalog so much as provide hyperlink pointers to distributed catalogs maintained by various MSN properties and those of business partners. Essentially, Microsoft is the e-marketmaker behind bCentral and has recruited a constellation of small-business-oriented e-commerce facilitators, per the framework we presented in Chapter 6.

We present MSN bCentral's small-business service offerings in Table 11-5.

Behind bCentral's membership model is MSN Passport, one of the "mega-services" touted by Steve Ballmer, Microsoft's chief executive officer. MSN Passport provides a service for users to consolidate account information at participating merchant sites into an online "wallet" that contains usernames, passwords, credit card information, shipping information, and other user profile information. The service allows users to avoid having to reenter this information at each participating Passport site (MSN and non-MSN) when shopping on the Web. Microsoft has implemented Passport in bCentral and all other MSN services. However, Passport has not gained universal support in the e-commerce world and, as noted in Chapter 6, competes with a growing range of similar services from other companies.

Table 11-5	*MSN bCentral Offerings*
Offering	**Description**
Obtain Internet access	High-speed Digital Subscriber Loop (DSL) connections from NorthPoint Communications
Develop and host e-commerce Web site	SiteManager online tool and hosting service (develop online store and begin accepting credit cards)
Sign up for free Web-based e-mail account	MSN Hotmail
Get a Web address	Domain registrations through Network Solutions
Advertise on the Web	LinkExchange Banner Network; AdStore (purchase advertising on leading Web sites)
List business in Web search engines and directories	SubmitIt! (submits to MSN Shopping Directory and more than 400 search engines)
Obtain memberships in Website-affiliate programs	Affiliate Program (revenue through referrals to and from other sites)
Create customer e-mail address lists	ListBot (capture and grow mailing list of customers to target future business)
Purchase keywords in major search engine	KeyWords in MSN Search
Obtain sales leads	RFQ (links to eShop business-to-business auctions and FairMarket auction network)
Obtain business loans and financing	Through link to LiveCapital.com and participating lenders
Recruit employees	MSN Careers
Compare shipping rates	Through link to iShip.com
Purchase office supplies	Through link to Staples.com
Purchase books	Through link to Barnesandnoble.com
Purchase other items	MSN eShop
Arrange business travel	MSN Expedia
Consult buyers' guides	MSN eShop; link to Verticalnet.com

11.5 Summary

Mega-services will very likely be a dominant theme for Microsoft as it migrates its business model toward addressing Web services architectures more completely. Microsoft product managers have discussed the company's ongoing direction of removing functional boundaries between its Windows

DNA 2000 products and MSN e-marketplace services. The day may soon come when Microsoft releases new Windows DNA 2000 offerings as linked software and service packages that either integrate tightly or can substitute for one another.

The company has provided few details on its plans in this regard, but it's quite likely that Microsoft will at some point in the not too distant future give customers the option either of licensing BizTalk Server 2000, Commerce Server 2000, and other products for internal deployment or subscribing to the same functionality as a service accessed over the Internet. Microsoft has made no secret of its plans to migrate away from software-license revenues as the mainstay of its business toward more of an application service provider, or "ASP," model (not to be confused, or maybe the confusion is fortuitous, with ASP, as in Microsoft's Active Server Pages technology).

Increasingly, users will access Microsoft application services through their browsers, interacting with ASPs rendered by Internet Information Server, which, in turns, fetches the contents and logic for them from Windows DNA 2000 application servers, such as BizTalk Server 2000, Commerce Server 2000, SQL Server 2000, and Host Integration Server 2000. These application servers, in turn, will pull data from a vast array of back-end data sources throughout the Internet, supply-chain extranets, and corporate intranets. E-commerce merchant sites and e-marketplaces will grow larger clustered Windows DNA 2000 server farms that provide the scalability and reliability necessary to compete in the new economy. Application service providers will be among the biggest consumers of BizTalk Server 2000 and its brethren application servers.

Microsoft's business emphasis is no longer merely on the knowledge worker desktop or the enterprise server. Its new operating environment is the Internet, its new killer application is e-commerce, and its new architecture is Windows DNA 2000. That architecture, and its many component technologies, is the focus of Part 4, to which we now proceed.

PART FOUR

BIZTALK TECHNOLOGIES

This part discusses the various technologies, standards, and products that support a full deployment of BizTalk Server 2000 in a corporate or service provider network. In particular, we discuss the Windows 2000 operating environment and its markup, document mapping and transformation, schema definition, database, directory, security, message brokering, transaction, application development, and system management technologies.

Microsoft E-Commerce Operating Environment

BizTalk, as we've seen, is an initiative that spans much more than the application server of that name. The term is in fact a shorthand for the many technologies, platforms, services, and standards that give substance to Microsoft's e-commerce strategy.

Windows 2000 is, of course, Microsoft's primary server operating environment. Windows 2000 is the platform on which BizTalk Server 2000 and kindred application server products run. However, Microsoft recognizes that the complete operating environment for e-commerce is not Windows 2000— or, for that matter, any other server or client operating system (OS)—but the Internet as a whole. Consequently, the vendor has defined an Internet-facing application model—called Windows Distributed interNetworking Architecture (DNA)—in which Microsoft and third-party software packages interoperate transparently through open, vendor-neutral, Internet standards such as the Extensible Markup Language (XML).

So we may regard Windows DNA as Microsoft's total operating environment for B2B and B2C e-commerce. Windows 2000 is the core platform of Windows DNA: the repository of application services on which all applications and services depend. Windows 2000 provides file, directory, security, object, Web, connector, transaction, development, administration, and other services for distributed computing. What Windows DNA services have in common are two things: They run only under Microsoft's proprietary OS, Windows 2000, and application developers can access them only through Microsoft's proprietary development technology, the Component Object Model (COM).

This chapter discusses Microsoft's network applications model, focusing on Windows DNA, Windows 2000, and core Windows 2000-based services. This chapter presents the grand architectural framework within which

Microsoft wants customers to implement BizTalk Server 2000 and other commerce-related products and services (both its own and those from business partners). Other chapters in Part Four focus on the core markup, development, object, connector, and transaction technologies on which Microsoft's Windows DNA services depend.

12.1 Windows Distributed interNetworking Architecture

Windows DNA is a bit like DNA of the double-helix variety. Windows DNA supplies the blueprint for a new breed of applications adapted to the online ecology of the Web. And it defines a hybrid gene pool of open industry standards and proprietary Microsoft technologies.

E-commerce, according to Microsoft's vision, will live in the Windows DNA environment. This architecture is Microsoft's attempt to shape the new world of browser-oriented applications as decisively as the vendor dominated the previous desktop-oriented paradigm. In Windows DNA, Microsoft has entwined its proprietary content, component, database, and transaction specifications into all levels of a Web-facing application model.

Windows DNA is also Microsoft's tacit admission that it will not be able to bring the whole world into its proprietary sphere of technologies. The Web's ascendancy has caused a progressive blurring of the boundaries between Microsoft's environment and that of the world at large. Windows applications have become presentation containers for a growing range of documents, objects, and components originated elsewhere, in other environments, and delivered transparently over the Web. Integration with the Web's namespace, filestores, directories, objects, and services is making Windows environments completely visible and searchable from anywhere. Microsoft integration with public key infrastructures and other industry standard security technologies paves the way for multiplatform e-marketplaces and extranets.

Essentially, the Windows DNA application model organizes Web-facing distributed services into three functional tiers: presentation, business logic, and data. The model associates these services/tiers with particular nodes in an Internet-centric distributed environment: the browser-based client, the application server, and the database server. The architecture relies on various Windows 2000 run-time system services, such as COM, Active Directory (AD), Distributed File Services, Distributed Security Services (DSS), Microsoft Management Console (MMC), and Microsoft Message Queue Server (MSMQ). And it includes COM development tools such as Microsoft Visual Studio.

Figure 12-1 presents a graphical overview of the Windows DNA application model. We will now discuss each of the tiers of this model at a high level, saving more detailed discussions for later in this chapter and throughout Part Four.

12.1.1 Presentation Tier

The presentation tier defines the user interface and interaction model in the Windows DNA environment.

Windows DNA provides a broad range of presentation options, supporting two types of clients: rich and thin. These categories correspond to traditional Windows desktops and to Web browsers (Windows- or non-Windows-based), respectively. As we all know, the Web browser is the dominant presentation paradigm for e-commerce and other Internet-based services, including those delivered from Microsoft Commerce Server 2000.

Microsoft supports both the Windows and Web presentation paradigms in its Visual family of development tools for the Visual Basic, VBScript, Java

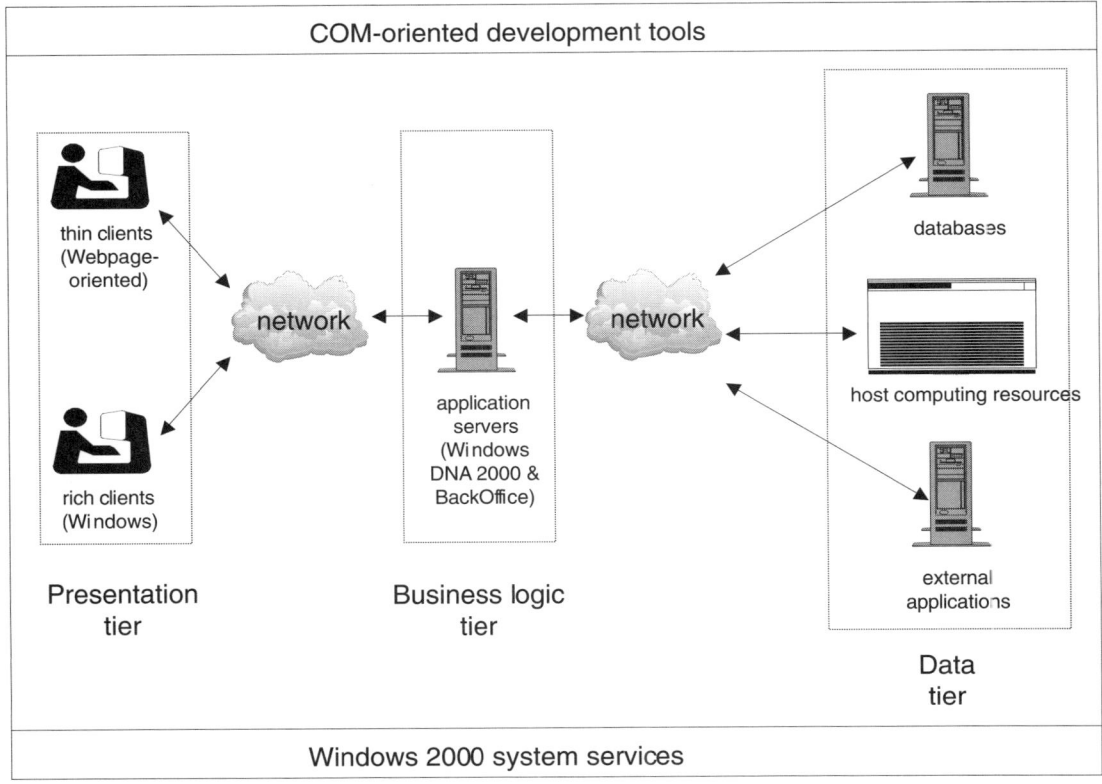

Figure 12-1	*Windows DNA organizes distributed services into three functional tiers—presentation, business logic, and data—and supports these tiers with Windows 2000 run-time system services and COM-oriented development tools.*

Script, C, C++, and Java programming languages. Likewise, Microsoft supports both presentation paradigms in Windows 2000, Windows NT Server, and Windows 98, so that administrators can, for example, view Active Directory entries through the Win32-based Microsoft Management Console or as scripted HTML pages from their Internet Explorer (IE) browsers.

Microsoft, of course, would prefer that you continue to develop applications for the rich presentation services of its ubiquitous desktop operating environment: Windows 9x. Windows is still the world's most popular content presentation platform. As an OS, Windows encompasses much more than simply a graphical user interface (GUI), but the GUI—its content-presentation front-end—represents the familiar face of that environment.

At the core of the Windows GUI are the long-established Win32 APIs and Windows Application Foundation Classes. These enable application developers to access such presentation objects as windows, menus, buttons, clipboards, dialogue boxes, controls, scrollbars, toolbars, and help screens. Developers can assign appearances and behaviors to these objects, such as the ability to respond in various ways to mouse-clicks. Applications generate output for a window using Win32's graphics device interface (GDI) functions. The GUI translates mouse movement, mouse button clicks, and keystrokes into input messages and places these messages in the message queue for the Windows-based application. Clipboard and dynamic data exchange functions allow user-driven or automatic data transfer between applications.

The Windows GUI supports development and display of applications incorporating 16-bit Unicode, as opposed to 8-bit ANSI, character-set encoding. Unicode support in the OS enables easier development of workstations, applications, and documents that use two or more alphabets or character sets, such as the Roman, Arabic, and Chinese character sets. A single version of a Unicode application can be compiled to display in any of several character sets supported by Windows.

Microsoft has also developed the DirectX APIs and associated COM class libraries to support presentation and interactive control of high-performance, real-time multimedia applications in Windows applications and its Internet Explorer 5.0 browser. DirectX APIs support hardware acceleration for streaming media, interactive playback, animation, 3-D modeling, and multiuser gaming applications. DirectX supports such multimedia presentation file formats as Motion Picture Experts Group (MPEG), Advanced Streaming Format (ASF), and QuickTime. DirectX is the basis for Microsoft's streaming and multimedia products such as NetMeeting.

When Microsoft refers to thin clients, it is speaking of Web browsers generally (Windows-based and non-Windows based) and of the new breed of thin wireless clients and network appliances. However, it is primarily referring to its own IE 5.0 browser. IE 5.0 is a thin client only with respect to the full Windows GUI but is in fact chock full of rich browsing functionality. Microsoft has developed IE 5.0 into a highly interactive, graphical, multimedia browser. It serves as an all-purpose presentation container for HTML pages, in-line graphics, URL hyperlinks, frames, forms, format-specific viewers, Java applets (via the embedded Java Virtual Machine), ActiveX components (via the embedded ActiveX Virtual Machine), Java Script and VBScript scripts, streaming audio and video, and other digital objects.

IE 5.0 is optimized for display of Active Server Pages (ASPs). ASPs consist of HTML plus VBScript, Cascading Stylesheets, and ActiveX components. ASP technology provides a language-neutral, compile-free, server-side scripting environment for generating and displaying interactive Web pages. Microsoft's Web server product, Internet Information Server, can detect the type of client accessing it and dynamically render Web pages in the most appropriate format (ASP and otherwise). However, Microsoft doesn t support Sun's competing Java Server Pages (JSP) technology.

IE 5.0 can display and manipulate documents and other objects appropriately based on Multipurpose Internet Mail Extensions (MIME) tags. MIME tags indicate the format of in which that object—such as an ASCII text file, Microsoft Word file, Group 3 facsimile—was encoded for transmission. MIME encoding provides an industry-standard method for tagging content transmitted over Web and enabling the appropriate viewers and applications to be invoked automatically upon receipt.

As implemented in IE 5.0 and ASPs, Dynamic HTML (DHTML) exposes Web page contents as collections of extensible, scriptable, dynamic presentation objects. Microsoft has declared that DHTML will be the basis for future presentation user interfaces on Windows platforms, with XML serving as the corresponding storage format, potentially replacing Microsoft-proprietary formats such as Word and Excel. Microsoft has based its DHTML implementation principally on the World Wide Web Consortium's HTML v. 3.2 specification plus some proprietary extensions. Microsoft's version of DHTML enables the complex multimedia effects described in Table 12-1.

Over the next several years, browser-based "thin" clients such as IE 5.0 will grow richer in functionality with each new product revision until they achieve functional parity with Windows and other traditional desktop operating environments (assuming that the browser doesn't merge completely with the desktop OS in the meantime). Since Windows 98, Microsoft has embedded IE 5.0's browsing functionality deeply within the OS's presentation environment. Browsing functionality is now available from within all Microsoft Office applications, from the Windows Explorer utility, and even from the "run" dialog box on the desktop. Indeed, it is getting increasingly difficult to tell where the traditional Win32 GUI leaves off and IE 5.0's DHTML/ASP browsing functionality picks up.

As most everyone knows by now, Microsoft's decision to "browserize" Windows caused much consternation in regulatory circles and among the company's competitors, since it effectively killed Netscape's original business model and hopes of toppling Windows' hegemony on the desktop. The

Table 12-1	Windows DNA Dynamic HTML Multimedia Effects

Feature	Description
Overlays	Content developers can design pages in three dimensions, as sets of overlaid subpages or frames that can be cascaded, tiled, revealed, and concealed in various ways. This feature reduces the need to fetch new pages from the originating server.
Dynamic stylesheets	Pages can be designed to automatically alter their own appearance, content, and windowing structure in response to user events, such as passing a cursor over a particular block of text. This feature reduces the need to communicate with the originating server in order to modify a page's appearance.
Cascading stylesheets	Pages can be set up to reuse design parameters such as margins, colors, and fonts. This feature reduces the need to transmit such information redundantly from the originating server.
Absolute positioning	Pages can be set up to control the exact positioning of all text and graphical elements on the user's display. This feature gives content developers the assurance that their creations are being viewed precisely in the intended layout.
Transition effects	Pages can be set up to download or exit with any of the transition effects found in a typical presentation package, such as dissolve, fade, wipe, cover, blinds, box, iris, checkerboard, random bars, split, and strips.
Drag and drop	Pages can be set up to support dragging and dropping of textual and graphical elements. This feature enables on-the-fly page revision and interactive input.
Data manipulation	Pages can be set up to allow data contained within them to be queried, sorted, and otherwise manipulated on the fly at the browser. This feature eliminates the need for the browser to invoke ActiveX components or Java applets for these functions.
Downloadable run-time fonts	Pages can be set up to use downloadable run-time fonts that disappear when the page is unloaded or browser session terminated.
Data binding	Data can be gathered from various local sources and cached, presented, and manipulated locally without a server round trip.
Scriptlets	Reusable components can be created from HTML pages and scripts.

stakes in the browser battle are very high for the rival software vendors, since the browser is the new universal client for all network services, including—especially—electronic commerce. If Microsoft can ensure universal deployment of IE on PCs and new wireless clients and network appliances, then it will effectively control the user interface for the online economy of the 21st century.

At the very thin end of the presentation spectrum, Windows DNA recognizes that Windows 2000 may sometimes be configured to serve Win32

GUI screens to network computers. Microsoft has designed Windows 2000's multi-user Terminal Server presentation technology for serving resource-poor computing platforms over networks. Windows Terminal technology essentially transforms client computers into new-fangled dumb terminals when communicating with Windows 2000. Dumb Windows terminals are not a new client technology for the age of e-commerce, but a throwback to the old days of host computing when terminals lacked local computing and storage resources. Dumb terminals have their niche applications, but they do not compete with browsers as a strategic platform for future network application development.

12.1.2 Business Logic Tier

The business logic tier defines the application development and run-time services model in the Windows DNA environment.

Microsoft has standardized on its proprietary COM technology as the basis for application development and run-time services across all three Windows DNA tiers, but with a special emphasis on the Windows DNA 2000 family of application servers (which we discussed in Part Three). Application servers are the primary repositories of programmable, COM-based business logic under Windows DNA. Application servers are platforms for projecting corporate data to browser-based clients under the control of programmable business rules. These servers—such as Internet Information Server, BizTalk Server, Commerce Server, and SQL Server 2000—constitute the middle tier in a three-tier services infrastructure. They are a critical technology for e-commerce, extranet, and intranet applications, and they all rely on the underlying system services of the Windows 2000 platform (which we will discuss shortly and which Microsoft has implemented as a set of COM components).

COM, which we'll discuss in greater detail later in Part Four, defines a consistent, language-independent framework under which reusable software objects point to and invoke one another's functions. COM components can encapsulate any type of application functionality, such as user interface or data access features. COM components can communicate with each other within memory on a single Windows machine or, via Distributed COM (DCOM) technology, across the local or wide-area network connecting multiple Windows machines. Developers can write COM components in any language, including C, C++, Visual Basic, and Java. These components may expose their methods and proproperties through multiple programmatic interfaces so that they may be queried and set by other components and applications.

COM is the most widely used component software model in the world, by virtue of its central role in the ubiquitous Windows family of operating environments. Its direct predecessor, the compound document technology known as Object Linking and Embedding (OLE), first brought the benefits of language-independent object-oriented computing to the Windows platform in the early 1990s. Through OLE, a user working in Microsoft Word could, for example, embed or link a spreadsheet file or graphic object, and later, by clicking on that object, bring the embedded object's application to life while remaining inside Word.

Microsoft developed ActiveX technology as a means of packaging downloadable COM component binaries for insertion into Web pages rendered by Internet Explorer. Developers can insert URL pointers to ActiveX components into their Web pages. When Internet Explorer accesses the page, it automatically connects to the source server, downloads the ActiveX component, and runs it. ActiveX uses a Microsoft-proprietary remote procedure call (RPC) protocol to interconnect the local COM libraries of communicating computers. ActiveX components register themselves with the receiving computer's Windows registry and execute as native Windows applications. Developers may write ActiveX components in such computer languages as C, Visual C++, Visual Basic, and Java. ActiveX technology uses Microsoft's Authenticode code-signing technology to ensure secure download of components over the network.

Java, developed by Sun Microsystems, competes directly with ActiveX as a programming language for Web applications. However, Microsoft, recognizing widespread user adoption of Java programming tools, has implemented a Win32 reference implementation of the Java Virtual Machine in Internet Explorer, Windows 2000, Windows NT Server 4.0, and Windows 98. Microsoft also supports Java development in its Visual Studio, Visual InterDev, and Visual J++ tools (though it has failed to support Enterprise JavaBeans technology, which directly competes with Microsoft's proprietary COM and DCOM technologies).

DCOM, introduced with Windows NT Server 4.0, is the distributed, network-enabled version of COM. DCOM supports remote location, invocation, and execution of COM objects across networks, between Windows-based desktops and application servers. Under Windows 2000, DCOM can support scalable object-oriented computing, thanks to the distributed Active Directory Class Store, a directory subtree that allows a remote object's current location to be maintained in one distributed directory rather than, as previously, in the local registries of every platform that might call that object. Client-based COM libraries consult the Class Store—maintained under Active Directory—when an object requested by the application is not found in the local registry.

Microsoft Transaction Server (MTS), also introduced with Windows NT Server 4.0, is a DCOM extension that ensures reliable transactions among COM components in a networked environment. MTS is essentially a transaction processing monitor for distributed Windows environments. The service provides a business rulebase, resource broker, and run-time middleware environment for processing high-performance, scalable, secure distributed enterprise transactions. Under MTS, work from multiple distributed COM objects can be composed into a single atomic transaction.

COM+ is a new technology under Windows 2000 that builds on, integrates, and improves the component development and run-time features of COM, DCOM, and MTS. COM+ reduces the amount of coding needed to access underlying COM, DCOM, and MTS services for distributed applications. It also provides a unified administration model, in the form of Windows 2000's Component Services Explorer, which replaces Windows NT Server 4.0's separate MTS Explorer and DCOM Configuration tools. Microsoft has designed COM+ component technology to support transparent interoperability with existing COM and DCOM components.

In addition to helping COM programmers be more productive, COM+ technology also introduces new object computing services to the Windows environment. For example, COM+ supports reliable program execution across linked COM components on separate machines that may occasionally disconnect from the network. It also provides a notification mechanism that allows components to "subscribe" to real-time event information that is "published" by other components on the network. Furthermore, it allows component-based applications to distribute their workload across a group of clustered application servers in a way that is invisible to clients accessing those services.

12.1.3 Data Tier

The data tier defines the content access and integration model in the Windows DNA environment.

Windows DNA defines an architecture in which applications primarily access data where it lives. Microsoft's has stressed the need for accessing existing applications and data on other platforms without requiring significant modifications or upgrades to those platforms. This is the content integration approach behind BizTalk Server 2000, Commerce Server 2000, SQL Server 2000, and Host Integration Server 2000, as discussed in Part Three.

This is a sound approach to harnessing and mining the rich vein of distributed data sources on legacy platforms in any large enterprise, and it's the only feasible solution to integrating applications among trading partners in extranets and hubbed e-marketplaces. So it's no accident that Microsoft also refers to the Windows DNA data tier as its "universal data access" architecture.

Microsoft's data tier rides on three main data-access programmatic interfaces—Open Database Connectivity (ODBC), OLE DB, and Active X Data Objects (ADO)—all of which are fundamental features of Windows 2000 and Windows NT Server.

ODBC "drivers" enable a single application to access different database management systems (DBMSs) directly without the need to modify application source code. Applications that access DBMSs only need to call APIs in a local ODBC interface, which communicates with ODBC software drivers installed in local or remote DBMSs.

OLE DB "providers" integrate with one or more data sources. OLE DB is a published specification for accessing all kinds of data, including XML, which is a native storage format in Windows 2000. The most commonly used OLE DB provider is Microsoft's OLE DB Provider for ODBC Drivers, which exposes ODBC data sources to ADO components. OLE DB providers enable data from heterogeneous sources—structured and unstructured, relational and nonrelational—to appear as if they reside in a single, logically unified data repository.

ADO "components" provide object-oriented programmatic access to OLE DB data providers. ADO is a language-neutral object model that exposes data raised by an underlying OLE DB Provider. ADO, currently in version 2.5, defines a COM "wrapper" for accessing OLE DB APIs and exposing OLE DB functionality to C, C++, Visual Basic, Java, and other programming languages. Remote Data Service (RDS) is a subset of the ADO object model that supports low-overhead, high-performance transfer of ADO object record sets from a server to a client computer. The resulting record set is cached on the client computer and available in online or offline mode from the source server.

In addition to these data access-oriented layers, Windows DNA's data tier also includes transaction services that bind heterogeneous, dispersed data stores into a unified application environment.

MTS, discussed above, plays a significant role in Windows DNA's data tier. Accessed via language-independent COM components, MTS integrates clients and resource managers to enable "two-phase commit" transaction processing, which spares database application developers from having to write transaction logic into their code. MTS is a basic facility of Windows 2000 and Windows NT Server. It supports server-based concurrency control, transaction logging, and rollback, which enables linked databases to be rolled back to their previous states in case a transaction is aborted.

Microsoft Message Queue Server, discussed in greater detail in Chapter 14, enables reliable, loosely coupled data-sharing among applications across local and wide-area networks. Accessed via language-independent COM components, MSMQ, a basic facility of Windows 2000 and Windows NT Server, uses an asynchronous message-brokering technology. It implements a "publish and subscriber" business-event notification model between applications and spares programmers from having to build networking logic into their applications.

COM Transaction Integrator (COMTI), also discussed in Part Three, enables developers to access mainframe-based transactional database applications from COM components. COMTI development tools and run-time services automatically "wrap" IBM mainframe transaction and business logic as

COM components that run under SNA Server 4.0 or Host Integration Server 2000. COMTI does not require configuration changes to the host computers being accessed or installation of new executables on those computers.

Distinct from multiplatform transaction integration is the issue of data-semantics interchange. Semantics interchange involves data transfer in a standard "self-describing" format that conveys the logical structure and application context or meaning of that data. XML is the industry-standard markup format for semantics interchange, and Microsoft is implementing XML at all tiers in the Windows DNA environment. Microsoft has equipped its entire software product family—from the client to the application server and database server—to generate and process documents and other objects in XML format. An embedded XML "parser" module is now a standard feature of most Microsoft software products for the enterprise and service provider markets. Windows 2000 includes a high-performance validating XML parser that implements the World Wide Web Consortium's XML 1.0 standard, as well as such related standards as the Document Object Model (DOM), XML Stylesheet Language (XSL), and XML Namespaces. This parser is available to all applications that run on Windows 2000. DOM support in Windows 2000, IIS, and IE enables XML documents to be used as objects, accessible through COM and scripts.

XML, of course, is central to the BizTalk initiative and serves as the markup format for BizTalk Messages and their contents. Microsoft has enabled Windows 2000, all Windows DNA 2000 servers (including, of course, BizTalk Server 2000), and all Microsoft Servers to generate, process, and store documents in BizTalk-compliant XML schemas. Microsoft is also extending BizTalk-enablement to its client products such as the Windows operating system and the Office productivity suite. Office 2000 already stores documents in native XML format (in addition to proprietary Microsoft file formats). The company also provides such developer resources as the Windows DNA XML Resource Kit, which includes sample code, demo applications, whitepapers, and tools that show how to use XML with Visual Studio, BizTalk Server 2000, SQL Server, Internet Explorer, and other Microsoft products and development technologies.

12.2 Windows 2000

Windows 2000 is Microsoft's flagship operating environment. Microsoft has designed, optimized, and packaged Windows 2000 to fit into any and all tiers of the Windows DNA environment: as a client OS, network OS, application-server OS, or scalable Web-farm OS.

However, Microsoft has focused Windows 2000 functionality primarily on the middle tier: as a robust, scalable platform for application servers, which host the business logic on which e-commerce and other distributed applications depend. The company's e-commerce product roadmap positions Windows 2000 as the platform providing critical system services for Windows DNA 2000 application servers. Windows DNA 2000 products include BizTalk Server 2000, Commerce Server 2000, SQL Server 2000, and Host Integration Server 2000. Windows 2000 also hosts other Microsoft Server application servers, including Internet Information Server, Exchange 2000, and System Management Server.

All of these Windows 2000-based application servers are important components of Microsoft's total software environment for e-commerce, extranet, and enterprise applications. For the uninitiated, it can be difficult to determine which of these servers and services are integral parts of Windows 2000 and which are optional add-on modules. Microsoft bundles many application servers with Windows 2000 as part of the Microsoft Server suite. And the company has embedded many important system services into Windows 2000 itself, including such features as COM, DCOM, MTS, MSMQ, AD, Kerberos, MMC, Microsoft Certificate Server, Microsoft Cluster Services, and Windows Terminal Services.

Call it feature cram or code bloat if you will, but the four-year Windows 2000 development effort was among the industry's most complex, high-stakes software-engineering projects ever. Microsoft has pumped Windows 2000 full of functionality. And it has the Godzilla-sized system "footprint" to show for it. The new OS contains approximately 40 million lines of source code, compared to 5 million lines in its immediate predecessor, Windows NT Server 4.0.

Windows 2000 comes in four varieties, each with its own feature set, minimum system requirements, and scalability profile. These versions are Windows 2000 Professional, Windows 2000 Server, Windows 2000 Advanced Server, and Windows 2000 Datacenter Server. Table 12-2 describes these versions at a high level.

Clearly, Windows 2000 is an exceedingly complex OS—some might argue that it attempts to be all things to all applications. One good way to gauge its complexity is to review the range of COM components, methods, and properties that expose its various system service capabilities to application developers. Another approach is to review the various Microsoft Management Console snap-in modules that expose these same run-time services to system administrators.

Yet another (more conceptual) approach for fathoming Windows 2000's complexity is to decompose its many features into logical service categories. At the most fundamental level are hardware-oriented system services. These include Windows 2000's microkernel architecture, preemptive multitasking, memory protection, virtual memory, symmetric multiprocessing, remote booting capability, "plug-and-play" device-driver support, power management, and hierarchical storage management features.

Table 12-2	Windows 2000 Versions

Version	Description
Windows 2000 Professional	Corporate desktop version of the operating system, though it can also run on high-performance notebook computers. Windows 2000 Professional succeeds Windows NT Workstation 4.0 in Microsoft's product family. The new workstation operating system offers better performance, reliability, manageability, and security than its predecessor. It includes such new features as support for DirectX 7.0 multimedia applications, mobile device power management, removable storage devices, and "plug and play" Universal Serial Bus (USB) devices. It includes out-of-the-box client connectivity to Windows 2000 Server's Active Directory, as well as to Windows NT domain services, Novell NetWare file and print services, and Unix Network File System (NFS) and printing services. Minimum system requirements for Windows 2000 Professional include a 133-megahertz (MHz) Pentium-compatible central processing unit (CPU), 64 megabytes (MB) of random-access memory (RAM), and a 1-gigabyte (GB) hard drive. Optimal performance requires at least 128 MB RAM and a 4-GB hard drive. It supports two-processor symmetric multiprocessing (SMP) per machine but not the ability to cluster machines running the operating system.
Windows 2000 Server	Small to mid-size enterprise server version of the operating system, supporting workgroup or branch-office network operating system (NOS) and Web server requirements. Windows 2000 Server succeeds Windows NT Server 4.0. The new server supports the same functionality as Windows 2000 Professional, plus such server functionality as file, print, and application sharing. It includes the full suite of Windows 2000 system services, including Active Directory, Kerberos authentication, X.509-based public key infrastructure, Internet Information Server, and Windows Terminal Server. Minimum system requirements for Windows 2000 Server include a 133-MHz Pentium-compatible CPU, 256 MB RAM, and 1-GB hard drive. Optimal performance requires at least 512 MB RAM. Windows 2000 Server supports four-processor SMP per machine and up to 4 GB RAM per machine, but does not support clustering.
Windows 2000 Advanced Server	Enterprise-class server version of the operating system, supporting high-performance departmental, application, or Web server requirements. Windows 2000 Advanced Server succeeds Windows NT Server 4.0 Enterprise Edition. It provides the same functionality as Windows 2000 Server. However, it supports more memory per machine (up to 64 GB) and more CPUs for symmetric multiprocessing (up to eight). It also supports the ability to cluster up to four machines, to balance network loads across up to 32 network nodes, and to failover a malfunctioning server automatically to a live backup machine. Minimum system requirements for Windows 2000 Advanced Server include a 133-MHz Pentium-compatible CPU, 256 MB RAM, and 1-GB hard drive. Optimal performance requires at least 512 MB RAM.

Table 12-2	*Windows 2000 Versions (cont.)*
Version	**Description**
Windows 2000 Datacenter Server	High-performance server version of the operating system. It supports mission-critical corporate applications, online transaction processing, data warehouses, large-scale scientific and engineering simulations, and application service providers. Windows 2000 Datacenter Server is more scalable than any previous version of Windows NT. Windows 2000 Datacenter Server supports the same functionality as Windows 2000 Advanced Server but scales to support very large server-farm installations that require reliable, high-performance, continuously available applications. It includes the Process Control Manager utility, which supports fine-grained administrative controls over allocation of critical server resources such as processors, memory, and job-scheduling priorities. This version of Windows 2000 supports up to 32-way SMP and 64 GB RAM per machine, four-way clustering, 32-node network load balancing, and cascading failover among four nodes.

Beyond the physical level are the many distributed software services that run across Windows 2000, Windows DNA 2000, and Windows DNA environments. (This may sound like three ways of saying the same thing, but, as we've seen, Windows DNA 2000 refers to particular application servers running on the Windows 2000 NOS, and Windows DNA environments can include non–Windows 2000 and non-Microsoft platforms). Table 12-3 presents a high-level listing of these distributed services, which we will then proceed to describe in greater detail (in this and other chapters in Part Four).

12.3 Core Windows 2000 System Services

We now examine Windows 2000's file, directory, security, and management services in detail. We have already discussed Windows 2000 middleware technologies at a high level and will save the detailed discussion for later chapters. (We point the reader to any number of Microsoft and third-party resources that describe Windows 2000's network protocol and routing options in greater detail than we can possibly provide in this book.)

12.3.1 Windows 2000 File Services

One of the most fundamental services of any OS is file sharing and management. File management services support user and application access to files

| Table 12-3 | *Windows 2000 Distributed Services* |

Service Category	Description
File	Supports Distributed File System (DFS), NT File System (NTFS), File Allocation Table 32-bit (FAT32), FAT 16-bit (FAT16), Virtual File Allocation Table (VFAT), Compact Disk File System (CDFS), and Installable File Systems (IFS). The OS uses the Server Message Block (SMB) protocol for client/server file-service operations and exposes the same operations to browsers via the Web-Distributed Authoring and Versioning (WebDAV) protocol.
Directory	Provides Active Directory services, as well as support for such naming services as Domain Name System (DNS), Dynamic DNS, Dynamic Host Configuration Protocol (DHCP), Windows Internet Name Service (WINS), and Information Locator Service (ILS). Windows 2000 interfaces Active Directory to external directories through Microsoft Meta-Directory Services (MMDS). The OS supports the Active Directory Services Interface (ADSI) and Lightweight Directory Access Protocol (LDAP).
Security	Provides Distributed Security Services, which includes support for single sign-on, public key certificate services, file-system encryption services, smartcard logon, code signing, and virtual private network (VPN) tunneling. The OS implements such authentication interfaces as Kerberos, NT LAN Manager (NTLM), Remote Authentication Dial-In User Service (RADIUS), Password Authentication Protocol (PAP), Challenge Handshake Authentication Protocol (CHAP), and MS-CHAP. It supports public key infrastructure interfaces such as X.509 certificates, S/MIME, Transport Layer Security (TLS), CryptoAPI, and Private Communications Technology (PCT) 1.0. For VPN services, it supports such tunneling protocols as Point-to-Point Tunneling Protocol (PPTP), Layer 2 Tunneling Protocol (L2TP), and IPSec.
Management	Provides a wide range of management and administration services and tools. These include Microsoft Management Console, Systems Management Server, IntelliMirror, Windows Management Instrumentation, and Windows Scripting Host.
Network	Provides many network protocol interfaces, including enhanced TCP/IP, Point-to-Point Protocol (PPP), Internet Packet Exchange/Sequenced Packet Exchange (IPX/SPX), H.323, and AppleTalk. Windows 2000's Remote Routing and Access Services (RRAS) supports several routing protocols, including Open Shortest Path First (OSPF), Routing Information Protocol (RIP) v2, and Internet Group Management Protocol (IGMP) v2. RRAS supports quality-of-service protocols such as Resource Reservation Setup Protocol (RSVP) and Differentiated Quality of Service (DiffServ). Through IIS, Windows 2000 supports HTTP and File Transfer Protocol (FTP). Through Exchange Server, it supports SMTP, Network News Transfer Protocol (NNTP), Post Office Protocol version 3 (POP3), and Internet Messaging Access Protocol version 4 (IMAP4).
Middleware	Provides DCOM, COM+, MTS, MSMQ, and Simple Object Access Protocol (SOAP) middleware services. It exposes these services as COM objects in Visual Studio, Visual InterDev, Visual Basic, Visual C++, and Visual J++.

on local devices, such as hard drives or CD-ROM drives, and on remote nodes, such as file or Web servers.

Windows 2000 relies on Microsoft-proprietary file services as well as the OS's interfaces to third-party file services, including the universal, distributed filestore we call the World Wide Web. Microsoft-proprietary file services primarily serve intranet deployments, while the Web is the lightweight, distributed file service for extranets and hubbed e-marketplaces.

DISTRIBUTED FILE SYSTEM

DFS—a Microsoft-proprietary technology—is the native 32-bit networked file system of both Windows 2000 and Windows NT Server 4.0.

DFS supports a unified, logical, hierarchical view of file servers and shared volumes across a local- or wide-area network. Network administrators can establish an arbitrary number of logical directories and then map physical servers and volumes to these directories. Users can look up files in logical directories, rather than the physical devices on which those files reside. Administrators can move files to new physical servers without users noticing any change. Behind the scenes, multimaster replication ensures consistency between local and remote copies of files across Windows 2000 network clients and servers.

DFS can also replicate volumes and direct users to the nearest, most accessible copy, based on DFS replica profiles in Active Directory. Windows 2000 and NT clients can automatically select the correct DFS replica by consulting Active Directory.

DFS, like previous Microsoft file systems, uses Universal Naming Convention (UNC) pathnames to point to files in specific remote physical volumes. UNC names are of the general form "\\machinename\sharename\dirname1\dirname2\dirname3\filename." In addition, DFS uses the SMB file access protocol implemented in previous versions of Windows NT. DFS is backward compatible with other Microsoft-proprietary file systems implemented in previous versions of Windows. It can read volumes running NTFS, FAT, VFAT, CDFS, and IFS.

SUPPORT FOR OTHER MICROSOFT-PROPRIETARY FILE SYSTEMS

What follows are a few words on each of these legacy Microsoft file systems.

NTFS is the native 32-bit file system on Windows NT 4.0 and previous versions. Windows NT can also read CDFS, VFAT, and FAT volumes.

FAT is the native, 16-bit, real-mode file system that was included in MS-DOS and Windows 3.x for managing local fixed and diskette drives. Local FAT volumes can be read by Windows 9x and NT.

VFAT is the native 32-bit file system in Windows 9x. It was first introduced in Windows for Workgroups version 3.11 as an optional FAT file system that processes file I/O in protected mode and supports native disk compression. VFAT can use 32-bit, protected-mode drivers or 16-bit real-mode drivers. Actual allocation on disk is still 12-bit or 16-bit (depending on the size of the volume), so FAT on the disk uses the same structure as previous versions of this file system. The VFAT and FAT file systems lack such DFS and NTFS features as file-level security, on-the-fly file compression, and disk quotas.

CDFS is also included as a native 32-bit file system in Windows 2000, NT, and 9x for managing files on local CD-ROMs. CDFS loads automatically if a local CD-ROM device is detected. CDFS performs the same functions on CD-ROMs that VFAT performs on local fixed and diskette drives.

IFS interfaces—supported in Windows 200, NT, and 9x—allow third parties to provide special file-sharing and management features that span networks of Windows and (possibly) non-Windows machines. Windows 2000 can support access to multiple, installable, third-party file systems in addition to its native DFS. In addition, Windows 2000 DFS supports a Microsoft IFS called "Web Store" that is a central feature of Exchange Server 2000.

INTERFACE TO THIRD-PARTY FILE SYSTEMS

In addition to working with these various file systems, Windows 2000 can also function as a client or server in third-party distributed file management services. All Windows versions (2000, NT, 9x, and 3.x) support NOS redirectors, such as Microsoft Client for NetWare Networks, which are file system drivers for specific third-party LAN file systems. Redirectors translate I/O requests into network protocols—such as Network Core Protocol (NCP) and Network File System (NFS)—that are understood by remote LAN file server volumes. Windows 2000, NT, and 9x clients can support multiple NOS redirectors simultaneously. Any volume that is accessible through a redirector can participate in the DFS name space.

INTERFACE WITH WEB-FACING FILESTORES

Furthermore, Windows 2000 participates fully in the Web, which, as we noted above, is the world's first truly open, cross-platform, distributed filestore. What distinguishes the Web from DFS and other traditional distributed file systems is its reliance on URL naming, rather than UNC and similar conventions. Microsoft's efforts to embed browser functionality in the Windows platforms have helped to blur the distinction between local and Web-based filestores to the point of irrelevance, especially for corporate users with high-speed, continuous Internet connectivity. Consequently, Microsoft's file systems must accommodate a world of non-Microsoft fileshares. One might argue that the availability of a ubiquitous, vendor-neutral distributed filestore (the Web), content presentation interface (HTML), and client (browser) shows that we already have what amounts to a worldwide operating environment not totally under Microsoft's thumb.

Microsoft recognizes this reality and has integrated a Web file management interface, WebDAV, into Windows 2000. WebDAV (IETF RFC 2518, a proposed standard) defines extensions to HTTP 1.1 that allow heterogeneous Web clients and servers to operate as a scalable, distributed document store. The specification defines mechanisms for naming, posting, saving, version control, and other functions on Web-resident documents in a way that is independent of underlying operating systems. It uses XML tags to define metadata applicable to documents and the collections to which they belong. However, it does not in itself define a new distributed file system, since it does not define core attribute sets beyond those necessary for basic distributed authoring and versioning.

12.3.2 Windows 2000 Directory Services

Directory services are an essential tool for finding and managing people, information, and resources in distributed computing environments. Directories support naming, location, and management of users, groups, servers, and other resources in network environments.

Microsoft has implemented directory services as a core feature of Windows NT Server since the product's introduction, and Windows 2000's dominant new feature is a radically redesigned directory service: Active Directory.

ACTIVE DIRECTORY

AD provides a distributed, hierarchical, replicated, multimaster X.500-based directory service. It is available to all users and applications under Windows 2000. It presents a unified logical view of network resources and supports centralized administration of all network resources, including files, peripherals, host connections, and databases. AD can scale up to manage 10 million entries (known as "objects") in a single domain. AD can be accessed through any of the following interfaces: LDAP, Microsoft's Active Directory Services Interface (ADSI) APIs for various high-level languages, or Active Directory Components (a set of COM objects for manipulating and querying multiple directory services).

AD's core function in an intranet, extranet, or e-marketplace is to provide identity and permission management services. AD directly supports Windows 2000's authentication, access control, and resource management features. Consequently, the directory helps organizations implement internal access controls across the enterprise network. When implemented in an extranet or e-marketplace environment, AD, which provides a repository for X.509 public key certificates, can also help define and enforce the virtual boundaries among trading partners communicating via a distributed network of BizTalk Servers.

AD comes into play the moment a user switches on his or her PC in a network running the Windows 2000 NOS. On bootup, the user's client automatically obtains its IP address from AD's Dynamic Domain Name System (DDNS) facility. The client automatically locates a Windows 2000 Domain Controller through AD's DNS mechanism. When the user logs into the DC, his or her client automatically obtains its Kerberos authentication credentials from a Windows 2000 Key Distribution Center integrated with AD. When users attempt to browse resources and access services in the Windows 2000 environment, their requests are granted—or denied—in accordance with access lists maintained under AD.

The older NT Directory Service (NTDS) has technical limitations that had hampered Microsoft's enterprise-distributed computing initiatives and left the company vulnerable to competition from other NOS vendors, especially Novell Directory Services. For starters, AD replaces NT's registry with a scalable, high-performance database able to hold millions of entries.

But NTDS's greatest limitation is its flat domain-name directory structure, which AD has replaced with a hierarchical, cross-domain, enterprise directory. Each NT domain is a group of machines for which accounts and access privileges are managed by the same administrator. NTDS directories are dedicated to particular domains, an architecture that requires significant manual intervention from network administrators when users require access to resources in other Windows NT domains. NT domain administrators must explicitly (in other words, manually) define domain-to-domain trust relationships and configure information about users or groups that require cross-domain privileges.

Microsoft has positioned AD as the central object repository for an organization that deploys Windows 2000 as its core NOS. Indeed, AD is central to all of Windows 2000's distributed services. In addition, AD, in conjunction with Microsoft's new family of "meta-directory" tools, can be the core directory for an extranet or e-marketplace. Meta-directory tools enable integration of user, group, resource, and policy information from the directories of trading partners (and the marketmaker's own internal directories), many of which may be using competing products such as Novell Directory Services or Critical Path's Global Directory Server.

In support of distributed file services, AD, as we noted earlier, maintains DFS replica profiles to facilitate replication of files across distributed storage volumes. More generally, AD manages the enterprise-wide namespace for identifying, joining, and locating shared volumes in a logically unified, location-independent fashion.

In support of distributed security services, AD maintains security policy, access control, and authentication information, including Kerberos credentials and X.509 public key certificates. AD supports single login authentication to file, print, and other application services for all users under Windows

2000. AD supports a sophisticated range of group policy and access controls applicable to users, applications, and services. Application permissions in the Windows 2000 environment rely on access control lists (ACLs) maintained centrally in AD.

To facilitate cross-domain authentication, AD replicates a Global Catalog (GC) throughout a Windows 2000 network, replicating such critical information as domain schemas, configuration information, replication topologies, and selected user and resource entries between domains. Selected Windows 2000 servers in each domain maintain GC information. Other uses for GC information include allowing users in different domains to browse for one another's names and addresses, and supporting lookup and retrieval of public key certificates for digital signatures and encryption on e-mail.

In support of distributed management services, AD maintains a master copy of directory information in each Windows 2000 domain controller (DC). This directory information implements the X.500 and DNS information models. AD stores application configuration, security, and user management information, replicating this information along with other directory objects. Figure 12-2 shows AD's replication scheme, which involves full multimaster replication among DCs in the same domain tree and replication of GC contents between DCs in different trees of the same forest.

AD combines application-specific objects and Windows 2000 objects into a single directory managed within a single GUI environment: Microsoft Management Console. IT administrators can use Microsoft Management Console's drag-and-drop facility to move users, servers, and other resources across AD domains in an organization. Moves, copies, renamings, deletions, and other changes to AD objects do not affect the underlying X.500 distinguished names (DNs) associated with these entities, since AD identifies all resources by, unchanging globally unique identifiers (GUIDs).

AD ensures consistency among distributed directory information through multimaster replication, which eliminates the need for primary and backup DCs (which are core features of NT Server 4.0's management model). Multimaster directory replication enables one Windows 2000 DC to take over logon, authorization, and access control functions from another, if necessary, and to accept changes. AD also enables more powerful policy administration through enterprise-wide searching for users, groups, and resources based on various criteria. And it supports administrative coexistence between Windows 2000, NT4, and NT3 servers during the upgrade and migration process, since it enables a Windows 2000 DC to appear as an NT primary or backup DC.

AD generates heavy, ongoing replication traffic between Windows 2000 servers within and between domains. Windows 2000 supports various domain and site configuration options aimed at optimizing replication topologies.

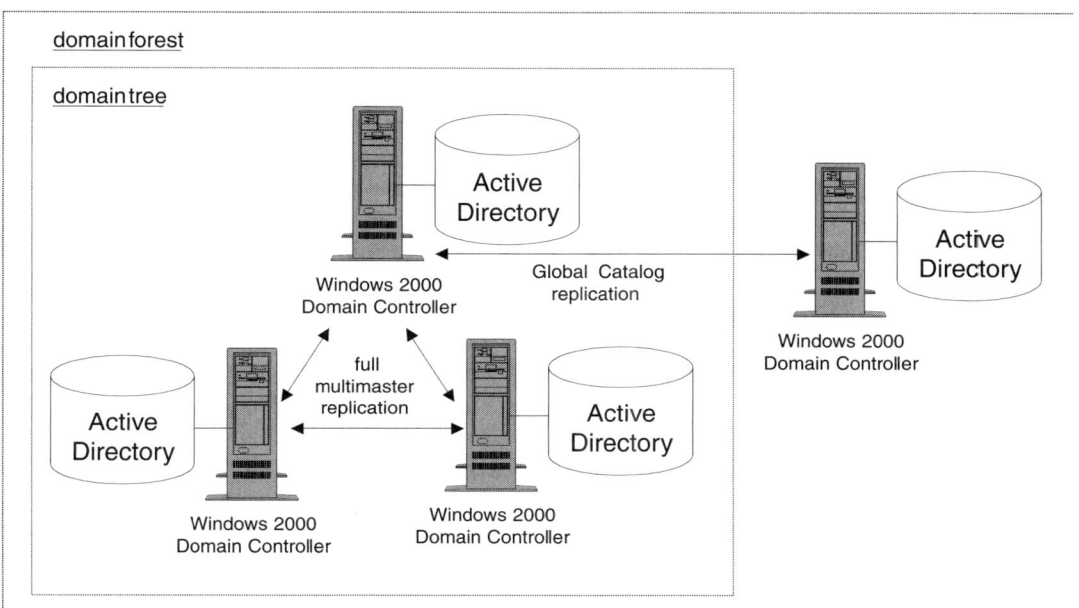

domain forest

domain tree

Active Directory

Windows 2000 Domain Controller

Global Catalog replication

Active Directory

Windows 2000 Domain Controller

full multimaster replication

Active Directory

Windows 2000 Domain Controller

Active Directory

Windows 2000 Domain Controller

Figure 12-2   *Windows 2000 maintains a full master copy of domain tree's AD at each domain controller in the domain tree and replicates incremental changes between all domain controllers in real time. Only changes in AD's Global Catalog are replicated between domain controllers in different trees of a Windows 2000 domain forest.*

And, finally, in support of DCOM, AD provides a namespace to locate network objects and resources across a large enterprise. Before AD, COM applications still ran mostly on single machines. AD provides a distributed service for COM components to expose their locations and methods to each other for the purpose of engaging in DCOM transactions.

DOMAIN NAME SYSTEM

DNS, the Internet's distributed address-resolution infrastructure, is also Windows 2000's core naming, TCP/IP address-resolution, and locator service. Windows 2000 domain names consist of DNS domain names and X.500 distinguished names. Active Directory servers publish their addresses so that clients can find them knowing only the domain name. Active Directory supports dynamic DNS updates, sparing administrators from having to manually configure records stored in DNS servers. Microsoft provides a DNS server under Windows 2000, but any standards-compliant DNS server can be configured to interoperate with Windows 2000. The DHCP client included in Windows 2000 will automatically register DHCP-issued TCP/IP addresses in Microsoft or third-party DNS servers.

DNS replaces WINS, the NetBIOS-to-Internet name-resolution service that was supported in NT Server 4.0. However, Windows 2000 still supports WINS to provide backward compatibility with 16-bit clients.

12.3.3 Windows 2000 Security Services

Security services are a critical infrastructure for fine-grained administrative control in a distributed computing environment. These services support authentication, access control, content confidentiality, content integrity, and nonrepudiation on files, applications, databases, and other dispersed resources.

Windows 2000's DSS includes a wide range of services carried over from Windows NT Server 4.0 as well as some significant new features that Microsoft has integrated tightly with AD. In support of single sign-on and other security features, AD maintains account profiles, passwords, access control lists, security policies, public key certificates, and other credentials.

Among Windows 2000's new security services are Kerberos-based authentication, smartcard authentication, security groups, Encrypting File System, and IPSec tunneling.

AUTHENTICATION

Kerberos-based authentication is the most important new security service in Windows 2000. Windows 2000 also supports three other authentication services carried over from Windows NT Server 4.0: NT LAN Manager, Secure Sockets Layer (SSL) v3 (also known as Transport Layer Security), and Distributed Password Authentication (DPA). Each authentication service supports a different range of clients, network environments, and applications.

Kerberos, a secret-key-based authentication technology developed at the Massachusetts Institute of Technology (MIT), supports single sign-on across multiple Windows 2000 domains. Users do not have to explicitly log on to separate Windows 2000 servers and applications in a given online session. Kerberos authentication (as defined in IETF RFCs 1510 and 1964) can provide single sign-on for transparent access to resources, where services, applications, and users are tied together by a Kerberos service acting as an authentication broker.

Kerberos version 5 supports strong authentication of Windows 2000 client requests for single sign-on access to Windows 2000–based services. Kerberos uses secret keys to provide "under the covers" authentication credentials for Windows 2000 users to transparently access services throughout a Windows 2000 environment. A Kerberos Key Distribution Center (KDC) running on a Windows 2000 server authenticates the user's encrypted password credentials against a trusted directory (under AD), and provides the user with a Ticket-Granting Ticket (TGT). The user's client caches the TGT locally. When the user attempts to access resources, the client uses the TGT to obtain a one-time Session Ticket (ST), which is a KDC-signed cryptographic credential for use in authenticating to the server that controls the desired resource. Kerberos technology encrypts all user passwords, session keys, and data transmissions over local- and wide-area networks. Figure 12-3 shows the basic Kerberos authentication steps.

Windows 2000 uses Kerberos to support implicit, two-way transitive trust relationships among servers within an AD "domain tree" (which consists of a set of hierarchically related domains in a contiguous X.500 namespace; all such domains share a common directory schema, global catalog, and configuration). Two-way transitive trusts exist when all "child" domains trust the parent domain, and all child domains within a tree trust one another. Kerberos also supports two-way transitive trust between Windows 2000

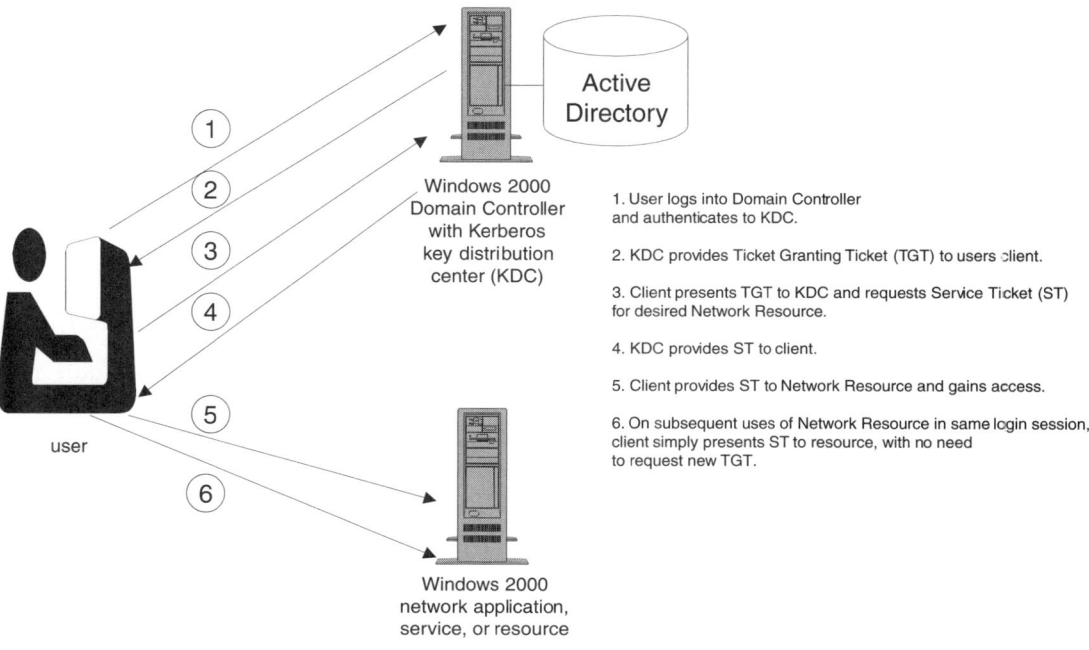

1. User logs into Domain Controller and authenticates to KDC.

2. KDC provides Ticket Granting Ticket (TGT) to users client.

3. Client presents TGT to KDC and requests Service Ticket (ST) for desired Network Resource.

4. KDC provides ST to client.

5. Client provides ST to Network Resource and gains access.

6. On subsequent uses of Network Resource in same login session, client simply presents ST to resource, with no need to request new TGT.

Figure 12-3   *Kerberos authentication involves Windows 2000 users logging in to their domain controller, obtaining (transparently) a Ticket Granting Ticket from the local Key Distribution Center, and caching the TGT in their client. When the user attempts to gain access to a Windows 2000 network application, service, or resource, his or her client presents the TGT to the KDC for a Session Ticket for that resource. Upon presenting the ST to the desired resource, the client is automatically granted access to the resource.*

domain trees in a "domain forest" (which is a set of noncontiguous, nonhier-archical domains that share a common schema, global catalog and configuration). However, administrators must establish explicit trust relationships among Windows 2000 domains that do not belong to the same forest, or between Windows 2000 and Windows NT Server domains. Figure 12-4 shows two-way, transitive, implicit trust relationships among Windows 2000 domains within a tree and a forest.

Trust among Windows 2000 domains is defined implicitly through the AD domain hierarchy, rather than (as under Windows NT 4.0) through explicit cross-domain trust relationships defined by administrators. Windows 2000 now requires explicit administrative setting of trust relationships only for disjoint domains or for backward compatibility to Windows NT Server 4.0 domains.

Whereas Kerberos only works among Windows 2000 clients and servers (and other Kerberos-enabled computing environments), NTLM supports Windows 2000 server authentication of down-level Windows clients and servers. NTLM is the primary authentication scheme supported in Windows NT. NTLM supports both weak and strong authentication. For weak authentication, it supports transmission of plaintext IDs and passwords to Windows NT server-based applications. NTLM credentials consist of the domain name, username, and encrypted password that is entered once during the initial logon to Windows NT. For strong authentication, NTLM supports a shared-key challenge/response dialogue, in which the Windows NT server sends an encrypted challenge to the client and the user's password is never sent over the wire.

NTLM is a less efficient protocol than Kerberos, which is one reason why Microsoft standardized on the latter technology in Windows 2000. NTLM requires that servers communicate with the DC before authenticating a client and granting its request. This is a step that Kerberos eliminates, since clients present their credentials directly to the server controlling the resource they seek. Consequently, Kerberos speeds up the authentication process and reduces network traffic.

Another NTLM disadvantage is that it authenticates the client but not the server. Kerberos authenticates the client and server to each other, thereby guarding against the possibility of a rogue server that spoofs an authentic network server.

Where Kerberos and NTLM authentication operate primarily in the intranet, SSLv3 is Windows 2000's primary authentication protocol for Web-based applications. SSLv3 supports user authentication, digital signatures, and transport-level encryption from Web browsers and other applications that access Windows 2000 and NT server applications over the Internet (through Internet Information Server). SSLv3 provides client-to-server security on HTTP, LDAPv3, POP3, NNTP, and IMAP4 connections to Windows 2000/NT-based applications. This security protocol uses server-side and (optional)

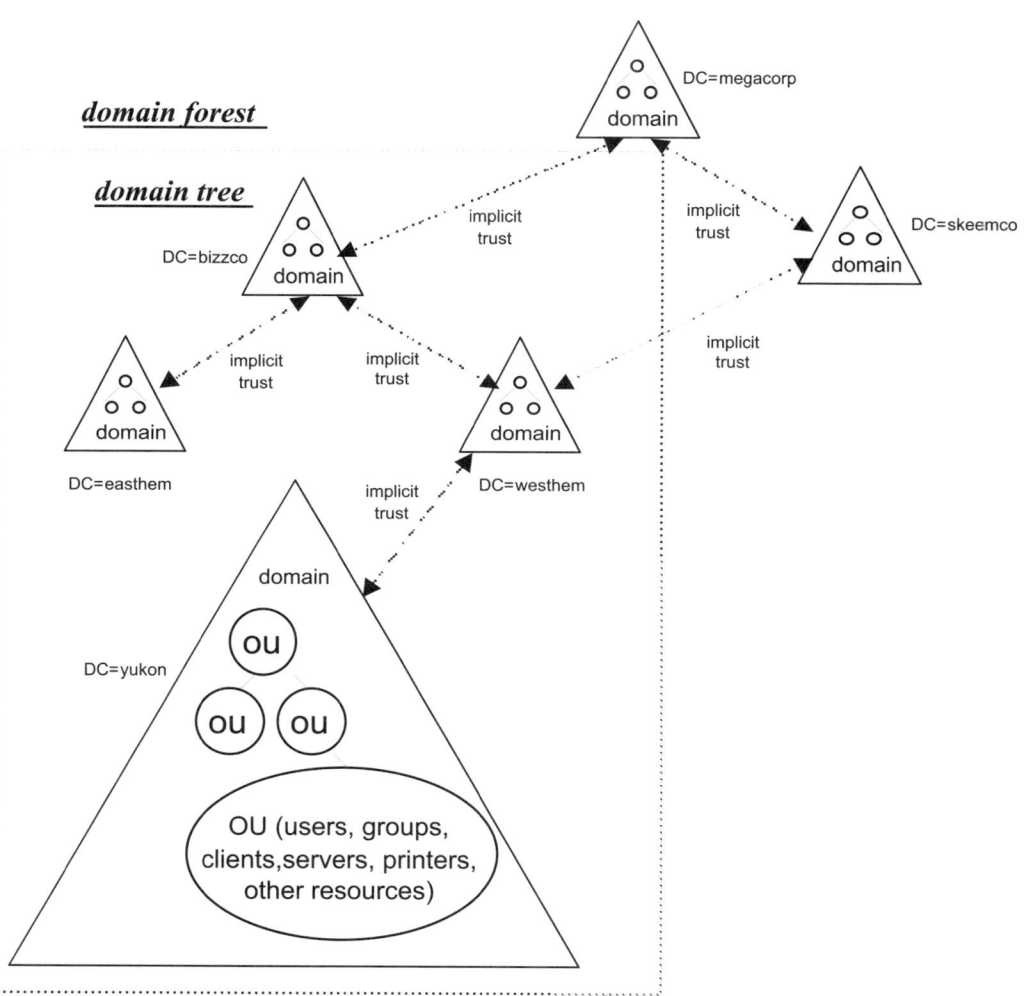

domain forest

domain tree

DC=bizzco

DC=megacorp

DC=skeemco

implicit trust

implicit trust

implicit trust

implicit trust

implicit trust

implicit trust

DC=easthem

DC=westhem

DC=yukon

domain

ou

ou ou

OU (users, groups, clients, servers, printers, other resources)

Figure 12-4   *Windows 2000 uses AD and Kerberos to establish two-way, transitive, implicit trust relationships among domains within "domain trees" and "domain forests." Implicit trust relationships support Windows 2000's single sign-on feature, which allows users to gain authorized access to resources in other domains without needing to establish accounts in those domains.*

client-side X.509 public key certificates (v3 or v1) stored under AD. The directory can store X.509 certificates that were issued by Microsoft Certificate Server 1.0 (which is a component of Windows 2000) or by any third-party certificate authority (CA).

Certificate Server is the core of the Windows DNA public key infrastructure (PKI) architecture (as shown in Figure 12-5). X.509 public key certificates, issued by Certificate Server and stored in AD, support authentication, encryption, message integrity, and nonrepudiation services within Windows 2000 applications. X.509 certificates are essential for security protocols such as SSLv3/v2 (also called Transport Layer Security), S/MIME, and IPSec, and to the new Encrypting File System feature of Windows 2000.

Administrators can use Certificate Server (or a third-party product) to issue X.509v3 certificates to employees or business partners, and also store these certificates in AD (or any third-party LDAP-accessible directory). Certificate Server supports central administration of certificates, certificate revocation lists, and trust policy information within AD. Windows 2000 administrators can specify which external CAs applications may trust for the purpose of verifying externally issued X.509 certificates.

X.509 certificates can extend enterprise single sign-on privileges to extranet users with SSL/TLS-enabled browsers. In this scenario, the external user comes into Microsoft's Internet Information Server outside the enterprise firewall and logs in with a username and password maintained in AD. IIS

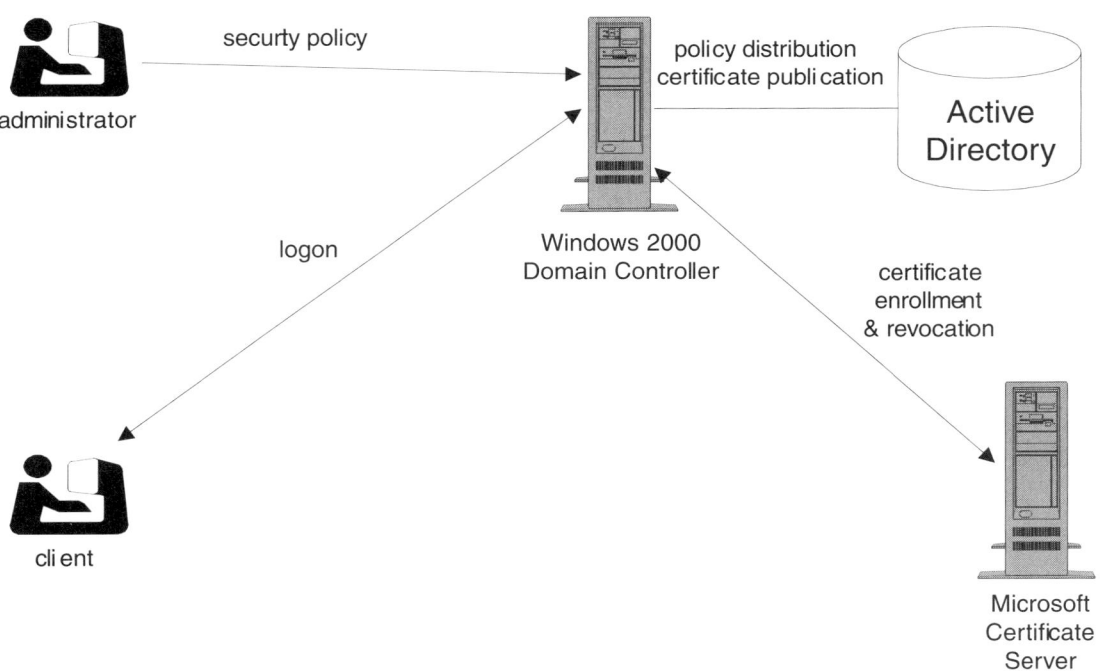

Figure 12-5   *Windows 2000's public key infrastructure includes Domain Controllers, Microsoft Certificate Server, Active Directory, and security administration snap-ins under Microsoft Management Console. Administrators use Certificate Server to issue and revoke X.509 certificates and Active Directory to store and publish the certificates.*

retrieves the user's X.509 certificate from AD, validates the certificate, and maps the certificate to a configured Windows 2000 account. IIS then attempts to access the requested resource using Kerberos and the privileges available to the mapped account.

In a similar fashion, BizTalk Server 2000 can retrieve X.509 certificates from AD to authenticate and decrypt incoming messages from trading partners, as well as to perform the reverse operations on outgoing messages. Consequently, trading partners can be set up with various levels of privileges in an extranet or e-marketplace environment riding on Windows 2000, thanks to X.509 PKI technologies embedded in the OS.

However, Microsoft does not use X.509-based PKI as its principal intranet authentication technology, because Kerberos offers better performance within domains. Kerberos-enabled applications can verify client Session Tickets more efficiently than they can verify X.509 credentials. Of course, one of PKI's great advantages for secure Web applications is its more scalable key-distribution model, based on public key certificates and CAs, as opposed to Kerberos's secret keys and KDCs.

Windows 2000 carries forward NT Server's support for secure storage of personal security credentials on disk. In addition, Windows 2000 adds native support for smartcard authentication. A smartcard contains a chip that stores a user's X.509 certificate and private key, thereby protecting these critical security data elements from theft or disclosure over the network. The user enters a password or personal identification number (PIN) after inserting the smartcard into a card reader at the client computer.

DPA is the shared-secret-key authentication protocol used by some of the largest Internet membership organizations, such as CompuServe. DPA authenticates users to any number of Internet sites that are part of the same membership organization without the need to reenter their passwords. Microsoft supports Windows 2000 server integration with third-party DPA providers via the published Security Service Provider Interface (SSPI). Separate from Windows 2000, Microsoft provides its own DPA technology in Microsoft Commercial Internet System (MCIS), a package that it markets to ISPs and other online services.

Windows 2000's support for multiple authentication schemes is a great advantage in distributed computing environments that include other operating systems (such as might be found in the average large company's intranet, extranet, or hubbed e-marketplace). Figure 12-6 shows the various client/server authentication configurations in which Windows 2000 clients and/or servers can participate.

SSPI, a Win32 API, enables Windows 2000 and NT servers to interface with alternate third-party authentication mechanisms. SSPI enables Windows 2000 applications to retrieve credentials from any Microsoft or third-party authentication service, including Kerberos KDCs, X.509 public key certificate stores, or DPA-compliant online service providers. SSPI allows distributed

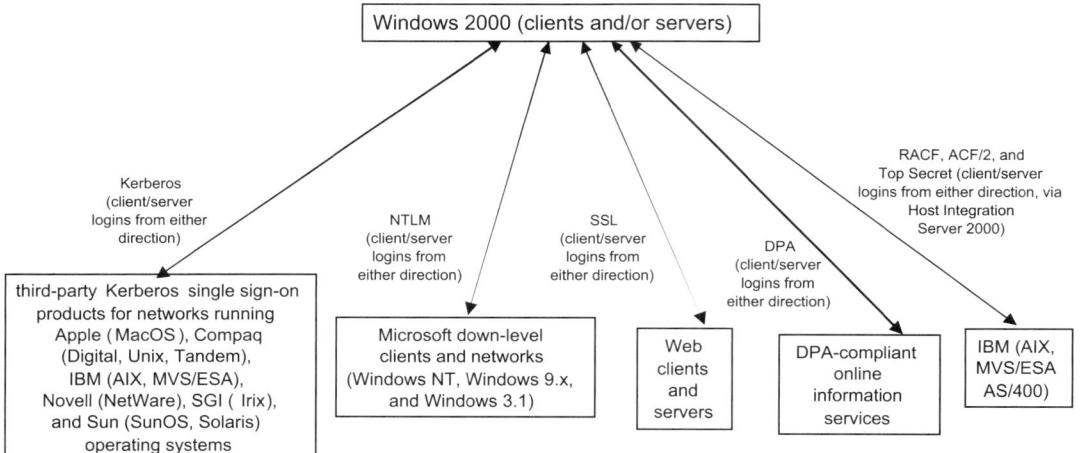

Figure 12-6   *Windows 2000 servers can authenticate non–Windows 2000 clients via Kerberos, NTLM, SSL, DPA, RACF, ACF/2, and TopSecret protocols. Windows 2000 clients can use any of these protocols to log into non–Windows 2000 operating environments.*

applications to call back-end service providers, including Microsoft's legacy NTLM account store, to obtain an authenticated connection without knowledge of the details of the security protocol. Security providers use SSPI as an abstraction layer to pass authentication, message integrity, message privacy, and security quality-of-service profile information to applications, system services, and protocols. However, SSPI doesn't yet provide interfaces to service providers' encryption functionality.

CryptoAPI 2.0, another Win32 API, supports access from Windows desktop applications to X.509-based public key technologies running under Windows 2000 and NT servers. CryptoAPI supports creation, management, retrieval, and deletion of public key certificates and certificate revocation lists (CRLs). CryptoAPI works with PKCS #10 and #7 security technologies, as well as X.509 v3 and v2 certificate and CRL syntaxes. The APIs support handling of X.509 certificates issued by either a commercial CA, third-party CA, or the Windows 2000 or NT Certificate Server.

ACCESS CONTROL

Windows 2000 relies on the access control list mechanism implemented in Windows NT Server.

ACLs are fundamental to the OS' security, policy, and account administration features. ACLs are lists of Windows 2000 user accounts and groups, stored in AD, that determine whether a user or process has authorized access to an object. These lists allow administrators to define and enforce access controls on objects down to the property level, controlling read, write, and delete privileges. Administrators can also grant access rights to individual properties on user objects—for example, allowing a specific individual or group to have the right only to reset passwords, but not to modify other account information.

A new concept in Windows 2000—the "security group"—enables more efficient administration of user permissions through ACLs. Security groups have ACLs associated with them and can also function as mailing lists. Administrators grant permissions for a particular resource to a group of users and then add or remove users as members of that group. This is usually a more productive approach than to assign resource access privileges explicitly to individual users.

AD's hierarchical namespace supports administration of user accounts and security groups by logical organizational units, rather than by the location-dependent domains supported in Windows NT Server. AD supports delegation of account administration privileges to the organizational unit level.

CONTENT CONFIDENTIALITY

Windows 2000 relies on NT's encryption options, including support for the SSLv3 (and v2) and Microsoft's proprietary Private Communications Technology (PCT) 1.0 channel-security protocol.

This release also adds support for the IPsec VPN tunneling protocol to Windows 2000's Routing and Remote Access Server (RRAS) module, in addition to the PPTP and L2TP stacks that were supported in NT Server 4.0.

IPSec tunneling—defined in RFCs 1826 and 1827—supports network-level authentication, data integrity, and encryption features under the broader IPv6 protocol specification. Tunneling enables companies to build secure VPNs over the Internet by encrypting packets so that they can be transmitted confidentially over an insecure virtual circuit, such as an Internet TCP/IP connection. Tunneling also enables new protocols to be encapsulated and delivered unmodified to a remote intranet that has been set up to handle them properly, such as when IP version 6 packets are tunneled over legacy IP version 4 wide-area networks, facilitating eventual transition to the new protocol. Tunneled packets are decrypted at the receiving end and then routed in the clear on the recipient's intranet to their ultimate destinations.   PPTP—introduced in Windows NT Server 4.0—is an extension to the Point-to-Point Protocol that was developed by Microsoft and leading manufacturers of firewalls, routers, and remote access servers to support tunneling of IP, IPX, or NetBEUI protocols inside IP packets.

Another new content-confidentiality feature in Windows 2000 is Encrypting File System (EFS), which builds encryption services into DFS. This new feature supports encryption of specific files and/or directories in local and remote DFS volumes. It uses a combination of public key and symmetric private key technologies for encryption and decryption. A user can read an encrypted DFS file only if he or she has the private key to that file. If the user encrypts a file, EFS also encrypts its temporary copies. EFS resides in the Windows 2000 kernel and uses the nonpaged pool to store file encryption keys, ensuring that they never make it to the paging file. However, EFS is based on DESX 128-bit encryption key technology, which is currently limited to North America due to existing U.S. national security policy.

CONTENT INTEGRITY

Windows 2000 carries forward NT's content-integrity services, including the tamper-proofing assurances associated with SSLv3 secure channels and S/MIME digital signatures on e-mail.

In addition, Windows 2000 supports Microsoft's established Authenticode technology for signing ActiveX controls, Java applets, and other downloadable executables. Authenticode is a Microsoft-proprietary code-signing technology that uses public-key-based digital signatures to verify the integrity of software downloaded from the Internet and to strongly authenticate the software publisher. Authenticode uses X.509 v.3 cryptography certificates as well as PKCS #7 and #10 signature standards.

12.3.4 Windows 2000 Management Services

Management services keep distributed environments optimized and operating around the clock. These services support configuration, fault, performance, security, and account management on desktops, servers, backbones, databases, and other online resources.

Windows 2000 provides a very compelling set of new management features. What administrators will notice first are the new management presentation options—Microsoft Management Console and Windows Scripting Host (WSH)—supporting interactive and automated tasks, respectively.

MMC is Windows 2000's new management GUI, and it's the administrative front-end to AD. MMC (which actually became available with Windows NT Server 4.0 service pack 4) is the unified face of Windows 2000 management and administration services. It presents a Windows Explorer–type management GUI and connects to the Windows 2000 DCs being administered. MMC's administrator-friendly GUI reduces the "hassle factor" in Windows 2000 network, system, and application management by means of a consolidated administrative user interface and toolset. MMC is a significant improvement over Windows NT's fragmented management toolset, which required administrators to work with tools in separate windows (such as Server Manager, User Manager, Domains, and DHCP Administration) and switch among these windows constantly.

MMC also allows administrators to build their own customized administrative consoles that contain only the tools they need, arranged according to their personal preferences. MMC can be tailored to individual administrator roles, by, for example, allowing a Commerce Server 2000 system administrator to see a "User Manager" administrative view of user accounts while giving the system architect a complete view of Commerce Server 2000 properties. MMC does not draw a topology map of the network being administered but simply organizes tasks into a hierarchical tree outline. And MMC does not, in and of itself, provide any management functionality, but it provides a common environment for application-specific snap-ins, which provide the actual management behavior.

Upon installation, a Windows 2000-based server application automatically plugs the appropriate management snap-ins into MMC. For example, BizTalk Server 2000's MMC snap-in displays, in a left-hand "scope pane," a hierarchical, expandable tree view of BizTalk Server objects that an administrator can manage. MMC displays the Microsoft BizTalk Server 1.0 folder as a subfolder of the console's root. Each BizTalk Server group displays as a separate subfolder of the Microsoft BizTalk Server folder. This subfolder, in turn, contains further subfolders for each of the BizTalk Server components associated with the server group: queues, pipeline components, parsers, receive services, and transport services. Within the MMC GUI, clicking on the text next to any of the component icons displays additional details about the associated object in the console's right-hand "result pane." Administrators manage an object by right-clicking that object in the console display to access the desired task.

In contrast to the interactive MMC GUI environment, WSH is the automation front-end to Windows 2000 servers, supporting sophisticated script-driven access to the platform's rich management functionality. WSH allows VBScript, Jscript, JavaScript, and other scripts to be run natively within the OS, rather than simply from within an HTML document. Scripts can be written in any appropriate scripting tool and then executed from within the Windows GUI or a command-line interface. Scripts can act on all native Windows 2000 management tasks, which have been exposed as COM objects. Scripts can automate actions in response to real-time events fed into the OS from external entity management systems via the new Windows Management Instrumentation (WMI) interface. Scripts can even access and use all information maintained in AD.

These presentation environments provide an administrative "dashboard" and "steering wheel" into the Windows 2000 management model, which is fundamentally different in several respects from the management environment of Windows NT Server.

First, Windows 2000's administrative domains coincide with DNS domains, unlike under Windows NT Server, which allowed separate administrative and DNS namespaces. Windows 2000 administrative domains are identified by their DNS names. Clients use DNS to locate the DCs for any given domain. And the DNS name of a Windows 2000 domain indicates its position in AD's X.500 tree/forest hierarchy. All of which means that enterprises must coordinate the planning of their OS administrative domains and DNS namespaces.

Next, a Windows 2000 administrative domain can span more than one physical location. An administrative domain does not have to be limited to a single physical location. It may include several locations and span a wide-area network (though such an administrative model must be squared with an enterprise's DNS domains, which often coincide with localities). This means that Windows 2000 administrative domain planning and site planning may follow separate tracks, but they should both be addressed in an integrated fashion.

Furthermore, Windows 2000 administrative domains nest within hierarchical trees and forests in AD's X.500/LDAP namespace. Domain trees and forests allow administrators to manage multiple domains with contiguous or disjoint namespaces. All Windows 2000 DCs maintain master copies of the directory, and some maintain copies of the Global Catalog for the domain forest. Windows 2000 uses AD's hierarchical namespace to automatically accomplish cross-domain replication of user, group, resource, and access control information. Consequently, an administrative domain plan can have serious impacts on the availability of the directory to clients, on client query traffic patterns, and on replication traffic patterns between DCs.

Finally, Windows 2000 uses AD's hierarchical domain structure to automatically set up Kerberos-authenticated, two-way, implicit, transitive trust relationships up and down the domain tree. As noted previously, a trust relationship allows users to access resources in a different domain without having to have user accounts defined in that domain. Trust relationships ensure that when a client has been authenticated by a DC anywhere in the tree, its Kerberos credentials and session tickets will be honored elsewhere in the tree. However, every domain can still maintain its own explicit trust relationships with other domains within the tree. And each domain may—indeed, must—maintain explicit trust relationships with domains outside the tree (including Windows NT Server domains). In these cases, administrators set up explicit trust relationships as cross-references in AD.

Consequently, Windows 2000 administrative domain planning must, of necessity, be a multidisciplinary exercise in any large or mid-sized enterprise. It involves coordination among several IT support groups that may rarely interact, including DNS administrators, NOS domain administrators, directory administrators, physical network managers, and security managers.

Within the new management presentation and domain models that we've just discussed, Windows 2000 administrators have access to a wide range of tools, both new and familiar. Microsoft organizes Windows 2000's management features into six broad functional categories, described in Table 12-4.

Microsoft is positioning Windows 2000's Change and Configuration Management (CCM) tools, integrated with AD, as its solution for lowering the total cost of owning and managing a distributed NOS environment. CCM was formerly known as "Zero Administration Windows," a label that seriously overstated its potential benefits. However, the zero administration slogan very succinctly characterizes one of Microsoft's dominant goals for Windows 2000. The company recognizes that total cost of ownership is proportional to the number of hardware nodes in a network (servers, clients, printers, etc.) and the number of times that human technicians must visit each of them to install, configure, administer, upgrade, and troubleshoot software. Microsoft's reasoning is that if it can automate many of these chores on Windows networks from a central, policy-driven configuration management console, then

Table 12-4	Windows 2000 Management Functionality Categories
Category	**Description**
Change and configuration management	Administrators can set, monitor, and enforce policies governing Windows 2000 server and client software configurations, using the existing Systems Management Server 2.0 toolset and Group Policy capability in conjunction with the new IntelliMirror and Remote OS Installation features.
Security management	Administrators can set, monitor, and enforce policies governing Windows 2000's authentication, access control, content confidentiality, content integrity, and nonrepudiation services, as implemented through Kerberos, Microsoft Certificate Server, AD ACLs, and other OS security features.
Storage management	Administrators can set, monitor, and enforce policies governing Windows 2000's file and storage management services, including DFS, hierarchical and removable storage, backup and recovery, and disk quotas.
Network quality of service	Administrators can set, monitor, and enforce policies governing network quality of service (QoS) delivered by Windows 2000's RRAS.
Health monitoring	Administrators can monitor the real-time performance of Windows 2000 networks and servers from a central console under SMS 2.0.
Problem tracking	Administrators can integrate SMS 2.0's health-monitoring features with third-party problem-tracking tools, to assist in diagnosing and troubleshooting network and server problems.

it can help customers administer larger networks with less staff. The CCM ideal is totally unattended, flawless remote desktop installation, configuration, administration, and troubleshooting (an ideal that Microsoft is not guaranteeing in Windows 2000).

New CCM features built into Windows 2000 include IntelliMirror and Remote OS Installation. These features supplement CCM-related functionality carried over from Windows NT Server, including the Systems Management Server 2.0 administration tool.

IntelliMirror, integrated with AD, supports robust desktop availability, roaming, backup, recovery, and remote booting throughout enterprise networks. And it enables Windows 2000 client software to be self-distributing, self-configuring, and self-healing.

IntelliMirror lets users log in to the Windows 2000 NOS from any other Windows 2000 client within their domain forest and have that client automatically configure itself to be their personal client while they're using it. Users' personal client applications, data, and configuration settings follow them to the new computer. Windows 2000 servers automatically distribute users' applications to and install them on the new client, according to administrator-defined policies maintained in AD. Administrators define client configurations centrally, according to group policy profiles maintained in AD and based on users' business roles, group memberships, and locations.

IntelliMirror also lets users recover automatically from inadvertent or accidental deletion of or corruption to system files and settings on their "home" clients. IntelliMirror can recover, restore, or replace users' data, applications, and personal settings in a Windows 2000–based environment.

IntelliMirror consists of three core features: user data management, software installation and maintenance, and user and computer settings management. Administrators can use these features jointly or separately.

The user data management feature automatically replicates selected user data to a network volume (which is often backed up regularly) and caches selected network data locally (where it is available offline). User data can be restored from the network if it has been deleted locally. Users can define which personal data may roam with them, and which may not.

The software installation and maintenance feature supports automatic, just-in-time client software installation and repair. It can be used to upgrade applications and operating systems or remove software that is obsolete or no longer required. Windows 2000 administrators define policies that specify which software is to be deployed, upgraded, or removed from a client. Administrators can define software installation policies for groups of users or computers, in accordance with sites, domains, and organizational units. Every time a Windows 2000 client is switched on or a user logs in, Windows 2000 compares the client's configuration against a group policy configuration maintained in AD. If a software installation or update is required, the server automatically pushes the software package to the client via Windows 2000's

Windows Installer service (though software must be authored or repackaged to use the Installer service). Windows Installer automates the process of software installation and configuration. In addition, each time an application is launched, Windows Installer make sure that all the required application files and components are available.

The user and computer settings management service allows administrators to centrally define and enforce standard client environments for groups of users and/or computers. The appropriate desktop settings automatically follow users to any other Windows 2000 computer they log into within their home domain forest. Administrators can also restore a user's settings if his or her PC fails. Administrators can apply group policies to any of the following settings:

- User interface settings
- Folder-data redirection settings
- Software configuration settings for applications and operating system components
- Script settings for client startup or shutdown, or user logon or logoff
- Security settings for local computers, domains, or the entire network

One limitation of IntelliMirror is that it is available to Windows 2000 Professional clients only on networks that have deployed the Windows 2000 NOS. These features are not available to Windows NT, 9x, or 3.1 clients, or to Windows 2000 Professional clients on the Windows NT Server NOS.

Another new CCM feature in Windows 2000, separate from IntelliMirror, is Remote OS Installation. Administrators can remotely and automatically distribute Windows 2000 and service packs to new client computers and install and configure the OS on these machines. One limitation of this feature is that it works only with client machines that include a Pre-Boot eXecution Environment (PXE) DHCP-based remote-boot Read-Only Memory (ROM) Basic Input/Output System (BIOS) chip. The PXE ROM BIOS (or a special remote boot floppy) enables a client machine to boot remotely and initiate OS installation from a remote source to a client's local hard drive. The remote source must be a Windows 2000 server running the new Remote Installation Services (RIS) functionality. Remote OS Installation provides the network equivalent of a CD-based installation of Windows 2000 Professional and preconfigured Sysprep desktop images (which clone a standard desktop configuration).

A remote OS installation would take place as follows. When a properly configured client requests a network service boot, the Windows 2000 DHCP service provides an IP address for that client. The client can download the remote OS installation wizard, which prompts the user to log on. The wizard may also display a menu of unattended operating system installation options customized per administrator-defined policies. Once the user selects the parameters of the remote OS installation, the download, installation, and configuration take place automatically.

IntelliMirror and Remote OS Installation supplement the CCM features of Systems Management Server (SMS) 2.0, which Microsoft licenses separately from Windows 2000.

SMS 2.0 allows network administrators to automatically maintain an up-to-date inventory of all hardware and software components on all connected servers and desktops. The tool also automates software distribution, installation, and configuration; monitors and enforces usage restrictions per application software licenses; and supports remote diagnostics across distributed Windows servers and desktops. SMS's remote diagnostics tools include real-time network and server monitors. The server monitor can track in minute detail the performance of the OS and the Microsoft Server family application processes running on it. Enterprise help desks can use this real-time performance information to assist in diagnosing and troubleshooting problems with Windows client and servers.

Where SMS 2.0 and IntelliMirror overlap functionally is in their support for policy-based automated software inventory, distribution, and installation. However, unlike IntelliMirror, SMS 2.0 is not tied exclusively to Windows 2000 and AD. SMS works across mixed-mode Windows deployments. It supports all Windows 16-bit and 32-bit desktops, from Windows 3.1 to Windows 2000, whether operating in a Windows 2000, Windows NT, NetWare 3.1, or NetWare NDS environment. SMS operates as a stand-alone desktop management tool or as the desktop management component of an integrated enterprise management environment.

When deployed on top of the Windows 2000 NOS, SMS 2.0, like IntelliMirror, uses the OS's new resource-information software scanners and Windows Management Instrumentation (WMI) interface to feed detailed hardware and software inventory information into a SQL Server–based repository.

WMI is Microsoft's implementation of the Desktop Management Task Force (DMTF) Web-Based Enterprise Management (WBEM) framework. WMI uses WBEM's Common Information Model (CIM) to represent managed objects in Windows-based environments. In addition to supporting automated inventory compilation, WMI also provides an interface through which software and hardware components provide fault, performance, and security management information and notifications to Windows 2000's management applications (MMC, WSH, and browser-based). WMI provides administrative access to hardware and software event logs and other system data in a Windows 2000 deployment.

To sum up Windows 2000's management services infrastructure, we can view it in terms of the Windows DNA framework presented at the beginning of this chapter. As shown in Figure 12-7, Windows 2000's management framework includes functionality at the presentation, business logic, and data tiers. In the presentation tier are the MMC and WSH interfaces, the former supporting interactive management and the latter automated management of

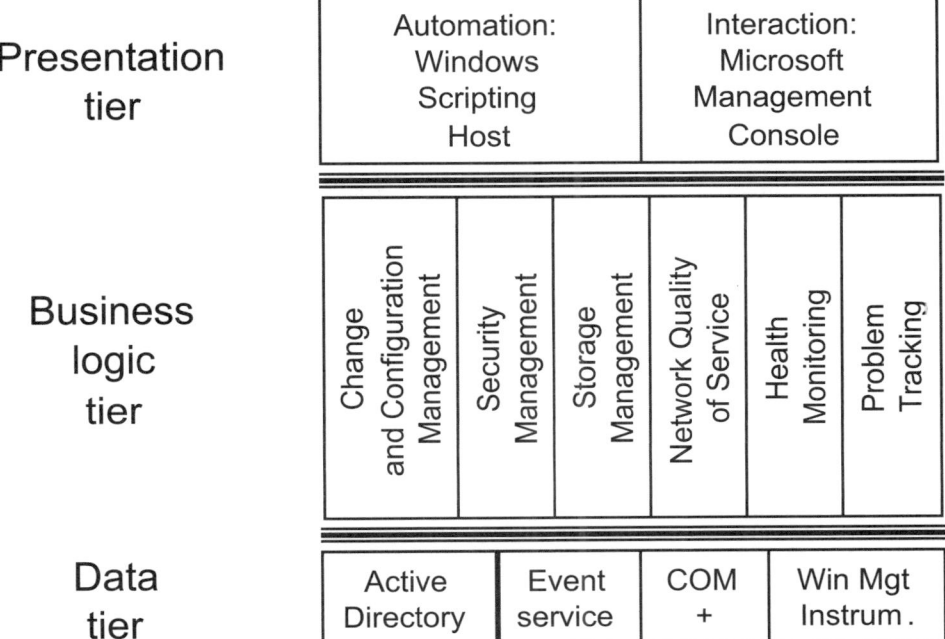

Presentation tier	Automation: Windows Scripting Host	Interaction: Microsoft Management Console

| Business logic tier | Change and Configuration Management | Security Management | Storage Management | Network Quality of Service | Health Monitoring | Problem Tracking |

| Data tier | Active Directory | Event service | COM + | Win Mgt Instrum. |

Figure 12-7 *Windows 2000's management infrastructure includes functionality in all three tiers of the Windows DNA framework: presentation, business logic, and data.*

Windows 2000 environments. In the business logic tier are the change and configuration management, security management, storage management, network quality of service, health monitoring, and problem tracking features of Windows 2000 and SMS 2.0. And the data tier includes such management features as AD (supplying user, group, server, resource, and policy information to Windows 2000 management tools), event service (supporting event data notification, delivery, and logging), COM+ (pulling real-time fault, performance, and management data from Windows-based applications), and WMI (integrating real-time fault, performance, and management data from external management systems).

12.4 Summary

BizTalk Server 2000 is a Windows 2000 application, so any BizTalk deployment must plumb the depths of this sophisticated, complex operating environment. Network administrators can scarcely hope to master BizTalk Server

2000 without a strong grounding in DFS, AD, PKI, MMC, and the other fundamental distributed services under the Windows DNA umbrella.

We now proceed to explore another fundamental BizTalk technology—XML—that we have mentioned at various points throughout the book. The next chapter presents a primer on XML and related standards and specifications. It then describes how Microsoft has implemented XML throughout its products generally, but with specific focus on XML's role in Windows 2000, BizTalk Server 2000, and the BizTalk Framework.

Microsoft E-Commerce Markup Technologies

*B*iz*Talk-enabled e-commerce applications rely heavily on the new lingua franca of network computing: the Extensible Markup Language (XML). As we discussed in Chapter 1, the BizTalk Framework specifies XML as the syntax for BizTalk Messages and their contents. And as we showed in Chapter 9, BizTalk Server 2000 processes these messages and other XML-formatted business contents (as well as flat files, ANSI X12 transaction sets, EDIFACT messages, and other document types).*

XML's applications are multifaceted, and Microsoft has implemented the standard throughout all three tiers—presentation, business logic, and data—of the Windows DNA application model. Indeed, Microsoft has made a critical piece of XML software technology—an XML "parser"—a component of all its enterprise server and client products. In so doing, Microsoft is simply keeping pace with the information technology (IT) world's near-universal embrace of XML. Nearly every IT industry group is mapping its interoperability hopes and dreams to this new markup standard.

It's important to remember that XML is not nirvana. And XML is not a protocol, programming interface, or framework for plug-and-play cross-platform interoperability, though many people have come to treat these three letters as a conceptual proxy for all the above. Rather, XML is simply a very versatile, developer-friendly markup language.

This chapter explains the core XML 1.0 standards plus supplementary core standards and other XML-based application, commerce, and middleware specifications. We then discuss how Microsoft has implemented XML throughout its products generally, but with specific focus on XML's role in Windows 2000, BizTalk Server 2000, and the BizTalk Framework. XML and related markup specifications are our sole focus in this chapter. We don't doubt for a moment the critical importance of the other major markup language—HyperText Markup Language (HTML)—but have chosen to discuss Microsoft's HTML implementations in Chapter 12 (under Windows DNA's presentation tier) and Chapter 14 (under Windows 2000's development technologies).

13.1 What's XML?

XML[1] is both a dry technical specification and a critical stepping stone in the Web's development as a universal service platform.

A few words of historical background will suffice. XML is a markup language that describes logical relations among data elements within a document. It is a subset of the older but now largely obsolete Standard Generalized Markup Language (SGML). XML is simpler and more network-oriented than SGML. And it is more flexible and focused on data structuring than its sister specification, the presentation-oriented HTML. Still, the sister specifications are complementary, not overlapping, since XML defines logical data structures and HTML defines how pages containing those data structures display at the client level.

XML version 1.0 is a published, controlled, open standard to which vendors may build. All XML documents are, by construction, conforming SGML documents. Like all conforming SGML profiles, XML supports flexible definition of new document structures and extension of existing structures. However, XML defines the logical interrelationships among data fields within the document, while SGML's traditional orientation has been toward defining relationships among document elements such as titles, headers, paragraphs, and footnotes.

XML is not so much a single standard as a growing suite of interoperability specifications that orbit around a core standard: XML 1.0. The World Wide Web Consortium ratified XML 1.0 in February 1998, labeling it an official "recommendation" (a term that the consortium applies to its published standards). Other XML-related W3C recommendations include Document Object Model (DOM), XML Schemas, XML Namespaces, Extensible Stylesheet Language (XSL), XSL Transformations (XSLT), XML Path Language (XPath), XML Linking Language (XLL), and XML Pointers. Hinging on these core standards, in turn, are a staggering range of application- and industry-specific interoperability specifications.

---

[1]The XML technical discussion in this chapter draws from my discussion in *Extensible Markup Language (XML): Foundation for Interoperable Electronic Commerce,* (Midvale, UT: Burton Group, June 28, 1999).

And XML is not a single, stand-alone language. Rather, we might describe it as a meta-language for crafting higher-level markup "vocabularies" or "schemas" for various applications. XML's purpose is to spawn a new generation of application-specific markup vocabularies, all of which share a common set of conventions for "tagging" content so that it can be processed by any standards-compliant XML parser. The BizTalk Framework specifies one such application-specific XML vocabulary, and the business documents wrapped within a BizTalk Message implement XML vocabularies specific to countless applications, industries, and companies. One important focus of XML-based standardization is in e-commerce-related schemas, an area where Microsoft has asserted itself forcefully with its BizTalk Framework.

But, first and foremost, XML is a flexible syntax for describing and structuring data separate from application and presentation logic. XML enables developers to define "self-describing content," which is data that specifies its own application context or processing requirements. In this regard, we may contrast XML with ASCII files, which contain raw information but no guidelines or instructions for validating, interpreting, rendering, and manipulating that information. Nevertheless, XML and ASCII share a common core purpose: providing an industry-wide data-sharing format that is independent of object models, network protocols, operating systems, databases, and programming languages. However, XML is Unicode-based, and provides a richer framework to work from than ASCII.

Ideally, a self-describing XML document would include all the content and context that two dissimilar applications—the sender and receiver—need for full interoperability. Applications would be able to exchange documents whose intended processing by the recipient is self-explanatory. As such, XML could potentially support full-fidelity computer-to-computer communications across diverse environments. As noted in Chapter 2, BizTalk and other XML-based e-commerce interoperability frameworks define business document contents and the workflows that provide the business policy context for those contents. None of these frameworks, however, can specify the entire processing context for any given business document, which is why these frameworks still presuppose an ongoing need for implementation-specific bilateral technical coordination between trading partners.

From a distributed computing standpoint, the broadest context is the object model—the service offerings—that a networked operating environment provides to applications. Potentially, XML could provide a standard syntax for describing all services and resources available within an intranet or extranet. Developers might register new applications by storing these XML-based service profiles in enterprise directories. Application servers, for their part, would access these service profiles for use in assembling and personalizing new applications on the fly from preexisting "service modules."

An XML document's application context resides both within the document itself and in one or more external documents and data sources (such as directories) to which it points. Inside the document are markup constructs, such as tags, declarations, and attributes, that frame the content elements and provide metadata that describes, in human-readable plaintext, what that content means and how it hangs together logically. At a minimum, each data element in an XML document declares its name, content, and rung within the document's logical hierarchy. Consequently, XML content is self-documenting and readily comprehensible to the average (markup-loving) human. In addition, XML documents often declare other metadata useful to receiving applications, including such properties as the document's encoding scheme, datatypes, display characteristics, programming interfaces, routing paths, and processing constraints.

Outside the content-bearing XML document are related entities—such as XML schemas, namespaces, stylesheets, transformation maps, and workflow definitions—that collectively instruct XML-enabled applications how to interpret, render, and process its content. The XML document may also contain hyperlinks to related data accessible across the Web, in which case receiving applications might follow these links to retrieve this information and assemble it all within composite objects.

Perhaps the most important of these external entities are schemas, or their close cousins: XML 1.0 Document Type Definitions (DTDs). The schema is essentially a logical template that defines the permissible vocabulary of elements and fields in a particular type of XML document. A "validating XML parser" uses the schema or DTD to determine whether an incoming document correctly implements the logical structure for a document of its type. Validating parsers might retrieve schemas or DTDs from public reference libraries and repositories of document schema and tags, such as the ones at www.biztalk.org or www.xml.org. Figure 13-1 shows the typical sequence of events for receiving, parsing, and processing an XML document.

One of the great features of XML is that a document can supply general processing instructions to receiving applications without dictating precisely how those applications perform that processing. Communicating applications need not share an object model, network protocol, operating system, database, or programming language. Instead they rely on their mutual ability to exchange and interpret messages formatted in XML. The recipient of an XML document is free to process that document as it wishes, without being tightly bound to the sending application's calling conventions.

Consequently, XML is a key enabler for "loosely coupled distributed computing" on the Internet. As an architectural ideal, this phrase has a multilayered meaning.

On one level, it harks back to the notion that communicating applications may reside on different hardware platforms, operating systems, and the like. They may need to communicate in much the same way that human beings who speak different languages often need each other to fathom some

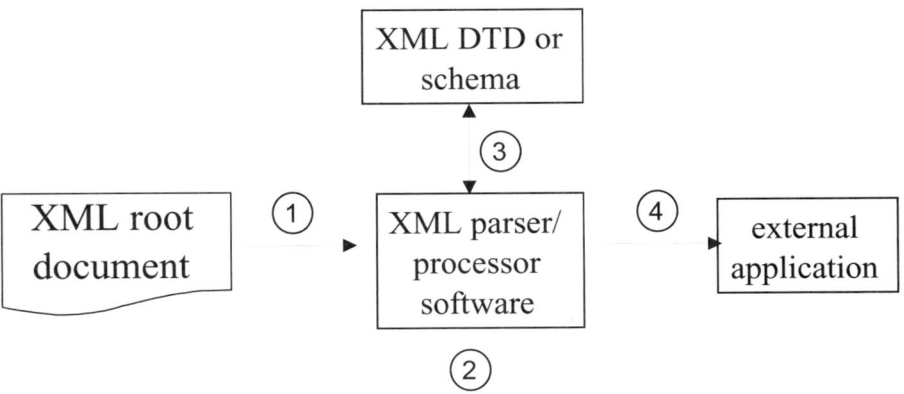

1. XML document received by XML processor software.

2. XML processor parses document and determines whether it contains well-formed XML.

3. XML processor validates document structure and contents against DTD or schema.

4. XML processor exposes document structure and contents to external application through Document Object Model (DOM) APIs.

Figure 13-1   *An XML processor/parser receives an inbound document, parses it, checks to see if it contains well-formed XML, validates it against a DTD or schema, and exposes its structure and content to external applications via Document Object Model (DOM) APIs.*

important point. In this scenario, XML is the common language to and from which everyone translates their native tongue.

On another level, loose coupling means that applications need not agree on the precise field-by-field layout of documents they exchange, so long as they generate and receive documents in valid XML vocabularies. Applications can respond on the fly to new XML-encoded data structures, ignoring fields that they do not recognize or understand. Or they may rely on an intermediate node to map an XML document from a schema that the sender understands to an equivalent schema comprehensible to the recipient.

On yet another level, the concept of loosely coupled computing recognizes that communicating applications may not always be connected to the network at the same time. After all, servers crash, desktop PCs get switched off at quitting time, and Internet-capable cell phones occasionally pass through patches of "dead air." In other words, most real-world computing nodes may not always be able to engage each other in "synchronous" conversations, so they must resort to store-and-forward or "asynchronous" communications mediated by proxies, inboxes, or queues. XML-formatted messages may be the objects that nodes exchange asynchronously, including just enough application context in the messages to eliminate the need for real-time coordination between sender and receiver.

Finally, loosely coupled computing may also refer to environments in which a client node may not be aware of a server node until such time as the former requests access to functions and data that just happen to be under the control of the latter. These environments usually depend on all nodes having access to a central directory, registry, or naming service for servers to publish their availability and clients to conduct searches. XML supports more efficient directory services, since distributed objects can use the syntax to expose their data structures and functionality down to a fine grain, enabling more powerful indexing, profiling, cataloguing, and searching.

As illustrated in Chapter 9, Microsoft enables loosely coupled computing through BizTalk Server 2000. BizTalk Server 2000's implementation of diverse protocol and middleware connectors allows Microsoft and non-Microsoft systems to exchange data and engage in distributed transactions. The server's document transformation engine enables interchange of documents in XML and non-XML formats, as well as efficient mapping between different XML vocabularies. Its support for synchronous protocols, such as DCOM, and asynchronous protocols—such as MSMQ—enables BizTalk Server 2000 to support applications with various connectivity scenarios. And its integration with the DCOM "class store" registry under Windows 2000's Active Directory (AD) allows BizTalk Server 2000 to broker connections between client and server components over local- and wide-area networks. When the day comes that Microsoft supports maintenance of Simple Object Access Protocol (SOAP)-accessible object descriptions in AD, this directory-resident application metadata will almost certainly be in XML format.

XML now has a life of its own in the development of the online economy. XML and related specifications are well on the road to eventual ubiquity in networked applications, across all architectural tiers and vendor platforms. Already, XML has achieved near-universal industry implementation in platform operating systems, application servers, database servers, commerce servers, groupware servers, and other networked applications. And vendors are constantly regaling the analyst community with tales of ever tighter XML integration into their product architectures.

XML is rapidly living up to its promise. In just a few years, it has become a universal standard for distributed computing. It is rapidly occupying most application niches in the n-tier architecture of intranets, extranets, and the Internet. And it fits into each of the three tiers of the Windows DNA environment, as illustrated in Figure 13-2.

In the presentation tier, XML enables delivery of structured data to browser, desktop applications, and mobile communications terminals. An

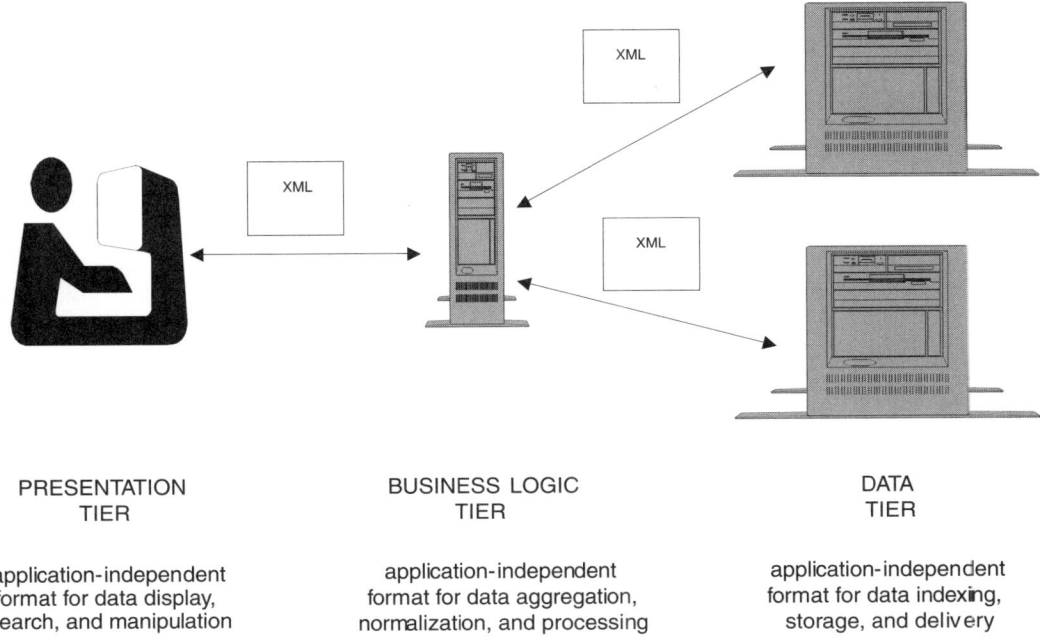

PRESENTATION TIER	BUSINESS LOGIC TIER	DATA TIER
application-independent format for data display, search, and manipulation	application-independent format for data aggregation, normalization, and processing	application-independent format for data indexing, storage, and delivery

Figure 13-2 *XML addresses core requirements in Windows DNA's presentation, business logic, and data tiers.*

XML-enabled client—in other words, one that incorporates XML parser/processor software—can do more effective searching, querying, and manipulation on tagged data elements without help from the server. Applying a stylesheet to the XML document, the client can display the information in HTML or other formats.

Both leading browsers—Microsoft Internet Explorer and Netscape Navigator—parse XML documents and support XML's DOM. Microsoft also supports XML as a native data storage format in its new Office 2000 desktop application suite. Many other client application vendors have pledged to support XML as either the primary or an alternate data-storage format, with either cascading stylesheet (CSS) or XSL as the principal presentation format.

In spite of all this, we're not likely to see much XML delivered straight to the universal client of the Internet age: the browser. There is a large installed base of desktop and server applications—including many Web browsers—that cannot yet read or write XML formats. For the foreseeable future, browsers will render HTML content fetched from Web and application servers. However, these servers will increasingly store that content in one format—XML—and use XSL stylesheets to render it on the fly into HTML. The average user will scarcely realize that, behind the scenes, XML processors have been working to deliver them with a data-rich, interactive browser-based view of the Internet.

In the business logic tier, XML provides a universal format for data interchange, aggregation, search, and manipulation. XML also represents a universal format for encoding, interchange, and reuse of business logic at the application server level.

The business logic tier is where XML will play its primary role in distributed environments. XML-enabled application servers can evaluate and handle incoming XML data objects by examining their self-describing tags. Servers can easily examine an object's internal structure. The XML DOM, facilitates granular access to data structures from server-side scripts, COM objects, and other business logic modules. Typically, an XML-enabled application server translates data from legacy databases into XML format and integrates diverse data objects into a logically unified view. It also transforms XML to HTML for delivery to non-XML-enabled clients through Web servers.

Each specialized application server can make good use of XML. Interchange servers such as BizTalk Server 2000 can read XML message tags and routing blocks, convert the messages to schema understood by recipients, and then route the messages. Commerce servers might view and compare vendors' online catalogs down to the field level if all catalog stores incorporate XML schema. Network security applications can view the structure and contents of incoming XML-formatted messages to apply access controls and content-filtering rules. Search engines and data repositories can parse, index, and catalog XML-formatted information objects.

In the data tier, XML provides an application-neutral data storage and interchange format for any highly structured information. Most major database vendors have either implemented XML natively in their products or have announced plans to add XML support in their next release. Initially, database vendors have supported XML as an alternative interchange format for data import and export. In the near future, many may also support XML as a native data storage format.

We will return later in this chapter to a fuller discussion of XML's role in Microsoft's server and client product architectures. Before we launch into a detailed discussion of XML 1.0 and each of the key supplementary core standards, we should stress that XML is in no way a Microsoft-proprietary specification, and that Microsoft has not implemented any proprietary twists in the core XML standards. Indeed, Microsoft doesn't control the direction of XML and XML-based standards (a notion that conspiracy theorists may find hard to believe).

XML is bigger than Microsoft. Therein lies the power of the standard.

13.1.1 Core Standard: XML 1.0

XML 1.0 should be required reading for all IT professionals, and not because of its winning prose style.

XML 1.0's importance lies in its familiarity, simplicity, and flexibility. XML notation should be familiar to anyone who has ever authored an HTML document, because it uses common markup conventions. It is simple enough so that someone can comprehend an XML document's high-level structure and contents with a quick glance. And it has the flexibility to be applied to a never-ending range of application domains. Before long, most IT professionals will need at least a basic understanding of XML 1.0 concepts, since the standard is finding its way into every niche of distributed computing.

Another XML 1.0 strength is stability. It has been a formal W3C Recommendation—a published standard—since February 1998, which is eons in Internet time. As a result, vendors don't worry that the core standard will change and render their applications incompatible with what others are building.

XML 1.0 also benefits from the fact that the industry had considerable input into its creation. Microsoft had a hand in writing XML 1.0, as did Sun, Netscape, Hewlett-Packard, Adobe, Vignette, and other vendors of platform, Web, document publishing, and sundry software solutions.

The W3C has pursued the right approach by defining new XML-related functionality, over and above version 1.0, through supplementary specifications rather than revisions to the core standard. Consequently, we find new XML-based standardization activities taking place on many fronts, both within the W3C, but increasingly within industry groups and vendor consortia, such as Microsoft and its BizTalk Steering Committee.

XML RIDES ON HTML'S CONSIDERABLE COATTAILS

As we noted, one of XML 1.0's core virtues is familiarity.

XML 1.0 has benefited greatly from HTML's ubiquity. By the time XML entered the scene in 1998, millions of people had already learned HTML, so such fundamental concepts as markup languages, tags, and stylesheets had already taken root in the popular mind. These and other fundamental XML concepts, terms, and notational conventions derive from SGML, of which XML is a subset (and HTML an even narrower slice). However, XML introduces many concepts that are unfamiliar to the average HTML content author, such as "trees," "nodes," "declarations," "entities," "elements," "attributes," "document type definitions," "schemas," and "namespaces." So developers must surmount a whole new learning curve when getting up to speed on XML.

The most fundamental XML concept is that of "markup," which is so important that we've made it the organizing topic of this chapter. XML (like HTML and SGML) is a markup language. Consequently, XML, by definition, provides text-based notational conventions—a.k.a. markup—for embedding within documents.

XML IS CONTENT THAT DESCRIBES ITS OWN APPLICATION CONTEXT

Markup is what developers use to define content that specifies its own application context.

In other words, markup describes the content elements within a document as well as those elements' logical hierarchy, constraints, and processing requirements. Marked-up content may consist of character data, text in various codings and formats, or references to binary information stored outside the XML document. Markup also specifies how the document is to be read and manipulated by specialized programs known as "XML processors," which pass content to external applications. XML processors operate on behalf of external applications, which access an XML document's logical "elements" or "nodes" through a set of APIs known as the XML DOM.

XML 1.0 and supplementary specifications provide a language for defining various levels of application context surrounding a piece of content. Table 13-1 discusses some of the many levels of application context expressible through XML.

We can understand a particular XML "vocabulary" only within the context of the applications that generate, consume, and process documents implementing that vocabulary. Since networked applications generally consist of particular objects (such as documents or database views) and the workflows under which these objects get processed and routed, we can group XML vocabularies into those that focus primarily on "object contexts" versus those that emphasize "workflow contexts." XML vocabulary, or "schema," standards generally fall into these two categories.

Some XML-based standards describe particular object types specific to particular applications. XML-based specifications exist for electronic forms (Extensible Forms Description Language), digital signatures (XML-Signature), interactive voice inputs (Voice Extensible Markup Language), wireless data displays (Wireless Markup Language), streaming media (Synchronized Multimedia Integration Language), vector graphics (Vector Markup Language), and mathematical formulas (Mathematical Markup Language). Many industry groups have used XML to define standard formats for particular electronic media or objects. Much of this standardization activity is taking place outside the W3C.

Other XML-based standards describe structured workflows for processing and routing of commerce-relevant documents. The BizTalk Framework is one good example of such a framework, as are cXML and RosettaNet. These XML-based B2B interoperability frameworks, managed outside the W3C, define commerce-relevant workflows to varying degrees of completeness and detail. The BizTalk Framework, for example, specifies message and document formats. The BizTalk initiative also includes an online repository for industry groups to post their vertical market XML schemas, which are designed for various industries' e-commerce or EDI transactions.

Table 13-1	*Levels of Application Context Expressible Through XML*
Application Context	**Discussion**
Encoding	Content must be encoded either as UTF-8 or UTF-16 character sets.
Typing	Content can be assigned data types for efficient programmatic processing, as defined under various XML schema definition specifications.
Language	Documents can include an identifier or code for the natural language in which document content is written, enabling content-processing applications to automatically apply appropriate stylesheets and other options.
Presentation	Documents can be transformed, rendered, and displayed through application of XSL stylesheets.
Hierarchy	Content items are wrapped in element and attribute tags, thereby defining their names, scopes, and positions within a document's logical content hierarchy.
Schema	Documents specify schemas or DTDs that define their validation against a prescribed logical structure and range of legal attribute values associated with their document type.
Namespace	Documents specify URLs, known as "namespaces," that uniquely identify the source of their document type's schema.
Hyperlinks	Documents can contain embedded hyperlinks using the XLL, pointing to other pages and resources, both local and remote.
Inheritance	Content items can use various schema definition languages to declare their inheritance of properties and behaviors from other documents and objects.
Processing	Documents can include implementation-specific instructions for automated processing by recipient applications and systems.
Commentary	Documents contain embedded commentary, in human-readable format, on the meaning, purpose, and use of content items.

Workflow contextual information rides primarily in the headers of BizTalk and other XML-based B2B message/document formats. BizTalk-enabled applications insert routing and state variables into BizTalk message/document headers. These variables trigger workflow execution rules on nodes within a BizTalk-enabled commerce environment. Ideally, an XML-based B2B message/document should define its full workflow context through routing and state variables in its header. However, BizTalk and other B2B frameworks fall short of supporting complete specification of commerce workflows within their respective headers.

Yet another application context for XML is in support of middleware protocols, such as Microsoft's SOAP. We will defer a detailed discussion of SOAP until Chapter 15. Arguably, one might regard SOAP as a cross between an object context and a workflow context for XML. The protocol uses the markup language to define specific object types (procedure invocation and response contents) transmitted within the context of specific workflow types (remote function calls).

XML IS EXTENSIBLE INTERNALLY AND EXTERNALLY

An XML document can define these many layers of application context because the document is extensible, both internally and externally. Internally, an XML document may implement a logical data structure of arbitrary complexity, as defined through "declarations" in its header and content elements in its body. Externally, it may implement a physical data structure of arbitrary complexity through one or more cross-referenced files, known as "entities." Figure 13-3 shows the high-level logical structure of an XML document.

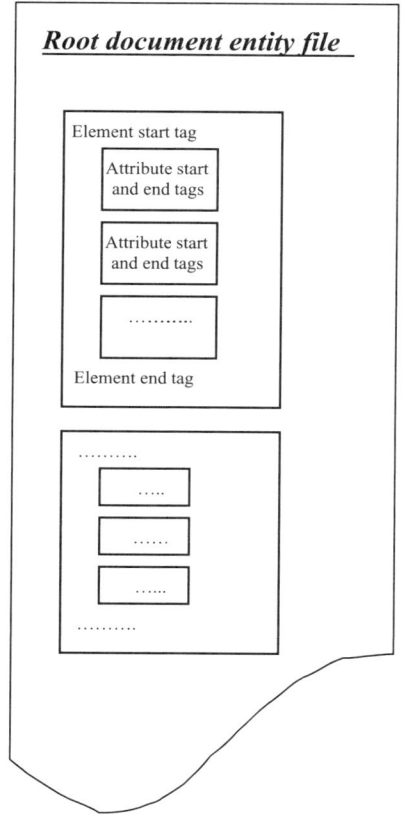

| Figure 13-3 | An XML document's high-level logical structure nests elements, attributes, and their values under a root document entity. |

Declarations define the logical, internal structure and properties of an XML document. Declarations specify the version of XML a document supports. They also specify the tags, character sets, data types, language, schemas, namespaces, stylesheets, attributes, default values, hyperlinks, and pointers that it contains or references. Tags instantiate the declared structure by framing content elements within an XML document. Together, declarations and tags define an XML document's metadata. Table 13-2 defines declarations, tags, and the other categories of markup defined under XML 1.0.

Tags (and the content they frame) populate most of the real estate within the average XML document. Start-tags and end-tags frame individual XML content elements and specify those elements' respective names and positions within a document's internal logical structure. Tags attach descriptive names to content items. Tag names should describe the semantics, or real-world meaning, of those items. We primarily distinguish one vertical market XML vocabulary (or "dialect") from another by the sets of tags each of them uses. All things considered, tag names should be terse but not obscure, to the point but nuanced, and easy for the average person to comprehend. An XML document cannot be self-describing if its tags read like some code language crafted by evil robots.

Tagged XML elements nest within a document in a hierarchical, logical structure known as an element tree. The element tree includes root, parent, child, and leaf elements, all of which are known as "nodes." A receiving application's XML processor can parse any well-formed XML document—in

Table 13-2	XML Markup Categories
Category	**Definition**
Declarations	Define the logical structure and properties of an XML document, including the version of XML that it supports; what character sets and human languages comprise its content; and what entities, elements, attributes, default values, data types, links, and pointers it contains or references.
Tags	Delimit the beginning and end of each content element and attribute within an XML document, as defined through prior element and attribute declarations.
References	Invoke, within the document, parameters that were previously defined through declarations.
Processing instructions	Contain specific procedures and rules to be invoked by applications that process XML content, bypassing the normal operation of an XML processor and delivering instructions directly to a downstream process whose responsibility it is to interpret the instruction and act accordingly.
Comments	Contain explanations of an XML document and its contents for use by human readers.

other words, any document that correctly implements the markup conventions defined in the XML 1.0 standard. An application that publishes an XML document can add new elements or attributes to that document dynamically, or rearrange the serial order of elements in the document. The receiving XML processor can ignore these changes safely, since it parses only to find specific elements. Alternately, receiving applications can detect new elements automatically and add them to their database schema. By contrast, traditional computer-to-computer data interchanges usually require a predetermined, rigid message format.

XML allows receiving applications to parse and process only the portion of an application's context that they find meaningful, such as specific elements, attributes, presentation instructions, document types, and encoding schemes. XML-compatible applications may ignore tags and declarations that they cannot process. Applications access XML document elements through the DOM. Typically, the DOM exposes its APIs through an interface definition language (IDL) with bindings to programming languages, such as C, C++, Visual Basic, and Java.

As we've seen, markup defines the logical internal structure of an XML document. Entities, on the other hand, define its physical, external structure. An XML document may be a single, stand-alone "root" entity (also known as the "document entity"), or the composite of the root entity plus one or more "external" entities declared within the root. Examples of external entities include Document Type Definitions, schemas, stylesheets, other XML-syntax documents, or external data sources. The XML processor reads and manipulates the XML root document and associated DTDs, schemas, stylesheets, and other entities through DOM APIs. Figure 13-4 shows the high-level physical structure of an XML document.

XML processors always start processing a document at its root entity. The document entity may contain the entire contents of the document. References to external entities may use local system pathnames or Uniform Resource Identifiers (URIs), depending on the network location of the entities in relation to the root.

XML IS SELF-VALIDATING VIA DTDS AND SCHEMAS

XML documents may conform with two kinds of constraints: well-formedness and validity. An XML document is well formed if it conforms to typographical, syntactic, and element-nesting constraints specified in XML 1.0. An XML document is valid if it conforms to "vocabulary" and data-typing constraints defined in its DTD (per XML 1.0) or schema (per XML Schemas, XML Data Reduced [XDR], and other schema-definition specifications).

To validate an incoming XML document as conforming to a specific DTD or schema associated with that document type, an application invokes a "validating XML processor." The validating processor compares the received

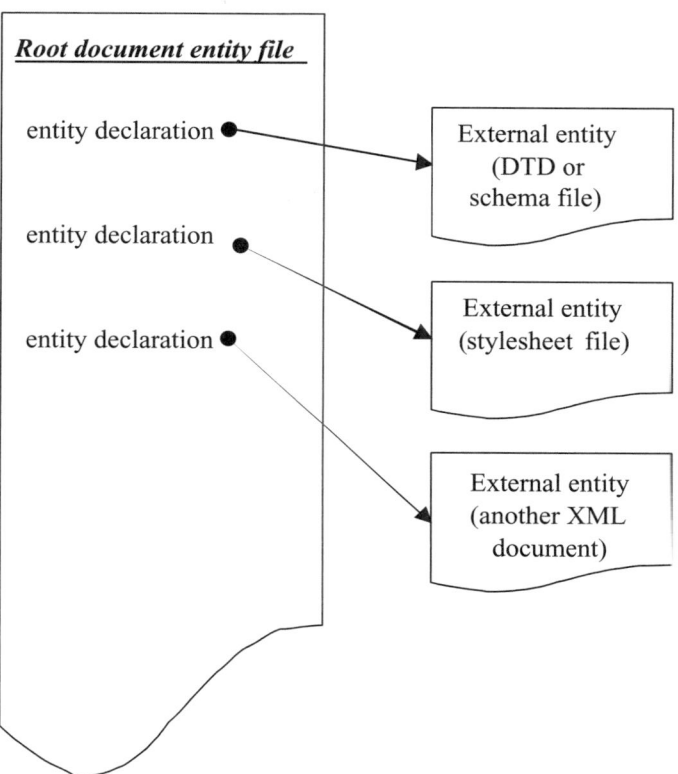

Root document entity file

entity declaration •————————➤ External entity (DTD or schema file)

entity declaration •

entity declaration •————————➤ External entity (stylesheet file)

External entity (another XML document)

Figure 13-4 *An XML document's high-level physical structure involves a root document entity referencing external entities, such as DTDs, schemas, and stylesheets.*

document to the structure prescribed in its DTD or schema, which are usually external entities referenced within the root document (though XML 1.0 allows DTDs and schemas to be contained entirely within the root document entity). An XML document is valid if it complies with the constraints expressed in its DTDs or schemas.

A DTD (as defined in the XML 1.0 standard) consists of a series of declarations that define the document's tags. The DTD defines the permissible structure and content of an XML document-type, by means of declarations for elements, attributes, and default attribute-values. Developers may use XML to define DTDs specific to various applications or to extend and modify preexisting DTDs. (HTML, by contrast with XML, specifies a single standard DTD, which can be extended only under the auspices of a W3C working group, not by document authors or application developers).

In lieu of DTDs, an XML document might declare a document schema, as defined under any of several specifications (separate from the core XML 1.0 standard, which only specifies DTDs). Alternate XML schema-definition specifications include XML Schemas, XDR, Document Content Description (DCD), and Schema for Object-Oriented XML (SOX). These supplementary specifications define document schema through XML tags, rather than the non-XML-syntax declarations of which DTDs consist. Schema definition languages also provide a vocabulary for defining richer, more elaborate object classes, data types, properties, interrelationships, and constraints applying to XML documents.

Microsoft has specified XDR as the schema definition language for the BizTalk Framework. However, industry momentum has shifted toward XML Schemas, which the W3C will almost certainly ratify as a published recommendation by the end of 2000. Microsoft has committed to supporting XML Schemas in the BizTalk Framework in addition to the older XDR. It's important to note that XDR is not a proprietary Microsoft specification and that Microsoft has never committed to it as a long-term solution. Rather, Microsoft has always regarded XDR, which it developed in 1998, as a necessary stop-gap until the W3C finished work on a robust XML schema definition standard. Indeed, Microsoft submitted the XDR specification to the W3C in 1998 as a reference point for discussion purposes.

Originating and receiving applications may reference local DTDs or schemas that have the same name but declare different elements, attributes, and default values. This condition is known as "namespace collision" and might cause receiving applications to misinterpret the logical structure and semantic meaning of elements within an XML document. For example, sending and receiving applications may inadvertently reference different versions of the same DTD or schema.

To avoid such misunderstandings, the sender may declare, within the XML document itself, one or more public "namespaces," denominated as Uniform Resource Names (URNs, which are essentially globally unique identifiers for entities on the Web). Public namespaces uniquely define the sources and versions of particular DTDs or schemas referenced within XML documents. Within any given XML document, the originator may combine elements declared through local DTDs/schemas with DTDs/schemas declared via public namespaces.

Public namespaces are how XML schema developers make sure the world validates documents according to the master copy of their schema definitions. The BizTalk Framework Document Specification 1.0, for example, states that all BizTalk Documents must begin and end with the XML tag "biztalk_1" and include a declaration of the BizTalk namespace.

Stylesheets are another type of external entity (apart from DTDs/schemas) that XML documents may declare. Stylesheets, usually conforming to the XSL specification, define how applications process XML documents for presentation and display. The receiving XML processor performs a "source-to-result tree transformation," which embeds formatting tags in the original XML document, in accordance with the applicable stylesheet. An XSL transformation enables the receiving processor to transform an XML document into an HTML document for display on a browser or other application. Applications may also perform source-to-result tree transformations to convert one XML document type to another.

Having presented the fundamental concepts that link XML 1.0 to supplementary core standards and specifications, we now present the highlights of these other specifications.

13.1.2 XML Supplementary Core Standards and Specifications

As we've noted, XML 1.0 is a stable, widely adopted standard, ratified by the W3C in February 1998. XML 1.0, however, does not stand alone. It relies on several supplementary core standards and specifications to define the broader application contexts discussed above.

The most important supplementary core specifications, cited in many object- and workflow-specific XML vocabularies, are presented in Table 13-3. We have already discussed some of these specifications within the context of our primer on XML 1.0. Shortly, we will examine each of them individually. Please note that this is not an exhaustive list of XML-related core specifications that have been accepted, considered, and/or ratified by the W3C. It is simply a list of those most frequently cited and supported in object- and workflow-specific XML vocabularies/schemas, including those supported by Windows 2000 and the Windows DNA 2000 products.

We now discuss the scope and status of each of these supplementary XML core specifications.

DOCUMENT OBJECT MODEL

The DOM provides a platform- and language-neutral software interface that external applications use to dynamically parse, read, create, update, and manipulate XML and HTML document elements and entities. It allows external programs and scripts to be portable across XML processors and Web browsers.

Applications can get and set attributes on in-memory XML document structures through standard DOM APIs exposed by XML processors. DOM APIs support programmatic access to XML documents so that applications can modify those documents' contents, structures, behaviors, and styles. Vendors may support interfaces to the DOM from their proprietary data struc-

Table 13-3	*XML Supplementary Core Standards and Specifications*	
Specification	**Definition**	**Specification URL**
DOM	Provides a platform- and language-neutral software interface that external applications use to dynamically read, create, update, and manipulate XML and HTML document elements and entities. It includes a DOM Level 1 (a W3C Recommendation) and a DOM Level 2 (a W3C Candidate Recommendation). The W3C has also begun to define requirements for a proposed DOM Level 3.	http://www.w3.org/TR/REC-DOM-Level-1/ http://www.w3.org/TR/DOM-Level-2/
XML Schema	Defines an object-oriented language for describing the structure and constraining the contents of XML documents. It consists of a Part 1 (Structures) and Part 2 (Datatypes), both of which were W3C Working Drafts at the time this book was published.	http://www.w3.org/TR/xmlschema-1/ http://www.w3.org/TR/xmlschema-2/
XML Namespaces	A W3C Recommendation, defines a facility for resolving XML tag and attribute name conflicts in the schemas utilized by document originators and recipients.	http://www.w3.org/TR/1999/REC-xml-names-19990114/
XSL	A W3C Recommendation, defines a vocabulary for specifying formatting semantics applicable to the elements within XML documents.	http://www.w3.org/TR/xsl/
XSLT	A W3C Recommendation, defines mechanisms for embedding formatting tags in XML documents and for transforming an XML document into another XML document.	http://www.w3.org/TR/xslt

tures and APIs. Content authors, in turn, may write to standard DOM interfaces rather than vendor-specific APIs.

The DOM consists of Level 1 and Level 2 specifications.

DOM Level 1 is a W3C Recommendation, ratified in October 1998. Level 1 provides a standard set of objects for representing both XML and HTML documents as element "trees" in the device memory accessible to an XML processor. DOM Level 1 also provides a standard model for defining how these objects can be combined and a standard interface for accessing and manipulating them. The standard uses the Object Management Group's Interface Definition Language (IDL) to provide a language-independent interface. It defines language-bindings to Java and ECMAScript (also known as JavaScript). However, third parties can define DOM IDL bindings to other programming and scripting languages, including C, C++, Visual Basic, and Perl, or via language-independent programming environments such as Common Object Request Broker Interface (CORBA) and Component Object Model (COM). Many parser vendors support DOM Level 1 APIs, as well as an API that falls outside the DOM standards documents: Simple API for XML (SAX). DOM Level 1 supports only those features needed to represent and manipulate document structure and content. It lacks facilities for controlling acccess to document structure and contents, or for validating documents against schemas.

DOM Level 2 was still a W3C Candidate Recommendation (as of April 2000). It builds on Level 1, adding interfaces for an XML event model, query interface, document ranges, filters, and generic stylesheets.

The W3C is discussing requirements for a planned DOM Level 3. Candidate requirements include moving nodes from one XML document to another, ordering nodes within documents, supporting whitespace in element content, exposing XML and text declarations, and looking up element namespaces.

XML SCHEMA

XML Schema provides a language for describing constraints on the structure and contents (the schema or "vocabulary") of a particular class of XML 1.0 documents. The specification, a W3C Working Draft, consists of a Part 1 (Structures) and Part 2 (Datatypes).

XML Schema Part 1 (Structures) defines a broader range of structure and content validation features than XML 1.0 DTDs. It provides XML 1.0–compliant markup for representing schemas and their various components, which include type definitions, element declarations, and attribute declarations, as well as default attribute and element values. It's possible that some applications may need to define XML document structure and content constraints not supported within XML Schema Part 1 (Structures). In this case, these applications would need to perform additional validations on their own (since XML processors would generally perform those validations only within the scope of the schema-definition language).

An XML Schema can be used by XML processors to validate well-formed element and attribute information items in an incoming document. The schema may also be used to "augment" those items and their descendants in the incoming document, which means making explicit various relationships that may have been implicit in the original document, such as the default values and datatypes of an attribute or element information item.

Developers define an XML Schema through one or more schema documents. Each schema document contains representations of schema components, such as datatype definitions and element declarations, that have a common namespace. A schema document may import one or more element information items from other documents and thereby reference more than one namespace.

Primary XML Schema components consist of type definitions, element declarations, and attribute declarations.

A type definition may involve either simple or complex data types. A simple type definition constrains attribute values and the text-only content of elements. A complex type definition constrains the attribute declarations and data types of an element and its child subelements.

An attribute declaration is an association between an attribute name and a simple type definition, in accordance with an optional namespace defined for that attribute name. These declarations specify whether particular attribute information items are required or must not occur in a particular document type. They also constrain attribute information item values to a simple type definition and provide default or fixed values for an attribute information item. An XML Schema may use an "attribute group" definition to reference multiple attribute declarations by a single name, such as when reusing the same set of attribute declarations in several complex data-type definitions.

An element declaration is an association between an element name, a type definition (simple or complex), a default value (optional), and identity-constraint definitions, in accordance with an optional namespace defined for that element name. An identity-constraint definition associates an element's value with the value of other information items in the same XML document. XML Schema uses another XML core specification, XML Path Language (XPath, a W3C Recommendation), to reference other elements and attributes in the same document.

XML Schema also allows "model group definitions" to be used in validating lists of element information items within a particular document. One type of model group definition specifies that particular element information items are to be listed in a particular sequence. Another type specifies that element information items need not be listed in any particular order, but that the list must contain particular elements. And a third type of model group specifies that at least one of the element information items must match one of the listed elements.

XML Schema Part 2 (Datatypes) defines specifications for explicitly declaring and checking datatypes in XML 1.0 documents. XML 1.0's native DTD specification, by contrast, defines limited facilities for applying datatypes to document content. XML Schema Part 2 (Datatypes) supports primitive data typing, including byte, date, integer, and sequence. It distinguishes requirements for lexical data representation from those governing an underlying information set. It allows creation of user-defined datatypes, such as datatypes that are derived from existing datatypes and that may constrain certain of its properties, such as range, precision, length, and format.

Microsoft has committed to supporting the XML Schema standard (both parts) in future revisions to the BizTalk Framework and all of its Windows DNA products. As noted earlier, though, Microsoft will also continue to support an older XML schema-definition language, XDR, that it co-developed and submitted to the W3C in 1998.

Just like XML Schema, XDR renders document schemas through tagged XML element name-tags, rather than DTD declaration statements. XDR schemas take the place of DTDs for document validation. XML processors must recognize XDR schemas in order to validate documents against them. XDR schemas include tags for declaring:

- Elements, attributes, entities, and notations
- Object classes, such as class hierarchies, properties, constraints, and relationships
- Data types, including all highly popular data types, all built-in data types of popular database and programming languages (even Web URIs), parsing rules, and implementation formats

XDR identifies data types for particular elements through references to URIs. The data type's URI refers to a part of the XML document's schema that declares the appropriate parser and storage format of the element.

XDR supports open content models in addition to the closed content models defined under XML 1.0. Open content models allow XML documents to contain subelements that were not explicitly listed in their schema declarations. A closed content model, by contrast, requires that all elements and attributes be listed explicitly and declares as invalid any XML document that includes undeclared content.

XDR is one of several industry-submitted schema-definition languages that the W3C considered in its development of the XML Schema standard. Other schema-definition specifications include SOX and DCD. All of these specifications overlap and propose similar content-model, data-typing, and inheritance features. XML Schema's success in gaining industry acceptance has caused developers to stop developing to these older schema formats. However, software vendors will continue to be able to write to the simpler DTDs defined in the basic XML 1.0 standard, which is stable and universally supported.

XML NAMESPACES

XML Namespaces (a W3C Recommendation ratified in January 1999) provides a mechanism for resolving XML tag and attribute name conflicts in the DTDs and schemas utilized by document originators and recipients. It provides a means for participants in an XML interchange to agree on the underlying semantics of a document's elements, attributes, and values. The namespace establishes a shared semantic context for all transactions involving XML documents that reference that namespace.

In accordance with this standard, a root XML document entity can declare as external entities one or more public "namespaces," in the form of unique Web URLs referencing those namespaces. The namespace declaration must be near the beginning of the root XML document, before all element and attribute tags. A namespace declaration also contains a short identifier that will be used to reference the namespace from within the root document. A namespace's URL may also reference remote DTDs or schemas that define permissible elements, attributes, and default values under that namespace. The root document may define one external namespace as its default and others as alternates that must be referenced explicitly by individual elements and attributes.

To define elements under an external namespace, an XML document's author must add the namespace's short identifier as a prefix to element name-tags wherever they appear in the document. The XML processor assumes that any element name-tags without namespace prefixes belong to the document's default namespace.

In practice, an XML document can reference external tag-sets from many public sources, including government agencies, industry consortia, and vendors. It may also reference the authoring organization's own externally published, proprietary tag-sets and, for good measure, some additional, document-specific element and attribute tags. In this way, XML documents can build an extensible, composite semantic context from public, private, and transaction-specific tag-sets and schemas.

XSL AND XSLT

XSL is a Working Draft of the W3C XSL Working Group. The supplementary XSLT, however, is a W3C Recommendation.

XSL is a language for expressing stylesheets. It enables flexible formatting and display of XML data. It incorporates all formatting options of the older CSS standard into a broader superset applicable to both XML and HTML documents. It also allows Web browsers and servers to translate XML documents into HTML on the fly.

XSL consists of two specifications: a language for embedding formatting tags in XML documents and a vocabulary for specifying formatting semantics. XSLT defines the former, and the base XSL document defines the latter.

XSLT has broader applicability than simply preparing XML documents for formatting and display. It defines a mechanism called "tree transformation," which specifies how XML processors can transform a document that embodies one DTD or schema (the "source tree") into a document conforming to an equivalent schema (the "result tree"). XSLT also defines how applications can filter, reorder, and add data elements to the XML source tree. For example, an application can use XSLT functionality to generate and append a table of contents, based on metadata contained in the source document's element tags.

XSL allows document authors to express formatting semantics in terms of a catalog of formatting objects and properties. Each element or attribute of the result tree is an instance of a formatting object, such as a page, paragraph, or horizontal rule. Associated with each formatting object are properties, such as pagination, indentation, word and letter spacing; and widow, orphan, and hyphenation control. Authors can define formatting properties specific to various presentation media, such as Web browsers, wireless handsets, or hardcopy printouts.

The author of an XML document specifies its XSL stylesheet through declarations in the beginning of the source document. An XML root document uses XML namespaces to distinguish between those tags that specify XSLT formatting semantics from those that refer to content elements in the result tree.

13.2 What Is XML's Role in Microsoft's Products?

XML pervades Microsoft's Windows DNA environment at all tiers and in many capacities.

Microsoft has integrated XML 1.0 and supplementary core specifications into Windows 2000, Windows DNA 2000 application servers, various middleware technologies, and client applications. Microsoft has actively participated in the W3C's development and standardization of XML and supplementary specifications, as attested by the names of Microsoft personnel as authors, editors, or contributors on several of the W3C standards documents.

And let's not forget the XML-based BizTalk Framework (as amply described in Chapter 1). XML is the syntax for BizTalk Messages, BizTalk Documents, and their Business Document contents.

The remainder of this chapter details Microsoft's implementation of these standards across its product line.

13.2.1 Windows 2000

Windows 2000 supports key XML standards, including XML 1.0, DOM, XML Namespaces, XSL, and XSLT (plus the Microsoft-developed XDR schema-definition language).

The operating system includes MSXML, a high-performance, multithreaded, componentized XML processor. MSXML enables Windows 2000 to support XML streaming and persistence, XML record-set translation, and generation and processing of XML "data islands" in HTML pages. These capabilities are available for integration with all Windows 2000 applications through the multilanguage COM programming model. Microsoft has also embedded MSXML technology within Internet Information Server 4.x, Windows NT Server 4.x, and Internet Explorer 5.x. Microsoft has engineered continual improvements in the MSXML parser's reliability and scalability under increasing loads and in multiprocessor scenarios.

Windows 2000's Internet Information Server supports the Web Distributed Authoring and Versioning (WebDAV) protocol. WebDAV (RFC 2518) is a set of standard extensions to HTTP 1.1 that enable browsers to read, write, and manipulate collections of documents over the Web, supporting basic distributed file-sharing functionality. WebDAV uses XML data encoding over HTTP transports. WebDAV allows users to share and work with server-based documents regardless of their authoring tools, platforms, or the type of Web server on which the documents are stored.

13.2.2 Windows DNA 2000 Application Servers

All Windows DNA 2000 application servers integrate with Windows 2000's MSXML processor. Each of these servers—BizTalk Server 2000, Commerce Server 2000, SQL Server 2000, and Host Integration Server 2000—puts XML to different uses.

BIZTALK SERVER 2000

As discussed in Chapter 9, BizTalk Server 2000 incorporates XML in several places:

- Various modules of the BizTalk Management Desk
- Server's parser, transformation, and transport run-time components

At the BizTalk Management Desk level, Microsoft's BizTalk Editor and BizTalk Mapper support creation and editing of XDR-based schemas and XSLT-based transformation "maps." Both BizTalk Mapper and BizTalk Editor can retrieve XML schemas from the BizTalk.org schema repository via the HTTP-based WebDAV protocol, or from Windows 2000 via normal file system operations.

BizTalk Editor allows programmers to build, modify, and inspect XML schema specifications. The tool interprets a document's structure as a set of records and fields. It presents the document's structure visually under a "tree control" view and provides a detailed property view that allows users to edit all the records and fields contained in a document specification. The tool allows developers to automatically create a BizTalk Framework–compliant XDR schema that describes the document's structure and contents. The tool allows developers to publish the schemas they create to standards-based schema repositories on the Web, such as BizTalk.org, and to corporate repositories on intranets or extranets as well. BizTalk Editor allows developers to build new XML document schema specifications from an existing XML schema specification, from an existing document instance (such as any well-formed XML document), or from a blank specification that contains no logical data structure.

BizTalk Mapper allows programmers to use XSLT to define element-level correspondences between one XML-based schema specification and another. Developers can graphically depict structural transformation relationships—in other words, XSLT "maps"—between source specification data elements and destination specification data elements. Developers build maps with simple visual links and with on-screen palettes of "functoids" and other programming objects. Consequently, XSLT maps are the pivot upon which trading partners, in a BizTalk environment, exchange structured data with a common understanding of its business semantics.

At the parser-component level, BizTalk Server 2000 uses Windows 2000's MSXML processor to extract basic BizTalk Message/Document header information that defines an interchange's specific document format. MSXML can also extract routing information from within a well-formed XML-formatted Business Document. The parser can validate the schemas of XML documents against XDR schemas and XML 1.0 DTDs. BizTalk Server 2000 also supports parsers for other formats, including flat files, hierarchical files, X12, EDIFACT, ERP, and CRM formats. Consequently, it's important to realize that BizTalk Server 2000 is a full-featured EDI-ready interchange server and not limited to processing just XML content.

At the transformation-component level, BizTalk Server 2000 uses XSLT-based maps that were generated in the BizTalk Mapper tool. These maps drive the server's engine in transforming document content from one structural form to another. Structural transformations take place between two XML representations of the same data, distinguishing the transformation process from the closely related process of translating content into and out of XML-based application file formats. By using XML to describe data structures in a general way, BizTalk Server can translate documents to both XML and non-XML business document formats consistently, depending on what formats destination applications can consume.

At the transport-component level, BizTalk Server 2000 routes an XML document by using its parser to extract from a BizTalk Message or other well-formed XML document the information needed to route the message or document appropriately. The required routing attributes, defined through XML markup in the message or document header, include the name of the document's schema and identifiers for the document's source and destination organization.

COMMERCE SERVER 2000

As discussed in Chapter 10, Commerce Server 2000 also makes heavy use of XML in several run-time and administration modules.

Commerce Server 2000's profiling system, a run-time module, aggregates user data from multiple back-end directories and other data stores into its Commerce Property Store, which it maintains under SQL Server 7 or 2000. It translates and maps all imported user data into XML syntax for storage and manipulation within its user profile repository.

At the level of the Commerce Desk administration tool, administrators can use an "expression builder" feature to define conditional rules that drive content targeting, service personalization, real-time recommendations, direct mailing, and order processing under Commerce Server 2000. The tool uses boolean operators and profile attributes to build conditional expressions in XML syntax. In addition to keying on user profile information, expressions can incorporate variables related to the contents of a customer's online "shopping basket" as well as other context variables such as the site section, page elements, and time associated with a user interaction through Commerce Server 2000.

Commerce Desk's catalog management tool supports interchange of catalog contents through BizTalk Server 2000 via a Catalog API (to a COM object) that exports and imports data in the Microsoft-defined Commerce Catalog XML format (an XDR schema that the vendor has published on the BizTalk.org schema repository), as well as in Comma Separated Value (CSV) format. Administrators can use the Catalog API to import and export catalog information on individual products, groups of products, and product categories. The Catalog XML format represents both catalog schemas and data. Objects exported via the Catalog XML format may be mapped using the BizTalk Mapper tool in the BizTalk Management Desk. Administrators who deploy BizTalk Server

2000 with Commerce Server 2000 may rely on the former for document transformation, or may use Commerce Server 2000 for this purpose.

SQL SERVER 2000

As noted in Chapter 11, SQL Server 2000 provides native support for XML. It supports BizTalk Framework specifications through its ability to read, write, and store documents in native XML format.

In addition, SQL Server 2000 and 7.0 both store and retrieve data contained in XML documents. They also allow queries to be sent directly to the server via URLs, with the results returned as XML-formatted documents.

HOST INTEGRATION SERVER 2000

As also noted in Chapter 11, Host Integration Server 2000, when deployed with BizTalk Server 2000, allows external applications to drive mainframe transactions via a loosely coupled, message-oriented COM Transaction Integrator (COMTI) interface. BizTalk Server 2000 can consume and parse XML documents and messages and, per "agreements" defined under BizTalk Management Desk, invoke COMTI objects on HIS 2000 via the COM+/COMTI "Ipipeline" interface. In some documents, Microsoft has referred to this capability as "XML-TI."

XML-TI allows developers to invoke transactions on a host with XML without having to change any existing host code or write any new code. XML-TI consists of a runtime proxy and a component builder that generates an XML document interface for executing legacy mainframe transactions.

13.2.3 Application Development Tools and Sites

Microsoft has also spread the XML gospel through its application development tools and Web-site resources.

Developers can use Visual Studio 6.0 to take full advantage of Windows 2000 features such as XML, COM+, Active Directory, and Internet Information Server 5.0. Developers can use Visual Studio 6.0 to integrate Windows 2000's MSXML parser with any Windows 2000-based application. They can XML-enable applications via such programming and scripting languages as C++, Visual Basic, Java, ECMAScript, VBScript, Perl, and Python. The parser is implemented as a COM component. As noted earlier, it supports XML 1.0 (including DTDs), DOM, XDR, XML Namespaces, XSL, and XSLT. Microsoft also provides a stand-alone, redistributable version of MSXML.

Microsoft provides XML schema development tools at BizTalk.org. It has also established the MSDN XML Developer Center (http://msdn.microsoft.com/xml/default.asp), which provides developers with tools and resources to help them take advantage of XML.

13.2.4 Middleware Technologies

Microsoft also supports XML in its middleware technologies, which will be discussed in greater detail in Chapter 14.

Microsoft Transaction Server (MTS) supports robust, high-performance, distributed transactions involving XML content.

Microsoft Message Queue Server supports and ensures reliable, asynchronous delivery of XML content.

Simple Object Access Protocol v.1.1 supports programmatic interfaces between programs that exchange XML content over HTTP. SOAP 1.1, authored by Microsoft and other vendors, defines mechanisms for distributed object invocation and data marshaling. Microsoft is implementing in Windows 2000, BizTalk Server 2000, and other Windows DNA 2000 application server products.

SOAP 1.1 specifies HTTP 1.1 as the default transport protocol and XML as the encoding scheme for programmatic invocation requests and responses. SOAP invocation parameters and data types can be scalars, numbers, strings, and dates, as well as complex array, record, and list structures. SOAP invocations can support stateless or stateful transactions. Within the HTTP envelope, the SOAP content is a single XML document that consists of two mandatory elements: a SOAP envelope and, within the envelope, a SOAP payload. The payload, in turn, consists of two "child" elements: an optional SOAP header and a mandatory SOAP body.

SOAP payload header elements contain transaction IDs and additional information that travel with the method call but are processed within the distributed transaction processing (TP) environment, rather than by the communicating applications. TP components—such as transaction monitors, message brokers, and object brokers—extract transaction IDs from the SOAP payload header. The TP middleware then passes the SOAP payload body, which contains the method call, through to the target object's SOAP adapter. The SOAP adapter, in turn, passes the SOAP payload body (an XML document containing method call or response data) to the target object.

A SOAP method request is the first child element within the SOAP payload-body element. The method request may, in turn, contain additional child elements for specific method-call parameters. The SOAP specification places no restrictions on the structure or contents of data in the method-call or method-response payload, apart from the requirement that it all be encoded in a well-formed XML document.

13.2.5 Client Applications

Microsoft has also made XML a native format supported in its Windows 2000 Professional desktop operating system, Office 2000 desktop application suite, and Internet Explorer (IE) browser.

Microsoft has implemented XML as a native data storage format in Windows 2000 and Office 2000, using the markup standard to encode data structures and metadata within documents saved to HTML presentation formats. Microsoft still retains Office's binary file formats, though the vendor will increasingly stress HTML/XML for cross-platform applications.

Office 2000 provides the ability to save files back and forth between standard Office document formats (such as .doc, .xls, and .ppt) and HTML. Users can open an HTML page in an Office 2000 application—Word, Excel, PowerPoint, or Access—without losing the HTML coding. Likewise, they can save an Office 2000 document to HTML without losing document properties (subject to several caveats). Office 2000 uses XML and other methods to ensure that Word formatting, macros, special characters, document properties, and similar information are preserved when the file is saved to HTML.

For example, if users save a Microsoft Word document in HTML format and then reopen it in Word, they do not lose Word document properties. When an Office document is saved to HTML, any macros in the document are stored in a separate file linked to the HTML file. PowerPoint and Excel files saved in HTML format use scripts to make slide shows and workbooks function similarly to the way they function in the original applications. When users open the resultant HTML file in an Office application, the macros are available and run correctly.

When an Office application is used to open an HTML file that was developed externally, the HTML code is preserved. Users can modify the HTML file from within the Office application and save it back to HTML without losing any HTML tags. However, the HTML tags are not preserved when the file is saved to a standard Office format (though scripting tags are preserved).

Some features are available only in Office formats (not HTML). Word's File menu Version command is available only in .doc format. Excel's scenarios, custom views, shared workbooks, templates, and add-ins are available only in .xls format. Only Access's data access pages, not the .mdb database file itself, can be saved to HTML format.

IE 4.x was the industry's first browser to support XML. IE 5.x provides significant enhancements to the browser's XML-related features, including support for DOM, XDR, Namespaces, and XSL. The browser's XML features are presented in Table 13-4.

As we noted in Chapter 12, WebDAV will become increasingly important in the Windows DNA environment as a means of extending Windows 2000's Distributed File System over the Internet to browsers and other client applications. WebDAV allows heterogeneous Web clients and servers to operate as a scalable, distributed document store. The specification defines mechanisms for naming, posting, saving, version control, and other functions on Web-resident documents in a way that is independent of underlying operat-

Table 13-4	Internet Explorer 5.x's XML Features
Feature	**Discussion**
High-performance, validating XML engine	Incorporates an enhanced MSXML parser that supports XML 1.0 and Namespaces.
Direct XML browsing	Users can view XML using XSL or CSS within the browser, just as they view HTML documents.
DOM support	Supports DOM Level 1 and exposes document elements and behaviors to scripts, Visual Basic, C++, and other languages.
XSL support	Can apply XSL stylesheets to XML data and display the data dynamically and flexibly. Applications can use the XSL Pattern syntax to programmatically find and extract information within an XML data set on the client or the server.
XDR support	Validates XML documents according to XDR schemas.
Channel Definition Format (CDF)	Uses the XML-based CDF to describe Active Channel content and desktop components. CDF can describe collections of pages and data about pages, such as channel-bar display, download behavior, Web-page usage, and page-hit logging.
Open Software Format (OSF)	Uses the XML-based OSD to advertise and install software components over the Internet. OSD provides a publishing mechanism to notify users of new versions of software. OSD can provide detailed descriptions of how to install ActiveX Controls and Java packages.
Vector Markup Language (VML)	Along with Office 2000, supports XML data islands that contain vector graphic data, as described in the XML-based VML. VML allows vector graphical information to be integrated with the text and other data in HTML pages. VML also facilitates description of business diagrams in documents created in Office 2000.
WebDAV	Along with Office 2000, implements the WebDAV (RFC 2518) standard, which supports distributed document read, write, concurrency control, and manipulation over the Web. WebDAV uses XML data encoding over HTTP transports.

ing systems. It uses XML tags to define metadata applicable to documents and the collections to which those documents belong.

WebDAV is to DFS what SOAP is to Microsoft's Distributed Component Object Model —the Internet-oriented next-generation technology. What WebDAV and SOAP share is a common reliance on HTTP as the standard transport protocol and XML as the standard content syntax.

13.3 Summary

WebDAV and SOAP are critical middleware technologies for the future of multiplatform e-commerce. We now move to Chapter 14, where we discuss these and the other middleware and application development technologies in Microsoft's e-commerce product architecture. BizTalk-enabled e-commerce applications can only be as strong as the connector technologies—the "glue"—that bind Microsoft's products into a unified family and help them play well in a world invented elsewhere.

Microsoft E-Commerce Application Development and Middleware Technologies

Modern business is a many-threaded network tapestry. Today's global B2B supply chains bind billions of software components into patterns of staggering complexity. Middleware is the warp and woof of the online economy. And application development tools provide templates upon which we weave new business processes from lines of modular program code.

Microsoft built the BizTalk initiative on preexisting middleware and application development technologies. The company recognizes that no new computing architecture can succeed if its proponent declares legacy invest-ments to be irrelevant. As we noted in Chapter 8, BizTalk Server 2000 is mid-dleware for "any-to-any" enterprise application integration (EAI) and elec-tronic data interchange (EDI). BizTalk Server 2000 is an EAI/EDI interchange server—in other words, one part workflow engine, one part format-transla-tion engine, and one part message broker. It provides a software-adaptability layer with translators and adapters that support transparent communications among otherwise incompatible applications.

We put ironic quotes around "any to any" because Microsoft has not broken from its long-standing practice of favoring its own proprietary tech-nologies, such as Component Object Model (COM), Distributed COM (DCOM), Microsoft Transaction Server (MTS), and Microsoft Message Queue Server (MSMQ). In BizTalk Server 2000, Microsoft adds to these technologies a new middleware framework, the Simple Object Access Protocol (SOAP), which it helped develop (but which is not truly proprietary to Microsoft, since other vendors have participated in developing it). BizTalk Server 2000 is notable for its lack of support for object-oriented computing environments that Microsoft had no hand in developing, such as Enterprise JavaBeans (EJB), Common Object Request Broker Architecture (CORBA), and the Internet Inter-ORB Protocol (IIOP). The server also lacks built-in adapters for some competing message brokers, transaction monitors, and XML-based B2B message formats (other than Microsoft's own BizTalk Message/Document format). Consequently, Microsoft's middleware and application development technologies primarily provide a framework within which you will build B2B and EAI applications for BizTalk Server 2000 and other Windows DNA products. Previous chapters (in particular, Chapters 8, 11, and 12) provide general overviews of these technologies and describe Microsoft's proprietary approaches to varying degrees. The present chapter consolidates these discussions into a panoramic tour of Microsoft's proprietary object-computing environment, drilling down into the technologies listed in Table 14-1.

In the following discussions, we provide as much detail on each standard, specification, and technology as is necessary to understand its role in Windows DNA environments generally and Windows DNA 2000 application servers specifically. We then close the chapter, and the book, with a discussion that brings the focus back from network "plumbing" to an examination of middleware as an integration environment for B2B and B2C e-marketplaces. In particular, we focus on BizTalk Server 2000's potential role as an integration hub for the diverse middleware environments that must mesh in the online economy of the 21st century.

14.1 Development Tools

Visual Studio 6.0 is the developmental glue for Microsoft's entire enterprise software product family. It is the integrated application development tool

Table 14-1	*Technologies in Microsoft's Object Computing Environment*
Category	**Technologies**
Development tools	Visual Studio
Object computing framework	COM, COM+, ActiveX Components, Active Server Pages (ASP)
Object brokering framework	DCOM
Message brokering framework	MSMQ
Distributed transaction processing monitor	MTS
XML-based remote procedure call (RPC) protocol	SOAP
Data access components, providers, and drivers	ActiveX Data Object (ADO), OLE DB, Open Database Connectivity (ODBC)

suite for Windows DNA environments. The suite includes the Visual Basic, Visual C++, Visual J++, Visual InterDev, and Visual FoxPro tools.

Visual Studio addresses all three tiers of the Windows DNA application model. It provides tools for user interface development (presentation tier), application server component development (business logic tier), and database programming and design (data tier). It also supports integration of Windows DNA applications with third-party COM-based applications, as well as third-party ERP, CRM, and supply-chain management applications running in host computing environments (and connected through COMTI interfaces to Host Integration Server 2000 or SNA Server, as discussed in Chapter 11).

Visual Studio supports graphical design, implementation, and analysis of components and applications for all Windows server and client environments. It allows programmers to integrate applications with data sources through ODBC, OLE DB, and ADO interfaces. And it enables integration of distributed components through programmatic access to Microsoft's principal middleware protocols and frameworks: DCOM, MSMQ, MTS, and SOAP.

BizTalk-enabled e-commerce applications take shape within the Visual Studio tool suite. Visual Studio provides programmatic access to the COM and COM+ component libraries that drive the functionality of BizTalk Server 2000, Commerce Server 2000, SQL Server 2000, and other Windows DNA 2000 and Microsoft Server products, plus all Microsoft Windows client environments. At run-time, COM and COM+ components share a common object model that enables developers to reuse components across tools in the Visual Studio suite. In addition, developers can combine COM/COM+ components that they created in Visual Studio with those created in any of the scores of third-party COM programming tools.

Developers can build rich applications from diverse program elements, including COM and COM+ components, ActiveX controls, Java applets, HTML and ASP pages, and source code. The toolset supports development in any of several programming and scripting languages, including C++, Basic, Java, VBScript, and ECMAscript. Components in any supported language may be reused by any other tool in the suite.

In Table 14-2, we discuss Visual Studio's support for development activities throughout the application life cycle.

Visual Studio also supports a Web-based collaboration environment for distributed development team members. This environments allows geographically scattered developers to share components, specifications, documentation, and other program elements. The fundamental infrastructure for the collaboration environment includes Visual Studio's Visual SourceSafe, Visual Component Manager, and Repository tools. All joint-authoring operations are HTTP-based, though the tool also supports offline operations. The project model is shared by Microsoft's FrontPage tool for Web-site creation and management. Consequently, nonprogramming content developers who use FrontPage may collaborate remotely with programmers who use Visual Studio.

Table 14-2	*Development Life-Cycle Activities Supported by Visual Studio*
Activity	**Discussion**
Design	Supports graphical design of multitier applications. It provides an on-screen "white-board" that serves as a shared architectural reference diagram for development teams. Its Visual Modeler tool enables developers to create detailed graphical descriptions of components, component relationships, methods, properties, and events. It automatically translates graphical models into logical program and component definitions using the industry-standard Unified Modeling Language (UML). In addition, the modeler supports automatic code generation from models into Visual Basic and Visual C++–based projects. Visual Studio also includes tools for designing Web-site applications to run on Internet Information Server and database applications to run on both SQL Server (version 6.5 and higher) and Oracle (version 7.x and higher) databases.
Development	Provides development tools for multiple programming languages (C++, Basic, Java, and FoxPro) and paradigms (desktop, multitier, and Web). All Visual Studio tools have a common look and feel and support COM-based component development and assembly. Visual Studio includes development/test editions of Microsoft application servers, including SQL Server, Internet Information Server, Transaction Server, Message Queue Server, Host Integration Server, Exchange Server, Systems Management Server, and Site Server. It also includes the freely redistributable Microsoft Data Engine, which developers can include as part of their stand-alone database applications that can scale up to run under SQL Server 7.0 or 2000.
Analysis	Allows developers to graphically visualize distributed solutions; understand their structure, interactions, and performance; and locate problems and bottlenecks. Its Visual Studio Analyzer tool displays the component flow of distributed applications. The tool monitors component processing graphically and provides developers with the low-level information they need to analyze the run-time behaviors, events, and performance of individual components as well as complex applications running across several nodes. Development teams can record typical debugging sessions, time-stamp events, and save the resulting event logs. The analyzer correlates component-level requests and responses and generates Gantt-style reports that present the timing and duration of events. Selected events from Windows 2000's performance monitor can be recorded and correlated with data from Visual Studio Analyzer.
Management	Provides tools for developers to manage any component or other program element developed in the suite. Its Microsoft Repository 2.0 stores project elements created by both Microsoft tools and third-party COM-oriented development tools. Its Visual Component Manager 2.0 allows teams of developers to publish, catalog, track, find, and reuse components and other project elements within Microsoft Repository. Its Visual SourceSafe 6.0 supports source-code version control and file locking across development teams. And Microsoft Management Console support integrated management of run-time COM components as well as Windows 2000 server and the full range of Windows DNA 2000 and Microsoft Server products.
Deployment	Provides tools for packaging, replicating, and deploying distributed components to staging and production servers, via Microsoft Site Server, or to client systems, via Microsoft Systems Management Server.

14.2 Object Computing Framework

An object is a discrete unit of computing functionality that exposes its behaviors through a set of fully described interfaces. Object-oriented computing binds two or more software components into a unified information service.

Object technologies enable software components to be created, instantiated, named, described, discovered, activated, and invoked. Object technologies may bind different applications on a single machine or across a local- or wide-area network. Object technologies use declarative interface specifications and separate these interfaces from implementation details on each network and operating environment. In this manner, developers can replace and update object implementations without requiring changes to existing applications that rely on them.

Many platform and application software vendors provide object models as basic development tools in their product environments. Object models expose software functions as reusable libraries so that developers can integrate, customize, control, and extend these capabilities. Typically, an object model exposes an interface definition language (IDL) that defines component capabilities as methods, properties, and events. The object model also maps its IDL to various programming languages, such as C, C++, Visual Basic, and Java. The object model's software components usually correspond to run-time services in the underlying platform, such as server operating system, groupware application, or commerce server.

On a single platform, object models usually support most of the functions necessary for component-oriented computing, from object creation to invocation. However, applications that span two or more dissimilar platforms require a layer of software adapters, or middleware, that bridge their dissimilar object models and support run-time component-level interoperability.

Introduced in 1993, COM technology provides the underlying object model and programming framework for all Windows DNA environments. It defines a consistent, language-independent framework under which software objects can point to one another and invoke one another's functions. Programmers can use C++, Basic, Java, and other languages to develop COM objects, as well as employ various scripting languages to access and manipulate this functionality.

Most of Microsoft's server and client applications are written as collections of interoperating COM components or objects. COM's direct predecessor, the compound-document technology known as Object Linking and Embedding (OLE), first brought the benefits of language-independent object-oriented computing to the Windows platform. Through OLE, a user working in Microsoft Word can, for example, embed or link a spreadsheet file, or graphic object, and later, by clicking on that object, bring the embedded object's application to life while remaining inside Word.

All Microsoft application development and middleware technologies
build on or use COM technology, as described in Table 14-3 (and discussed
in greater detail later in this chapter). Protocol capabilities, such as LDAP, are
exposed as COM components, and APIs, such as the Active Directory
Services Interface (ADSI), are accessed using COM libraries. Other COM
components can enable interoperability by acting as proxies to nonstandard
heterogeneous services.

COM allows two or more applications or ``components'' to interoperate
even if they were written by different developers at different times, in different programming languages, or running on different machines running different operating systems. COM incorporates Distributed Computing
Environment's (DCE) RPC, which, in Microsoft's implementation, is known as
"MS-RPC."

A COM component is a collection of related functions plus the interfaces (the "verbs" or "behaviors") that those functions present to other components. COM software infrastructure provides operations through which
client components may connect to multiple server components that provide
functions they require. COM infrastructure establishes connections between
client and server components and then drops out of the connection. After the

Table 14-3	*COM's Central Role in Microsoft Application Development and Middleware Technologies*
Technology	**Discussion**
COM+	Enables more efficient development and assembly of COM objects into applications
MTS	Enables application access to transactional services through COM programmatic interfaces
ActiveX Components	Enables packaging and transfer of downloadable COM component bina-ries for execution within HTML pages running under Web browsers, via page-embedded URL pointers to ActiveX components
Active Server Pages (ASPs)	Enables run-time Web page generation using server-side scripts to access COM objects and other program elements
DCOM	Enables remote location, invocation, and execution of COM objects across networks
MSMQ	Enables application access to message queuing services through COM programmatic interfaces
SOAP	Enables application access to XML-based remote procedure calls through COM programmatic interfaces
ActiveX Data Objects	Enables application access to structured data through COM programmatic interfaces

connection is established, client and server components communicate directly with one another, not via any intermediate component. COM infrastructure provides mechanisms for object creation, registry, interface negotiation, server component location, reference counting, memory allocation, and error reporting between server and client components.

COM supports a programming environment in which the functionality of each binary component can evolve independently. Server components can continue to support the interfaces through which they communicated with older clients while exposing new interfaces for communicating with newer clients. COM supports location-independent communication between client and server components, regardless of whether the server components are running in the same process, on the same machine, or on a different machine from the client.

In any discussion of object-oriented COM programming, it's important to keep straight some key terms that have interlocking definitions:

- COM interface: a group of related functions specifying a "contract" (a set of behaviors) that COM components expose to clients through verbs expressed in an IDL
- COM class: a named, concrete implementation of one or more interfaces
- COM object: the in-memory instantiation of a COM class
- COM component: a code module that loads on demand and creates COM objects

It's also important to keep straight the run-time services provided by the COM infrastructure to components, as presented in Table 14-4.

COM+ is a late 1990s upgrade to the programming environment that simplifies creation and management of COM components. COM+ is the underlying object model and programming environment for Windows 2000, and COM+ components are backward-compatible with existing COM components. Table 14-5 describes the value-added run-time services that this enhanced object and programming model provides to distributed COM applications.

COM+ also integrates MTS fully into the COM infrastructure. MTS, which Microsoft introduced in 1996 (prior to COM+), is a component-based transaction monitor for Windows-distributed environments. MTS enables work from multiple-distributed objects to be composed into a single atomic transaction. For example, BizTalk-enabled e-commerce applications might use MTS to link dispersed software modules and databases into a single unit of work. BizTalk application developers can write MTS application components in any of several languages as COM components. And COM client programs can access MTS-enabled applications remotely via DCOM.

MTS provides clients and resource managers with "two-phase commit" transaction-processing services, sparing database application developers from

| Table 14-4 | COM Infrastructure Runtime Services |

Service	Discussion
Object RPC	Supports interface marshalling, message filter/call control, and proxy/stub management
Service control manager	Supports maintenance of registry class information for locating classes implemented as libraries, local processes, or remote servers
Security	Supports authentication, authorization, and confidentiality on distributed transactions
Structured storage	Supports transaction-based, hierarchical file format for creating and sharing files across applications and platforms
Monikers	Supports persistent, intelligent names for referencing objects in persistent storage
Automation	Supports exposing component functionality to high-level programming environments, including visual development tools and scripting languages such as JScript and VBScript
Registry	Supports database of components and their configuration information
Error handling	Supports return of error codes to the client component
Uniform data transfer	Supports transfer of structured data between components
Persistent property sets	Supports attachment of structured information to objects in structured storage
Persistent objects	Supports saving objects' internal state when asked to do so by a client
Connectable objects	Supports ability of objects to express and enumerate "outgoing" interfaces, such as event sets; connect and disconnect "sinks" to the objects for those outgoing interfaces; and enumerate connections that exist to a particular outgoing interface
Type libraries	Supports interface repository database for data-driven cross-process and cross-machine interface marshalling
Security Service Provider Interface (SSPI)	Supports pluggable security providers

having to write transaction logic into their code. Without need for a "client foot-print" other than Windows itself, MTS supports server-based concurrency control, transaction logging, and rollback, in case a transaction is aborted and linked databases need to be rolled back to their previous states. MTS infrastructure includes a business rulebase, resource broker, and run-time middleware environment for processing high-performance, scalable, secure distributed enterprise transactions across linked data stores on intranets and the Internet.

MTS functionality, accessible through COM components, makes transaction management transparent to the component developer. MTS hides transactional concurrency, resource pooling, security, context management, and

Table 14-5	*Value-Added COM+ Infrastructure Run-time Services*
Service	**Discussion**
Publish and subscribe event mechanism	A general event mechanism that allows client components to subscribe to notifications for specific events published by server components
Fast transaction support	Fast transactions with an in-memory database, thereby avoiding the overhead associated with storing and accessing durable state to and from physical disk
Queued components	Client invocation of methods on server components via an asynchronous queuing model
Dynamic load balancing	Automatic balancing of client requests across multiple equivalent COM server components

other system-level complexities from the developer. It spares developers from having to write begin-transaction or end-transaction code into their applications. A programmer can declare that a particular set of COM components is to execute in transactional mode, in which case MTS manages transactional operations. A server component may participate in the transaction of the component calling it.

Table 14-6 describes the run-time infrastructure services that MTS provides to COM+ applications.

Many database vendors have implemented MTS technology in their products, including IBM, Sybase, and Informix. MTS can handle cross-platform distributed database commits, such as commits between DB2 on IBM's OS/390 and Microsoft SQL Server on Windows 2000 Datacenter.

Microsoft has tightly integrated MTS with Internet Information Server (IIS), thereby enabling any ASP to be managed as a transaction. IIS uses ASP technology to generate Web pages dynamically by means of server-side scripts that access COM objects and other program elements (in addition to supporting scripted Common Gateway Interface Web applications).

An ASP contains a script—which may be VBscript or ECMAScript—that is executed at IIS. ASP scripts can create and use COM objects, so they can access the entirety of the Windows DNA object model in generating dynamic Web content. ASP scripts can use MTS themselves to ensure that all scripted operations succeed or fail as a unit, or these scripts can access MTS-enabled transactional applications.

14.3 Object-Brokering Framework

Object-brokering technologies, also known as object request brokers (ORBs), support naming, discovery, invocation, and data-marshalling functions among networked components.

Table 14-6	*MTS Infrastructure Run-Time Services*
Service	**Discussion**
Automatic thread and resource pooling	Automatic thread and resource pooling to enable scalability for server-side components
Automatic transactions	Automatic configuration of a component's transactional requirements when that component is deployed
Configurable security	Administrator configuration of client components' roles and the interfaces and server components that may be accessed by clients in those roles
Database connection pooling	Reuse and pooling of existing component-to-database connections
Support for multiple databases and resource managers	Multiple databases and resource managers, including SQL Server, Oracle, and DB2 databases, as well as other resource managers such as Microsoft Message Queue Server
Automatic thread support	Automatic assignment of threads to single-threaded components as needed
Component state management	Requiring components to give up any in-memory state when each transaction ends, as well as providing a shared property manager for components that wish to store and later retrieve their in-memory states
Process isolation through packages	Grouping of individual applications into one or more packages, and allowing each package to run in its own process, thereby enabling greater fault tolerance
Integration with mainframe transactions	Through COMTI (as discussed in Chapter 11), initiation and control of CICS transactions on IBM mainframes

ORBs maintain addresses, identifiers, and attributes of all components in networked directories or registries. This feature ensures that the ORB infrastructure can easily locate and invoke components when needed. Several competing, overlapping object-computing standards have been proposed, each of which defines APIs, ORB mechanisms, RPC protocols, and registry/naming services. Leading networked ORB standards include CORBA and DCOM.

DCOM, introduced in 1996 under Windows NT Server 4.0 and carried forward in Windows 2000, is Microsoft's network-oriented extension to COM. DCOM enables COM clients to access server components on other systems over networks. DCOM supports remote location, invocation, and execution of COM server components. When client and server components reside on different machines, DCOM replaces the local interprocess communication with the synchronous Distributed Computing Environment RPC, also known as a "wire protocol." DCOM hides the locations of client and server components, enabling location-independent, distributed interprocess communication. DCOM requires no changes to COM source code and does not require that programs be recompiled; instead, a simple reconfiguration allows formerly colocated components to connect to each other remotely.

Figure 14-1 shows the key difference between COM and DCOM: The former integrates client and server components across different processes on the same machine, while the latter integrates components across different processes on different machines.

DCOM is the primary middleware approach that Windows DNA 2000 servers, such as BizTalk Server 2000 and Commerce Server 2000, use to communicate with each other in a data-center environment. Under Windows 2000, DCOM supports scalable, networkable object-oriented computing, thanks to Active Directory's Class Store. This feature allows a remote object's current location to be maintained in one distributed directory subtree rather than, as under Windows NT Server 4.x, in the local registries of every platform that might call that object. Client-based COM libraries consult the Class Store when an object requested by the application is not found in the local registry.

DCOM manages connections to server components that are dedicated to a single client, as well as server components that are shared by multiple clients, by maintaining a reference count on each component. When a client establishes a connection to a component, DCOM increments the component's reference count. When the client releases its connection, DCOM decre-

COM: connecting different processes on the same machine

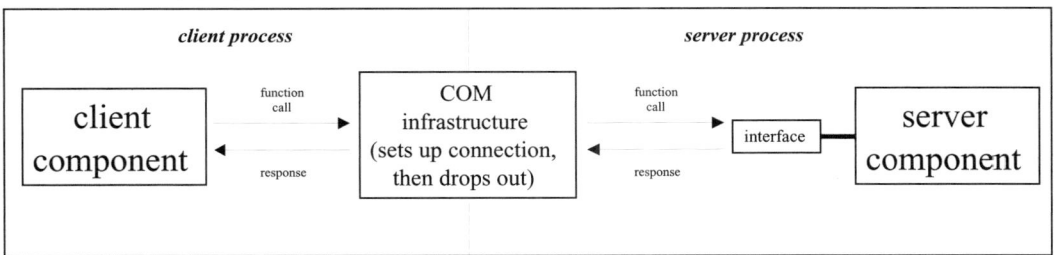

DCOM: connecting different processes on different machines

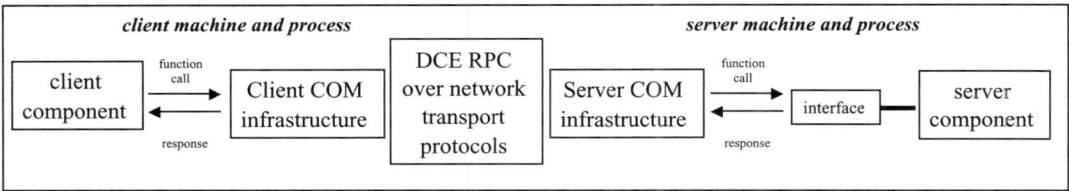

Figure 14-1   *COM integrates different components on the same machine. DCOM integrates COM components on different machines across networks.*

ments the component's reference count. If the count reaches zero, the component can free itself. This reference-counting feature is known in middleware lingo as "distributed garbage collection."

14.4 Message-Brokering Framework

Message-brokering services enable reliable, network-based, application-to-application communications using structured messages. This technology also goes by such names as "message-oriented middleware," "message queuing," and "business-quality messaging."

With message-brokering services, one or more sending applications can submit messages to one or more receiving applications, usually through broadcast, multicast, or publish/subscribe mechanisms. Leading message-brokering products include MSMQ, IBM MQ Series, TIBCO TIB/Rendezvous, Momentum X-IPC, BEA MessageQ, PeerLogic PIPES, and TIBCO. Sun's Java Messaging Service (JMS) specification also defines a message-brokering environment.

MSMQ is one of the middleware approaches that Windows DNA 2000 servers use to communicate with each other remotely in distributed intranet, extranet, and Internet environments. MSMQ—introduced under Windows NT and carried forward as an integrated feature of Windows 2000—provides a nonblocking, asynchronous, interprocess messaging service (in contrast to the blocking, synchronous, client/server conversations supported in DCOM). MSMQ messages can contain data in any format that makes sense to both the sender and the receiver, including BizTalk Messages, SOAP content, and other well-formed XML documents.

When an MSMQ-enabled application receives a request message, it processes the request by reading the contents of the message and acting accordingly. If required, the receiving application might send a response message back to the original requestor. Applications can use MSMQ to send messages to other applications without waiting for responses, in cases where, for example, the target application is not running. The sending application submits messages to queues, where they are stored until receiving applications remove them. The sender does need to stop sending other messages while it waits for responses to prior messages.

While messages are in transit between senders and receivers, MSMQ keeps the messages in intermediate queues. MSMQ holds messages in queues when network links or nodes are unavailable. When the network becomes available or the receiving application is ready to process requests, MSMQ will reliably deliver any waiting messages. MSMQ supports dynamic routing and configuration, multiple delivery and acknowledgment options, and integration with Windows 2000 security facilities. Programmers can

Table 14-7	*MSMQ Run-time Services*
Service	**Discussion**
Transactions	MTS-based applications can include the act of sending or receiving MSMQ messages in larger atomic units, enabling all operations in a transaction to succeed or fail as a group.
Automatic message journaling	Can use journals to keep copies of messages sent or received by applications, thereby providing audit trails and facilitating recovery from various kinds of network and node failures.
Automatic notification	Can notify sending applications of the success or failure of message delivery, receipt, and processing.
Data signing, confidentiality, and integrity	Can digitally sign, encrypt, and tamperproof messages for transfer across network.
Message priority support	Allows administrators to prioritize messages and queues for routing and delivery purposes.

access MSMQ features via COM components from within any Windows DNA 2000 application. Applications can send and receive MSMQ messages from within ASP scripts, MTS-based applications, or any software (Microsoft or otherwise) that supports COM programming.

Table 14-7 describes the various run-time services that MSMQ infra-structure provides to distributed applications.

Many non-Microsoft operating systems support MSMQ, including various Unix versions and IBM mainframes. Third-party vendors provide gate-ways between MSMQ and other message-brokering environments, as does Microsoft through BizTalk Server 2000 and Host Integration Server 2000.

14.5 XML-Based Remote Procedure Calls

An RPC is a protocol that allows a program to call a program on another machine.

To the calling and called programs, RPCs seem no different from local, machine-bound method calls. All the networking-oriented logic is hidden from programs by "stub" code, or RPC run-time libraries, on each platform. The stub code handles the encoding, compression, packaging, buffering, and transfer of method call and response data across the network. Traditional RPCs use compact binary encoding of data transmitted over the wire. RPC stub code integrates with an underlying network transport protocol, such as Transmission Control Protocol/Internet Protocol (TCP/IP) or Internet Packet Exchange/Sequenced Packet Exchange (IPX/SPX).

Traditional RPC technology is synchronous, which means that the calling program does not perform further processing until it receives a reply from the called program. Synchronous RPCs are among the oldest middleware technologies, having been developed initially at Xerox in the 1970s. More than a decade old, Sun Microsystems's Open Network Computing (ONC) is one of the more popular synchronous RPC technologies, though many other vendors provide RPC development toolkits. Object-brokering technologies incorporate synchronous RPCs as their wire protocols. CORBA's RPC is the Internet Inter-ORB Protocol. As noted above, DCOM provides an RPC to interface COM objects over networks.

Many platform and application vendors have implemented proprietary synchronous RPCs in their products. However, there are no open industry standards for synchronous RPCs, and the technology has largely receded in importance with the spread of other middleware approaches, as well as with the development of standards-based, loosely coupled, Internet-oriented distributed computing environments.

A new category of middleware—XML-based RPCs—differs from traditional RPCs in three principal ways. First, XML-based RPCs move interapplication method calls and responses over Internet-standard application-layer protocols, such as HTTP. Second, they are capable of operating asynchronously, which means that the calling program may continue further processing while waiting for responses. And third, they use XML markup rather than binary encoding on data transmitted over the wire.

The leading XML-based RPC initiative is SOAP. SOAP[1] provides an open, extensible way for applications to communicate using XML-based messages over the Web, regardless of what operating system, object model, or language particular applications may use. SOAP facilitates universal communication by defining a simple, extensible message format in standard XML and thereby providing a way to send that XML message over HTTP and other Internet standard protocols.

SOAP defines mechanisms for distributed object invocation and response. Microsoft, IBM/Lotus, UserLand Software, and DevelopMentor co-authored SOAP 1.1 and have submitted the specification to the World Wide Web Consortium and Internet Engineering Task Force (IETF) for consideration. Microsoft was the first platform vendor to commit firmly to SOAP. Microsoft provides a SOAP Toolkit for Visual Studio 6.0 and has announced plans to implement SOAP in Windows 2000, BizTalk Server 2000, and other Windows DNA 2000 application-server products. SOAP defines the BizTalk Message envelope. SOAP is also a fundamental middleware technology in the Microsoft.NET initiative. Other platform vendors, including IBM and Sun, are strongly evaluating the possibility of implementing SOAP in their products.

---

[1]The SOAP technical discussion in this chapter draws from my discussion in *XML-Based Remote Procedure Calls,* (Midvale, UT: Burton Group, May 2000.)

SOAP 1.1 specifies HTTP 1.1 as the default transport protocol and XML as the encoding scheme for programmatic invocation requests and responses. The SOAP 1.1 specification also indicates that future revisions will allow use of other protocols, including MSMQ and the Simple Mail Transfer Protocol (SMTP) to enable more loosely coupled, asynchronous client/server conversations.

A SOAP invocation consists of an action message and an optional response message. A successful SOAP invocation occurs when three events take place:

* The destination or target SOAP interface (or "listener") has been able to decode the input parameters in the payload body of the SOAP **action message**.
* The target SOAP interface has been able to dispatch the invocation to an appropriate back-end application server indicated by the server address in the SOAP message's HTTP envelope.
* The target SOAP interface has been able to invoke an application-level function that corresponds semantically to that indicated in the SOAP method call.

SOAP allows the client program to call a method without regard for the destination application's location, calling conventions, and object model, since these factors are hidden by the intervening SOAP listener at the destination (though the SOAP listener's location must be specified in the action message that the client posts).

SOAP implicitly defines a distributed application model that consists of the following processing layers: HTTP (version 1.1), RPC (SOAP), transaction processing (TP, which is implementation-specific), and application (which is also implementation-specific). Each of these layers corresponds to processes running in SOAP-enabled client and server software, and also to nested envelopes or elements in SOAP method call and response messages. The layering and nesting are as follows:

* HTTP layer: builds and processes the HTTP envelope with SOAP headers
* RPC layer: builds and processes the SOAP envelope, which is nested within the HTTP envelope
* TP layer: builds and processes the SOAP payload header, which is nested within the SOAP envelope
* Application layer: builds and processes the SOAP payload body, which is nested within the SOAP envelope as a "sibling" of the SOAP payload header

This layering approach enables TP software infrastructure—such as transaction monitors and message brokers—to manage end-to-end SOAP-enabled transactions without needing to maintain transaction "state variable" information at the SOAP or applications layer. Transaction state information cannot be maintained in the HTTP layer, which is stateless by design. Figure 14-2 shows the SOAP application model.

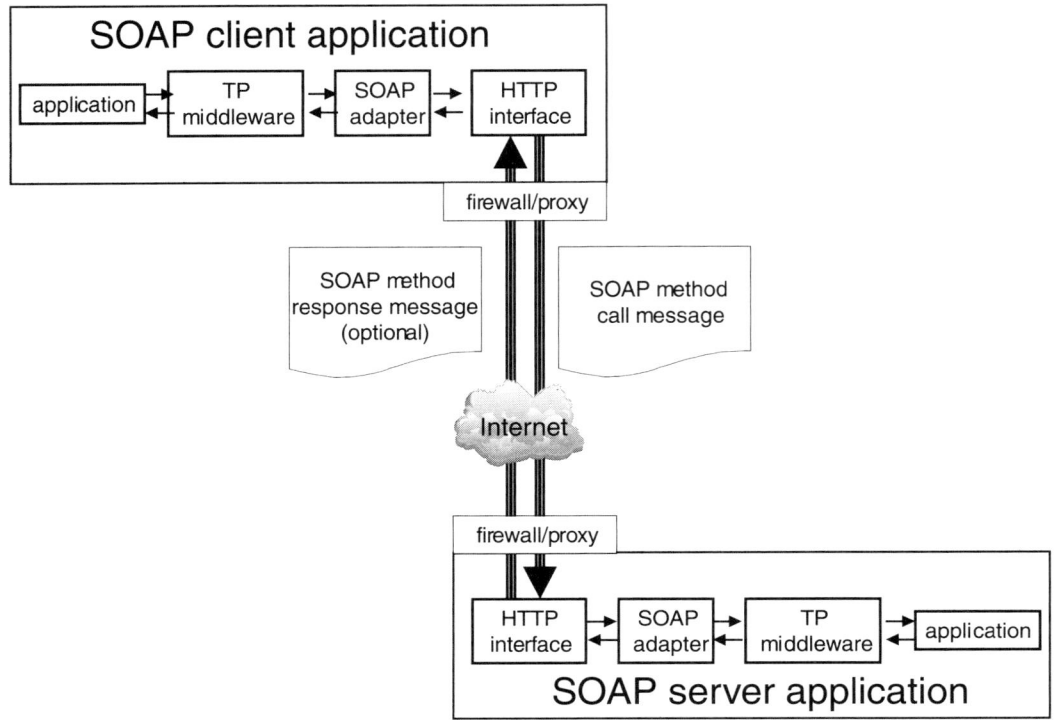

Figure 14-2   *SOAP implicitly defines a four-layered application model across distributed client and server components.*

A SOAP client can specify transactional handling of a function invocation. Within the invocation request's payload header, the SOAP client must define the XML namespace that uniquely identifies the semantics of the transaction ID. Within the payload header, the SOAP client must also define a "SOAP:mustUnderstand" attribute for the transaction ID, and set the value of that attribute to "1" (for true). The SOAP client must also supply, within the SOAP payload header, a value for the transaction ID (the SOAP specification places no restrictions on legal values, apart from global encoding rules, for transaction IDs, which are assumed to be platform- or implementation-specific).

These markup conventions require the destination's SOAP layer to understand that the SOAP client is passing a type of transaction ID that has particular semantics. The destination SOAP layer will (presumably) pass the value of the transaction ID, along with the contents of SOAP payload body, to a TP system for further processing. If the SOAP client passed a transaction ID header with SOAP:mustUnderstand="1", then the SOAP server should send back a fault message if it cannot process the transaction ID and comply with the transactional semantics.

The SOAP method call and response bodies are contained in HTTP request and response messages, respectively. In addition, SOAP-enabled applications insert SOAP-specific elements into HTTP message headers, defining these elements in conformance with the HTTP Extension Framework specification.

SOAP relies on existing HTTP request/response handling mechanisms, including redirection, connection management, and support for access authentication and security. SOAP also relies on existing HTTP security mechanisms for authentication (basic and digest access authentication) and channel security (HTTPS and Transport Layer Security), but doesn't define additional security mechanisms. SOAP's authors have indicated that future versions of the specification will address content confidentiality and integrity in XML payload, most likely through incorporation of the W3C's emerging XML-Signatures specification.

SOAP specifies unidirectional interactions between clients and servers, using HTTP's POST command for transmitting method calls and any associated responses. SOAP relies on the HTTP POST command because content that is posted generally avoids being cached at HTTP proxy servers, unlike content exchanged through HTTP's GET command. If the GET command were used, proxy caching and replay of SOAP messages could wreak havoc with SOAP applications that expect a single action message in one direction and a single, corresponding method-response message in the reverse direction. Application developers can approximate bidirectional program communications by passing the SOAP client's URL and methods as arguments in an action message.

Furthermore, SOAP relies on POST, rather than the similar HTTP PUT command, because POST allows the server of the target URI to route the method call to some other resource—in other words, to the destination application that uses SOAP to expose its methods. By contrast, the PUT command does not allow the server of the target URI to redirect the request.

A SOAP client program calls a SOAP server program by including the following information in the method call message's HTTP and/or SOAP envelope: the Uniform Resource Identifier (URI) and path of the target object, the method name, and method parameters.

In the HTTP envelope header, the target URI points to the network address of the SOAP server that the SOAP client is attempting to call. SOAP places no restriction on the form of a server network address, other than the requirement that it be a valid URI. Likewise, SOAP places no restrictions on the syntax or case-sensitivity of interface names, method names, or parameter names, though SOAP servers will respond to only those names they support.

The HTTP envelope on a SOAP client's action message includes a "SOAPMethodName" header, the value of which specifies the method an application wants to invoke on the target object. The method's value is specified by a concatenation of three character strings: the URI of the target object, a "#" sign, and the method name (which must not include the "#" sign).

Within the HTTP envelope, the SOAP content is a single XML encoding that consists of two mandatory elements: a SOAP envelope and, within the envelope, a SOAP payload. The payload, in turn, consists of two "child" elements: an optional SOAP header and a mandatory SOAP body.

SOAP payload header elements contain transaction IDs and additional information that travel with the method call but are processed within the distributed TP environment, rather than by the communicating applications. TP components—such as transaction monitors, message brokers, and object brokers—extract transaction IDs from the SOAP payload header. The TP middleware then passes the SOAP payload body, which contains the method call, through to the target object's SOAP adapter. The SOAP adapter, in turn, passes the SOAP payload body (an XML document containing method call or response data) to the target object.

SOAP makes use of (optional) XML namespaces at two levels: in the SOAP envelope and the SOAP payload.

The SOAP envelope references the SOAP namespace to define tags associated with the RPC mechanism. The SOAP namespace (currently, "urn:schemas-xmlsoap-org:soap.v1") indicates the version of SOAP supported by the SOAP client. The SOAP server must use the SOAP version specified in the method call to encode the response, or must send back a fault message indicating that the invocation has failed. If the server accepts a method call that specifies a SOAP version less than its maximum, the server must encode its response in the client's version.

The SOAP payload references implementation-specific namespaces to define tags associated with methods exposed and responses delivered by target programs. SOAP requires that applications specify the method namespace and name in the HTTP header. Applications must also repeat that information in the body element of the SOAP payload. The HTTP header's SOAPMethodName value must exactly match the corresponding values of the method namespace URI and method name specified in the body element of the SOAP payload. This requirement prevents a SOAP client from, for example, specifying a harmless-looking method in the HTTP header (such as "GetTimeOfDay") and a malicious method in the SOAP body (such as "FormatHardDrive").

SOAP's ability to traverse firewalls is a cause for concern among firewall administrators. It could potentially provide an open door for hackers, viruses, and other undesirable Internet visitors. However, SOAP has several security-oriented features that should assuage some of these concerns.

First, SOAP-enabled applications transmit all method call and response traffic over HTTP's (widely and easily monitored) port 80. Consequently, firewall administrators need not concern themselves, as they do with ORBs and synchronous RPCs, with having to open and monitor many nonstandard ports for external traffic.

In addition, when an HTTP message contains a SOAP method call, the HTTP header includes a declaration of the method being called. Consequently, firewalls will be able to determine from the HTTP message header alone whether a remote application is using SOAP to invoke a remote object's method, without needing to inspect the contents of the message. Firewall administrators would have to set up rules that flag incoming SOAP-based function calls and double-check HTTP header information against SOAP payload headers to fend off sneak attacks from hackers.

Furthermore, firewall administrators will be able to force use of the SOAP-specific M-POST command for method calls and responses, in lieu of POST. The M-POST extension enables SOAP-compliant programs to add header information to the HTTP protocol (per future revisions to the SOAP specification), thereby facilitating more fine-grained, rule-based filtering and handling of SOAP messages by firewalls and proxy servers. If an M-POST invocation fails (and produces an HTTP status of "501 Not Implemented" or "510 Not Extended", the SOAP client should fail the request. If the target returns any other error, the method call should be processed according to HTTP specifications. Of course, the SOAP-specific M-POST command will not work unless network administrators reconfigure their proxies, firewalls, Web servers, other HTTP infrastructure to recognize this new verb.

Firewall administrators will also be able to mandate M-POST and prohibit POST method calls for SOAP. They can block use of POST for SOAP by blocking traffic that has a MIME content-type "text/xml" and HTTP header attribute "SOAPMethodName." However, all SOAP clients must first try the POST command when sending action messages. If the POST-based method call fails (and produces an HTTP status of "405 Method Not Allowed"), the SOAP client retries the method call using the M-POST command.

Another security advantage of SOAP is that it, like other XML-based RPCs, encodes function call and response message bodies in plaintext XML. This approach makes such content potentially available for inspection and filtering at the firewall. However, there is no reason why SOAP payload cannot be encrypted, apart from the fact that SOAP 1.1 does not define how the protocol works with encryption, digital signature, or key management schemes. By contrast, each ORB and synchronous RPC technology uses its own specialized parser technology and encoding scheme for data marshalling. Use of different encoding schemes is a significant technical barrier to firewall-based content filtering of traditional middleware traffic, as well as to bridged interoperability among synchronous middleware environments.

Of course, this latter feature—plaintext content encoding—can also represent a security vulnerability of SOAP. It raises the possibility of packet "sniffers" being able to eavesdrop on RPC sessions and easily decode content over the wire, something that's not quite so straightforward with binary encodings based on Abstract Syntax Notation (ASN) 1 and similar techniques.

And these potential security advantages of SOAP are of little use unless firewall vendors support them and firewall administrators know how to use them. Administrators will need to be able to look into their logs and distinguish between regular HTTP traffic and SOAP traffic, as well as between different types of SOAP traffic. Firewall vendors will need to implement significant enhancements in their products' HTTP proxies to provide SOAP-aware filtering, audit, and logging features. One big caveat is that proxy rules necessary to distinguish unwanted and dangerous SOAP traffic from benign content could become extremely complex and difficult to define and administer.

Integration of SOAP with MSMQ and other message-brokering environments would have the added benefit of supporting enterprise-grade distributed transactional services that are lacking in the SOAP specification. SOAP defines an RPC for simple stateless transactions over HTTP (which is itself a stateless transport protocol). However, SOAP does provide some basic features that could support a more stateful end-to-end transactional infrastructure, if deployed with a transactional middleware environment such as MSMQ.

A future version of SOAP will introduce support for digital signatures on XML method call and response content via public key infrastructure (PKI) X.509 certificates. This is a critical security feature for enterprise-grade SOAP deployments, because unsigned SOAP method calls are fairly straightforward to spoof. Robust SOAP deployments will depend on digital signatures as a method of providing strong authentication on messages exchanged in a client/server function call.

In addition, a future SOAP version will probably support exchange of XML method call and response payloads within other Internet protocol envelopes, including SMTP and MSMQ. This will be an important enhancement in defining SOAP as a robust RPC specification for e-business, which relies on these standard messaging and file transfer protocols in addition to HTTP (though HTTP will remain the primary application-layer protocol for the Web and, hence, e-commerce).

14.6 Data Access Components, Providers, and Drivers

BizTalk-enabled e-commerce applications use such Microsoft connector technologies as ADO, OLE DB, and ODBC to tap into rich veins of enterprise data.

ADO, OLE DB, and ODBC are core features of Microsoft's "universal data access" strategy. Under this strategy, developers can use Visual Studio tools to build applications that access a wide range of data sources, relational and nonrelational, across multiple platforms (Windows and non-Windows). All Visual Studio 6.0 tools include new Microsoft-developed OLE DB providers and/or ODBC drivers for accessing Microsoft's SQL Server, Access, and FoxPro databases, as well as Oracle and IBM AS/400 VSAM databases. Third-party OLE DB providers and ODBC drivers are available for other database systems, such as Informix, Sybase, and IBM DB/2. Independent software vendors can create custom OLE DB providers for their own proprietary storage formats.

We discussed ADO, OLE DB, and ODBC previously in Chapter 12, as specifications that bind middle-tier business logic to back-end data sources under Windows DNA. Table 14-8 presents a high-level discussion of their relationship to COM and to one another.

As discussed earlier, Visual Studio programmers can use MTS middleware with ADO to bind multiple database operations into a single atomic

Table 14-8	Microsoft Data Access Components, Providers, and Drivers
Technology	**Discussion**
ADO	Defines a language-neutral set of COM components that access data exposed via underlying OLE DB provider and ODBC drivers. ADO completely isolates developers from the APIs of the underlying OLE DB providers and ODBC drivers. ADO allows developers to create business applications that link many types of data from many heterogeneous sources by abstracting the lower-layer services of OLE DB and ODBC. It enables applications to apply relational queries, joins, and other operations to objects, regardless of whether those objects are RDBMS tables or some other, nonrelational data entity. And it supports scalable data access through connection pooling, disconnected record sets, and synchronized remote record sets delivered over HTTP.
OLE DB	Defines "providers" that integrate data from one or more data sources. OLE DB is a published set of APIs for accessing all kinds of data, including XML. The most commonly used OLE DB provider is Microsoft's OLE DB Provider for ODBC Drivers, which exposes ODBC data sources to ADO components. OLE DB providers enable data from heterogeneous sources—structured and unstructured, relational and nonrelational—to appear as if they reside in a single, logically unified data repository. OLE DB goes beyond simple RDBMS access to support query, filter, navigation, aggregation, manipulation, update, joining, and storage of all types of data entities. OLE DB supports direct programmatic access to unstructured or structured data types, such as database tables, documents, address books, messages, recordsets, rowsets, queries, and access control lists.
ODBC	Defines "drivers" enable a single application to access different RDBMSs directly without the need to modify application source code. These ODBC software drivers isolate applications from RDBMS-specific calls. ODBC is supported in all Microsoft RDBMS products (including SQL Server, Access, and FoxPro) and by many other RDBMS vendors in all major operating environments. Applications that access RDBMSs only need to call APIs in a local ODBC interface, which communicates with ODBC software drivers installed in local or remote DBMSs.

transaction. MTS provides clients and resource managers with "two-phase commit" transaction processing services, sparing database application developers from having to write transaction logic into their code. Consequently, developers can build complex e-commerce and other applications that combine data from many back-end data sources and reliably update those sources in unison.

14.7 Middleware, BizTalk-Hubbed E-Marketectures, and the Future of E-Commerce

Beneath the complexity, middleware is just application-to-application messaging. And so are EDI and workflow, which, as we noted in Chapter 3, are foundation applications underlying BizTalk, Commerce XML (cXML), Electronic Business XML (ebXML), and other B2B interoperability frameworks.

The primary middleware distinction is between object invocation and object "data-marshaling" technologies. The former concept refers to interoperability specifications, such as DCOM and SOAP, that involve explicit invocation of methods on remote components. The latter refers to approaches, such as MSMQ and BizTalk Messages, that shuttle data back and forth between components but do not invoke their programmatic interfaces. When transmitting EDI documents within a structured B2B workflow, the sender is often implicitly triggering activation of procedures, programs, and methods in recipient applications, but does not explicitly call those remote functions.

EDI-like data marshaling is becoming the dominant middleware paradigm for B2B e-commerce (the BizTalk Framework, discussed in Part 1 of this book, is one such approach). Also known as loosely coupled B2B messaging, BizTalk and similar XML-based B2B message envelopes spare companies the trouble and expense of having to establish tight linkages between their respective operating environments and applications. Senders and recipients of XML-based B2B messages are free to process them as they wish, without being tightly bound to each other's service interfaces (a "tight coupling" feature of XML-based RPCs, ORBs, and other traditional middleware approaches). Over the next several years we will see the distinction between XML-based RPCs and other messaging-oriented technologies continue to blur, especially as SOAP's authors adapt it to run over SMTP, MSMQ, and other asynchronous protocols. Figure 14-3 shows BizTalk Server 2000's role as a master "message switch" in this more "loosely coupled" B2B environment.

However, robust e-commerce environments must bridge multiple middleware approaches, and Microsoft has wisely chosen to support both paradigms—tightly and loosely coupled program-to-program integration—in BizTalk Server 2000 and Windows DNA. Though loose coupling will be predominant in hubbed e-marketplaces, tightly coupled middleware will still be

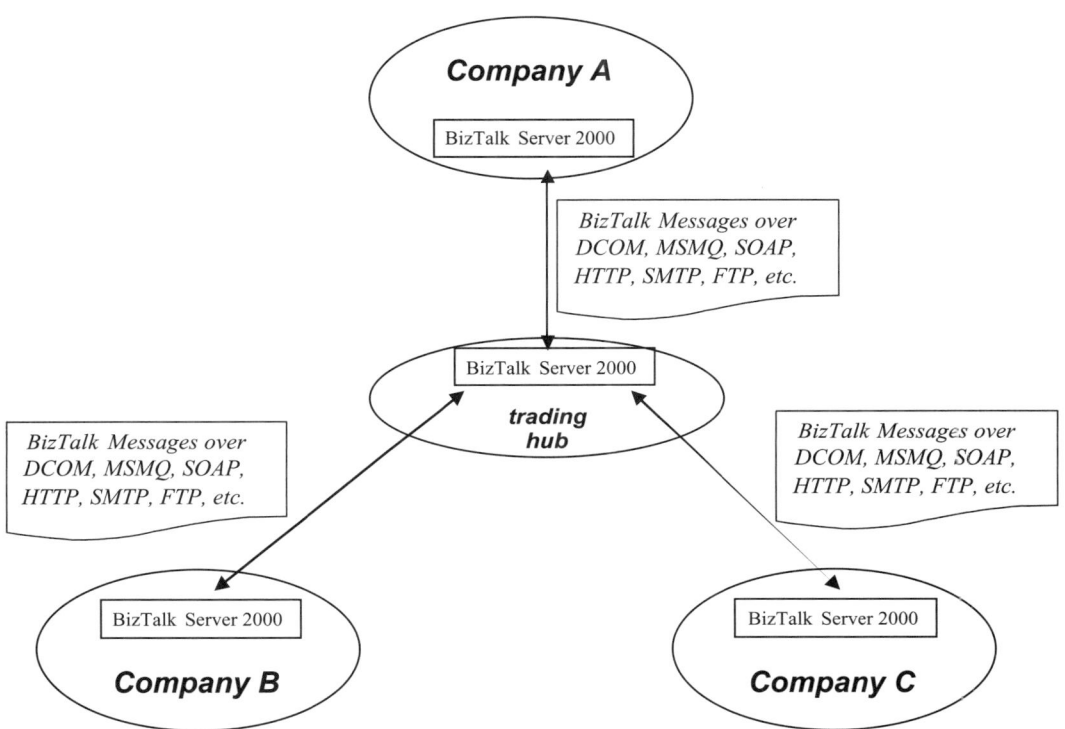

Figure 14-3 *BizTalk Server 2000 is a master B2B message switch that routes BizTalk-enveloped business data via various protocols, including MSMQ, SOAP, SMTP, and HTTP.*

used in B2B environments, especially for extranets among stable trading partners who require an extra level of end-to-end integration, throughput, and reliability. Both approaches—tightly and loosely coupled integration—will be implemented in intranets, depending on the heterogeneity, geographic distribution, and dynamism of each company's distributed computing environment. Figure 14-4 shows how Microsoft has addressed both middleware paradigms in its total middleware environment under the Windows DNA framework.

BizTalk Server 2000 does much more than simply route BizTalk Messages. It is Microsoft's application-integration "glue" for bridging the various middleware environments, transport protocols, message envelopes, and document formats that bind enterprises internally and externally. Interchange servers, such as BizTalk Server 2000, are all-purpose protocol gateways, message switches, workflow engines, and document translators for end-to-end e-commerce. Interchange servers are the new "meta-middleware" engines for B2B and EAI.

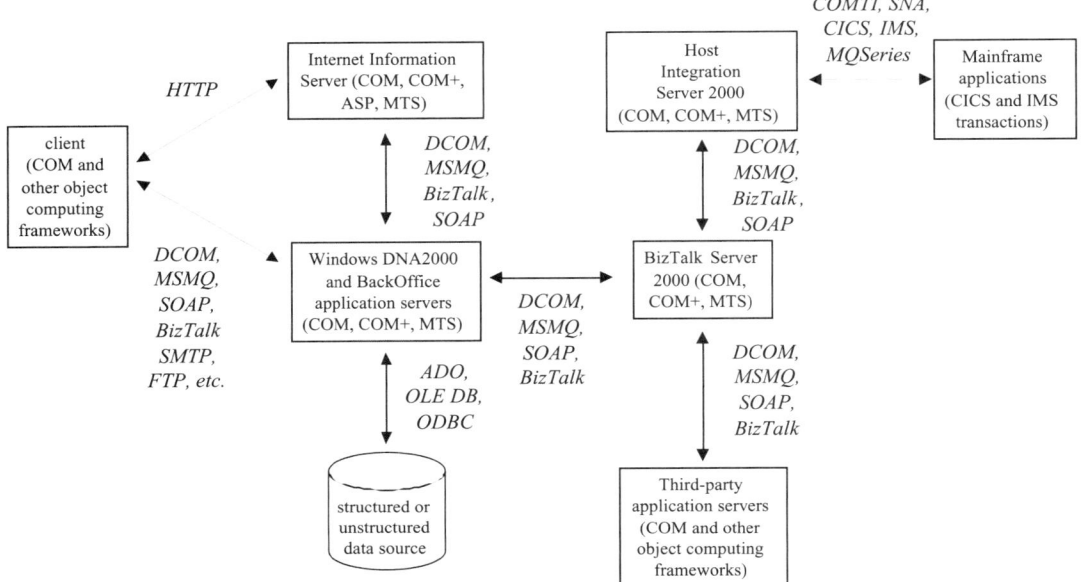

Microsoft's total middleware environment supports both tightly coupled application-to-application messaging (via DCOM) and loosely coupled messaging (via MSMQ). Tightly coupled SOAP function invocations and responses can potentially ride over various transport protocols, as will loosely coupled BizTalk Message exchanges.

BizTalk Server 2000 and other interchange servers will increasingly become the distributed operating environment for e-marketplaces of all sorts. E-marketmakers will use interchange servers as platforms to run the complex workflow business logic that integrates buyers with sellers and third-party trade facilitators. These platforms will support all seven layers of trading-exchange functionality: hosting, membership, aggregation, transaction, pricing, payment, and facilitation. And as industries realign their operations around e-marketplaces, interchange servers will become the primary repositories of business logic for the online economy.

Marketplace participants, in turn, will deploy interchange servers as external gateways for integrating back-end business processes with hubs and extranets. Interchange servers will also find ample applications within companies that seek middleware for bridging incompatible environments, or supporting ready integration with newly acquired, merged, or reorganized business operations. We discussed all three integration scenarios in Part Two, describing BizTalk Server 2000's role in them all. XML will increasingly permeate all layers of the online environment: as a universal, standard syntax for describing documents, messages, services, processes, workflows, and marketplaces. Microsoft's multilayered middleware environment will be the web that binds its products with an increasingly multivendor, standards-oriented, Web-facing world.

Microsoft provides a strong suite of application servers for e-commerce. Any organization seeking to establish itself as an e-marketmaker or participate in such an environment would need the functionality supplied by the Windows DNA 2000 and Microsoft Server products: distributed operating environment, interchange server, catalog server, database server, legacy integration server, Web server, and messaging server. We described this functionality in Parts Three and Four, showing how BizTalk Server 2000 is but one component in Microsoft's integrated e-commerce solution set.

Going forward, Windows 2000 and the Windows DNA 2000 servers are a strong foundation for Microsoft's e-commerce software strategy. We expect Microsoft to increasingly integrate these products into its MSN and bCentral e-marketplace services, as well as into other business-oriented application service provider offerings. Over the next several years, we expect that Microsoft will transform the Windows DNA 2000 servers into a scalable, standards-oriented platform for network services provided by application service providers (under the Microsoft.NET initiative).

And e-marketmakers, of course, are the premier application service providers in the new economy. They seek scalable, reliable, high-performance, standards-oriented products on which to build their communities. And they seek a rich development environment for integrating functionality and data from within their own organizations and with a myriad of buyers and sellers. Microsoft has architected BizTalk Server 2000 and the other Windows DNA 2000 products to meet those core requirements.

BizTalk is not the only message envelope, interchange server, or e-commerce software architecture in the B2B marketplace. However, the BizTalk initiative comes from a company that has established itself as a leader in so many spheres of distributed computing—from the desktop to the browser, from the workgroup server to the corporate data center—that eventual widespread implementation of BizTalk-enabled products and services seems a foregone conclusion.

Microsoft will survive and prosper in this new world of B2B and B2C e-commerce, even if it means splitting into several independent operating units. Whatever happens to the vendor that set it in motion, BizTalk will almost certainly become a dominant B2B dialect in the global economy.

BizTalk and the Buzz of the Modern Economy

We live in the age of network software, in which shapes fresh from someone's imagination can enrich—or imperil—our lives almost overnight.

This book was written in the year 2000. It is a year that some thought would arrive with a great network cataclysm triggered by a tiny little programming shortcut. It is also a year in which viruses, worms, zombies, and other invisible network beasties regularly made the headlines and showed just how vulnerable the online economy is to sabotage from anyone with a phone line.

But modern society has shown surprising resiliency in the face of these network-borne threats. This is also a time of unprecedented prosperity and economic growth, an era of grand plans. Two thousand is the tenth year of an economic expansion that has buoyed the United States and other developed nations. Almost spontaneously, the global economy has begun to reengineer itself around the World Wide Web, a computer networking architecture that was little more than a laboratory curiosity when the long expansion began. No one knows with any certainty how far the Web will penetrate and reshape everyday life. And no one really knows how far the demands of round-the-clock e-commerce will drive the Web's technical evolution. We race headlong into this new online marketplace, not fully understanding what makes it all tick or what can bring it crashing down. But here we sit, hands on mice, watching the possibilities unfurl and surfing a wave of continuous innovation.

Above all, it is the age of Microsoft, one of the most important private enterprises of this or any time. Love it or fear it, embrace or resist it, you have to admit that Microsoft is the most visible and influential purveyor of grand plans and new vistas in distributed computing. Microsoft—more than any other single company—drives the technical agenda for today's online economy. It has established itself as a dominant player in so many areas of distributed computing, in both the business and consumer spheres, that its every action and reaction draws tight scrutiny.

Microsoft's grand plan is to weave its DNA into the world's e-commerce infrastructures, and BizTalk is a central component of that plan. The company may not inspire, coax, or coerce everyone into adopting the BizTalk Framework, posting vertical market business document schemas to BizTalk.org, or buying the BizTalk Server 2000 product. Others may develop more popular message formats, schema repositories, and interchange servers than Bill Gates and company. But Microsoft is the king of the computing world at this stage in history, and its hegemony is now the legacy upon which we will build our new economy.

So no matter what B2B standards you adopt, there will probably be a major piece of Microsoft's technical environment that you'll need to glue into your commerce applications. And you very likely may implement BizTalk Server 2000 and other Microsoft Windows DNA 2000 servers in your e-marketplace, extranet, or intranet. The BizTalk Message envelope—supported in all Windows DNA 2000 products—will become a familiar presence in your trading environment.

Microsoft has shown itself to be quite resilient, flexible, and competitive. It has a way of moving from strength to strength. You'll certainly be hearing more about BizTalk products, services, and technical specifications in the years to come, no matter what becomes of the company that set the initiative in motion. The term, the philosophy, and the initiative have a life all their own.

BizTalk is the buzz of millions of firms, billions of people, and trillions of software components engaged in a never-ending network dialogue. It will be part of the background buzz of the modern economy.

Active Directory: Windows 2000's distributed directory service.

Active Server Page (ASP): Microsoft technology that enables run-time Web-page generation using server-side scripts to access COM objects and other program elements.

ActiveX Components: Enables packaging and transfer of downloadable COM component binaries for execution within HTML pages running under Web browsers, via page-embedded URL pointers to ActiveX components.

ActiveX Data Object (ADO): Microsoft specification that defines a language-neutral set of COM components that access data exposed via underlying OLE DB provider and ODBC drivers.

Aggregation model: Approaches for organizing buy and sell offers in an e-marketplace.

Agreement: Information that enables an organization to transmit or receive business documents with another organization, specifying the source and destination organizations, the source and destination documents, the document map, and the envelope information.

American Standard Code for Information Interchange (ASCII): Standard coding method used to convert letters, numbers, punctuation, special characters, and hardware control codes into digital form.

Application Center 2000: Web-farm management tool in Windows DNA 2000 product family.

Application programming interface (API): Well-defined statement that supports programmatic access to an external function.

Attribute: Name-value pair within a tagged XML element that modifies features of the element.

Authentication: Verification of a user's identity to a computer or network system.

BizTags: Set of XML tags, defined under the BizTalk Framework, that are used to create BizTalk Documents by enveloping Business Documents.

BizTalk: Microsoft initiative to support B2B application interoperability through XML-based interoperability specifications, a public repository for XML-based business document schemas, a standards-compliant interchange server product, e-commerce portal services, and alliances with third-party e-commerce software vendors and service providers.

BizTalk Document: Single well-formed XML document that envelopes BizTags around a Business Document.

BizTalk Editor: Tool for creating, editing, and managing XML-based Business Document specifications.

BizTalk Framework: Application model, document routing/handling XML tags, and other interoperability specifications defined in the BizTalk Framework Independent Document Specification.

BizTalk Management Desk: Administrative tool for BizTalk Server 2000.

BizTalk Mapper: Tool for mapping records and fields between two different Business Document formats.

BizTalk Message: Transport-specific envelope around a BizTalk Document, used as the unit of interchange between BizTalk servers.

BizTalk.org: Public XML business document schema repository Web site and hub of the BizTalk developer community.

BizTalk server: Server-side processing functionality defined in the BizTalk Framework's application model.

BizTalk Server 2000: Interchange server product in Microsoft's Windows DNA 2000 product family.

Broker-hosted marketplace: E-marketplace managed by an entity that is neither a buyer nor seller of the traded good or service.

Browser: Client software that facilitates online user access, viewing, and navigation of the World Wide Web.

Business Document: Per the BizTalk Framework, well-formed XML data exchanged between trading partners; examples include purchase orders, purchase order acknowledgments, ship notices, invoices, billing records, and receipts.

Business process: Set of interdependent business activities.

Buyer-hosted marketplace: E-marketplace managed by one of the sellers in the marketplace, often a dominant seller, or by a consortium of sellers.

Certificate authority (CA): Organization or agency that publishes authenticated certificates binding user identifiers to public keys.

Client/server: Partitioning of applications into separate software modules capable of operating on separate computers connected over a network.

COM+: Enables more efficient development and assembly of COM objects into applications.

Comments: Per XML 1.0, plain-English embedded explanations within an XML document of that document and its contents.

Commerce Business Library: Existing horizontal-market reference library of reusable XML element- and attribute-tags for generating EDI documents.

Commerce Desk: Administrative tool for Commerce Server 2000.

Commerce Interchange Pipeline (CIP): Specification of document handling and processing steps performed by BizTalk Server 2000.

Commerce Server 2000: Storefront server in Microsoft's Windows DNA 2000 product family.

Commerce XML (cXML): XML-based B2B interoperability framework defined by Ariba Technologies.

Common Object Request Broker Architecture (CORBA): Object management standard developed by the Object Management Group, an industry consortium, which provides high-level object "wrappers" that allow one application to locate and invoke data and functions internal to another application.

Communications gateway: Hardware and/or software that encapsulates, converts, or translates commands, messages, and information between dissimilar application environments to enable some basic level of service interoperability.

Component Object Model (COM): Microsoft's Windows-based object-management specification.

Component Object Model Transaction Integration (COMTI): Programming wrapper technology that provides access to IBM mainframe transaction environments from COM programming tools and languages.

Data mapping: Defining the logical correspondence—a "map"—between the elements and attributes of two well-formed XML documents for the purpose of automating transformation between the documents' logical data structures.

Data transformation: Conversion of a document from one logical data structure to another in accordance with a data map.

Declarations: Markup that defines the logical structure and properties of an XML document, including the version of XML that it supports; what character sets and human languages comprise its content; and what entities, elements, attributes, default values, data types, links, and pointers it contains or references.

Destination organization: Organization designated within a BizTalk agreement to receive documents.

Digital certificate: Certificate from a trusted source that contains identifying information about the organization, a public key, and a digital signature from the certificate authority (CA) attesting that the public key belongs to the named organization.

Digital signature: String of bits associated with a document that can be used to mathematically certify that the document was originated by a particular user and has not been altered or tampered with during transmission or storage.

Directory services: Services that support naming, locator, address lookup, and resolution functions for network applications.

Distributed Component Object Model (DCOM): Microsoft-proprietary object brokering environment that enables remote location, invocation, and execution of COM objects across networks.

Distributed File System (DFS): Network file system in Windows 2000 and Windows NT Server.

Distributed interNetworking Architecture (DNA): Microsoft interoperability framework specifying standards and specifications in the presentation, business logic, and data tiers.

Distributed transaction processing monitor (DTPM): Middleware technology supporting reliable atomic transactions among distributed databases.

Document: Logical container of information with a well-defined beginning and end.

Document Content Description (DCD): XML schema-definition language specification.

Document Object Model (DOM): W3C standard specifying how the elements of HTML and XML documents can be updated programmatically with scripts or other programs.

Document Tracking and Activity (DTA) database: SQL database associated with a BizTalk Server group that enables tracking of documents that pass through the server and recording of state engine activity against those documents.

Document Type Definition (DTD): Markup declarations, defined in XML 1.0, that describe the grammar for a class of documents.

Domain: Networked computers that share a common context within a directory information tree and can be administered as a group.

Domain Name System (DNS): Naming and address resolution service for the Internet and other TCP/IP-based networks.

Electronic Business Extensible Markup Language (ebXML): Industry initiative, sponsored by OASIS, to define XML-based, B2B e-commerce interoperability standards.

Electronic commerce: Business transactions conducted over data networks, utilizing Internet, messaging, EDI, public key cryptography, digital signature, encryption, and certification technologies.

Electronic Data interchange (EDI): Electronic exchange of standardized business documents among companies and their suppliers, distributors, customers, and other trading partners.

Electronic data Interchange for Administration, Commerce, and Transport (EDIFACT): EDI transaction-set standards developed by the United Nations's Electronic Data Interchange for Administration, Commerce, and Transport group.

Electronic forms: Computerized forms that replicate the layout of traditional paper forms while supporting value-added features such as autocalculation, mandatory field entry, database lookups, and structured routing.

Electronic mail: Application that supports interpersonal exchange of unstructured text messages and, sometimes, semistructured electronic forms and binary file attachments between networked users on a store-and-forward basis; also known as "e-mail" or "email."

Element: XML structural construct delimited by a start tag and end tag.

E-marketecture: Technical architecture of an e-marketplace.

E-marketecture reference model: Interpretive framework defining seven layers of functionality supported within an e-marketplace, including hosting, membership, aggregation, transaction, pricing, payment, and facilitation.

E-marketplace: Online environment supporting aggregation of commercial content and transactions among buyers, sellers, brokers, and other facilitators.

Encryption: Algorithmic transformation of plain text into an unintelligible string of bits that can be returned to its original form—or "decrypted"—only through application of a special algorithm and "key" string.

Enterprise application integration (EAI): Integration of applications and systems within an enterprise intranet.

Entity: XML structural construct that associates a name with a sequence of characters or well-formed XML hierarchy within a root document or external document.

Envelope: Data construct that encapsulates a document or group of documents for transmission from the source organization to the destination organization.

Extensible Markup Language (XML): Per W3C's XML 1.0 standard, a subset of SGML that provides a uniform method for describing and exchanging structured data in an open, text-based format.

Extensible Stylesheet Language (XSL): Per W3C's XSL standard, a language used to transform XML-based data into HTML or other presentation formats for display in a browser or browser-based application.

Extensible Stylesheet Language Transformations (XSLT): Per W3C's XSLT standard, a language for defining data maps between well-formed XML documents.

Facilitation model: Organization of third-party responsibilities for assisting buyers, sellers, and/or marketmakers in setting up, executing, and consummating transactions in an e-marketplace.

Facilitator: E-marketplace participant that provides services to buyers, sellers, and/or marketmakers.

File system: Software that supports organization, searching, retrieval, and administration of local or distributed files under the control of a computer or network operating environment.

File Transfer Protocol (FTP): Internet protocol providing a family of commands for performing file and directory operations over the network, including the uploading and downloading of files.

Firewall: Combination of hardware and software that supports prevention of unauthorized external access to a corporate intranet or subnet with an intranet.

Folder: Container of digital information that includes two or more files.

Forest: Collection of one or more Windows 2000 Active Directory trees organized as peers, sharing a common schema, configuration, and global catalog, and connected by two-way transitive trust relationships between the root domains of each tree, but not forming a contiguous namespace.

Functional acknowledgment: Receipt indicating that documents have been received by the destination organization and have been opened and verified as being functionally correct.

Horizontal marketplace: E-marketplace with all-inclusive membership model.

Hosting model: Structure of ownership, sponsorship, control, and management in an e-marketplace.

Host Integration Server 2000: Legacy integration server within Microsoft Windows DNA 2000 product family; successor to SNA Server 4.0.

Hubbed e-marketplace: E-marketplace with a central site and marketmaker.

Hypertext: Information access method that allows users to peruse information associatively through linking of related blocks of information called nodes.

HyperText Markup Language (HTML): Standard for tagging a document's internal structure and links to external files, servers, and Internet sites; an extension to SGML that has become the standard for the World Wide Web.

HyperText Transfer Protocol (HTTP): Standard communication protocols for connecting World Wide Web browsers to sites, using a standard addressing format referred to as an URL.

Industry-hosted marketplace: E-marketplace managed by an organization owned and/or controlled by a broad range of buyers and sellers in an industry.

Information and Content Exchange (ICE): XML-based standard for online content subscription and syndication between Web sites.

Internet: Worldwide network of data networks all connected using the TCP/IP suite of protocols, supporting application-level protocols such as SMTP (e-mail) and HTTP (World Wide Web), and functioning as a single virtual network.

Internet Engineering Task Force (IETF): Open community of network designers, operators, vendors, and researchers concerned with the evolution of Internet architecture, the smooth operation of the Internet, and development of interoperability standards for Internet infrastructure and applications.

Internet Explorer (IE): Microsoft's Web browser product.

Internet Information Server (IIS): Microsoft's Web server product.

Internet Inter-ORB Protocol (IIOP): Wire protocol for CORBA object brokering environment.

Internet Server Application Programming Interface (ISAPI): Programmatic interface between Microsoft Internet Information Server and back-end external applications.

Kerberos: Industry-standard authentication mechanism used as the default authentication service for Windows 2000.

Lightweight Directory Access Protocol (LDAP): Directory service protocol that runs directly over TCP/IP and is the primary access protocol for Active Directory.

Marketmaker: Organizer and/or operator of an e-marketplace.

Markup: Text in an XML document that does not represent character data, consisting of tags, declarations, references, comments, and processing instructions.

Map file: File that contains instructions on how to transform a source XML document with a particular logical structure and into a target document with a different logical structure.

Mapping: Process of creating a map file.

Membership agreement: Contractual relationship between a marketmaker and a participating organization.

Membership model: Policies determining eligibility, terms, and conditions for participating in an e-marketplace.

Message broker: Synonymous with message-oriented middleware, message queuing, and business-quality messaging

Message store: Database that retains inbound and outbound messages.

Message transfer agent (MTA): Server-based software that supports routing, delivery, forwarding, and communications functions on messaging systems; also known as a "mail router" or "message router."

Messaging Application Programming Interface (MAPI): Microsoft-developed APIs for interfacing Windows-based client applications to third-party message handling systems.

Microsoft Management Console (MMC): Windows 2000's framework for hosting administrative consoles for different applications, utilities, and tools.

Microsoft Message Queue Server (MSMQ): Messaging middleware for Microsoft Windows 2000 and NT Server that allows programs to send messages to other programs.

Microsoft Transaction Server (MTS): Microsoft middleware supporting atomic transactions among components, services, and applications within and between Windows environments.

Middleware: Layer of software adapters that support run-time component-level interoperability among dissimilar operating, object-computing, application-development, and/or application environments; enables dispersed applications to behave as if they were kindred software modules running on the same machine.

Multimaster replication: Replication model in which any domain controller accepts and replicates directory changes to any other domain controller.

Multipurpose Internet Mail Extensions (MIME): Standard for messaging over the Internet and other TCP/IP-based networks that supports transparent encoding, transport, and decoding of binary files alongside normal mail messages; supports descriptive tagging of binary file attachments and identifies the originating applications.

Namespace: Set of unique names for resources or items used in a shared computing environment.

Network operating system (NOS): Run-time software that allows network-connected devices to share files, disks, printers, communications links, and other facilities, and also supports centralized network administration, monitoring, and control.

Nonrepudiation: Basic security function of cryptography providing assurance that a party in a communication cannot falsely deny that a part of the communication occurred.

Object: Digital entity, such as a file, folder, shared folder, executable, or printer, described by a distinct, named set of attributes.

Object broker: Synonymous with object request broker

Object Linking and Embedding (OLE): Microsoft specification that defines "providers" for integrating data from one or more structured and/or semistructured data sources.

Object-oriented programming: Programming techniques that support rapid application development and modification by reusing existing software modules, each of which performs a well-defined set of functions and contains executable program code plus the data that may be manipulated by this code.

Object request broker (ORB): Functional entity that performs registry, directory, and locator functions for distributed objects in a network environment.

Open Applications Group Interface Specification (OAGIS): XML-based interoperability framework for integrating dissimilar enterprise resource planning applications.

Open Buying on the Internet (OBI): Non-XML-based B2B e-commerce interoperability framework supporting order submission and acknowledgment.

Open Database Connectivity (ODBC): Microsoft-developed APIs for interfacing applications to SQL-compliant local or networked database management systems.

Open Trading Protocol (OTP): XML-based B2B e-commerce interoperability framework supporting payment applications.

Order Processing Pipeline (OPP): Specification of processing steps performed by Commerce Server 2000.

Organization for Advancement of Structured Information Standards (OASIS): Nonprofit organization sponsoring the ebXML standardization effort and managing the public XML.org business document schema repository.

Parallel routing: Routing in which duplicate copies of a workflow item are sent over two or more paths at the same time.

Payment model: Procedures for submitting, processing, and settling payments in an e-marketplace.

Pricing model: Procedures for determining prices in an e-marketplace.

Private marketplace: E-marketplace with a membership model that requires preexisting business relationship with the marketmaker or another market member in order to participate.

Process definition: Flowchart or textual representation of a process that defines associated activities, routes, roles, rules, and documents.

Process definition tool: Software that supports development of computerized representations, including both the automated and manual process components

Process instance: Single run through a workflow process.

Processing instructions: XML markup that contains specific procedures and rules to be invoked by applications that process XML content, bypassing the normal operation of an XML processor and delivering instructions directly to a downstream process whose responsibility it is to interpret the instructions and act accordingly.

Protocol: Framework for a dialogue conducted between network devices in order to establish, maintain, and terminate communications sessions and exchange information successfully.

Public key cryptography: Cryptographic system that provides two different keys for encrypting and decrypting information, or for signing and verifying signatures on information; one key is held in private by a user and the other disclosed to other parties.

Public key infrastructure (PKI): System of digital certificates, certification authorities, and other registration authorities that verify and authenticate the validity of each party involved in an electronic transaction.

Record: Repeating structure that represents two or more logically related fields in a computer database.

Relational database management system (RDBMS): Database management system that organizes information into one or more tables, each of which contains multiple rows (records) and columns (fields).

Remote procedure call (RPC): Message-passing facility that allows a distributed application to call services that are available on various machines in a network while hiding the details of network connections from the applications.

Replication: Process of copying data from a data store or file system to multiple computers that store the same data for the purpose of synchronizing the data.

Role: Activities performed and privileges enjoyed by a specific workflow participant.

RosettaNet: XML-based B2B e-commerce interoperability framework and specifications supporting the information technology industry supply chain.

Route: Path that a workflow item takes through an organization.

Rule: Statement of the conditions that will trigger automatic execution of one or more computer and network functions.

Schema: Formal specification of element names that indicates which elements are allowed in an XML document, and in which combinations; functionally equivalent to a DTD, but written in XML markup.

Schema for Object-Oriented XML (SOX): An XML schema definition language specification.

Script: Set of interdependent rules defined in a procedural computing language.

Secure Sockets Layer (SSL): Specification, supporting secure connections between World Wide Web browsers and servers; standard version is known as TLS.

Segment: Data structure in an EDI transaction set that is a collection of fields, each with its own name and type.

Seller-hosted marketplace: E-marketplace managed by one of the sellers in the marketplace, often a dominant seller, or by a consortium of sellers.

Sequential routing: Route in which there are no parallel paths and in which predecessor activities must be completed prior to initiation of their successors.

Server: Network-connected computer that provides shared access to resources such as applications, files, disks, printers, message transfer agents, and communications links.

Shared Queue (SQ) database: SQL database that is shared by all servers within a BizTalk Server group and which stores all checkpoint information related to interchanges processed by BizTalk Server.

Simple Mail Transfer Protocol (SMTP): Standard, also referred to as RFC821, for electronic messaging over the Internet.

Simple Object Access Protocol (SOAP): XML-based RPC specification supported in Microsoft's Windows DNA 2000 application server products, including BizTalk Server 2000.

Source organization: Organization designated within a BizTalk agreement to send documents.

SQL Server 2000: Database server within Microsoft's Windows DNA 2000 application server product family.

Standard Generalized Markup Language (SGML): Standard language used to tag the structural elements in a document to facilitate organization and formatting by external desktop publishing, layout, and other applications.

Structured Query Language (SQL): Dominant data query, retrieval, update, and administration language for relational database management systems.

Tags: XML markup that delimits the beginning and end of each content element and attribute within an XML document, as defined through prior element and attribute declarations.

Transaction model: Procedures for establishing commercial contracts, bargaining, and processing transactions in an e-marketplace.

Transaction processing monitor: Software that ensures the security and integrity of end-to-end database operations.

Transaction set: Semantically meaningful unit of information exchanged between trading partners or between applications, containing records, fields, attributes, and codes.

Transitive trust relationship: Two-way trusts that exist between Windows 2000 domains within a domain tree or forest, enabling users with accounts in one domain to transparently log into and access resources in other domains.

Transmission Control Protocol/Internet Protocol (TCP/IP): Protocol suite for networking and internetworking that ensures that data packets are delivered to their destination in the order in which they were transmitted.

Transparency: Ability of a system or service to maintain a consistent, intuitive interface from the end user's point of view, thereby shielding the user from complexity, reconfigurations, modifications, failures, and other distracting technical details in the serving platform.

Transport Layer Security (TLS): Standard protocol, based on SSL, that enables Web clients to authenticate servers or, optionally, Web servers to authenticate clients; also supports secure, encrypted transmission channels between Web clients and servers.

Tree: Collection of Windows 2000 Active Directory domains that share a common contiguous namespace, schema, configuration, and global catalog.

Unicode: A superset of the ASCII character set that uses two bytes for each character rather than one. Unicode is able to handle 65,536 character combinations rather than only 256, and can house the alphabets of most of the world's languages.

Uniform Resource Identifier (URI): Generic set of all names and addresses that refer to Web resources, including URLs and URNs.

Uniform Resource Locator (URL): Standard addressing format for accessing sites, pages, and other resources on the Internet.

Uniform Resource Name (URN): Name identifying a persistent Internet resource.

Universal Naming Convention (UNC): Full pathname to server, share, directory, and file hosting a resource on a local- or wide-area network.

Valid XML: XML document that conforms to the vocabulary specified in a DTD or schema.

Vertical marketplace: E-marketplace with a membership model that requires participants to meet criteria specific to a particular segment of industry, business, or commerce.

Visual Basic Script (VBScript): Microsoft-proprietary scripting language.

Web-Distributed Authoring and Versioning (WebDAV): Extension to HTTP 1.1 that supports file system-like operations on document collections over the Web.

Well-formed XML: XML document that conforms to the syntax specified in XML 1.0.

Windows DNA 2000: Microsoft's application server product family that includes BizTalk Server 2000, Commerce Server 2000, SQL Server 2000, Host Integration Server 2000, and Application Center 2000.

Windows 2000: Microsoft's high-performance server and workstation operating system.

Workflow: Flow of information and control in a business process.

Workflow client application: Software that allows workflow participants to interact with workflow enactment services for the purpose of signing on and off the service, initiating processes, displaying worklists, invoking applications, and accessing workflow relevant, application, and control data.

Workflow control data: Real-time data on work-item status and locations used by the workflow enactment service to control an active process.

Workflow definition: Subset of a process definition that describes activities, routes, roles, and rules that can be supported by automated computer and network tools.

Workflow-enabled application: Application that utilizes document routing and tracking services provided through APIs on a workflow enactment service.

Workflow enactment service: Software that provides a run-time environment for initiating, executing, sequencing, and controlling instances of a process definition, adding work items to user worklists and invoking application tools as necessary; includes one or more workflow engines.

Workflow engine: Server-resident software that provides the run-time execution environment for a workflow instance, either individually or in communication with other workflow engines; component of a distributed workflow enactment service.

Workflow management: Ability of a system to support structured routing and tracking of documents, folders, and other information throughout a workgroup or enterprise.

Workflow management system: System that defines, manages, and executes automated workflows in accordance with a computerized process definition.

World Wide Web (WWW): Internet service that supports transparent, graphical, point-and-click navigation among distributed information services and resources, based on HTML (for document hyperlinking), HTTP (for connecting browsers to servers), and URLs (for naming and addressing resources).

World Wide Web Consortium (W3C): Nonprofit organization that develops interoperability standards for the World Wide Web.

XML Data Reduced (XDR): XML schema definition language specification supported in Microsoft's products.

XML document: Data object that is well formed, according to the XML 1.0 standard recommendation, and that may or may not correctly implement an XML vocabulary or grammar (DTD or schema); has a logical structure (composed of declarations, elements, comments, character references, and processing instructions) and a physical structure (composed of entities, starting with the root, or document entity).

XML/EDI Group: Nonprofit organization developing XML-based B2B e-commerce interoperability specifications.

XML Namespace: Standard defining a mechanism for XML validating parsers to uniquely identify the source of a document type's schema.

XML parser: Software component that reads an incoming XML document, determines the logical structure of that document, extracts data from the document, then hands off the data to external applications for processing.

XML processor: Software component that generates outgoing XML documents.

XML Schemas: W3C standard XML schema definition language.

X12: EDI transaction-set standards developed by ANSI.

X.500 Directory Services: Directory-services standards developed by the International Telecommunications Union's Telecommunications Standardization Sector.

X.509 Public Key Certificates: Public key certificate standard developed by the International Telecommunications Union's Telecommunications Standardization Sector.

INDEX